The East European and Soviet
Data Handbook

THE EAST EUROPEAN AND SOVIET DATA HANDBOOK:

POLITICAL, SOCIAL, AND DEVELOPMENTAL INDICATORS, 1945-1975

PAUL S. SHOUP

HOOVER INSTITUTION PRESS
STANFORD UNIVERSITY—STANFORD, CALIFORNIA

Columbia University Press
New York
1981

Library of Congress Cataloging in Publication Data

Shoup, Paul.
  The East European and Soviet data handbook.

  Includes bibliographical references and index.
  1. Russia—Statistics.   2. Europe, Eastern—
Statistics.   I. Title.
HA1446.S53   314.7   80-25682
ISBN 0-231-04252-3

Columbia University Press
New York   Guildford, Surrey

ACKNOWLEDGMENTS

The authors wishes to acknowledge the generous assistance of the Earhart Foundation, the Hoover Institution on War and Peace, and the University of Virginia, without whose help this volume could never have been written. A debt of gratitude is also owed all those individuals and institutions who helped the author with their suggestions and by supplying data. The author of course accepts full responsibility for any errors or omissions that may appear in the tables to follow.

CONTENTS

GENERAL INTRODUCTION   *1*

EXPLANATION OF SYMBOLS AND MANNER OF PRESENTING DATA   *37*

SECTION A: POPULATION

INTRODUCTION   *39*

TABLE A-1   TOTAL POPULATION, PREWAR AND POSTWAR BOUNDARIES, CENSUS
             YEARS: ALBANIA AND BULGARIA   *41*

TABLE A-2   TOTAL POPULATION, PREWAR AND POSTWAR BOUNDARIES, CENSUS
             YEARS: CZECHOSLOVAKIA AND GDR   *42*

TABLE A-3   TOTAL POPULATION, PREWAR AND POSTWAR BOUNDARIES, CENSUS
             YEARS: HUNGARY AND POLAND   *43*

TABLE A-4   TOTAL POPULATION, PREWAR AND POSTWAR BOUNDARIES, CENSUS
             YEARS: ROMANIA AND USSR   *44*

TABLE A-5   TOTAL POPULATION, PREWAR AND POSTWAR BOUNDARIES, CENSUS
             YEARS: YUGOSLAVIA   *45*

TABLE A-6   POPULATION GROWTH, COMPONENTS OF POPULATION CHANGE,
             AND VITAL RATES: ALBANIA, 1950-1975   *46*

TABLE A-7   POPULATION GROWTH, COMPONENTS OF POPULATION CHANGE,
             AND VITAL RATES: BULGARIA, 1950-1975   *47*

TABLE A-8   POPULATION GROWTH, COMPONENTS OF POPULATION CHANGE,
             AND VITAL RATES: CZECHOSLOVAKIA, 1950-1975   *48*

TABLE A-9   POPULATION GROWTH, COMPONENTS OF POPULATION CHANGE,
             AND VITAL RATES: GDR, 1950-1975   *49*

TABLE A-10   POPULATION GROWTH, COMPONENTS OF POPULATION CHANGE,
             AND VITAL RATES: HUNGARY, 1950-1975   *50*

TABLE A-11   POPULATION GROWTH, COMPONENTS OF POPULATION CHANGE,
             AND VITAL RATES: POLAND, 1950-1975   *51*

TABLE A-12   POPULATION GROWTH, COMPONENTS OF POPULATION CHANGE,
             AND VITAL RATES: ROMANIA, 1950-1975   *52*

TABLE A-13   POPULATION GROWTH, COMPONENTS OF POPULATION CHANGE,
             AND VITAL RATES: USSR, 1950-1975   *53*

TABLE A-14   POPULATION GROWTH, COMPONENTS OF POPULATION CHANGE,
             AND VITAL RATES: YUGOSLAVIA, 1950-1975   *54*

TABLE A-15   POPULATION BY AGE GROUPS AND SEX: ALBANIA, 1950-1975   *55*

TABLE A-16   POPULATION BY AGE GROUPS AND SEX: BULGARIA, 1950-1975   *56*

TABLE A-17   POPULATION BY AGE GROUPS AND SEX: CZECHOSLOVAKIA,
             1950-1975   *57*

TABLE A-18   POPULATION BY AGE GROUPS AND SEX: GDR, 1950-1975   *58*

TABLE A-19   POPULATION BY AGE GROUPS AND SEX: HUNGARY, 1950-1975   *59*

TABLE A-20   POPULATION BY AGE GROUPS AND SEX: POLAND, 1950-1976   *60*

TABLE A-21   POPULATION BY AGE GROUPS AND SEX: ROMANIA, 1950-1975   *61*

TABLE A-22 POPULATION BY AGE GROUPS AND SEX: USSR, 1950-1975   *62*

TABLE A-23 POPULATION BY AGE GROUPS AND SEX: YUGOSLAVIA, 1950-1975   *63*

TABLE A-24 URBAN AND RURAL BIRTHRATES: EASTERN EUROPE AND THE USSR, 1946-1975   *64*

TABLE A-25 URBAN AND RURAL INFANT MORTALITY RATES: EASTERN EUROPE AND THE USSR, 1946-1975   *66*

TABLE A-26 AGE SPECIFIC FERTILITY RATES: BULGARIA, 1946-1972   *68*

TABLE A-27 AGE SPECIFIC FERTILITY RATES: CZECHOSLOVAKIA, 1946-1972   *69*

TABLE A-28 AGE SPECIFIC FERTILITY RATES: GDR, 1946-1972   *70*

TABLE A-29 AGE SPECIFIC FERTILITY RATES: HUNGARY, 1946-1973   *71*

TABLE A-30 AGE SPECIFIC FERTILITY RATES: POLAND, 1946-1973   *72*

TABLE A-31 AGE SPECIFIC FERTILITY RATES: ROMANIA, 1946-1973   *73*

TABLE A-32 AGE SPECIFIC FERTILITY RATES: USSR, 1946-1972   *74*

TABLE A-33 AGE SPECIFIC FERTILITY RATES: YUGOSLAVIA, 1946-1972   *75*

TABLE A-34 TOTAL FERTILITY RATES: EASTERN EUROPE AND THE USSR, 1946-1973   *76*

TABLE A-35 PROJECTED POPULATION, BY AGE GROUPS AND SEX: EASTERN EUROPE AND THE USSR, 1980-2000   *77*

SECTION B: PARTY MEMBERSHIP

INTRODUCTION   *81*

TABLE B-1 TOTAL NUMBER OF PARTY MEMBERS: EASTERN EUROPE AND THE USSR, 1945-1976   *82*

TABLE B-2 SOCIAL COMPOSITION OF THE PARTY ACCORDING TO CURRENT OCCUPATION OR POSITION: ALBANIA, 1948-1976   *86*

TABLE B-3 SOCIAL COMPOSITION OF THE PARTY ACCORDING TO CURRENT OCCUPATION OR POSITION: BULGARIA, 1948-1976   *87*

TABLE B-4 SOCIAL COMPOSITION OF THE PARTY ACCORDING TO CURRENT OCCUPATION OR POSITION: CZECHOSLOVAKIA, 1947-1971   *88*

TABLE B-5 SOCIAL COMPOSITION OF THE PARTY ACCORDING TO CURRENT OCCUPATION OR POSITION: GDR, 1947-1976   *89*

TABLE B-6 SOCIAL COMPOSITION OF THE PARTY ACCORDING TO CURRENT OCCUPATION OR POSITION: HUNGARY, 1951-1975   *90*

TABLE B-7 SOCIAL COMPOSITION OF THE PARTY ACCORDING TO CURRENT OCCUPATION OR POSITION: POLAND, 1945-1975   *91*

TABLE B-8 SOCIAL COMPOSITION OF THE PARTY ACCORDING TO CURRENT OCCUPATION OR POSITION: ROMANIA, 1955-1974   *94*

TABLE B-9 SOCIAL COMPOSITION OF THE PARTY ACCORDING TO CURRENT OCCUPATION OR POSITION: USSR, 1925-1932   *96*

TABLE B-10 SOCIAL COMPOSITION OF THE PARTY ACCORDING TO CURRENT OCCUPATION OR POSITION: YUGOSLAVIA, 1948-1975   *97*

TABLE B-11 SOCIAL COMPOSITION OF THE PARTY ACCORDING TO ORIGINAL OCCUPATION OR POSITION: HUNGARY, 1951-1975   *101*

TABLE B-12 SOCIAL COMPOSITION OF THE PARTY ACCORDING TO OCCUPATION OR POSITION WHEN JOINING THE PARTY: USSR, 1927-1976   *102*

TABLE B-13   POSITION AND NUMBER OF PARTY MEMBERS WITH WHITE COLLAR
             OCCUPATIONS: CZECHOSLOVAKIA, 1958-1966   *104*

TABLE B-14   POSITION AND NUMBER OF PARTY MEMBERS WITH WHITE COLLAR
             OCCUPATIONS, POLAND, 1959-1973   *105*

TABLE B-15   POSITION AND NUMBER OF PARTY MEMBERS WITH WHITE COLLAR
             OCCUPATIONS: USSR, 1956-1973   *107*

TABLE B-16   POSITION AND NUMBER OF PARTY MEMBERS WITH WHITE COLLAR
             OCCUPATIONS: YUGOSLAVIA, 1964-1966   *108*

TABLE B-17   POSITION AND NUMBER OF PARTY MEMBERS WITH WHITE COLLAR
             OCCUPATIONS: YUGOSLAVIA, 1968-1975   *109*

TABLE B-18   NUMBER OF PARTY MEMBERS BY LEVEL OF EDUCATION: ALBANIA
             AND BULGARIA   *111*

TABLE B-19   NUMBER OF PARTY MEMBERS BY LEVEL OF EDUCATION: GDR,
             1962-1976   *112*

TABLE B-20   NUMBER OF PARTY MEMBERS BY LEVEL OF EDUCATION:
             CZECHOSLOVAKIA AND HUNGARY   *113*

TABLE B-21   NUMBER OF PARTY MEMBERS BY LEVEL OF EDUCATION: POLAND,
             1953-1975   *114*

TABLE B-22   NUMBER OF PARTY MEMBERS BY LEVEL OF EDUCATION: USSR,
             1922-1976   *116*

TABLE B-23   NUMBER OF PARTY MEMBERS EMPLOYED IN THE SOCIALIST
             SECTOR BY TYPE OF QUALIFICATION REQUIRED FOR THE JOB:
             YUGOSLAVIA, 1958-1972   *119*

TABLE B-24   NUMBER OF PARTY MEMBERS BY AGE: CZECHOSLOVAKIA AND
             ROMANIA   *120*

TABLE B-25   NUMBER OF PARTY MEMBERS BY AGE: GDR, 1947-1976   *121*

TABLE B-26   NUMBER OF PARTY MEMBERS BY AGE: POLAND, 1954-1976   *122*

TABLE B-27   NUMBER OF PARTY MEMBERS BY AGE: USSR AND HUNGARY   *123*

TABLE B-28   NUMBER OF PARTY MEMBERS BY AGE: YUGOSLAVIA, 1961-1975   *124*

TABLE B-29   NUMBER OF PARTY MEMBERS BY DATE OF JOINING PARTY AND
             LENGTH OF PARTY MEMBERSHIP: CZECHOSLOVAKIA, HUNGARY
             AND ROMANIA   *125*

TABLE B-30   NUMBER OF PARTY MEMBERS BY DATE OF JOINING PARTY AND
             LENGTH OF PARTY MEMBERSHIP: USSR, 1927-1976   *126*

TABLE B-31   NUMBER OF PARTY MEMBERS BY DATE OF JOINING PARTY AND
             LENGTH OF PARTY MEMBERSHIP: YUGOSLAVIA AND POLAND   *128*

TABLE B-32   NUMBER OF PARTY MEMBERS BY NATIONALITY: CZECHOSLOVAKIA
             AND ROMANIA   *129*

TABLE B-33   NUMBER OF PARTY MEMBERS BY NATIONALITY: USSR, 1927-1976   *130*

TABLE B-34   NUMBER OF PARTY MEMBERS BY NATIONALITY: YUGOSLAVIA,
             1957-1972   *131*

SECTION C: NATIONAL AND RELIGIOUS AFFILIATION

INTRODUCTION   *133*

TABLE C-1   NATIONAL COMPOSITION ACCORDING TO ETHNIC AFFILIATION:
             ALBANIA AND CZECHOSLOVAKIA   *135*

TABLE C-2   NATIONAL COMPOSITION ACCORDING TO LANGUAGE OR ETHNIC AFFILIATION: BULGARIA, 1934-1965   *136*

TABLE C-3   NATIONAL COMPOSITION ACCORDING TO LANGUAGE OR ETHNIC AFFILIATION: HUNGARY, 1930-1970   *137*

TABLE C-4   NATIONAL COMPOSITION ACCORDING TO LANGUAGE OR ETHNIC AFFILIATION: POLAND, 1931-1975   *138*

TABLE C-5   NATIONAL COMPOSITION ACCORDING TO ETHNIC AFFILIATION: ROMANIA, 1930-1977   *139*

TABLE C-6   NATIONAL COMPOSITION ACCORDING TO ETHNIC AFFILIATION: USSR, 1926-1979   *140*

TABLE C-7   NATIONAL COMPOSITION ACCORDING TO LANGUAGE OR ETHNIC AFFILIATION: YUGOSLAVIA, 1931-1971   *143*

TABLE C-8   NATIONAL COMPOSITION ACCORDING TO REPUBLIC: CZECHOSLOVAKIA, 1930-1970   *145*

TABLE C-9   NATIONAL COMPOSITION ACCORDING TO REPUBLIC: USSR, 1926-1979   *146*

TABLE C-10   NATIONAL COMPOSITION ACCORDING TO REPUBLIC: YUGOSLAVIA, 1948-1971   *156*

TABLE C-11   COMPARISON OF NATIONALITIES BY ETHNIC AFFILIATION AND LANGUAGE: EASTERN EUROPE   *160*

TABLE C-12   COMPARISON OF ETHNIC AFFILIATION AND LANGUAGE: USSR, 1926-1970   *161*

TABLE C-13   RELIGIOUS AFFILIATION: EASTERN EUROPE   *162*

TABLE C-14   COMPARISON OF RELIGIOUS AFFILIATION AND LANGUAGE: BULGARIA, 1934   *163*

TABLE C-15   COMPARISON OF RELIGIOUS AFFILIATION AND ETHNIC AFFILIATION OR LANGUAGE: HUNGARY AND CZECHOSLOVAKIA, 1930   *164*

TABLE C-16   COMPARISON OF RELIGIOUS AFFILIATION AND LANGUAGE: POLAND, 1931   *165*

TABLE C-17   COMPARISON OF RELIGIOUS AFFILIATION AND ETHNIC AFFILIATION OR LANGUAGE: YUGOSLAVIA, 1931-1953   *166*

SECTION D: EDUCATIONAL ATTAINMENT

INTRODUCTION   *167*

TABLE D-1   NUMBER OF ILLITERATES IN POPULATION: ALBANIA AND BULGARIA   *169*

TABLE D-2   NUMBER OF ILLITERATES IN POPULATION: HUNGARY, 1930-1970   *171*

TABLE D-3   NUMBER OF ILLITERATES IN POPULATION: POLAND, 1931-1970   *172*

TABLE D-4   NUMBER OF ILLITERATES IN POPULATION: ROMANIA, 1930-1956   *173*

TABLE D-5   NUMBER OF ILLITERATES IN POPULATION: USSR, 1926-1979   *174*

TABLE D-6   NUMBER OF ILLITERATES IN POPULATION: YUGOSLAVIA, 1931-1971   *175*

TABLE D-7   LEVEL OF EDUCATION OF POPULATION 25 AND OVER IN CENSUS YEARS: EASTERN EUROPE AND THE USSR   *176*

TABLE D-8   LEVEL OF EDUCATION OF POPULATION OVER A GIVEN AGE IN CENSUS YEARS: BULGARIA, 1934-1965   *177*

TABLE D-9   LEVEL OF EDUCATION OF POPULATION OVER A GIVEN AGE IN CENSUS YEARS: CZECHOSLOVAKIA AND GDR   178

TABLE D-10   LEVEL OF EDUCATION OF POPULATION OVER A GIVEN AGE IN CENSUS YEARS: HUNGARY AND ROMANIA   179

TABLE D-11   LEVEL OF EDUCATION OF POPULATION OVER A GIVEN AGE IN CENSUS YEARS: POLAND AND USSR   180

TABLE D-12   LEVEL OF EDUCATION OF POPULATION OVER A GIVEN AGE IN CENSUS YEARS: YUGOSLAVIA, 1948-1971   182

TABLE D-13   LEVEL OF EDUCATION OF POPULATION, ALTERNATIVE MINIMUM AGES: BULGARIA, 1956 and 1965   183

TABLE D-14   LEVEL OF EDUCATION OF POPULATION, ALTERNATIVE MINIMUM AGES: CZECHOSLOVAKIA, 1950 and 1961   184

TABLE D-15   LEVEL OF EDUCATION OF POPULATION, ALTERNATIVE MINIMUM AGES: CZECHOSLOVAKIA, 1970   185

TABLE D-16   LEVEL OF EDUCATION OF POPULATION, ALTERNATIVE MINIMUM AGES: GDR, 1964 and 1971   186

TABLE D-17   LEVEL OF EDUCATION OF POPULATION, ALTERNATIVE MINIMUM AGES: HUNGARY, 1949   187

TABLE D-18   LEVEL OF EDUCATION OF POPULATION: ALTERNATIVE MINIMUM AGES: HUNGARY, 1960   188

TABLE D-19   LEVEL OF EDUCATION OF POPULATION: ALTERNATIVE MINIMUM AGES: HUNGARY, 1970   189

TABLE D-20   LEVEL OF EDUCATION OF POPULATION: ALTERNATIVE MINIMUM AGES: POLAND, 1960   190

TABLE D-21   LEVEL OF EDUCATION OF POPULATION: ALTERNATIVE MINIMUM AGES: POLAND, 1970 and 1974   191

TABLE D-22   LEVEL OF EDUCATION OF POPULATION: ALTERNATIVE MINIMUM AGES: ROMANIA, 1956   192

TABLE D-23   LEVEL OF EDUCATION OF POPULATION: ALTERNATIVE MINIMUM AGES: ROMANIA, 1966   193

TABLE D-24   LEVEL OF EDUCATION OF POPULATION: ALTERNATIVE MINIMUM AGES: USSR, 1959-1979   194

TABLE D-25   LEVEL OF EDUCATION OF POPULATION, ALTERNATIVE MINIMUM AGES: YUGOSLAVIA, 1948 and 1953   196

TABLE D-26   LEVEL OF EDUCATION OF POPULATION, ALTERNATIVE MINIMUM AGES: YUGOSLAVIA, 1961 and 1971   197

TABLE D-27   LEVEL OF EDUCATION OF POPULATION IN CENSUS YEARS, INTERNATIONAL STANDARD CLASSIFICATION: EASTERN EUROPE AND THE USSR   198

SECTION E: CLASSES

INTRODUCTION

203

TABLE E-1   CLASS STRUCTURE OF POPULATION: ALBANIA, 1950-1973   207

TABLE E-2   CLASS STRUCTURE OF POPULATION: BULGARIA, 1956-1965   208

TABLE E-3   CLASS STRUCTURE OF POPULATION: CZECHOSLOVAKIA, 1930-1970   210

TABLE E-4   CLASS STRUCTURE OF POPULATION: GDR, 1950-1964   213

TABLE E-5   CLASS STRUCTURE OF POPULATION: HUNGARY, 1949-1973   *216*

TABLE E-6   CLASS STRUCTURE OF POPULATION: POLAND, 1931-1974   *220*

TABLE E-7   CLASS STRUCTURE OF POPULATION: ROMANIA, 1956-1966   *223*

TABLE E-8   CLASS STRUCTURE OF POPULATION: USSR, 1926-1979   *224*

TABLE E-9   CLASS STRUCTURE OF POPULATION: YUGOSLAVIA, 1953-1971   *229*

TABLE E-10   CLASS STRUCTURE OF ACTIVE EARNERS: BULGARIA, 1956-1975   *230*

TABLE E-11   CLASS STRUCTURE OF ACTIVE EARNERS: CZECHOSLOVAKIA, 1950-1970   *232*

TABLE E-12   CLASS STRUCTURE OF ACTIVE EARNERS: GDR, 1946-1975   *233*

TABLE E-13   CLASS STRUCTURE OF ACTIVE EARNERS: HUNGARY, 1930-1973   *236*

TABLE E-14   CLASS STRUCTURE OF ACTIVE EARNERS: POLAND, 1950-1974   *239*

TABLE E-15   CLASS STRUCTURE OF ACTIVE EARNERS: ROMANIA, 1956-1966   *241*

TABLE E-16   CLASS STRUCTURE OF ACTIVE EARNERS: USSR, 1926-1970   *243*

TABLE E-17   CLASS STRUCTURE OF ACTIVE EARNERS: YUGOSLAVIA, 1953-1971   *246*

TABLE E-18   MANUAL, NONMANUAL AND INDEPENDENT POPULATION: HUNGARY, 1949-1970   *248*

TABLE E-19   CLASSES BY LEVEL OF EDUCATION: BULGARIA, 1956   *249*

TABLE E-20   CLASSES BY LEVEL OF EDUCATION: BULGARIA, 1965   *250*

TABLE E-21   CLASSES BY LEVEL OF EDUCATION: HUNGARY, 1949-1970   *251*

TABLE E-22   CLASSES BY LEVEL OF EDUCATION: POLAND, 1970   *253*

TABLE E-23   CLASSES BY LEVEL OF EDUCATION: ROMANIA, 1956   *254*

TABLE E-24   CLASSES BY LEVEL OF EDUCATION: USSR, 1939-1974   *255*

TABLE E-25   MANUAL, NONMANUAL AND OTHER ACTIVE EARNERS: LEVEL OF EDUCATION: HUNGARY, 1949-1970   *257*

TABLE E-26   MANUAL AND NONMANUAL EMPLOYEES, LEVEL OF EDUCATION: POLAND, 1958-1973   *259*

TABLE E-27   MANUAL AND NONMANUAL ACTIVE EARNERS, LEVEL OF EDUCATION: USSR, 1939-1970   *261*

TABLE E-28   AGRICULTURAL POPULATION BY CLASS AND AGE: BULGARIA, 1956-1965   *263*

TABLE E-29   AGRICULTURAL POPULATION BY CLASS AND AGE: CZECHOSLOVAKIA, 1950-1970   *264*

TABLE E-30   AGRICULTURAL POPULATION BY CLASS AND AGE: GDR, 1950-1964   *265*

TABLE E-31   AGRICULTURAL POPULATION BY CLASS, AGE, AND SIZE OF HOLDING: HUNGARY, 1949-1970   *267*

TABLE E-32   AGRICULTURAL POPULATION BY CLASS, AGE, AND SIZE OF HOLDING: POLAND, 1950-1974   *269*

TABLE E-33   AGRICULTURAL POPULATION BY CLASS AND AGE: ROMANIA, 1956-1966   *272*

TABLE E-34   AGRICULTURAL POPULATION BY CLASS AND AGE: USSR, 1926-1970   *273*

TABLE E-35   AGRICULTURAL POPULATION BY CLASS, AGE, AND SIZE OF HOLDING: YUGOSLAVIA, 1948-1971   *274*

TABLE E-36   CLASS STRUCTURE OF THE POPULATION OF EASTERN EUROPE
             AND THE USSR: CMEA DATA   *276*

TABLE E-37   POPULATION BY TYPE OF ECONOMIC ACTIVITY ACCORDING TO
             INTERNATIONAL STANDARD CLASSIFICATION: EASTERN EUROPE
             AND THE USSR   *277*

SECTION F: PARTY LEADERS

INTRODUCTION   *281*

TABLE F-1   BACKGROUND OF PARTY LEADERS: ALBANIA, 1948-1976   *285*

TABLE F-2   BACKGROUND OF PARTY LEADERS: BULGARIA, 1945-1976   *288*

TABLE F-3   BACKGROUND OF PARTY LEADERS: CZECHOSLOVAKIA, 1946-1976   *292*

TABLE F-4   BACKGROUND OF PARTY LEADERS: GDR, 1946-1976   *296*

TABLE F-5   BACKGROUND OF PARTY LEADERS: HUNGARY, 1948-1975   *301*

TABLE F-6   BACKGROUND OF PARTY LEADERS: POLAND, 1945-1975   *305*

TABLE F-7   BACKGROUND OF PARTY LEADERS: ROMANIA, 1948-1974   *309*

TABLE F-8   BACKGROUND OF PARTY LEADERS: USSR, 1917-1939   *314*

TABLE F-9   BACKGROUND OF PARTY LEADERS: USSR AFTER WORLD WAR II   *317*

TABLE F-10   BACKGROUND OF PARTY LEADERS: YUGOSLAVIA, 1948-1974   *322*

TABLE F-11   ESTIMATED LEVEL OF EDUCATION OF PARTY LEADERS: ALBANIA
             AND BULGARIA   *330*

TABLE F-12   ESTIMATED LEVEL OF EDUCATION OF PARTY LEADERS:
             CZECHOSLOVAKIA   *331*

TABLE F-13   ESTIMATED LEVEL OF EDUCATION OF PARTY LEADERS: GDR AND
             HUNGARY   *332*

TABLE F-14   ESTIMATED LEVEL OF EDUCATION OF PARTY LEADERS: POLAND   *333*

TABLE F-15   ESTIMATED LEVEL OF EDUCATION OF PARTY LEADERS: ROMANIA   *334*

TABLE F-16   ESTIMATED LEVEL OF EDUCATION OF PARTY LEADERS: USSR
             1917-1939 and USSR AFTER WORLD WAR II   *335*

TABLE F-17   ESTIMATED LEVEL OF EDUCATION OF PARTY LEADERS:
             YUGOSLAVIA   *336*

SECTION G: OCCUPATIONS

INTRODUCTION   *337*

TABLE G-1   MAJOR OCCUPATIONS: BULGARIA, 1956-1965   *339*

TABLE G-2   MAJOR OCCUPATIONS: CZECHOSLOVAKIA, 1961   *341*

TABLE G-3   MAJOR OCCUPATIONS: GDR, 1950-1964   *342*

TABLE G-4   MAJOR OCCUPATIONS: HUNGARY, 1960-1970   *344*

TABLE G-5   MAJOR OCCUPATIONS: POLAND, 1960-1974   *347*

TABLE G-6   MAJOR OCCUPATIONS: ROMANIA, 1956-1966   *349*

TABLE G-7   MAJOR OCCUPATIONS: USSR, 1926-1970   *351*

TABLE G-8   MAJOR OCCUPATIONS: YUGOSLAVIA, 1953-1971   *354*

TABLE G-9   OCCUPATION AND EDUCATION: BULGARIA, 1956   *358*

TABLE G-10   OCCUPATION AND EDUCATION: BULGARIA, 1965   *360*

TABLE G-11   OCCUPATION AND EDUCATION: HUNGARY, 1960   *361*

TABLE G-12   OCCUPATION AND EDUCATION: HUNGARY, 1970   *362*

TABLE G-13   OCCUPATION AND EDUCATION: ROMANIA, 1956   *363*

TABLE G-14   OCCUPATION AND EDUCATION: ROMANIA, 1966   *365*

TABLE G-15   OCCUPATION AND EDUCATION, MAJOR NONMANUAL OCCUPATIONS:
             USSR, 1939-1970   *367*

TABLE G-16   OCCUPATION AND EDUCATION, SELECTED NONMANUAL
             OCCUPATIONS: USSR, 1959-1970   *368*

TABLE G-17   OCCUPATION AND EDUCATION: YUGOSLAVIA, 1953   *370*

TABLE G-18   OCCUPATION AND EDUCATION: YUGOSLAVIA, 1961   *372*

TABLE G-19   OCCUPATION AND EDUCATION: YUGOSLAVIA, 1971 (EMPLOYEES)   *374*

TABLE G-20   OCCUPATIONS ACCORDING TO INTERNATIONAL STANDARD
             CLASSIFICATION OF OCCUPATIONS: EASTERN EUROPE, 1961-1971   *376*

SECTION H: DEVELOPMENTAL INDICATORS AND THE STANDARD OF LIVING

INTRODUCTION   *379*

TABLE H-1   SELECTED INDICATORS OF DEVELOPMENT: EASTERN EUROPE AND
             THE USSR, PREWAR AND 1950-1975   *382*

TABLE H-2   INDEXES OF GROWTH IN NATIONAL INCOME: EASTERN EUROPE
             AND THE USSR, 1950-1977   *384*

TABLE H-3   ESTIMATES OF GROSS NATIONAL PRODUCT: EASTERN EUROPE
             AND THE USSR, 1960-1977   *385*

TABLE H-4   ESTIMATES OF GROSS NATIONAL PRODUCT PER CAPITA: EASTERN
             EUROPE AND THE USSR, 1960-1977   *386*

TABLE H-5   NUMBER OF PERSONS IN AGRICULTURE: BULGARIA, 1934-1965   *387*

TABLE H-6   NUMBER OF PERSONS IN AGRICULTURE: CZECHOSLOVAKIA,
             1930-1970   *388*

TABLE H-7   NUMBER OF PERSONS IN AGRICULTURE: GDR, 1950-1975   *389*

TABLE H-8   NUMBER OF PERSONS IN AGRICULTURE: HUNGARY, 1930-1975   *391*

TABLE H-9   NUMBER OF PERSONS IN AGRICULTURE: POLAND, 1931-1974   *393*

TABLE H-10   NUMBER PERSONS IN AGRICULTURE: ROMANIA, 1930-1966   *394*

TABLE H-11   NUMBER OF PERSONS IN AGRICULTURE: USSR, 1926-1970   *395*

TABLE H-12   NUMBER OF PERSONS IN AGRICULTURE: YUGOSLAVIA, 1931-1976   *396*

TABLE H-13   URBAN POPULATION: ALBANIA, 1923-1973   *397*

TABLE H-14   URBAN POPULATION: BULGARIA, 1934-1975   *398*

TABLE H-15   URBAN POPULATION: CZECHOSLOVAKIA, 1921-1975   *399*

TABLE H-16   URBAN POPULATION: GDR, 1939-1975   *401*

TABLE H-17   URBAN POPULATION: HUNGARY, 1920-1975   *402*

TABLE H-18   URBAN POPULATION: POLAND, 1931-1975   *403*

TABLE H-19   URBAN POPULATION: ROMANIA, 1930-1977   *404*

TABLE H-20   URBAN POPULATION: USSR, 1926-1979   *406*

TABLE H-21   URBAN POPULATION: YUGOSLAVIA, 1921-1971   *407*

TABLE H-22   HOUSING: BULGARIA, 1956-1975   *408*

TABLE H-23   HOUSING: CZECHOSLOVAKIA, 1950-1970   *409*

TABLE H-24   HOUSING: GDR, 1961-1971   *410*

TABLE H-25   HOUSING: HUNGARY, 1949-1970   *411*

TABLE H-26   HOUSING: POLAND, 1950-1970   *412*

TABLE H-27   HOUSING: ROMANIA, 1966   *413*

TABLE H-28   HOUSING: YUGOSLAVIA, 1951-1971   *414*

TABLE H-29   PER CAPITA CONSUMPTION OF SELECTED FOODS: EASTERN
             EUROPE AND THE USSR, 1950-1975   *415*

TABLE H-30   CALORIES, PROTEINS, AND FATS AVAILABLE PER CAPITA:
             EASTERN EUROPE AND THE USSR, 1961-1974   *417*

TABLE H-31   INDICATORS OF DEVELOPMENT IN THE FIELDS OF
             COMMUNICATIONS AND TRANSPORT: EASTERN EUROPE AND THE
             USSR, 1950-1975   *418*

TABLE H-32   INDICATORS OF DEVELOPMENT IN THE FIELDS OF HEALTH AND
             CULTURE: EASTERN EUROPE AND THE USSR, 1950-1975   *419*

APPENDICES

APPENDIX 1   DATES OF CENSUSES IN EASTERN EUROPE AND THE USSR   *421*

APPENDIX 2   DIVISIONS UTILIZED IN CLASSIFYING LEVELS OF EDUCATION IN
             APPENDICES 3 THROUGH 9   *422*

APPENDIX 3   CLASSIFICATION OF LEVELS OF EDUCATION: BULGARIA AND THE
             USSR   *423*

APPENDIX 4   CLASSIFICATION OF LEVELS OF EDUCATION: CZECHOSLOVAKIA   *424*

APPENDIX 5   CLASSIFICATION OF LEVELS OF EDUCATION: GDR   *425*

APPENDIX 6   CLASSIFICATION OF LEVELS OF EDUCATION: HUNGARY   *426*

APPENDIX 7   CLASSIFICATION OF LEVELS OF EDUCATION: POLAND   *427*

APPENDIX 8   CLASSIFICATION OF LEVELS OF EDUCATION: ROMANIA   *428*

APPENDIX 9   CLASSIFICATION OF LEVELS OF EDUCATION: YUGOSLAVIA   *429*

APPENDIX 10 COMPARISON OF INTERNATIONAL STANDARD CLASSIFICATION OF
             EDUCATION WITH STANDARD CLASSIFICATION USED IN THE
             HANDBOOK   *430*

APPENDIX 11 LEVELS OF EDUCATION IN THE SOVIET UNION AND THEIR
             RELATION TO THE STANDARD FORM USED IN THE HANDBOOK   *432*

APPENDIX 12 GUIDE TO NUMBER OF ACTIVE   *434*

APPENDIX 13 CLASSIFICATION OF SOCIAL CLASSES IN EASTERN EUROPE AND
             THE USSR   *437*

APPENDIX 14 EXECUTIVE COMMITTEE MEMBERS NOT ELECTED AT PARTY
             CONGRESSES: USSR   *443*

APPENDIX 15 ALPHABETICAL LISTING OF POLITICAL LEADERS INCLUDED IN
             SECTION F   *444*

APPENDIX 16 DATES OF PARTY CONGRESSES CHOOSING POLITBUROS INCLUDED
             IN SECTION F   *451*

APPENDIX 17 ABBREVIATIONS   *452*

BIBLIOGRAPHY   *455*

SUMMARY OF SOURCES   *467*

SOURCES FOR INDIVIDIUAL TABLES   *471*

The East European and Soviet
Data Handbook

GENERAL INTRODUCTION

I.

The East European and Soviet Data Handbook is designed to make available to scholars and other interested persons basic social science data on Eastern Europe and the Soviet Union, ordered in such fashion as to facilitate cross-national and historical comparisons. The time frame is the period 1945 to 1975, although relevant data from the period prior to World War II are also included, notably on the Soviet Union, and on nationalities in Eastern Europe.

The Handbook differs from others dealing with this area in that it presents data for all the Communist countries of Eastern Europe, and also for the Soviet Union.[1] Further, it includes data on subjects that were either incomplete or not covered at all in other texts. These subjects include party membership, social classes, occupations, and levels of educational attainment. It also provides data on political leaders. Economic statistics, except for national income data presented in Section H of *The Handbook*, are not included here, on the grounds that these are generally available in other sources.

A major objective of *The Handbook* is to give an overview of social change and elite development in Eastern Europe and the Soviet Union since World War II, with the data presented in such a way as to facilitate comparisons. With this goal in mind, tables are grouped according to the manner of presentation of the data, not by country. Within each table data are presented in a way designed to facilitate cross-national comparisons. Where possible (for example, in respect to levels of education), uniform criteria have been developed to make comparisons more precise. Cross-national comparisons of the data must nevertheless be made with care, as these introductory remarks will make clear.

Most data are presented as they appeared in censuses or other original sources. Corrections were made in cases where there were obvious and correctable errors in official data. In addition, in Section A it has proven advisable to substitute corrected figures for official statistics on the population in noncensus years in cases where the census data were published after the official estimates for noncensus years were made. Information on the backgrounds of party leaders was drawn from a variety of official and secondary sources, as well as from information made available to the author by individuals familiar with the personalities in question. Cases where official and nonofficial sources of information on party leaders conflict are indicated in the footnotes.

Every effort is made in *The Handbook* to inform the reader of the limits of the data and, insofar as is humanly possible, to provide guidelines to the data's use. Where the meaning of the data differs from that given by the categories in the tables, the footnotes will indicate this fact. Each section of *The Handbook* is preceded by an introduction containing comments on the type of data utilized in each table, and their comparability, as well as an explanation of the abbreviations for terms used in that section. Appendices provide additional information on such matters as the terms used in *The Handbook* and the manner in which data were presented in original census materials. Sources used in preparing *The Handbook* are listed in the bibliography, which is followed by a bibliographical essay dealing with the sources for each section. An explanation of the symbols used in the tables precedes Section A. Finally, the General Introduction is designed to aid the reader in evaluating the data and in appreciating their limitations. It also explains the terminology developed for use in *The Handbook*.

While the data are presented in as comprehensive a fashion as possible, the reader should be aware that the collection of aggregative statistics of this kind is an ongoing process; that the publication of *The Handbook* will undoubtedly reveal areas where gaps can be filled; and that there are certain subjects which, for reasons of time and space, could

---

1. Handbooks of data on Eastern Europe and the Soviet Union include Ellen Mickiewicz, ed., *Handbook of Soviet Social Science Data* (New York: The Free Press, 1973); John L. Scherer, ed., *USSR: Facts and Figures Annual* (Gulf Breeze, Florida: Academic International Press, 1978); Bundesministerium für innerdeutsche Beziehungen, *DDR Handbuch* (Cologne: Verlag Wissenschaft und Politik, 1975); Zev Katz, ed., *Handbook of Major Soviet Nationalities* (New York: The Free Press, 1975). The original, and in many ways still unsurpassed, handbooks on Eastern Europe and the Soviet Union are those edited by Werner Markert: *Osteuropa Handbuch: Jugoslawien* (Cologne: Bohlau Verlag, 1959); *Osteuropa Handbuch: Polen* (Cologne: Bohlau Verlag, 1959); and *Osteuropa Handbuch: Sowjetunion* (Cologne: Bohlau Verlag, 1965). Reference should also be made to CIA, National Foreign Assessment Center, *Handbook of Economic Statistics, 1978* (Washington, D.C.: GPO, 1978). For an excellent handbook covering the 1950s and 1960s in which economic data on Eastern Europe and Western Europe can be compared, see United Nations, Economic Commission for Europe, *The ECE Region in Figures* (New York: United Nations, 1972).

not be included.[2] It is the author's hope that the data presented here will in fact encourage the collection of further statistics in areas related to those presented in *The Handbook* and promote a more intensive use of the basic census data on which *The Handbook* is based. If the volume achieves no more than this it will have amply justified the effort involved in its completion.

II.

The data appearing in *The Handbook* present many challenges in respect to analysis and interpretation. Large gaps exist for certain periods, and the amount of data available varies greatly from country to country and subject to subject. Questions arise concerning reliability, including the possibility of outright falsification of the data. Problems also exist in respect to the use of the data for comparative purposes, given the fact that data are seldom presented in exactly the same manner, or for the same years, for the countries in question.

These problems are familiar to the users of Eastern Europe and Soviet statistics, and a sizeable literature is available on the dangers and pitfalls of the use of such materials.[3] These introductory remarks will therefore be limited to acquainting the reader with some of the general issues that arise in connection with the use of Eastern European and Soviet statistics, especially in respect to their availability and reliability.

The availability of data on Eastern Europe and the Soviet Union has varied greatly, from the almost complete absence of regularly published statistics in the Soviet Union in the 1930s, to the relatively large output of statistical materials in Eastern Europe and the Soviet Union from the late 1950s to the present. Variations exist not only in the quantity and quality of statistics, but also in the subjects they covered.[4]

2. Included in this category are statistics on the labor force by economic branch, population migration data, more comprehensive data on education and the standard of living, and data on career tracks of political leaders.

3. See Colin Clark, *A Critique of Russian Statistics* (London: MacMillan, 1939); Naum Jasny, *The Soviet 1956 Statistical Handbook: A Commentary* (East Lansing: The Michigan State University Press, 1957); Vladimir Treml and John Hardt, eds., *Soviet Economic Statistics* (Durham: Duke University Press, 1972); Hans-Werner Gottinger, "Sowjetstatistik im Rückblick," *Osteuropa Wirtschaft*, vol. 13, no. 2 (June, 1968), pp. 147–61; Wlodzimierz Brus, "To Count or Not to Count," *Eastern European Economics*, vol. 1, no. 1 (Fall, 1962), pp. 41–48.

4. The availability of statistics on Eastern Europe has been admirably covered in articles by Leszek Kosinski. See his "Statistical Yearbooks in East Central Europe," *Zeitschrift für Ostforschung*, vol. 23, no. 1, (March, 1974), pp. 137–47; "Population Censuses in East-Central Europe in the Twentieth Century," *East European Quarterly*, vol. 5, no. 3, pp. 279–301; and other of his works cited below. An excellent resume of the statistical literature on Eastern Europe has been prepared by Elizabeth

These gaps are apparent in the pages to follow. For example, data on the early years after World War II is generally scarce. Statistics on Albania are extremely limited. The last reported census in Albania took place in 1960, while statistical annuals were published in the late 1950s and 1960s but ceased to appear in the early 1970s. (In the spring of 1980 the preliminary results of a census held in January 1979 were announced by the Albanians. These figures are included in Section A, Table 1 of *The Handbook*.) Data on nationalities in Eastern Europe also show major gaps. The Poles have published only estimates of their minority population after World War II, while the Bulgarians have yet to publish statistics on the national composition of the Bulgarian population in 1975, the date of the last Bulgarian census. The 1970 Hungarian census results do not include statistics on the minority population. Data on occupations have been made available for only one of the four postwar Czech censuses, and exist only in incomplete form for Poland. Data on housing have been gathered in connection with most of the postwar censuses in Eastern Europe; in the Soviet Union, on the other hand, censuses since 1926 have not included statistics on this subject.

Furthermore, data may be selectively suppressed if they are thought embarrassing, or if they might reveal some unfavorable trend. A case in point is the failure of the Soviet Union to publish statistics on infant mortality rates since the figure began to rise in the early 1970s. Since 1959, no statistics have been published on the age of the agricultural population in the Soviet Union, presumably because they would reflect unfavorably on the age structure of persons employed in that sector. A more serious omission is the failure of the Romanians to publish statistics on literacy since 1956; the reasons for this will be discussed shortly. When examining the statistics on party membership in Section B, the reader will encounter selective omissions in otherwise complete data—for example, in respect to the number of party members. Presumably this is meant to conceal instances in which party membership declined significantly.

Obtaining published statistics can also be a problem. While all the countries included in *The Handbook*, with the exception of Albania, now publish statistical annuals on a regular basis, and in most cases also issue demographic annuals, census results are not always made public. When published they often have extremely limited circulation. For example, the results of the 1966 Romanian census are very difficult to obtain; for a number of years,

Marbury Bass. See her "East European Statistical Materials: Publications and Collections: A Report on a Short Term Survey Submitted to the Joint Committee on Eastern Europe of the American Council of Learned Societies" (Mimeographed, 1973).

no copies of this census were available in the United States. The results of the 1971 GDR census have not been made public, except in selective statistics published in East German statistical annuals, and in one volume which can only be found in the libraries of the statistical services of Eastern Europe. To the best of the author's knowledge, the final results of none of the three censuses held in Eastern Europe since 1970 (in the GDR in 1971, Bulgaria in 1975, and Romania in 1977) have been published, with the exception of the volume on the GDR mentioned above.

Problems also exist with respect to locating data on party leaders and on party membership. While *Who's Whos* are available for a number of Eastern European countries,[5] and biographical data on the Soviet leadership is abundant, other countries have published little information about the leadership group. This is particularly true of Albania, and to a somewhat lesser extent, Romania. In general, data on the background of the younger party leaders is more difficult to obtain than on the revolutionaries who became prominent before, or immediately after, World War II. The availability of data on party membership, meanwhile, varies greatly from country to country, and tends to decline for Eastern Europe generally after 1970.

Since data are made available by the East European governments to international agencies, such as the United Nations and the International Labour Organization, it might be anticipated that the statistics published by these organizations could be used to fill some of the gaps in the data just alluded to. Statistics published by the international agencies do in fact provide additional information on certain subjects covered in *The Handbook*. This is especially true in respect to the data presented in Sections A and H on population and on developmental indicators. In other areas, however, the reader will discover that the statistics published by the UN and other international agencies, included in *The Handbook*, do not exceed in quantity or quality those given in censuses and other national sources. Where gaps exist in national statistics, they usually exist in the statistics of the international organization as well.

The problem of the absence of data therefore remains a serious one, notwithstanding the vast increase in the publication of statistics that has taken place in Eastern Europe and the Soviet Union over the past two decades. At the same time, the amount of data that has appeared on Eastern Europe and the Soviet Union since World War II is impressive. Gaps in the data do not appear as serious as they otherwise might in the light of this record. Furthermore, not all Eastern European countries are reluctant to publish data. Hungarian,

Polish, and Yugoslav statistics, while not free of deficiencies, have generally been available in great quantities since the mid-1950s, and have not been affected by the cut-back in the publishing of data evident in other East European countries.

In concluding these brief remarks on the problem of the availability of the data, the reader should be aware that the gaps alluded to earlier do give *The Handbook* a certain temporal focus—namely, the period from about 1955 to 1970, during which the bulk of the census data and data on party membership made its appearance. Our ability to extend the data back in time is hindered in part by the scarcity of statistics, but also by the unsettled conditions surrounding the early postwar period in Eastern Europe, and of course by the disruptions of World War II. On the other hand, it is to be hoped that the unavailability of certain types of data from 1970 to the present is only a temporary phenomenon, and that the data appearing in *The Handbook* will in the future be updated, broadened, and improved.

The reliability and accuracy of the data presented in *The Handbook* vary greatly, depending on the subject matter, country, and time of publication. At one extreme, there exists the possibility of outright falsification of data. Western scholars working with economic statistics tend to discount this possibility,[6] and the evidence surrounding the data presented in *The Handbook* appears to bear out this contention. While the data may be presented in a highly selective fashion, there is no evidence in *The Handbook* of methodical and deliberate falsification of statistics on a large scale.

There are, nevertheless, isolated instances where the data appearing in *The Handbook* are not correct, under circumstances which suggest some degree of deliberate distortion. The most striking case occurs in the data on the national income reported for Romania, in the figures supplied to the World Bank by the Romanian government (see table H-3). More will be said about this in connection with the data in Section H. Also, data on the national and social backgrounds of several of the political leaders in Eastern Europe included in Section F appear to have been altered in official pub-

---

5. See the bibliography for a complete listing of these sources.

6. On this issue see the remarks of Peter Wiles in Samuel Hendel, ed., *The USSR After 50 Years* (New York: Alfred Knopf, 1967), pp. 65–66; Jasny, *The Soviet 1956 Statistical Handbook*, pp. 13–15; Nicholas DeWitt, *Education and Professional Employment in the USSR* (Washington, D.C.: National Science Foundation, 1961), p. 49, who quotes Abram Bergson that "despite many harassing deficiencies it seems that the Soviet government does not falsify those statistics which it elects to publish." On the other hand, we have the account of Antoni Gutowski, who claims that the statistical administration in Poland was forced to alter whole series of data to make them consistent with figures on personal incomes which the politburo had forced the statistical administration to accept. See his "Statystycy i statyści [Statistics and Statisticians]," *Kultura* (Paris), no. 4/271 (1970), p. 73.

lications; such instances are noted in the footnotes to the appropriate tables.

There is also the possibility of deliberate official distortion or falsification in the data on nationalities reported in Section C. A large share of the distortions that do arise in this data may be attributed to the bias of the census takers and the pressures put on respondents to report their nationalities in predetermined ways. Nonetheless, some of the statistics reported on nationality—both from before World War II as well as after—may indeed reflect an element of outright falsification. As an example, one could cite the results of the Yugoslav census of 1931, which reported nationality by language; members of the Bulgarian minority included in this census were reported as speaking Serbo-Croatian. One would also have reason to question the results of the Soviet censuses of 1959 and 1970 in reporting the number of Moldavians speaking that language as their native tongue—95 percent in both 1959 and 1970. In both of these cases, however, it is also possible that the central statistical offices did not alter the census results; rather, the data on nationality and language were already hopelessly biased by the refusal of the census enumerators to record answers which ran counter to official policy.

Most of the inaccurate or unreliable data that appear in *The Handbook* can be traced either to failures in the data-collecting process; to unsettled conditions prevailing at the time a census was taken; or to distortions arising from the misreporting of data to the authorities. When these data occur in the text and are liable to mislead the reader, the problem is indicated in a footnote or in the comments in the introduction to the section in question.

Examples of data that must be approached with caution because of unsettled conditions in a country are the 1946 census figures for the GDR and Poland. In both cases, large transient elements were present in the population; the censuses themselves were undertaken hurriedly; and conditions generally were in a state of flux. These factors influenced data on urbanization, and even the total population. The same could probably be said of the Albanian census of 1945, about which, unfortunately, we know virtually nothing. The Soviet census of 1939 must also be approached cautiously because of the unusual circumstances of the time, including large numbers of persons in forced labor camps not identified in the census results.[7]

Defects in census reporting procedures and in the classification of data in connection with the 1948 Yugoslav census have frequently been cited by Yugoslav census publications.[8] The data from this census are included in *The Handbook* with suitable warnings concerning their use. About other censuses, we know less. Because of alleged defects in implementation, the results of the 1937 Soviet census were never published, although the fact that the census reported a lower population figure than anticipated may have played a part in its suppression.[9] In Eastern Europe, the results of agricultural censuses conducted in Poland in the late 1950s were considered so unreliable that they were never made public.[10] Overcounting of the population may have occurred in a number of censuses reported in *The Handbook*. This criticism has been made of the Albanian census of 1930, the Romanian census of 1941, and the Yugoslav census of 1948.[11] Since the degree of possible overcounting has not been reported, the original data from these censuses are reported without change in *The Handbook*.

Other instances could be cited where defects in procedures for gathering statistics appear to have affected their reliability. The increase in infant mortality rates reported in Albania in the early and mid-1960s is apparently the result of improved reporting of vital statistics, suggesting that the true level of infant mortality in Albania in the 1940s and 1950s has been understated in Albanian statistics. In both Eastern Europe and the Soviet Union, population registers have not always been successful in keeping track of population movements between urban and rural areas, and in certain cases, notably Czechoslovakia in 1968 and the GDR up to 1961, in accurately reporting emigration abroad. As a consequence, official estimates of the total population between censuses and the distribution of the population between urban and rural areas have on occasion been in error. In cases where the countries in question have not issued revised statistics, corrected population data are supplied in *The Handbook*, based on estimates prepared by the Foreign Demographic Analysis Division of the U.S. Bureau of the Census (hereafter

7. An excellent discussion of Soviet censuses and their accuracy is contained in J. A. Newth, "The 1970 Soviet Census," *Soviet Studies*, vol. 24, no. 2 (Oct., 1972), pp. 200–22. On the problem of the reporting of forced labor in Soviet censuses, see the remarks of W. E. Eason, in Abram Bergson and Simon Kuznets, eds., *Economic Trends in the Soviet Union* (Cambridge: Harvard University Press, 1963), pp. 83–85.

8. On the 1948 Yugoslav census, see references cited below in respect to the overcounting of the population.

9. On the 1937 census, see Michael Roof, "The Russian Population Enigma Reconsidered," *Population Studies*, vol. 14 (1960 and (1961), p. 3.

10. Michał Pohoski, *Migracje ze wsi do miast* [Migrations from the Villages to the Cities] (Warsaw: PWE, 1963), p. 33.

11. See Andre Blanc, "Problemes de Geographie urbaine en Roumanie," *Revue Geographique de L'Est*, vol. 3, no. 3 (July–Sept., 1963), p. 307; Institut Društvenih nauka, *Migracije stanovništva Jugoslavije* [Migration of the Yugoslav Population] (Belgrade: Institut Društvenih Nauka, 1974), pp. 39–40; Stavro Skendi, ed., *East Central Europe Under the Communists: Albania* (New York: Praeger, 1956), p. 263.

referred to as the FDAD). Official estimates of urban and rural population for noncensus years, on the other hand, appear in *The Handbook* in their original, unadjusted, form; the reader should bear this in mind when using the data on urbanization in Section H of *The Handbook*.

These examples by no means cover all the cases in which the methods used to collect data appearing in *The Handbook* could be criticized, or found wanting in some respect. On the other hand, there is no reason not to accept the position that the statistical services of Eastern Europe and the Soviet Union, with the possible exception of Albania, are at a level at which errors in statistical procedures are no longer the primary source of inaccuracies that may appear in *The Handbook*.

Evidence of false or misleading reporting of data may show up in a number of ways, ranging from the misreporting of age in censuses, to the concealing of nonproletarian origins of party members or party leaders, or the false reporting of ethnic affiliation by minority groups. A well-known and oft-reported source of misleading reporting in the economic field in Eastern Europe and the Soviet Union is the tendency of economic enterprises and organizations to conceal information from higher authorities concerning economic performance.

There can be no doubt that some of the most difficult questions relating to the accuracy of data in *The Handbook* arise in connection with false or misleading reporting of information, whether it be given to the statistical organs, party organizations, or census enumerators. There are several areas where inaccuracies are apparent. Statistics on the nationalities given in Section C contain a number of examples, especially from the period before World War II, of data which have been falsely reported or distorted by the fear of the respondent to give his proper nationality.[12] A partial corrective to distortions of this kind exists in the statistics on religion, and in comparisons of the statistics on ethnic affiliation with those on native tongue. Such data, when reported by the census, have been included in Section D. There nevertheless remain a number of instances where the true size of a national group is difficult to determine from the census data, or where its number varies from census to census, not as a result of population growth or decline, but as a consequence of shifting official attitudes towards the nationality or minority in question, or the manner in which the question of nationality is posed. A striking example of this is to be found in the case of the Slav Moslems of

Yugoslavia, whose number has varied greatly in the postwar censuses as the official definition of this group has undergone modifications; this and other examples will be cited in the discussion of Section D to follow.

Data on social origins and class affiliation may also reflect misleading or distorted reporting.[13] In all walks of life in Eastern Europe and the Soviet Union there are important advantages to be gained from claiming working-class membership or working-class background. Thus it is possible that the number of workers reported in the class data in Section E is overstated. Further, by examining establishment statistics (for example, from cadre censuses), and comparing them with the results of population censuses, it is possible to ascertain that political and trade-union functionaries tend to report themselves as workers in the censuses. In reporting one's class for party purposes, the same tendency probably exists. Finally, in the data on political leaders in Section F, one can anticipate that there are cases where nonproletarian origins are not reported or are concealed.

How great a distortion is introduced into the data on social origins and class affiliation in *The Handbook* because of these factors is difficult to determine. Much depends on the detail with which data are presented, as well as how they were collected. Statistics on the social composition of the CPSU, because they are given in terms of class or status when joining the party, are less prone to this type of distortion than are statistics on the social composition of the parties of Eastern Europe, which are reported in terms of current occupation or status. In the footnotes to Section F on party leaders, several instances are cited where data on social background have been misrepresented in official sources, and more information would undoubtedly reveal additional instances. On the other hand, when data on social backgrounds are examined in conjunction with data showing levels of education, a fairly high degree of consistency emerges. Persons who report themselves to be of working-class origin are those, in the main, with a poorer education who joined the party as workers. There remain two categories, meanwhile, where social class remains in doubt or may not be correctly reported. The first is the group of postwar leaders who give no information on social origin; while the majority may come from working-class

12. On the problem in the prewar period, see Dudley Kirk, *Europe's Population in the Interwar Years* (Princeton: League of Nations, 1946), pp. 224–25; for the postwar years, see Robert King, *Minorities Under Communism* (Cambridge, Mass.: Harvard University Press, 1973), Chapter 5.

13. The problem has been discussed in a number of sources dealing with the Soviet Union; see, for example, Robert A. Feldmesser, "The Persistence of Status Advantages in Soviet Russia," *The American Journal of Sociology*, vol. 59, no. 1 (July, 1953), p. 23 and p. 27. For the problem of misreporting data on occupations and social origins as reported in an East German source, see Kurt Lungwitz, *Über die Klassenstruktur der Deutschen Demokratischen Republik* (Berlin: Verlag Die Wirtschaft Berlin, 1962), p. 129.

families, some may also be of nonproletarian origin.[14] The second category of persons whose social origins are suspect are those whose claim to a working-class background is not authenticated by concrete information on the occupation of the father, and who, at the same time, received a secondary or higher education before the war. The data on the Romanian and Hungarian leaders in Section F reveal a number of cases of such persons whose social origins must, as a consequence, be considered uncertain.

In respect to political leaders in Section F, there is also the possibility of distortion arising over the reporting of data on education. It was possible, immediately after the war, to receive a university degree or its equivalent in less than the four or five years normally required. Ljubomir Brokl has reported how, in Czechoslovakia, party officials were sometimes awarded a university diploma after only a year of study.[15] Cases of this kind, when they can be identified, are reported in the footnotes to Section F, and are ranked as "Higher Education, Political or Part-Time," in Tables F-11 through F-17, where data are given on the level of education of party leaders.

Data on levels of educational attainment of the population which appear in Section E and C of *The Handbook* are also susceptible to error as a result of respondent bias. Much depends in this case upon the care with which the census was administered, how questions relating to levels of education were phrased, and whether proof of completion of a given level of education was required. Since differences do exist in these respects among the countries for which data are reported, one cannot assume that the statistics on levels of educational attainment are completely comparable, either cross-nationally or over time. Some evidence of distortion in the data on education has been reported by the Polish statistical office, which found that there existed a tendency to confuse vocational and secondary levels of education at the time of the 1970 census, resulting in an over-reporting by some 15 percent of persons with a secondary education in Poland at that time.[16] Yugoslav investigations into the accuracy of the data on levels of educational

attainment recorded by the censuses, meanwhile, have shown that errors occur both in respect to understating and overstating education, the former error being more widely encountered in rural areas, the latter in more urbanized parts of the country.[17]

In conclusion, it should be noted that no one standard of accuracy can be applied to the data that follow, nor can a final judgment be made on the reliability of these statistics. It is a fact that the data presented here are, in certain cases, subject to manipulation or include distortions introduced by respondent bias and misreporting. Every effort is made, in the footnotes and the commentary that accompany each section, to warn the reader of these dangers.

Difficulties in the use of data are in any case not restricted to Eastern Europe and the Soviet Union. Whatever their possible shortcomings, the data published here are the product of statistical systems which are well established and which in several cases enjoy a long and respected tradition of statistical reporting. It is hoped that the present level of reporting and disseminating of this data will be maintained in the future, and that results of recent censuses will be published in as great detail as were those of the preceding two decades. Building on this foundation, the analysis of social statistics can become more and more significant as a tool for understanding social and political change in Eastern Europe and the Soviet Union.

III.

The manner of classifying the data in *The Handbook*, and terminology employed, adhere closely to Eastern Europe usage, or to international usage in the case of data presented according to international standard classifications. In those cases where the system of classifying the data is devised especially for *The Handbook*, an explanation is provided in the introduction to the relevant section as well as in the appendices.

Meanwhile, there are two areas where the method of classifying the data and the terms employed require special explanation. These are, first, statistics on labor force and classes appearing in Sections E, G, and H; and, second, statistics on levels of educational attainment, appearing primarily in Section D, but also in Sections E and G. Both areas are of great importance for *The Handbook*, and both pose special problems in respect to terminology and the manner in which the data are presented and compared.

Data on the labor force in *The Handbook* are primarily census results reported for the active population. (In certain cases, they are supplemented by

14. George Fischer, in his work *The Soviet System and Modern Society* (New York: Atherton Press, 1968), pp. 166–67, reports on a sample of first party secretaries in the Soviet Union who did not give information on social backgrounds in their official biographies, but on whom additional data could be gathered concerning their class origins. Out of 23 in the sample, 12 turned out to have nonproletarian origins (52 percent). In the larger sample with which Fischer was working, only 19 percent had nonproletarian backgrounds.

15. Lubomir Brokl, "Power and Social Stratification," *International Journal of Sociology*, vol. 1, no. 3 (Fall, 1971), p. 235.

16. Główny urząd statystyczny, *Rocznik demograficzny 1974* [Demographic Annual 1974], p. 28.

17. From conversations of the author with experts from the Yugoslav statistical office.

statistics on the civilian labor force reported by economic establishments on an annual basis.) Because national and international usage have changed over time, the question of how the active population is defined, and what groups are included or excluded, can be extremely confusing. Prior to World War II, the active group as reported in census data included many persons who were unemployed or retired, listed under their former or "usual" occupation.[18] After World War II, both international usage and Eastern European and Soviet practice changed, and the active group became divided into those who were economically active and those who were not. Presently, in international usage, all who are not active are grouped together as "not economically active." Included in this category are pensioners, dependents, and housewives. In the data reported in Eastern European and Soviet censuses, the population is broken down into three groups: those earning an income from work (active earners), those with unearned income (pensioners, students on scholarships, and related groups), and dependents. Those distinctions are reflected in the tables on classes in Section E, in which data on class divisions are distinguished from data on "Other Earners" (those with unearned income), and data on dependents.

There remain, nevertheless, great differences in the way statistics on the labor force are reported by the countries of Eastern Europe and the Soviet Union. Data on those receiving an income from work are identified by the Soviet Union as "Persons with Occupations"; by Bulgaria as "Economically Active"; and by Hungary as "Active Earners." In Poland this group is classified as either "Occupationally Active" (*Czynni zawodowo*) or as "Supported from Work" (*Utrzymujacy sie z pracy*). In Yugoslavia, persons with both earned and unearned incomes are reported as persons "With Personal Incomes." These differences in terminology are accompanied by different approaches to who is or is not included in the active group. The usual practice in Eastern Europe and the Soviet Union is to exclude the unemployed from those with incomes from work; however, Yugoslavia, following international definitions of the economically active, includes the unemployed with those having occupations. Those helping on private plots, and helping family members, are in some cases excluded and in others included with data on the active. In Poland, before 1970, the military was excluded from the data on the active, but since 1970, it has been included. Census data on the labor force in Poland are particularly confusing. They include, among

the occupationally active, pensioners with supplementary incomes, but exclude these pensioners from data on those "supported from work."[19]

According to United Nations definitions the economically active include the military, apprentices, helping family members, and the unemployed, as well as those with occupations.[20] As noted earlier, the remaining groups in the population, following international usage, are grouped together in the category "not economically active."

Footnotes to Sections E, G, and H, show which of the many possible approaches is being used to the data on the labor force.[21] In an effort to maintain a distinction between data presented according to international standard classifications, and that reflecting East European or Soviet usage, the term, "economically active" is used in this text solely in reference to statistics presented by the international standard classification of occupations adopted by the United Nations. Labor force statistics presented according to East European or Soviet usage, regardless of differences among these countries, are broken down according to the categories "Active Earners," "Other Earners" (pensioners and related), and "Dependents." To avoid confusion, the reader should bear in mind the following points: (1) Data on Active Earners are not always comparable; definitions of the Active Earners in Eastern Europe and the Soviet Union have changed over time, and differ from country to country; (2) Data on Economically Active, and on Not Economically Active, while restricted to labor force statistics published by the United Nations or the International Labour Office, may in fact reflect national usage and may therefore be identical to figures published in national sources; (3) Data on Active Earners may in certain instances correspond closely to the United Nations definition of the economically active, as in the case of Yugoslavia; (4) Data on Other Earners and Not Economically Active

18. For a discussion of this problem relating to prewar Hungarian statistics on the active population, see Alexander Eckstein, "National Income and Capital Formation in Hungary 1900–1950," *Income and Wealth*, vol. 5 (London: Bowes and Bowes, 1955), pp. 178–79.

19. In practice this category "occupationally active" prior to 1970 appears to have corresponded closely to that of persons "supported from work" after that date, disregarding the problem of the military and its exclusion from the data prior to 1970. This was because of the restrictive definition of persons with unearned but supplementary incomes from work which was in effect prior to 1970.

20. See Henry S. Shrycock and Jacob S. Siegel, *The Methods and Materials of Demography*, 3rd ed., vol. 1 (Washington, D.C.: GPO, 1975), p. 336; United Nations Department of Economic and Social Affairs, *Methods of Analyzing Census Data on Economic Activities of the Population* (New York: United Nations, 1968).

21. Footnotes and introductory comments to these sections also indicate which data are census data and which are data on the civilian labor force. The latter, it should be borne in mind, are establishment statistics, and exclude military and security personnel. Data on *zaposleno*, given for Yugoslavia in Section G, are census data from which the military, but not security personnel, have been excluded.

are not identical in scope; the latter include dependents while the former do not.

To aid the reader, Appendix 12 summarizes the manner in which data on the active are presented in various tables in *The Handbook*. The same figure, it should be remembered, may appear under Economically Active in one table, and under Active Earners in another, depending on its source.

Since the bulk of the data on the labor force appearing in *The Handbook* is given in the form of data on Active Earners, the reader should bear in mind the following: the phrase "active earners" is used here as a convenient way of covering various approaches to defining those who are active in Eastern Europe and the Soviet Union; it is used in conjunction with the threefold distinction between Active Earners, Other Earners, and Dependents in the data on classes appearing in the censuses of Eastern Europe and the Soviet Union; and, while its definition differs from country to country, it does, in the majority of cases, comprise those with income from work, including the military, but excluding the unemployed and auxiliary personnel working on private plots.

The terminology employed in *The Handbook* with respect to levels of educational attainment also requires a brief explanation. A major objective of *The Handbook* is to present data on education in terms of a single, uniform system, thus allowing comparisons to be made as to levels of education among the countries under study as well as comparisons of social classes and occupational groups cross-nationally and over time. In order to realize this objective, a standard form for measuring levels of education has been devised, based on Eastern European and Soviet practices in reporting data on levels of educational attainment. This standard form includes eleven categories and is used in Sections B, D, E, and G to measure levels of educational attainment both of party members, and of the population, classes, and occupational groups.

In addition, data on educational attainment are given in Table D-27 according to the international classification of levels of education developed by UNESCO; Appendix 10 compares the standard form used in *The Handbook* with the UNESCO system; and, in Section F on political elites, the standard form used in *The Handbook* is applied in a modified version to take into account the special problems of measuring and comparing elite levels of education (these modifications are explained in the introduction to Section F).

The precise relationship between the eleven categories used in the standard form and the classification systems used in Eastern European and Soviet census data in measuring levels of educational attainment are set forth in Appendices 3 through 9. The reader will also find it useful to consult Appendix 2, in which the complexities of the systems of measuring educational attainment in Eastern

Europe and the Soviet Union are simplified by identifying five major educational levels: (1) No Schooling and Incomplete Elementary Education; (2) Elementary and Incomplete Basic Education; (3) Basic School, Trade School, and Incomplete Secondary Education; (4) Secondary, Specialized Secondary and Incomplete Higher Education; (5) Higher Education. These categories are distinguished by dotted lines in Appendices 3 through 9, thus enabling the reader to understand better how educational achievement is reported in the census data. The first level includes persons with three or less years of education. With the exception of the GDR and Czechoslovakia, data on this category exist for all the countries of Eastern Europe. The second level, Elementary and Incomplete Basic, includes persons who have finished a four-year school, but have not received a diploma at the next higher level. This level in Appendix 2 is not reported in the census data on the GDR or Czechoslovakia, but can be identified in the censuses of the remaining Eastern European countries and the Soviet Union. The next level, Basic School, Trade School, and Incomplete Secondary Education, includes persons who have completed a basic school of seven or eight years, but have not received a diploma at the next higher level. It is this level of education which is now compulsory in Eastern Europe and the Soviet Union, and to which all classes and groups can now aspire. Persons with this level of education can be identified in the educational data for all the countries in Section D including the GDR, whose ten-year compulsory basic school is considered to fall into this category.

The fourth and fifth levels include persons who have received a secondary or higher education, respectively. The former category includes those who have graduated from basic school and completed an additional two to four years of secondary education. The latter category includes those who have completed their higher education, either at a faculty, a technical institute, a military academy, or some other institution of higher learning. By the time the student reaches the fourth level, he will have completed ten to twelve years of school, and will be 17 to 19 years of age. Higher education should, but often is not, completed by age 25. The number of persons with a secondary or higher education—almost all of whom belong to the white-collar class—can be determined in the census data for all the countries given in Section D.

In light of the preceding remarks, the more detailed categories used in the Standard Form for measuring levels of educational achievement should be largely self-explanatory. Two distinctions made in the standard form nevertheless require further explanation; namely, the difference between lower and higher levels of specialized secondary education and lower and higher levels of higher education.

The former distinction is used to differentiate

between those specialized secondary schools which grant a leaving certificate (permitting the student to enter the university, or at least certain faculties in the university), and those that do not. Notable among secondary schools in the first category are the German *Fachschule* and the Czech *Stredni odborna skola*, both of which are included in the Standard Form under Specialized Secondary, Higher Level. Elsewhere such schools exist, but are not distinguished from other types of secondary institutions whose diplomas do not entitle one to enter institutions of higher learning.

The distinction between the two levels of higher education is designed to accommodate post-secondary education received in institutions other than those of higher learning. Education received in this manner is classified as Higher Education, Lower Level. Examples of institutions offering this type of education are the pedagogical schools of Czechoslovakia, institutions of "semi-higher" learning in Poland, and the very highly developed system of "higher" schools in Yugoslavia.[22] It should be noted that practice in Eastern Europe varies in respect to whether persons with this level of education will be included in the census data with those having a higher education, or with those having a secondary education. The tables in Section D, meanwhile, are designed in such a fashion that these differences in approach can be identified in the data.

The classification of levels of education used in *The Handbook* attempts to simplify an extremely diverse set of educational experiences. The resulting standard form cannot pretend to set up exact equivalence in terms of years of education completed but seeks rather to compare common stages of the educational process. While the categories used in the standard form are flexible, and can accommodate systems of reporting data on education employed in all the countries of Eastern Europe, there are problems that arise when the system is applied to the Soviet Union. This is so both because of the way in which educational levels are distinguished in Soviet data—the seven-eight year school, for example, is referred to by the Soviets as "incomplete secondary"—and because Soviet higher education normally commences after only ten years of basic and secondary schooling. The Soviet student may therefore be entering the university at the same time the German student is beginning his secondary education. The approach taken in *The Handbook* is to consider higher education in the Soviet Union the equivalent of higher education in the countries of Eastern Europe; to do otherwise would create hopeless confusion when making comparisons between levels of edu-

cation in the Soviet Union and other countries. At the same time it was found necessary, if comparability of levels of educational attainment was to be maintained at lower levels, to arbitrarily choose one category in the standard form which would be considered nonapplicable to the data reported on the Soviet Union. This approach has been applied to the category of Incomplete Secondary reported in the standard form. In Section D and elsewhere in *The Handbook* this category is therefore not considered to have a Soviet equivalent. For those readers who wish to explore this matter further, Appendix 11 examines the problem of comparing Eastern European and Soviet data on levels of educational attainment in greater detail.

IV.

In the remarks to follow, the data presented in each section will be reviewed briefly in terms of their availability, reliability, and general suitability for purposes of comparison. Areas which seem to present no problem of interpretation will not be subjected to analysis. In the case of data drawn from United Nations or International Labour Office publications, the reader is referred to these sources for a more detailed treatment of the data and their method of presentation.

Section A

The data in Section A embrace basic population statistics for Eastern Europe and the Soviet Union for the period 1945 to 1975.[23] Total population, by sex, is given for prewar and postwar census years in Tables A-1 through A-5. Estimates of the population of Eastern Europe and the Soviet Union to the year 2000 are included in Table A-35. The reader should encounter relatively few problems in this section. The United Nations *Demographic Yearbook* has classified the population data from the postwar censuses as *de jure* for Yugoslavia and the GDR and as *de facto* for the remaining countries in *The Handbook*. In practice, the censuses reported in *The Handbook* appear to use a combination of both approaches. In the case of Yugoslavia, as the tables in Section A note, data on pop-

---

22. This type of education should not be confused with higher education first or second degree, which is sometimes used in connection with data on levels of educational attainment, for example, in the case of Poland.

23. The numerous studies of population problems relating to Eastern Europe and the Soviet Union need not be cited here. The reader is referred in particular to studies prepared by the FDAD cited in the bibliography, and to the outstanding account of demographic and population problems contained in the United Nations, Economic Commission for Europe, *Economic Survey of Europe in 1974, Part II: Post-War Demographic Trends in Europe and the Outlook Until the Year 2000* (New York: United Nations, 1975). Many of the problems encountered in using population data from Eastern Europe are discussed in Leszek Kosinski, ed., *Demographic Developments in Eastern Europe* (New York: Praeger, 1974). For the prewar period, see Dudley Kirk, *Europe's Population in the Interwar Years*, and the classic work by Frank Lorimer on the Soviet Union, *The Population of the Soviet Union* (Geneva: League of Nations, 1946).

ulation include those temporarily abroad, unless otherwise indicated. In using the statistics on Yugoslavia in Table A-14 (on population growth) and Table A-23 (on population by age group and sex), it should be borne in mind that the estimates for noncensus years are based on census data which include those temporarily abroad, and that the figures do not therefore accurately represent the number of persons residing in any given year within the boundaries of Yugoslavia. Also, as indicated earlier, census data on total population cited in Section A are subject to error in certain instances.

In Tables A-1 through A-5, the reader will note that an effort has been made to provide estimates of the population in postwar boundaries at the time of the prewar censuses. In the case of Czechoslovakia, Hungary, Romania, the Soviet Union, and Yugoslavia, these estimates are taken from official publications. The estimate of the population of Poland in 1931 in its present boundaries has been taken from a Western source,[24] no official estimates having been published. The estimate of Bulgaria's population in 1934 according to the country's present boundaries is the author's own.

Statistics on population presented in Tables A-6 through A-12 are adjusted official estimates prepared by the FDAD. Data on the population by age group and sex in Tables A-15 through A-22 are drawn from statistics published by the International Labour Office, adjusted to accord with midyear population estimates given in Tables A-6 through A-12, and supplemented by data from national sources for 1975 (1976 in the case of Poland). The projections included in Table A-35 were prepared by the FDAD; they are estimates, made in 1978, based on a "middle variant" projection of population growth for Eastern Europe and the Soviet Union.[25]

Data on infant mortality rates and on birth rates by urban-rural population have been gathered from national statistics and report the latest statistics available from these sources. Data on infant mortality in the Soviet Union, as noted earlier, ceased to be published in 1974; Murray Feshbach of the FDAD estimates that in 1976, infant mortality rates in the Soviet Union rose to 31 per thousand.[26] In making comparisons of the data presented in Tables A-24 and A-25, the reader should keep in mind that these statistics do not reflect uniform definitions of urban and rural areas. For the problems that arise in making comparisons

of data on urban and rural areas, the reader is referred to the discussion of Section H to follow.

The statistics on population in Section A are relatively complete and, with a few exceptions (such as the data on urban and rural birth rates and infant mortality rates) pose no special problems in respect to comparability. Nevertheless, these data must be used with care, keeping in mind that total population figures, even for census years, are not always completely accurate, and that improvements in the data are always possible (for example, in respect to the estimates on population by age and sex in Tables A-15 through A-23). In their totality, nevertheless, the data available are more than adequate to meet the basic needs of the social scientist, and serve as indispensable reference points for the data presented in the remaining sections of *The Handbook*.

Section B

In Section B the reader will find assembled for the first time data on party membership in Eastern Europe and the Soviet Union by social composition, age, nationality, and length of time in the party. (Data on the sex of party members are not included.) All data refer to full and candidate members unless otherwise indicated.

Because these data have been gathered from a number of disparate sources, including reports of party congresses, articles in party journals and newspapers, and statistical annuals,[27] there can be no guarantee that some of the relevant data have not been overlooked. Nevertheless, the absence of figures (indicated by the three dots in the tables) is in most cases a reliable indication of where gaps in the data do indeed exist.

The tables on total party membership, on age and length of service in the party, and on the nationality of the party members do not present any special methodological difficulties and can be passed over without comment. In using the data in Table B-1, the reader should keep in mind that party membership is limited to those 18 years and over, and in the case of Hungary between 1957 and 1970, to those 21 and over. These differences in respect to minimum age influence the ratio between party members and total population given in the table. It should also be remembered that data on the Polish party do not include party members in the military.

The data on the social composition of the parties presented in Section B have proven to be among the most difficult in *The Handbook*[28] to classify. Without some appreciation of these problems, seri-

24. FDAD, *The Population of Poland*, p. 75.

25. For population projections prepared by the Polish and Yugoslav statistical authorities, see Główny Urząd Statystyczny, *Perspektywy rozwoju ludności do 2000 r.* [Perspectives on the Development of the Population to the Year 2000] (Warsaw: GUS, 1973); Savezni Zavod za Statistiku, *Projekcije stanovništva Jugoslavije 1970–2000 godine* [Projections of the Population of Yugoslavia 1970–2000] (Belgrade: SZS, 1973).

26. *Wall Street Journal*, June 20, 1978, p. 20.

27. See the bibliography for a complete listing of these sources.

28. For a more detailed discussion of the problem of comparing party membership data, the reader is referred to the author's paper, "The Social Structure of the Communist Parties of Eastern Europe and the Soviet Union," delivered to the 1976 annual meeting of the American Political Science Association.

ous errors can be made in interpreting and reporting on the data.

The Handbook employs four major social categories in presenting the relevant statistics: Workers, Peasants and Collective Farmers, White Collar Employees and Intellectuals, and Others. These categories correspond to the classes utilized in Section E and elsewhere in *The Handbook*; the reader is referred in particular to Appendix 13 for a detailed description of these groups.[29] In using the data in Section B, it should nevertheless be remembered that party data on social classes are not always comparable to data on classes for the population as a whole, and that the presentation of class data on the party has been accompanied in several cases by manipulations, usually with the aim of increasing the share of workers in the total.

As an example of manipulation of the data, the reader is referred to the statistics in Table B-5 dealing with the SED (the German party). Statistics on the social composition of the SED have progressively included greater numbers of lower level white-collar employees with Workers. In addition, after 1966, workers on pension (placed among Others up to that time), are included with Workers. Since 1962 Hungary has lumped together all manual laborers (Workers and Collective Farmers) in the data on social composition by current occupation or position; then, in the early 1970s, pensioned workers were included with the newly designated manual group.

A further obstacle that presents itself in making comparisons of the data is the practice of presenting statistics on social composition of the party in terms of current occupation or social status, or in terms of occupational status at some other specific moment in time, usually when joining the party. In most cases, data presented according to current occupation or status will show a lower percentage of Workers and a higher percentage of Others (especially pensioners) than will data on occupation or status when joining the party.[30] If the data are

presented in terms of the party members' first, or original occupations, as in the case of Hungary in Table B-11, still another pattern will emerge in respect to social composition.

These differences in presentation of the data on the social composition of the parties are evident in Table I. The table, which gives data from the 1927 Soviet party census, shows that the number of workers in the party measured by current occupation was 343,147, or 32.3 percent. When measured by social class at the time of joining the party, workers numbered 599,111 or 56.4 percent of the total. In this case, less than half of the white-collar employees had white-collar occupations when first becoming party members. This was the result of the upward social mobility of worker and peasant party members into the white-collar group.

Appreciation of the importance of this factor— the moment used to determine class or occupation of the party member in statistics on the social composition of the party—is basic to the reading of the data in Section B. Statistics on the social composition of the party by current occupation exist for all the countries included in *The Handbook*, but in the case of the Soviet Union, data of this type ceased to be published in 1932. Since that time, figures for the Soviet Union have been published in terms of occupation or status when joining the party. As a result, the number of workers in the CPSU is greater, by approximately 10 to 15 percent, than if the data were given in terms of the current position or occupation of party members.

In the case of Eastern Europe, the Hungarian party has published data on the class composition of the party by original position, meaning the first job held by the party member, and also by current position (see Tables B-6 and B-11). The data on Czechoslovakia, Poland, and Yugoslavia are, it appears, consistently presented in terms of current position or occupation.[31]

The Bulgarian, Romanian, and Albanian data also appear, *in the main*, to be presented according to current occupation or status of the party member. However, it remains unclear to what extent these countries applied these standards consistently. In the case of Bulgaria, there is evidence of complaints by local party officials that party record-keeping involves freezing certain persons in the status they occupied when entering the party.[32] If this is true, an undetermined number of persons reported as Workers in Table B-3 on Bulgaria may actually belong in the white collar group. In addi-

---

29. The category Intellectuals has no precise equivalent in Appendix 13. As used in Section B, the term refers to anyone *so described* in the original source. Usually, it cannot be determined precisely what the critieria for Intellectuals are. The term is normally used in statistics on Eastern European social classes to refer to those who have completed a secondary education, or who occupy positions that require such an education (or its equivalent). Data on Intellectuals, in this sense, appear in Table B-23, on Yugoslavia, where those party members occupying positions that require a secondary education (not necessarily persons with this level of education) constituted over 47 percent of the party in 1972. In Romania in 1965, on the other hand, only 10 percent of the party were termed Intellectuals, suggesting a more restrictive definition of the term.

30. This is because party members who are workers when joining the party are often subsequently promoted to white-collar positions; also, as the labor force ages, workers with pensions begin to constitute a significant percentage of the party. On the other hand, a party in a predominantly peasant society will show a higher percentage of workers when current occupational status is used as a measure of the class makeup of the party.

31. There is some reference in the literature to the Czech party presenting data on social composition in the 1950s in terms of position when joining the party. These data could not be located and do not appear in the tables in Section B.

32. For evidence of this practice, see *Za nauchnost v partiino-organizatsionnata rabota* [For a Scientific Approach to Party-Organizational Work] (Sofia: 1975), p. 220.

TABLE I
SOCIAL COMPOSITION OF THE VKP(B), 1927:
BY CURRENT OCCUPATION AND OCCUPATION
OR SOCIAL POSITION WHEN JOINING PARTY

Current Occupation	Position When Joining Party				
	Total	Workers	Peasants	Employees	Others
TOTAL PARTY MEMBERSHIP[a]	1,061,860	599,111	195,608	237,912	29,229
Percent	100.0%	56.4%	18.4%	22.4%	2.8%
Workers	343,147	319,580	11,474	9,309	2,784
Percent	100.0%	93.1%	3.3%	2.7%	0.8%
In Industry	215,559	203,994	4,167	5,626	1,772
Percent	100.0%	94.6%	1.9%	2.6%	0.8%
In Transport	94,300	90,682	1,364	1,742	512
Percent	100.0%	96.2%	1.4%	1.8%	0.5%
In Agriculture	15,765	9,634	4,850	1,051	230
Percent	100.0%	61.1%	30.8%	6.7%	1.5%
Other Branches	17,523	15,270	1,093	890	270
Percent	100.0%	87.1%	6.2%	5.1%	1.5%
Peasants	116,169	10,128	103,241	2,167	663
Percent	100.0%	8.7%	88.9%	1.9%	0.5%
Peasant Landowners	88,392	6,427	80,673	928	364
Percent	100.0%	7.3%	91.3%	1.0%	0.4%
In Collective Farms	7,226	1,419	5,519	163	125
Percent	100.0%	19.6%	76.4%	2.3%	1.7%
Others	20,551	2,282	17,049	1,076	144
Percent	100.0%	11.1%	83.0%	5.2%	0.7%
White Collar Employees	438,832	184,184	56,070	187,746	10,832
Percent	100.0%	42.0%	12.8%	42.8%	2.5%
Young Service Personnel	28,777	16,182	3,375	8,128	1,092
Percent	100.0%	56.2%	11.7%	28.2%	3.8%
Artisans	5,466	1,672	1,690	166	1,938
Percent	100.0%	30.6%	30.9%	3.0%	35.5%
Students & Pupils	57,995	29,367	12,314	12,956	3,358
Percent	100.0%	50.6%	21.2%	22.3%	5.8%
Others	71,474	37,998	7,444	17,440	8,592
Percent	100.0%	53.2%	10.4%	24.4%	12.0%

Note: a Data exclude military and party members abroad.

Source: Vsesoiuznaia Kommunisticheskaia Partiia (Bol'sh), <u>Vsesoiuznaia perepis 1927</u>, pp. 22-23.

tion, an examination of the data in Table B-3 reveals that the number of Others in the Bulgarian party fails to rise significantly over time, a normal occurrence in parties in which the working class ages and workers retire. This suggests the possibility that pensioners who were formerly workers are still being included in the data on Workers in the party in a manner analogous to the German and Hungarian parties. In the case of the Albanian and Romanian parties, the high percentage of Workers recorded in the statistics on party membership raises questions as to how this group is distinguished from other social class in party statistics.[33]

33. It should be kept in mind that farm workers belong in the Worker category in party statistics and that the increase in the number of state farmers in the 1960s, especially in Bulgaria and Albania, is reflected in party

Section B also contains available data on the education of party members, and on the number of White Collar Employees who are party members, broken down by occupation, up to 1975. In the former case, the reader should be aware of the possibility that the criteria used to measure educational attainment in the party may be more lax than those for the population as a whole. Concretely, this could mean that data on levels of education of party members do not, as in the case of census data, measure the highest level of education actually *completed*, but rather the highest *attended*. The approach taken by *The Handbook* is

statistics by an increase in the number of workers in the party. This in itself might account for the large number of workers in the two parties.

to assume that the data measure the highest level of education completed, noting obvious exceptions in the footnotes. Even if this assumption is not always correct, the data do appear to be broadly comparable with data for the population as a whole, and also suitable for cross-national comparisons.[34]

Data on the occupations of White Collar Employees in the party are to be found in Tables B-13 through B-17. The classifications utilized in these tables vary widely, and are not generally comparable. In the case of the Soviet data, special care must be taken not to confuse the data on persons who were White Collar Employees at the time of joining the party with the total number of White Collar Employees in the party at any given time. The data in Table B-15 refer to the former group. Furthermore, because the categories of White Collar Employees and Others are lumped together in the Soviet data on the social composition of the party, it is impossible to derive an absolute figure for any of the occupational groups given in Table B-15. This fact has sometimes been overlooked by writers on the Soviet Union who have published absolute figures for the number of party members having occupations listed in Table B-13.[35]

The preceding remarks indicate the need to exercise caution in using the data in Section B, but leave open the possibility for making cross-national comparisons in cases where the data are presented in a compatible mode. The existence of gaps in the data is to be regretted. At the same time, the statistics on party membership are complete enough to allow some simple exercises in model building, in which factors such as age, time spent in the party, and social composition can be related to one another and to the data on the population at large. Combined with data on regional party membership (not included in *The Handbook*) the statistics given here could lead to a considerably more sophisticated view of the variables which determine a party's composition and size, as well as the role of deliberate party policy in shaping a party's membership characteristics.

Section C

Section C presents data on nationalities and religion in Eastern Europe and the Soviet Union. Data draw on both prewar and postwar censuses, and are given as they were published without ad-

justments or corrections. Estimates which differ from official census results are provided in the introduction to Section C.[36] In contrast to other sections of *The Handbook*, a number of estimates appear in the tables in Section C. These include estimates on the number of postwar Polish minorities and the breakdown of the Albanian population by religion. In the former case estimates differ greatly in respect to the number of Germans in the population in Poland after World War II. These figures are obviously influenced by whether they originate in Polish or German sources and must be approached with extreme caution.[37]

In evaluating the data in Section C, the reader should bear in mind certain shortcomings in the data. As previously noted, there are gaps in the statistics on the number of nationalities and minorities for the postwar period, while official figures, both from before and after the war, can be misleading and may in certain cases have been falsified. Even when such problems are not present, care should be taken when making comparisons over time of the number of nationalities, or minorities, in any given country. There are a number of reasons for this: (1) Nationality may be defined by language in one census, and by ethnic affiliation in another; the two types of data may not be completely comparable. (2) The definition of nationality or ethnic affiliation may change from one census to the next, resulting in a sharp increase or decrease in the number of the nationalities or minorities affected by this change. (3) The definition of language may be altered, with the same results. (4) The attitude toward national groups may change, with resulting changes in the number of persons who are willing to be identified with the nationalities or minorities in question.

The effect on the data of changes in the manner in which a nationality is defined can be seen most dramatically in the case of the Yugoslav Moslem population (Table C-7). In 1948, the bulk of this group were recorded as "Moslems Undeclared (by nationality)." In 1953, the majority of the Slav Moslems chose the category "Yugoslavs nationally undeclared" when registering their nationality. In 1961 they were permitted to declare themselves as "Moslems in the Ethnic Sense." Finally, in 1971, they were officially recognized as "Moslems in the National Sense." The elevation of the Slav Moslems to the status of a nation in 1971 significantly con-

34. The Yugoslav party is an exception, presenting data on the types of jobs held by party members according to the levels of education or training required for the job in question. This should not be confused with the actual level of training or education of the party member holding the job, which is often less than the job requires.

35. See Merle Fainsod, *How Russia is Ruled*, Rev. ed. (Cambridge, Mass.: Harvard University Press, 1963), p. 278; Abdurkhan Avtorkhanov, *The Communist Party Apparatus* (Chicago: H. Regnery Co., 1966), p. 88; Phillip Steward, *Political Power in the Soviet Union* (Indianapolis: Bobbs Merrill, 1968), p. 41.

36. For general discussions of the data on minorities in Eastern Europe and the Soviet Union, see King, *Minorities Under Communism*; Edward Allworth, ed., *Soviet Nationality Problems* (New York: Columbia University Press, 1971); and Leszek Kosinski, "Changes in the Ethnic Structure in East-Central Europe, 1930–1960," *Geographical Review*, vol. 59, no. 3 (July, 1969), pp. 388–402.

37. Kosinski has remarked that "It is nearly impossible to estimate the present size of the German minority in Poland. The result would depend on the criteria applied." *Demographic Developments in Eastern Europe*, p. 330.

tributed to the increase in numbers of this group recorded in the census data from 1961 to 1971. Another case in which a change in the definition of nationality may have affected the data is cited by Robert Lewis. In the 1926 Soviet census, persons were asked to give their ethnic affiliation or "narodnost." After World War II persons were required to state their nationality, that is, "natsional'-nost," a status to which the smaller ethnic minorities in the Soviet Union could not always lay claim.[38]

The results on the data of a change in attitudes by authorities towards a nationality or minority can be seen in the case of the Macedonian minority in Bulgaria. Table C-2 reveals that in 1956 the number of Macedonians was given as 188,000. The number dropped to 9,362 in 1965. The 1975 census reported that there were no longer any persons of Macedonian nationality in Bulgaria. Changing attitudes toward the Gypsies, the Vlachs, and the Jews have also affected their number in the census results for Eastern Europe and the Soviet Union.[39]

Comparing data on language is also not a completely reliable approach to determining the size of a nationality or minority and its growth or decline over time. Statistics gathered in this fashion may be distorted by the tendency of individuals to claim the dominant language as that normally spoken. Also, the types of questions asked in respect to language may differ, and may include reference to (1) the national language, that is, the language of the ethnic group to which the individual belongs; (2) the language which the individual grew up speaking; (3) the language of everyday discourse; and (4) the language or languages which the individual can speak fluently. "Native tongue," the most frequently used standard of language in censuses, should refer to the second of these alternatives, but can easily be confused by the respondent with the language of one's nationality, to which native tongue usually but not always corresponds. With certain exceptions, the Soviet and East European censuses, when gathering data on language, have used the criterion of native tongue. However, the Bulgarian census of 1965 reported data on the language customarily spoken; presumably the number reporting a minority language was slightly less than would have been the case if the criterion of native tongue had been used.

Table II gives data on the use of language of ethnic affiliation as one's native tongue in cases where this has been recorded in the census statistics. In the case of Bulgaria in 1965, the language "customarily spoken" is reported here. The data on Hungary compare native tongue to nationality as reported in several secondary sources; the exact criteria for determining nationality in this case are not clear.[40] As can be expected, the table shows a high degree of correspondence between native tongue and ethnic affiliation, except for those partially assimilated groups lacking a strong national identity (Jews, Gypsies, Vlachs).

Estimates of the total number of minorities in Eastern Europe are provided in Table III. The estimates can be considered only approximate because of the lack of up-to-date data, and because of the difficulty in estimating the number of semiassimilated minorities in the area, such as Germans, Jews, Vlachs, and Gypsies. The table gives two variants. Variant A is a minimum figure, based on official data for the early 1970s. Variant B is our own estimate for the mid-1970s which includes Gypsies, the Sorbs of East Germany, and the Pomaks of Bulgaria. As can be seen from the table, the greatest difference between official data and that given according to the maximum variant is for Bulgaria, which shows 12.1 percent and 23.1 percent, respectively. This is the result of the inclusion in the latter figures of an estimated 1 million Turks, 200,000 Macedonians, 200,000 Pomaks, and 500,000 Gypsies.

In concluding these remarks on the data in Section C, a cautionary word is in order concerning the data on nationalities by republic to be found in Tables C-8, C-9, and C-10. These data may understate the number of persons not of the dominant nationality residing in a republic in cases where a temporary work force made up of persons from outside the republic is known to be present. These persons may not be reported as residing in the republic where they are working. Evidence of this can be seen in the case of Yugoslavia, where it appears that the census of 1971 seriously undercounted those of non-Slovenian nationality residing in the republic—largely persons who were part of the temporary work force there.[41]

Section D

Section D assembles, for the first time, a complete set of data on levels of educational attainment

---

38. Allworth, *Soviet Nationality Problems*, p. 127.
39. The number of Jews in Eastern Europe is, like the number of Germans, very difficult to estimate. The largest number are to be found in Romania and Hungary where, in the mid-1970s, there were from 50,000 to 100,000 in each of these countries. The total number of Jews in the mid-1970s in Eastern Europe did not exceed 275,000. In the Soviet Union, Soviet estimates of the number of persons holding internal passports which identified the bearer as Jewish were, in the late 1960s, 3 million. This can be compared to the figure of 2.1 million Jews identified in the 1971 census. See Katz, *Handbook of Major Soviet Nationalities*, p. 364.

40. See the introduction to Section C for further details.
41. A special census of economic establishments in Slovenia in 1974 discovered that Slovenian industry employed about 100,000 workers from other republics, or 18 percent of the work force in the industrial sector in Slovenia. In the 1971 census, only 103,108 persons of non-Slovenian nationality were reported in the republic, including dependents and persons not working in the industrial sector of the economy.

TABLE II
USE OF LANGUAGE OF ETHNIC AFFILIATION
AS NATIVE TONGUE (in Percents)

Ethnic Affiliation	USSR 1926	USSR 1959	USSR 1970	Romania 1956	Romania 1966	Bulgaria 1965	Yugo. 1953	Czech 1970	Hung. 1970
Russian	99.7	99.8	99.8	...	92.1	...	...	...	...
Ukrainian	87.1	87.7	85.7	...	96.1[a]	...	...	...	...
Uzbek	98.1	98.4	98.6	...	...	...	...	...	...
Belorussian	71.8	84.2	80.6	...	...	...	...	...	...
Tatar	96.8	92.1	89.2	...	95.0	...	...	...	...
Kazakh	99.6	98.4	98.0	...	...	...	...	...	...
Azerbaidzan	93.5	97.6	98.2	...	...	...	...	...	...
Armenian	92.4	89.9	91.4	...	...	...	...	...	...
Georgian	96.5	98.6	98.4	...	...	...	...	...	...
Moldavian	92.3	95.2	95.0	...	...	...	...	...	...
Lithuanian	46.9	97.8	97.9	...	...	...	...	...	...
Latvian	78.5	95.1	95.2	...	...	...	...	...	...
Estonian	88.4	95.2	95.5	...	...	...	...	...	...
Tadzhik	98.3	98.1	98.5	...	...	...	...	...	...
Turkmen	97.3	98.9	98.9	...	...	...	...	...	...
Kirghiz	99.0	98.7	98.8	...	...	...	...	...	...
Jewish	72.6	21.5	17.7	22.0	11.0	...	...	...	...
German	94.9	75.0	66.8	96.2	97.4	...	...	...	14.9
Polish	42.9	45.2	32.5	...	...	...	...	...	...
Romanian	...	...	...	99.3	99.6	...	...	...	33.0
Hungarian	...	...	...	98.6	98.9	...	...	...	99.0
Gypsy	...	...	...	46.0	59.0	34.2	...	...	...
Serb	...	...	...	...	⎤	...	97.3	...	⎤
Croat	...	...	...	...	→93.3	...	99.4	...	→25.4
Slovene	...	...	...	...	⎦	...	98.8	...	⎦
Macedonian	...	...	...	...	...	4.8	98.5	...	...
Montenegrain	...	...	...	...	...	...	98.6	...	...
Czech	...	...	...	...	...	...	...	99.7	...
Slovak	...	...	...	...	...	...	...	96.3	16.2
Bulgarian	...	...	...	...	89.7	99.7	...	...	...
Turk	...	...	...	...	93.4	91.8	...	...	...

Notes: a Ukrainians, Ruthenians, and Hutani.

Source: Section C.

for Eastern Europe and the Soviet Union, classified in terms of the standard form devised for *The Handbook*.[42] In addition, Table D-27 presents these data according to the International Standard Classification devised by UNESCO.[43] Finally, Tables D-1 through D-6 present available census data from the prewar and postwar periods on the number of illiterates in the population.[44]

42. Among the many volumes on international education, several of which are useful for understanding data on educational attainment, are Nigel Grant, *Society, Schools, and Progress in Eastern Europe* (Oxford: Pergamon Press, 1969); Martena Tenney Sasnett, *Educational Systems of the World: Interpretations for Use in Evaluation of Foreign Credentials* (Los Angeles: University of Southern California Press, 1952); Dewitt, *Education and Professional Employment in the USSR*. For data on levels of educational attainment, see also FDAD studies on the population of Eastern Europe and the Soviet Union cited in the bibliography.

43. UNESCO, *International Standard Classification of Education* (Paris: UNESCO, 1976).

44. Data on literacy are available for Czechoslovakia for the prewar years but are not included in these tables. The data show that illiterates accounted for 7.1 percent of the population in 1921 and 4.1 percent in 1930. (For Ruthenia, meanwhile, the data showed 31 percent illiterate in 1930.)

TABLE III
ESTIMATED SIZE OF MINORITY POPULATION
IN EASTERN EUROPE (in Percents)

Country	A. Minimum Figure[a]	B. Maximum Figure[b]
Albania	...	2
Bulgaria	12.1	23.1
Czechoslovakia	5.7	8.2
GDR	...	0.6
Hungary	1.0	8.6
Poland	1.2	2.2
Romania	11.8	12.9
Yugoslavia	11.4[c]	12.7[c]

Notes: a Early 1970s; estimates based on official
census data and official definitions of
minorities. b Mid-1970s; estimates include
Gypsies, Jews, and Sorbs. c Includes
Albanians.

Source: Tables C-1 through C-7 and sources cited in
Summary of Sources for Section C.

Data presented in Section D are census data, and apply to the total population.[45] Data on levels of educational attainment of Active Earners have also appeared in census results, but are not given in *The Handbook*, except in summary form, in connection with data on occupations and levels of education (see Tables D-11 through D-18). All data refer to levels of education completed unless otherwise indicated.

The standard form used to compare levels of educational attainment has already been explained. It should be noted once more that this method of classifying levels of educational attainment, and the methods of classifying the data in each country from which the standard form is derived, do not attempt to measure and compare years of schooling, but rather stages in the educational process.[46] Because the educational systems of Eastern Europe and the Soviet Union have been reformed on several occasions after World War II, and because compulsory schooling has been extended to 8 years or more, it is perfectly possible for an individual who completed 7 years of schooling immediately

45. An exception is Table D-8, giving levels of education of the population in Bulgaria between 1934 and 1965. In the data for 1934 and 1946 the illiterate population is not included and must be added to the data given in the table to make the results comparable with other years.

46. An exception to this rule is the data on educational attainment for the GDR for 1971, which give data on those with 10 years of schooling, regardless of how obtained. All these persons, regardless of whether they were graduates of the present 10-year unified school, or products of a secondary school from before or immediately after the war, are classified as having a Secondary Incomplete level of education in Table D-9 and Table D-16.

after the war to be included in census data with the group of persons with a 7-8 Year Basic Complete Education, while an individual finishing the same number of years today would be listed as having received an Incomplete Basic Education. There are other apparent anomalies which result from the manner in which the data on educational attainment are recorded. Thus, no distinction is made in the censuses, in respect to those with a vocational education, between individuals who have completed a 7-8 year school prior to entering a vocational school, and those who have not. As a result, all persons with a vocational education are recorded in the census data as having completed a basic education, even though this may not necessarily be the case.

It should also be noted that distinctions made in the census data among levels of education at the postsecondary and higher levels are often minimal, and categories may, in fact, overlap. A Specialized Secondary Education at a higher level, such as in the German Fachschule, can last for three years and be the equivalent of a secondary education plus one year of higher education. Postsecondary education, or Higher Education, Lower Level, in the standard form, is very similar in terms of length of schooling to that offered in technical or pedagogical institutes, the completion of which may be considered the equivalent of a higher education at the faculty level in some countries (Hungary, Romania).

These examples illustrate the unavoidable complexities in comparing levels of educational attainment in Eastern Europe and the Soviet Union. As

TABLE IV
LEVELS OF EDUCATIONAL ATTAINMENT IN EASTERN EUROPE AND
THE USSR, PERSONS 15 AND OVER, 1950-1970 (in Percents)

Year and Level of Education	Albania	Bulgaria[a]	Czecho-slovakia[b]	GDR[c]	Hungary	Poland[d]	Romania[e]	USSR[f]	Yugo-slavia[g]
1950									
Illiterate	53.8	...	...	...	4.7	6.2	...	...	27.1
Level I	...	...		...	6.5	...	...	...	14.6
Level II	...	...	} 86.9h	...	68.3	...	...	...	45.2
Level III	...	...		...	15.4	...	...	...	9.2
Level IV	...	...	11.1	...	3.6	...	...	...	3.0
Level V	...	...	0.9	...	1.6	...	...	...	0.7
Unknown	...	...	1.1	...	...	...	...	...	0.3
1960									
Illiterate	...	11	...	...	3.1	2.8	10i	...	22.5
Level I	...	10		...	5.6	} 42.4	} 70	34	10.2
Level II	...	33	} 82.5h	...	58.4			30	46.7
Level III	...	31		...	24.5		12	21	15.1
Level IV	...	11	14.9	...	5.9	} 52.7	6	12	3.8
Level V	...	3	1.8	1.8j	2.4	2.1	2	3	1.5
Unknown	...	...	0.5	...	...	...	...	...	0.1
1970									
Illiterate	...	...	...	...	2.0	1.7	...	...	16.5
Level I	...	...			3.9	} 22.5	...	23	6.7
Level II	...	...	} 76.5h	} 82.2h	42.4		...	27	39.3
Level III	...	...			37.1	58.9	...	24	27.0
Level IV	...	...	19.2	14.9	10.9	12.2	...	21	7.0
Level V	...	...	3.3	2.9	3.7	3.8	...	5	3.1
Unknown	...	...	...	...	...	0.8	...	...	0.3

Level I - Incomplete Elementary or Less (less than 4 years of schooling)
Level II - Elementary and Incomplete Basic (4 - 6-7 years of schooling)
Level III - Basic, Trade School, and Incomplete Secondary
Level IV - Secondary and Incomplete Higher
Level V - Higher

Notes: a Data for Bulgaria, 1960, are average of 1956 and 1965 (16 and over in 1965). b Data for 1960 are for March, 1961. c Data for 1960 are for 1964, persons 21 and over. For 1970, data are for persons 18 and over. d Data for 1960 are for persons 14 and over. e Data for 1960 are average of 1956 and 1966. f Data for 1960 are for 1959. Data for 1970 are average of data for persons 10 and over and persons 20 and over. g Data for 1950 are for 1953; for 1960, for 1961; and for 1970, for 1971. h All but a small percentage completed Level III. i Estimate. j Data for 1964, persons 21 and over.

Source: Section D.

indicated earlier, Appendix A-11 explores these problems in greater detail. Clearly the approach taken in *The Handbook* to measuring levels of education is not the last word on the subject. Nevertheless, it should adequately serve as a basic guide to educational achievement in Eastern Europe and the Soviet Union, if used with care and in consultation with the original census classifications given for each of the Eastern European countries and the Soviet Union in appendices 3 through 9.

Direct comparisons of the data in Section D on levels of educational achievement are hampered by differences in respect to the dates on which the censuses were taken, the age groups for which data are presented, and the levels of educational achievement reported. Data relate to levels of education completed, and in this respect are compatible. However, not enough is known about the manner in which the censuses were conducted and how questions on educational achievement were phrased,

to rule out misreporting of the data. The Polish census of 1970, cited earlier, exemplifies the problem. Because respondents did not clearly understand the classifications used in the census, persons with only a basic education were sometimes reported as having had a secondary education, and this resulted in an error of 15 percent in respect to the size of the latter group.

In Table IV, an attempt is made to summarize the data on educational attainment for those 15 and over, using the five categories given in Appendix 2 and described earlier in the Introduction. The percentages are meant to serve only as guidelines and have been estimated from census data and age groups given in Section D which do not always correspond to those given in the table. The data reveal clearly how the more advanced countries of Eastern Europe have an advantage at the level of basic and secondary education (Levels III and IV) relative to the lesser developed countries.

The data also show the gains made in higher education in all the East European countries and the Soviet Union in the 1950s and 1960s. The percentage of the population with higher education in Eastern Europe and the Soviet Union has doubled over two decades and, in the cases of Yugoslavia and Poland, doubled, or almost doubled, in the course of one decade.

The data on literacy presented in Section D, Tables D-1 through D-6, are the most comprehensive yet assembled on Eastern Europe and the Soviet Union.[47] Still, the data have gaps, some of which have already been described. Albania has not published data on the subject of literacy since 1955, and Romania since 1956. Since 1939, data on literacy in the Soviet Union have appeared only for the age groups from 9 to 49. Data on literacy for the urban and rural population are often lacking, or are not available for the age group 15 and over.

In respect to the formal criteria used to measure literacy in Eastern Europe and the Soviet Union, variations in approach do not seem to pose any significant obstacles to comparing the data in Section D. Ability to read has been the measure of literacy before World War II and after. Following this approach, those who could read but not write, that is, the semiliterate, have been included among the literate population. Two exceptions to this rule are Yugoslavia and Bulgaria. In the former case, the test of literacy since 1953 has been the ability to read and write. Bulgaria has followed the same approach, except in 1956, when only the ability to read was required as a test of literacy.[48]

On the other hand, because of loose application of criteria for literacy, the number of illiterates may be understated, often by a very substantial amount. Where this is the case, and the extent to which it affects the data in Table D-1 through D-7, cannot be determined with precision. The Yugoslavs have been frank to admit that the census of 1948 gave a distorted picture of the number of illiterates in the population. No test of literacy was required at a time when reduction of illiteracy was being given a high priority. The resultant underreporting of the number of illiterates in 1948 can be seen in table D-7, where the number of illiterates shows no change between 1948 and 1953.[49]

Other cases of underreporting of illiteracy are less easy to document. The rapid drop in illiteracy in Albania from 1950 to 1955, from 67.0 percent to 28.3 percent, is certainly some kind of a record and suggests a high degree of underreporting in 1955. The fact that 1955 was the last year for which data on literacy were published for Albania tends to support this conclusion, for if more accurate data were gathered in 1960, and compared with the underreported data for 1955, very little progress would appear to have been made between the two censuses in reducing illiteracy. Soviet data for 1939 should be approached with caution, for they show an extremely rapid decline in the percentage of illiterates among those nine and over, from 48.8 percent to 18.8 percent (see Table D-5). Romanian data for 1948, and especially for 1956, appear to suffer from an undercounting of illiterates. This would explain the reluctance of the Romanians to publish data relating to illiteracy in connection with the 1966 census, assuming that these results would be more accurate than those of 1956.[50]

Although problems of reliability do make exact comparisons of data concerning levels of education among the countries of Eastern Europe and the Soviet Union difficult, the absolute orders of magnitude reflected in the data and summarized in Table IV seem to be sufficiently accurate to allow distinctions to be made in terms of the overall levels of educational achievement in these countries. Furthermore, these figures may serve as a guide to the progress each country has made in educating its population.

The data on education also serve as benchmarks against which the educational levels of classes, occupational groups, party members, and political elites can be measured. Cross-cutting comparisons of this kind may be made with confidence when they involve only census data; greater care must be exercised when comparing data on party members, or elites, with data on the population as a whole, for some of the reasons already discussed. Nevertheless, comparisons of the data, however incomplete, when considered in conjunction with all other available data, do serve as useful tools for analyzing the impact of education on the class structure, understanding the status and social prestige of specific occupations, and establishing the relationship between political and educational elites

47. On the problem of measuring illiteracy, see UNESCO, *Progress of Literacy in Various Countries* (Paris: UNESCO, 1953).

48. In the 1956 Bulgarian census, including semiliterates (those able to read but not write) with illiterates adds some 30,000 to the illiterate population, and increases the percentage of illiterates overall from 13.1 percent to 13.6 percent.

49. The extreme case of enthusiastic underreporting of illiterates took place in the Republic of Montenegro, where the percentage of illiterates fell from 56.1 percent in 1931 to 26.4 percent in 1948, then rose in 1953, and by 1961 still had not been reduced to the level reported in 1948!

50. It can be noted in this connection that literacy rates before the war in Yugoslavia and Romania were approximately the same, and were also almost identical in 1948, even though the Yugoslav figures for that year were overstated by a significant amount. By 1956 the Romanian level of illiteracy had dropped again, dramatically, to 10.1 percent, while illiteracy in Yugoslavia was over 20 percent. While overall levels of educational attainment in Romania do seem higher than those in Yugoslavia in the postwar period, the possibility that the difference in levels of illiteracy between the two countries is the result of underreporting in Romania in 1956 cannot be excluded.

in Eastern Europe and the Soviet Union. The data on education of the population should not, then, be considered in isolation from the data in the remainder of *The Handbook* with which they are closely related, and in combination with which they gain their full significance.

Section E

Section E presents data on the population according to class distinctions, as these are recorded in Eastern European and Soviet censuses. Data on class by level of education are also included, as are data on the agricultural population by class, age, and size of holding.

This is the first occasion on which a data handbook on either Eastern Europe or the Soviet Union has included extensive statistics on classes.[51] While there are gaps in the data and problems in respect to the manner in which class divisions are defined, the statistics appearing in Section E do give a broad picture of the social structure of Eastern Europe and the Soviet Union, as well as illustrate the changes that have taken place in the class structure of the countries of the area since World War II.

Tables E-1 through E-9 present statistics on the total population and its class composition. In these tables a distinction is made between Active Earners, Other Earners, and Dependents. Data on class divisions in these tables may relate to the population as a whole, to Active Earners and their dependents, or to Active Earners alone; these differences are indicated in the column headings. This method of presenting the data corresponds to that followed in the censuses in Eastern Europe and the Soviet Union. By following this approach, the comparability of the data is enhanced (similar types of data may be grouped together), and data are provided for the categories of Other Earners (pensioners, students with scholarships, and related groups) and Dependents.

It should be noted that distinctions between the Active Earners and Other Earners, discussed earlier,

apply to Section E. Thus the data on Active Earners may include or exclude helping family members, apprentices, or even the military, depending on the definition of Active Earners being followed in the census in question. This in turn will affect the distribution of the population in the tables in Section E between Active Earners and Other Earners. Thus in Table E-8 on the Soviet Union, members of families of collective farmers, workers, and employees tending private plots in agriculture are included among the dependent population in accordance with Soviet census practices; this in turn affects the number and distribution among classes of the Active Earners for the census years in question. In Table E-27, on the other hand, an effort is made to order all the data in accord with the International Standard Classification of Occupations; in this case, helping family members, apprentices, and family members tending private plots are included among the economically active. This is also the approach taken in Table H-11 on the size of the agricultural population, discussed below.

The basic class divisions used in Eastern European and Soviet censuses are broad and, on occasion, have been flexibly applied, particularly the distinction between Workers and Other Employees. A striking example of this is the data in Table E-3 on Czechoslovakia, where statistics on the total population according to class for 1950 are given in two variants. In the first, Workers make up 56.4 percent of the population and Other Employees, 16.4 percent. In the second variant for the same year Workers account for 46 percent of the population and Other Employees, 22.6 percent.

The extreme example of Czechoslovakia in 1950 notwithstanding, the class distinctions reported in the censuses in Eastern Europe and the Soviet Union are not totally arbitrary. In all cases, manual workers employed in the socialist sector, regardless of branch, are classified as Workers, while nonmanual employees in the socialist sector are placed in a separate category, here referred to as Other Employees. In addition, distinctions are normally made between Collective Farmers, Private Peasantry, "Capitalist Classes," those in the free professions, and Artisans on their Own Account. These basic class divisions appear in all the statistics reported in Section E with the exception of Yugoslavia, where the censuses have reported on "Position in Occupation," which is restricted to Active Earners or Active Earners and their Dependents. (The categories used when reporting on Position in Occupation can be seen by examining Table E-9 on the class composition of the Yugoslav population). A brief description of the composition of these basic classes can be found in the introduction to Section E, while Appendix 13 gives the original census classifications appearing in Eastern Europe and Soviet sources and their equivalent as they are given in Section E.

51. There is a growing literature on classes in Eastern Europe and the Soviet Union. Among those useful for understanding the data in Section E may be cited Cyril Black, ed., *The Transformation of Russian Society* (Cambridge, Mass.: Harvard University Press, 1967); Miloslav Janićijević, ed., *Promene klasne strukture savremenog jugoslovenskog društva* [Changes in the Class Structure of Contemporary Yugoslav Society] (Belgrade: JUS, 1967); Jaroslav Krejci, *Social Change and Stratification in Postwar Czechoslovakia* (New York: Columbia University Press, 1972); Lungwitz, *Über die Klassenstruktur*; Pavel Machonin, ed., *Československá společnost* [Czechoslovak Society] (Bratislava: Epocha, 1969); Adam Sarapata, ed., *Przemiany społeczne w Polsce Ludowej* [Social Change in Peoples' Poland] (Warsaw: PWN, 1969); S. L. Seniavskii, *Izmeniia v stosial'noi strukture sovetskogo obshchestva 1938-1970* [Changes in the Social Structure of Soviet Society 1938-1970] (Moscow: Mysl', 1973); D. Storbeck, *Soziale Strukturen in Mitteldeutschland* (Berlin: Duncker and Humblot, 1964); Zdeněk Valenta, *Fyzická a duševní práce za socialismu* [Physical and Mental Work in Socialism] (Prague: Nakladatelství Politické, 1965).

Of all the class distinctions appearing in Section E, that between Workers and Other Employees is certainly the hardest to draw, if also the most interesting for purposes of analysis and comparison. The basis of this difference rests, as just indicated, on the distinction between manual and nonmanual occupations (or to use the East European and Soviet terms, mental and physical work). How this distinction is drawn varies from country to country, and is often not clear in the explanations that accompany census statistics. In some cases the distinction clearly rests on the difference between salaried employees and wage workers. Thus, in the case of Poland, a truck driver receiving a salary (possibly because of employment in a state security institution) would be classified as a nonmanual employee, while a technician, or any professional person, receiving a wage would be placed in the group of manual workers (a very rare occurrence). In other cases, including the Soviet Union and Bulgaria, the distinction between manual and nonmanual employees for the purposes of the census appears to be based on classifications of occupations used primarily in connection with the gathering of census data. In these occupational classification systems, all jobs are identified as either manual or nonmanual, and persons are assigned either to the class of Workers or Other Employees[52] on the basis of whether their occupations fall into the first or second of these categories.

In still other countries, the distinction between Workers and Other Employees has been dropped entirely. This is true of the GDR and Yugoslavia. In the former case a new class, that of the Intelligentsia, appears in the census data for 1964, while all other employees, both manual and nonmanual, are placed in the category of Workers.[53]

In using the data on Workers and on Other Employees the reader should also remember that East European and Soviet practice is to include agricultural workers in the working class, while nonmanual workers in the collective farm sector are excluded from the category of Other Employees. (Other Employees may, to repeat, include a number of persons with manual occupations in establishments concerned with security, or defense.) The number of persons classified as workers is therefore influenced by the number of persons employed as agriculturalists on state farms, and this number has grown as collective farms have been transformed into state farms in Eastern Europe and the Soviet Union. In order to determine the importance of state farmers in the growth of the working class, it is necessary to refer to the data provided in Tables E-10 through E-17, which give data on Active Earners by class, broken down by occupation and branch. Further data are provided in Tables E-28 through E-35 on the number of workers in agriculture and their dependents; these data can be used in conjunction with those in Tables E-2 through E-9 to calculate the size of the working class outside the agricultural sector if so desired.

Data on manual and nonmanual earners appear in Tables E-18, and E-25 through E-27. In these tables, class distinctions are ignored and all persons with the exception of Independents (those with their own source of income) are grouped according to their occupations into the manual or nonmanual categories. The nonmanual category, in this case, corresponds closely to what might be considered white collar employees in a broader sense, including both collective farm members and persons employed in the socialist sector with nonmanual occupations. The manual category includes both workers and peasants who are not in the private sector. (In examining these tables, it should be remembered that the very valuable data on manual and nonmanual employees in Poland given in table E-26 are not census data but rather data on the civilian labor force, drawn from establishment statistics and relating only to the socialist sector.)

Data on the agricultural population in tables E-28 through E-37 are largely self-explanatory, and do not require extended comment. It should be noted that the total number of agriculturalists is a *branch* figure, including different social groups, and that this branch figure is in turn not always the same as that given for the agricultural population in Section H, where data on Active Earners include apprentices, helping family members, and family members working on private plots.

The data on classes are subject to criticism on the grounds that they do not accurately delineate the class structure of Eastern Europe and the Soviet Union, that the basis of class distinctions remains unclear in certain cases, or that the data themselves are not always accurately reported. Obviously, in the light of the uncertainty which surrounds the distinction between manual and nonmanual categories, it would be unwise to compare absolute magnitudes in respect to Workers and Other Employees, except in general terms. The measurement of trends over time must also be approached care-

52. The term Other Employees is used in *The Handbook* to avoid giving the impression that the category is restricted solely to white-collar employees (see the discussion to follow). The Soviet term *sluzhashchie* (or its East European equivalent) has also been avoided because of its misleading connotation, in translation, as "official."

53. See Lungwitz, *Über die Klassenstruktur*, p. 125, for a discussion of the class of Intelligentsia. It appears, from this discussion, that the group includes all white-collar workers with at least a secondary education or higher, or white-collar workers in positions which require such a level of education. Lungwitz, p. 39, also reveals that the distinction between manual and nonmanual workers in the GDR is, as in Poland, based on the distinction between salaried and wage employees. In a trial census in the late 1950s, it was determined that of a total of 180,872 persons queried, 141,686 belonged in the category of employees; of these, 109,541 were workers and the remaining were white-collar employees (that is, salaried employees).

fully and with reference to groups, such as state farmers, whose transfer from one class to another can influence the data significantly.

Nevertheless the data, with all their shortcomings, provide a picture of the social structure of Eastern Europe and the Soviet Union in which basic class differences can be distinguished and measured, especially when combined with the data on education and class given in Section E, and the data on occupations and education presented elsewhere in *The Handbook*. It should be noted that while the categories used by each country differ in detail, they follow a similar approach in broad outline, and that, while the data may include a degree of respondent bias, the possibilities for distortions in this respect are fewer than in the case of data reported on a number of other subjects, especially nationalities. Comparisons can even be made between the number of manual and nonmanual employees in different countries if care is taken to limit the comparison to those cases where all occupations are divided into one or the other of these two categories, and points of divergence between the censuses in question can be established, using the data on manual and nonmanual occupations given in Section G.

The reader should also be aware that the data in Section E can be supplemented by other types of data, not presented in *The Handbook*, in order to gain a more complete picture of the class structure of Eastern Europe and the Soviet Union. Additional sources of data include labor force statistics (including data on persons with pensions), sample survey data on income differences where available, and data on social mobility and occupational prestige. Many of those data have been analyzed by Western scholars[54] and serve as indispensable complements to the census data presented in Section E.

Section F

Section F includes data on age, nationality, and other background characteristics of party leaders. Tables F-1 through F-10, in which data are coded for individual party leaders, are supplemented by Tables F-11 through F-17, in which estimates of levels of education are aggregated according to those Executive Committees chosen for comparison in the first ten tables of the section.[55]

The criterion for party leadership chosen for Section F is membership in the leading decision-making body of the party, referred to here as the

Executive Committee, regardless of its actual name (Executive Committee, Politburo, or Presidium). Only those persons are included in Section F who were members of the Executive Committee at the times indicated at the bottom of each table—normally, the date of the election of the Executive Committee by a party congress. If an individual served only briefly on the Executive Committee—more precisely for a period of time between any two of the dates utilized in the tables—he will not appear in the list of Executive Committee members. With the exception of the Soviet Union prior to 1952, and Hungary and Czechoslovakia during their respective revolutions in 1956 and 1968, the number of Executive Committee members excluded in this fashion is minimal.[56] Data for Soviet politburo members not elected at party congresses prior to 1952 is given in Appendix 14.

For most of the countries studied in Section F, it is relatively clear which organ should be considered the leading decision-making body of the party. However, in the case of the Yugoslav League of Communists, there is some question as to whether the Executive Committee or the broader Presidium is the real decision-making group. This problem has been solved by including party leaders belonging to both bodies in Table F-10.[57]

In respect to order of appearance, Executive Committee members are listed according to the Executive Committee in which they first appear. Within each Executive Committee, they are listed alphabetically, with full members preceding candidate members. For a full list of the political leaders appearing in Section F, arranged in alphabetical order, the reader is referred to Appendix 15.

Analysis of the material appearing in Section F is sometimes difficult because of problems relating to reliability and coding of data. Not all issues can be addressed here; several words on these subjects will nevertheless assist the reader in the use of the data.

The manner in which the data are coded is explained in the introduction to Section F. Most of the twelve columns in which the data are presented in Tables F-1 through F-10 are self-explanatory. However, the very important entries dealing with formal education and advanced training (columns 6 and 7), as well as the entries dealing with status prior to party work (column 5) and revolutionary type (column 9) require some explanation.

The data in columns 6 and 7 on education distinguish between formal education received on a

54. See, for example, Walter D. Connor, *Socialism, Politics, and Equality* (New York: Columbia University Press, 1979).

55. For a better understanding of the problems of comparative elite analysis, the reader is referred to Carl Beck et al, *Comparative Communist Political Leadership* (New York: David McKay, 1973); George Fischer, *The Soviet System and Modern Society*; Federic Fleron, ed., *Communist Studies and the Social Sciences* (Chicago: Rand McNally, 1969).

56. Omitting such persons was necessitated by the difficulty of confirming precisely who was a member, and especially a candidate member, of the Executive Committees in Eastern Europe between the congresses of the party.

57. The October, 1952, Soviet Executive Committee is the "Bureau" of the Presidium of the CPSU as reconstructed by Robert Conquest, no official list of persons in this body having been published.

full-time basis, and other types of educational experience, which are here included under advanced training. In contrast to some elite studies, column 6 does not include education received on a part-time basis, or education received in party schools. An individual who received a diploma from a higher educational institution may not have this fact recorded in the entry in column 6 if the degree was received on a part-time basis. (The fact that he or she received the degree will, meanwhile, appear in the footnotes.) Column 7 records the type of advanced training received in technical and professional fields; the humanities are excluded.[58] If an individual attended a party school, this is also recorded in column 7.

On the basis of these data, a final estimate of overall levels of education of Executive Committee members, aggregated by Executive Committee, is given in Tables F-11 through F-17. In these tables, all types of education, including full-time and part-time, as well as party schools, are considered part of the educational experience. The data appearing in Tables F-11 through F-17 should therefore approximate those figures for levels of education of party leaders which have appeared in other elite studies.

The data in column 5, on status or position prior to full-time party work, are designed to give the reader information on the individual's occupation or position at the point of transition into a revolutionary or political career. It should be noted that the criteria for determining this moment are not the same for all party leaders. For those who were revolutionaries before the seizure of power, the date of joining the party (or earlier, if the individual was actively engaged in youth work) is taken as evidence of a full-time commitment to a revolutionary, or political career. After the seizure of power (1945 in Eastern Europe, 1917 in the USSR), joining the party is no longer considered an adequate measure of a commitment to a career in party work. In such cases, column 5 gives the occupation or status of the individual prior to assuming a full-time career in the party.

Column 5 should therefore be read in conjunction with column 8 on party membership. Those who joined the party before 1945 will, in respect to status, usually be students, workers, or even in some cases "youth," reflecting their entry into the revolutionary movement at an early age. The status of those in column 5 who joined the party after 1945 (1917 in the USSR) may be that of student or worker, but may also be that of professor, engineer, state official, or other category

reflecting a high position. In such cases, the individual did not enter a full-time political career until rising to some high post in administration, the military, or some other field. The entry "State Official" in column 5 usually indicates that the party leader in question does not show any record of full-time political activity until joining the Executive Committee itself.

Column 9, on revolutionary types, attempts to distinguish between prewar revolutionary leaders and party leaders who came of age during the postwar period, or could be considered, because of their educational experience, part of the postwar generation. The basic criterion is that of age in distinguishing between the two major groups, but education is also a factor. Those born in 1921 (1896 in the USSR) can still be included in the postwar generation if they received a full-time higher education after World War II (World War I in the case of the Soviet Union). If the individual party leader did not receive such an education, he had to have been born in 1927 (1899 in the USSR) or after to qualify as part of the postwar generation. As the introduction to Section F explains, the prewar leadership group is in turn broken down into subcategories: Worker Revolutionary, Student Revolutionary, Intellectual Revolutionary, and Those with No Revolutionary Experience (in effect, individuals who did not join the party until 1945, but were too old or poorly educated to be included in the postwar generation). These categories are all fully explained in the introduction to Section F.

In considering the implications of the coding system for column 9, the reader should first and foremost be aware of the fact that those designated as Postwar exclude a certain group born after 1921 (1896 in the USSR) who did receive a higher education after World War II (World War I in the USSR), but not on a full-time basis. It is at this point that the approach to the coding of education in column 6 has a critical effect on the data presented elsewhere in the tables. Concretely, the restrictive definition of education given in column 6 results in a reduction of the number of persons who might be considered part of the postwar generation in column 9.

Table V indicates the results of the method of coding just explained in respect to the number of party leaders who could be considered as belonging to the postwar generation. (Only those countries are included in Table V for which there are complete or nearly complete data.) Row 4 gives the measure of postwar status used by *The Handbook*. The effect of omitting from this group persons with a part-time postwar education born in or after 1921 can be seen in row 5, where such individuals are included in the postwar generation of leaders. The difference is particularly marked in the case of Czechoslovakia, where only 5 persons out of 59 qualify as postwar by the standards used

---

58. In theory, it is possible that a person with a degree in the humanities, obtained on the basis of part-time study, would not be recorded in columns 6 and 7 as receiving a higher education. In practice, a complete picture of the educational experience of all the leaders in Section F can be gained from a careful reading of these two entries and the accompanying footnotes.

TABLE V
ALTERNATIVE APPROACHES TO MEASURING THE
POSTWAR LEADERSHIP CATEGORY

Measures of Postwar Status	Bulgaria	Czecho.	GDR	Poland	USSR 1917–39	USSR 1945–75	Yugo.
1) All Leaders	47	59	61	47	34	56	103
2) Those Born in 1921 or After	7	20	19	14	2[a]	44[a]	49
3) Those Born in 1927 or After	4	3	13	9	1[b]	40[b]	17
4) Postwar as defined in Handbook	5	5	13	11	0	40	28
5) Postwar as Defined in Row 4 plus Those with a Postwar Higher Educ. Received Part-Time	6	10	15	13	1	40	29
6) All Those with a Post-war Higher Education	6	19	9	17	2	56	44

Notes: a 1896 or after.   b 1899 or after.

Source: Tables F-1 through F-10.

in *The Handbook*, but 10 out of 59, if those born in 1921 or after, with a part-time postwar education, are included. It can also be seen from Table V that the criteria which result in the greatest number of persons being identified as postwar are not the same for all the countries in question. In the majority of cases the postwar group is largest if defined in terms of age alone (born in 1921 or after in Eastern Europe or 1896 or after in the case of the USSR). In respect to Poland and the USSR, meanwhile, the criterion of a postwar education (World War II in the case of Poland, World War I in the case of the USSR) produces the greatest number of persons with a claim to belonging in the postwar generation of political leaders.

In both columns 5 and 9, participation in the resistance movements in Eastern Europe is not considered a revolutionary experience, and does not therefore enter into determining when an individual entered into full-time party work, or what type of revolutionary he was. It should be noted, therefore, that for those whose prepolitical status in column 5 is given as "Partisan" there is always another change of status involved, explained in the footnotes. Usually this change is associated with assuming responsibilities as a political commissar, here considered as full-time party work. (For a complete record of who was or was not in the resistance, the reader is referred to column 10, which gives the individual party leader's status during World War II.)

A number of problems arise with respect to the accuracy and reliability of the data in Section F. Sources may not always agree with one another. There is the danger that party leaders have misreported data or concealed information. Not infre-

quently, sources are imprecise in respect to such matters as the type of education the individual has received, or whether the date of joining the Central Committee refers to full or candidate status (to cite only two examples). While the data on the Soviet leadership are fairly complete, there are serious gaps in the data on the Eastern European leaders, as a glance at the tables will reveal.

These problems are not new.[59] An attempt has been made to resolve these difficulties over the accuracy of data on Eastern European political leaders by checking a number of sources. Where this did not lead to a resolution of the problem, the footnotes indicate the presence of conflicting information. Not infrequently, a clearly unreasonable figure has been discarded for a clearly more reasonable one (especially in respect to conflicting data over the dates of joining the party). Where official data are challenged by informed observers in respect to nationality, social origins, or education, this fact is indicated in the footnotes.

The data in Section F must be approached with a degree of caution, given the possibilities for concealment, or misrepresentation. At the same time, it is possible to exaggerate the effects of misreporting of the data. Those who claim working class origins are as a rule poorly educated, and were workers before joining the revolutionary movement prior to World War II. Among the Soviet political leaders included in Section F, there are probably no more than two or three whose social

59. For an extremely useful summary of the problems that arise in using the Soviet data on the political leadership, see T. H. Rigby, "The Soviet Politburo, A Comparative Profile," *Soviet Studies*, vol. 24, no. 1 (July, 1972), p. 8.

origins as given in official data are open to doubt.[60] In the case of the Eastern European leaders, it appears that Henryk Jabłoński, who, official Polish sources report, was of working class origin, was in fact the son of a middle-class government employee. In addition, there are instances of persons among the East European leadership who report working-class origins but were educated in prewar gymnasiums or were even university graduates, a rare occurrence in those days. In some cases there is enough data to confirm this combination of working-class origins and advanced education as correct. In other cases the absence of supporting data creates doubts concerning the social origins of those involved. Emil Bodnaras and Iosif Chisinevski, in the Romanian leadership, are examples of persons whose lower-class social origins appear suspect for this reason.

In respect to education, one can also assume that a bias exists in the data, based on political leaders exaggerating their level of education (while playing down nonworking class origins). As we have suggested earlier, a higher degree could be obtained in several years or less in the years immediately after World War II. Meanwhile, careful examination of the data in columns 6 and 7 will reveal most of these cases in which higher education was received under doubtful circumstances. In Tables F-11 through F-17, furthermore, an effort is made to take these differences in educational experience into account. In these tables, party leaders with a higher education are broken down according to the manner in which education was obtained, and a distinction is made between a higher education received in a party school, or as a result of a part-time education, and that received in other ways.

Data on age, birthplace, and dates of joining party bodies given in Section F are less prone to distortion than data on social origin and education. In respect to nationality, there appear to be several cases in which an individual's true nationality was not recorded; these are indicated in the footnotes. The data on nationality, meanwhile, suffer from the defect that nationality is frequently not reported in official data, and must be deduced from names, place of birth, and other information. In the case of the Soviet Union, the data available are not always sufficient to allow an independent judgment on an individual's nationality; in these cases, The Handbook relies on information on nationality provided in other elite studies, as well as on opinions of experts on the Soviet Union. Data on the nationality of the Albanian leaders, on the other hand, is based on a regional distinction—

between Ghegs and Tosks—rather than on nationality per se. Those born north of the Shkumbi river are considered Ghegs, and those south of the river, Tosks.

In closing, it must be emphasized that the data given in Section F deal with a small number of persons. Distributions in percentage terms among different categories can be greatly influenced by slight changes in coding or interpretation of the data. Misreported information or gaps in the data can have the same effect. It is for this reason that the percentages given in Tables F-11 through F-17 must be considered as the broadest of guidelines to levels of education of political leaders in Eastern Europe and the Soviet Union.

The value of the data in Section F therefore lies in its ordering of information on education and other background attributes of political leaders in easily comparable categories, rather than providing a precise data base for quantitative measurement of the interrelationship of elite attributes. From these data, it is possible to extract valuable insights into trends in the leadership group in Eastern Europe and the Soviet Union and to experiment with typologies of political elites. Data on career tracks would facilitate this type of comparative analysis greatly; unfortunately, for reasons alluded to earlier, it has not proven possible to include such data in The Handbook.

Section G

Section G presents census data on occupations. This is the first time most of these data have appeared in print outside the census results themselves.[61] The data are arranged in terms of twelve major categories, closely following the method of

---

60. Soviet sources disagree over whether Shelepin's father was a railway worker or a railway official; Bulganin's father has been described as both a worker and white-collar employee. These cases are discussed by Rigby, p. 8.

61. Because of limitations of space, data on the civilian labor force are not included in The Handbook. The reader should bear in mind the existence of this alternative source of data, as well as the fact that in most cases such data cannot be compared with the occupational statistics presented in Section G because of differences in scope, in method of collection, and in the categories used to distinguish different groups in the labor force.

Discussions of the occupational data from a methodological viewpoint are relatively rare outside the introductions to the relevant censuses. Several useful noncensus sources include Vojin Milić, "Problemi klasifikacije zanimanja u ispitivanju društvene strukture [The Problem of Classifying Occupations in Research on the Social Structure]," Statistička revija, vol. 11, no. 4, pp. 295–321; Zenon Rajewski, "Zmiany w strukturze społecznej i zawodowej ludności Polski na tle wybranych krajów europejskich [Changes in the Social and Occupational Structure of Poland on the Basis of Selected European Countries]," Wiadomości statystyczne, vol. 16, no. 9 (Sept., 1971), pp. 2–4; Krzysztof Zagórski, "Podział ludności na 'grupy społeczno zawodowe' w NSP 1970–zródłem informacji dla polityki społecznej [The Division of the Population into 'Socio-Economic Groups' in the General Census of 1970–A Source of Information for Social Policy]," Wiadomości statystyczne, vol. 16, no. 5 (May, 1971), pp. 6–9; Sotsiologiia v SSSR [Sociology in the USSR], 2 vols. (Moscow: Mysl, 1965).

presentation used in the East European and Soviet censuses. (Poland follows a different approach, about which more will be said shortly). The sub-categories used in Section G, on the other hand, cannot be standardized, even for one country. All census subcategories for all years for which there are data are listed in the stub of each table. For any given year, data will be given only for those subcategories which appeared in that census. A blank entry indicates that the subcategory was not used in the census of that year; if the category was used, but no data were published, the entry will show three dots (no information).

Where possible, the tables distinguish between occupations classified as manual and nonmanual. When the term Worker is used, the occupation was classified as manual in the original census. Use of the term Personnel indicates that the occupation was classified as nonmanual. In Tables G-1 through G-8 all occupations in the first four major categories (Agriculture and Forestry, Mining, Manufacturing, Construction) are always manual. All occupations in the major categories of Leading and Supervisory Personnel; Technical Personnel; and Education, Scientific, and Cultural Personnel, are always nonmanual. With the exception of the data for Hungary for 1970, all occupations relating to health personnel are also nonmanual.

Albania excepted, all the countries of Eastern Europe, and the Soviet Union, have published some census data on occupations. Nevertheless, these data are far from complete. The GDR has published only meagre data from the 1950 census and, to the best of our knowledge, none from the census of 1971. In respect to occupations, Czechoslovakia has made public only the results of the 1961 census. The data on Poland are restricted largely to 1970 and the microcensus of 1974, although some very rudimentary data from the census of 1960 have appeared, in percentages, and are included in Table G-5.

The data on occupations as a result tend to cluster around the period of the early and mid-1960s. Data are available for Bulgaria for 1965, for Czechoslovakia for 1961, for the GDR for 1964, for Hungary for 1960, for Romania for 1966, for the Soviet Union for 1959, and for Yugoslavia for 1961. For the 1950s, data on occupations are practically nonexistent, while for the early 1970s they are limited to the Soviet Union, Poland, Hungary, and Yugoslavia.

The amounts of data published have varied from census to census and country to country. In most cases, the data in Section G refer to "second level" occupational categories, roughly comparable to the 284 Unit Groups of the International Standard Classification of Occupations (ISCO).[62]

The twelve categories in which the data are grouped in Tables G-1 through G-12 are largely self-explanatory, and no effort will be made to provide a detailed analysis of each of them here. It should be remembered that these categories do not constitute a grouping of occupations by branch of the economy, but rather by similar type of occupation. Thus engineers in the branch of manufacturing are reported in the category Technical Personnel, not under the category of Manufacturing. Occupations that cannot be identified in terms of one of the first eleven categories are placed in the category Other Occupation. While this category is easy to overlook, it often includes a number of important occupations, such as unskilled workers, quality controllers, and power equipment operators. In some cases, white-collar occupations which cannot be classified in any other way are also included in this group of occupations. The tendency for this category to expand or contract from census to census is one major source of difficulty in making comparisons of occupational groups from one census to another.

The data in Section G are, for a number of reasons, difficult to compare. Definitions of major occupational groups change from census to census, as does the scope of the subcategories into which occupations are grouped. Systematic lists of occupations and accompanying descriptions of each are rare and difficult to obtain; in any case, attempting to reconcile differences among the systems of classifying occupations in Eastern Europe and the Soviet Union on the basis of such systematic lists would be a task of gigantic proportions. Data permitting comparison of occupations between two or more consecutive censuses are limited to the cases of the Soviet Union (1959 and 1970) and Poland (1970 and 1974).

Two tables, G-5 and G-20, differ from the others in the manner in which the data on occupations are presented. A brief comment on each is in order. Table G-5 gives data on occupations in Poland. Data on occupations were first gathered in Poland in connection with the 1960 census. Since there were difficulties in classifying the results, they were never published. For the 1970 census an ambitious scheme was adopted for gathering and classifying data on classes and occupations.[63] However, these data, too, were never published in full. The Polish figures for 1970, dealing with occupa-

---

62. The Czech census of 1961 published data on 295 occupations. The Bulgarian census of 1956 distinguished

570 separate occupations; in the 1965 census this number was reduced to 287. The census of 1964 in the GDR listed 480 separate occupations. The Hungarian census of 1960 included 295 occupations, while the 1970 census reported data on 176. Romania provided data on 330 occupations in 1956, and 352 in 1966. The Soviet census of 1959 listed 192 occupations; this number increased to 287 in 1970. In the Yugoslav censuses, data were reported on 305 occupations in 1953, 469 in 1961, and 243 in 1971.

63. Zagórski, pp. 6-9.

tions, differ considerably from those available in other East European countries. In Table G-5 the data on Poland have been reordered to correspond as closely as possible to the twelve categories used in the remainder of the section. Still, the reader should bear in mind that major differences remain between Table G-5 and other tables in the section, especially in respect to the inclusion of branch data in Table G-5.

In Table G-20 data are presented on occupations as they appear in the International Labour Office *Yearbook*, classified according to the International Standard Classification of Occupations. The data in most cases are adjusted to conform to ISCO classifications. The figures given in Table G-20 are nevertheless not fully comparable. For one thing, the ISCO system has itself undergone modifications; for another, some of the data in G-20 match those given in census results and reported in the remainder of the tables in Section G. This fact suggests that at least in some cases no attempt has been made by the ILO to modify national data to meet ISCO criteria.[64]

Data on manual and nonmanual (or mental and physical) occupations given in Section G vary in respect to the manner in which individual occupations are classified and the thoroughness with which the distinction between manual and nonmanual occupations is applied to the data. In Soviet, Czech, and Bulgarian census data, *all* occupations are divided into one or another of these two groups. This has had the result that two closely related occupations (for example in the area of transport and communications) may be placed in quite different categories in the census data, reflecting their manual or nonmanual status. In Section G, such occupations have been grouped together; they can be distinguished in most cases by their designation as Worker, or Personnel, occupations. Tables on the remaining East European countries do not attempt to classify all jobs according to their manual or nonmanual character. Nevertheless, the tables do indicate into which category most occupations are considered to fall: as noted earlier, in Tables G-1 through G-8 the first four major categories include only manual occupations, while the five other categories mentioned earlier are limited to persons with nonmanual occupations.

Not only are there differences in approach to the problem of distinguishing manual and nonmanual occupations on the countries reporting data in Section G, but also criteria for determining the category of each occupation are frequently altered from one census to the next. Sales clerks, post-

men, and communications personnel tend to be shifted about between the manual and nonmanual categories. These changes do not reveal an obvious trend toward including more nonmanual occupations in the manual category, or the reverse: between 1959 and 1970 the Soviet Union broadened the manual category through the device of shifting sales clerks from nonmanual to manual status; meanwhile, between 1960 and 1970 Hungary shifted sales clerks from the manual to nonmanual category. This suggests that the approach taken in the censuses to the question of which occupations are manual or nonmanual is not necessarily that reflected in the theoretical literature in Eastern Europe and the Soviet Union, where stress has been placed upon enlarging the concept of the working class to include more and more nonmanual occupations.[65]

Tables G-9 through G-19 provide data on the level of educational attainment of various occupational categories and groups. In approaching these data, it should be remembered that the groups whose educational levels are being measured are not necessarily homogeneous. This fact is illustrated in Table VI. The table gives data on leadership groups in the Soviet Union in 1970, broken down by level of government (village, district, and higher level posts) or type of position (heads of enterprises, heads of sections, etc.). The importance of the level of government or type of position on the education of the leadership group in question is immediately obvious. In the case of those in state administration, 78.7 percent in okrug positions had a higher education in 1970, compared to 40.4 percent at the district level, and only 5.8 percent at the village level. The data given in Table VI represent an extreme case; nevertheless they do point to the need for caution when generalizing about the levels of education of occupational groups, especially for the broader categories of occupations on which data are presented in the upper section of the tables on occupation and education in Section G.

Data on occupations, regardless of their quality, have certain drawbacks for use in the comparative mode. As noted earlier, such data are rarely comparable over time, or from country to country, except for highly specialized professions, and, on oc-

---

64. In the case of Yugoslavia, meanwhile, the overlap in the data reported in Tables G-20 and G-8 (on occupations) reflects the close adherence to ISCO standards by the Yugoslavs in reporting census data on occupations.

65. See Michał Sadowski *Przemiany społeczne a system partyjny PRL* [Social Changes and the Party System of the PRP] (Warsaw: Książka i Wiedza, 1969); Włodzimierz Wesołowski, "Przemiany strukturalne w współczesnym socjalizmie (Structural Changes in Contemporary Socialism]," *Studia socjologiczne*, no. 2 (1969), pp. 43–62; M. N. Rutkevich and F. P. Filippov, *Sotsial'nye peremeshcheniia* [Social Transformations] (Moscow: 1970); Miroslav Pečujlić, "Socijalna struktura i razvojne tendencije [Social Structure and Developmental Tendencies], *Sociologija*, vol. 14, no. 3 (1972), pp. 601–12; Lungwitz, *Über die Klassenstruktur.*

TABLE VI

EDUCATION OF LEADERS BY LEVEL OF GOVERNMENT OR
POSITION IN ORGANIZATION: USSR, 1970

Level of Education	State Administration			Political Organization			Technical Leaders		
	Okrug Level & Above	District Level	Village Level	Okrug Level & Above	District Level	Basic Org.	Heads of Enterpr.	Heads of Sections	Heads of Depts.
TOTAL	52,276	70,314	88,234	24,571	74,934	95,455	300,843	392,599	581,893
Percent	100.0%	100.0%	100.0%	100.0%	100.0%	100.0%	100.0%	100.0%	100.0%
Elem. or Less									
Percent									
Inc. Basic	[470]	[980]	[5,100]	[320]	[750]	[1,900]	[1,400]	[4,300]	[28,500]
Percent	0.9%	1.4%	5.8%	1.3%	1.0%	2.0%	3.8%	1.1%	4.9%
Basic									
Percent									
Trade School	[840]	[6,700]	[26,700]	[1,200]	[3,700]	[11,300]	[31,900]	[20,000]	[71,000]
Percent	1.6%	9.5%	30.6%	5.1%	5.0%	11.8%	10.6%	5.2%	12.2%
Inc. Second.									
Percent									
Second. & Spec. Second.	[9,800]	[34,200]	[51,000]	[8,800]	[34,800]	[59,900]	[139,300]	[165,300]	[310,700]
Percent	18.8%	48.7%	57.8%	35.8%	46.5%	62.7%	46.3%	42.1%	53.4%
Inc. Higher									
Percent									
Higher	[41,100]	[28,400]	[5,100]	[14,200]	[35,600]	[22,400]	[118,200]	[202,600]	[171,700]
Percent	78.7%	40.4%	5.8%	57.8%	47.5%	23.5%	39.3%	51.6%	29.5%

Source: Itogi vsesoiuznoi perepisi naseleniia 1970, vol. 6, Table 68, pp. 620-31.

casion, certain larger well-defined groups such as those with agricultural occupations.[66] Nor do these data on occupations include figures on groups, such as the secret police or those engaged in censorship activities, which might be of special interest to the Western observer.

These drawbacks to the data are nevertheless understandable if the purpose of the data on occupations is kept in mind—namely, to provide an accurate breakdown of the population according to type of economic activity and function at a given moment in time, in as detailed a fashion as possible. In performing this function, the data on Eastern Europe and the Soviet Union vary in quality, but at their best, have certain advantages over data on occupations published in the United States.[67]

These data are in turn enhanced in value by other data in *The Handbook* on social classes, and education, as well as by the breakdown of the oc-

cupational data themselves in terms of sex. Unfortunately, scarcity of data made it inadvisable to include statistics on occupation and branch, another important cross-cutting measure of value in determining the nature of the occupational structure of the population. Finally, considerations of time and space prevented the preparation and inclusion in *The Handbook* of the census data on "Specialists"—that is, on persons by the type of education and training received, which can be very profitably compared with the data on occupations and education.

Section H

Section H includes statistics on basic developmental indicators and the standard of living on Eastern Europe and the Soviet Union. Data for the tables in this section are taken from census results, statistical annuals, and from statistics published by U.S. and international agencies and institutions (United Nations, World Bank, CIA, and others).

While most major developmental indicators of importance are included in Section H, gaps do exist in the data. There are problems also in respect to the reliability and utility of a number of the in-

66. The Soviet data on occupations for 1959 and 1970 stand out as an exception, since they are characterized by a high degree of comparability among individual occupational categories.

67. For example, they identify supervisory or leadership occupations, something not done in U.S. statistics on occupations.

dicators on which data are given. Although great progress has been made in the past decade in publishing data on development and the standard of living in Eastern Europe and the Soviet Union, many difficulties remain. These include the problem of finding a way of measuring qualitative as well as quantitative changes in living standards in Eastern Europe and the Soviet Union; developing more accurate ways of measuring national income; and collecting comparative statistics on personal incomes, consumption patterns, and other indexes of the standard of living for which sample survey techniques must be used in addition to aggregative statistics.

Tables H-2 through H-4 present data on national income in the form of indexes of growth of GNP and NMP between 1950 and 1977, as well as data on absolute levels of GNP and per capita GNP (in dollars). Data on the growth of NMP, despite their deficiencies as a measure of national income,[68] are included in Table H-2 for purposes of comparison with the indexes on the growth of GNP. As might be expected, the NMP indexes, with the exception of Yugoslavia, show a higher rate of growth of national income than those based on GNP.

Data on GNP in Table H-3 are calculated in constant prices by sector of origin. The GNP on Eastern Europe link two indexes of national income growth prepared by the Research Project on National Income in East Central Europe. The GNP index of Soviet national income growth is a single series with the base year adjusted from 1970 to 1965, originating with the CIA, published in a report of the U.S. Congress Joint Economic Committee.

Data on GNP in dollars in Table H-3 are given in the form of two estimates; the first (Series I) is that of the World Bank, while the second was prepared by the CIA and the Research Project on National Income in East Central Europe (Series II). World Bank estimates, with the exception of Romania and Yugoslavia, utilize data on the growth of selected physical indicators as a basis for estimating national income, a method first developed and subsequently refined by the United Nations. CIA estimates are based on statistics on the economic performance of the countries of Eastern Europe and the Soviet Union as reported in Eastern European and Soviet sources, following methods for estimating national income developed by Western scholars over the past several decades.[69] Data

in the two series cannot be directly compared. Each series employs a different year in calculating the constant dollar value of GNP, and each converts national income as measured in local currencies into dollars in a different fashion. As noted earlier in the introduction, the data presented by the World Bank grossly understates Romanian GNP. This is the result of the Romanian practice of submitting data to the World Bank which show Romania as a lesser-developed country with low levels of national income.

While the data in Table H-3 are not directly comparable, they should, if they accurately measure national income, show a reasonably high degree of compatability in respect to the ranking of the individual countries involved. Table VII gives indexes of levels of GNP calculated in the two ways just described, with the national income of Poland taken as the basis for comparison. As the table indicates, there are significant differences in the relative standing of the states of Eastern Europe, and the Soviet Union, using these two methods of determining absolute levels of national income (disregarding the clearly erroneous data presented in the World Bank figures for Romania). Differences between the two measures are most striking in the case of the Soviet Union, whose total national income, using the physical indicators approach of the World Bank, is much lower relative to Poland than national income measured according to the methods developed by the CIA and the Research Project on National Income in Eastern Europe referred to earlier. Differences in the two approaches in respect to Yugoslavia are also evident, perhaps reflecting the fact that the CIA data are in this case an estimate, probably less accurate than the data presented by the World Bank.

Data on the number of persons in agriculture, presented in Tables H-5 through H-12, are branch data; they differ from similar data given in Section E by virtue of the fact that they include prewar statistics on the agricultural population, and include, among the Active Earners, helping family members, apprentices, and, where the data are provided, persons working on private plots.

Data on the agricultural population are presented in these tables in three ways: (1) in terms of the total population currently or previously employed in agriculture, and their dependents; (2) in terms of Active Earners and their Dependents currently engaged in agriculture; (3) in terms of Active Earners alone. The first of these measures of the agricultural population includes Other Earners (pensioners and related groups) as well as Active Earners and their Dependents in agriculture. Figures for the total population in agriculture have, where necessary, been estimated by determining the ratio between the number of Active Earners and the total population for each class given in the census

68. For a clear account of the problem of interpreting national income statistics in Communist countries, see Martin Hoffman, "How to Read National Income Statistics," *East Europe*, vol. 2, no. 11 (Nov., 1962), pp. 11–18.

69. For the methodology involved in calculating national income in terms of GNP for Eastern Europe, see Thad Alton et al., "Statistics on East European Economic Structure and Growth," *Occasional Papers of the Research Project on National Income in East Central Europe*, No. 48 (New York: L. W. International Financial Research Inc., 1977).

TABLE VII

INDEXES OF LEVELS OF GNP, CALCULATED
IN DOLLARS, FOR EASTERN EUROPE
AND THE SOVIET UNION (Poland=100)

Country	1960 I	1960 II	1970 I	1970 II	1975 I	1975 II
Bulgaria	20.3	20.9	24.0	25.3	21.9	23.2
Czechoslovakia	77.7	86.1	68.2	76.3	58.9	65.9
GDR	102.6	94.9	90.3	86.8	61.3	75.1
Hungary	31.9	37.5	30.2	35.1	26.2	30.5
Poland	100	100	100	100	100	100
Romania	14.8	46.6	22.8	56.6	28.5	57.1
USSR	744.6	1,044.4	820.9	1,207.6	724.8	1,064.1
Yugoslavia	30.0	41.9	36.3	49.2	37.2	47.9

Series I: World Bank estimates of GNP.   Series II: CIA estimates of GNP.

Source: Table H-3.

data and then applying these ratios to the data on Active Earners, by class, in agriculture, to obtain estimates of the total number of each class in the agricultural sector.[70]

Data on Active Earners and their Dependents can, if the reader wishes, be treated as data on the economically active, keeping in mind that the figures for Active Earners given in Tables H-5 through H-12 do not necessarily conform to United Nations or Western definitions of the economically active. Data on the Active Earners and their Dependents are census data; in the case of Table H-7 on the GDR and Table H-8 on Hungary, these data have been supplemented by data on the civilian labor force. While the two types of data in most cases show a similar percentage of persons in agriculture, they differ in respect to method of reporting and the groups included among Active Earners, and should not therefore be treated as part of a single series on the number active in agriculture.

Efforts at calculating the number of persons in agriculture in Eastern Europe and the Soviet Union have encountered numerous difficulties. Because of a lack of data, estimates of the agricultural population (either in terms of the total population

in agriculture, or Active Earners and their Dependents in agriculture) differ widely.[71] Data on the number of Active Earners (or economically active) in agriculture are more plentiful, but difficult to compare, either cross-nationally or over time, chiefly because definitions of helping family members in agriculture differ from census to census and country to country.[72] Data on the number of active earners in agriculture, it should also be noted, do not necessarily give an accurate picture of employment in the agricultural sector, since many persons in agricultural occupations work less than full time, while persons outside agriculture contribute their labor to the agricultural sector in significant amounts, through working on private plots, or by participating in seasonal labor on the collective farms.[73]

70. The accuracy of these estimates depends on the degree to which differences exist between dependency ratios for the class as a whole and for the agricultural branch. In the case of Romania in 1956, the actual number of Active Earners and Dependents in agriculture was 8,613,622. The estimated number of Active Earners and Dependents in agriculture was 8,556,000, using the approach just outlined, or 0.6% less than the actual figure. The difference between the two figures can be attributed to the fact that workers and white-collar employees in agriculture had a greater number of dependents than did workers and white-collar employees as a whole, and therefore had a higher dependency ratio.

71. See various editions of the FAO *Production Yearbook*, where estimates of the size of the agricultural population in Eastern Europe and the Soviet Union have varied considerably. The CMEA handbook also publishes data on employment by branch, including agriculture, by percent; the data are not comparable to those published in Section H.

72. See Andrew Elias, in Joint Economic Committee, *Economic Development in the Countries of Eastern Europe* (Washington, D.C.: GPO, 1970), p. 156. Note his remarks that "The category 'helping family members' accounts, particularly in agriculture, for the lion's share of conceptual differences in reporting on the economically active population among the six countries [of Eastern Europe]. Unfortunately, the information available on the coverage of this category is too scanty to permit meaningful intercensal or international comparisons." Ten years later, this judgment is still basically correct.

73. For an excellent discussion of the differences between employment and labor force statistics on agriculture in the Soviet Union, see FDAD, *Estimates and Projections of the Labor Force and Civilian Employment in the U.S.S.R.* (Washington, D.C.: GPO, 1967), pp. 1–5.

Data are also affected by the profound changes which the agricultural population has experienced in Eastern Europe and the Soviet Union over the past several decades or more, having passed from a system of private ownership in agriculture to one in which collective farming predominates. In the course of this change, helping family members have ceased to play a decisive role in agriculture, except in the case of Yugoslavia and Poland, where private farming still prevails. At the same time, older persons have increasingly come to play a major role in agriculture. The number of such persons among the active is, in turn, influenced by the presence or absence of pension systems for collective farmers in Eastern Europe and the Soviet Union. Where such pension plans have been introduced, the number of older collective farmers considered part of the labor force has declined, although these persons continue to contribute their labor to the collective farms, if only on a part-time basis.

These considerations must be kept in mind when using the data in Tables H-5 through H-12. Special care should be exercised in making comparisons between the data on Active Earners. The data include helping family members, but the criteria used to measure this group differ. For example, in Yugoslavia, those between ten and fifteen years of age are considered helping family members if they do not attend school and are involved in some agricultural work.[74] In Poland, those under fourteen are excluded entirely from the category of helping family members.[75] In the Yugoslav case, females whose *primary* occupation is household work are not included among the active in agriculture, while in Poland, housewives are included among the active in agriculture unless occupied *exclusively* in household work. The effect of these differences in the data on the number of Active Earners in agriculture in Yugoslavia and Poland has never been fully determined. The fact that among those of working age in Poland the percentage of Active Earners relative to the total population in agriculture approaches 100 percent, while in Yugoslavia the data show much lower participation rates, suggests that most wives of agriculturalists in Poland are included among the active. As a result the number of persons active in agriculture in Poland appears to be overstated both in respect to Yugoslavia and the remaining states of Eastern Europe and the Soviet Union.

In making comparisons of the number of Active

74. Zagorka Aničić, "Neka metodološka pitanja 'poljoprivrednog stanovništva' [Some Methodological Problems of the Active Agricultural Population]," *Stanovništvo*, vol. 10–11, no. 3–4 and 1–2 (1972–1973), pp. 88–100.

75. Główny Urząd Statystyczny, *Narodowy spis powszechny 8 XII 1970* [National Census 8 XII 1970] (Warsaw: GUS, 1972), p. xx.

Earners in agriculture over time it should once more be borne in mind that with the introduction of collective farming the number of helping family members dropped drastically in Eastern Europe and the Soviet Union. While many of these persons became collective farm members, and thus continued to be counted among the active in agriculture, others were reclassified as dependents, thus contributing to the rapid decline in the number of those in agriculture which accompanied collectivization.

Some former helping family members have reappeared in the census data, in those countries with collectivized agriculture, as persons working on private plots. This group, when its number is known, is included among the Active Earners in Tables H-5 through H-12. There are nevertheless many difficulties associated with the data on this category of persons in agriculture. Since many of this group are older, their number has been reduced as pension systems have been introduced in the collective farm sector in Eastern Europe and the Soviet Union; as noted, differences in the implementation of these plans results in differences among the number of older persons included among the active in agriculture. Secondly, the data on persons tending private plots are not reported in the same manner in all the countries with collectivized agriculture. In some cases, these data are not reported at all. This further complicates the task of making comparisons among the number of Active Earners in agriculture in Eastern Europe and the Soviet Union.

Fewer difficulties arise in comparing the number of persons in agriculture, when using either the data on the total population, or Active Earners and their Dependents (the first two of the three methods outlined above). Each of these two measures of the number of persons in agriculture has its advantages and disadvantages. In both cases, it should be borne in mind, the percentages used to indicate the proportion of the population in agriculture in Tables H-5 through H-12 are derived from comparisons between each category and the total number of persons, including those in other branches of the economy, in that category. This approach differs from that in which Active Earners (or economically active) and their Dependents are compared to the total population. In Table H-1, in which the data on developmental indicators are summarized, it is this latter approach to measuring the proportion of the population in agriculture which is used. The difference between the two methods for measuring the percentage of the population in agriculture can be seen in Table VIII, which gives the percentage of the population in agriculture in Eastern Europe and the Soviet Union in the 1960s. The percentage of the population in agriculture is of course lower in the first variant

TABLE VIII
PERCENTAGE OF POPULATION IN AGRICULTURE
EASTERN EUROPE AND THE USSR, 1960s

Measures of Agric. Population	Bulg. 1965	Czecho. 1961	GDR 1964	Hung. 1960	Pol. 1960	Rom. 1966	USSR 1970	Yugo 1961
Active Earners & Dependents in Agric. as a Percentage of the Total Population	33.3	19.3	12.4	34.8	37.8	45.1	22.8	49.6
Active Earners & Dependents in Agric. as a Percentage of the Total Number of Active Earners & Dependents	39.2	22.6	15.6	37.3	40.9	50.3	27.1	52.9

Source: Tables H-5 through H-12.

presented in the table; that is, when Active Earners and their Dependents are compared to the total population. (It should be added that the difference between these two measures of the percentage of the population in agriculture has tended to grow with time and with the aging of the population generally.)

Data on urbanization are presented in Tables H-13 through H-21.[76] Here all available census data are assembled on the total number and distribution of the urban population by size of urban settlement. Official estimates are used for noncensus years.[77] Boundaries of urban settlements are those of the year in question, unless otherwise indicated in the footnotes. In the case of Hungary, it has been the practice to publish retrospective data on urbanization in terms of the most recent boundaries of urban areas. This approach, while it facilitates the identification of natural increases of the urban population and migrations to urban areas as factors in urban growth, can be misleading for purposes of comparison. Data on the urban population in Hungary, given in Table H-17, have been made available by the Hungarian Statistical Office. In this table, urbanization is measured according

to the boundaries of urban areas for the years in question, or as near to these years as possible. The data in Table H-17 are therefore comparable to the data in the remainder of Section H.

Official definitions of urbanization are given in the introduction to Section H. These definitions differ greatly from country to country. As a consequence, data on the total percentage of the population residing in urban areas can be compared only with extreme care. In Table H-1, urbanization in Eastern Europe and the Soviet Union is measured in terms of urban settlements of 20,000 and over; settlements of this size are uniformly considered urban in Eastern Europe and Soviet Union, with the exception of some large agrarian settlements included in the data on the rural population in Hungary.

In tracing the growth of the urban population in Eastern Europe and the Soviet Union in Tables H-13 through H-21, attention must be paid to those cases in which the definition of urban settlements changed from one census to the next; where the annexation of rural areas led to the rapid growth of cities over a relatively short period of time; or where data on the urban population include communities of a semiurban type. In the case of Yugoslavia, the definition of urban settlements prior to 1953 was a legal one, and the boundaries of urban settlements embraced rural as well as urban areas. In 1953, a set of uniform criteria for defining urbanization was adopted, with the result that data on levels of urbanization became comparable from 1953 onward. Czechoslovakia has, since 1961, employed two measures of urbanization. The first includes all settlements of 2,000 and over, while the second represents a complex formula using density of population and other criteria. To complicate matters, data on urbanization in Czechoslovakia since 1961 have not always specified which of these

76. On problems of measuring urbanization in Eastern Europe and the Soviet Union, see Leszek Kosinski, "Urbanization in East-Central Europe After World War II," *East European Quarterly*, vol. 8, no. 2 (June, 1974), pp. 129–45; Maria Kielczewska-Zaleska, "The Definition of Urban and Non-Urban Settlements in East Central Europe," *Geographia Polonica*, vol. 7 (1965), pp. 5–15; Robert A. Lewis and Richard H. Rowland, "Urbanization in Russia and the USSR, 1897–1966," *Annals of the Association of American Geographers*, vol. 59, no. 4 (Dec., 1969), pp. 776–96; United Nations, Department of Economic and Social Affairs, *Growth of the World's Urban and Rural Population, 1920–2000* (New York: United Nations, 1969).

77. As noted earlier, these official estimates are not adjusted to take into account census results appearing after the estimates were made.

TABLE IX

POPULATION IN URBAN AND OTHER SETTLEMENTS,
BULGARIA, 1956-1975

Settlements by Size	1956	1965	1975
2,000 - 4,999			
Urban Settlements	67,123	127,327	171,673
All Settlements	1,551,296	1,410,545	1,175,499
5,000 - 9,999			
Urban Settlements	267,483	500,550	512,813
All Settlements	529,702	647,236	586,836
10,000 - 24,999			
Urban Settlements	508,040	523,281	780,523
All Settlements	541,106	523,281	780,523

Source: Statisticheskii ezhegodnik 1977, Table 3, p. 28.

two measures is being employed.[78] In the case of the Soviet Union, the definition of urban settlements is based on formal criteria, including city size and the percentage of the population in urban areas in agriculture. These criteria differ by republic and vary from census to census. Comparisons of levels of urbanization in the Soviet Union over time are therefore best limited to cities of 20,000 and over.[79]

Rapid urbanization in Eastern Europe and the Soviet Union has been accompanied by the expansion of urban settlements through the annexation of surrounding territories, and by the elevation of villages to urban status. In certain cases this has led to an artificial inflation of the rates of growth of urban areas. An example of this may be seen in Table IX, which gives data on the number of persons in urban and other settlements in Bulgaria according to size between 1956 and 1975. As the table shows, there was a great increase in Bulgaria in the 1960s in the percentage of the population considered urban residing in settlements of between 5,000 and 10,000. While only half of the population residing in settlements of this size were considered urban in 1956, by 1975, 87 percent were to be found in settlements defined as urban. In Poland a great many villages were given urban status in the early 1950s, contributing to a sharp increase in the urban population in Poland between 1950 and 1960 (see Table H-18). In the case of the GDR, comparisons of the data on levels of urbanization in 1946 with those for other years must be made with caution in light of the practice at that time of enlarging cities through the annexation of

surrounding areas. This was in a period when the larger urban areas in the GDR were in fact experiencing a decline in population. In Hungary, on the other hand, the 1950s witnessed a redrawing of municipal boundaries which in some cases resulted in a decrease in urban population as rural areas were detached from urban settlements.[80]

The practice of including persons residing in semiurban areas in the data on the urban population should also be noted. Such areas are of a mixed urban-rural character, and typically show a large percentage of the population engaged in agriculture. Semiurban areas have been included with the data on urban settlements in Poland, Bulgaria, and Romania. In Poland after World War II such areas were supposed to have, at a minimum, 1,000 persons, no more than 50 percent of whom could be engaged in agriculture.[81] The number of persons to be found in these "urban settlements" reached 679,200 in 1960, then declined in subsequent years. In Bulgaria in 1965, the number of persons in "villages of a city type" amounted to 207,408; all were included in the data on the urban population for that year. Data on "assimilated urban areas" in Romania can be found in Table H-19. Here it can be seen that the number in such semiurban areas has kept pace with the growth of urbanization, making up 7 to 8 percent of the total urban population in Romania over the years. In the case of individual cities in Romania, assimilated urban areas may constitute a large percentage of the urban population; thus, in Ploiesti in 1970, 25 percent were to be found in assimilated urban areas sur-

78. Data on urbanization in Czechoslovakia for 1974 appearing in the 1977 *United Nations Yearbook* are mistakenly identified as based on the formal definition of urbanization adopted in 1961. In *The Handbook* the 1974 data are presumed, on the basis of other data in Table H-15, to measure the population residing in settlements of 2,000 and over.

79. Lewis and Rowland, p. 778.

80. The above notwithstanding, the effect on the data of using the most recent urban boundaries to measure city size is to increase the total number of persons in urban areas for earlier years in Hungary.

81. Jan Malanowski, "Procesy urbanizacji [Processes of Urbanization]," in Włodzimierz Wesołowski, ed., *Struktura i dynamika społeczeństwa polskiego* [The Structure and Dynamics of Social Change in Poland] (Warsaw: Państwowe Wydawnictwo Naukowe, 1970), p. 75.

rounding the city.[82] A strong rural influence on these assimilated urban areas in Romania is suggested by the fact that in 1966, 52 percent of the active population in these areas were employed in agriculture, compared to 15.7 percent for urban areas proper.

Data on housing, appearing in Tables H-22 through H-28, are taken directly from the pathbreaking work, *A Statistical Survey of the Housing Situation in Europe*, published in 1978 by the UN Economic Commission for Europe. These housing statistics are drawn from census data, and therefore do not include the Soviet Union, which has not included data on housing in its postwar censuses. The data in Tables H-22 through H-28 give the distribution by number of persons, and by number of dwellings, for a number of key indicators relating to housing—the number of families per dwelling, facilities to be found in dwellings, and age of dwellings. The data conform to United Nations recommendations on the classification of statistics on housing, buildings, and planning drawn up in 1969. Departures from these practices, in the case of the Eastern European countries, are not enumerated in *The Handbook*, but can be found in Appendix II of the ECE volume.

Data in Tables H-22 through H-28 are in most cases presented in terms of the number of "conventional occupied dwellings." Table X shows the types of living quarters on which data were reported to the United Nations, and the number of each in the East European countries. Living quarters include all dwellings used for habitation, subdivided into Housing Units and Other Living Quarters (hotels, institutions, and the like). Housing Units are in turn subdivided into Conventional Dwellings and Other Housing Units, as indicated in Table X. As can be seen from the table, all of the East European countries reported data on the number of Conventional Occupied Dwellings. It is this category which serves as the basis for comparisons of housing stock which emerge from the ECE data.

The data on housing gathered by the ECE are a significant improvement over those available on Eastern Europe in the past. Furthermore, they have the advantage that they can be compared with data on the rest of Europe contained in the ECE volume. The reader should nevertheless keep in mind that there are departures from UN recommendations in respect to the manner in which the data are presented, and that the data were not originally gathered in precisely the same way or under the same conditions. These factors could influence the comparability of the statistics given in Tables H-22 through H-28.

Tables H-29 through H-32 present statistics on patterns of food consumption, growth in the stock of selected consumer goods, and other indicators of development in the fields of health and culture.[83] Although the best available, these statistics have definite shortcomings as measures of the standard of living in Eastern Europe and the Soviet Union. Great differences among the countries of the region in respect to the quality and availability of foodstuffs and consumer goods items are not revealed in the data. Statistics on *per capita* consumption of foodstuffs are not, strictly speaking, comparable. Only when aggregative statistics are supplemented by sample survey data gathered in a uniform fashion can it be expected that accurate comparisons of the standard of living in Eastern Europe and the Soviet Union will be possible. The statistics given in Tables H-29 through H-32 are nevertheless important indicators of development, and in certain cases are broadly comparable.

Table H-29 presents data on food consumption published in the statistical annuals of the countries of Eastern Europe and the Soviet Union, as assembled by the Economics, Statistics, and Cooperative Services Division of the U.S. Department of Agriculture, for the period 1950-1975. These food consumption schedules are not comparable, nor do they measure actual consumption.[84] They do serve as indicators of shifts in consumption habits, but the reader must be cautioned that even in this respect the data must be used with care because of abrupt changes resulting from the redefinition of a product being reported in the data. (For example, in the case of the GDR, Table H-29 shows that consumption of fruits fell from 80.1 kilos *per capita* in 1960 to 46.5 kilos in 1965.) Among the major differences in the manner of presentation of the data there can be noted the Soviet practice of including edible fats and internal organs in the data on meat consumption; the Bulgarian practice of measuring cereals in terms of whole grain, not flour; and the Soviet practice of including melons with vegetables.

Table H-30 presents the results of food balance sheets published by the FAO. The table estimates food available at the retail level on a *per capita* basis in terms of calories per day, and in the case of proteins and fats, in terms of grams per day. The data do not measure food actually consumed and their accuracy depends on the accuracy and re-

83. On the standard of living, see the reports of the Joint Economic Committee of the U.S. Congress dealing with Eastern Europe cited in the bibliography. In addition, note M. Mod et al., *The Standard of Living: Some Problems of Analysis and International Comparison* (Budapest: Akademiai Kiado, 1962); Maria Elisabeth Ruban, *Die Entwicklung des Lebensstandards in der Sowjetunion* (Berlin: Duncker and Humblot, 1965); Gertrude Schroeder, "Consumption in the USSR: A Survey," *Studies on the Soviet Union*, vol. 10, no. 4 (1970), pp. 1–40; Radio Liberty, "Indicators of Living Standards in the USSR and Eastern Europe," *Radio Liberty Research*, no. 101/77 (May 4, 1977).

84. See the remarks on food balance sheets below.

82. *Anuarul Statistic* [Statistical Annual], 1971, Table 18, p. 69.

TABLE X

TYPES OF HOUSING (LIVING QUARTERS) IN EASTERN EUROPE

(Number of Dwellings, in Thousands)

Types of Living Quarters	Bulgaria 1956	1965	1975	Czechoslovakia 1950	1961	1970	GDR 1964	1971	Hungary 1949	1960	1970
TOTAL	...	2,103	2,526	...	...	...	...	6,062	...	...	...
Housing Units	1,733	2,100	2,523	...	...	...	5,575[a]	6,057[a]	2,477	2,786	3,169
Conventional Dwellings	1,722	2,077	2,498	...	...	4,277[b]	...	...	2,467	2,758	3,150
Occupied	1,688	2,019	2,339	3,613	3,820	4,239	5,427[a]	5,933[a]	2,425	2,711	3,034
Vacant	34	58	159	...	...	38[c]	148	124[a]	42[c]	47[c]	116[c]
Other Housing Units (Mobile Homes, etc.)	11	23	25	...	...	...	...	...	11	28	19
Living Quarters Other Than Housing Units (Hotels, Institutions, etc.)	...	3	3	...	...	...	...	...	...	...	...

Types of Living Quarters	Poland 1950	1960	1970	Romania 1966	Yugoslavia 1953	1961	1971
TOTAL	...	...	8,313	5,481	...	4,191	5,206
Housing Units	...	...	8,303	5,461	3,497	4,189	5,200
Conventional Dwellings	...	...	8,295	5,380	...	...	5,110
Occupied	5,851	7,026	8,081	5,250	3,490	4,082	4,935
Vacant	...	...	214[c]	130[c]	...	...	175[c]
Other Housing Units (Mobile Homes, etc.)	64	22	8	81	7	107	90
Living Quarters Other Than Housing Units (Hotels, Institutions, etc.)	11	14	10	20	...	2	6

Notes: a Includes occupied housing units and dwellings in residential buildings used for non-residential purposes. b Includes approximately 9,000 housing units in semi-permanent buildings. c Vacant and reserved for seasonal and secondary use.

Source: United Nations, Economic Commission for Europe, A Statistical Survey of the Housing Situation in Europe, Table I.2, pp. 28-38.

liability of the food balance sheets prepared by the individual countries and submitted to the FAO. While Table H-30 does give an approximate picture of the overall food situation in Eastern Europe and the Soviet Union, the data must be used with care and reserved primarily for purposes of comparing trends rather than orders of magnitude in food consumption.[85]

Tables H-30 and H-31 provide data on the stock of certain consumer goods, on health, and on culture. The data are available in the *United Nations Statistical Yearbooks* and have frequently been cited in studies on Eastern Europe and the Soviet Union. They therefore require no special comment here. While the data should be broadly comparable in most cases, they cannot, in the nature of things, be considered extremely precise. Thus, the number of radio sets per 1,000 is probably considerably larger in actual fact than the number given here, which is for registered sets only. Data on the number of books published, to cite another example, are not comparable due to differences in definitions of books in the case of the countries reporting data.

In conclusion, it should be pointed out that the variety of the data present in Section H precludes an overall judgment concerning their reliability and comparability. In some cases, the data are comparable insofar as trends are concerned, but must be used with caution if absolute magnitudes are in question. This would seem to be true in the case of the data on national income, and on food consumption. In other instances, for example, urbanization or the number of persons in agriculture, proper choice of criteria allow one to compare absolute magnitudes as well as trends.

Much the same can be said for the data as a whole. With proper care, they allow us to measure trends in the Soviet Union and Eastern Europe, trends which in most cases can be successfully compared. Absolute magnitudes can also be compared cross-nationally in selected cases, and over time in the case of any single country if proper precautions are taken to note changes in methods of gathering and presenting the data from census to census. Data utilized strictly on a country-by-country basis of course pose fewer problems in respect to the method of collection and presentation. But even in this case, as we have seen, comparing the data with other countries can be useful, and sometimes reveals omissions or distortions which otherwise would not be evident.

Whatever their imperfections, the statistics presented in the tables to follow help satisfy an obvious need for more empirical data on Eastern Europe and the Soviet Union. Without these data there can be no starting point for understanding the processes of change which have so profoundly altered the societies of Eastern Europe and the Soviet Union. It is hoped that the data appearing here will, through comments and criticisms, be improved and enlarged upon, with the goal of providing a broad base of statistical information upon which an authentically empirical, although not necessarily exclusively quantitative, mode of comparing Communist societies and political systems will emerge.

85. Note the remark of the OECD publication, *Food Consumption Statistics 1955-1973*, p. v, that "food balance sheets cover data on production, foreign trade, utilization, etc. and are therefore subject to all the shortcomings which might occur in the compilation of all these statistics." Organization for Economic Cooperation and Development, *Food Consumption Statistics, 1955-1973* (Paris: OECD, 1975).

EXPLANATION OF SYMBOLS AND MANNER OF PRESENTING DATA

. . .	Data not available.
(Space left blank)	Entry inapplicable.
I, II	Series (see explanation below).
[ ]	Brackets. Data within brackets are derived from percents or from data obtained in this manner.

Percents: Unless otherwise indicated, all percents relate to totals given in the first row of the table. This rule applies to subentries as well as major entries in the table.

Rounding: As the result of rounding, subtotals may not always add up to totals.

Rounded data: Data rounded in the original source will be shown, in any given column, by zeros: 00 if rounded to hundreds, 000 if rounded to thousands, and so forth.

Unaccounted for: Data in the Unaccounted for row indicate the difference between the total, in the first row of the table, and the sum of the remaining entries in the column. In most cases the total is established independently of the data given in the remainder of the column; if the data provided in the original source do not add up to the total, the entry in the Unaccounted for row will reflect the difference. A footnote will indicate if the total is arrived at by summing the remaining entries in any given column; in such cases the Unaccounted for entry is inapplicable and is left blank. Inspection of the table may suggest that the data in the Unaccounted for entry can be substituted for entries in the table for which no data are available.

Series: Series notations (I, II) are used when data for a given year are presented in two versions and data for remaining years may be associated with either of these two versions, or when it is otherwise necessary to distinguish one series from another in the table. Data not having a series notation may still be part of a series. For the comparability of data in different years, regardless of whether identified as a series or not, see the introduction to each section and comments in the General Introduction.

Data in Brackets: Data in brackets have been rounded to reflect the lack of precision which results from obtaining absolute figures indirectly from percents.

Explanations of Data: Explanations of the data are to be found in footnotes and in the introduction to each section. Footnotes relate to individual entries in the table while the introduction to each section deals with questions of the comparability and reliability of the data. For further explanations of the classifications used in each section the reader should consult the General Introduction and the appendices.

Census and Noncensus Data: Where appropriate, the introduction to each section will indicate whether data are census or noncensus data, or official estimates. When data are based on nonofficial estimates, this fact is indicated either in the footnotes or by reference in the title of the table to the fact that the data are estimates.

Abbreviations: Abbreviations for Tables F-1 through F-10 are explained in each table following presentation of the data. Abbreviations used in column headings are explained in the introduction to each section. For a list of all abbreviations used in *The Handbook* arranged in alphabetical order, see Appendix 17.

Entries in East European Languages and Russian: For technical reasons, entries in East European languages in the tables and in most appendices are given without diacritical marks. Transliteration of Russian and Bulgarian entires in the bibliography follows the Library of Congress system. In the tables, Russian and Bulgarian names, nationalities, and expressions are rendered in a simplified form based on customary Western usage.

SECTION A: POPULATION

Introduction

Table A-1   Population for Southern Dobrudja in 1934 is derived from an official Bulgarian estimate of the population in the region for Jan. 1, 1941, of 318,772. For comments on the possible over-counting of the Albanian population in 1930, see the General Introduction.

Table A-3   Data for Hungary for 1941 reflect the annexation of Ruthenia and parts of Slovakia and Transylvania in the period 1938 to 1940.

Table A-4   Data for Romania for 1941 reflect the secession of parts of Transylvania to Hungary in 1940, and the loss of Northern Bukovina to the Soviet Union and Southern Dobrudja to Bulgaria in the same year. For comments on the possible overcounting of the population in Romania in 1941, see the General Introduction.

Table A-5   Data in the footnotes for Yugoslavia for 1948 and 1953 reflect formal annexation of portions of Trieste by Yugoslavia in 1954. Those "temporarily abroad" in 1971 are citizens of Yugoslavia working abroad who were expected to return to the country.

Table A-6   Data for 1950-1974 are taken from publications of the Foreign Demographic Analysis Division of the U.S. Bureau of the Census (here-after referred to as the FDAD). Data for 1975 are estimates of the International Labour Office. The last official Albanian population estimates are for 1971; figures after this date are projected esti-mates of the FDAD and ILO.

Table A-7   Data are from FDAD sources for the years 1950-1974; for 1975, data are taken from official Bulgarian sources.

Table A-8   Data are from FDAD sources for the years 1950-1974; for 1975, data are taken from official Czech sources. Official Czech estimates of the population for 1961-1970 have been revised by the FDAD in light of the 1970 census results.

Table A-9   Data are from FDAD sources for the years 1950-1975; for 1975, data are taken from official East German sources. Official East German estimates of the population for 1950-1964 have been revised by the FDAD in light of the 1964 census results.

Table A-10   Data are from FDAD sources for the years 1950-1974; for 1975, data are taken from official Hungarian sources.

Table A-11   Data are from FDAD sources for the years 1950-1974; for 1975, data are taken from official Polish sources.

Table A-12   Data are from FDAD sources for the years 1950-1974; for 1975, data are taken from official Romanian sources.

Table A-13   Data are from FDAD sources.

Table A-14   Data are from FDAD sources for the years 1950-1974. For 1975, data are taken from official Yugoslav sources.

Table A-15   Data are midyear estimates published by the International Labour Office. These figures have been adjusted to correspond to population data given in Table A-6. Data for 1975 are esti-mates.

Table A-16   Data are midyear estimates published by the International Labour Office.

Table A-17   Data are midyear estimates published by the International Labour Office. These figures have been adjusted to correspond to population data given in Table A-8. Data for 1975 are taken from official Czech sources.

Table A-18   Data are midyear estimates published by the International Labour Office. These figures have been adjusted to correspond to population data given in Table A-9. Data for 1975 are taken from official East German sources.

Table A-19   Data are midyear estimates published by the International Labour Office. Data for 1975 are taken from official Hungarian sources.

Table A-20   Data are midyear estimates published by the International Labour Office. These figures have been adjusted to correspond to population data given in Table A-11. Data for 1976 are taken from official Polish sources.

Table A-21   Data are midyear estimates published by the International Labour Office. These figures have been adjusted to correspond to population data given in Table A-12. Data for 1975 are taken from official Romanian sources.

Table A-22   Data are midyear estimates published by the International Labour Office. These figures have been adjusted to correspond to population data given in Table A-13. Data for 1975 are estimates.

Table A-23   Data are midyear estimates published by the International Labour Office, and include persons temporarily abroad. Data for 1975 are estimates.

Table A-24   Rates are those given in official statistical publications, and may differ slightly from those given in Tables A-6 through A-14, as well as from those appearing in United Nations publications.

Table A-25   Rates are those given in offical statistical publications, and may differ slightly from those appearing in United Nations publications.

Tables A-26 through A-33   United Nations data. See the General Introduction for further comments.

Table A-34   Total Fertility Rates—sum of the age-specific fertility rates.

Table A-35   Population projections are those of the FDAD, "medium variant." For further information see comments in *Summary of Sources* on Section A.

TABLE A-1   TOTAL POPULATION, PREWAR AND POSTWAR BOUNDARIES, CENSUS YEARS:
ALBANIA AND BULGARIA

Albania

Date of Census	Prewar Boundaries[a]			Postwar Boundaries		
	Total	Male	Female	Total	Male	Female
May 1930	1,003,097[b]	...	...			
Sept. 1945				1,122,044	570,361	551,683
Sept. 1950				1,218,943	625,935	593,008
Oct. 1955				1,391,499	713,316	678,183
Oct. 1960				1,626,315	835,294	791,021
Jan. 1979				2,594,600	...	...

Bulgaria

Date of Census	Prewar Boundaries			Postwar Boundaries		
	Total	Male	Female	Total	Male	Female
Dec. 1920	4,846,971	2,420,784	2,426,187	...	...	...
Dec. 1926	5,483,125	2,748,060	2,735,065	...	...	...
Dec. 1934	6,077,939	3,053,893	3,024,046	6,382,000[c]	...	...
Dec. 1946	...	...	...	7,029,349	3,516,774	3,512,575
Dec. 1956	...	...	...	7,613,709	3,799,356	3,814,353
Dec. 1965	...	...	...	8,227,866	4,114,167	4,113,699
Dec. 1975	...	...	...	8,727,771	4,357,820	4,369,951

Notes: a Prewar boundaries identical to postwar boundaries.   b Not cited in Albanian sources,
which utilizes 1938 data in estimating the prewar population.   According to these
estimates, total population in 1938 was 1,040,353.   c Estimate based on the
assumption that there were approximately 304,000 persons in Southern Dobrudja (those
portions falling within Romania) in 1934.

TABLE A-2   TOTAL POPULATION, PREWAR AND POSTWAR BOUNDARIES,
CENSUS YEARS: CZECHOSLOVAKIA AND GDR

Czechoslovakia

	Prewar Boundaries			Postwar Boundaries		
Date of Census	Total	Male	Female	Total	Male	Female
Feb. 1921	13,613,172	6,559,503	7,053,669	13,006,604	6,261,163	6,745,441
Dec. 1930	14,729,536	7,143,116	7,586,420	14,004,179	6,788,098	7,216,081
1946 - 1947	...	...	...	a	...	...
March 1950	...	...	...	12,338,450	5,996,783	6,341,667
March 1961	...	...	...	13,745,577	6,704,674	7,040,903
Dec. 1970	...	...	...	14,361,557	6,989,486	7,372,071

GDR

	Prewar Boundaries			Postwar Boundaries		
Date of Census	Total	Male	Female	Total	Male	Female
May 1939				16,745,300	8,190,800	8,554,600
Oct. 1946				18,488,316[b]	7,859,545[c]	10,628,771[d]
Aug. 1950				18,388,172	8,161,189	10,226,983
Dec. 1964				17,003,631	7,748,134	9,255,497
Jan. 1971				17,068,318	7,865,265	9,203,053

Notes: a Census taken in Slovakia Oct. 4, 1946 and in Czech lands May 22, 1947. Population
of the two regions: Slovakia--3,327,803, Czech lands--8,762,361. b 18,355,000 excluding transients and persons in labor and refugee camps. c 7,796,200 excluding transients
and persons in labor and refugee camps. d 10,558,800 excluding transients and persons
in labor and refugee camps.

TABLE A-3   TOTAL POPULATION, PREWAR AND POSTWAR BOUNDARIES, CENSUS YEARS:
HUNGARY AND POLAND

Hungary

	Prewar Boundaries			Postwar Boundaries		
Date of Census	Total	Male	Female	Total	Male	Female
Dec. 1920	7,990,202	3,875,904	4,114,298	7,986,875	3,874,111	4,112,764
Dec. 1930	8,688,319	4,250,110	4,438,209	8,685,109	4,248,452	4,436,657
Jan. 1941	14,683,323	7,227,680	7,455,643	9,316,074	4,560,875	4,755,199
Jan. 1949	...	...	...	9,204,799	4,423,420	4,781,379
Jan. 1960	...	...	...	9,961,044	4,804,043	5,157,001
Jan. 1970	...	...	...	10,322,099	5,003,651	5,318,448

Poland

	Prewar Boundaries			Postwar Boundaries		
Date of Census	Total	Male	Female	Total	Male	Female
Sept. 1921	27,177,000	13,133,000	14,044,000	...	...	...
Dec. 1931	32,107,252	15,619,000	16,488,000	30,019,400	...	...
Feb. 1946	...	...	...	23,930,000	10,954,000	12,976,000
Dec. 1950	...	...	...	25,008,179	11,927,988	13,080,191
Dec. 1960	...	...	...	29,775,508	14,404,218	15,371,290
Dec. 1970	...	...	...	32,642,270	15,853,618	16,788,652
March, 1974	...	...	...	33,635,933	16,312,730	17,323,203

TABLE A-4   TOTAL POPULATION, PREWAR AND POSTWAR BOUNDARIES,
             CENSUS YEARS: ROMANIA AND THE USSR

Romania

Date of Census	Prewar Boundaries			Postwar Boundaries		
	Total	Male	Female	Total	Male	Female
Dec. 1930	18,057,028	8,886,883	9,170,195	14,280,729	7,015,771	7,264,958
April 1941	16,126,063	...	...	...	...	...
Jan. 1948	...	...	...	15,872,624	7,671,983	8,200,641
Feb. 1956	...	...	...	17,489,450	8,503,420	8,986,030
March 1966	...	...	...	19,103,163	9,351,075	9,752,088
Jan. 1977	...	...	...	21,559,416	10,626,771	10,932,645

USSR

Date of Census	Prewar Boundaries			Postwar Boundaries		
	Total	Male	Female	Total	Male	Female
Dec. 1926	147,027,915	71,043,352	75,984,563	...	...	...
Jan. 1939	170,557,093	81,694,889	88,862,204	190,677,890	91,404,452	99,273,438
Jan. 1959	...	...	...	208,826,650	94,050,303	114,776,347
Jan. 1970	...	...	...	241,720,134	111,399,377	130,320,757
Jan. 1979	...	...	...	262,436,000	122,300,000	140,100,000

TABLE A-5   TOTAL POPULATION, PREWAR AND POSTWAR BOUNDARIES, CENSUS YEARS:
YUGOSLAVIA

Date of Census	Prewar Boundaries			Postwar Boundaries[a]		
	Total	Male	Female	Total	Male	Female
Jan. 1921	11,984,911	5,879,691	6,105,220	12,545,000	6,154,452	6,390,548
March 1931	13,934,038	6,891,627	7,042,411	14,534,000	7,188,371	7,345,629
March 1948	15,326,200	7,368,500	7,957,700	15,772,098[b]	7,582,461[b]	8,189,637[b]
March 1953	...	...	...	16,936,573[c]	8,204,595[c]	8,731,978[c]
March 1961	...	...	...	18,549,291	9,043,424	9,505,867
March 1971	...	...	...	20,522,972[d]	10,077,282[d]	10,445,690[d]

Notes: [a] Boundaries after Sept. 10, 1954, except where otherwise indicated.   [b] Population at time of census. In the present territory of Yugoslavia, the population
was 15,841,566 total, of which 7,615,023 were males, 8,226,543 were females.
[c] Population at time of census. In the present territory of Yugoslavia, the
population was 16,991,449, of which 8,231,936 were males, 8,759,513 females.
[d] Includes 674,449 persons temporarily abroad, of whom 458,963 were males,
215,486 were females.

TABLE A-6   POPULATION GROWTH, COMPONENTS OF POPULATION CHANGE, AND VITAL
RATES: ALBANIA, 1950-1975 (Absolute Numbers in Thousands; Rates
per Thousand Population)

Year	Estimated Population Jan. 1	July 1	Births	Deaths	Natural Increase	Rates Birth	Death	Nat. Increase
1950	1,199	1,215	47	17	30	38.9	14.2	24.7
1951	1,229	1,242	48	19	29	38.5	15.2	23.3
1952	1,256	1,270	45	20	25	35.2	15.6	19.6
1953	1,286	1,302	53	18	35	40.9	13.7	27.2
1954	1,321	1,340	55	18	37	40.8	13.1	27.7
1955	1,359	1,379	61	21	41	44.5	15.1	29.4
1956	1,400	1,420	60	16	43	41.9	11.5	30.4
1957	1,441	1,462	57	17	40	39.1	11.8	27.4
1958	1,482	1,507	63	14	49	41.8	9.3	32.5
1959	1,531	1,556	65	15	50	41.9	9.8	32.1
1960	1,581	1,607	70	17	53	43.4	10.4	32.9
1961	1,634	1,660	68	15	53	41.2	9.3	31.9
1962	1,686	1,711	67	18	49	39.3	10.7	28.6
1963	1,736	1,762	69	18	51	39.1	10.0	29.1
1964	1,788	1,814	69	16	53	37.8	8.7	29.1
1965	1,841	1,865	66	17	49	35.2	9.0	26.2
1966	1,890	1,914	65	16	49	34.0	8.6	25.4
1967	1,938	1,965	69	17	53	35.3	8.4	26.9
1968	1,991	2,019	72	16	56	35.6	8.0	27.6
1969	2,047	2,080	73	16	58	35.3	7.5	27.8
1970	2,105	2,136	70	20	50	32.5	9.2	23.3
1971	2,157	2,188	73	18	55	33.3	8.1	25.2
1972	2,210	2,238	74	18	55	32.9	8.1	24.8
1973	2,266	2,297	70	18	52	30.4	7.9	22.5
1974	2,323	2,352	78	19	59	33.0	8.0	25.0
1975	2,417	2,482	...	...	...	...	...	...

TABLE A-7   POPULATION GROWTH, COMPONENTS OF POPULATION CHANGE, AND VITAL
             RATES: BULGARIA, 1950-1975 (Absolute Numbers in Thousands;
             Rates per Thousand Population)

Year	Estimated Population Jan. 1	Estimated Population July 1	Births	Deaths	Natural Increase	Rates Birth	Rates Death	Rates Nat. Increase
1950	7,228	7,250	183	74	108	25.2	10.2	15.0
1951	7,273	7,258	153	77	75	21.0	10.6	10.4
1952	7,243	7,275	154	84	70	21.2	11.6	9.6
1953	7,307	7,346	153	68	85	20.9	9.3	11.6
1954	7,386	7,423	150	68	82	20.2	9.2	11.0
1955	7,461	7,499	151	68	83	20.1	9.0	11.1
1956	7,538	7,576	148	71	77	19.5	9.4	10.1
1957	7,616	7,651	141	66	75	18.4	8.6	9.8
1958	7,689	7,728	138	61	78	17.9	7.9	10.0
1959	7,766	7,798	137	74	63	17.6	9.5	8.1
1960	7,829	7,867	140	64	76	17.8	8.1	9.7
1961	7,906	7,943	138	63	75	17.4	7.9	9.5
1962	7,981	8,013	134	70	65	16.7	8.7	8.0
1963	8,045	8,078	132	66	66	16.4	8.2	8.2
1964	8,111	8,144	131	64	66	16.1	7.9	8.2
1965	8,178	8,201	126	67	59	15.3	8.1	7.2
1966	8,231	8,258	123	68	55	14.9	8.3	6.6
1967	8,285	8,310	125	75	50	15.0	9.0	6.0
1968	8,335	8,370	141	72	69	16.9	8.6	8.3
1969	8,404	8,434	143	80	63	17.0	9.5	7.5
1970	8,464	8,490	139	77	62	16.3	9.1	7.2
1971	8,515	8,536	135	83	53	15.9	9.7	6.2
1972	8,558	8,576	131	84	47	15.3	9.8	5.5
1973	8,594	8,621	140	81	58	16.2	9.5	6.7
1974	8,647	8,679	149	85	64	17.2	9.8	7.4
1975	8,710	8,722	145	90	55	16.6	10.3	6.3

TABLE A-8   POPULATION GROWTH, COMPONENTS OF POPULATION CHANGE, AND VITAL
RATES: CZECHOSLOVAKIA, 1950-1975 (Absolute Numbers in Thousands;
Rates per Thousand Population)

Year	Estimated Population Jan. 1	July 1	Births	Deaths	Increase	Rates Birth	Death	Nat. Increase
1950	12,340	12,389	288	143	145	23.3	11.5	11.8
1951	12,464	12,532	286	143	143	22.8	11.4	11.4
1952	12,607	12,683	281	135	146	22.2	10.6	11.6
1953	12,754	12,820	272	134	137	21.2	10.5	10.7
1954	12,892	12,952	267	135	132	20.6	10.4	10.2
1955	13,024	13,093	265	126	139	20.3	9.6	10.7
1956	13,162	13,229	262	126	136	19.8	9.6	10.2
1957	13,296	13,358	253	134	118	18.9	10.1	8.8
1958	13,414	13,474	235	126	109	17.4	9.3	8.1
1959	13,523	13,565	217	131	86	16.0	9.7	6.3
1960	13,608	13,654	217	125	92	15.9	9.2	6.7
1961	13,698	13,779	218	126	92	15.8	9.2	6.7
1962	13,822	13,858	217	139	79	15.7	10.0	5.7
1963	13,899	13,948	236	133	103	16.9	9.5	7.4
1964	13,999	14,052	241	135	106	17.2	9.6	7.6
1965	14,097	14,147	232	141	91	16.4	10.0	6.4
1966	14,179	14,224	223	142	80	15.7	10.0	5.7
1967	14,252	14,277	216	144	72	15.1	10.1	5.0
1968	14,298	14,323	214	153	61	14.9	10.7	4.2
1969	14,282	14,284	223	161	62	15.6	11.3	4.3
1970	14,309	14,319	229	166	63	16.0	11.6	4.4
1971	14,350	14,390	237	165	72	16.5	11.5	5.0
1972	14,419	14,465	251	161	91	17.4	11.1	6.3
1973	14,510	14,561	274	168	107	18.8	11.5	7.3
1974	14,618	14,686	291	171	120	19.8	11.7	8.1
1975	14,738	14,797	289	170	120	19.5	11.5	8.0

TABLE A-9   POPULATION GROWTH, COMPONENTS OF POPULATION CHANGE, AND VITAL
             RATES: GDR, 1950-1975 (Absolute Numbers in Thousands; Rates per
             Thousand Population)

Year	Estimated Population Jan. 1	Estimated Population July 1	Births	Deaths	Natural Increase	Rates Birth	Rates Death	Rates Nat. Increase
1950	18,388	18,388	304	220	84	16.5	11.9	4.6
1951	18,355	18,344	311	209	102	16.9	11.4	5.6
1952	18,334	18,303	306	222	84	16.7	12.1	4.6
1953	18,271	18,164	299	213	86	16.5	11.7	4.8
1954	18,057	17,993	294	220	74	16.3	12.2	4.1
1955	17,929	17,832	293	214	79	16.4	12.0	4.4
1956	17,736	17,607	281	213	69	16.0	12.1	3.9
1957	17,478	17,370	273	225	48	15.7	13.0	2.8
1958	17,263	17,206	271	221	50	15.8	12.9	2.9
1959	17,149	17,132	292	230	62	17.0	13.4	3.6
1960	17,114	17,058	293	234	59	17.2	13.7	3.5
1961	17,002	16,938	301	223	78	17.8	13.2	4.6
1962	16,875	16,903	298	234	64	17.6	13.8	3.8
1963	16,930	16,951	301	222	79	17.8	13.1	4.7
1964	16,972	16,983	292	226	66	17.2	13.3	3.9
1965	17,004	17,020	281	230	51	16.5	13.5	3.0
1966	17,040	17,058	268	226	42	15.7	13.2	2.5
1967	17,071	17,082	253	227	26	14.8	13.3	1.5
1968	17,090	17,084	245	242	3	14.3	14.2	0.2
1969	17,087	17,076	239	244	-5	14.0	14.3	-0.3
1970	17,075	17,070	237	241	-4	13.9	14.1	-0.2
1971	17,068	17,061	235	235	0	13.8	13.8	0.0
1972	17,054	17,043	200	234	-34	11.8	13.8	-2.0
1973	17,011	16,980	180	232	-52	10.6	13.7	-3.0
1974	16,951	16,925	179	229	-50	10.6	13.5	-2.9
1975	16,891	16,850	182	240	-59	10.8	14.3	-3.5

TABLE A-10   POPULATION GROWTH, COMPONENTS OF POPULATION CHANGE, AND VITAL
             RATES: HUNGARY, 1950-1975 (Absolute Numbers in Thousands; Rates
             per Thousand Population)

Year	Estimated Population		Births	Deaths	Natural Increase	Rates		
	Jan. 1	July 1				Birth	Death	Nat. Increase
1950	9,293	9,338	196	107	89	20.9	11.4	9.5
1951	9,383	9,423	191	110	81	20.2	11.7	8.5
1952	9,463	9,504	186	107	78	19.6	11.3	8.3
1953	9,545	9,595	207	112	95	21.6	11.7	9.9
1954	9,645	9,706	223	107	117	23.0	11.0	12.0
1955	9,767	9,825	210	98	113	21.4	10.0	11.4
1956	9,883	9,911	193	104	89	19.5	10.5	9.0
1957	9,829	9,839	167	104	64	17.0	10.5	6.5
1958	9,850	9,882	158	98	61	16.0	9.9	6.1
1959	9,913	9,937	151	104	47	15.2	10.5	4.7
1960	9,961	9,984	146	102	45	14.7	10.2	4.5
1961	10,007	10,029	140	96	44	14.0	9.6	4.4
1962	10,052	10,063	130	108	22	12.9	10.8	2.1
1963	10,074	10,091	132	100	32	13.1	9.9	3.2
1964	10,108	10,124	132	101	31	13.1	10.0	3.1
1965	10,140	10,153	133	108	25	13.1	10.7	2.4
1966	10,166	10,185	138	102	37	13.6	10.0	3.6
1967	10,203	10,223	149	110	39	14.6	10.7	3.9
1968	10,244	10,264	154	115	39	15.1	11.2	3.9
1969	10,284	10,303	154	117	38	15.0	11.4	3.6
1970	10,322	10,338	152	120	32	14.7	11.6	3.1
1971	10,354	10,368	151	123	28	14.5	11.9	2.6
1972	10,381	10,398	153	119	34	14.7	11.4	3.3
1973	10,416	10,432	156	123	33	15.0	11.8	3.2
1974	10,448	10,473	186	126	61	17.8	12.0	5.8
1975	10,509	10,541	194	131	63	18.4	12.4	6.0

TABLE A-11   POPULATION GROWTH, COMPONENTS OF POPULATION CHANGE, AND VITAL
              RATES: POLAND, 1950-1975 (Absolute Numbers in Thousands; Rates
              per Thousand Population)

Year	Estimated Population Jan. 1	Estimated Population July 1	Births	Deaths	Natural Increase	Rates Birth	Rates Death	Rates Nat. Increase
1950	24,613	24,824	763	289	474	30.7	11.6	19.1
1951	25,035	25,271	784	312	471	31.0	12.4	18.6
1952	25,507	25,753	779	287	492	30.2	11.1	19.1
1953	25,999	26,255	779	267	512	29.7	10.2	19.5
1954	26,511	26,761	778	276	502	29.1	10.3	18.8
1955	27,012	27,281	794	262	532	29.1	9.6	19.5
1956	27,550	27,815	780	250	530	28.1	9.0	19.1
1957	28,080	28,310	782	269	513	27.6	9.5	18.1
1958	28,540	28,770	755	241	514	26.3	8.4	17.9
1959	29,000	29,240	723	252	470	24.7	8.6	16.1
1960	29,480	29,561	669	224	445	22.6	7.6	15.0
1961	29,795	29,978	628	228	400	20.9	7.6	13.3
1962	30,161	30,329	600	239	360	19.8	7.9	11.9
1963	30,497	30,663	588	230	358	19.2	7.5	11.7
1964	30,829	30,976	563	236	327	18.2	7.6	10.6
1965	31,124	31,261	546	232	314	17.5	7.4	10.0
1966	31,399	31,528	530	233	297	16.8	7.4	9.4
1967	31,657	31,780	520	248	273	16.4	7.8	8.6
1968	31,903	32,031	524	244	280	16.4	7.6	8.7
1969	32,158	32,277	531	263	268	16.5	8.1	8.3
1970	32,397	32,526	546	267	279	16.8	8.2	8.6
1971	32,658	32,805	562	284	279	17.1	8.6	8.5
1972	32,909	33,068	576	265	310	17.4	8.0	9.4
1973	33,202	33,363	599	277	321	17.9	8.3	9.6
1974	33,512	33,691	621	277	344	18.4	8.2	10.2
1975	33,846	34,015	644	297	346.9	18.9	8.7	10.2

TABLE A-12   POPULATION GROWTH, COMPONENTS OF POPULATION CHANGE, AND VITAL
             RATES: ROMANIA, 1950-1975 (Absolute Numbers in Thousands; Rates
             per Thousand Population)

Year	Estimated Population Jan. 1	Estimated Population July 1	Births	Death	Natural Increase	Rates Birth	Rates Death	Rates Nat. Increase
1950	16,198	16,311	427	202	225	26.2	12.4	13.8
1951	16,400	16,464	413	210	203	25.1	12.8	12.3
1952	16,547	16,630	413	195	218	24.8	11.7	13.1
1953	16,738	16,847	402	195	207	23.8	11.6	12.2
1954	16,944	17,040	422	195	227	24.8	11.5	13.3
1955	17,182	17,325	443	168	275	25.6	9.7	15.9
1956	17,457	17,583	426	175	251	24.2	9.9	14.3
1957	17,706	17,829	408	182	226	22.9	10.2	12.7
1958	17,943	18,056	390	157	234	21.6	8.7	12.9
1959	18,141	18,226	368	187	181	20.2	10.2	10.0
1960	18,315	18,403	352	161	192	19.1	8.7	10.4
1961	18,495	18,567	325	162	163	17.5	8.7	8.8
1962	18,624	18,681	302	172	130	16.2	9.2	7.0
1963	18,747	18,813	295	156	139	15.7	8.3	7.4
1964	18,870	18,927	287	152	135	15.2	8.1	7.1
1965	18,977	19,027	278	163	115	14.6	8.6	6.0
1966	19,084	19,141	274	157	116	14.3	8.2	6.1
1967	19,195	19,285	528	179	349	27.4	9.3	18.1
1968	19,542	19,721	526	189	338	26.7	9.6	17.1
1969	19,879	20,010	466	201	265	23.3	10.1	13.2
1970	20,140	20,253	427	193	234	21.1	9.5	11.6
1971	20,361	20,470	400	194	206	19.5	9.5	10.0
1972	20,562	20,663	389	190	199	18.8	9.2	9.6
1973	20,754	20,828	379	204	175	18.2	9.8	8.4
1974	20,917	21,030	427	191	236	20.3	9.1	11.2
1975	21,137	21,245	418	198	221	19.7	9.3	10.4

TABLE A-13   POPULATION GROWTH, COMPONENTS OF POPULATION CHANGE, AND VITAL
RATES: USSR, 1950-1975 (Absolute Numbers in Thousands; Rates
per Thousand Population)

Year	Estimated Population Jan. 1	Estimated Population July 1	Births	Deaths	Natural Increase	Rates Birth	Rates Death	Rates Nat. Increase
1950	178,547	180,075	4,805	1,745	3,060	26.7	9.7	17.0
1951	181,603	183,191	4,954	1,777	3,177	27.0	9.7	17.3
1952	184,778	186,378	4,984	1,749	3,199	26.5	9.4	17.1
1953	187,977	189,491	4,754	1,724	3,030	25.1	9.1	16.0
1954	191,004	192,710	5,135	1,715	3,420	26.6	8.9	17.7
1955	194,415	196,159	5,047	1,613	3,435	25.7	8.2	17.5
1956	197,902	199,658	5,023	1,517	3,505	25.2	7.6	17.6
1957	210,414	203,170	5,164	1,585	3,579	25.4	7.8	17.6
1958	204,925	206,806	5,240	1,491	3,749	25.3	7.2	18.1
1959	208,686	210,529	5,265	1,604	3,661	25.0	7.6	17.4
1960	212,372	214,329	5,341	1,529	3,812	24.9	7.1	17.8
1961	216,286	218,145	5,192	1,563	3,629	23.8	7.2	16.6
1962	220,003	221,730	4,959	1,667	3,292	22.4	7.5	14.9
1963	223,457	225,063	4,758	1,627	3,131	21.2	7.2	13.9
1964	226,669	228,149	4,457	1,581	2,875	19.5	6.9	12.6
1965	229,628	230,936	4,253	1,690	2,563	18.4	7.3	11.1
1966	232,243	233,533	4,242	1,711	2,351	18.2	7.3	10.9
1967	234,823	235,994	4,093	1,799	2,294	17.3	7.6	9.7
1968	237,165	238,317	4,088	1,833	2,254	17.2	7.7	9.5
1969	239,468	240,554	4,087	1,957	2,130	17.0	8.1	8.9
1970	241,640	242,757	4,226	1,996	2,229	17.4	8.2	9.2
1971	243,873	245,091	4,372	2,015	2,356	17.8	8.2	9.6
1972	246,300	247,450	4,404	2,105	2,299	17.8	8.5	9.3
1973	248,600	249,700	4,386	2,164	2,222	17.6	8.7	8.9
1974	250,900	252,100	4,546	2,191	2,355	18.0	8.7	9.3
1975	253,300	254,300	4,612	2,363	2,248	18.1	9.3	8.8

TABLE A-14   POPULATION GROWTH, COMPONENTS OF POPULATION CHANGE, AND VITAL
               RATES: YUGOSLAVIA, 1950-1975 (Absolute Numbers in Thousands;
               Rates per Thousand Population)

Year	Estimated Population		Births	Deaths	Natural Increase	Rates		
	Jan. 1	July 1				Birth	Death	Nat. Increase
1950	16,240	16,346	494	212	282	30.2	13.0	17.2
1951	16,467	16,588	447	235	213	27.0	14.1	12.9
1952	16,693	16,798	499	198	302	29.7	11.8	17.9
1953	16,923	17,048	484	212	272	28.4	12.4	16.0
1954	17,166	17,284	494	188	306	28.6	10.9	17.7
1955	17,402	17,519	471	200	271	26.9	11.4	15.5
1956	17,602	17,685	460	198	262	26.0	11.2	14.8
1957	17,772	17,859	427	190	236	23.9	10.7	13.2
1958	17,938	18,018	432	167	266	24.0	9.3	14.7
1959	18,116	18,214	424	181	244	23.4	9.9	13.5
1960	18,308	18,402	433	183	250	23.5	9.9	13.6
1961	18,507	18,612	422	167	255	22.7	9.0	13.7
1962	18,716	18,819	413	187	226	21.9	9.9	12.0
1963	18,924	19,029	407	170	238	21.4	8.9	12.5
1964	19,126	19,222	401	181	220	20.8	9.4	11.4
1965	19,328	19,434	408	171	238	21.0	8.8	12.2
1966	19,539	19,644	400	160	240	20.4	8.1	12.3
1967	19,742	19,840	390	174	216	19.6	8.8	10.8
1968	19,934	20,029	383	175	208	19.1	8.7	10.4
1969	20,119	20,209	383	189	194	18.9	9.3	9.6
1970	20,290	20,371	363	182	181	17.8	8.9	8.9
1971	20,471	20,572	376	179	197	18.3	8.7	9.6
1972	20,670	20,772	381	191	190	18.3	9.2	9.1
1973	20,860	20,956	377	182	195	18.0	8.7	9.3
1974	21,055	21,155	379	177	202	17.9	8.4	9.5
1975	21,253	21,352	388	185	203	18.2	8.7	9.5

TABLE A-15   POPULATION BY AGE GROUPS AND SEX: ALBANIA, 1950-1975
(in Thousands)

Age Groups	1950			1955			1960		
	Total	Male	Female	Total	Male	Female	Total	Male	Female
TOTAL POPULATION	1,215	609	606	1,379	692	687	1,607	807	800
Percent	100.0%	100.0%	100.0%	100.0%	100.0%	100.0%	100.0%	100.0%	100.0%
0-9	330	168	162	388	198	190	493	251	242
Percent	27.2%	27.6%	26.8%	28.1%	28.5%	27.8%	30.7%	31.0%	30.4%
10-14	147	74	73	153	78	75	168	85	83
Percent	12.1%	12.2%	12.0%	11.1%	11.3%	11.0%	10.5%	10.5%	10.4%
15-19	123	63	60	145	73	72	154	78	76
Percent	10.1%	10.3%	10.0%	10.5%	10.6%	10.4%	9.6%	9.7%	9.4%
20-24	108	55	53	121	62	59	145	73	72
Percent	8.8%	9.0%	8.7%	8.8%	8.9%	8.7%	9.0%	9.1%	9.0%
25-44	278	140	138	324	163	161	373	188	185
Percent	22.8%	23.0%	22.7%	23.5%	23.6%	23.4%	23.2%	23.3%	23.1%
45-54	91	45	46	98	49	49	118	59	59
Percent	7.5%	7.4%	7.6%	7.1%	7.1%	7.1%	7.3%	7.3%	7.4%
55-64	64	30	34	69	33	36	77	38	39
Percent	5.3%	5.0%	5.6%	5.0%	4.8%	5.1%	4.8%	4.7%	4.9%
65 & over	74	34	40	81	36	45	78	35	43
Percent	6.1%	5.6%	6.6%	5.9%	5.2%	6.6%	4.9%	4.4%	5.4%

Age Groups	1965			1970			1975[a]		
	Total	Male	Female	Total	Male	Female	Total	Male	Female
TOTAL POPULATION	1,865	940	925	2,136	1,079	1,057	2,482	1,256	1,226
Percent	100.0%	100.0%	100.0%	100.0%	100.0%	100.0%	100.0%	100.0%	100.0%
0-9	588	300	288	632	324	308	698	358	339
Percent	31.5%	31.9%	31.1%	29.6%	30.0%	29.2%	28.1%	28.5%	27.7%
10-14	214	108	106	273	139	134	314	160	153
Percent	11.5%	11.5%	11.4%	12.8%	12.9%	12.7%	12.7%	12.7%	12.5%
15-19	167	84	83	213	107	106	276	140	135
Percent	8.9%	9.0%	8.9%	10.0%	9.9%	10.0%	11.1%	11.1%	11.0%
20-24	152	77	75	165	84	81	214	108	106
Percent	8.1%	8.2%	8.0%	7.7%	7.8%	7.7%	8.6%	8.6%	8.6%
25-44	440	222	218	512	259	253	578	293	285
Percent	23.6%	23.6%	23.6%	24.0%	24.0%	24.0%	23.3%	23.3%	23.2%
45-54	132	67	65	141	71	70	174	86	87
Percent	7.1%	7.1%	7.1%	6.6%	6.6%	6.6%	7.0%	6.8%	7.1%
55-64	88	43	45	106	52	54	122	61	62
Percent	4.7%	4.6%	4.9%	5.0%	4.8%	5.1%	4.9%	4.9%	5.1%
65 & over	84	39	45	94	43	51	107	50	57
Percent	4.5%	4.2%	4.9%	4.4%	4.0%	4.7%	4.3%	4.0%	4.6%

Notes: a Projected Population.

TABLE A-16   POPULATION BY AGE GROUPS AND SEX: BULGARIA, 1950-1975
(in Thousands)

Age Groups	1950 Total	1950 Male	1950 Female	1955 Total	1955 Male	1955 Female	1960 Total	1960 Male	1960 Female
TOTAL POPULATION	7,251	3,624	3,627	7,499	3,739	3,760	7,867	3,927	3,940
Percent	100.0%	100.0%	100.0%	100.0%	100.0%	100.0%	100.0%	100.0%	100.0%
0-9	1,343	686	657	1,401	715	686	1,347	688	659
Percent	18.5%	18.9%	18.1%	18.7%	19.1%	18.2%	17.1%	17.5%	16.7%
10-14	599	302	297	591	300	291	703	358	345
Percent	8.3%	8.3%	8.2%	7.9%	8.0%	7.7%	8.9%	9.1%	8.7%
15-19	682	344	338	581	292	289	591	300	291
Percent	9.4%	9.5%	9.3%	7.7%	7.8%	7.7%	7.5%	7.6%	7.4%
20-24	690	350	340	660	332	328	580	291	289
Percent	9.5%	9.7%	9.4%	8.8%	8.9%	8.7%	7.4%	7.4%	7.3%
25-44	2,140	1,083	1,057	2,233	1,123	1,110	2,363	1,185	1,178
Percent	29.5%	30.0%	29.1%	29.8%	30.0%	29.5%	30.0%	30.2%	29.9%
45-54	794	397	397	907	459	448	986	498	488
Percent	10.9%	10.9%	10.9%	12.1%	12.3%	11.9%	12.5%	12.7%	12.4%
55-64	515	236	279	570	271	299	706	346	360
Percent	7.1%	6.5%	7.7%	7.6%	7.2%	7.9%	9.0%	8.8%	9.1%
65 & over	488	226	262	556	247	309	591	261	330
Percent	6.7%	6.2%	7.2%	7.4%	6.6%	8.2%	7.5%	6.6%	8.4%

Age Groups	1965 Total	1965 Male	1965 Female	1970 Total	1970 Male	1970 Female	1975 Total	1975 Male	1975 Female
TOTAL POPULATION	8,201	4,098	4,102	8,490	4,244	4,246	8,722	4,354	4,368
Percent	100.0%	100.0%	100.0%	100.0%	100.0%	100.0%	100.0%	100.0%	100.0%
0-9	1,296	664	632	1,279	656	623	1,303	668	634
Percent	15.8%	16.2%	15.4%	15.1%	15.5%	14.7%	14.9%	15.3%	14.5%
10-14	686	350	336	659	337	323	617	319	299
Percent	8.4%	8.5%	8.2%	7.8%	7.9%	7.6%	7.1%	7.3%	6.8%
15-19	700	356	344	681	347	333	650	332	318
Percent	8.5%	8.7%	8.4%	8.0%	8.2%	7.8%	7.5%	7.6%	7.3%
20-24	587	298	290	688	349	339	671	339	332
Percent	7.1%	7.3%	7.1%	8.1%	8.2%	8.0%	7.7%	7.8%	7.6%
25-44	2,526	1,266	1,260	2,448	1,231	1,217	2,452	1,230	1,223
Percent	30.8%	30.9%	30.7%	28.8%	29.0%	28.7%	28.1%	28.2%	28.0%
45-54	881	442	439	1,011	503	508	1,265	629	635
Percent	10.7%	10.8%	10.7%	11.9%	11.8%	12.0%	14.5%	14.4%	14.5%
55-64	835	416	420	910	451	459	811	400	411
Percent	10.2%	10.1%	10.2%	10.7%	10.6%	10.8%	9.3%	9.2%	9.4%
65 & over	688	307	382	814	370	444	953	437	516
Percent	8.4%	7.5%	9.3%	9.6%	8.7%	10.5%	10.9%	10.0%	11.8%

TABLE A-17   POPULATION BY AGE GROUPS AND SEX: CZECHOSLOVAKIA, 1950-1975
(in Thousands)

Age Groups	1950			1955			1960		
	Total	Male	Female	Total	Male	Female	Total	Male	Female
TOTAL POPULATION	12,389	6,021	6,368	13,093	6,368	6,725	13,654	6,662	6,992
Percent	100.0%	100.0%	100.0%	100.0%	100.0%	100.0%	100.0%	100.0%	100.0%
0-9	2,343	1,195	1,148	2,586	1,319	1,267	2,481	1,269	1,212
Percent	18.9%	19.8%	18.0%	19.7%	20.7%	18.8%	18.2%	19.0%	17.3%
10-14	870	440	430	1,047	531	516	1,267	645	622
Percent	7.0%	7.3%	6.7%	8.0%	8.3%	7.7%	9.3%	9.7%	8.9%
15-19	930	469	461	861	435	426	1,045	530	515
Percent	7.5%	7.8%	7.2%	6.6%	6.8%	6.3%	7.6%	7.9%	7.4%
20-24	988	492	496	918	461	457	859	433	426
Percent	7.9%	8.2%	7.9%	7.0%	7.2%	6.8%	6.3%	6.5%	6.1%
25-44	3,591	1,763	1,828	3,546	1,739	1,807	3,504	1,726	1,778
Percent	29.0%	29.3%	28.7%	27.1%	27.3%	26.9%	25.7%	25.9%	25.4%
45-54	1,657	792	865	1,811	883	928	1,845	900	945
Percent	13.4%	13.1%	13.6%	13.8%	13.9%	13.8%	13.5%	13.5%	13.5%
55-64	1,071	467	604	1,256	564	692	1,479	685	794
Percent	8.6%	7.7%	9.5%	9.6%	8.9%	10.3%	10.8%	10.3%	11.3%
65 & over	939	403	536	1,068	436	632	1,174	474	700
Percent	7.6%	6.7%	8.4%	8.1%	6.8%	9.4%	8.6%	7.1%	10.0%

Age Groups	1965			1970			1975		
	Total	Male	Female	Total	Male	Female	Total	Male	Female
TOTAL POPULATION	14,147	6,905	7,242	14,319	6,977	7,342	14,797	7,209	7,588
Percent	100.0%	100.0%	100.0%	100.0%	100.0%	100.0%	100.0%	100.0%	100.0%
0-9	2,279	1,168	1,111	2,173	1,112	1,061	2,360	1,208	1,152
Percent	16.1%	16.9%	15.3%	15.2%	15.9%	14.4%	15.9%	16.8%	15.2%
10-14	1,304	665	638	1,127	575	552	1,097	563	534
Percent	9.2%	9.6%	8.8%	7.9%	8.2%	7.5%	7.4%	7.8%	7.0%
15-19	1,264	644	620	1,278	651	627	1,157	591	566
Percent	8.9%	9.3%	8.6%	8.9%	9.3%	8.5%	7.8%	8.2%	7.5%
20-24	1,041	528	514	1,254	637	617	1,285	656	629
Percent	7.4%	7.6%	7.1%	8.7%	9.1%	8.4%	8.7%	9.1%	8.3%
25-44	3,740	1,850	1,890	3,674	1,832	1,842	3,916	1,960	1,956
Percent	26.4%	26.8%	26.1%	25.6%	26.2%	25.1%	26.5%	27.2%	25.8%
45-54	1,482	717	765	1,566	755	811	1,872	898	974
Percent	10.5%	10.4%	10.5%	10.9%	10.8%	11.0%	12.7%	12.5%	12.8%
55-64	1,646	777	869	1,629	765	864	1,316	610	706
Percent	11.6%	11.3%	12.0%	11.4%	11.0%	11.8%	8.9%	8.5%	9.3%
65 & over	1,391	556	835	1,618	650	968	1,792	721	1,071
Percent	9.8%	8.0%	11.5%	11.3%	9.3%	13.2%	12.1%	10.0%	14.1%

TABLE A-18   POPULATION BY AGE GROUPS AND SEX: GDR, 1950-1975 (in Thousands)

Age Groups	1950			1955			1960		
	Total	Male	Female	Total	Male	Female	Total	Male	Female
TOTAL POPULATION	18,387	8,160	10,227	17,832	7,968	9,864	17,058	7,679	9,379
Percent	100.0%	100.0%	100.0%	100.0%	100.0%	100.0%	100.0%	100.0%	100.0%
0-9	2,482	1,268	1,214	2,409	1,232	1,177	2,645	1,357	1,288
Percent	13.5%	15.5%	11.9%	13.5%	15.5%	11.9%	15.5%	17.7%	13.7%
10-14	1,718	874	844	1,348	685	663	950	483	467
Percent	9.3%	10.7%	8.3%	7.6%	8.6%	6.7%	5.6%	6.3%	5.0%
15-19	1,339	669	670	1,589	805	784	1,237	626	611
Percent	7.3%	8.2%	6.6%	8.9%	10.1%	7.9%	7.2%	8.2%	6.5%
20-24	1,177	523	654	1,206	596	610	1,386	701	685
Percent	6.4%	6.4%	6.4%	6.8%	7.5%	6.2%	8.1%	9.1%	7.3%
25-44	4,665	1,830	2,835	4,037	1,609	2,428	3,744	1,620	2,124
Percent	25.4%	22.4%	27.7%	22.6%	20.2%	24.6%	21.9%	21.1%	22.6%
45-54	2,876	1,258	1,618	2,786	1,197	1,589	2,379	953	1,426
Percent	15.6%	15.4%	15.8%	15.6%	15.0%	16.1%	13.9%	12.4%	15.2%
55-64	2,187	905	1,282	2,270	935	1,335	2,384	1,017	1,367
Percent	11.9%	11.1%	12.5%	12.7%	11.7%	13.5%	14.0%	13.2%	14.6%
65 & over	1,943	833	1,110	2,187	909	1,278	2,333	922	1,411
Percent	10.6%	10.2%	10.8%	12.3%	11.4%	13.0%	13.7%	12.0%	15.0%

Age Groups	1965			1970			1975		
	Total	Male	Female	Total	Male	Female	Total	Male	Female
TOTAL POPULATION	17,019	7,762	9,257	17,070	7,857	9,213	16,850	7,823	9,027
Percent	100.0%	100.0%	100.0%	100.0%	100.0%	100.0%	100.0%	100.0%	100.0%
0-9	2,751	1,410	1,341	2,669	1,368	1,301	2,214	1,134	1,080
Percent	16.2%	18.2%	14.5%	15.6%	17.4%	14.1%	13.1%	14.5%	12.0%
10-14	1,306	670	636	1,318	676	642	1,429	732	697
Percent	7.7%	8.6%	6.9%	7.7%	8.6%	7.0%	8.5%	9.3%	7.7%
15-19	923	471	452	1,307	671	636	1,322	678	644
Percent	5.4%	6.1%	4.9%	7.7%	8.5%	6.9%	7.8%	8.7%	7.1%
20-24	1,170	588	582	926	474	452	1,311	673	638
Percent	6.9%	7.6%	6.3%	5.4%	6.0%	4.9%	7.8%	8.6%	7.1%
25-44	4,315	2,018	2,297	4,539	2,237	2,302	4,441	2,238	2,203
Percent	25.3%	26.0%	24.8%	26.6%	28.5%	25.0%	26.4%	28.6%	24.4%
45-54	1,690	647	1,043	1,534	584	950	1,863	783	1,080
Percent	9.9%	8.3%	11.3%	9.0%	7.4%	10.3%	11.1%	10.0%	12.0%
55-64	2,380	1,004	1,376	2,125	833	1,292	1,528	571	957
Percent	14.0%	12.9%	14.9%	12.4%	10.6%	14.0%	9.1%	7.3%	10.6%
65 & over	2,484	954	1,530	2,652	1,014	1,638	2,742	1,014	1,728
Percent	14.6%	12.3%	16.5%	15.5%	12.9%	17.8%	16.3%	12.9%	19.2%

TABLE A-19   POPULATION BY AGE GROUPS AND SEX: HUNGARY, 1950-1975
(in Thousands)

Age Groups	1950			1955			1960		
	Total	Male	Female	Total	Male	Female	Total	Male	Female
TOTAL POPULATION	9,338	4,490	4,848	9,825	4,745	5,080	9,984	4,816	5,168
Percent	100.0%	100.0%	100.0%	100.0%	100.0%	100.0%	100.0%	100.0%	100.0%
0-9	1,605	818	787	1,752	897	855	1,724	882	842
Percent	17.2%	18.2%	16.2%	17.8%	18.9%	16.8%	17.3%	18.3%	16.3%
10-14	739	373	366	767	389	378	804	409	395
Percent	7.9%	8.3%	7.5%	7.8%	8.2%	7.4%	8.1%	8.5%	7.6%
15-19	765	384	381	733	370	363	750	377	373
Percent	8.2%	8.5%	7.9%	7.5%	7.8%	7.1%	7.5%	7.8%	7.2%
20-24	788	389	399	756	379	377	684	333	351
Percent	8.4%	8.7%	8.2%	7.7%	8.0%	7.4%	6.8%	6.9%	6.8%
25-44	2,729	1,295	1,434	2,766	1,323	1,443	2,698	1,301	1,397
Percent	29.2%	28.8%	29.6%	28.2%	27.9%	28.4%	27.0%	27.0%	27.0%
45-54	1,210	574	636	1,299	620	679	1,351	639	712
Percent	13.0%	12.8%	13.1%	13.2%	13.1%	13.4%	13.5%	13.3%	13.8%
55-64	817	359	458	946	425	521	1,070	498	572
Percent	8.7%	8.0%	9.4%	9.6%	9.0%	10.3%	10.7%	10.3%	11.1%
65 & over	685	298	387	806	342	464	903	377	526
Percent	7.3%	6.6%	8.0%	8.2%	7.2%	9.1%	9.0%	7.8%	10.2%

Age Groups	1965			1970			1975		
	Total	Male	Female	Total	Male	Female	Total	Male	Female
TOTAL POPULATION	10,153	4,906	5,247	10,338	5,012	5,326	10,541	5,113	5,427
Percent	100.0%	100.0%	100.0%	100.0%	100.0%	100.0%	100.0%	100.0%	100.0%
0-9	1,439	739	700	1,355	698	658	1,501	772	729
Percent	14.2%	15.1%	13.3%	13.1%	13.9%	12.3%	14.2%	15.1%	13.4%
10-14	922	471	451	796	409	387	642	330	312
Percent	9.1%	9.6%	8.6%	7.7%	8.2%	7.3%	6.1%	6.5%	5.7%
15-19	803	407	396	927	475	452	794	407	387
Percent	7.9%	8.3%	7.5%	9.0%	9.5%	8.5%	7.5%	8.0%	7.1%
20-24	745	375	370	797	405	392	922	472	451
Percent	7.3%	7.6%	7.1%	7.7%	8.0%	7.4%	8.7%	9.2%	8.3%
25-44	2,884	1,396	1,488	2,853	1,402	1,451	2,890	1,433	1,457
Percent	28.4%	28.5%	28.4%	27.6%	28.0%	27.2%	27.4%	28.0%	26.8%
45-54	1,140	534	606	1,188	560	628	1,430	682	748
Percent	11.2%	10.9%	11.5%	11.5%	11.2%	11.8%	13.6%	13.3%	13.8%
55-64	1,172	547	625	1,228	567	661	1,030	470	560
Percent	11.5%	11.1%	11.9%	11.9%	11.3%	12.4%	9.8%	9.2%	10.3%
65 & over	1,048	437	611	1,194	496	698	1,332	548	784
Percent	10.3%	8.9%	11.6%	11.5%	9.9%	13.1%	12.6%	10.7%	14.4%

TABLE A-20   POPULATION BY AGE GROUPS AND SEX: POLAND, 1950-1976 (in Thousands)

Age Groups	1950			1955			1960		
	Total	Male	Female	Total	Male	Female	Total	Male	Female
TOTAL POPULATION	24,824	11,830	12,994	27,281	13,123	14,158	29,561	14,301	15,260
Percent	100.0%	100.0%	100.0%	100.0%	100.0%	100.0%	100.0%	100.0%	100.0%
0-9	4,972	2,522	2,450	6,448	3,293	3,155	6,992	3,570	3,422
Percent	20.0%	21.3%	18.8%	23.6%	25.1%	22.3%	23.6%	25.0%	22.4%
10-14	2,323	1,171	1,152	2,000	1,014	986	2,900	1,475	1,425
Percent	9.4%	9.9%	8.9%	7.3%	7.7%	7.0%	9.8%	10.3%	9.3%
15-19	2,412	1,204	1,208	2,297	1,158	1,139	1,949	985	964
Percent	9.7%	10.2%	9.3%	8.4%	8.8%	8.0%	6.6%	6.9%	6.3%
20-24	2,369	1,159	1,210	2,393	1,200	1,193	2,220	1,124	1,096
Percent	9.5%	9.8%	9.3%	8.8%	9.1%	8.4%	7.5%	7.8%	7.2%
25-44	7,022	3,283	3,739	7,459	3,519	3,940	7,966	3,836	4,130
Percent	28.3%	27.8%	28.8%	27.3%	26.8%	27.8%	26.9%	26.8%	27.1%
45-54	2,781	1,274	1,507	3,224	1,505	1,719	3,358	1,566	1,792
Percent	11.2%	10.8%	11.6%	11.8%	11.5%	12.1%	11.4%	10.9%	11.7%
55-64	1,647	704	943	1,956	847	1,109	2,470	1,097	1,373
Percent	6.6%	5.9%	7.3%	7.2%	6.4%	7.8%	8.3%	7.7%	9.0%
65 & over	1,298	513	785	1,504	587	917	1,706	648	1,058
Percent	5.2%	4.3%	6.0%	5.5%	4.5%	6.5%	5.8%	4.5%	6.9%

Age Groups	1965			1970			1976		
	Total	Male	Female	Total	Male	Female	Total	Male	Female
TOTAL POPULATION	31,261	15,173	16,088	32,526	15,803	16,723	34,356	16,719	17,637
Percent	100.0%	100.0%	100.0%	100.0%	100.0%	100.0%	100.0%	100.0%	100.0%
0-9	6,242	3,197	3,045	5,324	2,715	2,609	5,514	2,827	2,687
Percent	20.0%	21.1%	18.9%	16.4%	17.2%	15.6%	16.0%	16.9%	15.2%
10-14	3,462	1,765	1,697	3,437	1,751	1,686	2,685	1,373	1,311
Percent	11.1%	11.6%	10.5%	10.6%	11.1%	10.1%	7.8%	8.2%	7.4%
15-19	2,870	1,460	1,410	3,433	1,749	1,684	3,308	1,688	1,621
Percent	9.2%	9.6%	8.8%	10.6%	11.1%	10.1%	9.6%	10.1%	9.2%
20-24	1,924	972	952	2,822	1,427	1,395	3,465	1,763	1,702
Percent	6.1%	6.4%	5.9%	8.7%	9.0%	8.3%	10.1%	10.5%	9.7%
25-44	8,790	4,278	4,512	8,619	4,273	4,346	9,238	4,625	4,613
Percent	28.1%	28.2%	28.0%	26.5%	27.0%	26.0%	26.9%	27.7%	26.2%
45-54	2,921	1,342	1,579	3,186	1,468	1,718	4,181	1,969	2,212
Percent	9.3%	8.8%	9.8%	9.8%	9.3%	10.3%	12.2%	11.8%	12.5%
55-64	2,923	1,339	1,584	3,013	1,360	1,653	2,616	1,159	1,457
Percent	9.3%	8.8%	9.8%	9.3%	8.6%	9.8%	7.6%	6.9%	8.3%
65 & over	2,129	820	1,309	2,692	1,060	1,632	3,349	1,314	2,035
Percent	6.8%	5.4%	8.1%	8.3%	6.7%	9.8%	9.7%	7.9%	11.5%

TABLE A-21 POPULATION BY AGE GROUPS AND SEX: ROMANIA, 1950-1975
          (in Thousands)

Age Groups	1950 Total	1950 Male	1950 Female	1955 Total	1955 Male	1955 Female	1960 Total	1960 Male	1960 Female
TOTAL POPULATION	16,311	7,867	8,444	17,325	8,413	8,912	18,403	8,979	9,424
Percent	100.0%	100.0%	100.0%	100.0%	100.0%	100.0%	100.0%	100.0%	100.0%
0-9	3,004	1,527	1,477	3,410	1,737	1,673	3,622	1,851	1,771
Percent	18.4%	19.4%	17.5%	19.7%	20.6%	18.8%	19.7%	20.6%	18.8%
10-14	1,630	807	823	1,353	687	666	1,562	794	768
Percent	10.0%	10.2%	9.7%	7.8%	8.2%	7.5%	8.5%	8.8%	8.1%
15-19	1,638	826	812	1,598	793	805	1,348	683	665
Percent	10.0%	10.5%	9.6%	9.2%	9.4%	9.0%	7.3%	7.6%	7.0%
20-24	1,589	798	791	1,596	805	791	1,587	785	802
Percent	9.7%	10.1%	9.4%	9.2%	9.6%	8.9%	8.6%	8.7%	8.5%
25-44	4,574	2,170	2,404	4,876	2,333	2,543	5,260	2,567	2,693
Percent	28.0%	27.6%	28.5%	28.1%	27.7%	28.5%	28.6%	28.6%	28.6%
45-54	1,807	863	944	2,012	988	1,024	2,193	1,046	1,147
Percent	11.1%	11.0%	11.2%	11.6%	11.7%	11.5%	11.9%	11.6%	12.2%
55-64	1,200	521	679	1,374	616	758	1,595	748	847
Percent	7.4%	6.6%	8.0%	7.9%	7.3%	8.5%	8.7%	8.3%	9.0%
65 & over	869	355	514	1,106	454	652	1,236	505	731
Percent	5.3%	4.5%	6.1%	6.4%	5.4%	7.3%	6.7%	5.6%	7.7%

Age Groups	1965 Total	1965 Male	1965 Female	1970 Total	1970 Male	1970 Female	1975 Total	1975 Male	1975 Female
TOTAL POPULATION	19,027	9,316	9,711	20,253	9,946	10,307	21,245	10,460	10,785
Percent	100.0%	100.0%	100.0%	100.0%	100.0%	100.0%	100.0%	100.0%	100.0%
0-9	3,216	1,647	1,569	3,451	1,767	1,684	3,948	2,020	1,928
Percent	16.9%	17.7%	16.1%	17.0%	17.8%	16.3%	18.6%	19.3%	17.9%
10-14	1,794	915	879	1,794	917	877	1,413	724	689
Percent	9.4%	9.8%	9.1%	8.9%	9.2%	8.5%	6.6%	6.9%	6.4%
15-19	1,546	785	761	1,808	921	887	1,785	911	874
Percent	8.1%	8.4%	7.8%	8.9%	9.3%	8.6%	8.4%	8.7%	8.1%
20-24	1,330	673	657	1,503	766	737	1,795	914	880
Percent	7.0%	7.2%	6.8%	7.4%	7.7%	7.2%	8.4%	8.7%	8.2%
25-44	5,931	2,930	3,001	5,897	2,951	2,946	5,842	2,935	2,907
Percent	31.2%	31.4%	30.9%	29.1%	29.7%	28.6%	27.5%	28.1%	27.0%
45-54	1,892	868	1,024	2,053	949	1,104	2,718	1,312	1,406
Percent	9.9%	9.3%	10.5%	10.1%	9.5%	10.7%	12.8%	12.5%	13.0%
55-64	1,810	872	938	2,006	930	1,076	1,705	762	943
Percent	9.5%	9.4%	9.6%	9.9%	9.3%	10.4%	8.0%	7.3%	8.7%
65 & over	1,508	626	882	1,741	745	996	2,040	881	1,158
Percent	7.9%	6.7%	9.1%	8.6%	7.5%	9.6%	9.6%	8.4%	10.7%

TABLE A-22   POPULATION BY AGE GROUPS AND SEX: USSR, 1950-1975 (in Thousands)

Age Groups	1950			1955			1960		
	Total	Male	Female	Total	Male	Female	Total	Male	Female
TOTAL POPULATION	180,075	79,053	101,022	196,159	87,291	108,868	214,329	96,878	117,451
Percent	100.0%	100.0%	100.0%	100.0%	100.0%	100.0%	100.0%	100.0%	100.0%
0-9	32,119	16,404	15,715	41,448	21,120	20,328	47,244	24,109	23,135
Percent	17.8%	20.7%	15.5%	21.1%	24.2%	18.7%	22.0%	24.9%	19.7%
10-14	22,037	11,057	10,980	13,166	6,667	6,499	18,510	9,396	9,114
Percent	12.2%	14.0%	10.9%	6.7%	7.6%	6.0%	8.6%	9.7%	7.7%
15-19	17,530	8,718	8,812	21,824	10,893	10,931	13,134	6,646	6,488
Percent	9.7%	11.0%	8.7%	11.1%	12.5%	10.0%	6.1%	6.9%	5.5%
20-24	19,669	9,377	10,292	17,323	8,557	8,766	21,736	10,818	10,918
Percent	10.9%	11.9%	10.2%	8.8%	9.8%	8.0%	10.1%	11.2%	9.3%
25-44	48,372	19,349	29,023	55,470	23,471	31,999	60,258	26,985	33,273
Percent	26.9%	24.5%	28.7%	28.3%	26.9%	29.4%	28.1%	27.8%	28.3%
45-54	17,706	6,483	11,223	20,733	7,796	12,937	22,870	8,744	14,126
Percent	9.8%	8.2%	11.1%	10.6%	8.9%	11.9%	10.7%	9.0%	12.0%
55-64	11,668	4,398	7,270	13,490	4,843	8,647	16,093	5,548	10,545
Percent	6.5%	5.6%	7.2%	6.9%	5.5%	7.9%	7.5%	5.7%	9.0%
65 & over	10,974	3,267	7,707	12,705	3,944	8,761	14,484	4,632	9,852
Percent	6.1%	4.1%	7.6%	6.5%	4.5%	8.0%	6.8%	4.8%	8.4%

Age Groups	1965			1970			1975[a]		
	Total	Male	Female	Total	Male	Female	Total	Male	Female
TOTAL POPULATION	230,936	105,600	125,336	242,757	111,797	130,960	254,300	118,105	136,195
Percent	100.0%	100.0%	100.0%	100.0%	100.0%	100.0%	100.0%	100.0%	100.0%
0-9	47,857	24,458	23,399	44,469	22,645	21,824	41,704	21,239	20,465
Percent	20.7%	23.2%	18.7%	18.3%	20.3%	16.7%	16.4%	18.0%	15.0%
10-14	22,707	11,560	11,147	25,068	12,778	12,290	23,855	12,150	11,704
Percent	9.8%	10.9%	8.9%	10.3%	11.4%	9.4%	9.4%	10.3%	8.6%
15-19	18,478	9,381	9,097	22,465	11,455	11,010	24,909	12,683	12,226
Percent	8.0%	8.9%	7.2%	9.2%	10.2%	8.4%	9.8%	10.7%	9.0%
20-24	13,083	6,610	6,473	18,107	9,133	8,974	22,269	11,329	10,940
Percent	5.7%	6.3%	5.2%	7.5%	8.2%	6.8%	8.8%	9.6%	8.0%
25-44	71,237	33,415	37,822	69,921	33,818	36,103	67,648	33,334	34,314
Percent	30.8%	31.6%	30.2%	28.8%	30.2%	27.6%	26.6%	28.2%	25.2%
45-54	21,508	8,105	13,403	21,906	8,397	13,509	31,271	13,337	17,934
Percent	9.3%	7.7%	10.7%	9.0%	7.5%	10.3%	12.3%	11.3%	13.2%
55-64	19,031	6,780	12,251	21,878	7,778	14,100	19,573	6,932	12,640
Percent	8.2%	6.4%	9.8%	9.0%	6.9%	10.8%	7.7%	5.9%	9.3%
65 and over	17,035	5,291	11,744	18,943	5,793	13,150	23,071	7,100	15,971
Percent	7.4%	5.0%	9.4%	7.8%	5.2%	10.0%	9.1%	6.0%	11.7%

Note: a Projected population.

TABLE A-23   POPULATION BY AGE GROUPS AND SEX: YUGOSLAVIA, 1950-1975
              (in Thousands)

Age Groups	1950			1955			1960		
	Total	Male	Female	Total	Male	Female	Total	Male	Female
TOTAL POPULATION	16,346	7,880	8,466	17,519	8,519	9,000	18,402	8,996	9,406
Percent	100.0%	100.0%	100.0%	100.0%	100.0%	100.0%	100.0%	100.0%	100.0%
0-9	3,310	1,682	1,628	3,825	1,956	1,869	3,905	2,006	1,899
Percent	20.2%	21.3%	19.2%	21.8%	23.0%	20.8%	21.2%	22.3%	20.2%
10-14	1,776	904	872	1,496	764	732	1,711	875	836
Percent	10.9%	11.5%	10.3%	8.5%	9.0%	8.1%	9.3%	9.7%	8.9%
15-19	1,784	903	881	1,694	860	834	1,426	728	698
Percent	10.9%	11.4%	10.4%	9.7%	10.0%	9.3%	7.7%	8.1%	7.4%
20-24	1,603	781	822	1,773	900	873	1,633	830	803
Percent	9.8%	9.9%	9.7%	10.1%	10.6%	9.7%	8.9%	9.2%	8.5%
25-44	4,176	1,938	2,238	4,570	2,127	2,443	5,152	2,474	2,678
Percent	25.5%	24.6%	26.4%	26.1%	25.0%	27.1%	28.0%	27.5%	28.5%
45-54	1,697	810	887	1,917	936	981	1,948	926	1,022
Percent	10.4%	10.3%	10.5%	10.9%	11.0%	10.9%	10.6%	10.3%	10.9%
55-64	1,074	464	610	1,190	534	656	1,464	684	780
Percent	6.6%	5.9%	7.2%	6.8%	6.3%	7.3%	7.9%	7.6%	8.3%
65 & over	926	398	528	1,054	442	612	1,163	473	690
Percent	5.7%	5.0%	6.2%	6.0%	5.2%	6.8%	6.3%	5.3%	7.3%

Age Groups	1965			1970			1975[a]		
	Total	Male	Female	Total	Male	Female	Total	Male	Female
TOTAL POPULATION	19,434	9,510	9,924	20,371	10,001	10,370	21,352	10,508	10,844
Percent	100.0%	100.0%	100.0%	100.0%	100.0%	100.0%	100.0%	100.0%	100.0%
0-9	3,784	1,938	1,846	3,682	1,885	1,797	3,635	1,865	1,770
Percent	19.5%	20.4%	18.6%	18.1%	18.8%	17.3%	17.0%	17.7%	16.3%
10-14	1,984	1,014	970	1,906	975	931	1,854	949	905
Percent	10.2%	10.7%	9.8%	9.3%	9.7%	9.0%	8.7%	9.0%	8.3%
15-19	1,709	871	838	1,983	1,015	969	1,904	974	930
Percent	8.8%	9.2%	8.4%	9.7%	10.1%	9.3%	8.9%	9.3%	8.6%
20-24	1,407	709	698	1,640	839	801	1,977	1,010	967
Percent	7.2%	7.4%	7.0%	8.0%	8.4%	7.7%	9.3%	9.6%	8.9%
25-44	5,899	2,871	3,028	5,959	2,962	2,997	6,089	3,061	3,028
Percent	30.3%	30.2%	30.5%	29.2%	29.6%	28.9%	28.5%	29.1%	27.9%
45-54	1,621	742	879	1,830	819	1,011	2,585	1,202	1,383
Percent	8.3%	7.8%	8.6%	9.0%	8.2%	9.7%	12.1%	11.4%	12.7%
55-64	1,728	823	905	1,785	828	957	1,472	653	819
Percent	8.9%	8.6%	9.1%	8.8%	8.3%	9.2%	6.9%	6.2%	7.6%
65 & over	1,302	542	760	1,586	678	908	1,836	794	1,042
Percent	6.7%	5.7%	7.6%	7.8%	6.8%	8.7%	8.6%	7.6%	9.6%

Note: a Projected population.

TABLE A-24 URBAN AND RURAL BIRTHRATES: EASTERN EUROPE AND THE USSR, 1946-1975 (Rates per Thousand Population)

Country	1946	1947	1948	1949	1950	1951	1952	1953	1954	1955	1956	1957	1958	1959	1960
Albania															
Total Popul.	27.1	35.8	36.1	38.6	38.5	39.0	35.5	40.7	40.2	43.8	41.2	38.5	41.0	41.0	43.3
Urban Popul.	...	...	...	...	...	...	...	...	...	...	...	...	...	...	30.9
Rural Popul.	...	...	...	...	...	...	...	...	...	...	...	...	...	...	48.4
Bulgaria															
Total Popul.	25.6	24.1	24.6	24.7	25.2	21.0	21.2	20.9	20.2	20.1	19.5	18.4	17.9	17.6	17.8
Urban Popul.	24.6	23.2	23.1	23.9	24.9	22.5	21.0	20.8	19.0	18.7	17.5	17.0	16.4	16.0	16.1
Rural Popul.	25.9	24.4	25.2	25.0	25.3	20.5	21.2	20.9	20.7	20.8	20.5	19.2	18.7	18.4	18.8
Czechoslovakia															
Total Popul.	...	24.2	23.4	22.4	23.3	22.8	22.2	21.2	20.6	20.3	19.8	18.9	17.4	16.0	15.9
Urban Popul.	...	...	...	...	...	...	...	...	...	...	...	...	...	...	...
Rural Popul.	...	...	...	...	...	...	...	...	...	...	...	...	...	...	...
GDR															
Total Popul.	10.4	13.1	12.8	14.5	16.5	16.9	16.7	16.4	16.3	16.3	15.9	15.6	15.6	16.9	17.0
Urban Popul.	...	...	...	...	...	...	...	...	...	...	...	...	...	...	...
Rural Popul.	...	...	...	...	...	...	...	...	...	...	...	...	...	...	...
Hungary															
Total Popul.	18.7	20.6	21.0	20.6	20.9	20.2	19.6	21.6	23.0	21.4	19.5	17.0	16.0	15.2	14.7
Urban Popul.	...	...	...	...	...	...	...	...	...	...	15.3	12.6	12.5	11.9	11.6
Rural Popul.	...	...	...	...	...	...	...	...	...	...	22.6	20.1	18.9	17.3	16.7
Poland															
Total Popul.	26.2	28.7	29.4	29.7	30.7	31.0	30.2	29.7	29.1	29.1	28.1	27.6	26.3	24.7	22.6
Urban Popul.	25.2	27.8	28.5	28.6	30.0	30.7	29.7	29.2	28.7	28.6	26.8	26.0	24.5	22.4	19.9
Rural Popul.	26.7	29.2	29.8	30.3	31.2	31.2	30.6	30.0	29.3	29.5	29.1	29.0	27.8	26.8	24.9
Romania															
Total Popul.	24.8	23.4	23.9	27.6	26.2	25.1	24.8	23.8	24.8	25.6	24.2	22.9	21.6	20.2	19.1
Urban Popul.	17.5	16.5	16.4	19.7	20.1	20.4	19.4	19.9	20.1	20.6	19.5	18.1	16.7	15.0	14.6
Rural Popul.	26.9	25.4	26.2	30.1	28.1	26.6	26.8	25.2	26.5	27.4	26.3	25.1	24.0	22.6	21.3
USSR															
Total Popul.	...	...	...	...	26.7	27.0	26.5	25.1	26.6	25.7	25.2	25.4	25.3	25.0	24.9
Urban Popul.	...	...	...	...	26.0	26.2	25.4	23.9	25.1	23.5	22.3	22.4	22.5	22.0	21.9
Rural Popul.	...	...	...	...	27.1	27.6	27.3	26.0	27.8	27.4	27.5	27.9	27.9	27.8	27.8
Yugoslavia															
Total Popul.	...	26.6	28.1	30.0	30.2	27.0	29.7	28.4	28.6	26.9	26.0	23.9	24.0	23.4	23.5
Urban Popul.	...	...	...	...	...	...	...	...	...	...	...	...	...	18.9	...
Rural Popul.	...	...	...	...	...	...	...	...	...	...	...	...	...	24.7	...

TABLE A-24   (CONCLUDED)

Country	1961	1962	1963	1964	1965	1966	1967	1968	1969	1970	1971	1972	1973	1974	1975
Albania															
Total Popul.	41.2	39.3	39.1	37.8	35.2	34.0	35.3	35.6	35.3	32.5	33.3	...	...	...	...
Urban Popul.	...	...	...	...	29.4	...	...	...	26.0	23.6	25.7	...	...	...	...
Rural Popul.	...	...	...	...	37.8	...	...	...	39.5	36.7	36.8	...	...	...	...
Bulgaria															
Total Popul.	17.4	16.7	16.4	16.1	15.3	14.9	15.0	16.9	17.0	16.3	15.9	15.3	16.2	17.2	16.6
Urban Popul.	15.8	15.3	15.5	15.6	14.7	15.5	15.9	18.0	18.7	18.0	17.4	17.0	18.4	19.8	19.1
Rural Popul.	18.3	17.7	17.0	16.4	15.9	14.4	14.2	15.9	15.2	14.6	14.1	13.3	13.4	13.6	13.0
Czechoslovakia															
Total Popul.	15.8	15.7	16.9	17.2	16.4	15.6	15.1	14.9	15.5	15.9	16.5	17.4	18.9	19.8	19.5
Urban Popul.	...	...	...	...	...	...	...	...	...	...	...	...	...	...	...
Rural Popul.	...	...	...	...	...	...	...	...	...	...	...	...	...	...	...
GDR															
Total Popul.	17.6	17.4	17.6	17.2	16.5	15.7	14.8	14.3	14.0	13.9	13.8	11.8	10.6	10.6	10.8
Urban Popul.	...	...	...	...	...	...	...	...	...	...	...	...	...	...	...
Rural Popul.	...	...	...	...	...	...	...	...	...	...	...	...	...	...	...
Hungary															
Total Popul.	14.0	12.9	13.1	13.1	13.1	13.6	14.6	15.1	15.0	14.7	14.5	14.7	15.0	17.8	18.4
Urban Popul.	11.0	10.4	10.8	11.1	11.3	12.1	13.5	13.9	14.3	13.7	13.4	13.8	14.1	17.3	18.4
Rural Popul.	16.0	14.7	14.8	14.5	14.5	14.8	15.6	16.0	15.8	15.4	15.5	15.6	15.8	18.2	18.4
Poland															
Total Popul.	20.9	19.8	19.2	18.1	17.4	16.7	16.3	16.2	16.3	16.6	17.2	17.4	17.9	18.4	18.9
Urban Popul.	18.1	16.9	16.3	15.5	14.9	14.4	14.0	13.8	14.1	14.7	15.0	15.6	15.9	16.4	17.2
Rural Popul.	23.6	22.4	21.9	20.5	19.7	19.1	18.6	18.7	18.7	18.8	19.5	19.5	20.4	20.9	21.0
Romania															
Total Popul.	17.5	16.2	15.7	15.2	14.6	14.3	27.4	26.7	23.3	21.1	19.5	18.8	18.2	20.3	...
Urban Popul.	13.9	13.2	13.3	12.7	12.1	11.4	26.9	25.8	21.5	18.9	17.3	16.8	16.4	...	...
Rural Popul.	19.2	17.6	16.8	16.4	15.9	16.1	27.6	27.2	24.5	22.6	21.1	20.3	19.5	...	...
USSR															
Total Popul.	23.8	22.4	21.2	19.5	18.4	18.2	17.3	17.2	17.0	17.4	17.8	17.8	17.6	18.0	18.1
Urban Popul.	21.1	19.9	18.5	17.3	16.1	16.0	15.4	15.3	15.6	16.4	16.9	16.9	16.6	16.9	17.0
Rural Popul.	26.5	24.9	24.0	22.1	21.1	20.8	19.8	19.5	18.7	18.7	19.2	19.0	19.0	19.6	19.8
Yugoslavia															
Total Popul.	22.7	21.9	21.4	20.8	21.0	20.4	19.6	19.1	18.9	17.8	18.3	18.3	18.1	18.1	18.1
Urban Popul.	...	...	...	...	...	...	...	...	...	...	...	...	...	...	...
Rural Popul.	...	...	...	...	...	...	...	...	...	...	...	...	...	...	...

TABLE A-25   URBAN AND RURAL INFANT MORTALITY RATES: EASTERN EUROPE AND THE USSR, 1946-1975 (Rates per Thousand Live Births)

Country	1946	1947	1948	1949	1950	1951	1952	1953	1954	1955	1956	1957	1958	1959	1960
Albania															
Total Popul.	...	...	...	...	...	...	...	...	...	103.9	81.5	87.0	68.3	76.5	83.0
Urban Popul.	...	...	...	...	...	...	...	...	...	...	...	...	...	...	...
Rural Popul.	...	...	...	...	...	...	...	...	...	...	...	...	...	...	...
Bulgaria															
Total Popul.	...	...	118.2	115.7	94.5	108.2	97.7	80.8	86.3	82.4	72.0	66.3	52.2	55.9	45.1
Urban Popul.	...	...	94.5	92.4	74.3	85.0	78.0	67.5	70.8	60.8	55.1	48.3	38.6	40.7	34.6
Rural Popul.	...	...	125.9	123.7	101.9	118.1	105.5	86.4	92.6	91.4	79.1	74.5	58.5	63.2	50.4
Czechoslovakia															
Total Popul.	...	88.9	83.5	82.6	77.7	73.0	55.5	45.0	37.6	34.1	31.4	33.5	29.5	25.7	23.5
Urban Popul.	...	...	...	...	...	...	...	...	...	...	...	...	...	...	...
Rural Popul.	...	...	...	...	...	...	...	...	...	...	...	...	...	...	...
GDR															
Total Popul.	131	114	89	78	72	64	59.2	53.5	50.3	48.8	46.5	45.5	43.8	40.7	38.8
Urban Popul.	...	...	...	...	...	...	...	...	...	...	...	...	...	...	...
Rural Popul.	...	...	...	...	...	...	...	...	...	...	...	...	...	...	...
Hungary															
Total Popul.	...	...	...	91.0	85.7	83.9	69.9	70.8	60.7	60.0	58.8	63.1	58.1	52.4	47.6
Urban Popul.	...	...	...	...	...	...	...	...	...	...	...	...	...	...	...
Rural Popul.	...	...	...	...	...	...	...	...	...	...	...	...	...	...	...
Poland															
Total Popul.	119.8	114.7	112.1	108.4	111.2	117.6	96.4	88.4	83.3	82.2	70.9	77.2	72.1	71.4	54.8
Urban Popul.	108.3	103.3	98.6	96.0	102.6	106.3	88.2	80.1	75.5	73.3	64.8	70.0	64.2	64.4	49.7
Rural Popul.	125.3	120.4	119.2	115.0	116.0	124.6	101.7	94.0	88.7	88.9	75.4	82.6	78.2	76.6	58.5
Romania															
Total Popul.	164.1	198.8	142.7	136.3	116.7	118.1	104.7	96.3	88.8	78.2	81.5	80.9	69.4	75.7	74.6
Urban Popul.	141.1	158.5	115.1	106.4	112.2	132.0	90.2	76.4	74.8	60.3	68.8	69.1	60.5	67.2	67.5
Rural Popul.	168.6	206.6	148.0	142.5	117.7	114.4	108.4	101.9	92.7	83.2	85.8	84.9	72.4	78.1	76.9
USSR															
Total Popul.	...	...	...	...	80.7	83.7	74.8	67.6	68.2	59.6	47.4	45.3	40.6	40.6	35.3
Urban Popul.	...	...	...	...	...	...	...	...	...	...	...	...	...	...	...
Rural Popul.	...	...	...	...	...	...	...	...	...	...	...	...	...	...	...
Yugoslavia															
Total Popul.	...	...	...	102.1	118.4	139.8	105.0	116.1	101.6	112.8	98.3	101.5	86.4	92.0	87.7
Urban Popul.	...	...	...	...	...	...	...	...	...	...	...	...	...	...	...
Rural Popul.	...	...	...	...	...	...	...	...	...	...	...	...	...	...	...

Country	1961	1962	1963	1964	1965	1966	1967	1968	1969	1970	1971	1972	1973	1974	1975
Albania															
Total Popul.	79.5	92.1	90.6	81.5	86.8	...	...	...	...	...	...	...	...	...	...
Urban Popul.	...	...	...	...	...	...	...	...	...	...	...	...	...	...	...
Rural Popul.	...	...	...	...	...	...	...	...	...	...	...	...	...	...	...
Bulgaria															
Total Popul.	37.8	37.3	35.7	32.9	30.8	32.2	33.1	28.3	30.5	27.3	24.9	26.2	26.2	25.5	23.1
Urban Popul.	31.2	29.4	28.0	27.2	25.6	26.4	26.6	24.8	26.5	22.7	21.0	22.6	23.0	22.3	19.9
Rural Popul.	41.4	41.7	40.4	36.9	35.0	37.7	39.9	32.1	35.6	33.5	30.6	31.7	31.7	31.8	29.7
Czechoslovakia															
Total Popul.	22.7	22.8	22.1	21.4	25.5	23.8	22.9	22.2	23.1	22.1	21.7	21.6	21.3	20.4	20.9
Urban Popul.	...	...	...	...	...	...	...	...	...	...	...	...	...	...	...
Rural Popul.	...	...	...	...	...	...	...	...	...	...	...	...	...	...	...
GDR															
Total Popul.	33.7	31.6	31.2	28.6	24.8	22.9	21.4	20.2	20.3	18.5	18.0	17.6	15.6	15.9	15.9
Urban Popul.	...	...	...	...	...	...	...	...	...	18.3	18.0	17.6	...	...	...
Rural Popul.	...	...	...	...	...	...	...	...	...	19.1	18.0	17.9	...	...	...
Hungary															
Total Popul.	44.1	47.9	42.9	40.0	38.8	38.4	37.0	35.8	35.7	35.9	35.1	33.2	33.8	34.3	32.8
Urban Popul.	...	...	...	...	...	39.4	38.3	37.0	36.8	36.5	37.5	34.2	34.2	...	...
Rural Popul.	...	...	...	...	...	37.7	36.1	34.9	34.9	35.4	33.3	32.3	33.4	...	...
Poland															
Total Popul.	53.2	54.2	48.5	47.2	41.4	38.6	37.9	33.4	34.4	33.4	29.7	28.6	26.1	23.7	25.1
Urban Popul.	47.0	47.8	44.2	41.6	38.7	35.2	35.7	31.4	33.1	31.6	29.0	28.0	25.7	23.6	24.8
Rural Popul.	57.7	58.8	51.6	51.3	43.4	41.2	39.5	34.9	35.4	34.8	30.3	29.2	26.4	23.9	25.3
Romania															
Total Popul.	69.4	58.8	55.2	48.6	44.1	46.6	46.6	59.5	54.9	49.4	42.4	40.0	38.1	35.0	...
Urban Popul.	56.3	49.4	44.6	39.8	39.0	41.3	42.6	56.2	51.4	46.4	38.9	35.8	33.3	...	...
Rural Popul.	73.9	62.2	59.3	52.0	46.0	48.9	49.0	61.6	57.0	51.2	44.4	42.5	41.1	...	...
USSR															
Total Popul.	32.3	32.3	30.9	28.8	27.2	26.1	26.0	26.4	25.8	24.7	22.9	24.7	26.4	27.9	...
Urban Popul.	...	...	...	...	...	...	...	...	...	...	...	...	...	...	...
Rural Popul.	...	...	...	...	...	...	...	...	...	...	...	...	...	...	...
Yugoslavia															
Total Popul.	82.0	84.2	77.5	75.8	71.8	62.1	62.1	58.6	57.3	55.5	49.5	44.4	44.0	40.9	39.9
Urban Popul.	...	...	...	...	...	...	...	...	...	...	...	...	...	...	...
Rural Popul.	...	...	...	...	...	...	...	...	...	...	...	...	...	...	...

TABLE A-26   AGE SPECIFIC FERTILITY RATES: BULGARIA, 1946-1972
(Births per Thousand Women of Given Age)

Age	1946	1947	1948	1949	1950	1951	1952	1953	1954
Under 20	50.7	48.3	49.9	53.2	54.9	54.0	54.1	57.0	60.4
20-24	199.8	188.1	195.9	195.2	200.1	171.0	175.5	174.6	168.4
25-29	178.8	166.2	163.8	163.0	162.2	132.4	135.2	132.7	129.2
30-34	108.2	98.3	95.5	92.8	99.5	78.3	74.6	70.0	67.4
35-39	53.2	49.3	50.4	48.6	49.2	38.1	35.3	33.6	32.6
40-44	16.6	15.1	15.4	14.9	16.8	12.4	11.5	11.8	10.8
45 & over	4.1	3.6	3.5	3.5	4.1	2.8	2.4	2.4	1.9

Age	1955	1956	1957	1958	1959	1960	1961	1962	1963
Under 20	59.7	61.1	62.9	63.4	70.9	74.5	71.8	68.5	68.0
20-24	180.3	181.7	179.8	177.5	180.6	187.1	185.2	182.4	181.7
25-29	130.8	125.4	119.1	118.7	115.7	120.0	119.3	114.8	113.5
30-34	65.0	61.5	54.5	54.9	50.2	51.3	52.1	51.6	49.9
35-39	33.5	30.4	26.4	22.1	20.7	19.7	19.3	19.2	18.1
40-44	10.6	9.8	7.5	7.3	6.2	7.2	6.4	6.3	5.4
45 & over	2.0	1.8	1.5	1.1	1.2	0.9	0.8	0.8	0.6

Age	1964	1965	1966	1967	1968	1969	1970	1971	1972
Under 20	70.4	67.4	65.0	68.0	75.3	74.2	71.5	69.7	69.3
20-24	183.9	175.1	175.2	176.8	197.3	194.3	189.2	186.4	181.1
25-29	107.7	105.7	102.1	102.3	118.3	120.3	111.6	106.1	101.8
30-34	48.2	45.7	41.7	40.3	45.1	47.1	45.0	42.3	39.3
35-39	16.9	16.8	15.3	14.6	15.5	15.8	14.8	13.5	12.4
40-44	5.0	4.4	3.8	3.8	3.9	3.4	3.1	3.1	3.0
45 & over	0.7	0.7	0.7	0.6	0.5	0.6	0.4	0.4	0.3

TABLE A-27   AGE SPECIFIC FERTILITY RATES: CZECHOSLOVAKIA,
1946-1972 (Births per Thousand Women of Given Age)

Age	1946	1947	1948	1949	1950	1951	1952	1953	1954
Under 20	...	40.1	44.8	45.5	50.7	52.7	51.7	48.3	45.1
20-24	...	178.8	182.5	183.6	194.1	196.4	195.2	193.5	197.5
25-29	...	181.6	170.2	165.4	169.1	168.4	165.8	159.7	158.4
30-34	...	120.7	109.5	100.0	108.8	106.5	104.7	101.1	97.4
35-39	...	72.9	67.4	60.7	62.5	58.4	55.4	51.3	49.6
40-44	...	23.6	23.2	21.2	21.5	20.4	19.1	18.8	17.5
45 & over	...	1.8	1.7	1.8	1.8	1.7	1.6	1.5	1.3

Age	1955	1956	1957	1958	1959	1960	1961	1962	1963
Under 20	44.6	47.0	48.2	46.2	45.9	46.0	45.2	44.9	47.3
20-24	201.0	206.0	205.3	200.3	196.6	198.7	198.7	198.4	206.8
25-29	159.0	156.8	149.8	141.8	130.5	131.7	130.7	130.8	142.6
30-34	94.5	91.0	86.5	76.5	65.1	63.8	64.4	60.8	68.2
35-39	51.7	50.6	47.4	39.4	30.9	29.1	28.1	25.8	28.1
40-44	16.9	14.4	12.1	9.3	7.8	8.8	8.5	7.8	7.4
45 & over	1.4	1.1	1.1	0.8	0.6	0.6	0.4	0.3	0.4

Age	1964	1965	1966	1967	1968	1969	1970	1971	1972
Under 20	46.4	45.1	45.0	44.8	42.9	45.3	45.5	47.0	49.0
20-24	204.8	193.4	184.8	177.2	173.5	176.7	180.5	184.0	194.0
25-29	144.0	134.8	124.8	114.7	109.7	111.6	113.9	119.0	124.0
30-34	70.2	68.8	59.0	53.5	50.3	50.7	51.5	54.0	54.0
35-39	28.8	27.2	24.4	21.6	20.0	19.7	18.6	19.0	18.0
40-44	7.5	6.9	5.8	5.2	4.8	4.6	4.5	4.3	4.2
45 & over	0.4	0.5	0.5	0.4	0.3	0.3	0.3	0.2	0.2

TABLE A-28   AGE SPECIFIC FERTILITY RATES: GDR, 1946-1972
(Births per Thousand Women of Given Age)

Age	1946	1947	1948	1949	1950	1951	1952	1953	1954
Under 20	...	23.7	23.4	27.6	35.7	41.2	42.4	42.5	42.1
20-24	...	109.5	109.0	126.0	149.6	159.7	162.1	163.7	163.4
25-29	...	99.0	97.4	119.1	139.0	139.8	136.1	132.7	132.0
30-34	...	61.3	57.8	68.8	83.5	85.7	84.1	82.1	80.1
35-39	...	33.3	30.1	33.9	40.3	43.0	42.5	41.0	40.8
40-44	...	10.4	9.3	9.6	11.0	12.7	12.4	11.9	11.9
45 & over	...	...	...	...	...	...	...	...	...

Age	1955	1956	1957	1958	1959	1960	1961	1962	1963
Under 20	43.8	42.6	42.3	43.1	47.9	50.7	54.4	57.3	60.8
20-24	163.5	161.1	157.7	157.3	168.7	167.1	175.2	178.8	181.0
25-29	131.5	127.2	126.3	126.1	134.5	132.0	133.2	132.2	134.6
30-34	79.4	73.1	71.6	70.8	73.8	72.3	73.1	72.3	74.2
35-39	39.7	37.1	34.2	34.3	35.0	34.1	34.2	33.2	33.9
40-44	11.4	10.6	9.6	9.0	9.1	9.4	9.2	9.0	9.2
45 & over	...	...	...	...	...	...	...	...	...

Age	1964	1965	1966	1967	1968	1969	1970	1971	1972
Under 20	63.9	66.1	64.2	61.9	59.8	60.0	60.9	62.0	55.5
20-24	182.0	182.6	182.6	182.6	185.1	183.0	181.9	177.2	153.6
25-29	135.0	131.9	129.0	122.5	117.9	113.7	108.9	104.0	85.3
30-34	76.8	74.1	71.1	66.1	63.4	59.5	57.2	54.1	41.0
35-39	34.3	33.0	31.1	28.6	28.1	26.4	25.1	24.3	18.1
40-44	9.4	8.7	6.7	5.8	5.1	4.4	4.3	4.4	3.8
45 & over	...	...	...	...	...	...	...	...	...

TABLE A-29   AGE SPECIFIC FERTILITY RATES: HUNGARY, 1946-1973
              (Births per Thousand Women of Given Age)

Age	1946	1947	1948	1949	1950	1951	1952	1953	1954
Under 20	36.3	45.0	47.8	47.9	52.5	52.2	49.2	50.7	54.0
20-24	132.0	154.7	162.1	161.4	168.4	166.5	163.4	177.4	129.9
25-29	123.6	133.0	138.3	138.6	141.5	137.8	135.3	152.1	165.2
30-34	91.2	93.9	91.2	86.4	86.8	82.3	82.5	96.9	105.9
35-39	56.1	58.4	55.9	52.4	50.5	47.3	45.6	54.7	56.9
40-44	19.9	20.5	19.8	18.9	18.5	17.3	16.1	18.1	18.2
45 & over	1.8	1.7	1.7	1.7	1.6	1.5	1.3	1.4	1.3

Age	1955	1956	1957	1958	1959	1960	1961	1962	1963
Under 20	55.9	57.0	58.9	57.2	55.6	54.3	52.3	46.8	44.7
20-24	188.6	183.7	172.4	167.3	161.3	157.6	152.6	141.7	142.4
25-29	151.5	137.6	116.0	110.7	107.7	105.9	101.5	95.6	100.9
30-34	96.5	84.1	67.0	61.3	56.7	53.5	50.4	47.2	46.9
35-39	50.5	43.2	34.3	30.2	27.4	25.2	23.1	20.5	21.3
40-44	16.7	13.6	10.5	9.0	8.2	7.3	6.8	6.3	5.7
45 & over	1.3	1.0	0.7	0.9	0.6	0.5	0.5	0.4	0.3

Age	1964	1965	1966	1967	1968	1969	1970	1971	1972	1973
Under 20	45.2	46.5	48.9	52.8	54.3	55.3	54.1	50.3	53.5	57.5
20-24	143.2	145.8	151.2	159.3	162.6	160.5	157.0	157.7	157.4	157.0
25-29	100.5	100.6	104.4	112.0	116.2	111.8	108.4	103.8	105.2	105.1
30-34	48.4	48.0	49.0	53.5	54.9	54.2	51.4	49.8	47.8	48.1
35-39	19.3	18.4	18.9	19.8	20.0	19.8	18.7	17.9	17.4	17.9
40-44	5.4	4.9	4.7	4.7	4.6	4.6	4.4	4.1	...	...
45 & over	0.4	0.3	0.4	0.3	0.3	0.3	0.3	0.2	...	...

TABLE A-30   AGE SPECIFIC FERTILITY RATES: POLAND, 1946-1973
(Births per Thousand Women of Given Age)

Age	1946	1947	1948	1949	1950	1951	1952	1953	1954
Under 20	...	...	...	...	39.0	39.0	38.0	37.0	39.0
20-24	...	...	...	...	194.0	198.0	197.0	200.0	202.0
25-29	...	...	...	...	209.0	211.0	206.0	203.0	201.0
30-34	...	...	...	...	157.0	158.0	156.0	152.0	146.0
35-39	...	...	...	...	100.0	100.0	95.0	90.0	90.0
40-44	...	...	...	...	38.0	39.0	38.0	36.0	34.0
45 & over	...	...	...	...	4.0	4.0	4.0	3.0	4.0

Age	1955	1956	1957	1958	1959	1960	1961	1962	1963
Under 20	42.0	43.0	46.0	47.0	48.0	45.0	42.0	37.0	34.0
20-24	208.0	207.0	214.0	211.0	207.0	199.0	195.0	193.0	194.0
25-29	203.0	198.0	197.0	188.0	178.0	165.0	157.0	152.0	153.0
30-34	144.0	136.0	131.0	123.0	114.0	103.0	96.0	91.0	91.0
35-39	89.0	84.0	80.0	75.0	69.0	60.0	54.0	49.0	48.0
40-44	32.0	30.0	26.0	24.0	24.0	22.0	20.0	19.0	18.0
45 & over	3.0	3.0	3.0	3.0	3.0	2.0	2.0	2.0	1.0

Age	1964	1965	1966	1967	1968	1969	1970	1971	1972	1973
Under 20	34.0	32.0	32.0	31.0	30.0	30.0	30.0	29.0	27.0	28.0
20-24	185.0	184.0	177.0	170.0	164.0	164.0	165.0	171.0	168.0	169.0
25-29	148.0	144.0	140.0	134.0	128.0	125.0	126.0	130.0	134.0	136.0
30-34	87.0	84.0	81.0	77.0	74.0	71.0	71.0	72.0	71.0	71.0
35-39	46.0	43.0	42.0	40.0	39.0	37.0	36.0	36.0	35.0	35.0
40-44	16.0	15.0	13.0	12.0	12.0	12.0	11.0	11.0	11.0	11.0
45 & over	2.0	2.0	1.0	1.0	1.0	1.0	1.0	1.0	1.0	1.0

TABLE A-31   AGE SPECIFIC FERTILITY RATES: ROMANIA, 1946-1973
(Births per Thousand Women of Given Age)

Age	1946	1947	1948	1949	1950	1951	1952	1953	1954
Under 20	...	...	36.1	...	...	...	...	...	...
20-24	...	...	167.6	...	...	...	...	...	...
25-29	...	...	174.3	...	...	...	...	...	...
30-34	...	...	94.6	...	...	...	...	...	...
35-39	...	...	73.5	...	...	...	...	...	...
40-44	...	...	27.5	...	...	...	...	...	...
45 & over	...	...	3.7	...	...	...	...	...	...

Age	1955	1956	1957	1958	1959	1960	1961	1962	1963
Under 20	...	52.5	54.3	55.9	59.4	59.1	62.6	58.4	61.5
20-24	...	180.4	180.1	176.7	168.4	164.1	155.4	147.4	144.0
25-29	...	155.9	145.4	136.8	125.8	121.2	110.1	105.0	102.9
30-34	...	103.5	92.8	84.2	73.9	67.6	60.1	54.9	53.1
35-39	...	58.8	54.6	48.2	42.6	39.0	32.4	29.5	28.2
40-44	...	23.8	17.2	14.0	14.4	14.5	13.2	11.4	10.7
45 & over	...	2.7	2.2	1.8	1.6	1.4	0.9	0.8	0.7

Age	1964	1965	1966	1967	1968	1969	1970	1971	1972	1973
Under 20	56.8	52.4	51.7	79.8	82.4	72.6	65.7	62.1	61.6	60.6
20-24	144.0	140.7	143.0	251.8	251.4	215.7	201.4	190.9	185.9	182.4
25-29	102.6	99.8	98.2	198.1	193.9	171.7	151.6	138.1	131.6	124.2
30-34	52.2	53.5	53.4	124.1	126.5	108.0	94.9	82.7	76.9	71.6
35-39	26.2	25.1	25.1	59.7	63.9	54.7	48.8	44.3	40.7	37.6
40-44	9.5	8.9	8.3	16.6	17.3	15.0	13.8	13.1	12.0	10.3
45 & over	0.8	0.8	0.9	1.2	1.2	1.0	0.9	0.8	0.8	0.6

TABLE A-32   AGE SPECIFIC FERTILITY RATES: USSR, 1946-1972
(Births per Thousand Women of Given Age)

Age	1946	1947	1948	1949	1950	1951	1952	1953	1954
Under 20	...	...	...	...	...	...	...	...	...
20-24	...	...	...	...	...	...	...	...	...
25-29	...	...	...	...	...	...	...	...	...
30-34	...	...	...	...	...	...	...	...	...
35-39	...	...	...	...	...	...	...	...	...
40-44	...	...	...	...	...	...	...	...	...
45 & over	...	...	...	...	...	...	...	...	...

Age	1955	1956	1957	1958	1959	1960	1961	1962	1963
Under 20	16.0	17.9	22.0	25.9	31.8	35.8	35.4	24.4	22.7
20-24	148.1	151.4	157.1	161.4	163.1	159.7	162.5	161.5	164.4
25-29	169.1	167.5	172.4	168.0	163.2	165.5	162.0	155.3	149.8
30-34	122.7	117.2	112.7	112.0	109.0	112.5	106.4	105.8	101.5
35-39	75.9	72.8	72.0	67.3	65.4	63.9	56.6	53.5	52.1
40-44	32.5	28.3	24.7	24.0	23.8	25.5	24.0	24.2	22.7
45 & over	9.1	8.3	7.5	6.6	5.9	5.7	5.1	4.7	5.1

Age	1964	1965	1966	1967	1968	1969	1970	1971	1972
Under 20	22.8	24.8	26.9	26.7	29.7	29.4	31.6	32.0	32.4
20-24	159.8	158.8	162.3	153.6	152.5	158.7	167.6	170.2	173.9
25-29	142.7	134.1	134.2	131.7	129.5	127.8	132.6	132.1	137.1
30-34	97.4	97.1	102.6	97.4	95.4	91.3	86.7	87.1	84.3
35-39	49.9	51.0	50.1	49.3	48.8	47.9	48.2	49.6	49.4
40-44	21.5	19.5	18.4	16.6	16.6	15.3	16.3	14.9	14.6
45 & over	5.1	6.5	5.6	5.1	4.6	3.8	3.2	2.4	2.0

TABLE A-33   AGE SPECIFIC FERTILITY RATES: YUGOSLAVIA,
1946-1972 (Births per Thousand Women of
Given Age)

Age	1946	1947	1948	1949	1950	1951	1952	1953	1954
Under 20	...	...	...	...	39.6	34.6	38.7	39.1	40.6
20-24	...	...	...	...	201.9	180.7	198.9	190.3	198.4
25-29	...	...	...	...	206.3	179.6	199.1	189.1	187.4
30-34	...	...	...	...	153.0	135.9	148.1	129.8	126.4
35-39	...	...	...	...	94.5	80.2	85.8	82.5	78.8
40-44	...	...	...	...	43.5	37.8	39.7	36.9	33.6
45 & over	...	...	...	...	13.6	11.2	10.5	9.7	8.4

Age	1955	1956	1957	1958	1959	1960	1961	1962	1963
Under 20	41.3	40.7	41.3	42.2	46.4	48.9	50.4	51.5	51.2
20-24	186.5	182.2	170.2	174.1	173.9	178.2	177.6	177.5	178.0
25-29	175.8	168.8	154.9	156.6	151.9	155.5	151.4	148.6	148.6
30-34	112.4	106.3	96.1	94.6	91.9	93.7	90.1	87.9	86.4
35-39	78.6	72.0	61.7	58.2	54.9	51.8	48.1	45.1	44.3
40-44	30.3	27.1	22.9	23.9	24.4	26.4	24.3	21.6	19.1
45 & over	9.1	7.6	5.9	5.7	4.9	5.3	5.3	5.1	5.6

Age	1964	1965	1966	1967	1968	1969	1970	1971	1972
Under 20	50.3	53.4	57.3	55.7	56.2	56.1	51.6	53.8	56.1
20-24	180.7	188.1	183.5	177.6	173.8	170.6	161.3	170.3	167.4
25-29	147.1	152.5	148.0	142.3	136.4	134.5	124.6	129.6	130.1
30-34	84.7	85.7	82.5	80.0	76.7	75.7	71.9	73.2	71.8
35-39	43.5	42.7	41.2	40.2	37.9	37.0	34.0	33.5	33.1
40-44	17.3	14.9	13.5	12.7	12.2	11.5	10.8	10.9	10.3
45 & over	5.5	5.7	4.8	3.9	3.3	2.7	2.4	1.9	1.5

TABLE A-34   TOTAL FERTILITY RATES: EASTERN EUROPE AND THE USSR, 1946-1973
(Average Births per Woman)

Country	1946	1947	1948	1949	1950	1951	1952	1953	1954	1955	1956	1957	1958	1959
Albania	...	...	...	...	...	...	...	...	...	...	...	...	...	...
Bulgaria	3.06	2.84	2.87	2.86	2.94	2.45	2.44	2.41	2.35	2.41	2.36	2.26	2.23	2.23
Czechoslovakia	...	3.10	3.00	2.89	3.04	3.02	2.97	2.87	2.83	2.85	2.84	2.75	2.57	2.39
GDR	...	1.69	1.64	1.93	2.30	2.41	2.40	2.37	2.35	2.35	2.26	2.21	2.20	2.35
Hungary	2.30	2.54	2.58	2.54	2.60	2.53	2.47	2.76	2.97	2.81	2.60	2.30	2.18	2.09
Poland	...	...	...	...	3.71	3.75	3.67	3.61	3.58	3.61	3.51	3.49	3.36	3.22
Romania[a]	...	...	2.89	3.34	3.17	3.03	3.00	2.88	3.00	3.09	2.89	2.73	2.59	2.43
USSR	...	...	...	...	2.88	2.92	2.87	2.73	2.97	2.87	2.82	2.76	2.83	2.81
Yugoslavia	...	...	...	...	3.74	3.29	3.60	3.38	3.36	3.16	3.02	2.84	2.77	2.74

Country	1960	1961	1962	1963	1964	1965	1966	1967	1968	1969	1970	1971	1972	1973
Albania	...	...	...	...	...	...	...	...	...	...	...	...	...	...
Bulgaria	2.30	2.28	2.22	2.19	2.16	2.08	2.02	2.03	2.28	2.28	2.18	2.11	2.04	...
Czechoslovakia	2.39	2.38	2.34	2.50	2.51	2.37	2.22	2.09	2.01	2.05	2.07	2.14	2.23[a]	...
GDR	2.33	2.40	2.41	2.47	2.51	2.48	2.42	2.34	2.30	2.24	2.19	2.13	1.79	1.58
Hungary	2.02	1.94	1.79	1.81	1.82	1.82	1.89	2.01	2.06	2.03	1.97	1.92	1.93	1.95
Poland	2.98	2.83	2.72	2.70	2.59	2.52	2.43	2.33	2.24	2.20	2.20	2.25	2.24	2.26
Romania[a]	2.34	2.17	2.04	2.01	1.96	1.91	1.90	3.66	3.63	3.19	2.89	2.66	2.55	2.44
USSR	2.84	2.76	2.65	2.59	2.50	2.46	2.50	2.40	2.39	2.37	2.43	2.44	2.47	...
Yugoslavia	2.80	2.73	2.68	2.66	2.64	2.71	2.65	2.56	2.48	2.44	2.28	2.37	2.35	...

Note: a Estimates.

TABLE A-35   PROJECTED POPULATION, BY AGE GROUPS AND SEX: EASTERN EUROPE AND THE USSR, 1980-2000
(in Thousands)

Country and Age Groups	1980			1985			1990			2000		
	Total	Male	Female	Total	Male	Female	Total	Male	Female	Total	Male	Female
Albania	2,655	1,363	1,292	2,965	1,522	1,444	3,298	1,692	1,606	3,962	2,029	1,933
Percent	100.0%	100.0%	100.0%	100.0%	100.0%	100.0%	100.0%	100.0%	100.0%	100.0%	100.0%	100.0%
0-14	981	504	477	1,046	539	507	1,126	580	546	1,248	644	604
Percent	36.9%	37.0%	36.9%	35.3%	35.4%	35.1%	34.1%	34.3%	34.0%	31.5%	31.7%	31.2%
15-19	303	157	146	309	159	150	323	166	157	373	192	181
Percent	11.4%	11.5%	11.3%	10.4%	10.4%	10.4%	9.8%	9.8%	9.8%	9.4%	9.5%	9.4%
20-44	900	470	429	1,062	552	510	1,221	630	591	1,514	778	736
Percent	33.9%	34.5%	33.2%	35.8%	36.3%	35.3%	37.0%	37.2%	36.8%	38.2%	38.3%	38.1%
45-54	201	106	95	237	126	111	269	142	127	342	176	166
Percent	7.6%	7.8%	7.3%	8.0%	8.3%	7.7%	8.2%	8.4%	7.9%	8.6%	8.7%	8.6%
55-64	131	64	67	154	77	77	185	95	90	249	128	121
Percent	4.9%	4.7%	5.2%	5.2%	5.0%	5.3%	5.6%	5.6%	5.6%	6.3%	6.3%	6.3%
65 & over	139	61	78	158	72	87	174	79	97	237	111	125
Percent	5.2%	4.5%	6.0%	5.3%	4.7%	6.0%	5.3%	4.7%	6.0%	6.0%	5.5%	6.5%
Bulgaria	8,914	4,444	4,470	9,102	4,529	4,572	9,252	4,597	4,655	9,555	4,736	4,819
Percent	100.0%	100.0%	100.0%	100.0%	100.0%	100.0%	100.0%	100.0%	100.0%	100.0%	100.0%	100.0%
0-14	1,989	1,022	967	2,027	1,039	988	2,009	1,028	981	2,007	1,027	980
Percent	22.3%	23.0%	21.6%	22.3%	22.9%	21.6%	21.7%	22.4%	21.1%	21.0%	21.7%	20.3%
15-19	624	320	304	625	321	304	666	342	324	664	339	325
Percent	7.0%	7.2%	6.8%	6.9%	7.1%	6.6%	7.2%	7.4%	7.0%	6.9%	7.2%	6.7%
20-44	3,105	1,563	1,543	3,136	1,582	1,553	3,188	1,614	1,572	3,202	1,630	1,573
Percent	34.8%	35.2%	34.5%	34.5%	34.9%	34.0%	34.5%	35.1%	33.8%	33.5%	34.4%	32.6%
45-54	1,255	627	628	1,179	586	593	1,097	542	555	1,271	630	641
Percent	14.1%	14.1%	14.0%	13.0%	12.9%	13.0%	11.9%	11.8%	11.9%	13.3%	13.3%	13.3%
55-64	906	440	466	1,133	550	583	1,155	561	592	1,016	489	526
Percent	10.2%	9.9%	10.4%	12.4%	12.1%	12.8%	12.5%	12.2%	12.7%	10.6%	10.3%	10.9%
65 & over	1,036	473	563	1,002	451	551	1,137	508	629	1,393	619	774
Percent	11.6%	10.6%	12.6%	11.0%	10.0%	12.1%	12.3%	11.1%	13.5%	14.6%	13.1%	16.1%
Czechoslovakia	15,291	7,454	7,839	15,726	7,670	8,056	16,079	7,851	8,228	16,882	8,257	8,626
Percent	100.0%	100.0%	100.0%	100.0%	100.0%	100.0%	100.0%	100.0%	100.0%	100.0%	100.0%	100.0%
0-14	3,706	1,895	1,810	3,932	2,010	1,922	3,907	1,998	1,910	3,743	1,917	1,826
Percent	24.2%	25.4%	23.1%	25.0%	26.2%	23.9%	24.3%	25.4%	23.2%	22.2%	23.2%	21.2%
15-19	1,088	557	531	1,065	545	521	1,245	635	610	1,294	661	633
Percent	7.1%	7.5%	6.8%	6.8%	7.1%	6.5%	7.7%	8.1%	7.4%	7.7%	8.0%	7.3%
20-44	5,432	2,743	2,691	5,686	2,878	2,808	5,749	2,913	2,835	5,883	2,982	2,900
Percent	35.5%	36.8%	34.3%	36.2%	37.5%	34.9%	35.8%	37.1%	34.5%	34.8%	36.1%	33.6%
45-54	1,765	856	909	1,632	796	836	1,719	843	877	2,367	1,176	1,192
Percent	11.5%	11.5%	11.6%	10.4%	10.4%	10.4%	10.7%	10.7%	10.7%	14.0%	14.2%	13.8%
55-64	1,382	638	743	1,693	779	914	1,600	744	855	1,574	742	832
Percent	9.0%	8.6%	9.5%	10.7%	10.2%	11.3%	10.0%	9.5%	10.4%	9.3%	9.0%	9.6%
65 & over	1,920	765	1,154	1,718	662	1,054	1,860	718	1,142	2,023	779	1,244
Percent	12.6%	10.3%	14.7%	10.9%	8.6%	13.1%	11.6%	9.1%	13.9%	12.0%	9.4%	14.4%

Country and Age Groups	1980			1985			1990			2000		
	Total	Male	Female	Total	Male	Female	Total	Male	Female	Total	Male	Female
GDR	16,803	7,864	8,939	16,984	8,036	8,947	17,229	8,251	8,978	17,606	8,585	9,021
Percent	100.0%	100.0%	100.0%	100.0%	100.0%	100.0%	100.0%	100.0%	100.0%	100.0%	100.0%	100.0%
0-14	3,324	1,703	1,621	3,336	1,711	1,626	3,614	1,854	1,760	3,576	1,835	1,740
Percent	19.8%	21.7%	18.1%	19.6%	21.3%	18.2%	21.0%	22.4%	19.6%	20.3%	21.4%	19.3%
15-19	1,429	731	698	1,249	639	609	1,004	514	490	1,263	647	616
Percent	8.5%	9.3%	7.8%	7.4%	8.0%	6.8%	5.8%	6.2%	5.5%	7.2%	7.5%	6.8%
20-44	5,978	3,033	2,944	6,102	3,104	2,998	6,114	3,117	2,995	6,008	3,065	2,945
Percent	35.6%	38.6%	32.9%	35.9%	38.6%	33.5%	35.5%	37.8%	33.3%	34.1%	35.7%	32.6%
45-54	1,955	924	1,030	2,258	1,125	1,134	2,433	1,211	1,222	2,088	1,053	1,035
Percent	11.6%	11.7%	11.5%	13.3%	14.0%	12.7%	14.1%	14.7%	13.6%	11.9%	12.3%	11.5%
55-64	1,399	517	882	1,719	693	1,026	1,811	837	974	2,261	1,098	1,163
Percent	8.3%	6.6%	9.9%	10.1%	8.6%	11.5%	10.5%	10.1%	10.8%	12.8%	12.8%	12.9%
65 & over	2,720	956	1,765	2,319	764	1,555	2,255	717	1,538	2,410	886	1,524
Percent	16.2%	12.2%	19.7%	13.7%	9.5%	17.4%	13.1%	8.7%	17.1%	13.7%	10.3%	16.9%
Hungary	10,755	5,221	5,534	10,899	5,297	5,601	10,971	5,340	5,631	11,204	5,469	5,736
Percent	100.0%	100.0%	100.0%	100.0%	100.0%	100.0%	100.0%	100.0%	100.0%	100.0%	100.0%	100.0%
0-14	2,346	1,204	1,140	2,431	1,246	1,186	2,395	1,225	1,170	2,273	1,164	1,110
Percent	21.8%	23.1%	20.6%	22.3%	23.5%	21.2%	21.8%	22.9%	20.8%	20.3%	21.3%	19.4%
15-19	647	332	315	698	359	339	765	393	373	787	402	385
Percent	6.0%	6.4%	5.7%	6.4%	6.8%	6.1%	7.0%	7.4%	6.6%	7.0%	7.4%	6.7%
20-44	3,884	1,951	1,931	3,846	1,948	1,899	3,801	1,932	1,868	3,753	1,912	1,841
Percent	36.1%	37.4%	34.9%	35.3%	36.8%	33.9%	34.6%	36.2%	33.2%	33.5%	35.0%	32.1%
45-54	1,386	666	720	1,311	628	683	1,333	644	689	1,594	793	801
Percent	12.9%	12.8%	13.0%	12.0%	11.9%	12.2%	12.2%	12.1%	12.2%	14.2%	14.5%	14.0%
55-64	1,056	483	574	1,295	596	699	1,260	586	674	1,222	572	650
Percent	9.8%	9.3%	10.4%	11.9%	11.3%	12.5%	11.5%	11.0%	12.0%	10.9%	10.5%	11.3%
65 & over	1,438	584	854	1,316	521	795	1,419	560	858	1,577	627	950
Percent	13.4%	11.2%	15.4%	12.1%	9.8%	14.2%	12.9%	10.5%	15.2%	14.1%	11.5%	16.6%
Poland	35,571	17,328	18,244	37,295	18,202	19,093	38,717	18,930	19,787	41,115	20,137	20,978
Percent	100.0%	100.0%	100.0%	100.0%	100.0%	100.0%	100.0%	100.0%	100.0%	100.0%	100.0%	100.0%
0-14	8,571	4,391	4,181	9,360	4,800	4,560	9,660	4,955	4,705	9,022	4,634	4,388
Percent	24.1%	25.3%	22.9%	25.1%	26.4%	23.9%	25.0%	26.2%	23.8%	21.9%	23.0%	20.9%
15-19	2,818	1,439	1,379	2,515	1,283	1,232	2,785	1,426	1,359	3,306	1,693	1,613
Percent	7.9%	8.3%	7.6%	6.7%	7.0%	6.5%	7.2%	7.5%	6.9%	8.0%	8.4%	7.7%
20-44	13,486	6,791	6,693	14,088	7,111	6,979	14,648	7,396	7,251	14,619	7,404	7,215
Percent	37.9%	39.2%	36.7%	37.8%	39.1%	36.5%	37.8%	39.1%	36.6%	35.6%	36.8%	34.4%
45-54	4,322	2,083	2,239	4,254	2,081	2,173	3,878	1,896	1,982	5,748	2,841	2,906
Percent	12.1%	12.0%	12.3%	11.4%	11.4%	11.4%	10.0%	10.0%	10.0%	14.0%	14.1%	13.9%
55-64	2,816	1,249	1,567	3,661	1,652	2,009	3,967	1,848	2,120	3,577	1,689	1,887
Percent	7.9%	7.2%	8.6%	9.8%	9.1%	10.5%	10.2%	9.8%	10.7%	8.7%	8.4%	9.0%
65 & over	3,559	1,374	2,185	3,415	1,275	2,140	3,779	1,408	2,370	4,843	1,875	2,968
Percent	10.0%	7.9%	12.0%	9.2%	7.0%	11.2%	9.8%	7.4%	11.9%	11.8%	9.3%	14.1%

Country and Age Groups	1980 Total	1980 Male	1980 Female	1985 Total	1985 Male	1985 Female	1990 Total	1990 Male	1990 Female	2000 Total	2000 Male	2000 Female
Romania	22,151	10,932	11,219	22,968	11,358	11,611	23,699	11,743	11,956	25,325	12,593	12,731
Percent	100.0%	100.0%	100.0%	100.0%	100.0%	100.0%	100.0%	100.0%	100.0%	100.0%	100.0%	100.0%
0-14	5,857	3,000	2,858	5,771	2,958	2,814	5,678	2,911	2,768	5,781	2,964	2,817
Percent	26.4%	27.4%	25.5%	25.1%	26.0%	24.2%	24.0%	24.8%	23.2%	22.8%	23.5%	22.1%
15-19	1,439	737	702	1,932	987	946	1,917	981	937	1,850	947	903
Percent	6.5%	6.7%	6.3%	8.4%	8.7%	8.1%	8.1%	8.4%	7.8%	7.3%	7.5%	7.1%
20-44	7,830	3,956	3,874	7,680	3,894	3,785	8,295	4,216	4,078	8,957	4,561	4,396
Percent	35.3%	36.2%	34.5%	33.4%	34.3%	32.6%	35.0%	35.9%	34.1%	35.4%	36.2%	34.5%
45-54	2,908	1,439	1,469	2,977	1,473	1,504	2,728	1,346	1,381	3,060	1,535	1,525
Percent	13.1%	13.2%	13.1%	13.0%	13.0%	13.0%	11.5%	11.5%	11.6%	12.1%	12.2%	12.0%
55-64	1,844	829	1,014	2,458	1,154	1,304	2,674	1,292	1,382	2,519	1,215	1,304
Percent	8.3%	7.6%	9.0%	10.7%	10.2%	11.2%	11.3%	11.0%	11.6%	9.9%	9.6%	10.2%
65 & over	2,273	972	1,300	2,148	891	1,258	2,408	997	1,411	3,157	1,371	1,787
Percent	10.3%	8.9%	11.6%	9.4%	7.8%	10.8%	10.2%	8.5%	11.8%	12.5%	10.9%	14.0%
USSR	265,049	123,726	141,323	277,743	130,493	147,250	289,206	136,671	152,535	308,050	146,554	161,496
Percent	100.0%	100.0%	100.0%	100.0%	100.0%	100.0%	100.0%	100.0%	100.0%	100.0%	100.0%	100.0%
0-14	64,891	32,983	31,909	69,733	35,453	34,281	73,589	37,426	36,163	73,045	37,209	35,838
Percent	24.5%	26.7%	22.6%	25.1%	27.2%	23.3%	25.4%	27.3%	23.7%	23.7%	25.4%	22.2%
15-19	24,371	12,393	11,977	20,275	10,273	10,001	21,057	10,676	10,380	25,127	12,748	12,379
Percent	9.2%	10.0%	8.5%	7.3%	7.9%	6.8%	7.3%	7.8%	6.8%	8.2%	8.7%	7.7%
20-44	97,079	48,238	48,842	99,826	49,819	50,008	105,703	52,750	52,953	110,357	54,923	55,432
Percent	36.6%	39.0%	34.6%	35.9%	38.2%	34.0%	36.5%	38.6%	34.7%	35.8%	37.5%	34.3%
45-54	33,640	15,475	18,165	35,054	16,521	18,533	31,870	14,905	16,965	35,359	16,889	18,471
Percent	12.7%	12.5%	12.9%	12.6%	12.7%	12.6%	11.0%	10.9%	11.1%	11.5%	11.5%	11.4%
55-64	19,268	6,927	12,341	27,349	10,954	16,395	30,013	13,008	17,005	28,456	12,522	15,934
Percent	7.3%	5.6%	8.7%	9.8%	8.4%	11.1%	10.4%	9.5%	11.1%	9.2%	8.5%	9.9%
65 & over	25,800	7,711	18,089	25,505	7,472	18,034	26,974	7,906	19,067	35,706	12,262	23,442
Percent	9.7%	6.2%	12.8%	9.2%	5.7%	12.2%	9.3%	5.8%	12.5%	11.6%	8.4%	14.5%
Yugoslavia	22,274	10,977	11,298	23,256	11,484	11,771	24,175	11,966	12,209	25,824	12,829	12,996
Percent	100.0%	100.0%	100.0%	100.0%	100.0%	100.0%	100.0%	100.0%	100.0%	100.0%	100.0%	100.0%
0-14	5,493	2,822	2,670	5,580	2,873	2,707	5,693	2,931	2,761	5,694	2,934	2,760
Percent	24.7%	25.7%	23.6%	24.0%	25.0%	23.0%	23.5%	24.5%	22.6%	22.0%	22.9%	21.2%
15-19	1,853	948	905	1,813	926	887	1,792	922	870	1,902	979	924
Percent	8.3%	8.6%	8.0%	7.8%	8.1%	7.5%	7.4%	7.7%	7.1%	7.4%	7.6%	7.1%
20-44	8,298	4,199	4,100	8,579	4,357	4,223	9,012	4,585	4,427	9,138	4,660	4,478
Percent	37.3%	38.3%	36.3%	36.9%	37.9%	35.9%	37.3%	38.3%	36.3%	35.4%	36.3%	34.4%
45-54	2,933	1,423	1,510	3,026	1,494	1,532	2,784	1,374	1,410	3,369	1,694	1,676
Percent	13.2%	13.0%	13.4%	13.0%	13.0%	13.0%	11.5%	11.5%	11.5%	13.0%	13.2%	12.9%
55-64	1,646	717	928	2,334	1,050	1,284	2,705	1,280	1,424	2,574	1,238	1,335
Percent	7.4%	6.5%	8.2%	10.0%	9.1%	10.9%	11.2%	10.7%	11.7%	10.0%	9.7%	10.3%
65 & over	2,051	867	1,184	1,923	784	1,139	2,191	873	1,316	3,147	1,324	1,823
Percent	9.2%	7.9%	10.5%	8.3%	6.8%	9.7%	9.1%	7.3%	10.8%	12.2%	10.3%	14.0%

SECTION B: PARTY MEMBERSHIP

Introduction

Table B-1 Data on party members relate to those 18 and over with the exception of Hungary between 1957 and 1970, which are for those 21 and over. Data on Poland do not include the military.

Table B-2 Data for 1948 appear to measure occupation at the time of joining the party, and are not comparable to data for subsequent years. Unaccounted for, 1966, 1971, and 1976, are White Collar Employees and Intellectuals, as well as a small number of Others. See the General Introduction for further comments on the Albanian data.

Table B-3 The failure in the number of Others to grow from 1962 to 1971 suggests the possibility that certain groups, such as workers with pensions, may be excluded from this category. See the General Introduction for further comments.

Table B-4 See the General Introduction for further comments on the data for the 1950s.

Table B-5 Data for 1961 and 1966 are not comparable for Workers and White Collar Employees; in 1966 a portion of the White Collar category was transferred to the Worker category. Data for 1961 and 1971 are not comparable for Workers and for Others; in 1971 a portion of the Others category (probably Workers with pensions) was transferred to the category of Workers. See the General Introduction for further comments. For 1971, those Unaccounted for can be considered as Others (pensioners, students, and housewives).

Table B-8 Data on the number of workers may be exaggerated. See comments in the General Introduction.

Table B-10 Series I includes all party members; in Series II, the military and party members on temporary military duty are excluded. Noncomparability of the data for 1952 and 1954 is prob-

ably the result of a shift of military and security personnel, students, and housewives from Worker or Peasant categories to the category of Others. Between 1960 and 1962 it appears that 15,000 to 20,000 Others were transferred to the category of White Collar Employees. Between 1970 and 1971, the military was shifted back to the Others category in Series I.

Table B-11 Original occupation or position—that when first employed.

Table B-12 The discrepency between the data in the table and in the footnotes arises largely from the fact that the Central Committee data determined social position by the job held longest before joining the party, while the party census measured social class according to the job held at the time of joining the party.

Table B-15 Data do not include persons who became white collar employees after joining the party—see fn. *a* and the General Introduction.

Table B-17 Figures cited in fn. *b* through *d* are estimates derived from percents.

Table B-18 For 1971, data on 7-8 Year Basic Incomplete Education for Bulgaria probably include those with a 4 Year Elementary Incomplete education.

Table B-19 Those completing a *Fachschule* are given here as having a Specialized Secondary Complete education. Note the rapid growth of those with Specialized Secondary and Higher education between 1962 and 1963, suggesting possible inaccuracies in the data.

Table B-23 Data exclude private peasantry and artisans, as well as housewives, pensioners, and others not active.

TABLE B-1 TOTAL NUMBER OF PARTY MEMBERS: EASTERN EUROPE AND THE USSR, 1945-1976

Total Party Membership	1945	1946	1947	1948	1949	1950	1951	1952
Albania				Nov.				March
Total Party Mbrship.	...	...	...	45,382	...	...	...	44,418
Percent of Popul.	...	...	...	3.9%	...	...	...	3.5%
Bulgaria	Jan.	"Over		Dec.	Jan.			
Total Party Mbrship.	254,140	490,000"	...	496,000	495,658	...	...	...
Percent of Popul.	3.7%	7.0%	...	6.9%	6.9%	...	...	...
Czechoslovakia	July	March 15	End	Oct.	May	Feb.	Jan.	
Total Party Mbrship.	475,304[a]	1,159,164[b]	1,393,778[c]	2,674,838	2,311,066	1,982,315	1,677,000	...
Percent of Popul.	3.4%	9.4%	11.4%	21.7%	18.6%	16.1%	13.5%	...
GDR			May	June	June	April	June	
Total Party Mbrship.	...	...	1,786,138	1,797,316	1,773,689	1,750,000	1,221,300	...
Percent of Popul.	...	...	9.4%	9.4%	9.4%	9.5%	6.7%	...
Hungary	May		Midyear	July		Jan.	Jan.	Jan.
Total Party Mbrship.	150,000	...	700,000	1,128,130	...	828,695	862,114	945,606
Percent of Popul.	1.7%	...	7.7%	12.0%	...	8.9%	9.1%	10.0%
Poland	Dec.	Dec.	Dec.	Dec.	April	Dec.	Dec.	Dec.
Total Party Mbrship.	235,296	555,888	820,786	1,460,000	1,368,759	1,241,000	1,138,000	1,147,000
Percent of Popul.	1%	2.4%	3.5%	6.0%	5.5%	5.0%	4.5%	4.4%
Romania	Oct.	Nov.		End "About		July		
Total Party Mbrship.	256,083	675,000	714,000	900,000"	...	720,000	...	...
Percent of Popul.	1.6%	4.3%	4.5%	5.7%	...	4.4%	...	...
USSR	Jan.	Jan.	Jan.	Jan.	Jan.	Jan.	Jan.	Jan.
Total Party Mbrship.	5,760,369	5,510,862	6,051,901	6,390,281	6,352,572	6,340,183	6,462,975	6,707,539
Percent of Popul.	...	...	...	...	...	3.6%	3.6%	3.6%
Yugoslavia		End	End	End	End	End	End	End
Total Party Mbrship.	161,880	258,303	285,147	482,938	530,812	607,443	704,617	772,920
Percent of Popul.	1.0%		1.8%	3.0%	3.3%	3.7%	4.2%	4.6%

Total Party Membership	1953	1954	1955	1956	1957	1958	1959	1960
Albania		March "Around						
Total Party Mbrship.	...	43,000"	...	48,644	...	...	...	...
Percent of Popul.	...	3.3%	...	3.5%	...	...	...	...
Bulgaria	Dec.			Jan.		June		
Total Party Mbrship.	455,251	...	...	482,300	...	484,255	...	...
Percent of Popul.	6.1%	...	...	6.4%	...	6.3%	...	...
Czechoslovakia						Jan.		Jan.
Total Party Mbrship.	...	...	...	1,417,989	...	1,422,199	...	1,559,082
Percent of Popul.	...	...	...	10.8%	...	10.5%	...	11.4%
GDR	Sept.	April 15			Dec.			
Total Party Mbrship.	1,230,000	1,413,313	...	...	1,472,932	...	...	...
Percent of Popul.	6.8%	7.8%	...	...	8.5%	...	...	...
Hungary				Jan.	Jan.	Midyear	Nov.	
Total Party Mbrship.	...	...	...	859,037	125,088	410,000[d]	437,956[d]	...
Percent of Popul.	...	...	...	8.7%	1.3%	4.4%	4.4%	...
Poland	Dec.		Dec.			Dec.	Dec.	Dec.
Total Party Mbrship.	1,226,718	1,293,000	1,343,837[e]	...	1,276,000	1,023,577[f]	1,108,466	1,154,672
Percent of Popul.	4.6%	4.8%	4.9%	...	4.5%	3.5%	3.5%	3.9%
Romania								
Total Party Mbrship.	...	...	595,398	...	...	720,000	...	834,600
Percent of Popul.	...	...	3.4%	...	...	4.0%	...	4.5%
USSR	Jan.	Jan.	Jan.	Jan.	Jan.	Jan.	Jan.	Jan.
Total Party Mbrship.	6,897,224	6,864,863	6,957,105	7,173,521	7,494,573	7,843,196	8,239,131	8,708,667
Percent of Popul.	3.7%	3.6%	3.6%	3.6%	3.7%	3.8%	3.9%	4.1%
Yugoslavia	End	End	End	End	End	End	End	End
Total Party Mbrship.	700,030	654,669	624,806	648,616	755,066	829,953	935,856	1,006,235
Percent of Popul.	4.1%	3.8%	3.6%	3.7%	4.2%	4.6%	5.1%	5.5%

Total Party Membership	1961	1962	1963	1964	1965	1966	1967	1968
Albania	Jan.							
Total Party Mbrship.	53,659	...	60,701	...	...	66,327	...	...
Percent of Popul.	3.2%	...	3.4%	...	...	3.5%	...	...
Bulgaria		Jan.	Dec.			Jan. 1	Dec.	Dec.
Total Party Mbrship.	...	520,118	550,384	...	...	593,529	613,393	637,265
Percent of Popul.	...	6.5%	6.8%	...	...	7.2%	7.4%	7.6%
Czechoslovakia		Jan.		Jan.	Jan. 1	Jan.	July	Jan.
Total Party Mbrship.	...	1,657,021[g]	...	1,676,509	1,684,416	1,698,002	1,689,207	1,690,977
Percent of Popul.	...	12.0%	...	11.9%	11.9%	11.9%	11.8%	11.8%
GDR	Dec.		Jan.			Dec.		
Total Party Mbrship.	1,610,769	...	1,610,679	1,750,000	...	1,769,912	...	...
Percent of Popul.	9.5%	...	9.5%	10.3%	...	10.5%	...	...
Hungary	Jan. 1	Nov.	Dec.		April	Nov.		
Total Party Mbrship.	478,000	511,965[d]	520,000[d]	...	540,000[d]	584,849[d]	...	...
Percent of Popul.	4.8%	5.1%	5.2%	...	5.3%	5.7%	...	...
Poland	Dec.	Dec.		Dec.	Dec.	Dec.	Dec.	Dec.
Total Party Mbrship.	1,306,215	1,397,001	...	1,640,700	1,775,049	1,894,895	1,931,345	2,104,331
Percent of Popul.	4.3%	4.6%	...	5.2%	5.6%	6.0%	6.0%	6.5%
Romania	May	April		Dec.	Dec.		Dec.	Oct.
Total Party Mbrship.	869,759	919,873	...	1,377,847	1,518,000	...	1,730,000	1,800,000
Percent of Popul.	4.7%	4.9%	...	7.3%	8.0%	...	9.0%	9.1%
USSR	Jan.	Jan.	Jan.	Jan.	Jan.	Jan.	Jan.	Jan.
Total Party Mbrship.	9,275,826	9,891,068	10,387,196	11,022,369	11,758,169	12,357,308	12,684,133	13,180,225
Percent of Popul.	4.3%	4.5%	4.6%	4.9%	5.1%	5.3%	5.4%	5.6%
Yugoslavia	End	End	End	End	End	End	End	End
Total Party Mbrship.	1,035,033	1,108,331	1,019,013	1,031,634	1,046,202	1,046,018	1,013,500	1,146,084
Percent of Popul.	5.6%	5.4%	5.3%	5.4%	5.2%	5.3%	5.1%	5.7%

Total Party Membership	1969	1970	1971	1972	1973	1974	1975	1976
Albania			Oct.		Dec.		Nov.	Fall
Total Party Mbrship.	...	75,637	86,985	...	87,000	...	"Over 100,000"	101,500
Percent of Popul.	...	3.6%	4.0%	...	3.7%	...	4.2%	4.1%
Bulgaria	End		Jan.		Dec.	April		Spring
Total Party Mbrship.	"Over 672,000"	...	696,156	...	700,000	755,679	...	780,796
Percent of Popul.	7.9%	...	8.2%	...	8.1%	8.7%	...	8.9%
Czechoslovakia	April	Dec.	Spring		May			
Total Party Mbrship.	1,650,567	1,225,946	"About 1,200,000"	...	1,250,000	...	...	1,382,860
Percent of Popul.	11.4%	8.6%	8.4%	...	8.6%	...	...	9.3%
GDR			June	Dec.	Dec.	July	June 6	May
Total Party Mbrship.	...	...	1,909,859	1,950,421	1,951,924	1,954,130	1,900,000	2,043,697
Percent of Popul.	...	...	11.2%	11.5%	11.5%	11.5%	11.3%	12.2%
Hungary	Jan.	June	June		Dec.		Jan.	
Total Party Mbrship.	627,000[f]	662,397[f]	693,000	...	760,000	...	754,353	765,566
Percent of Popul.	6.1%	6.4%	6.7%	...	7.3%	...	7.2%	7.2%
Poland	Dec.	Dec.	Dec.	Dec.	Dec.		June	Dec.
Total Party Mbrship.	2,203,553	2,319,963	2,254,112	2,322,531	2,322,531	...	2,359,000	2,568,400
Percent of Popul.	6.7%	7.1%	6.8%	7.0%	6.9%	...	6.9%	7.5%
Romania	Aug.	Dec.	Dec.	Dec.	Dec.	Nov.	Dec.	
Total Party Mbrship.	1,924,500	2,089,085	"Over 2,175,000"	2,260,000	2,386,819	2,480,000	2,500,000	...
Percent of Popul.	9.6%	10.3%	10.6%	10.9%	11.4%		11.8%	...
USSR		Jan.	Jan.	Jan.	Jan.	March	Jan.	Jan.
Total Party Mbrship.	13,639,891	14,011,784	14,372,563	14,631,289	14,821,031	14,970,000	15,000,000	15,638,891
Percent of Popul.	5.7%	5.8%	5.9%	5.9%	6.0%	6.0%	5.9%	6.1%
Yugoslavia	End	End	End	End	End	End	End	End
Total Party Mbrship.	1,111,682	1,049,184	1,025,476	1,009,947	1,076,711	1,192,466	1,302,843	1,460,267
Percent of Popul.	5.5%	5.1%	5.0%	4.8%	5.1%	5.7%	6.1%	6.7%

Notes: [a] End, 1945: 826,527. [b] Other figures for spring, 1946 include 1,050,081 and 1,081,544. [c] June, 1947: 1,109,967; August, 1947: 1,899,423. [d] 21 and over. [e] The figure of 1,440,144 has also been cited for December, 1955; this somewhat higher figure may include party members in the military. [f] Figure is for January, 1959, but given here as December, 1958, for purposes of comparison with other years. [g] October, 1962: 1,680,819.

TABLE B-2 SOCIAL COMPOSITION OF THE PARTY ACCORDING TO CURRENT OCCUPATION OR
          POSITION: ALBANIA, 1948-1976

Current Occupation or Position	Nov. 1948[a]	March 1952	Spring 1956	Jan. 1961	1966	Oct. 1971	Fall 1976
TOTAL PARTY MEMBERSHIP	45,382	44,418	48,644	53,659	66,327	86,985	101,500
Percent	100.0%	100.0%	100.0%	100.0%	100.0%	100.0%	100.0%
Workers	[9,100]	[5,000]	[9,600]	[15,900]	[21,900]	[31,700]	[38,000]
Percent	[20.1%]	11.5%	19.76%	29.66%	32.9%	36.41%	37.5%
Nonfarm Workers	...	...	...	...	...	...	...
Percent	...	...	...	...	...	...	...
Farm Laborers	...	...	...	...	...	...	...
Percent	...	...	...	...	...	...	...
Peasants & Collective Farmers	[30,190]	...	[15,300]	[14,400]	[19,200]	[25,800]	[29,000]
Percent	[66.5%]	...	31.44%	26.77%	28.95%	29.7%	29%
Peasants	[30,190]	...	[10,400]	[1,700]	...	...	...
Percent	[66.5%]	...	21.42%	3.15%	...	...	...
Collective Farmers	...	...	[4,900]	[12,700]	[19,200]	[25,800]	[29,000]
Percent	...	...	10.02%	23.62%	28.95%	29.7%	29%
White Collar Employees & Intellectuals	[1,690]	...	[22,000]	[22,500]	...	...	...
Percent	[3.7%]	...	45.2%	41.94%	...	...	...
Intellectuals	...	...	...	...	...	...	...
Percent	...	...	...	...	...	...	...
White Collar Empl.	...	...	...	...	...	...	...
Percent	...	...	...	...	...	...	...
Others	...	...	[1,700]	[900]	...	...	...
Percent	...	...	3.58%	1.62%	...	...	...
Students	[1,800]	...	...	...	...	...	...
Percent	[4.0%]	...	...	...	...	...	...
Housewives	...	...	...	...	...	...	...
Percent	...	...	...	...	...	...	...
Pensioned	...	...	...	...	...	...	...
Percent	...	...	...	...	...	...	...
Self-Employed	[1,100]	...	...	...	...	...	...
Percent	[2.4%]	...	...	...	...	...	...
Others	[1,300]	...	...	...	...	...	...
Percent	[2.9%]	...	...	...	...	...	...
Unknown	...	...	...	...	...	...	...
Percent	...	...	...	...	...	...	...
Unaccounted for	0	[39,300]	0	0	[25,300]	[29,500]	[34,000]
Percent	0%	88.5%	0%	0%	38.12%	33.89%	33.5%

Note: a Not comparable to subsequent years. Data appears to measure occupation or position at time of
       joining party.

TABLE B-3   SOCIAL COMPOSITION OF THE PARTY ACCORDING TO CURRENT OCCUPATION
OR POSITION: BULGARIA, 1948-1976

Current Occupation or Position	Fall 1948	Dec. 1953	June 1958	Oct. 1962	Oct. 1966	April 1971	Spring 1976
TOTAL PARTY MEMBERSHIP	464,000[a]	455,251	484,255	528,674	611,179	699,476	780,796
Percent	100.0%	100.0%	100.0%	100.0%	100.0%	100.0%	100.0%
Workers	122,896	155,081	[175,000]	196,449	[235,000]	[280,000]	[323,000]
Percent	26.5%	34.06%	36.09%	37.16%	38.41%	40.10%	41.4%
Nonfarm Workers	...	...	...	...	...	...	...
Percent	...	...	...	...	...	...	...
Farm Laborers	...	...	...	...	...	...	...
Percent	...	...	...	...	...	...	...
Peasants & Collective Farmers	207,490	180,998	[166,000]	169,601	[177,000]	[183,000]	...
Percent	44.74%	39.76%	34.16%	32.08%	29.21%	26.06%	...
Peasants	184,722	67,066	...	...	...	...	...
Percent	39.8%	14.7%	...	...	...	...	...
Collective Farmers	22,768	113,932	...	...	...	...	...
Percent	4.9%	25.0%	...	...	...	...	...
White Collar Employees & Intellectuals	75,501	81,664	[105,000]	124,587	...	[197,000]	...
Percent	16.28%	17.94%	21.72%	23.57%	...	28.19%	...
Intellectuals	...	...	...	...	...	...	...
Percent	...	...	...	...	...	...	...
White Collar Empl.	...	...	...	...	...	...	...
Percent	...	...	...	...	...	...	...
Others	57,895	37,508	[39,000]	38,037	...	...	...
Percent	12.48%	8.24%	8.03%	7.19%	...	...	...
Students		...	...	...	...	...	...
Percent		...	...	...	...	...	...
Housewives	28,000[b]	...	...	...	...	...	...
Percent	6%	...	...	...	...	...	...
Pensioned		...	...	...	...	...	...
Percent		...	...	...	...	...	...
Self-Employed	30,000[c]	...	...	...	...	...	...
Percent	6%	...	...	...	...	...	...
Others	[d]	...	...	...	...	...	...
Percent		...	...	...	...	...	...
Unknown	...	...	...	...	...	...	...
Percent	...	...	...	...	...	...	...
Unaccounted for	0	0	0	0	[198,000]	[39,000]	[458,000]
Percent	0%	0%	0%	0%	32.38%	5.65%	58.6%

Notes: a Excludes 32,000 former Social Democrats and military. b Includes students, housewives, those
on pension, and others. c Private artisans. d See fn. b.

TABLE B-4 SOCIAL COMPOSITION OF THE PARTY ACCORDING TO CURRENT OCCUPATION OR POSITION: CZECHOSLOVAKIA, 1947-1971

Current Occupation or Position	Beginning 1947	May 1949	Feb. 1950	Jan. 1958	Jan. 1962	Jan. 1966	Beginning 1968	Jan. 1971
TOTAL PARTY MEMBERSHIP	...	2,311,066	1,982,315	1,422,199	1,657,021	1,698,002	1,690,977	1,200,000
Percent	100.0%	100.0%	100.0%	100.0%	100.0%	100.0%	100.0%	100.0%
Workers	...	...	[761,000]	496,243	597,825	557,999	[514,000]	[313,000]
Percent	45.7%	...	38.4%	34.9%	36.0%	32.9%	30.4%	26.1%
Nonfarm Workers	...	...	...	...	554,084	511,917	...	...
Percent	...	...	...	...	33.4%	30.2%	...	...
Farm Laborers	...	...	...	...	43,741	46,082	...	...
Percent	...	...	...	...	2.6%	2.7%	...	...
Peasants & Collective Farmers	...	...	[192,000]	103,269	109,311	93,208	[88,000]	...
Percent	7.9%	...	9.7%	7.3%	6.6%	5.5%	5.2%	...
Peasants	...	...	...	14,062	2,938	2,099	...	...
Percent	...	...	...	1.0%	0.2%	0.1%	...	...
Collective Farmers	...	...	...	89,207	106,373	91,109	...	...
Percent	...	...	...	6.3%	6.4%	5.4%	...	...
White Collar Employees & Intellectuals	...	...	...	[565,000]	558,704	603,862	...	...
Percent	16.4%	...	...	39.7%	33.7%	35.6%	...	...
Administrative Staff (Urednici)	...	[358,000]	[262,000]	...	126,393	113,350	[105,000]	...
Percent	6.2%	15.5%	13.2%	...	7.6%	6.7%	6.2%	...
Others	...	...	...	...	432,311	490,512	...	...
Percent	10.2%	...	...	...	26.1%	28.9%	...	...
Others	...	...	...	[257,000]	391,181	442,933	...	...
Percent	...	...	...	18.1%	23.6%	26.1%	...	...
Students	...	...	...	...	8,044	6,372	...	...
Percent	...	...	...	...	0.5%	0.4%	...	...
Housewives	...	...	...	...	93,797	68,659	...	...
Percent	...	...	...	...	5.7%	4.0%	...	...
Pensioned	...	...	...	...	214,054	293,577	...	...
Percent	...	...	...	...	13.0%	17.3%	...	...
Self-Employed	...	...	...	...	...	...	...	...
Percent	4.5%	...	...	...	...	...	...	...
Others (Military)	...	...	...	...	75,286	74,325	...	...
Percent	...	...	...	...	4.6%	4.4%	...	...
Unknown	...	...	...	...	...	...	...	...
Percent	...	...	...	...	...	...	...	...
Unaccounted for	...	[1,953,000]	[767,000]	[1,000]	0	0	[984,000]	[887,000]
Percent	25.5%	[84.5%]	[38.7%]	0%	0%	0%	58.2%	73.9%

TABLE B-5 SOCIAL COMPOSITION OF THE PARTY ACCORDING TO CURRENT OCCUPATION OR POSITION: GDR, 1947-1976

Current Occupation or Position	May 1947	End 1957	End 1961	Dec. 1966	June 1971	Dec. 1972	May 1976
TOTAL PARTY MEMBERSHIP	1,786,138	1,472,932	...	1,769,912	1,909,859	1,950,421	2,043,697
Percent	100.0%	100.0%	100.0%	100.0%	100.0%	100.0%	100.0%
Workers	[859,000]	[498,000]	...	807,000	1,080,980	[1,104,000]	[1,147,000]
Percent	48.1%	33.8%	33.8%	45.6%	56.6%	56.6%	56.1%
Nonfarm Workers	...	...	...	...	...	...	...
Percent	...	...	...	...	...	...	...
Farm Laborers	...	...	...	...	...	...	...
Percent	...	...	...	...	...	...	...
Peasants & Collective Farmers	[168,000]	[74,000]	...	[113,000]	[113,000]	[111,000]	[106,000]
Percent	9.4%	5.0%	6.2%	6.4%	5.9%	5.7%	5.2%
Peasants	...	[31,000]	...	...	...	...	...
Percent	...	2.1%	...	...	...	...	...
Collective Farmers	...	[43,000]	...	[113,000]	[113,000]	[111,000]	[106,000]
Percent	...	2.9%	6.2%	6.4%	5.9%	5.7%	5.2%
White Collar Employees & Intellectuals	[393,000]	[623,000]	...	502,862	...	[599,000]	...
Percent	22.0%	42.3%	41.3%	28.4%	...	[30.7%]	...
Intellectuals	...	...	...	[218,000]	[327,000]	[349,000]	[409,000]
Percent	...	...	8.7%	12.3%	17.1%	17.9%	20%
White Collar Empl.	...	...	...	[285,000]	...	[249,654]	...
Percent	...	...	32.6%	16.1%	...	12.8%	...
Others	[366,000]	[278,000]	...	[347,000]	...	...	...
Percent	20.5%	18.9%	18.7%	19.6%	...	...	...
Students	...	...	...	28,323	...	...	...
Percent	...	...	1.6%	1.6%	...	...	...
Housewives	...	...	...	77,121	...	...	...
Percent	...	...	...	4.4%	...	...	...
Pensioned	...	...	...	214,049	...	...	...
Percent	...	...	...	12.1%	...	...	...
Self-Employed	...	...	...	12,218	...	...	...
Percent	...	...	...	0.7%	...	...	...
Others	...	...	...	15,029[a]	...	...	...
Percent	...	...	...	0.8%	...	...	...
Unknown	...	...	...	...	...	...	...
Percent	...	...	...	...	...	...	...
Unaccounted for	0	0	0	0	[390,000]	[137,000]	[382,000]
Percent	0%	0%	0%	0%	20.4%	7.0%	18.7%

Notes: a Members of nonagricultural production cooperatives.

TABLE B-6   SOCIAL COMPOSITION OF THE PARTY ACCORDING TO CURRENT OCCUPATION OR
POSITION: HUNGARY, 1951-1975

Current Occupation or Position	Jan. 1951	Nov. 1962	Nov. 1966	1968	June 1970	Jan. 1975[a]
TOTAL PARTY MEMBERSHIP	862,114	511,965	584,849	...	662,397	754,353
Percent	100.0%	100.0%	100.0%	100.0%	100.0%	100.0%
Workers	348,630	[177,000]				
Percent	40.5%	34.6%				
Nonfarm Workers	...	...				
Percent	...	...				
Farm Laborers	...	...				
Percent	...	...				
Peasants & Collective Farmers	100,585	[45,000]	"Manual" [249,000]	"Manual" ...	"Manual" [252,000]	[339,000]
Percent	11.7%	8.7%	42.5%	42.7%	38.0%	45.0%
Peasants	...	...				
Percent	...	...				
Collective Farmers	...	...				
Percent	...	...				
White Collar Employees & Intellectuals	...	[200,000]	[218,000]	...	[266,000]	[348,000][b]
Percent	...	[39.0%]	37.3%	38.1%	40.1%	46.1%
Intellectuals	...	[53,000]	...	...	...	...
Percent	...	10.3%	...	...	...	...
White Collar Empl.	226,760	[147,000]	...	...	...	...
Percent	26.3%	28.7%	...	...	...	...
Others	...	[91,000]	[118,000]	...	[145,000]	...
Percent	...	17.7%	20.2%	19.2%	21.9%	...
Students	...	...	...	...	...	...
Percent	...	...	...	...	...	...
Housewives	...	...	...	...	...	...
Percent	...	...	...	...	...	...
Pensioned[c]	...	...	[70,000]	...	[94,000]	d
Percent	...	...	[11.9%]	...	[14.2%]	
Self-Employed	...	...	...	...	...	...
Percent	...	...	...	...	...	...
Others	...	...	[49,000][e]	...	[51,000]	...
Percent	...	...	8.3%	...	7.7%	...
Unknown	...	...	...	...	...	...
Percent	...	...	...	...	...	...
Unaccounted for	186,139	0	0	0	0	[67,000]
Percent	21.6%	0%	0%	0%	0%	8.9%

Notes: a Social composition as of Jan. 1, 1975; total party membership as of March, 1975.
b Includes those who are in "direct production" (6.1%). c Includes pensioners and
Dependents; pensioners alone numbered 54,000 (9.3%) in 1966. d Included among
Workers or White Collar Employees and Intellectuals. e Includes 46,000 (7.9%)
professional military personnel.

TABLE B-7   SOCIAL COMPOSITION OF THE PARTY ACCORDING TO CURRENT OCCUPATION OR
            POSITION: POLAND, 1945-1975

Current Occupation or Position	Dec. 1945 I	Dec. 1948 II[a]	April 1949 I	Dec. 1951 I	Dec. 1952 I	Dec. 1953 I	Dec. 1954 I
TOTAL PARTY MEMBERSHIP	235,296	1,460,000	1,368,759	1,138,000	1,147,000	1,227,000	1,293,000
Percent	100.0%	100.0%	100.0%	100.0%	100.0%	100.0%	100.0%
Workers	[146,000]	876,000	838,277	[561,000]	[553,000]	[585,000]	[622,000]
Percent	62.2%	60.0%	61.3%	49.3%	48.2%	47.7%	48.1%
Nonfarm Workers	...	...	[781,000]	...	...	...	...
Percent	...	...	57.1%	...	...	...	...
Farm Laborers	...	...	[57,000]	...	...	...	...
Percent	...	...	4.2%	...	...	...	...
Peasants & Collective Farmers	[66,000]	263,000	197,436	[151,000]	[154,000]	[160,000]	[178,000]
Percent	28.2%	18.0%	14.4%	13.3%	13.4%	13.0%	13.8%
Peasants	...	...	...	...	...	...	...
Percent	...	...	...	...	...	...	...
Collective Farmers	...	...	...	...	...	...	...
Percent	...	...	...	...	...	...	...
White Collar Employees & Intellectuals	[23,000]	248,000	[312,000]	[401,000]	415,214	[455,000]	[468,000]
Percent	9.6%	17.0%	22.8%	35.2%	36.2%	37.1%	36.2%
Intellectuals	...	...	...	[179,000]	[194,000]	[221,000]	[239,000]
Percent	...	...	...	15.7%	16.9%	18.0%	18.5%
White Collar Empl.	...	...	...	[222,000][b]	[221,000][b]	[234,000][b]	[229,000][b]
Percent	...	...	...	19.5%	19.3%	19.1%	17.7%
Others	0	73,000	21,274	[25,000]	[25,000]	[27,000]	[26,000]
Percent	0%	5.0%	1.5%	2.2%	2.2%	2.2%	2.0%
Students	...	...	...	...	...	...	...
Percent	...	...	...	...	...	...	...
Housewives	...	...	...	...	...	...	...
Percent	...	...	...	...	...	...	...
Pensioned	...	...	...	...	...	...	...
Percent	...	...	...	...	...	...	...
Self-Employed	...	...	...	...	...	...	...
Percent	...	...	...	...	...	...	...
Others	...	...	...	...	...	...	...
Percent	...	...	...	...	...	...	...
Unknown	...	...	...	...	...	...	...
Percent	...	...	...	...	...	...	...
Unaccounted for	0	0	0	0	0	0	0
Percent	0%	0%	0%	0%	0%	0%	0%

Notes: a Figures for Series II, 1948 and 1955, are compatible with Series I. b Urzednicy. c Figures
       for Series II, 1960, are compatible with Series I in respect to Workers, Peasants and (cont'd.)

Current Occupation or Position	Dec. 1955 II[a]	Dec. 1956 I	1958	Dec. 1959 II[c]	Dec. 1960 II[c]	Dec. 1962 I	Dec. 1964 I
TOTAL PARTY MEMBERSHIP	1,343,837	...	1,023,577	1,018,466	1,154,672	1,397,001	1,640,700
Percent	100.0%	100.0%	100.0%	100.0%	100.0%	100.0%	100.0%
Workers	605,982	...	427,238	407,869	465,225	[556,000]	[660,000]
Percent	45.1%	44.6%	41.8%	40.0%	40.3%	39.8%	40.2%
Nonfarm Workers	...	...	...	...	415,788	...	...
Percent	...	...	...	...	36.0%	...	...
Farm Laborers	...	...	...	...	49,437	...	...
Percent	...	...	...	...	4.3%	...	...
Peasants & Collective Farmers	175,358	...	125,015	117,460	136,133	[161,000]	[187,000]
Percent	13.0%	12.8%	12.2%	11.5%	11.8%	11.5%	11.4%
Peasants	...	...	...	...	...	...	...
Percent	...	...	...	...	...	...	...
Collective Farmers	...	...	...	...	...	...	...
Percent	...	...	...	...	...	...	...
White Collar Employees & Intellectuals	527,350	...	431,178	438,576	494,915	[610,000]	[706,000]
Percent	39.2%	39.5%	42.1%	43.1%	42.9%	43.7%	43.0%
Intellectuals	[317,000]	...	...	...	...	...	...
Percent	23.6%	23.5%	...	...	...	...	...
White Collar Empl.	[210,000][b]	...	...	...	...	...	...
Percent	15.6%	16.0%	...	...	...	...	...
Others	35,147	...	40,146	54,561	58,399	[70,000]	[89,000]
Percent	2.7%	3.1%	3.9%	5.3%	5.0%	5%	5.4%
Students	...	...	...	...	...	...	...
Percent	...	...	...	...	...	...	...
Housewives	...	...	...	...	...	...	...
Percent	...	...	...	...	...	...	...
Pensioned	...	...	...	...	...	...	...
Percent	...	...	...	...	...	...	...
Self-Employed	...	...	...	...	...	...	...
Percent	...	...	...	...	...	...	...
Others	...	...	...	...	...	...	...
Percent	...	...	...	...	...	...	...
Unknown	...	...	...	...	...	...	...
Percent	...	...	...	...	...	...	...
Unaccounted for	0	0	0	0	0	0	0
Percent	0%	0%	0%	0%	0%	0%	0%

Notes: (cont'd.) Collective Farmers only. In Series I, the number of White Collar Employees and Intellectuals for 1959 was 443,000 (43.5%); for 1960, 495,000 (42.9%); for 1970, (cont'd.)

TABLE B-7 (CONCLUDED)

Current Occupation or Position	Dec. 1966 I	Dec. 1968 I	Dec. 1970 I	Dec. 1971 I	1972	June 1973 I	Dec. 1973 I	June 1975 I
TOTAL PARTY MEMBERSHIP	1,894,895	2,104,331	2,319,913	2,254,112	...	2,298,000	2,322,531	2,359,000
Percent	100.0%	100.0%	100.0%	100.0%	...	100.0%	100.0%	100.0%
Workers	760,039	[846,000]	934,425	894,362	...	[910,000]	912,798	965,000
Percent	40.1%	40.2%	40.3%	39.7%	...	39.6%	39.4%	[40.9%]
Nonfarm Workers	...	[789,000]	[873,363]	[836,000]	...	...	[849,000]	...
Percent	...	37.5%	[37.6%]	[37.1%]	...	...	[36.6%]	...
Farm Laborers	...	56,453	61,062	58,219	...	...	63,620	...
Percent	...	2.7%	2.6%	2.6%	...	...	2.7%	...
Peasants & Collective Farmers	224,373	[240,000]	265,708	238,691	...	[232,000]	237,876	225,000
Percent	11.8%	11.4%	11.5%	10.6%	...	10.1%	10.2%	[9.5%]
Peasants	...	...	[257,000]	[231,000]	...	...	228,515	215,775
Percent	...	...	[11.1%]	[10.2%]	...	...	9.8%	9.1%
Collective Farmers	...	...	8,688	7,999	...	...	9,361	9,225
Percent	...	...	0.4%	0.4%	...	...	0.4%	[0.4%]
White Collar Employees & Intellectuals	806,620	[905,000]	[981,000]	[983,000]	...	[1,009,000]	...	...
Percent	42.6%	43.0%	42.3%	43.6%	...	43.9%	...	...
Intellectuals	[363,000]	...	...	...	...	...	...	...
Percent	[19.2%]	...	...	...	...	...	...	...
White Collar Empl.	[444,000][d]	...	...	...	...	...	...	...
Percent	[23.4%]	...	...	...	...	...	...	...
Others	[104,000]	[114,000]	[137,000]	[138,000]	...	[147,000]	...	...
Percent	5.5%	5.4%	5.9%	6.1%	...	6.4%	...	...
Students	...	...	...	...	...	...	...	...
Percent	...	...	...	...	...	...	...	...
Housewives	...	...	...	...	...	...	...	...
Percent	...	...	...	...	...	...	...	...
Pensioned	...	80,082	102,483	108,235	...	...	144,334	...
Percent	...	3.8%	4.4%	4.8%	...	...	6.2%	...
Self-Employed	...	...	...	...	...	...	...	...
Percent	...	...	...	...	...	...	...	...
Others	...	...	...	...	...	...	...	...
Percent	...	...	...	...	...	...	...	...
Unknown	...	...	...	...	...	...	...	...
Percent	...	...	...	...	...	...	...	...
Unaccounted for	0	0[e]	0	0	...	0	1,027,523	1,169,000
Percent	0%	0%	0%	0%	...	0%	44.2%	49.6%

Notes: (cont'd.) 981,000 (42.3%). The number of "Others" for 1959 was 51,000 (5.0%); for 1960 58,000 (5.0%); for 1970, 137,000 (5.9%). d Kancilisti. e Subtotals exceed total party membership by 50.

TABLE B-8 SOCIAL COMPOSITION OF THE PARTY ACCORDING TO CURRENT OCCUPATION OR POSITION: ROMANIA, 1955-1974

Current Occupation or Position	1955	1960	May 1961	May[b] 1962	Dec. 1964	July 1965	Dec. 1965	May 1967[c]
TOTAL PARTY MEMBERSHIP[a]	595,398	834,600	869,759	919,873	1,377,847	1,450,000	1,518,000	1,676,000
Percent	100.0%	100.0%	100.0%	100.0%	100.0%	100.0%	100.0%	100.0%
Workers	253,000	426,000	[444,400]	[470,000]	[608,000]	630,000	"Over 600,000"	671,000
Percent	42.6%	51.05%	51.09%	51.1%	44.16%	44%	39.6%	41%
Nonfarm Workers	...	...	...	...	...	...	...	...
Percent	...	...	...	...	...	...	...	...
Farm Laborers	...	...	...	...	...	...	...	...
Percent	...	...	...	...	...	...	...	...
Peasants & Collective Farmers	...	[184,000]	...	[209,000]	[454,000]	500,000	"Over 480,000"	483,000
Percent	...	22%	...	22.7%	32.98%	34%	31.8%	30%
Peasants	...	...	...	...	...	...	...	...
Percent	...	...	...	...	...	...	...	...
Collective Farmers	...	...	...	...	...	...	...	...
Percent	...	...	...	...	...	...	...	...
White Collar Employees & Intellectuals	...	[195,000]	...	[215,000]	...	...	"Over 330,000"	...
Percent	...	[23.3%]	...	23.4%	...	...	21.7%	...
Intellectuals	70,000	93,000	[96,700]	...	[130,000]	145,000	...	...
Percent	11.8%	11.1%	11.12%	...	9.43%	10%	...	...
White Collar Empl.	...	[102,000]	...	...	...	...	...	...
Percent	...	[12.2%]	...	...	...	...	...	...
Others	...	[30,000]	[37,000]	[26,000]	...	...	...	...
Percent	...	3.59%	4.25%	2.8%	...	...	...	...
Students	...	...	...	...	...	...	...	...
Percent	...	...	...	...	...	...	...	...
Housewives	...	...	...	...	...	...	...	...
Percent	...	...	...	...	...	...	...	...
Pensioned	...	...	...	...	...	...	...	...
Percent	...	...	...	...	...	...	...	...
Self-Employed	...	...	...	...	...	...	...	...
Percent	...	...	...	...	...	...	...	...
Others	...	...	...	...	...	...	...	...
Percent	...	...	...	...	...	...	...	...
Unknown	...	...	...	...	...	...	...	...
Percent	...	...	...	...	...	...	...	...
Unaccounted for	[272,000]	0	[291,700]	0	[185,000]	175,000	108,000	522,000
Percent	45.7%	0%	33.5%	0%	13.43%	12%	7.1%	31.1%

TABLE B-8   (CONCLUDED)

Current Occupation or Position	March 1968	Aug. 1969	Dec. 1970	June 1972	Nov. 1974
TOTAL PARTY MEMBERSHIP	1,761,000	1,924,500	2,089,085	"Over 2,230,000"	2,480,000
Percent	100.0%	100.0%	100.0%	100.0%	100.0%
Workers	740,000	[820,000]	926,440	1,023,000	[1,120,000]
Percent	42.0%	42.6%	44.3%	45.9%	48.37%
Nonfarm Workers	...	...	...	...	...
Percent	...	...	...	...	...
Farm Laborers	...	...	...	...	...
Percent	...	...	...	...	...
Peasants & Collective Farmers	505,000	[539,000]	533,917	"Over 534,000"	[546,000]
Percent	28.7%	28%	25.6%	23.9%	22%
Peasants	...	...	...	...	...
Percent	...	...	...	...	...
Collective Farmers	...	...	...	...	...
Percent	...	...	...	...	...
White Collar Employees & Intellectuals	397,000	[443,000]	...	"Over 511,000"	[521,000]
Percent	22.6%	23%	...	22.9%	21%
Intellectuals	...	...	...	...	...
Percent	...	...	...	...	...
White Collar Empl.	...	...	...	...	...
Percent	...	...	...	...	...
Others	118,000	...	...	"Around 162,000"	...
Percent	6.7%	...	...	7.3%	...
Students	...	...	...	...	...
Percent	...	...	...	...	...
Housewives	...	...	...	...	...
Percent	...	...	...	...	...
Pensioned	...	...	...	...	...
Percent	...	...	...	...	...
Self-Employed	...	...	...	...	...
Percent	...	...	...	...	...
Others	...	...	...	...	...
Percent	...	...	...	...	...
Unknown	...	...	...	...	...
Percent	...	...	...	...	...
Unaccounted for	1,000	[123,000]	628,728	0	[214,000]
Percent	0%	6.4%	30.1%	0%	8.63%

Notes: a In 1946, total party membership was 675,000, 46% of whom (270,000) were reported as Workers; in 1948, 720,000, 42% of whom (336,000) were reported as Workers. b Party size as of April, 1962. c Percents as given in original source.

95

TABLE B-9   SOCIAL COMPOSITION OF THE PARTY ACCORDING TO CURRENT OCCUPATION OR POSITION: USSR , 1925-1932

Current Occupation or Position	1925	1926	1927[a]	1928	1929	1930	1931	1932
TOTAL PARTY MEMBERSHIP	801,804	1,079,814	1,212,505	1,305,854	1,535,362	1,677,910	2,212,225	3,117,25
Percent	100.0%	100.0%	100.0%	100.0%	100.0%	100.0%	100.0%	100.0
Workers	[331,000]	[450,000]	[480,000]	[530,000]	[676,000]	[777,000]	[976,000]	[1,360,00
Percent	41.3%	42.0%	39.4%	40.8%	44.0%	46.3%	44.1%	43.8
Peasants	[76,200]	[140,000]	[170,000]	[160,000]	[200,000]	[200,000]	[360,000]	[580,00
Percent	9.5%	13.4%	13.7%	12.3%	13.0%	12.0%	16.3%	18.5
Others	...	...	...	...	...	...	...	...
Percent	...	...	...	...	...	...	...	...
Unknown	...	...	...	...	...	...	...	...
Percent	...	...	...	...	...	...	...	...
Unaccounted for	[394,000]	[482,000]	[569,000]	[612,000]	[660,000]	[700,000]	[876,000]	[1,170,00
Percent	49.2%	44.6%	46.9%	46.9%	43.0%	41.7%	39.6%	37.7
Of Above, Those in Military	60,704	77,325	81,249	85,018	96,330	105,749	154,825	234,08
Percent	7.6%	7.2%	6.7%	6.5%	6.3%	6.3%	7.0%	7.5
Workers	[25,100]	[32,400]	[32,500]	[35,500]	[41,700]	[49,500]	[67,000]	[102,80
Percent	[41.4%]	[41.9%]	[40.0%]	[41.8%]	[43.3%]	[46.8%]	[43.3%]	[43.9
Peasants	[5,600]	[10,000]	[11,500]	[10,500]	[11,700]	[12,300]	[24,800]	[42,20
Percent	[9.3%]	[13.0%]	[14.2%]	[12.4%]	[12.2%]	[11.6%]	[16.0%]	[18.0
Others	[29,900]	[34,900]	[37,200]	[39,000]	[42,900]	[44,000]	[63,000]	[89,10
Percent	[49.3%]	[45.1%]	[45.8%]	[45.8%]	[44.5%]	[41.6%]	[40.7%]	[38.1

Notes: a For 1927, party census gave the following breakdown of the party by current occupation or position: total, 1,144,053;
Workers, 343,202 (30.0%); Peasants, 116,189 (10.1%), of which 88,408 (7.7%) were Private Peasantry, 7,226 (0.6%) were
Collective Farmers, and 20,555 (1.8%) were in leading posts; White Collar Employees, 440,501 (38.5%); Younger Service
Personnel (Mladshii obsluzhivaiushchii personal), 28,789 (2.5%); Artisans, 5,466 (0.5%); Students and Pupils, 58,004 (5.1
Military and Others, 151,902 (13.3%).

TABLE B-10   SOCIAL COMPOSITION OF THE PARTY ACCORDING TO CURRENT OCCUPATION OR POSITION: YUGOSLAVIA, 1948-1975

Current Occupation or Position	Dec. 1948 I	Dec. 1950 I	Dec. 1952 I	Dec. 1954 I	Dec. 1956 I	Dec. 1958 I	Dec. 1960 I	Dec. 1962 I	Dec. 1964 I
TOTAL PARTY MEMBERSHIP	482,938	607,443	772,920	654,669	648,616	829,953	1,006,285	1,018,331	1,031,634
Percent	100.0%	100.0%	100.0%	100.0%	100.0%	100.0%	100.0%	100.0%	100.0%
Workers	145,226	189,412	249,110	185,280	206,697	271,100	363,420	373,491	371,628
Percent	30.1%	31.2%	32.2%	28.3%	31.9%	32.7%	36.1%	36.7%	36.0%
Nonfarm Workers	...	...	...	...	...	...	...	...	...
Percent	...	...	...	...	...	...	...	...	...
Farm Laborers	...	...	...	...	...	...	...	...	...
Percent	...	...	...	...	...	...	...	...	...
Peasants & Collective Farmers	231,032	263,474	330,454	148,277	111,915	121,684	131,206	97,932	77,906
Percent	47.8%	43.4%	42.8%	22.6%	17.2%	14.7%	13.0%	9.6%	7.6%
Peasants	...	...	...	...	...	...	...	...	...
Percent	...	...	...	...	...	...	...	...	...
Collective Farmers	...	...	...	...	...	...	...	...	...
Percent	...	...	...	...	...	...	...	...	...
White Collar Employees & Intellectuals	65,665	115,318	146,033	195,153	211,325	289,099	321,800	371,069	402,632
Percent	13.6%	19.0%	18.9%	29.8%	32.6%	34.8%	32.0%	36.4%	39.0%
Intellectuals[a]	...	...	...	...	...	...	...	...	...
Percent	...	...	...	...	...	...	...	...	...
White Collar Empl.	...	...	...	...	...	...	...	...	...
Percent	...	...	...	...	...	...	...	...	...
Empl. in Leading Posts	...	...	...	...	...	...	...	...	...
Percent	...	...	...	...	...	...	...	...	...
Others	41,015	39,239	47,323	125,959	118,679	148,070	189,859	175,739	179,468
Percent	8.5%	6.5%	6.1%	19.2%	18.3%	17.8%	18.9%	17.3%	17.4%
Students[b]	...	...	...	...	...	...	...	41,062	33,858
Percent	...	...	...	...	...	...	...	4.0%	3.3%
Housewives	...	...	...	...	...	...	...	...	32,553
Percent	...	...	...	...	...	...	...	...	3.2%
Pensioned[c]	...	...	...	...	...	...	...	...	47,648
Percent	...	...	...	...	...	...	...	...	4.6%
Self-Employed	...	...	...	...	...	...	...	...	...
Percent	...	...	...	...	...	...	...	...	...
Others	...	...	...	...	...	...	...	134,677	65,409[d]
Percent	...	...	...	...	...	...	...	13.2%	6.3%
Unaccounted for	0	0	0	0	0	0	0	100	0
Percent	0%	0%	0%	0%	0%	0%	0%	0%	0%

Notes: a Technical Intelligentsia and Intelligentsia in the Areas of Education, Science, Culture, Public Health and Other Activities. b Series I: Students and Pupils. Series II: Students and Pupils, including pupils in workers' training institutions. c Series I, 1964 and 1966: Pensioners. Series I, 1968 and 1970: Pensioners and disabled persons. Series II: Pensioners. d Of whom, 56,685 were military in 1964, 52,842 military in 1966. (cont'd.)

Current Occupation or Position	Dec. 1966 I	Dec. 1968 I	Dec. 1968 II	Dec. 1969 II	Dec. 1970 I	Dec. 1970 II	Dec. 1971 I	Dec. 1971 II
TOTAL PARTY MEMBERSHIP	1,046,018	1,146,084	1,062,268	1,029,807	1,049,184	974,048	1,025,476	957,218
Percent	100.0%	100.0%	100.0%	100.0%	100.0%	100.0%	100.0%	100.0%
Workers	355,022	361,790	337,939	332,311	313,652[e]	304,039	291,493	286,862
Percent	33.9%	31.5%	31.9%	32.3%	29.9%	31.2%	28.4%	30.0%
Nonfarm Workers	...	...	...	...	...	...	...	...
Percent	...	...	...	...	...	...	...	...
Farm Laborers	...	...	...	...	...	...	...	...
Percent	...	...	...	...	...	...	...	...
Peasants & Collective Farmers	77,134	84,329	82,206	79,015	68,425	66,982	64,867	64,052
Percent	7.4%	7.4%	7.8%	7.7%	6.5%	6.9%	6.3%	6.7%
Peasants	...	...	...	...	...	...	...	...
Percent	...	...	...	...	...	...	...	...
Collective Farmers	...	...	...	...	...	...	...	...
Percent	...	...	...	...	...	...	...	...
White Collar Employees & Intellectuals	408,378	491,147	396,598	388,432	473,128	383,724	387,246	384,645
Percent	39.0%	42.9%	37.3%	37.7%	45.1%	39.4%	37.8%	40.2%
Intellectuals[a]	...	178,663	174,828	183,667	187,100	184,131	186,477	184,253
Percent	...	15.6%[f]	16.5%	17.7%	17.8%	18.9%	18.2%	19.2%
White Collar Empl.	...	229,543[f]	139,052	137,661	211,958	125,634	124,344	124,037
Percent	...	20.0%	13.1%	13.3%	20.2%	12.9%	12.1%	12.9%
Empl. in Leading Posts	...	82,941	82,718	67,104	74,070	73,959	76,425	76,355
Percent	...	7.2%	7.8%	6.5%	7.1%	7.6%	7.5%	8.0%
Others	205,484	208,818[f]	245,525	230,049	189,472[f]	219,303	...	221,659
Percent	19.6%	18.2%	23.1%	22.2%	18.0%	22.5%	...	23.1%
Students[b]	34,657	69,333	76,633	63,831	51,331	53.149	56,791	56,005
Percent	3.3%	6.0%	7.2%	6.1%	4.9%	5.4%	5.5%	5.8%
Housewives	31,604	33,526[g]	29,994	28,993	...	25,506	...	25,318
Percent	3.0%	2.9%	2.8%	2.8%	...	2.6%	...	2.6%
Pensioned[c]	74,610	90,238	90,238	91,364	91,067	91,067	91,325	91,325
Percent	7.1%	7.9%	8.5%	8.8%	8.7%	9.3%	8.9%	9.5%
Self-Employed	...	[h]	4,958[i]	4,641[i]	...	4,507	...	4,505[i]
Percent	...[d]	...[j]	0.5%[k]	0.4%[l]	...	0.5%[m]	...	0.5%[o]
Others	64,613[d]	15,721[j]	43,702[k]	41,220[l]	47,074	45,074[m]	[59,000][n]	44,506[o]
Percent	6.2%	1.4%	4.1%	4.0%	4.5%	4.6%	5.8%	4.6%
Unaccounted for	0	0	0		4,507		[75,000]	
Percent	0%	0%	0%		0.4%		7.3%	

Notes (cont'd.): e The original figure of 324,459 has been adjusted to correspond to 29.9% in the original source and to make subtotals consistent with total party membership. f In Series I for 1968 and 1970, military included with White Collar Employees. The number of party members in the permanent military in 1968 was 65,565. g Housewives and Others. h 4,956 Private Artisans included with Workers. (cont'd.)

Current Occupation or Position	Dec. 1972 I	II	Dec. 1973 I	II	Dec. 1974 I	II	Dec. 1975 I	II
TOTAL PARTY MEMBERSHIP	1,009,947	944,628	1,076,711	1,008,053	1,192,466	1,115,332	1,302,843	1,220,352
Percent	100.0%	100.0%	100.0%	100.0%	100.0%	100.0%	100.0%	100.0%
Workers	285,522	281,111	306,908	301,204	...	337,245	366,272	366,272
Percent	28.3%	29.8%	28.5%	29.9%	...	30.2%	28.1%	29.9%
Nonfarm Workers	...	...	...	...	...	...	...	...
Percent	...	...	...	...	...	...	...	...
Farm Laborers	...	...	...	...	...	...	...	...
Percent	...	...	...	...	...	...	...	...
Peasants & Collective Farmers	60,233	59,743	60,570	59,967	...	62,178	65,910	65,910
Percent	6.0%	6.3%	5.6%	6.0%	...	5.6%	5.1%	5.4%
Peasants	...	...	...	...	...	...	...	...
Percent	...	...	...	...	...	...	...	...
Collective Farmers	...	...	...	...	...	...	...	...
Percent	...	...	...	...	...	...	...	...
White Collar Employees & Intellectuals	389,432	386,732	...	413,652	...	457,444	542,248	506,962
Percent	38.6%	40.9%	...	41.0%	...	41.0%	41.6%	41.5%
Intellectuals[a]	190,565	188,184	209,927	206,773	...	231,394	...	258,991
Percent	18.9%	19.9%	19.5%	20.5%	...	20.7%	...	21.2%
White Collar Empl.	124,525	124,277	...	128,918	...	141,383	...	154,042
Percent	12.3%	13.1%	...	12.8%	...	12.7%	...	12.6%
Empl. in Leading Posts	74,342	74,271	77,135	76,633	...	84,667	...	93,929
Percent	7.4%	7.9%	7.2%	7.6%	...	7.6%	...	7.7%
Others	...	217,032	...	233,230	...	258,465	...	285,210
Percent	...	23.0%	...	23.1%	...	23.2%	...	23.4%
Students[b]	55,006	54,358	64,322	63,201	...	81,751	96,130	96,139
Percent	5.4%	5.7%	6.0%	6.3%	...	7.3%	7.4%	7.9%
Housewives	...	22,461	...	21,412	...	21,127	...	20,680
Percent	...	2.4%	...	2.1%	...	1.9%	...	1.7%
Pensioned[c]	91,789	91,789	94,682	94,682	...	98,320	...	100,251
Percent	9.1%	9.7%	8.8%	9.4%	...	8.8%	...	8.2%
Self-Employed	...	4,323[i]	...	4,394[i]	...	4,470[i]	...	8,429[i]
Percent	...	0.5%	...	0.4%	...	0.4%	...	0.7%
Others	...	44,101[p]	...	49,541[q]	...	52,797[r]	...	59,711[s]
Percent	...	4.7%	...	4.9%	...	4.7%	...	4.9%
Unaccounted for	127,965	10	263,167		...		232,283	t
Percent	12.7%	0%	24.4%		...		17.8%	

Notes (cont'd.): <u>i</u> Artisans. <u>j</u> Unemployed. <u>k</u> Includes 24,449 in Occupations Related to Protection, 15,721 Unemployed, and 3,532 not identified. <u>1</u> Includes 2,423 in Occupations Related to Protection, 14,136 Unemployed, and 2,661 not identified. <u>m</u> Includes 24,506 in Occupations Related to Protection, 11,318 Unemployed, 6,769 temporarily abroad, and 2,481 not identified. <u>n</u> Includes military personnel. (cont'd.)

TABLE B-10 (CONCLUDED)

Notes (cont'd.): o̲ Includes 23,724 in Occupations Related to Protection, 10,661 Unemployed, 8,145 temporarily abroad, and 1,976 not identified. p̲ Includes 24,198 in Occupations Relating to Protection, 9,955 Unemployed, 8,429 temporarily abroad, and 1,519 not identified. q̲ Includes 25,907 in Occupations Relating to Protection, 13,023 Unemployed, 8,689 temporarily abroad, and 1,922 not identified. r̲ Includes 28,472 in Occupations Relating to Protection, 15,625 Unemployed, and 8,700 temporarily abroad. s̲ Includes 30,850 in Occupations Relating to Protection, 20,923 Unemployed, and 7,938 temporarily abroad. t̲ Subcategories exceed total for party membership by 4,002.

TABLE B-11 SOCIAL COMPOSITION OF THE PARTY ACCORDING TO ORIGINAL OCCUPATION OR
POSITION: HUNGARY, 1951-1975

Original Occupation or Position	Jan. 1951	1954	June 1957	Nov. 1959	1960	Jan. 1961	June 1970	Jan. 1975[a]
TOTAL PARTY MEMBERSHIP	862,114	...	346,000	437,956	...	478,000	662,397	754,353
Percent	100.0%	100.0%	100.0%	100.0%	100.0%	100.0%	100.0%	100.0%
Workers	490,046	...	[197,000]	[261,000]	...	[281,000]	[464,000][b]	[447,000]
Percent	56.9%	60.5%	"Around	[59.7%]	59.3%	58.8%	70.0%	59.2%
Nonfarm Workers	...	...	57%"	...	...	...	...	...
Percent	...	...	...	...	...	...	...	...
Farm Laborers	...	...	...	...	...	...	...	...
Percent	...	...	...	...	...	...	...	...
Peasants & Collective Farmers	132,187	...	[58,000]	[63,000]	...	[72,000]	...	[98,000]
Percent	15.4%	14.45%	16.7%	[14.4%]	14.2%	15.0%	...	13.0%
Peasants	...	...	...	...	...	...	...	...
Percent	...	...	...	...	...	...	...	...
Collective Farmers	...	...	...	...	...	...	...	...
Percent	...	...	...	...	...	...	...	...
White Collar Employees & Intellectuals	...	...	...	...	...	...	...	[190,000]
Percent	...	...	...	...	...	...	...	[25.2%]
Intellectuals	[34,000]	...	...	...	...	[43,000]	...	[67,000]
Percent	4%	4.99%	...	...	...	9.1%	...	8.9%
White Collar Empl.	...	...	...	...	...	...	...	[123,000]
Percent	...	...	...	...	...	...	...	16.3%
Others	...	...	...	...	...	...	...	[19,000]
Percent	...	...	...	...	...	...	...	2.6%
Students	...	...	...	...	...	...	...	...
Percent	...	...	...	...	...	...	...	...
Housewives	...	...	...	...	...	...	...	...
Percent	...	...	...	...	...	...	...	...
Pensioned	...	...	...	...	...	...	...	...
Percent	...	...	...	...	...	...	...	...
Self-Employed	...	...	...	...	...	...	...	...
Percent	...	...	...	...	...	...	...	...
Others	...	...	...	...	...	...	...	...
Percent	...	...	...	...	...	...	...	...
Unknown	...	...	...	...	...	...	...	...
Percent	...	...	...	...	...	...	...	...
Unaccounted for	[206,000]	...	[91,000]	[115,000]	...	[82,000]	[198,000]	0
Percent	23.8%	20.06%	26.3%	25.9%	26.5%	17.1%	30.0%	0%

Notes: a Social composition as of Jan. 1, 1975; total party membership as of March, 1975. b May include Collective Farmers.

TABLE B-12   SOCIAL COMPOSITION OF THE PARTY ACCORDING TO OCCUPATION OR POSITION WHEN JOINING THE PARTY: USSR, 1927-1976

Occupation or Position	Jan. 1927[a]	1928	1929	1930	1932	Jan. 1946	Jan. 1952	Jan. 1956	Jan. 1957
TOTAL PARTY MEMBERSHIP	1,144,053	1,305,854	1,535,362	1,677,910	3,117,250	5,510,862	6,707,539	7,173,521	7,494,5
Percent	100.0%	100.0%	100.0%	100.0%	100.0%	100.0%	100.0%	100.0%	100.
Workers	637,768	740,731	940,136	[1,090,000]	[2,030,000]	1,865,126	2,162,059	2,291,455	[2,400,0
Percent	55.7%	56.8%	61.4%	65.3%	65.2%	33.8%	32.2%	32.0%	32.
Nonfarm Workers	...	...	...	...	...	...	...	...	..
Percent	...	...	...	...	...	...	...	...	..
Farm Laborers	...	...	...	...	...	...	...	...	..
Percent	...	...	...	...	...	...	...	...	..
Peasants & Collective Farmers	217,411	299,091	333,287	[340,000]	[840,000]	1,023,903	1,206,668	1,227,767	[1,300,0
Percent	19.0%	22.9%	21.7%	20.2%	26.9%	18.6%	18.0%	17.1%	17.
Peasants	...	...	...	...	...	...	...	...	..
Percent	...	...	...	...	...	...	...	...	..
Collective Farmers	...	...	...	...	...	1,023,903	1,206,668	1,227,767	[1,300,0
Percent	...	...	...	...	...	18.6%	18.0%	17.1%	17.
White Collar Employees & Intellectuals	258,125								
Percent	22.6%								
Intellectuals	...								
Percent	...								
White Collar Empl.	...								
Percent	...								
Others	30,749	264,649	258,924	[240,000]	[250,000]	2,621,833	3,338,812	3,654,299	[3,800,0
Percent	2.7%	20.3%	16.9%	14.5%	7.9%	47.6%	49.8%	50.9%	50.
Students	...								
Percent	...								
Housewives	...								
Percent	...								
Pensioned	...								
Percent	...								
Self-Employed	...								
Percent	...								
Others	...								
Percent	...								
Unknown	...	...	...	...	...	...	...	...	..
Percent	...	...	...	...	...	...	...	...	
Unaccounted for	0	1,383	3,015	0	0	0	0	0	
Percent	0%	0.1%	0.2%	0%	0%	0%	0%	0%	

TABLE B-12   (CONCLUDED)

Occupation or Position	Jan. 1961	Jan. 1964	Jan. 1966	Jan. 1967	Jan. 1968	Jan. 1971	Jan. 1973	Jan. 1976
TOTAL PARTY MEMBERSHIP	9,275,826	11,022,369	12,357,308	12,684,133	13,180,225	14,372,563	14,821,031	15,638,891
Percent	100.0%	100.0%	100.0%	100.0%	100.0%	100.0%	100.0%	100.0%
Workers	3,146,135	[4,110,000]	4,675,879	[4,830,000]	[5,110,000]	5,759,379	6,037,771	6,509,312
Percent	33.9%	37.3%	37.8%	38.1%	38.8%	40.1%	40.7%	41.6%
Nonfarm Workers	...	...	...	...	...	...	...	...
Percent	...	...	...	...	...	...	...	...
Farm Laborers	...	...	...	...	...	...	...	...
Percent	...	...	...	...	...	...	...	...
Peasants & Collective Farmers	1,632,847	[1,820,000]	1,999,138	[2,030,000]	[2,080,000]	2,169,437	2,169,764	2,169,813
Percent	17.6%	16.5%	16.2%	16.0%	15.8%	15.1%	14.7%	13.9%
Peasants	...	...	...	...	...	...	...	...
Percent	...	...	...	...	...	...	...	...
Collective Farmers	1,632,847	[1,820,000]	1,999,138	[2,030,000]	[2,080,000]	2,169,437	2,169,764	2,169,813
Percent	17.6%	16.5%	16.2%	16.0%	15.8%	15.1%	14.7%	13.9%
White Collar Employees & Intellectuals								
Percent								
Intellectuals								
Percent								
White Collar Empl.								
Percent								
Others	4,496,844	[5,090,000]	5,682,291	[5,820,000]	[5,980,000]	6,443,747	6,613,496	6,959,766
Percent	48.5%	46.2%	46.0%	45.9%	45.4%	44.8%	44.6%	44.5%
Students								
Percent								
Housewives								
Percent								
Pensioned								
Percent								
Self-Employed								
Percent								
Others								
Percent								
Unknown	...	...	...	...	...	...	...	...
Percent	...	...	...	...	...	...	...	...
Unaccounted for	0	0	0	0	0	0	0	0
Percent	0%	0%	0%	0%	0%	0%	0%	0%

Note: a Results of the 1927 party census. The party's social composition as shown in figures gathered by the Central Committee for Jan. 1, 1927: Workers, 55.1%; Peasants, 27.3%; Others, 17.6%.

TABLE B-13   POSITION AND NUMBER OF PARTY MEMBERS WITH WHITE
COLLAR OCCUPATIONS: CZECHOSLOVAKIA, 1958-1966

Occupation	1958	1962	1966
TOTAL NUMBER OF WHITE COLLAR WORKERS (EMPLOYEES) IN PARTY[a]	565,000	558,704	603,862
Percent of Total Party Membership	39.7%	33.7%	35.6%
Percent of Total No. of Empl. in Party	100.0%	100.0%	100.0%
Engineers, Technical & Economic Workers	165,592	241,218	293,277
Percent of Total Party Membership	11.6%	14.6%	17.3%
Percent of Total No. of Empl. in Party	29.3%	43.2%	48.6%
Those in Agriculture	15,823	...	...
Percent of Total Party Membership	1.1%	...	...
Percent of Total No. of Empl. in Party	2.8%	...	...
Those not in Agriculture	149,769	...	...
Percent of Total Party Membership	10.5%	...	...
Percent of Total No. of Empl. in Party	26.5%	...	...
Public Workers	...	31,750	27,246
Percent of Total Party Membership	...	1.9%	1.6%
Percent of Total No. of Empl. in Party	...	5.7%	4.5%
Scientific Workers	...	3,778	3,796
Percent of Total Party Membership	...	0.2%	0.2%
Percent of Total No. of Empl. in Party	...	0.7%	0.6%
Artists & Cultural Workers	...	8,192	9,218
Percent of Total Party Membership	...	0.5%	0.5%
Percent of Total No. of Empl. in Party	...	1.5%	1.5%
Teachers, Professors & Directors of Schools	...	56,267	64,787
Percent of Total Party Membership	...	3.3%	3.8%
Percent of Total No. of Empl. in Party	...	10.1%	10.7%
White Collar Functionaries & Office Workers (Urednici)	...	126,393	113,350
Percent of Total Party Membership	...	7.6%	6.7%
Percent of Total No. of Empl. in Party	...	22.6%	18.8%
Doctors	...	...	8,778
Percent of Total Party Membership	...	...	0.5%
Percent of Total No. of Empl. in Party	...	...	1.5%
Service Workers	...	69,218	62,491
Percent of Total Party Membership	...	4.2%	3.7%
Percent ot Total No. of Empl. in Party	...	12.4%	10.3%
Unaccounted for	339,408	21,888	20,919
Percent of Total Party Membership	28.1%	1.3%	1.2%
Percent of Total No. of Empl. in Party	70.7%	3.9%	3.5%

Note: a Excludes professional military. In 1962, there were 75,286 professional military in the party; in 1966, 74,325.

TABLE B-14 POSITION AND NUMBER OF PARTY MEMBERS WITH WHITE COLLAR OCCUPATIONS: POLAND, 1959-1973

Occupation	1959 I	1960 I	1960 II	1965 I	1965 II	1966 II
TOTAL NUMBER OF WHITE COLLAR WORKERS (EMPLOYEES) IN PARTY	[443,000][a]	[495,000][a]	[495,000]	[758,000]	[758,000]	806,620
Percent of Total Party Membership	43.5%	42.9%	42.9%	42.7%	42.7%	42.6%
Percent of Total No. of Empl. in Party	100.0%	100.0%	100.0%	100.0%	100.0%	100.0%
Engineers, Technical Personnel and Supervisory Personnel	"Around 60,000"	96,907	89,837	195,484	169,226	213,000[b]
Percent of Total Party Membership	5.9%	8.4%	7.7%	11.0%	9.5%	11.2%
Percent of Total No. of Empl. in Party	[13.5%]	[19.6%]	[18.1%]	[25.8%]	[22.3%]	26.4%
Agronomists and Other Specialists in Agriculture and Forestry	"Over 10,000"	12,288	12,733	26,972	19,924	...
Percent of Total Party Membership	1.0%	1.1%	1.1%	1.5%	1.1%	...
Percent of Total No. of Empl. in Party	[2.3%]	[2.5%]	[2.6%]	[3.6%]	[2.6%]	...
Teachers	"Over 35,000"	43,803	43,803	97,362	97,362	...
Percent of Total Party Membership	3.4%	3.8%	3.8%	5.5%	5.5%	...
Percent of Total No. of Empl. in Party	[7.9%]	[8.8%]	[8.8%]	[12.8%]	[12.8%]	...
Doctors	2,500	3,689	3,228	9,521	8,113	...
Percent of Total Party Membership	0.2%	0.3%	0.3%	0.5%	0.5%	...
Percent of Total No. of Empl. in Party	[0.6%]	[0.7%]	[0.7%]	[1.3%]	[1.1%]	...
Middle Level Health Personnel	...	5,211	5,211	12,571	12,571	13,790
Percent of Total Party Membership	...	0.5%	0.5%	0.7%	0.7%	0.7%
Percent of Total No. of Empl. in Party	...	[1.1%]	[1.1%]	[1.7%]	[1.7%]	1.7%
Scientists, Professors, Docents, Adjuncts and Assistants[c]	...	3,514	3,514	6,269	6,269	6,907
Percent of Total Party Membership	...	0.3%	0.3%	0.4%	0.4%	0.3%
Percent of Total No. of Empl. in Party	...	[0.7%]	[0.7%]	[0.8%]	[0.8%]	0.8%
Newspapermen, Artists and Writers	...	3,029	3,029	4,443	4,443	4,521
Percent of Total Party Membership	...	0.3%	0.3%	0.2%	0.2%	0.2%
Percent of Total No. of Empl. in Party	...	[0.6%]	[0.6%]	[0.6%]	[0.6%]	0.6%
Juridical Personnel and Lawyers	...	3,744	3,744	5,916	5,916	6,239
Percent of Total Party Membership	...	0.3%	0.3%	0.3%	0.3%	0.3%
Percent of Total No. of Empl. in Party	...	[0.8%]	[0.8%]	[0.8%]	[0.8%]	0.8%
Economists, Planners and Bookkeepers	"Over 38,000"	45,802	45,802	79,289	79,289	82,446
Percent of Total Party Membership	3.7%	4.0%	4.0%	4.5%	4.5%	4.4%
Percent of Total No. of Empl. in Party	[8.6%]	[9.2%]	[9.2%]	[10.5%]	[10.5%]	10.2%
Unaccounted for	[298,000]	[277,000]	[284,000]	[320,000]	[355,000]	479,717
Percent of Total Party Membership	29.2%	24.0%	[24.6%]	[18.0%]	[20.0%]	25.3%
Percent of Total No. of Empl. in Party	[67.2%]	[56.0%]	[57.4%]	[42.2%]	[46.8%]	59.5%

TABLE B-14 (CONCLUDED)

Occupation	1968 I	1969 I	1970 II	1971 II	1973 II
TOTAL NUMBER OF WHITE COLLAR WORKERS (EMPLOYEES IN PARTY	[905,000]	[943,000]	[981,000][a]	[983,000]	...
Percent of Total Party Membership	43.0%	42.8%	42.3%	43.6%	...
Percent of Total No. of Empl. in Party	100.0%	100.0%	100.0%	100.0%	...
Engineers, Technical Personnel and Supervisory Personnel	258,829	281,990	246,346	251,168	255,693
Percent of Total Party Membership	12.3%	12.8%	10.6%	11.2%	11.0%
Percent of Total No. of Empl. in Party	[28.6%]	[29.9%]	[25.1%]	[25.6%]	...
Agronomists and Other Specialists in Agriculture and Forestry	35,834	38,232	28,628	27,925	35,433
Percent of Total Party Membership	1.7%	1.7%	1.2%	1.2%	1.5%
Percent of Total No. of Empl. in Party	[4.0%]	[4.1%]	[2.9%]	[2.8%]	...
Teachers	126,512	132,892	141,485	141,105	144,062
Percent of Total Party Membership	6.0%	6.0%	6.1%	6.3%	6.2%
Percent of Total No. of Empl. in Party	[14.0%]	[14.1%]	[14.4%]	[14.4%]	...
Doctors	12,122	13,064	11,904	12,061	13,740
Percent of Total Party Membership	0.6%	0.6%	0.5%	0.5%	0.6%
Percent of Total No. of Empl. in Party	[1.3%]	[1.4%]	[1.2%]	[1.2%]	...
Middle Level Health Personnel	16,840	17,756	18,784	18,693	...
Percent of Total Party Membership	0.8%	0.8%	0.8%	0.8%	...
Percent of Total No. of Empl. in Party	[1.9%]	[1.9%]	[1.9%]	[1.9%]	...
Scientists, Professors, Docents, Adjuncts and Assistants[c]	8,273	9,611	11,397	12,161	15,889
Percent of Total Party Membership	0.4%	0.4%	0.5%	0.5%	0.7%
Percent of Total No. of Empl. in Party	[0.9%]	[1.0%]	[1.2%]	[1.2%]	...
Newspapermen, Artists and Writers	4,668	5,010	5,066	5,187	...
Percent of Total Party Membership	0.2%	0.2%	0.2%	0.2%	...
Percent of Total No. of Empl. in Party	[0.5%]	[0.5%]	[0.5%]	[0.5%]	...
Juridical Personnel and Lawyers	6,818	7,126	7,580	8,009	...
Percent of Total Party Membership	0.3%	0.3%	0.3%	0.4%	...
Percent of Total No. of Empl. in Party	[0.7%]	[0.8%]	[0.8%]	[0.8%]	...
Economists, Planners and Bookkeepers	104,380	109,324	117,300	117,316	115,689
Percent of Total Party Membership	5.0%	5.0%	5.1%	5.2%	5.0%
Percent of Total No. of Empl. in Party	[11.5%]	[11.6%]	[12.0%]	[11.9%]	...
Unaccounted for	[331,000]	[328,000]	[393,000]	[389,168]	
Percent of Total Party Membership	[15.8%]	[14.9%]	[16.9%]	[17.3%]	
Percent of Total No. of Empl. in Party	[36.5%]	[34.8%]	[40.0%]	[39.6%]	

Notes: a Totals for this table differ slightly from totals for White Collar Employees and Intellectuals given in Table B-7. See footnotes to Table B-7 for further details.
b Includes the following subcategories: Engineers, 46,000; Technical Personnel, 120,000; Supervisory Personnel, 47,000. c Up to 1971, "Scientists."

TABLE B-15 POSITION AND NUMBER OF PARTY MEMBERS WITH WHITE COLLAR OCCUPATIONS: USSR, 1956-1973

Occupation at Time of Joining Party	1956 I	1956 II	1957	1961	1962	1965	1966	1967	1971	1972	1973
TOTAL NUMBER OF WHITE COLLAR WORKERS (EMPLOYEES) IN PARTY[a]	...	...	...	...	...	...	...	...	...	...	...
Percent of Total Party Membership	...	...	...	...	...	...	...	...	...	...	...
Percent of Total No. of Empl. in Party	100.0%	100.0%	100.0%	100.0%	100.0%	100.0%	100.0%	100.0%	100.0%	100.0%	100.0%
Heads of Organizations, Institutions, Enterprises, Construction Projects, State Farms & their Subdivisions	...	...	...	...	...	...	...	...	...	...	...
Percent of Total Party Membership	...	...	...	...	...	...	...	...	...	...	...
Percent of Total No. of Empl. in Party	14.1%	14.0%	13.1%	10.2%	10.0%	7.8%	7.8%	7.9%	8.4%	8.5%	8.7%
Engineers, Technicians, Agricultural Specialists	...	...	...	...	...	...	...	...	...	...	...
Percent of Total Party Membership	...	...	...	...	...	...	...	...	...	...	...
Percent of Total No. of Empl. in Party	20.1%	18.2%	19.3%	29.2%	28.2%	32.5%	33.6%	34.9%	38.2%	38.5%	38.9%
Personnel in Science, Education, Public Health, Literature & the Arts	...	...	...	...	...	...	...	...	...	...	...
Percent of Total Party Membership	...	...	...	...	...	...	...	...	...	...	...
Percent of Total No. of Empl. in Party	18.8%	18.9%	19.3%	21.5%	21.6%	23.3%	23.4%	23.6%	23.8%	24.0%	24.1%
Personnel in Trade & Public Catering, Supply & Marketing	...	...	...	...	...	...	...	...	...	...	...
Percent of Total Party Membership	...	...	...	...	...	...	...	...	...	...	...
Percent of Total No. of Empl. in Party	4.7%	...	4.8%	4.9%	4.9%	5.8%	...	5.5%	...	...	...
Personnel in Inspection, Accounting & Clerical Work	...	...	...	...	...	...	...	...	...	...	...
Percent of Total Party Membership	...	...	...	...	...	...	...	...	...	...	...
Percent of Total No. of Empl. in Party	13.2%	...	...	11.9%	11.8%	10.8%	...	...	...	...	...
Other Employees (Communications, Utilities, etc.)	...	...	...	...	...	...	...	...	...	...	...
Percent of Total Party Membership	...	...	...	...	...	...	...	...	...	...	...
Percent of Total No. of Empl. in Party	29.1%	...	...	22.3%	23.5%	19.8%	...	...	...	...	...
Unaccounted for	0	...	...	0	0	0	...	...	...	...	...
Percent of Total Party Membership	0%	...	...	0%	0%	0%	...	...	...	...	...
Percent of Total No. of Empl. in Party	0%	48.9%	43.5%	0%	0%	0%	35.2%	28.1%	29.6%	29.0%	28.3%

Note: a Limited to those who were white collar workers at time of joining the party.

TABLE B-16   POSITION AND NUMBER OF PARTY MEMBERS WITH WHITE
             COLLAR OCCUPATIONS: YUGOSLAVIA, 1964-1966

Occupation or Position	1964	1965	1966
TOTAL NUMBER OF WHITE COLLAR WORKERS (EMPLOYEES) IN PARTY[a]	402,632	409,264	408,378
Percent of Total Party Membership	39.0%	39.1%	39.0%
Percent of Total No. of Empl. in Party	100.0%	100.0%	100.0%
Engineers & Technical Personnel	51,032	56,191	60,669
Percent of Total Party Membership	4.9%	5.4%	5.8%
Percent of Total No. of Empl. in Party	12.7%	13.7%	14.9%
Educational Workers	59,075	62,357	65,054
Percent of Total Party Membership	5.7%	6.0%	6.2%
Percent of Total No. of Empl. in Party	14.7%	15.2%	15.9%
Healthworkers	13,082	13,840	14,892
Percent of Total Party Membership	1.3%	1.3%	1.4%
Percent of Total No. of Empl. in Party	3.2%	3.4%	3.6%
Lawyers & Economists	25,363	30,227	33,862
Percent of Total Party Membership	2.5%	2.9%	3.2%
Percent of Total No. of Empl. in Party	6.3%	7.4%	8.3%
Other Employees with "High" and Higher Education	24,183	24,587	24,280
Percent of Total Party Membership	2.3%	2.4%	2.3%
Percent of Total No. of Empl. in Party	6.0%	6.0%	5.9%
Other Employees with Secondary Education	85,973	88,274	86,400
Percent of Total Party Membership	8.3%	8.4%	8.3%
Percent of Total No. of Empl. in Party	21.3%	21.6%	21.2%
Other Employees with Basic Educ. or Less	143,924	133,788	123,221
Percent of Total Party Membership	14.0%	12.8%	11.8%
Percent of Total No. of Empl. in Party	35.7%	32.7%	30.2%
Unaccounted for	0	0	0
Percent of Total Party Membership	0%	0%	0%
Percent of Total No. of Empl. in Party	0%	0%	0%

Notes: a Military excluded. In 1964 there were 56,685 professional military
        in the party; in 1965, 55,214; in 1966, 52,842.

TABLE B-17 POSITION AND NUMBER OF PARTY MEMBERS WITH WHITE COLLAR OCCUPATIONS: YUGOSLAVIA, 1968-1975

Occupation or Position	1968	1968 I	1969	1969 I	1970	1970 I
TOTAL NUMBER OF WHITE COLLAR WORKERS (EMPLOYEES) IN PARTY	491,147	396,598[a]	481,626	388,432[a]	473,128	383,724[a]
Percent of Total Party Membership	42.8%	37.3%	43.3%	34.9%	45.2%	36.6%
Percent of Total No. of Empl. in Party	100.0%	100.0%	100.0%	100.0%	100.0%	100.0%
Technical Intelligentsia	49,000[b]		54,765		52,758	
Percent of Total Party Membership	4.3%		4.9%		5.0%	
Percent of Total No. of Empl. in Party	10.0%		11.4%		11.2%	
Intelligentsia in Education, Science, Culture, Public Health & Other Activities	128,763[c]	174,828	132,853	183,667	134,342	184,131
Percent of Total Party Membership	11.3%	15.3%	11.9%	16.5%	12.9%	17.5%
Percent of Total No. of Empl. in Party	26.2%	44.1%	27.6%	47.3%	28.4%	48.0%
Administrative Personnel	139,529	139,052	138,217	137,661	125,987	125,634
Percent of Total Party Membership	12.2%	12.1%	12.4%	12.4%	12.0%	12.0%
Percent of Total No. of Empl. in Party	28.4%	35.1%	28.7%	35.4%	26.6%	32.7%
Management Personnel (Persons in Leading Posts)	82,941	82,718	67,250	67,104	74,070	73,959
Percent of Total Party Membership	7.2%	7.2%	6.1%	6.0%	7.1%	7.0%
Percent of Total No. of Empl. in Party	16.9%	20.9%	14.0%	17.3%	15.7%	19.3%
Civilian Security Personnel & Professional Military	90,014[d]		88,541		85,971	
Percent of Total Party Membership	7.9%		8.0%		8.2%	
Percent of Total No. of Empl. in Party	18.3%		18.4%		18.2%	
Unaccounted for	900		0		0	
Percent of Total Party Membership	0%		0%		0%	
Percent of Total No. of Empl. in Party	0.2%		0%		0%	

TABLE B-17   (CONCLUDED)

Occupation or Position	1971 I	Oct. 1972	1972 I	1973 I	1974 I	1975 I
TOTAL NUMBER OF WHITE COLLAR WORKERS (EMPLOYEES) IN PARTY	384,645[a]	[470,000]	386,732[a]	413,652[a]	457,444[a]	506,962[a]
Percent of Total Party Membership	37.5%	...	38.3%	38.4%	38.4%	38.9%
Percent of Total No. of Empl. in Party	100.0%	100.0%	100.0%	100.0%	100.0%	100.0%
Technical Intelligentsia		[53,000]				
Percent of Total Party Membership		5.2%				
Percent of Total No. of Empl. in Party		[11.3%]				
Intelligentsia in Education, Science, Culture, Public Health & Other Activities	184,253	[133,000]	188,184	206,773	231,394	258,991
Percent of Total Party Membership	18.0%	13.0%	18.6%	19.2%	19.4%	19.9%
Percent of Total No. of Empl. in Party	47.9%	[28.3%]	48.7%	50.0%	50.6%	51.1%
Administrative Personnel	124,037	[124,000]	124,277	128,918	141,383	154,042
Percent of Total Party Membership	12.1%	12.1%	12.3%	12.0%	11.9%	11.8%
Percent of Total No. of Empl. in Party	32.2%	[26.4%]	32.1%	31.2%	30.9%	30.4%
Management Personnel (Persons in Leading Posts)	76,355	[77,000]	74,271	77,961	84,667	93,929
Percent of Total Party Membership	7.4%	7.5%	7.4%	7.2%	7.1%	7.2%
Percent of Total No. of Empl. in Party	19.9%	[16.3%]	19.2%	18.9%	18.5%	18.5%
Civilian Security Personnel & Professional Military		[83,000]				
Percent of Total Party Membership		8.1%				
Percent of Total No. of Empl. in Party		[17.6%]				
Unaccounted for						
Percent of Total Party Membership						
Percent of Total No. of Empl. in Party						

Notes: a Military and security personnel excluded. The numbers of civilian security personnel in sources used for Series I were as follows: in 1968, 24,500; in 1969, 24,423; in 1970, 24,506; in 1971, 23,724; in 1972, 24,198; in 1973, 25,907; in 1974, 28,472; in 1975, 30,850. Sources used in this table for Series I provide no data for professional military personnel. b Includes 38,600 Engineers and 10,300 "Remaining" (Chemists, Physicists, Mathematicians and Others). c Includes 64,500 Teachers, 19,300 Party Members in the Field of Health, 19,000 Economists and Lawyers, 5,000 Scientific Workers, 4,400 Cultural Workers, 901 Artists, and 15,600 Not Accounted For. d Includes 65,500 professional military and 24,500 civilian security personnel.

TABLE B-18 NUMBER OF PARTY MEMBERS BY LEVEL OF EDUCATION: ALBANIA AND BULGARIA

Level of Education	Albania				Bulgaria	
	March 1952	Spring 1956	1963	Fall 1971	Dec. 1948	1971
TOTAL PARTY MEMBERSHIP	44,418	48,644	60,701	86,985	496,000	699,476
Percent	100.0%	100.0%	100.0%	100.0%	100.0%	100.0%
Illiterate	...	...	...	...	[34,700]	...
Percent	...	...	...	...	7%	...
4 Yr. Element. Incomplete	...	...	...	...	...	...
Percent	...	...	...	...	...	...
4 Yr. Element. Complete			...	...	[223,200]	
Percent			...	...	45%	
7-8 Yr. Basic Incomplete	29,155	34,100	...	...	...	[154,000]
Percent	65.6%	70.1%	...	...	...	22%
7-8 Yr. Basic Complete					[148,800]	
Percent					30%	
Trade School	...	...			...	[266,000]
Percent	...	...			...	38%
Inc. Second.	...	...			[29,800]	
Percent	...	...			6%	
General Second. Complete	2,800	3,360	[34,300]	[60,900]	[34,700]	
Percent	6.3%	6.9%	56.5%	70.0%	7%	
Specialized Second. Comp.	...	...			...	[280,000]
Percent	...	...			...	40%
Incomplete Higher	...	...			[9,900]	
Percent	...	...			2%	
Higher Complete	119	626			[12,400]	
Percent	0.3%	1.3%			2.5%	
Unknown	...	...	...	...	...	...
Percent	...	...	...	...	...	...
Unaccounted for	12,344	10,558	[26,400]	[26,100]	[2,400]	0
Percent	27.8%	21.7%	43.5%	30.0%	0.5%	0%

TABLE B-19 NUMBER OF PARTY MEMBERS BY LEVEL OF EDUCATION: GDR , 1962-1976

Level of Education	1962	Jan. 1963	1964	April 1967	1970	Dec. 1972
TOTAL PARTY MEMBERSHIP	1,590,000[a]	1,610,679	1,750,000	1,909,859	1,870,000[a]	1,950,421
Percent	100.0%	100.0%	100.0%	100.0%	100.0%	100.0%
Illiterate	...	...	...	...	...	...
Percent	...	...	...	...	...	...
4 Yr. Element. Incomplete	...	...	...	...	...	...
Percent	...	...	...	...	...	...
4 Yr. Element. Complete	...	...	...	...	...	...
Percent	...	...	...	...	...	...
7-8 Yr. Basic Incomplete	...	...	...	...	...	...
Percent	...	...	...	...	...	...
7-8 Yr. Basic Complete	...	...	...	...	...	...
Percent	...	...	...	...	...	...
Trade School	...	...	...	...	...	...
Percent	...	...	...	...	...	...
Inc. Second.	...	...	...	...	...	...
Percent	...	...	...	...	...	...
General Second. Complete	...	...	...	...	...	...
Percent	...	...	...	...	...	...
Specialized Second. Comp.			57,000			
Percent			3.3%			
Incomplete Higher	[95,000]	"Around 190,000"	...	283,000	[354,000]	[482,000]
Percent	6%	11.8%	...	14.8%	18.9%	24.7%
Higher Complete			132,000			
Percent			7.6%			
Unknown	...	...	...	...	...	...
Percent	...	...	...	...	...	...
Unaccounted for	[1,496,000]	[1,421,000]	1,561,000	[1,630,000]	[1,516,000]	[1,469,000]
Percent	94%	88.2%	89.2%	85.2%	81.1%	75.3%

Notes: a Estimates of party membership.

TABLE B-20   NUMBER OF PARTY MEMBERS BY LEVEL OF EDUCATION:
CZECHOSLOVAKIA AND HUNGARY

Level of Education	Czechoslovakia			Hungary	
	1957	Summer 1962	Jan. 1966	Nov. 1966	June 1970
TOTAL PARTY MEMBERSHIP	1,420,000[a]	1,662,000[a]	1,698,002	584,849	662,397
Percent	100.0%	100.0%	100.0%	100.0%	100.0%
Illiterate	...	...	...		
Percent	...	...	...		
4 Yr. Element. Incomplete	...	...	...		
Percent	...	...	...		
4 Yr. Element. Complete	...	...	...	[187,000]	[168,000]
Percent	...	...	...	32.0%	25.4%
7-8 Yr. Basic Incomplete	...	...	...		
Percent	...	...	...		
7-8 Yr. Basic Complete	[1,268,000]	[1,263,000]	[1,192,000]		
Percent	89.3%	76.0%	70.2%		
Trade School	...	...	...	[234,000]	[262,000]
Percent	...	...	...	40%	39.5%
Inc. Second	...	[158,000]	[170,000]		
Percent	...	9.5%	10.0%		
General Second. Complete	[111,000]	[170,000]	[236,000]	[109,000]	[153,000]
Percent	7.8%	10.2%	13.9%	18.7%	23.1%
Specialized Second. Comp.	...	...	...	...	...
Percent	...	...	...	...	...
Incomplete Higher	...	...	...	...	...
Percent	...	...	...	...	...
Higher Complete	[41,000]	[75,000]	[100,000]	[54,000]	[79,000]
Percent	2.9%	4.5%	5.9%	9.3%	12.0%
Unknown	...	...	...	...	...
Percent	...	...	...	...	...
Unaccounted for	0		0	0	0
Percent	0%	b	0%	0%	0%

Notes: a Estimate of party membership.   b Percents in original source total
102.0%.

TABLE B-21   NUMBER OF PARTY MEMBERS BY LEVEL OF EDUCATION: POLAND, 1953-1975

Level of Education	1953	1955	1958	Dec. 1960	Dec. 1962	Dec. 1965	Dec. 1966
TOTAL PARTY MEMBERSHIP	1,230,000[a]	1,343,837[a]	1,023,425	1,154,672	1,397,001	1,775,049	1,894,895
Percent	100.0%	100.0%	100.0%	100.0%	100.0%	100.0%	100.0%
Illiterate	...	...	...	...	...	...	...
Percent	...	...	...	...	...	...	...
4 Yr. Element. Incomplete	...	...	...	...	...	...	...
Percent	...	...	...	...	...	...	...
4 Yr. Element. Complete	...	...	...	...	...	...	...
Percent	...	...	...	...	...	...	...
7-8 Yr. Basic Incomplete[b]	[503,000]	507,735	322,246	301,701	...	285,633	276,288
Percent	40.9%	37.8%	31.5%	26.1%	...	16.1%	14.6%
7-8 Yr. Basic Complete	...	562,375	459,926	432,114	...	681,483	
Percent	...	41.8%	44.9%	37.5%	...	38.3%	
Trade School	...				...	130,758	1,039,117
Percent	...				...	7.4%	54.8%
Inc. Second.	...			134,299	...	150,685	
Percent	...			11.6%	...	8.5%	
General Second. Complete	...			97,475		119,125	
Percent	...			8.4%		6.7%	
Specialized Second. Comp.	...	231,626	194,626	113,258	[293,000]	245,066	453,587
Percent	...	17.2%	19.0%	9.8%	"Around 21%"	13.8%	24.0%
Incomplete Higher	...			14,943		47,495	
Percent	...			1.3%		2.7%	
Higher Complete	[28,000]	42,101	46,779	60,891	[84,000]	114,804	125,903
Percent	2.3%	3.1%	4.6%	5.3%	"Over 6%"	6.5%	6.6%
Unknown	...	...	...	...	...	...	...
Percent	...	...	...	...	...	...	...
Unaccounted for	[699,000]	0	c	d	1,020,000	0	0
Percent	56.9%	0%			73.0%	0%	0%

114

TABLE B-21   (CONCLUDED)

Level of Education	Dec. 1967	Dec. 1968	Dec. 1969	Dec. 1970	Dec. 1971	Dec. 1973	June 1975
TOTAL PARTY MEMBERSHIP	1,931,345	2,104,331	2,203,553	2,319,963	2,254,112	2,322,531	2,359,000
Percent	100.0%	100.0%	100.0%	100.0%	100.0%	100.0%	100.0%
Illiterate	...	...	...	...	...	...	...
Percent	...	...	...	...	...	...	...
4 Yr. Element. Incomplete	...	...	...	...	...	...	...
Percent	...	...	...	...	...	...	...
4 Yr. Element. Complete	...	...	...	...	...	...	...
Percent	...	...	...	...	...	...	...
7-8 Yr. Basic[b] Incomplete	247,032	239,853	230,427	220,868	194,852	177,751	[140,000]
Percent	12.8%	11.4%	10.5%	9.5%	8.6%	7.7%	6.0%
7-8 Yr. Basic Complete	736,112	803,464	834,014	870,011	822,243	806,665	...
Percent	38.1%	38.1%	37.8%	37.6%	36.6%	34.7%	...
Trade School	165,383	200,907	227,179	255,786	257,794	291,585	...
Percent	8.6%	9.5%	10.3%	11.0%	11.4%	12.6%	...
Inc. Second. Percent	162,563	167,846	164,406	163,415	149,548	140,048	...
	8.4%	8.0%	7.5%	7.0%	6.6%	6.0%	...
General Second. Complete	129,911	142,419	150,745	160,667	160,545	185,699	⎤
Percent	6.7%	6.8%	6.8%	6.9%	7.1%	8.0%	
Specialized Second. Comp.	285,963	321,299	347,629	376,914	385,408	399,414	
Percent	14.8%	15.3%	15.8%	16.2%	17.1%	17.2%	
Incomplete Higher	67,467	76,890	83,304	90,117	90,203	98,990	▶ [960,000]
Percent	3.5%	3.7%	3.8%	3.9%	4.0%	4.3%	40.7%
Higher Complete	136,914	151,653	165,759	182,185	193,519	222,379	
Percent	7.1%	7.2%	7.5%	7.9%	8.6%	9.6%	⎦
Unknown	...	...	...	...	...	...	...
Percent	...	...	...	...	...	...	...
Unaccounted for	0	0	90	0	0	0	[1,259,000]
Percent	0%	0%	0%	0%	0%	0%	53.4%

Notes: a Total party membership for 1953 and 1955 is end of year data. Dates of data for education of party members not known. b Data for 7-8 Year Basic Incomplete probably include those party members with lower levels of education. c Subcategories total 152 more than figure for total party membership. d Subcategories total 9 more than figure for total party membership.

TABLE B-22   NUMBER OF PARTY MEMBERS BY LEVEL OF EDUCATION: USSR, 1922-1976

Level of Education	1922[a]	Jan. 1927	1937	1939	Jan. 1946	1947
TOTAL PARTY MEMBERSHIP	410,430	1,144,053	1,981,697	2,306,973	5,510,862	6,051,901
Percent	100.0%	100.0%	100.0%	100.0%	100.0%	100.0%
Illiterate	...	26,010	...	...	...	...
Percent	...	2.3%	...	...	...	...
4 Yr. Element. Incomplete	...	283,512[b]	...	467,517	449,822	...
Percent	...	24.8%	...	20.3%	8.2%	...
4 Yr. Element. Complete	...		...			...
Percent	...		...			...
7-8 Yr. Basic Incomplete	...		...	1,062,859	1,894,939	...
Percent	...		...	46.1%	34.4%	...
7-8 Yr. Basic Complete	...	720,203[c]	...			...
Percent	...	63.0%	...			...
Trade School	...		...	314.058	1,356,029	...
Percent	...		...	13.6%	24.6%	...
Inc. Second.[d]						
Percent						
General Second. Complete						
Percent						
Specialized Second. Comp.	25,857	104,714[e]	227,612	289,185	1,284,924	1,324,896
Percent	6.3%	9.1%	11.5%	12.5%	23.3%	21.9%
Incomplete Higher			48,563	45,603	120,981	136,149
Percent			2.5%	2.0%	2.2%	2.3%
Higher Complete	2,463	9,614[f]	108,256	127,751	404,167	453,288
Percent	0.6%	0.8%	5.5%	5.5%	7.3%	7.5%
Unknown	...	...	...	...	...	...
Percent	...	...	...	...	...	...
Unaccounted for	382,110	0	1,597,266	0	0	4,137,568
Percent	93.1%	0%	80.6%	0%	0%	68.4%

116

TABLE B-22   (CONTINUED)

Level of Education	Jan. 1952	Jan. 1956	Jan. 1957	Jan. 1961	Jan. 1962	Jan. 1965
TOTAL PARTY MEMBERSHIP	6,707,539	7,173,521	7,494,573	9,275,826	9,891,068	11,758,169
Percent	100.0%	100.0%	100.0%	100.0%	100.0%	100.0%
Illiterate	...	...	...	...	...	...
Percent	...	...	...	...	...	...
4 Yr. Element. Incomplete	473,378	357,169	...	299,088	...	...
Percent	7.1%	5.0%	...	3.2%	...	...
4 Yr. Element. Complete			...			
Percent			...			
	2,107,872	2,036,745		2,394,836	2,754,307	2,874,623
7-8 Yr. Basic Incomplete	31.4%	28.4%		25.8%	27.8%	24.4%
Percent			...			
7-8 Yr. Basic Complete			...			
Percent	1,854,125	2,127,862	...	2,649,114	2,811,708	3,277,024
	27.6%	29.6%	...	28.6%	28.4%	27.9%
Trade School			...			
Percent			...			
Inc. Second.[d]						
Percent						
General Second. Complete						
Percent						
	1,486,469	1,593,505	1,696,114	2,427,837	2,693,457	3,542,005
Specialized Second. Comp.	22.2%	22.2%	22.6%	26.2%	27.2%	30.1%
Percent						
Incomplete Higher	188,157	256,856	267,158	278,806	282,061	301,255
Percent	2.8%	3.6%	3.6%	3.0%	2.9%	2.6%
Higher Complete	597,538	801,384	869,582	1,226,145	1,349,535	1,763,262
Percent	8.9%	11.2%	11.6%	13.2%	13.7%	15.0%
Unknown	...	...	...	...	...	...
Percent	...	...	...	...	...	...
Unaccounted for	0	0	4,661,719	0	0	0
Percent	0%	0%	62.2%	0%	0%	0%

TABLE B-22   (CONCLUDED)

Level of Education	Jan. 1966	Jan. 1967	Jan. 1968	Jan. 1971	Jan. 1973	Jan. 1976
TOTAL PARTY MEMBERSHIP	12,357,308	12,684,133	13,180,225	14,372,563	14,821,031	15,639,000
Percent	100.0%	100.0%	100.0%	100.0%	100.0%	100.0%
Illiterate	...	...	...	...	...	...
Percent	...	...	...	...	...	...
4 Yr. Element. Incomplete	0.0	...	...	0.0	0.0	...
Percent	0%	...	...	0%	0%	...
4 Yr. Element. Complete		...	...			
Percent		...	...			
	2,889,138			2,708,600	2,532,292	2,251,000
	23.4%			18.8%	17.1%	14.4%
7-8 Yr. Basic Incomplete		...	...			
Percent		...	...			
7-8 Yr. Basic Complete		...	...			
Percent	3,402,057	...	...	3,573,368	3,406,208	3,175,000
	27.5%			24.9%	23.0%	20.3%
Trade School		...	...			
Percent		...	...			
Inc. Second.[d]						
Percent						
General Second. Complete						
Percent						
	3,816,180	3,993,119	4,226,026	4,932,958	5,344,433	6,022,000
	30.9%	31.5%	32.1%	34.3%	36.1%	38.5%
Specialized Second. Comp. Percent						
Incomplete Higher	315,366	325,985	335,113	337,995	328,493	383,000
Percent	2.5%	2.6%	2.5%	2.4%	2.2%	2.5%
Higher Complete	1,934,567	2,097,055	2,274,182	2,819,642	3,209,605	3,808,000
Percent	15.7%	16.5%	17.2%	19.6%	21.6%	24.3%
Unknown	...	...	...	...	...	...
Percent	...	...	...	...	...	...
Unaccounted for	0	6,267,974	6,344,904	0	0	0
Percent	0%	49.4%	48.1%	0%	0%	0%

Notes: a   Full members only.   b   Domashnee .   c   Nizshee.   d   No equivalent Soviet category.
e   Srednee .   f   Vysshee

TABLE B-23   NUMBER OF PARTY MEMBERS EMPLOYED IN THE SOCIALIST SECTOR BY TYPE OF
             QUALIFICATION REQUIRED FOR THE JOB: YUGOSLAVIA, 1958-1972

Level of Job Qualifi- cations of Party Members	1958 I	1964 I	1964 II	1965 II	1966 II	1968	1972
TOTAL PARTY MEMBERSHIP, SOCIALIST SECTOR	...	...	774,260	775,920	763,400	1,080,519	1,009,947
Percent	...	...	100.0%	100.0%	100.0%	100.0%	100.0%
Manual Jobs not Requiring Training (Unskilled Workers)	45,100	63,422	50,494	55,791	50,555	64,202	[50,000]
Percent	8.5%	8.3%	6.5%	7.2%[a]	6.6%	5.9%	5%
Manual Jobs Requiring Semi- Skilled Training	62,233	67,588	67,087	64,762	59,125	57,891	[50,000]
Percent	11.7%	8.8%	8.6%[b]	8.3%	7.7%	5.4%	5%
Manual Jobs Requiring Skilled Training	133,270	178,304	179,376	176,060	172,924	209,236	[210,000]
Percent	25.0%	23.2%	23.2%	22.7%	22.7%	19.4%	21%
Manual Jobs Requiring High- ly Skilled Training	27,789	62,734	64,121	69,271	71,716	82,392	[90,000]
Percent	5.2%	8.1%	8.3%	8.9%[c]	9.4%	7.6%	9%
Nonmanual Positions Requir- ing Lower Grade of Education[d]	133,316	147,000	143,924	133,788	123,221	254,877	[90,000]
Percent	25.0%	19.2%	18.6%	17.2%	16.1%	23.6%	9%
Nonmanual Positions Requir- ing Secondary Education	98,509	156,800	161,544	166,518	167,321	244,178	[250,000]
Percent	18.5%	20.4%	20.9%	21.5%	21.9%	22.6%	25%
Nonmanual Positions Requir- ing Higher Education[e]	32,804	91,476	98,164	108,958	117,836	155,636	[228,000]
Percent	6.1%	11.9%	12.7%[f]	14.0%[g]	15.4%	14.4%	22.8%
Unknown	...	...	...	...	...	3,532	...
Percent	...	...	...	...	...	0.3%	...
Unaccounted for			9,550	772	0	8,575	[32,000]
Percent			1.2%	0.1%	0%	0.8%	3.2%

Notes: a 7.8% in original source. b 8.7% in original source. c 8.7% in original source. d Lower than
        secondary. e Visoke and više .   f 12.6% in original source. g 14.1% in original source.

TABLE B-24   NUMBER OF PARTY MEMBERS BY AGE: CZECHOSLOVAKIA AND ROMANIA

Age	Czechoslovakia					Romania	
	March 1946	May 1949	Feb. 1950	Jan. 1958	Jan. 1966	1965	1969
TOTAL PARTY MEMBERSHIP	1,159,164	2,311,066	1,982,315	1,422,199	1,698,002	1,450,000	1,924,000
Percent	100.0%	100.0%	100.0%	100.0%	100.0%	100.0%	100.0%
Twenties & Under							
Age	18-25	18-25	18-25	18-25	18-25		
Number	100,000	[335,000]	[220,000]	[92,000]	152,812		
Percent	8.6%	14.5%	11%	6.5%	9.0%		
Late Twenties							
Age	...	...			...	26-34	Under 40	18-30
Number	...	...			...	309,053	[930,000]	[460,000]
Percent	...	...			...	18.2%	64%	24%
Thirties							
Age	...	...	26-45	...			31-40
Number	...	...	[1,030,000]	...			[690,000]
Percent	...	...	52%	...			36%
Forties							
Age	...	...		...	35-44	...	...
Number	...	...		...	452,901	...	...
Percent	...	...		...	26.7%	...	...
Fifties							
Age	...	...	Over 45	...	45-59	...	...
Number	...	...	[730,000]	...	487,486	...	...
Percent	...	...	37%	...	28.7%	...	...
Sixties & Over							
Age	...	...		...	60 & Over	...	...
Number	...	...		...	295,750	...	...
Percent	...	...		...	17.4%	...	...
Unknown Age							
Number	...	...	...	...	...	...	...
Percent	...	...	...	...	...	...	...
Number Unaccounted for	1,059,164	[1,980,000]	0	[1,330,000]	0	[520,000]	[770,000]
Percent	91.4%	85.5%	0%	93.5%	0%	36%	40%

TABLE B-25 NUMBER OF PARTY MEMBERS BY AGE: GDR, 1947-1976

Age	May 1947	April 1954	Dec. 1957	Jan. 1963	Dec. 1966	1971	May 1976
TOTAL PARTY MEMBERSHIP	1,786,138	1,413,313	1,472,932	1,610,679	1,769,912	1,909,859	2,043,697
Percent	100.0%	100.0%	100.0%	100.0%	100.0%	100.0%	100.0%
Twenties & Under							
Age	18-20	"Youth"	"Youth"	18-25	18-25		18-24
Number	[121,000]	[76,000]	[113,000]	[158,000]	145,121		[249,000]
Percent	6.8%	5.4%	7.7%	9.8%	8.2%		12.2%
Late Twenties							
Age	21-30	...	...	...	26-30		...
Number	[243,000]	...	...	...	214,527		...
Percent	13.6%	...	...	...	12.1%		...
Thirties							
Age	31-40	...	...	...	31-40	18-45	...
Number	[423,000]	...	...	...	443,384	[859,000]	...
Percent	23.7%	...	...	...	25.1%	45%	...
Forties							
Age	41-50	...	...	...	41-50		...
Number	[488,000]	...	...	...	305,217		...
Percent	27.3%	...	...	...	17.2%		...
Fifties							
Age		...	...	...	51-60	...	...
Number		...	...	...	286,079	...	...
Percent		...	...	...	16.2%	...	...
Sixties & Over							
Age	51 & Over	...	...	...	61 & Over[a]	...	...
Number	[522,000]	...	...	...	375,584	...	...
Percent	29.2%	...	...	...	21.2%	...	...
Unknown Age							
Number	...	...	...	...	...	...	...
Percent	...	...	...	...	...	...	...
Number Unaccounted for		[1,337,000]	[1,360,000]	[1,453,000]	0	[1,050,000]	[1,790,000]
Percent	b	94.6%	92.3%	90.2%	0%	55%	87.8%

Notes: a 61-65 years, 147,304 (8.3%); over 65, 228,280 (12.9%). b Totals 100.6% in original source.

TABLE B-26   NUMBER OF PARTY MEMBERS BY AGE: POLAND, 1954-1976

Age	Dec. 1954	1955[a]	Dec. 1959	Dec. 1960	Dec. 1965	Dec. 1969	Dec. 1970	Dec. 1973	Dec. 1976
TOTAL PARTY MEMBERSHIP[b]	1,293,000	1,343,837	1,023,600	1,154,672	1,775,049	2,203,500	2,319,963	2,322,531	2,568,366
Percent	100.0%	100.0%	100.0%	100.0%	100.0%	100.0%	100.0%	100.0%	100.0%
Twenties & Under									
Age	18-24	18-25	18-25	18-24	18-24	18-25	18-24	18-24	18-24
Number	[184,000]	214,043	69,400	99,159	160,038	289,200	257,001	129,024	146,397
Percent	14.2%	15.9%	6.8%	8.6%	9.0%	10.9%	11.1%	5.6%	5.7%
Late Twenties									
Age	...			25-29	25-29		25-29	25-29	25-29
Number	...			201,010	282,351		328,652	344,371	394,244
Percent	...			17.4%	15.9%		14.2%	14.8%	15.4%
Thirties									
Age	...	26-40	26-40	30-39	30-39	26-40	30-39	30-39	30-39
Number	...	589,710	507,900	390,202	597,277	1,023,000	726,974	668,354	705,273
Percent	...	43.9%	49.7%	33.8%	33.6%	46.4%	31.3%	28.8%	27.4%
Forties									
Age	...	41-50	41-50	40-49	40-49	41-50	40-49	40-49	40-49
Number	...	305,774	234,600	215,649	383,151	503,000	583,691	655,876	707,328
Percent	...	22.8%	22.9%	18.7%	21.6%	24.6%	25.2%	28.2%	27.5%
Fifties									
Age					50-59		50-59	50-59	50-59
Number					231,349		255,760	319,861	407,086
Percent					13.0%		11.0%	13.8%	15.9%
Sixties & Over									
Age	50 & over	51 & over	51 & over	50 & over	60 & over	51 & over	60 & over	60 & over	60 & over
Number	[213,000]	234,310	211,700	248,652	120,883	398,300	167,885	205,045	208,038
Percent	16.5%	17.4%	20.6%	21.5%	6.8%	18.1%	7.2%	8.8%	8.1%
Unknown Age									
Percent	...	...	...	...	...	...	...	...	...
Number Unaccounted for	[896,000]	0	0	0	0	c	0	0	0
Percent	69.3%	0%	0%	0%	0%		0%	0%	0%

Notes: a Total party membership is for Dec., 1955; data on age published in June, 1956, and appear to relate to the end of 1955.   b Military excluded.   c Subcategories exceed total by 10,000.

TABLE B-27   NUMBER OF PARTY MEMBERS BY AGE: USSR AND HUNGARY

	USSR					Hungary		
Age	1927	1941	Jan. 1965	Jan. 1967	Jan. 1973	Jan. 1951	June 1966	June 1970
TOTAL PARTY MEMBERSHIP	1,144,053	3,872,465	11,758,169	12,684,133	14,821,031	862,114	560,000[a]	662,397
Percent	100.0%	100.0%	100.0%	100.0%	100.0%	100.0%	100.0%	100.0%
Twenties & Under								
Age	18-24	18-25	18-25	18-25	18-25	18-24	21-26	21-26
Number	289,002	[350,000]	[820,000]	[634,000]	834,166	111,493	[28,000]	[39,000]
Percent	25.3%	9.0%	7%	5.0%	5.7%	12.9%	5.0%	5.9%
Late Twenties								
Age	25-29	...			26-30	25-35		
Number	325,567	...			1,101,794	243,646		
Percent	28.5%	...			7.4%	28.3%		
Thirties								
Age	30-39	...	26-40	26-40	31-40		27-49	27-49
Number	365,514	...	[5,530,000]	[5,900,000]	4,588,939		[374,000]	[447,000]
Percent	32.0%	...	47%	46.5%	31.0%		66.8%	67.5%
Forties								
Age	40-49	...	41-50	41-50	41-50	36-50		
Number	130,862	...	[2,940,000]	[3,250,000]	4,329,005	[321,000]		
Percent	11.4%	...	25%	25.6%	29.2%	37.2%		
Fifties								
Age	50-59	...			51-60			
Number	28,822	...			2,425,048			
Percent	2.5%	...			16.3%			
Sixties & Over								
Age	60 & Over	...	51 & Over	51 & Over	61 & Over	51 & Over	50 & Over	50 & Over
Number	3,906	...	[2,470,000]	[2,900,000]	1,542,079	188,362	[158,000]	[176,000]
Percent	0.3%	...	21%	22.9%	10.4%	21.6%	28.2%	26.6%
Unknown Age								
Number	380	...	...	...	...	...	...	...
Percent	0%	...	...	...	...	...	...	...
Number Unaccounted for	0	[3,520,000]	0	0	0	0	0	0
Percent	0%	91.0%	0%	0%	0%	0%	0%	0%

Note: a Estimate.

TABLE B-28   NUMBER OF PARTY MEMBERS BY AGE: YUGOSLAVIA, 1961-1975

Age	End 1961	End 1963	End 1965	1966	End 1968	End 1969	End 1970	End 1971	End 1973	End 1975
TOTAL PARTY MEMBERSHIP	1,035,000	1,109,000	1,046,202	1,046,018	1,146,084	1,111,682	1,049,184	1,025,476	1,076,711	1,302,8
Percent	100.0%	100.0%	100.0%	100.0%	100.0%	100.0%	100.0%	100.0%	100.0%	100.
Twenties & Under										
Age	18-25	18-25	18-25	18-25						
Number	224,077	156,367	131,749	120,234						
Percent	21.6%	15.3%	12.6%	11.5%						
Late Twenties										
Age					18-27	18-27	18-27	18-27	18-27	18-
Number					281,713	259,115	218,967	212,434	258,124	371,4
Percent					24.6%	23.3%	20.9%	20.7%	24.0%	28.
Thirties										
Age	26-40	26-40	26-40	26-40	28-40	28-40	28-40	28-40	28-40	28-
Number	627,281	631,262	623,051	614,689	496,108	472,999	433,956	407,787	391,078	448,7
Percent	60.6%	61.9%	60.0%	58.8%	43.3%	42.5%	41.4%	39.8%	36.3%	34.
Forties										
Age					41-50	41-50	41-50	41-50	41-50	41-
Number					267,950	276,608	283,731	282,196	285,119	302,3
Percent					23.4%	24.9%	27.0%	27.5%	26.5%	23.
Fifties[a]										
Age	41-55	41-55	41-55	41-55						
Number	157,385	196,363	241,388	261,025						
Percent	15.2%	19.3%	23.1%	24.9%						
Sixties & Over										
Age	56 & Over	56 & Over	56 & Over	56 & Over	50 & Over	50 & Over	50 & Over	50 & Over	50 & Over	50 & Ov
Number	26,260	35,021	45,014	50,070	100,313	102,960	112,530	123,059	142,390	180,3
Percent	2.5%	3.4%	4.3%	4.8%	8.7%	9.3%	10.7%	12.0%	13.2%	13.
Unknown Age	...	...	...	...	...	...	...	...	...	..
Percent	...	...	...	...	...	...	...	...	...	..
Number Unaccounted for	b	b	5,000	0	0	0	0	0	0	0
Percent			0.5%	0%	0%	0%	0%	0%	0%	0

Notes: a In original source, data for 1968-1975 include age 50 in two age groups (41-50 and 50 & over). b For 1961, subcateg total 3 more than total party membership in line 1; for 1963, subcategories total 13 more than total party membership.

TABLE B-29   NUMBER OF PARTY MEMBERS BY DATE OF JOINING PARTY AND LENGTH OF PARTY
MEMBERSHIP: CZECHOSLOVAKIA, HUNGARY AND ROMANIA

Date of Joining Party	Czechoslovakia				Hungary		Romania[a]
	Jan. 1958	Jan. 1962	Jan. 1966	1968	June 1966	June 1970	March 1968
TOTAL PARTY MEMBERSHIP	1,422,199	1,657,021	1,698,002	1,690,977	[560,000][b]	662,397	1,761,000
Percent	100.0%	100.0%	100.0%	100.0%	100.0%	100.0%	100.0%
Early 1940s							
Date Joined	Pre-1945	Pre-1945	...	...	Pre-1944	Pre-1944	
Years in Party	14 & Over	18 & Over	...	...	23 & Over	27 & Over	
Number	18,000	15,929	...	...	[7,000]	[9,000]	
Percent	1.3%	1.0%	...	...	1.3%	1.4%	
Mid 1940s							
Date Joined	...	1945-1947	1945-1947		1944-1945	1944-1945	Pre-1949
Years in Party	...	15-17	19-21		21-22	25-26	20 & Over
Number	...	615,618	[606,000]		[96,000]	[87,436]	[404,700]
Percent	...	37.2%	35.7%		17.2%	13.2%	22.98%
Late 1940s							
Date Joined	...	1948-1952	1948	1945-1948			
Years in Party	...	10-14	18	20-23			
Number	...	475,717	[372,000]	919,500			
Percent	...	28.7%	21.9%	54.4%			
Early 1950s							
Date Joined	1953-1957	1953-1957			...	1946-1956	1946-1956
Years in Party	1-5	5-9			...	10-20	14-24
Number	209,000	182,833			...	[185,000]	[181,496]
Percent	14.7%	11.0%			...	33.1%	27.4%
Late 1950s							
Date Joined	...		1949-1965				1951-1960
Years in Party	...		1-17				8-17
Number	...		706,369				[391,600]
Percent	...		41.6%				22.2%
Early 1960s							
Date Joined	...	1958-1961		1958-1968	1957-Pres.	1957-Pres.	1961-1964
Years in Party	...	1-4		0-10	9 or Less	13 or Less	4-7
Number	...	366,924		521,800	[271,000]	[384,190]	[712,500]
Percent	...	22.1%		30.9%	48.4%	58.0%	40.46%
Late 1960s							
Date Joined	...	...	...				1965-1967
Years in Party	...	...	...				1-3
Number	...	...	...				[252,000]
Percent	...	...	...				14.31%
Date Unknown							
Number	...	...	...	...	...	...	...
Percent	...	...	...	...	...	...	...
Number Unaccounted for	1,195,199	0	13,633	249,677	0	0	0
Percent	84.0%	0%	0.8%	14.8%	0%	0%	0%

Notes: a Original data do not account for 1949 and 1950.   b Estimate.

125

TABLE B-30 NUMBER OF PARTY MEMBERS BY DATE OF JOINING PARTY AND LENGTH OF PARTY MEMBERSHIP: USSR, 1927-1976

Date of Joining Party	Jan. 1927	Jan. 1952	Jan. 1956	Jan. 1957	Jan. 1961
TOTAL PARTY MEMBERSHIP	1,144,053	6,707,539	7,173,521	7,494,573	9,275,826
Percent	100.0%	100.0%	100.0%	100.0%	100.0%
Before 1920					
Date Joined	Before 1917				
Years in Party	Over 10				
Number	8,955				
Percent	0.8%				
Early 1920s					
Date Joined	1917-1921	Before 1926	Before 1930	Before 1926	
Years in Party	6-10	Over 25	Over 25	Over 30	
Number	289,695	[300,000]	[500,000]	[290,000]	
Percent	25.3%	5%	7%	3.9%	
Late 1920s					
Date Joined	1922-1927				Before 1936
Years in Party	5 or Less				Over 25
Number	843,592				[700,000]
Percent	73.7%				8%
Early 1930s					
Date Joined		1927-1941		1927-1936	
Years in Party		11-25		21-30	
Number		[1,900,000]		[520,000]	
Percent		29%		6.9%	
Late 1930s					
Date Joined			1931-1945		
Years in Party			11-25		
Number			[3,700,000]		
Percent			51%		
Early 1940s					
Date Joined				1937-1946	1936-1950
Years in Party				11-20	11-25
Number				[3,370,000]	[4,800,000]
Percent				45.0%	52%
Late 1940s					
Date Joined		1942-1951			
Years in Party		10 or Less			
Number		[4,400,000]			
Percent		66%			
1950s					
Date Joined			1946-1955	1947-1956	1951-1960
Years in Party			10 or Less	10 or Less	10 or Less
Number			[3,000,000]	[3,310,000]	3,700,000
Percent			42%	44.2%	40%
Date Unknown					
Number	1,811	...	...	...	...
Percent	0.2%	...	...	...	...
Number Unaccounted for	0	0	0	0	0
Percent	0%	0%	0%	0%	0%

TABLE B-30   (CONCLUDED)

Date of Joining Party	Jan. 1967	Jan. 1971	Jan. 1973 I	Jan. 1973 II	Jan. 1976
TOTAL PARTY MEMBERSHIP	12,684,133	14,372,600	14,821,031	14,821,031	15,638,900
Percent	100.0%	100.0%	100.0%	100.0%	100.0%
Before 1920					
Date Joined		Before 1921	Before 1923	Before 1922	
Years in Party		Over 50	Over 50	Over 51	
Number		38,800	[40,000]	37,551	
Percent		0.3%	0.3%	0.2%	
1920s					
Date Joined	Before 1937		1923–1932	1922–1924	Before 1926
Years in Party	Over 30		41–50	40–51	Over 50
Number	[630,000]		[430,000]	16,136	63,000
Percent	5.0%		2.9%	0.1%	0.4%
1930s					
Date Joined		1921–1940	1933–1942	1925–1940	1926–1945
Years in Party		31–50	31–40	33–48	31–50
Number		956,300	[920,000]	860,424	2,611,300
Percent		7.0%	6.2%	5.8%	16.7%
1940s					
Date Joined	1937–1946	1941–1950	1943–1951	1941–1945	1946–1955
Years in Party	21–30	21–30	21–30	28–32	21–30
Number	[3,290,000]	3,257,100	[3,280,000]	2,033,719	2,255,600
Percent	25.9%	23.7%	22.1%	13.7%	14.4%
1950s					
Date Joined	1947–1956	1951–1960	1952–1962		1956–1965
Years in Party	11–20	11–20	11–20		11–20
Number	[2,640,000]	3,192,700	[3,990,000]		4,925,100
Percent	20.8%	23.2%	26.9%		31.5%
1960s					
Date Joined	1957–1966	1961–1965	1963–1967	1946–1972[a]	1966–1970
Years in Party	10 or Less	6–10	6–10	27 or Less	6–10
Number	[6,130,000]	3,375,700	[3,330,000]	11,382,695	2,778,500
Percent	48.3%	24.7%	22.5%	76.8%	17.8%
1970s					
Date Joined		1966–1970	1968–1972		1971–1976
Years in Party		5 or Less	5 or Less		5 or Less
Number		2,905,300	[2,830,000]		2,396,000
Percent		21.1%	19.1%		15.3%
Date Unknown					
Number	...	...	...	...	...
Percent	...	...	...	...	...
Number Unaccounted for	0	646,700	0	490,506	609,400
Percent	0%	4.5%	0%	3.4%	3.9%

Notes: a   "Postwar years."

TABLE B-31   NUMBER OF PARTY MEMBERS BY DATE OF JOINING PARTY AND LENGTH OF PARTY MEMBERSHIP: YUGOSLAVIA AND POLAND

Date of Joining Party	Yugoslavia					Poland	
	March 1957	1964	End 1965	End 1966	End 1968	Dec. 1958	Dec. 1969
TOTAL PARTY MEMBERSHIP	686,387	1,030,041[a]	1,046,202	1,046,018	1,146,084	983,199[a]	2,203,553
Percent	100.0%	100.0%	100.0%	100.0%	100.0%	100.0%	100.0%
Early 1940s							
Date Joined	Pre-1941	Pre-1941	Pre-1941	Pre-1941	Pre-1941		
Years in Party	17 & Over	24 & Over	25 & Over	26 & Over	28 & Over		
Number	2,985	3,030	2,919	2,900	2,940		
Percent	0.4%	0.3%	0.3%	0.3%	0.2%		
Mid 1940s							
Date Joined	1941-1944	1941-1944	1941-1944	1941-1944	1941-1944	Pre-1949	Pre-1949
Years in Party	13-16	21-23	22-24	23-25	25-27	10 & Over	21 & Over
Number	70,824	65,892	64,184	63,756	61,849	545,799	368,826
Percent	10.3%	6.4%	6.1%	6.1%	5.4%	55.5%	16.7%
Late 1940s							
Date Joined	1945-1948	1945-1948	1945-1948	1945-1948	1945-1948		
Years in Party	9-12	17-20	18-21	19-22	21-24		
Number	227,226	199,205	191,930	187,020	175,322		
Percent	33.1%	19.3%	18.3%	17.9%	15.3%		
Early 1950s							
Date Joined	1949-1952	1949-1952	1949-1952	1949-1952	1949-1952	1949-1953	1949-1953
Years in Party	5-8	13-16	14-17	15-18	17-20	5-9	16-20
Number	228,936	188,811	179,744	173,553	158,722	176,500	122,200
Percent	33.4%	18.3%	17.2%	16.6%	13.8%	18.0%	5.5%
Late 1950s							
Date Joined	1953-1957	1953-1957	1953-1957	1953-1957	1953-1957	1954-1958	1954-1958
Years in Party	4 or Less	8-12	9-13	10-14	12-16	4 or Less	11-15
Number	154,492	188,897	178,990	171,034	154,416	260,900	225,200
Percent	22.5%	18.4%	17.1%	16.3%	13.5%	26.5%	10.3%
Early 1960s							
Date Joined	...	1958-1962	1958-1962	1958-1962	1958-1962		...
Years in Party	...	3-7	4-8	5-9	7-11		...
Number	...	319,724	292,367	278,095	239,634		...
Percent	...	31.0%	28.0%	26.6%	20.9%		...
Mid 1960s							
Date Joined	...	1963-1964	1963-1965	1963-1966	1963-1968[b]		...
Years in Party	...	2 or Less	3 or Less	4 or Less	6 or Less		...
Number	...	64,482	136,068	169,660	353,201		...
Percent	...	6.3%	13.0%	16.2%	30.8%		...
Date Unknown	1,924	...	...	...	...	...	...
Percent	0.3%	...	...	...	...	...	...
Number Unaccounted for	0		0	0	0		1,487,327
Percent	0%		0%	0%	0%		67.5%

Notes: a Total of subcategories. b Of whom, 171,918 joined in 1968.

TABLE B-32   NUMBER OF PARTY MEMBERS BY NATIONALITY: CZECHOSLOVAKIA AND
ROMANIA

| Nationality | Czechoslovakia | | | Romania | | |
	Jan. 1958	Jan. 1962	Jan. 1968	1965	1969	1972
TOTAL PARTY MEMBERSHIP	1,422,199	1,657,021	1,698,002	1,450,000	1,924,000	"Over 2,230,000"
Percent	100.0%	100.0%	100.0%	100.0%	100.0%	100.0%
Czechs	1,172,783	1,323,917	[1,340,000]	...	...	...
Percent	82.5%	79.9%	79.2%	...	...	...
Slovaks	217,272	289,252	[310,000]	...	...	...
Percent	15.3%	17.5%	18.1%	...	...	...
Romanians	...	...	...	[1,300,000]	[1,710,000]	[2,000,000]
Percent	...	...	...	87%	88.8%	88%
Hungarians	15,130	24,311	...	[100,000]	[160,000]	[200,000]
Percent	1.0%	1.5%	...	"Over 9%"	8.4%	8%
Germans	978	1,651	...	...	[30,000]	[100,000]
Percent	0.1%	0.1%	...	...	1.3%	3%
Ukrainians	9,084	10,305	...	...	...	...
Percent	0.6%	0.6%	...	...	...	...
Poles	5,215	5,907	...	...	...	...
Percent	0.4%	0.3%	...	...	...	...
Others	1,737	1,678	45,846	[44,000]	[30,000]	[20,000]
Percent	0.1%	0.1%	2.7%	"Over 3%"	1.5%	1%
Unknown	...	...	...	...	...	...
Percent	...	...	...	...	...	...
Unaccounted for	978	0	0	[10,000]	0	0
Percent	0.1%	0%	0%	1%	0%	0%

TABLE B-33   NUMBER OF PARTY MEMBERS BY NATIONALITY: USSR, 1927-1976

Nationality	Jan. 1927	Jan. 1946	July 1961	Jan. 1967	Jan. 1973	Jan. 1976
TOTAL PARTY MEMBERSHIP	1,144,053	5,513,649	9,626,700	12,684,133	14,821,031	15,638,891
Percent	100.0%	100.0%	100.0%	100.0%	100.0%	100.0%
Russians	743,167	3,736,165	6,116,700	7,846,292	9,025,363	9,481,536
Percent	65.0%	67.8%	63.5%	61.9%	60.9%	60.6%
Ukrainians	134,030	667,481	1,412,200	1,983,090	2,369,200	2,505,378
Percent	11.7%	12.1%	14.7%	15.6%	16.0%	16.0%
Belorussians	36,420	114,799	287,000	424,360	521,544	563,408
Percent	3.2%	2.1%	3.0%	3.3%	3.5%	3.6%
Uzbeks	13,585	61,467	142,700	219,381	291,550	321,458
Percent	1.2%	1.1%	1.5%	1.7%	2.0%	2.1%
Kazakhs	12,041	92,354	149,200	199,196	254,667	282,471
Percent	1.1%	1.7%	1.5%	1.6%	1.7%	1.8%
Armenians	19,019	100,449	161,200	200,605	225,132	234,253
Percent	1.7%	1.8%	1.7%	1.6%	1.5%	1.5%
Georgians	16,985	107,910	170,400	209,196	246,214	259,520
Percent	1.5%	2.0%	1.8%	1.6%	1.7%	1.7%
Azerbaidzani	...	55,448	106,100	162,181	212,122	232,223
Percent	...	1.0%	1.1%	1.3%	1.4%	1.5%
Lithuanians	2,781	3,704	42,800	71,316	96,558	106,967
Percent	0.2%	0.1%	0.4%	0.6%	0.7%	0.7%
Moldavians	931	2,913	26,700	46,562	59,434	67,707
Percent	0.1%	0.1%	0.3%	0.4%	0.4%	0.4%
Latvians	13,336	8,408	33,900	49,559	61,755	65,116
Percent	1.2%	0.1%	0.4%	0.4%	0.4%	0.4%
Kirghiz	2,690	14,039	27,300	39,053	46,049	49,542
Percent	0.2%	0.3%	0.3%	0.3%	0.3%	0.3%
Tadzhiks	1,370	13,757	32,700	46,593	58,668	63,611
Percent	0.1%	0.2%	0.3%	0.4%	0.4%	0.4%
Turkmenians	2,998	12,675	27,300	35,781	44,218	48,021
Percent	0.3%	0.2%	0.3%	0.3%	0.3%	0.3%
Estonians	4,044	7,976	24,400	37,705	46,424	49,739
Percent	0.3%	0.1%	0.3%	0.3%	0.3%	0.3%
Jews	49,511	...	...	...	...	294,774
Percent	4.3%	...	...	...	...	1.9%
Tatars	15,646	...	...	...	...	300,714
Percent	1.4%	...	...	...	...	1.9%
Others	71,315	514,104	866,100	1,113,263	1,262,133	712,453
Percent	6.2%	9.3%	9.0%	8.8%	8.5%	4.5%
Unknown	655	...	...	...	...	...
Percent	0.1%	...	...	...	...	...
Unaccounted for	3,529	0	0	0	0	0
Percent	0.3%	0%	0%	0%	0%	0%

TABLE B-34 NUMBER OF PARTY MEMBERS BY NATIONALITY: YUGOSLAVIA , 1957-1972

Nationality	1957	1964	End 1966	End 1968	1972
TOTAL PARTY MEMBERSHIP	687,387[a]	1,031,031[a]	1,046,018	1,146,084	1,016,300[a]
Percent	100.0%	100.0%	100.0%	100.0%	100.0%
Serbs	374,329	530,119	541,526	582,126	507,000
Percent	54.5%	51.5%	51.8%	50.8%	49.4%
Croats	130,662	191,500	189,605	198,685	173,000
Percent	19.0%	18.6%	18.1%	17.3%	17.4%
Macedonians	43,206	68,042	67,603	74,555	63,000
Percent	6.4%	6.6%	6.5%	6.5%	6.2%
Montenegrins	46,108	63,876	65,986	72,140	65,000
Percent	6.7%	6.1%	6.3%	6.3%	6.4%
Slovenians	53,730	73,105	70,516	70,027	65,000
Percent	7.7%	7.1%	6.74%	6.1%	6.4%
Moslems in Ethnic Sense	b	36,470	37,433	45,047	46,000
Percent		3.5%	3.6%	3.9%	4.6%
Albanians	16,727	28,460	31,780	37,455	35,000
Percent	2.4%	2.8%	3.0%	3.3%	3.4%
Yugoslavs-Nationally Undeclared	b	12,984	14,969	37,000	...
Percent		1.3%	1.4%	3.2%	...
Hungarians	7,469	12,865	12,683	13,966	11,000
Percent	1.1%	1.2%	1.2%	1.2%	1.1%
Bulgarians	2,062	3,283	3,462	3,790	3,400
Percent	0.3%	0.3%	0.3%	0.3%	0.3%
Czechs				1,026	900
Percent	1,346	3,035	3,099	0.1%	0%
Slovaks	0.2%	0.3%	0.3%	2,273	1,700
Percent				0.2%	0.2%
Romanians	934	1,584	1,557	1,646	1,300
Percent	0.1%	0.1%	0.15%	0.1%	0.1%
Italians	672	712	719	703	600
Percent	0.1%	0.1%	0.1%	0.1%	0%
Others	10,142	4,996	5,080	5,645	43,400
Percent	1.5%	0.5%	0.5%	0.5%	4.3%
Unknown	...	...	...	...	...
Percent	...	...	...	...	...
Unaccounted for			0	0	
Percent			0%	0%	

Notes: a Total of subcategories. b In 1957, not recognized in party data as distinct nationality; party members of Slav Moslem ethnicity to be found among "Others."

SECTION C: NATIONAL AND RELIGIOUS AFFILIATION

Introduction

Table C-1 It is assumed here that the data on nationalities relate to ethnic affiliation, not native tongue. The original source does not indicate which of these measures was used in determining nationality. Data on the Greek minority in Albania have been disputed by the Greeks, who have claimed that as many as 300,000 persons of Greek origin reside in Albania. In the data on Czechoslovakia, Jews are treated as a nationality in the 1930 census but are not recorded as a nationality in subsequent censuses; for the number of Jews by religious affiliation in 1930, see Table C-13. The data for the number of Ruthenians in Czechoslovakia in 1930 have been disputed; Ruthenian sources have claimed that 587,000 Ruthenians resided in Czechoslovakia at that time. For the postwar period, the number of Hungarians in Czechoslovakia has been disputed, with Hungarian sources claiming that official figures understate the number of Hungarians by some 150,000.

Table C-2 Series I is taken from the final results of the census of 1934. Data in Series II are from the preliminary results of the 1965 census. Data for Series III are from the final results of the 1965 census. Data on the national composition of the population of Bulgaria for 1975 are not available but Bulgarian sources have stated that the census of that year did not record any Macedonians in the population.

Table C-3 Data for January, 1941, include areas annexed by Hungary between 1938 and 1941. Data for 1970 are given according to native tongue, and by criteria of nationality not specified, but including an "interest in the nationality's education and cultural activities." See Radio Free Europe, "Selected Demographic Data on Eastern Europe," Appendix C, reporting data from the Hungarian journal *Kritika*, June, 1975. Data on the number of Jews for 1930 were not recorded by nationality, but the number of Jews by religious affiliation for that year can be found in Table C-13.

Table C-4 For 1930, data on *Tutejszy* refer to persons residing in the province of Polesie, the majority of whom were Belorussian. The number of Germans in Poland in 1930 was unofficially estimated at from 780,000 to over one million. An American source has estimated the national composition of the population of Poland in 1930 as follows: Poles, 20,418,000; Ukrainians, 5,099,000; Belorussians, 2,020,000; Germans, 970,000; Jews, 3,115,000; Others and Unknown, 294,000. See U.S. Department of Commerce, Bureau of the Census, *The Population of Poland*, Table VIIA, p. 75. Estimates of the national composition of the population for 1956 are those of the Polish author Siekierska, as given by George Geilke. For 1958, estimates are those of the German author Richard Breyer, and for 1961, those of the Pole, Andrzej Kwilecki. For further comments on these estimates, see the General Introduction.

Table C-5 Series I is based on data from the Romanian census of 1930; Series II, from the census of 1966. For 1930, Hungarian sources have estimated the number of Hungarians at around 1.9 million, including Magyarized Jews.

Table C-6 For the number of Jews in the Soviet Union after World War II, and for comments on the reliability of the postwar data on the size of the Romanian minority in the Soviet Union, see the General Introduction.

Table C-7 Census data for 1931 include Serbs, Croats, Montenegrins, Macedonians, and Bulgarians among those speaking Serbo-Croatian. See Table C-17, on religion and language, which gives the number of Catholics speaking Serbo-Croatian as 3,186,295, and the number of Moslems speaking Serbo-Croatian as 908,167. In postwar censuses, Moslem Slavs are recorded as "Moslems Undeclared" and "Religious Moslems of Slav Ethnicity" (1948); and "Yugoslavs Undeclared" (1953); as "Moslems in the Ethnic Sense" (1961); and as "Moslems in the National Sense" (1971). Recognition of the Slav Moslems as a nationality in 1971 contributed to their rapid increase as recorded in the 1971 census. The number of Vlachs in Yugoslavia is disputed; note the data in Table C-11 which show 209,636 persons speaking Vlach in 1953, but only 36,728 of Vlach nationality in that year.

Table C-8 For remarks on the possible underreporting of persons making up the temporary labor force in a republic, and not of the dominant nationality of that republic, see the General Introduction.

Table C-9 See remarks on Table C-8.

Table C-10   See remarks on Table C-8.

Table C-11   For Bulgaria, 1965, language is "language customarily spoken"; for remaining countries, language is native tongue. Data on language spoken include those who may not be of that nationality or ethnic group; for example, Bulgarian speaking Gypsies. For data on languages spoken by individual nationalities or ethnic groups, given in percents, see Table II in the General Introduction.

Table C-12   Language is native tongue. Data on language include those who may not be of that nationality or ethnic group; see comments on Table C-11.

Table C-13 Sectarian Protestant—Baptists, Seventh Day Adventists. *Jednoty Bratrske*—Church of the Brethren.

Table C-15   Discrepencies between this table and Table C-13 on the total number of Catholics and Lutherans in Hungary in 1930 are to be found in the orginal sources.

Table C-16   For *Tutejszy*, see the remarks on Table C-4 above.

Albania

Ethnic Affiliation	1945	1950	1955
TOTAL POPULATION	1,122,044	1,218,943	1,391,499
Percent	100.0%	100.0%	100.0%
Albanian	1,075,467	1,186,123	1,349,051
Percent	95.8%	97.3%	97.0%
Greek	26,535	28,997	35,345
Percent	2.4%	2.4%	2.5%
Yugoslav	14,415	3,474	5,770
Percent	1.3%	0.3%	0.4%
Other	5,627	349	1,333
Percent	0.5%	0%	0.1%
Undetermined	...	...	...
Percent	...	...	...
Unaccounted for	0	0	0
Percent	0%	0%	0%

Czechoslovakia

Ethnic Affiliation	1930[a]	1930[b]	1950	1961	1970
TOTAL POPULATION	14,729,536	13,998,497	12,338,450	13,745,577	14,361,557
Percent	100.0%	100.0%	100.0%	100.0%	100.0%
Czech		7,426,284	8,383,923	9,069,222	9,344,210
Percent	9,756,604	53.0%	67.9%	66.0%	65.1%
Slovak	66.2%	2,295,067	3,240,549	3,836,213	4,193,892
Percent		16.4%	26.3%	27.9%	29.2%
German	3,318,445	3,306,099	165,117	140,402	85,582
Percent	22.5%	23.6%	1.3%	1.0%	0.6%
Hungarian	719,569	596,861	367,733	533,934	572,569
Percent	4.9%	4.3%	3.0%	3.9%	4.0%
Russian					
Percent		118,440	67,615	54,984	58,668
Ukrainian	568,941	0.8%	0.6%	0.4%	0.4%
Percent	3.9%				
Ruthenian		...	...	...	...
Percent		...	...	...	...
Polish	100,322	99,712	72,624	67,552	66,777
Percent	0.7%	0.7%	0.6%	0.5%	0.5%
Jewish	204,779	...	...	...	...
Percent	1.4%	...	...	...	...
Gypsy	32,857	...	...	...	c
Percent	0.2%	...	...	...	
Other				30,045	
Percent	28,019[d]	156,034	40,889	0.2%	39,859
Undetermined	0.2%	1.2%	0.3%	13,225	0.2%
Percent				0.1%	
Unaccounted for	0	0	0	0	0
Percent	0%	0%	0%	0%	0%

Notes: a Prewar boundaries. b Postwar boundaries. c Gypsy population estimated at 221,525 in 1966. d 14,170 Romanians, 6,026 Yugoslavs, and 7,823 Others and Undetermined.

TABLE C-2   NATIONAL COMPOSITION ACCORDING TO LANGUAGE OR ETHNIC AFFILIATION: BULGARIA, 1934-1965

Native Tongue or Ethnic Affil.	1934 I[a]	1934 II[a]	1946 II[b]	1956 II[b]	1965 II[b]	1965 III[b]
TOTAL POPULATION	6,077,939	6,077,939	7,029,349	7,613,709	8,226,564	8,227,866
Percent	100.0%	100.0%	100.0%	100.0%	100.0%	100.0%
Bulgarian	5,274,854	5,204,217	6,073,124	6,506,541	7,259,147	7,231,243
Percent	86.8%	85.6%	86.4%	85.4%	88.2%	87.9%
Pomak	c	...	...	...	...	...
Percent		...	...	...	...	...
Turk	618,268	591,193	675,500	656,025	746,755	780,928
Percent	10.2%	9.7%	9.6%	8.6%	9.1%	9.5%
Jewish	28,026	...	...	...	...	5,108
Percent	0.5%	...	...	...	...	0.1%
Russian	11,928	...	...	...	...	10,815
Percent	0.2%	...	...	...	...	0.1%
Greek	9,601	...	...	...	...	8,241
Percent	0.2%	...	...	...	...	0.1%
Serb	172	...	...	...	...	577
Percent	0.0%	...	...	...	...	0.0%
German	4,171	...	...	...	...	795
Percent	0.1%	...	...	...	...	0.0%
Macedonian	...	...	...	187,789	8,750	9,632
Percent	...	...	...	2.5%	0.1%	0.1%
Armenian	23,045	...	...	...	...	20,282
Percent	0.4%	...	...	...	...	0.2%
Romanian	16,405	...	...	...	...	763
Percent	0.3%	...	...	...	...	0%
Tatar	4,377	...	...	...	...	6,430
Percent	0.1%	...	...	...	...	0.1%
Gypsy	80,532	...	...	...	...	148,874
Percent	1.3%	...	...	...	...	1.8%
Other	6,560	...	...	...	...	4,178
Percent	0.1%	...	...	...	...	0.0%
Undetermined	0	282,529	280,725	263,354	211,912	0
Percent	0%	4.7%	4.0%	3.5%	2.6%	0%
Unaccounted for	0	0	0	0	0	0
Percent	0%	0%	0%	0%	0%	0%

Notes: a Nationality determined by native tongue.   b Nationality determined by ethnic affiliation.   c In 1934, 134,125 Moslems spoke Bulgarian; the majority of these persons were Pomaks. The 1926 census recorded 102,351 persons of Pomak ethnicity.

Native Tongue or Ethnic Affil.	1930[a]	1941[a]	1941[b]	1941[a,c]	1949[a]	1960[a]	1970[d]	1970[a]
TOTAL POPULATION	8,685,109	14,683,323	14,683,323	9,316,074	9,204,799	9,961,044	10,322,099	10,322,099
Percent	100.0%	100.0%	100.0%	100.0%	100.0%	100.0%	100.0%	100.0%
Hungarian	8,000,335	11,364,839	11,884,947	8,655,798	9,076,041	9,786,038	...	10,166,237
Percent	92.1%	77.4%	80.9%	92.9%	98.6%	98.2%	...	98.5%
German	477,153	720,291	532,868	475,491	22,455	50,765	235,600	35,594
Percent	5.5%	4.9%	3.6%	5.1%	0.2%	0.5%	2.3%	0.3%
Slovak	104,786	270,467	173,514	75,877	25,988	30,690	131,200	21,176
Percent	1.2%	1.8%	1.2%	0.8%	0.3%	0.3%	1.3%	0.2%
Czech	2,913	...	...	775	e	538	...	...
Percent	0.0%	...	...	0.0%		0.0%	...	...
Ruthenian	e	563,910	547,177	e	e	e	...	...
Percent		3.8%	3.7%				...	...
Croat	26,768	128,740	12,630	21,395	9,946	25,262	⎤	17,609
Percent	0.3%	0.9%	0.0%	0.2%	0.1%	0.2%		0.2%
Serb	7,031	164,755	159,346	5,442	5,158	4,583	134,000	12,235
Percent	0.1%	1.1%	1.1%	0.1%	0.1%	0.0%	▶ 1.3%	0.1%
Other South Slav Nationalities	26,028	149,309[f]	75,875[g]	21,306	14,950	7,752	⎦	4,205
Percent	0.3%	1.0%	0.5%	0.2%	0.2%	0.1%		0.0%
Rumanian	16,221	1,100,290	1,052,067	14,142	14,713	15,787	37,300	12,624
Percent	0.2%	7.5%	7.2%	0.1%	0.2%	0.2%	0.4%	0.1%
Gypsy	7,841	57,776	76,738	18,640	21,387	25,633[h]	h	34,957
Percent	0.1%	0.4%	0.4%	0.2%	0.2%	0.3%		0.3%
Others	16,033	162,946[i]	168,161[j]	27,208	14,161	13,996	52,800	17,462
Percent	0.2%	1.1%	1.1%	0.3%	0.1%	0.1%	0.5%	0.2%
Unaccounted for	0	0	0	0	0	0		0
Percent	0%	0%	0%	0%	0%	0%		0%

Notes: a Nationality determined by language. b Nationality determined by ethnic affiliation. c Postwar boundaries. d. Nationality determined by ethnic affiliation as measured by culture, language, and other factors. See introduction for additional comments. e Included with "Other South Slav." f Includes 70,315 Wends and Slovenes, and 55,532 Bunjevaci, Dalmatians, and Illyrians. g Includes 20 Wends and Slovenes, and 55,532 Bunjevaci, Dalmatians, and Illyrians. h Total number of gypsies estimated by Hungarian sources as 200,000 in 1960 and 320,000 in 1971. i Of whom, 132,325 were Jews. j Of whom 139,455 were Jews.

TABLE C-4 NATIONAL COMPOSITION ACCORDING TO LANGUAGE OR ETHNIC AFFILIATION: POLAND, 1931-1975

Native Tongue or Ethnic Affil.	1931[a]	1946[b]	1956[c]	1958[c]	1961[c]	1975[c]
TOTAL POPULATION	31,915,779	23,929,800	27,550,000	28,537,000	29,795,000	33,846,000
Percent	100.0%	100.0%	100.0%	100.0%	100.0%	100.0%
Polish	21,993,444	20,520,200	...	26,887,000	29,342,000	33,142,000
Percent	68.9%	85.8%	...	94.2%	98.5%	97.9%
Ukrainian	3,221,975	...	150,000	200,000	180,000	...
Percent	10.1%	...	0.5%	0.7%	0.6%	...
Ruthenian	1,219,647	...	...	...	...	...
Percent	3.8%	...	...	...	...	...
"Tutejszy"[d]	707,088	...	...	...	...	...
Percent	2.2%	...	...	...	...	...
Belorussian	989,852	...	...	120,000	165,000	...
Percent	3.1%	...	...	0.4%	0.6%	...
Jewish	2,732,573[e]	...	45,000	60,000	31,000	...
Percent	8.6%	...	0.2%	0.2%	0.1%	...
German	740,992	2,288,300	65,000	950,000[f]	3,000	Over 284,000
Percent	2.3%	9.6%	0.2%	3.3%	0.0%	0.8%
Lithuanian	83,116	...	...	10,000	10,000	...
Percent	0.3%	...	...	0.0%	0.0%	...
Russian	138,713	...	...	150,000	19,000	...
Percent	0.4%	...	...	0.5%	0.1%	...
Czech & Slovak	38,097[g]	...	20,000[h]	100,000	23,000	...
Percent	0.1%	...	0.0%	0.3%	0.1%	...
Gypsy	...	...	30,000	...	12,000	...
Percent	...	...	0.1%	...	0.0%	...
Other	11,119	399,600	...	60,000	10,000	420,000
Percent	0.0%	1.7%	...	0.2%	0.0%	1.2%
Undetermined	39,163	417,400	...	...	...	...
Percent	0.1%	1.7%	...	...	...	...
Unaccounted for	0	304,300	27,240,000[i]	...	0	0
Percent	0%	1.3%	98.9%	...	0%	0%

Notes: a Nationality determined by native tongue. b Nationality determined by ethnic affiliation. c Estimate. See introduction to this section for sources. d Persons reporting place of residence, not native tongue. e 2,489,034 spoke Yiddish; 243,539 spoke Hebrew. f 850,000 were autochthons, that is, former German citizens of Polish descent. g Czechs. h Slovaks. i Includes Poles and smaller minority groups such as Greeks and Macedonians.

TABLE C-5   NATIONAL COMPOSITION ACCORDING TO ETHNIC AFFILIATION:
ROMANIA, 1930-1977

Ethnic Affiliation	1930		1956	1966	1977[c]
	I[a]	II[b]	II	II	
TOTAL POPULATION	18,057,028	14,280,729	17,489,450	19,103,163	21,559,416
Percent	100.0%	100.0%	100.0%	100.0%	100.0%
Romanian	12,981,324	11,118,170	14,996,114	16,746,510	19,001,721
Percent	71.9%	77.8%	85.7%	87.7%	88.1%
Hungarian	1,425,507	1,423,459	1,587,675	1,619,592	1,706,874[d]
Percent	7.9%	10.0%	9.1%	8.5%	7.9%
German	745,421	633,488	384,708	382,595	358,732[e]
Percent	4.1%	4.4%	2.2%	2.0%	1.7%
Jewish	728,115	451,892	146,264	42,888	25,686
Percent	4.0%	3.2%	0.8%	0.2%	0.1%
Gypsy	262,501	242,656	104,216	64,197	229,986
Percent	1.5%	1.7%	0.6%	0.3%	1.1%
Ukrainian & Ruthenian	582,115	45,875	60,479	54,705	55,397
Percent	3.2%	0.3%	0.3%	0.3%	0.3%
Serb, Croat & Slovene	51,062	50,310	46,517	44,236	42,358
Percent	0.3%	0.4%	0.3%	0.2%	0.2%
Russian	409,150	50,725	38,731	39,483	20,653
Percent	2.3%	0.4%	0.2%	0.2%	0.1%
Czech			11,821	9,978	7,756
Percent	51,842	50,772	0.1%	0.1%	0.0%
Slovak	0.3%	0.4%	23,331	22,221	22,037
Percent			0.1%	0.1%	0.1%
Tatar	22,141	15,580	20,469	22,151	23,107
Percent	0.1%	0.1%	0.1%	0.1%	0.1%
Turk	154,772	26,080	14,329	18,040	23,303
Percent	0.9%	0.2%	0.1%	0.1%	0.1%
Gagauz	105,750	...	...	...	...
Percent	0.6%	...	...	...	...
Bulgarian	366,384	66,348	12,040	11,193	10,467
Percent	2.0%	0.5%	0.1%	0.1%	0.0%
Polish	48,310		7,627	5,860	4,756
Percent	0.3%		0.0%	0.0%	0.0%
Greek	26,495		11,166	9,080	6,607
Percent	0.1%		0.1%	0.0%	0.0%
Other	89,025	105,374	19,798	8,117	19,894
Percent	0.5%	0.7%	0.1%	0.0%	0.1%
Undetermined	7,114		4,165	2,309	62
Percent	0.0%		0.0%	0.0%	0.0%
Unaccounted for	0	0	0	8	20
Percent	0%	0%	0%	0%	0.0%

Notes: a Prewar boundaries. b Postwar boundaries. c Preliminary results
of 1977 census. d Includes 1,064 Szeklers. e Includes 5,930 Saxons
and 4,358 Swabians.

TABLE C-6   NATIONAL COMPOSITION ACCORDING TO ETHNIC AFFILIATION: USSR, 1926-1979 (in Thousands)

Ethnic Affiliation	1926[a]	1939	1959	1970	1979
TOTAL POPULATION	147,028	170,557	208,827	241,720	262,085
Percent	100.0%	100.0%	100.0%	100.0%	100.0%
Russian	77,791	99,591	114,114	129,015	137,397
Percent	52.9%	58.3%	54.6%	53.4%	52.4%
Ukrainian	31,195	28,111	37,253	40,753	42,347
Percent	21.2%	16.4%	17.8%	16.9%	16.2%
Uzbek	3,989	4,845	6,015	9,195	12,456
Percent	2.7%	2.8%	2.9%	3.8%	4.8%
Belorussian	4,739	5,275	7,913	9,052	9,463
Percent	3.2%	3.1%	3.8%	3.7%	3.6%
Tatar	3,311	4,314	4,968	5,931	6,317
Percent	2.2%	2.5%	2.4%	2.4%	2.4%
Kazakh	3,968	3,101	3,622	5,299	6,556
Percent	2.7%	1.8%	1.7%	2.2%	2.5%
Azerbaidzan	1,713	2,276	2,940	4,380	5,477
Percent	1.2%	1.3%	1.4%	1.8%	2.1%
Armenian	1,568	2,153	2,787	3,559	4,151
Percent	1.1%	1.3%	1.3%	1.5%	1.6%
Georgian	1,821	2,250	2,692	3,245	3,571
Percent	1.2%	1.3%	1.3%	1.3%	1.4%
Moldavian	279	260	2,214	2,698	2,968
Percent	0.2%	0.0%	1.1%	1.1%	1.1%
Lithuanian	41	33	2,326	2,665	2,851
Percent	0.0%	0.0%	1.1%	1.1%	1.1%
Jewish	2,672	3,029	2,268	2,151	1,811
Percent	1.8%	1.8%	1.1%	0.9%	0.7%
Tadzhik	981	1,229	1,397	2,136	2,898
Percent	0.7%	0.7%	0.7%	0.9%	1.1%
German	1,239	1,427	1,620	1,846	1,936
Percent	0.8%	0.8%	0.8%	0.9%	0.7%
Chuvash	1,117	1,370	1,470	1,694	1,751
Percent	0.8%	0.8%	0.7%	0.8%	0.7%
Turkmen	764	812	1,002	1,525	2,028
Percent	0.5%	0.4%	0.5%	0.6%	0.8%
Kirghiz	763	885	969	1,452	1,906
Percent	0.5%	0.5%	0.5%	0.6%	0.7%
Latvian	151	128	1,400	1,430	1,439
Percent	0.1%	0.1%	0.7%	0.6%	0.5%
Nationalities of Dagestan	698	...	944	1,365	1,657
Percent	0.5%	...	0.4%	0.6%	0.6%
Mordvin	1,340	1,456	1,285	1,263	1,192
Percent	0.9%	0.8%	0.6%	0.5%	0.5%
Bashkir	714	844	989	1,240	1,371
Percent	0.5%	0.5%	0.5%	0.6%	0.5%
Polish	782	630	1,380	1,168	1,151
Percent	0.5%	0.4%	0.7%	0.6%	0.4%
Estonian	155	144	989	1,007	1,020
Percent	0.1%	0.1%	0.5%	0.5%	0.4%
Udmurt	514	606	625	704	714
Percent	0.4%	0.4%	0.3%	0.3%	0.3%
Chechen	319	408	419	613	756
Percent	0.2%	0.2%	0.2%	0.3%	0.3%

TABLE C-6 (CONTINUED)

Ethnic Affiliation	1926[a]	1939	1959	1970	1979
Mary	428	482	504	599	622
Percent	0.3%	0.3%	0.2%	0.3%	0.2%
Ossetian	272	355	413	488	542
Percent	0.2%	0.2%	0.2%	0.2%	0.2%
Komi and Permyak	376	422	431	475	478
Percent	0.2%	0.2%	0.2%	0.2%	0.2%
Korean	87	182	314	358	389
Percent	0.1%	0.1%	0.1%	0.2%	0.1%
Bulgarian	111	113	324	351	361
Percent	0.1%	0.1%	0.2%	0.2%	0.1%
Greek	214	286	309	337	344
Percent	0.1%	0.2%	0.1%	0.2%	0.1%
Gypsy	61	88	132	175	209
Percent	0.0%	0.1%	0.1%	0.1%	0.1%
Hungarian	5	...	155	166	171
Percent	0.0%	...	0.1%	0.1%	0.1%
Romanian	5	...	106	119	129
Percent	0.0%	...	0.0%	0.1%	0.0%
Kurd	55	...	59	89	116
Percent	0.0%	...	0.0%	0.0%	0.0%
Finnish	19	...	93	85	77
Percent	0.0%	...	0.0%	0.0%	0.0%
Iranian	53[b]	...	21	27	...
Percent	0.0%	...	0.0%	0.0%	...
Czech		...	25	21	...
Percent	27	...	0.0%	0.0%	...
Slovak	0.0%	...	15	12	...
Percent		...	0.0%	0.0%	...
Albanian	3	...	5	4	...
Percent	0.0%	...	0.0%	0.0%	...
Afghan	5	...	2	5	...
Percent	0.0%	...	0.0%	0.0%	...
French	2	...	1	3	...
Percent	0.0%	...	0.0%	0.0%	...
Yugoslav	3[c]	...	5	...	...
Percent	0.0%	...	0.0%	...	...
Spanish	...	...	2	...	...
Percent	...	...	0.0%	...	...
Japanese	0	...	1	...	...
Percent	0.0%	...	0.0%	...	...
Chinese	10	...	26	...	...
Percent	0.0%	...	0.0%	...	...
Turk	1,716	...	35	...	93
Percent	1.2%	...	0.0%	...	0.0%
Italian	2	...	1	...	...
Percent	0.0%	...	0.0%	...	...
Others	951	3,452	2,250	3,021	3,370
Percent	0.6%	2.0%	1.9%	1.2%	1.3%
Undetermined	0	...	0	...	...
Percent	0.0%	...	0.0%	...	...
Unaccounted for	0	...	0	...	...
Percent	0.0%	...	0.0%	...	...

Notes: For notes, see next page.

TABLE C-6 (CONCLUDED)

Notes: a Boundaries are those of 1926; the classification of nationalities is that used in postwar censuses. The original 1926 census results differ from these as follows: (i) Azerbaidzani were not listed as a separate nationality; (ii) Udmurts were not listed as a separate nationality; (iii) Tatars totaled 2,917 thousand; (iv) Uzbeks totaled 3,905 thousand; (v) Tadzhiks totaled 979 thousand; (vi) Latvians totaled 142 thousand; (vii) in addition to 19 thousand Finns, the 1926 census listed 115 thousand Leningrad Finns; (viii) those nationalities subsequently identified as Nationalities of Dagestan numbered 142 thousand. b Includes 43,971 Persians and 9,188 Iranians. c Serbs.

TABLE C-7   NATIONAL COMPOSITION ACCORDING TO LANGUAGE OR ETHNIC AFFILIATION: YUGOSLAVIA, 1931-1971

Native Tongue or Ethnic Affil.	1931[a]	1948[b]	1953[b]	1961[b]	1971[b]
TOTAL POPULATION	13,934,038	15,772,098	16,936,573	18,549,264	20,522,972
Percent	100.0%	100.0%	100.0%	100.0%	100.0%
Serb		6,386,081	7,065,923	7,806,209	8,143,246
Percent		40.5%	41.7%	42.1%	39.7%
Croat		3,755,282	3,975,550	4,293,852	4,526,782
Percent		23.8%	23.5%	23.1%	22.1%
Macedonian	10,730,823	773,030	893,247	1,045,529	1,194,784
Percent	77.01%	4.9%	5.3%	5.6%	5.8%
Montenegrin		425,703	466,093	513,833	508,843
Percent		2.7%	2.8%	2.8%	2.5%
Moslem		1,036,124[c]	...	972,953[d]	1,729,932[e]
Percent		6.6%	...	5.2%	8.4%
Bulgarian	f	61,140	61,708	62,624	58,627
Percent		0.4%	0.3%	0.3%	0.3%
Slovene	1,135,410	1,415,432	1,487,100	1,589,176	1,678,032
Percent	8.15%	9.0%	8.8%	8.6%	8.2%
Albanian	505,259	750,431	754,245	914,760	1,309,523
Percent	3.63%	4.8%	4.5%	4.9%	6.4%
Hungarian	468,185	496,492	502,175	504,368	477,374
Percent	3.36%	3.1%	3.0%	2.7%	2.3%
Czech	52,909	39,015	34,517	30,329	24,620
Percent	0.38%	0.2%	0.2%	0.2%	0.1%
Slovak	76,411	83,626	84,999	86,432	83,656
Percent	0.55%	0.5%	0.5%	0.5%	0.4%
Italian	9,370	79,575	35,874	25,614	21,791
Percent	0.07%	0.5%	0.2%	0.1%	0.1%
Romanian		64,095	60,364	60,862	58,570
Percent	137,879	0.4%	0.4%	0.3%	0.3%
Vlach	0.98%	102,953	36,728	...	21,990
Percent		0.7%	0.2%	...	0.1%
Ruthenian	...		37,353	...	24,640
Percent	...		0.2%	...	0.1%
Ukrainian	27,681	37,140	...	...	13,972
Percent	0.20%	0.2%	...	...	0.0%
Turk	132,924	97,954	259,535	182,964	127,920
Percent	0.95%	0.6%	1.5%	1.0%	0.6%
German	499,969	55,337	60,536	...	12,785
Percent	3.59%	0.4%	0.4%	...	0.0%
Gypsy	70,424	72,736	84,713	...	78,485
Percent	0.51%	0.5%	0.5%	...	0.3%
Russian	36,333	20,069	12,426	...	7,427
Percent	0.26%	0.1%	0.0%	...	0.0%
Jewish	18,044	...	2,307	...	4,811
Percent	0.12%	...	0.0%	...	0.2%
Austrian	...	...	1,459	...	852
Percent	...	...	0.0%	...	0.0%
Greek	...	...	2,304	...	1,564
Percent	...	...	0.0%	...	0.0%
Polish	...	...	4,440	...	3,033
Percent	...	...	0.0%	...	0.0%
Yugoslav	...	...	998,698[g]	317,125[h]	273,077[i]
Percent	...	...	5.9%	1.7%	1.3%
Other	32,417	19,883	7,890		69,498[j]
Percent	0.23%	0.1%	0.0%	142,634	0.3%
Undetermined	...	...	6,389	0.8%	67,138
Percent	...	...	0.0%		0.3%
Unaccounted for	0	0	0	0	0
Percent	0%	0%	0%	0%	0%

Notes: For notes, see next page.

TABLE C-7 (CONCLUDED)

Notes: <u>a</u> Nationality determined by native tongue. <u>b</u> Nationality determined by ethnic affiliation. <u>c</u> Includes 227,203 "Religious Moslems of Slav Ethnicity" and 808,921 "Moslems Undeclared." <u>d</u> "Moslems in the Ethnic Sense." <u>e</u> "Moslems in the National Sense." <u>f</u> Included under those speaking Serbo-Croatian. <u>g</u> "Yugoslavs Undeclared." Almost all of this group are Slav Moslems. <u>h</u> "Yugoslavs Nationally Undeclared." <u>i</u> "Yugoslavs - Not a Nationality." <u>j</u> Includes 32,774 who did not declare nationality under Article 41.

TABLE C-8   NATIONAL COMPOSITION ACCORDING TO REPUBLIC: CZECHOSLOVAKIA, 1930-1970

Ethnic Affiliation	Czech Lands				Slovakia				Ruthenia
	1930	1950	1961	1970	1930	1950	1961	1970	1930
TOTAL POPULATION	10,674,386	8,896,133	9,571,531	9,818,465	3,329,793	3,442,317	4,174,046	4,543,092	725,357
Percent	100.0%	100.0%	100.0%	100.0%	100.0%	100.0%	100.0%	100.0%	100.0%
Czech		8,343,558	9,023,501	9,296,263		40,365	45,721	47,947	
Percent	7,349,039	93.8%	94.3%	94.7%	2,373,054	1.2%	1.1%	1.1%	34,511
Slovak	68.8%	258,025	275,997	308,699	71.3%	2,982,524	3,560,216	3,885,193	4.8%
Percent		2.9%	2.9%	3.1%		86.6%	85.3%	85.6%	
German	3,149,820	159,938	134,143	80,256	154,821	5,179	6,259	...	13,804
Percent	29.5%	1.8%	1.4%	0.8%	4.6%	0.1%	0.2%	...	1.9%
Hungarian	11,427	13,201	15,152	...	592,337	354,532	518,782	553,911	115,805
Percent	0.1%	0.2%	0.1%	...	17.8%	10.3%	12.4%	12.2%	16.0%
Russian				...					
Percent		19,384	19,549	...		48,231	35,435	42,147	
Ukrainian	22,657	0.2%	0.2%	...	95,359	1.4%	0.8%	0.9%	450,925
Percent	0.2%			...	2.9%				62.2%
Ruthenian		...	...	...		...	...	...	
Percent		...	...	...		...	...	...	
Polish	92,689	70,816	66,540	65,273	7,023	1,808	1,012	...	610
Percent	0.9%	0.8%	0.7%	0.7%	0.2%	0.1%	0%	...	0.1%
Jewish	37,093	...	...	...	72,678	...	...	...	95,008
Percent	0.3%	...	...	...	2.2%	...	...	...	13.1%
Gypsy	227	...	...	...	31,188	...	...	...	1,442
Percent	0.0%	...	...	...	0.9%	...	...	...	0.2%
Other	11,434		26,554	...	3,333		3,491	...	13,252
Percent	0.1%	31,211	0.3%	...	0.1%	9,678	0.1%	...	1.8%
Undetermined	...	0.3%	10,095	...	...	0.3%	3,130	...	...
Percent	...		0.1%	...	...		0.1%	...	...
Unaccounted for	0	0	0	67,974	0	0	0	13,894	0
Percent	0%	0%	0%	0.7%	0%	0%	0%	0.3%	0%

145

TABLE C-9   NATIONAL COMPOSITION ACCORDING TO REPUBLIC: USSR, 1926-1979 (in Thousands)

Ethnic Affiliation	RSFSR 1926	1939[a]	1939[b]	1959	1970	1979
TOTAL POPULATION	100,623	108,264	108,377	117,534	130,079	137,410
Percent	100.0%	100.0%	100.0%	100.0%	100.0%	100.0%
Russian	74,072	[90,300]	...	97,864	107,748	113,522
Percent	73.6%	83.4%	...	83.3%	82.8%	82.6%
Ukrainian	7,873	...	...	3,359	3,344	3,658
Percent	7.8%	...	...	2.9%	2.6%	2.7%
Belorussian	638	...	...	844	964	1,052
Percent	0.6%	...	...	0.7%	0.7%	0.8%
Moldavian	21	...	...	62	88	102
Percent	0.0%	...	...	0.1%	0.1%	0.1%
Tatar	2,847	...	...	4,075	4,758	5,011
Percent	2.8%	...	...	3.5%	3.6%	3.6%
Jewish	589	...	...	875	808	701
Percent	0.6%	...	...	0.7%	0.6%	0.5%
Polish	198	...	...	118	107	...
Percent	0.2%	...	...	0.1%	0.1%	...
German	806	...	...	820	762	...
Percent	0.8%	...	...	0.7%	0.6%	...
Romanian	3	...	...	...	...	...
Percent	0.0%	...	...	...	...	...
Gagauz	1	...	...	...	...	...
Percent	0.0%	...	...	...	...	...
Bulgarian	19	...	...	25	...	...
Percent	0.0%	...	...	0.0%	...	...
Gypsy	41	...	...	72	98	121
Percent	0.0%	...	...	0.1%	0.1%	0.1%
Hungarian	4	...	...	...	...	...
Percent	0.0%	...	...	...	...	...
Greek	51	...	...	47	58	...
Percent	0.0%	...	...	0.0%	0.0%	...
Chuvash	1,115	...	...	1,436	1,637	1,690
Percent	1.1%	...	...	1.2%	1.2%	1.2%
Mordvin	1,335	...	...	1,211	1,177	1,111
Percent	1.3%	...	...	1.0%	0.9%	0.8%
Bashkir	712	...	...	954	1,181	1,291
Percent	0.7%	...	...	0.8%	0.9%	0.9%
Finnish	134	...	...	72	62	...
Percent	0.1%	...	...	0.1%	0.0%	...
Central Asian Nationality	1,025	...	...	...	82	...
Percent	1.0%	...	...	...	0.1%	...
Caucasian Nationality	216	...	...	385	463	...
Percent	0.1%	...	...	0.3%	0.4%	...
Kazakh	3,852	...	...	382	478	518
Percent	3.8%	...	...	0.3%	0.4%	0.4%
Baltic Nationality	304	...	...	...	199	...
Percent	0.3%	...	...	...	0.2%	...
Other	4,770	[18,000]	...	4,009	6,063	8,633
Percent	4.7%	16.6%	...	3.4%	4.7%	6.3%
Unaccounted for	0	0	...	923	0	0
Percent	0%	0%	...	0.8%	0%	0%

TABLE C-9   (CONTINUED)

Ethnic Affiliation	Belorussia					
	1926	1939[a]	1939[b]	1959	1970	1979
TOTAL POPULATION	4,983	5,569	8,912	8,055	9,002	9,532
Percent	100.0%	100.0%	100.0%	100.0%	100.0%	100.0%
Russian	384	[362]	...	659	938	1,134
Percent	7.7%	6.5%	...	8.2%	10.4%	11.9%
Ukrainian	35	...	...	133	191	231
Percent	0.7%	...	...	1.7%	2.1%	2.4%
Belorussian	4,017	[4,617]	...	6,532	7,290	7,568
Percent	80.6%	82.9%	...	81.1%	81.0%	79.4%
Moldavian	0	...	...	...	2	...
Percent	0.0%	...	...	...	0.0%	...
Tatar	4	...	...	9	10	...
Percent	0.1%	...	...	0.1%	0.1%	...
Jewish	407	...	...	150	148	135
Percent	8.2%	...	...	1.9%	1.6%	1.4%
Polish	97	...	...	539	383	403
Percent	2.0%	...	...	6.7%	4.2%	4.2%
German	7	...	...	...	...	...
Percent	0.1%	...	...	...	...	...
Romanian	0	...	...	...	...	...
Percent	0.0%	...	...	...	...	...
Gagauz	...	...	...	...	...	...
Percent	...	...	...	...	...	...
Bulgarian	0	...	...	...	...	...
Percent	0.0%	...	...	...	...	...
Gypsy	2	...	...	5	7	...
Percent	0.0%	...	...	0.1%	0.1%	...
Hungarian	0	...	...	...	...	...
Percent	0.0%	...	...	...	...	...
Greek	0	...	...	...	...	...
Percent	0.0%	...	...	...	...	...
Chuvash	1	...	...	...	2	...
Percent	0.0%	...	...	...	0.0%	...
Mordvin	1	...	...	1	2	...
Percent	0.0%	...	...	0.0%	0.0%	...
Bashkir	0	...	...	...	...	...
Percent	0.0%	...	...	...	...	...
Finnish	0	...	...	...	...	...
Percent	0.0%	...	...	...	...	...
Central Asian Nationality	0	...	...	...	...	...
Percent	0.0%	...	...	...	...	...
Caucasian Nationality	0	...	...	...	2	...
Percent	0.0%	...	...	...	0.0%	...
Kazakh	0	...	...	...	...	...
Percent	0.0%	...	...	...	...	...
Baltic Nationality	22	...	...	8	11	...
Percent	0.4%	...	...	0.1%	0.1%	...
Other	5	[590]	...	19	18	61
Percent	0.1%	10.6%	...	0.2%	0.2%	0.7%
Unaccounted for	0	0	...	0	0	0
Percent	0%	0%	...	0%	0%	0%

TABLE C-9   (CONTINUED)

Ethnic Affiliation	Ukraine					
	1926	1939[a]	1939[b]	1959	1970	1979
TOTAL POPULATION	28,995	31,785	40,469	41,869	47,127	49,609
Percent	100.0%	100.0%	100.0%	100.0%	100.0%	100.0%
Ukrainian	23,219	[23,400]	...	32,158	35,284	36,489
Percent	80.1%	73.5%	...	76.8%	74.9%	73.6%
Moldavian	258	...	...	242	266	294
Percent	0.9%	...	...	0.6%	0.6%	0.6%
Russian	2,677	[4,100]	...	7,091	9,126	10,472
Percent	9.2%	12.9%	...	16.9%	19.4%	21.1%
Belorussian	76	...	...	291	386	406
Percent	0.3%	...	...	0.7%	0.8%	0.8%
Tatar	22	...	...	62	76	...
Percent	0.1%	...	...	0.1%	0.2%	...
Jewish	1,574	...	...	840	777	634
Percent	5.4%	...	...	2.0%	1.6%	1.3%
Polish	476	...	...	363	295	258
Percent	1.6%	...	...	0.9%	0.6%	0.5%
German	394	...	...	...	...	...
Percent	1.3%	...	...	...	...	...
Romanian	2	...	...	101	112	...
Percent	0.0%	...	...	0.2%	0.2%	...
Gagauz	0	...	...	24	26	...
Percent	0.0%	...	...	0.1%	0.1%	...
Bulgarian	92	...	...	219	234	238
Percent	0.3%	...	...	0.5%	0.5%	0.5%
Gypsy	14	...	...	23	30	...
Percent	0.0%	...	...	0.1%	0.1%	...
Hungarian	1	...	...	149	158	...
Percent	0.0%	...	...	0.4%	0.3%	...
Greek	105	...	...	104	107	...
Percent	0.4%	...	...	0.2%	0.2%	...
Chuvash	1	...	...	...	14	...
Percent	0.0%	...	...	...	0.0%	...
Mordvin	1	...	...	11	15	...
Percent	0.0%	...	...	0.0%	0.0%	...
Central Asian Nationality	0	...	...	...	11	...
Percent	0.0%	...	...	...	0.0%	...
Caucasian Nationality	12	...	...	28	59	...
Percent	0.0%	...	...	0.1%	0.1%	...
Kazakh	0	...	...	...	7	...
Percent	0.0%	...	...	...	0.0%	...
Baltic Nationality	18	...	...	20	23	...
Percent	0.1%	...	...	0.0%	0.0%	...
Other	53	[4,320]	...	143	120	818
Percent	0.2%	13.6%	...	0.3%	0.2%	1.6%
Unaccounted for	0	0	...	0	0	0
Percent	0%	0%	...	0%	0%	0%

TABLE C-9   (CONTINUED)

Ethnic Affiliation	Moldavia				
	1939[a]	1939[b]	1959	1970	1979
TOTAL POPULATION	599	2,452	2,884	3,569	3,950
Percent	100.0%	100.0%	100.0%	100.0%	100.0%
Ukrainian	[305]	...	421	507	561
Percent	51.0%	...	14.6%	14.2%	14.2%
Moldavian	[171]	...	1,887	2,304	2,526
Percent	28.5%	...	65.4%	64.5%	63.9%
Russian	[61]	...	293	414	506
Percent	10.2%	...	10.2%	11.6%	12.8%
Belorussian	...	...	6	10	14
Percent	...	...	0.2%	0.3%	0.4%
Tatar	...	...	1	2	...
Percent	...	...	0.0%	0.0%	...
Jewish	...	...	95	98	80
Percent	...	...	3.3%	2.7%	2.0%
Polish	...	...	5	5	...
Percent	...	...	0.2%	0.1%	...
German	...	...	...	...	...
Percent	...	...	...	...	...
Romanian	...	...	2	...	...
Percent	...	...	0.1%	...	...
Gagauz	...	...	96	125	138
Percent	...	...	3.3%	3.5%	3.5%
Bulgarian	...	...	62	74	81
Percent	...	...	2.1%	2.1%	2.0%
Gypsy	...	...	7	9	...
Percent	...	...	0.3%	0.3%	...
Hungarian	...	...	...	...	...
Percent	...	...	...	...	...
Greek	...	...	...	...	...
Percent	...	...	...	...	...
Chuvash	...	...	...	...	...
Percent	...	...	...	...	...
Mordvin	...	...	...	...	...
Percent	...	...	...	...	...
Central Asian Nationality	...	...	...	...	...
Percent	...	...	...	...	...
Caucasian Nationality	...	...	1	1	...
Percent	...	...	0.0%	0.0%	...
Kazakh	...	...	...	...	...
Percent	...	...	...	...	...
Baltic Nationality	...	...	...	...	...
Percent	...	...	...	...	...
Other	[62]	...	...	20	44
Percent	10.3%	...	...	0.5%	1.2%
Unaccounted for	0	...	10	0	0
Percent	0%	...	0.3%	0%	0%

TABLE C-9 (CONTINUED)

Ethnic Affiliation	Transcaucasia			Georgia		
	1926	1939[a]	1939[b]	1959	1970	1979
TOTAL POPULATION	5,793	3,540	3,540	4,044	4,686	4,993
Percent	100.0%	100.0%	100.0%	100.0%	100.0%	100.0%
Georgian	1,798	[2,170]	...	2,601	3,131	3,433
Percent	31.0%	61.4%	...	64.3%	66.8%	68.8%
Armenian	1,333	[414]	...	443	452	448
Percent	23.0%	11.7%	...	11.0%	9.6%	9.0%
Azerbaidzan	...	...	...	154	218	256
Percent	...	...	...	3.8%	4.6%	5.1%
Russian	336	[308]	...	408	397	372
Percent	5.8%	8.7%	...	10.1%	8.5%	7.4%
Ukrainian	35	...	...	52	50	45
Percent	0.6%	...	...	1.3%	1.1%	0.9%
Ossetian	114	...	...	141	150	160
Percent	2.0%	...	...	3.5%	3.2%	3.2%
Abkhaz	57	...	...	63	79	85
Percent	1.0%	...	...	1.6%	1.7%	1.7%
Greek	58	...	...	73	89	95
Percent	1.0%	...	...	1.8%	1.9%	1.9%
Jewish	62	...	...	52	55	28
Percent	1.1%	...	...	1.3%	1.2%	0.6%
Kurd	52	...	...	16	21	26
Percent	0.9%	...	...	0.4%	0.4%	0.5%
Tatar	11	...	...	5	6	...
Percent	0.2%	...	...	0.1%	0.1%	...
Other	1,937	[644]	...	15	38	45
Percent	33.4%	18.2%	...	0.3%	0.8%	0.9%
Unaccounted for	0	0	...	21	0	0
Percent	0%	0%	...	0.5%	0%	0%

TABLE C-9 (CONTINUED)

Ethnic Affiliation	Armenia					Azerbaidzan				
	1939[a]	1939[b]	1959	1970	1979	1939[a]	1939[b]	1959	1970	1979
TOTAL POPULATION	1,282	1,282	1,763	2,492	3,037	3,205	3,205	3,698	5,117	6,027
Percent	100.0%	100.0%	100.0%	100.0%	100.0%	100.0%	100.0%	100.0%	100.0%	100.0%
Georgian	...	...	1	1	...	...	...	10	14	...
Percent	...	...	0.0%	0.0%	...	...	...	0.3%	0.3%	...
Armenian	[1,060]	...	1,552	2,208	2,725	...	...	442	484	475
Percent	82.8%	...	88.0%	88.6%	89.7%	...	...	12.0%	9.4%	7.9%
Azerbaidzan	...	...	108	148	161	[1,870]	...	2,494	3,777	4,709
Percent	...	...	6.1%	5.9%	5.3%	58.4%	...	67.5%	73.8%	78.1%
Russian	[51]	...	56	66	70	[529]	...	501	510	475
Percent	4.0%	...	3.2%	2.7%	2.3%	16.5%	...	13.6%	10.0%	7.9%
Ukrainian	...	...	6	8	...	...	...	26	29	...
Percent	...	...	0.3%	0.3%	...	...	...	0.7%	0.6%	...
Ossetian	...	...	...	...	...	...	...	2	2	...
Percent	...	...	...	...	...	...	...	0.1%	0.0%	...
Abkhaz	...	...	...	...	...	...	...	...	...	...
Percent	...	...	...	...	...	...	...	...	...	...
Greek	...	...	...	6	...	...	...	...	...	...
Percent	...	...	...	0.2%	...	...	...	...	...	...
Jewish	...	...	1	1	...	...	...	40	41	35
Percent	...	...	0.0%	0.0%	...	...	...	1.1%	0.8%	0.6%
Kurd	...	...	26	37	51	...	...	1	5	...
Percent	...	...	1.5%	1.5%	1.7%	...	...	0.0%	0.1%	...
Tatar	...	...	...	...	...	...	...	30	32	31
Percent	...	...	...	...	...	...	...	0.8%	0.6%	0.5%
Other	[169]	...	4	15	30	[804]	...	126	223	302
Percent	13.2%	...	0.2%	0.6%	1.0%	25.1%	...	3.4%	4.4%	5.0%
Unaccounted for	0	...	10	0	0	0	...	25	0	0
Percent	0%	...	0.6%	0%	0%	0%	...	0.6%	0%	0%

TABLE C-9   (CONTINUED)

Ethnic Affiliation	Lithuania				Latvia				Estonia			
	1939[b]	1959	1970	1979	1939[b]	1959	1970	1979	1939[b]	1959	1970	1979
TOTAL POPULATION	2,880	2,711	3,128	3,392	1,885	2,093	2,364	2,503	1,052	1,197	1,356	1,465
Percent	100.0%	100.0%	100.0%	100.0%	100.0%	100.0%	100.0%	100.0%	100.0%	100.0%	100.0%	100.0%
Lithuanian	...	2,151	2,507	2,712	...	32	41	38	...	2	2	...
Percent	...	79.3%	80.1%	80.0%	...	1.5%	1.7%	1.5%	...	0.1%	0.2%	...
Latvian	...	6	5	...	...	1,298	1,342	1,344	...	3	3	...
Percent	...	0.2%	0.2%	...	...	62.0%	56.8%	53.7%	...	0.2%	0.2%	...
Estonian	...	...	...	...	...	5	4	...	...	893	925	948
Percent	...	...	...	...	...	0.2%	0.2%	...	...	74.6%	68.2%	64.7%
Russian	...	231	268	303	...	556	705	821	...	240	335	409
Percent	...	8.5%	8.6%	8.9%	...	26.6%	29.8%	32.8%	...	20.1%	24.7%	27.9%
Belorussian	...	30	45	58	...	62	95	112	...	11	19	23
Percent	...	1.1%	1.4%	1.7%	...	2.9%	4.0%	4.5%	...	0.9%	1.4%	1.6%
Jewish	...	25	24	15	...	37	37	28	...	5	5	5
Percent	...	0.9%	0.7%	0.4%	...	1.7%	1.5%	1.1%	...	0.5%	0.4%	0.3%
Polish	...	230	240	247	...	60	63	63	...	2	3	...
Percent	...	8.5%	7.7%	7.3%	...	2.9%	2.7%	2.5%	...	0.2%	0.2%	...
Ukrainian	...	18	25	32	...	29	53	67	...	16	28	36
Percent	...	0.7%	0.8%	0.9%	...	1.4%	2.3%	2.7%	...	1.3%	2.1%	2.5%
Finnish	...	...	...	...	...	...	...	...	...	17	19	...
Percent	...	...	...	...	...	...	...	...	...	1.4%	1.4%	...
Gypsy	...	1	2	...	...	4	5	...	...	...	...	...
Percent	...	0.0%	0.1%	...	...	0.2%	0.2%	...	...	...	...	...
Other	...	19	12	25	...	10	19	30	...	8	17	44
Percent	...	0.7%	0.4%	0.8%	...	0.5%	0.8%	1.2%	...	0.7%	1.3%	3.0%
Unaccounted for	...	0	0	0	...	0	0	0	...	0	0	0
Percent	...	0%	0%	0%	...	0%	0%	0%	...	0%	0%	0%

TABLE C-9   (CONTINUED)

Ethnic Affiliation	Turkmenistan						Kirghizia				
	1926	1939[a]	1939[b]	1959	1970	1979	1939[a]	1939[b]	1959	1970	1979
TOTAL POPULATION	976	1,252	1,252	1,516	2,159	2,765	1,458	1,458	2,066	2,933	3,523
Percent	100.0%	100.0%	100.0%	100.0%	100.0%	100.0%	100.0%	100.0%	100.0%	100.0%	100.0%
Turkmen	720	[741]	...	924	1,417	1,892	...	...	...	...	...
Percent	73.8%	59.2%	...	60.9%	65.6%	68.4%	...	...	...	...	...
Russian	75	[233]	...	263	313	349	[303]	...	624	856	912
Percent	7.7%	18.6%	...	17.3%	14.5%	12.6%	20.8%	...	30.2%	29.2%	25.9%
Uzbek	105	[106]	...	125	179	234	...	...	219	333	426
Percent	10.8%	8.5%	...	8.3%	8.3%	8.5%	...	...	10.6%	11.3%	12.1%
Kazakh	9	...	...	70	69	80	...	...	20	22	27
Percent	1.0%	...	...	4.6%	3.2%	2.9%	...	...	1.0%	0.7%	0.8%
Kirghiz	...	...	...	...	...	...	[754]	...	837	1,285	1,687
Percent	...	...	...	...	...	...	51.7%	...	40.5%	43.8%	47.9%
Tadzhik	1	...	...	...	...	...	...	...	15	22	23
Percent	0.0%	...	...	...	...	...	...	...	0.7%	0.7%	0.7%
Ukrainian	7	...	...	21	35	37	...	...	137	120	109
Percent	0.7%	...	...	1.4%	1.6%	1.3%	...	...	6.6%	4.1%	3.1%
Belorussian	1	...	...	3	4	...	...	...	5	7	...
Percent	0.1%	...	...	0.2%	0.2%	...	...	...	0.2%	0.2%	...
Jewish	2	...	...	4	4	...	...	...	9	8	...
Percent	0.2%	...	...	0.3%	0.2%	...	...	...	0.4%	0.3%	...
Tatar	5	...	...	30	36	40	...	...	56	69	72
Percent	0.5%	...	...	2.0%	1.7%	1.5%	...	...	2.7%	2.4%	2.0%
Other	51	[174]	...	46	101	133	[401]	...	46	212	267
Percent	5.2%	13.9%	...	3.1%	4.7%	4.8%	27.5%	...	2.2%	7.2%	7.6%
Unaccounted for	0	0	...	30	0	0	0	...	99	0	0
Percent	0%	0%	...	2.0%	0%	0%	0%	...	4.8%	0%	0%

TABLE C-9   (CONTINUED)

Ethnic Affiliation	Tadzhikistan					Uzbekistan					
	1939[a]	1939[b]	1959	1970	1979	1926	1939[a]	1939[b]	1959	1970	1979
TOTAL POPULATION	1,484	1,485	1,980	2,900	3,806	5,268	6,271	6,347	8,106	11,799	15,389
Percent	100.0%	100.0%	100.0%	100.0%	100.0%	100.0%	100.0%	100.0%	100.0%	100.0%	100.0%
Tadzhik	[884]	...	1,051	1,630	2,237	968	...	...	311	449	595
Percent	59.6%	...	53.1%	56.2%	58.8%	18.4%	...	...	3.8%	3.8%	3.9%
Kazakh	...	...	13	8	...	107	...	...	335	476	620
Percent	...	...	0.6%	0.3%	...	2.0%	...	...	4.1%	4.0%	4.0%
Uzbek	[353]	...	454	666	873	3,475	[4,040]	...	5,038	7,725	10,569
Percent	23.8%	...	23.0%	23.0%	22.9%	66.0%	64.4%	...	62.2%	65.5%	68.7%
Russian	[135]	...	263	344	395	247	[721]	...	1,091	1,473	1,666
Percent	9.1%	...	13.3%	11.9%	10.4%	4.7%	11.5%	...	13.5%	12.5%	10.8%
Turkmen	...	...	7	11	14	26	...	...	55	71	92
Percent	...	...	0.4%	0.4%	0.4%	0.5%	...	...	0.7%	0.6%	0.6%
Kirghiz	...	...	26	35	48	91	...	...	93	111	142
Percent	...	...	1.3%	1.2%	1.3%	1.7%	...	...	1.1%	0.9%	0.9%
Ukrainian	...	...	27	32	36	26	...	...	88	112	114
Percent	...	...	1.4%	1.1%	0.9%	0.5%	...	...	1.1%	0.9%	0.7%
Belorussian	...	...	3	4	...	4	...	...	10	17	...
Percent	...	...	0.1%	0.1%	...	0.1%	...	...	0.1%	0.1%	...
Tatar	...	...	57	71	80	28	...	...	445	574	649
Percent	...	...	2.9%	2.4%	2.1%	0.5%	...	...	5.5%	4.9%	4.2%
Jewish	...	...	12	15	15	38	...	...	94	103	100
Percent	...	...	0.6%	0.5%	0.4%	0.7%	...	...	1.2%	0.9%	0.6%
Other	[111]	...	12	84	108	259	[1,510]	...	154	689	842
Percent	7.5%	...	0.6%	2.9%	2.8%	4.9%	24.1%	...	1.9%	5.8%	5.5%
Unaccounted for	0	...	55	0	0	0	0	...	391	0	0
Percent	0%	...	2.8%	0%	0%	0%	0%	...	4.8%	0%	0%

TABLE C-9   (CONCLUDED)

Ethnic Affiliation	Kazakhstan				
	1939[a]	1939[b]	1959	1970	1979
TOTAL POPULATION	6,094	6,081	9,310	13,009	14,684
Percent	100.0%	100.0%	100.0%	100.0%	100.0%
Tadzhik	...	...	8	16	...
Percent	...	...	0.1%	0.1%	...
Kazakh	[2,330]	...	2,795	4,234	5,289
Percent	38.2%	...	30.0%	32.5%	36.0%
Uzbek	...	...	137	216	263
Percent	...	...	1.5%	1.7%	1.8%
Russian	[2,460]	...	3,974	5,522	5,991
Percent	40.3%	...	42.7%	42.4%	40.8%
Turkmen	...	...	...	...	...
Percent	...	...	...	...	...
Kirghiz	...	...	7	10	...
Percent	...	...	0.1%	0.1%	...
Ukrainian	[658]	...	762	933	898
Percent	10.8%	...	8.2%	7.2%	6.1%
Belorussian	...	...	107	198	181
Percent	...	...	1.2%	1.5%	1.2%
Tatar	...	...	192	288	313
Percent	...	...	2.1%	2.2%	2.1%
Jewish	...	...	28	28	...
Percent	...	...	0.3%	0.2%	...
Other	[652]	...	272	1,564	1,749
Percent	10.7%	...	2.9%	12.0%	11.9%
Unaccounted for	0	...	1,028	0	0
Percent	0%	...	11.0%	0%	0%

Notes: a Prewar boundaries. b Postwar boundaries.

155

Ethnic Affiliation	Bosnia-Hercegovina				Montenegro			
	1948	1953	1961	1971	1948	1953	1961	1971
TOTAL POPULATION	2,565,277	2,847,790	3,277,948	3,746,111	377,189	419,873	471,894	529,604
Percent	100.0%	100.0%	100.0%	100.0%	100.0%	100.0%	100.0%	100.0%
Serb	1,064,125	1,264,372	1,406,057	1,393,148	5,994	13,864	14,087	39,512
Percent	41.5%	44.4%	42.9%	37.2%	1.6%	3.3%	3.0%	7.5%
Croat	588,828	654,229	711,665	772,491	6,784	9,814	10,664	9,192
Percent	23.0%	23.0%	21.7%	20.6%	1.8%	2.3%	2.3%	1.7%
Ethnic Moslem	97,286[a]	...	842,248[b]	1,482,430[c]	737[d]	...	30,665[b]	70,236[c]
Percent	3.8%	...	25.7%	39.6%	0.2%	...	6.5%	13.3%
Moslem – Other	788,403[e]	891,800[f]	...	...	387[e]	6,424[f]	...	...
Percent	30.7%	31.3%	...	...	0.1%	1.5%	...	...
Macedonian	675	1,884	2,391	1,773	133	362	593	723
Percent	0.0%	0.1%	0.1%	0.0%	0.0%	0.1%	0.1%	0.1%
Slovene	4,338	6,300	5,939	4,053	484	642	819	658
Percent	0.2%	0.2%	0.2%	0.1%	0.1%	0.2%	0.2%	0.1%
Montenegrin	3,094	7,336	12,828	13,021	342,009	363,686[g]	383,988	355,632
Percent	0.1%	0.3%	0.4%	0.3%	90.7%	86.7%	81.4%	67.1%
Albanian	755	1,578	3,642	3,764	19,425	23,460	25,803	35,671
Percent	0.0%	0.1%	0.1%	0.1%	5.2%	5.6%	5.5%	6.7%
Yugoslav	...	...	275,883[h]	43,796[i]	...	...	1,559[h]	10,943[i]
Percent	...	...	8.4%	1.2%	...	...	0.3%	2.1%
Other	17,773[j]	20,291[j]	17,295[j]	31,635[j]	1,236	1,621	3,716[k]	7,037
Percent	0.7%	0.7%	0.5%	0.8%	0.3%	0.4%	0.8%	1.3%

Ethnic Affiliation	Slovenia				Serbia			
	1948	1953	1961	1971	1948	1953	1961	1971
TOTAL POPULATION	1,391,873	1,466,425	1,591,523	1,727,137	6,527,966	6,979,154	7,642,227	8,446,591
Percent	100.0%	100.0%	100.0%	100.0%	100.0%	100.0%	100.0%	100.0%
Serb	6,980	11,225	13,609	20,521	4,736,093	5,152,939	5,704,686	6,016,811
Percent	0.5%	0.8%	0.9%	1.2%	72.5%	73.8%	74.6%	71.2%
Croat	15,995	17,978	31,429	42,657	169,420	173,246	196,409	184,913
Percent	1.1%	1.3%	2.0%	2.5%	2.6%	2.5%	2.6%	2.2%
Ethnic Moslem	142[l]	...	465[b]	3,231[c]	88,081[m]	...	93,467[b]	154,330[c]
Percent	0.0%	...	0.0%	0.2%	1.3%	...	1.2%	1.8%
Moslem – Other	179[e]	1,617[f]	...	...	17,315[e]	81,081[f]	...	...
Percent	0.0%	0.1%	...	...	0.3%	1.2%	...	...
Macedonian	366	640	1,009	1,613	17,917	27,277	36,288	42,675
Percent	0.0%	0.0%	0.1%	0.1%	0.3%	0.4%	0.5%	0.5%
Slovene	1,350,149	1,415,448	1,522,248	1,624,029	20,998	20,717	19,957	15,957
Percent	97.0%	96.5%	95.6%	94.0%	0.3%	0.3%	0.3%	0.2%
Montenegrin	521	1,356	1,384	1,978	74,860	86,061	104,753	125,260
Percent	0.0%	0.1%	0.1%	0.1%	1.1%	1.2%	1.4%	1.5%
Albanian	216	169	282	1,281	532,011	565,513	699,772	984,761
Percent	0.0%	0.0%	0.0%	0.1%	8.2%	8.1%	9.2%	11.7%
Yugoslav	...	...	2,784[h]	6,744[i]	...	...	20,079[h]	123,824[i]
Percent	...	...	0.2%	0.4%	...	...	0.3%	1.5%
Other	17,325	17,992	18,313	25,083	871,271	872,320	766,816	798,060
Percent	1.2%	1.2%	1.1%	1.4%	13.3%	12.5%	10.0%	9.4%

TABLE C-10 (CONTINUED)

Ethnic Affiliation	Lesser Serbia			
	1948	1953	1961	1971
TOTAL POPULATION	4,136,934	4,458,394	4,823,264	5,250,365
Percent	100.0%	100.0%	100.0%	100.0%
Serb	3,810,573	4,088,724	4,459,953	4,699,415
Percent	92.1%	91.7%	92.6%	89.5%
Croat	30,342	38,991	43,817	38,088
Percent	0.7%	0.9%	0.9%	0.7%
Ethnic Moslem	...	...	83,811[b]	124,482[c]
Percent	...	...	1.7%	2.4%
Moslem – Other	6,586[e]	64,303[f]	...	...
Percent	0.2%	1.5%	...	...
Macedonian	8,301	14,616	19,956	25,100
Percent	0.2%	0.3%	0.4%	0.5%
Slovene	13,492	14,281	13,814	10,926
Percent	0.3%	0.3%	0.3%	0.2%
Montenegrin	16,221	24,157	32,383	57,289
Percent	0.4%	0.5%	0.7%	1.1%
Albanian	33,289	39,989	51,173	65,507
Percent	0.8%	0.9%	1.1%	1.2%
Hungarian	4,686	6,403	6,816	6,279
Percent	0.1%	0.1%	0.1%	0.1%
Czech	2,755	2,432	2,015	1,341
Percent	0.1%	0.1%	0.0%	0.0%
Slovak	1,106	1,546	3,986	3,912
Percent	0.0%	0.0%	0.1%	0.0%
Vlach	93,440	28,022	1,330	14,653
Percent	2.3%	0.6%	0.0%	0.3%
Romanian	3,849	2,453	2,233	4,412
Percent	0.1%	0.1%	0.0%	0.1%
Bulgarian	55,894	56,440	54,391	49,791
Percent	1.4%	1.3%	1.1%	0.9%
Italian	632	419	354	330
Percent	0.0%	0.0%	0.0%	0.0%
German	9,442	10,864	3,046	1,825
Percent	0.2%	0.3%	0.1%	0.0%
Yugoslav	...	...	11,699[h]	75,976[i]
Percent	...	...	0.2%	1.4%
Others	46,326	64,754	32,487	71,039
Percent	1.1%	1.5%	0.7%	1.4%
Unaccounted for	0	0	10	0
Percent	0%	0%	0%	0%

157

TABLE C-10   (CONTINUED)

Ethnic Affiliation	Croatia				Vojvodina			
	1948	1953	1961	1971	1948	1953	1961	1971
TOTAL POPULATION	3,756,807	3,918,817	4,159,696	4,426,221	1,663,212	1,712,619	1,854,965	1,952,533
Percent	100.0%	100.0%	100.0%	100.0%	100.0%	100.0%	100.0%	100.0%
Serb	543,521	588,411	624,985	626,789	841,246	874,346	1,017,717	1,089,132
Percent	14.5%	15.0%	15.0%	14.2%	50.6%	51.1%	54.9%	55.8%
Croat	2,972,187	3,117,513	3,339,841	3,513,647	134,232	128,054	145,341	138,561
Percent	79.1%	79.6%	80.3%[b]	79.4%[c]	8.1%	7.5%	7.8%[b]	7.1%[c]
Ethnic Moslem	3,486[h]	...	3,113[b]	18,457[c]	...	...	1,630[b]	3,491[c]
Percent	0.1%	...[f]	0.1%	0.4%	...[e]	...[f]	0.1%	0.2%
Moslem - Other	1,077[e]	16,185[f]	...	...	1,050[e]	10,537[f]	...	...
Percent	0.0%	0.4%	...	...	0.1%	0.6%	...	...
Macedonian	1,387	2,385	4,381	5,625	9,090	11,689	15,190	16,527
Percent	0.0%	0.1%	0.1%	0.1%	0.6%	0.7%	0.8%	0.8%
Slovene	38,734	43,010	39,101	32,497	7,223	6,025	5,633	4,639
Percent	1.0%	1.1%	0.9%	0.7%	0.4%	0.4%	0.3%	0.2%
Montenegrin	2,871	5,128	7,465	9,706	30,589	30,561	34,782	36,416
Percent	0.1%	0.1%	0.2%	0.2%	1.8%	1.8%	1.9%	1.9%
Albanian	635	1,001	2,126	4,175	480	965	1,994	3,086
Percent	0.0%	0.0%	0.0%	0.1%	0.0%	0.1%	0.1%	0.2%
Hungarian	51,399	47,711	42,347	35,488	428,932	435,345	442,561	423,866
Percent	1.4%	1.2%	1.0%	0.8%	25.8%	25.4%	23.9%	21.8%
Czech	28,991	25,954	23,391	19,001	3,976	3,480	3,086	2,771
Percent	0.8%	0.7%	0.6%	0.4%	0.2%	0.2%	0.2%	0.1%
Slovak	10,097	9,570	8,182	6,482	72,032	73,460	73,830	72,795
Percent	0.3%	0.2%	0.2%	0.1%	4.3%	4.3%	4.0%	3.7%
Vlach	1	2	34	13	0	25	37	66
Percent	0.0%	0.0%	0.0%	0.0%	0.0%	0.0%	0.0%	0.0%
Romanian	743	418	1,053	792	59,263	57,236	57,259	52,987
Percent	0.0%	0.0%	0.0%	0.0%	3.6%	3.3%	3.1%	2.7%
Bulgarian	637	464	593	676	3,501	3,706	3,852	3,745
Percent	0.0%	0.0%	0.0%	0.0%	0.2%	0.2%	0.2%	0.2%
Italian	76,093	33,316	21,103	17,433	192	196	214	211
Percent	2.0%	0.9%	0.5%	0.4%	0.0%	0.0%	0.0%	0.0%
German	10,144	11,242	4,214	2,791	31,821	35,290	11,432	7,243
Percent	0.3%	0.3%	0.1%[h]	0.1%[i]	1.9%	2.1%	0.6%[h]	0.4%[i]
Yugoslav	...	...	15,559[h]	84,118[i]	...	...	3,174[h]	46,928[i]
Percent	...	...	0.4%	1.9%	...	...	0.2%	2.4%
Other	14,804	16,507	22,208	48,531	39,585	41,704	37,233	50,069
Percent	0.4%	0.4%	0.5%	1.1%	2.4%	2.4%	2.0%	2.6%
Unaccounted for	0	0	0	0	0	0	0	0
Percent	0%	0%	0%	0%	0%	0%	0%	0%

TABLE C-10 (CONCLUDED)

Ethnic Affiliation	Macedonia				Kosovo			
	1948	1953	1961	1971	1948	1953	1961	1971
TOTAL POPULATION	1,152,986	1,304,514	1,406,003	1,647,308	727,820	808,141	963,988	1,243,693
Percent	100.0%	100.0%	100.0%	100.0%	100.0%	100.0%	100.0%	100.0%
Macedonian	752,552	860,699	1,000,854	1,142,375	526	972	1,142	1,048
Percent	65.3%	66.0%	71.2%	69.3%	0.1%	0.1%	0.1%	0.1%
Albanian	197,389	162,524	183,108	279,871	498,242	524,559	646,605	916,168
Percent	17.1%	12.4%	13.0%	17.0%	68.5%	64.9%	67.1%	73.7%
Serb	29,369	35,112	42,728	46,465	171,911	189,869	227,016	228,264
Percent	2.5%	2.7%	3.0%	2.8%	23.6%	23.5%	23.5%	18.3%
Croat	2,060	2,770	3,801	3,882	5,290	6,201	7,251	8,264
Percent	0.2%	0.2%	0.3%	0.2%	0.7%	0.8%	0.8%	0.7%
Ethnic Moslem	37,470[o]	...	3,002[b]	1,248[c]	...	...	8,026[b]	26,357[c]
Percent	3.2%	...	0.2%	0.1%	...	...	0.8%	2.1%
Moslem – Other	1,560[e]	1,591[f]	...	...	9,679[e]	6,241[f]	...	...
Percent	0.1%	0.1%	...	...	1.3%	0.8%	...	...
Slovene	729	983	1,147	838	283	411	510	392
Percent	0.1%	0.1%	0.1%	0.0%	0.0%	0.1%	0.1%	0.0%
Montenegrin	2,348	2,526	3,414	3,246	28,050	31,343	37,588	31,555
Percent	0.2%	0.2%	0.2%	0.2%	3.9%	3.9%	3.9%	2.5%
Turk	95,940	203,938	131,481	108,552	1,315	34,583	25,764	12,244
Percent	8.3%	15.6%	9.3%	6.6%	0.2%	4.3%	2.7%	1.0%
Bulgarian	889	920	3,087	3,334	77	36	32	37
Percent	0.1%	0.1%	0.2%	0.2%	0.0%	0.0%	0.0%	0.0%
Vlach	9,511	8,668	8,046	7,190	0	0	1	5
Percent	0.8%	0.7%	0.6%	0.4%	0%	0%	0.0%	0.0%
Yugoslav	...	...	1,260[h]	3,652[i]	...	...	5,206[h]	920[i]
Percent	...	...	0.1%	0.2%	...	...	0.5%	0.1%
Other	23,161	24,783	24,075	46,655	12,447	13,926	4,847	18,439
Percent	2.0%	1.9%	1.7%	2.8%	1.7%	1.7%	0.5%	1.5%
Unaccounted for	8	0	0	0	0	0	0	0
Percent	0%	0%	0%	0%	0%	0%	0%	0%

Notes: a Of whom, 71,991 Serb Moslems, 25,295 Croat Moslems. b "Moslems in the Ethnic Sense." c "Moslems in the National Sense." d Of whom, 713 Serb Moslems, 24 Croat Moslems. e "Moslems Undeclared." f "Yugoslavs Undeclared." g Including 52,929 Montenegrins of Moslem faith. h "Yugoslavs – Nationally Undeclared." i "Yugoslavs – Not a Nationality." j Of whom Jews made up 1,174 in 1948, 1,111 in 1953, 347 in 1961 and 408 in 1971. k Subcategories add up to 5 more than total. l Of whom, Serb Moslems 68, Croat Moslems, 74. m Of whom, Serb Moslems 87,637, Croat Moslems, 444. n Of whom, 274 Serb Moslems, 3,212 Croat Moslems. o Of whom, Macedonian Moslems 37,096, Croat Moslems, 22.

Nationality	Yugoslavia 1953 Ethnic Affil.	Language	Romania 1930 Ethnic Affil.	Language	Romania 1956 Ethnic Affil.	Language	Romania 1966 Ethnic Affil.	Language	Bulgaria 1965 Ethnic Affil.	Language
Serb	12,506,264	12,382,713							577	...
Croat									...	...
Montenegrin			51,062	47,724	46,517	43,057	44,236	41,897	...	...
Slav Moslem									...	...
Slovene	1,487,100	1,477,440	...	...	...	...	...	...	...	...
Macedonian	893,247	926,431	...	...	...	...	...	...	9,632	...
Albanian	754,245	778,088	...	...	...	...	...	...	...	...
Bulgarian	61,708	60,398	366,384	364,373	12,040	13,189	11,193	10,439	7,231,243	7,382,394
Czech	34,517	27,977	51,842	43,141	11,821	6,196	9,978	6,339	...	...
Slovak	84,999	82,378			23,331	18,935	22,221	19,797	...	...
Italian	35,874	39,926	...	...	...	...	...	...	...	...
Hungarian	502,175	500,184	1,425,507	1,554,525	1,587,675	1,653,700	1,619,592	1,651,873	...	...
German	60,536	63,040	745,421	760,687	384,708	395,374	382,595	387,547	...	...
Vlach	36,728	209,636	...	...	...	...	...	...	795	...
Romanian	60,364	70,385	12,981,324	13,180,936	14,996,114	15,080,686	16,746,510	16,770,628	763	...
Turk	259,535	181,887	154,772	a	14,329	14,228	18,040	17,453	780,928	758,832
Gypsy	84,713	76,379	262,501	101,015	104,216	66,882	64,197	49,086	148,874	58,873
Ruthenian	37,353	27,122	582,115	641,485	60,479	68,252	54,705	59,803	...	...
Ukrainian	...	...							...	...
Polish	4,440	2,988	48,310	38,265	7,627	5,494	5,860	4,699	5,108	...
Jewish	2,307	...	728,115	518,754	146,264	34,337	42,888	5,143	5,143	...
Armenian	...	...	15,544	11,377	6,441	4,716	3,436	2,617	20,282	...
Tatar	...	...	22,141	288,073[b]	20,469	20,574	22,151	21,224	6,430	...
Russian	12,426	10,485	409,150	450,981	38,731	45,029	39,483	40,526	10,815	...

Notes: a Included with Tatars. b Turks and Tatars.

TABLE C-12   COMPARISON OF ETHNIC AFFILIATION AND LANGUAGE: USSR, 1926-1970

Nationality	1926 Ethnic Affil.	Language	1959 Ethnic Affil.	Language	1970 Ethnic Affil.	Language
Russian	77,791,124	84,195,653	114,113,579	124,118,999	129,015,140	141,830,564
Ukrainian	31,194,976	27,570,081	37,252,930	33,224,939	40,753,246	35,400,944
Uzbek	3,904,622	4,062,859	6,015,416	6,007,520	9,195,093	9,154,704
Belorussian	4,738,923	3,465,651	7,913,488	6,952,123	9,051,755	7,630,007
Tatar	2,916,536	3,569,811	4,967,701	4,945,719	5,930,670	...
Kazakh	3,968,289	3,965,764	3,621,610	3,579,633	5,298,818	5,213,694
Azerbaidzan	...	...	2,939,728	2,917,548	4,379,937	4,347,089
Armenian	1,567,568	1,475,250	2,786,912	2,510,338	3,559,151	3,261,053
Georgian	1,821,184	1,610,458	2,691,950	2,765,013	3,245,300	3,310,917
Moldavian	278,905	263,638	2,214,139	2,128,821	2,697,994	2,607,367
Lithuanian	41,463	21,816	2,326,094	2,286,776	2,664,944	2,625,608
Jewish	2,672,499	1,884,245	2,267,814	407,900	2,150,707	...
Tadzhik	978,680	1,012,853	1,396,939	1,459,355	2,135,883	2,202,671
German	1,238,549	1,193,210	1,619,655	1,215,455	1,846,317	...
Chuvash	1,117,419	1,104,445	1,469,766	1,335,154	1,694,351	...
Turkmen	763,940	745,859	1,001,585	996,527	1,525,284	1,514,980
Kirghiz	762,736	757,517	968,659	964,889	1,452,222	1,445,213
Latvian	141,703	116,002	1,399,539	1,360,282	1,429,844	1,390,162
Polish	782,334	362,904	1,380,282	641,601	1,667,523	...
Estonian	154,666	139,486	988,616	953,019	1,007,356	974,649
Gypsy	61,234	41,562	132,014	78,344	175,335	...

TABLE C-13   RELIGIOUS AFFILIATION: EASTERN EUROPE

Religious Affiliation	Albania Prewar[a]	Bulgaria 1934	Czechoslovakia 1930	GDR 1950	GDR 1964	Hungary 1930	Poland 1931	Romania 1930	Yugoslavia 1931	Yugoslavia 1953
TOTAL POPULATION	...	6,077,939	14,729,536	17,199,098	17,003,633	8,688,319	31,915,779	18,057,028	13,934,038	16,936,573
Percent	...	100.0%	100.0%	100.0%	100.0%	100.0%	100.0%	100.0%	100.0%	100.0%
Orthodox	...	5,128,890	145,598	...	...	39,839	3,762,484	13,108,227	6,785,501	6,984,686
Percent	20%	84.4%	1.0%	...	...	0.5%	11.8%	72.6%	48.7%	41.2%
Uniate	...	...	585,041[b]	...	...	201,093	3,336,164	1,427,391	44,608	...
Percent	...	...	4.0%	...	...	2.3%	10.5%	7.9%	0.3%	...
Roman Catholic	...	45,704	10,854,408[c]	1,907,711[d]	1,375,237	5,634,103	20,670,051[e]	1,234,151	5,217,847	5,370,760
Percent	10%	0.8%	73.7%	11.1%	8.1%	64.9%	64.8%	6.8%	37.4%	31.7%
Moslem	...	821,298	...	...	...	...	...	185,486	1,561,166	2,090,380
Percent	70%	13.5%	...	...	...	...	...	1.0%	11.2%	12.3%
Lutheran	...	...	884,752[f]	13,980,100	10,091,907	534,065	424,216	398,759	175,279	...
Percent	...	...	6.0%	81.3%[h]	59.4%	6.1%	1.3%	2.2%	1.3%	...
Calvinist	...	...	219,108[g]	...	...	1,813,162	33,295	710,706	55,890	...
Percent	...	...	1.5%	...	...	20.9%	0.1%	3.9%	0.4%	...
Unitarian	...	8,371 ▲	...	...	...	...	269,531	69,257	...	157,702 ▲
Percent	...	0.1%	...	...	...	...	0.8%	0.4%	...	0.9%
Methodist	...	...	7,361	[i]	...	...	...	...	...	...
Percent	...	...	0%	...	...	...	...	...	...	...
Sectarian Protestant	...	...	4,445[j]	111,152[k]	...	...	...	76,664[l]	...	...
Percent	...	...	0%	0.6%	...	...	...	0.4%	...	...
Other Christian Denominations	...	23,476[m]	815,367[n]	...	107,353	...	253,634	...	23,544	61,274
Percent	...	0.4%	5.5%	...	0.6%	...	0.8%	...	0.2%	0.4%
Jewish	...	48,398	356,830	1,334	...	444,567	3,113,933	756,930	68,405	2,565
Percent	...	0.8%	2.4%	0%	...	5.1%	9.8%	4.2%	0.5%	0%
Other Denominations	...	1,802	362	28,443[o]	12,322	21,490[p]	6,750	76,167[q]	1,798	495
Percent	...	0%	0%	0.2%	0.1%	0%	0%	0.4%	0%	0%
Without Religion	...	...	856,264 ▲	1,170,358	5,416,814	...	...	6,604	...	2,127,875
Percent	...	...	5.8%	6.8%	31.9%	...	...	0%	...	12.6%
Undetermined	...	...	...	...	...	...	45,721[r] ▲	6,686	...	140,836
Percent	...	...	...	...	...	...	0.1%	0%	...	0.8%
Unaccounted for	0	0	0	0	0	0	0	0	0	0
Percent	0%	0%	0%	0%	0%	0%	0%	0%	0%	0%

Notes: [a] Estimate. [b] Includes Armenian Catholics. [c] Includes 22,712 Old Catholics. [d] Includes 7,619 Catholics Free of Rome. [e] Includes Armenian Catholics. [f] Includes 297,977 Ceskobratrske, 46,884 Augsburg Evangelical, and 132,333 German Evangelical. [g] Reform Church in Ruthenia and Slovakia. [h] Protestant Reform. [i] Included with Sectarian Protestant. [j] Czechoslovak Baptists. [k] Includes 69,015 Apostolic and New Apostolic, 27,455 Methodists and Baptists, and 14,682 Adventists. [l] 60,562 Baptists and 16,602 Adventists. [m] Armenian-Georgian. [n] Includes 5,682 Jednoty Bratrske, 6,813 Jednoty Ceskobratrske, 1,597 Other Evangelical Denominations, 7,890 Other Christians, and 793,385 of the Czechoslovak Faith. [o] Includes 26,787 of undetermined religion and 1,656 Other Religions. [p] Includes Undetermined. [q] Includes 57,288 Lipovani, 10,005 of Armenian Georgian Faith, 1,440 Armenian Catholics, and 7,434 Others. [r] Includes 6,058 unknown and those without religion, and 39,663 for whom there is no data.

TABLE C-14   COMPARISON OF RELIGIOUS AFFILIATION AND LANGUAGE: BULGARIA,
1934

Native Tongue	Orthodox	Catholic	Protestant	Armenian-Georgian	Moslem	Jewish	Other
TOTAL	5,128,890	45,704	8,371	23,476	821,298	48,398	1,802
Percent	100.0%	100.0%	100.0%	100.0%	100.0%	100.0%	100.0%
Bulgarian	5,072,608	40,679	4,983	1,689	134,125	19,263	1,507
Percent	98.9%	89.0%	59.5%	7.2%	16.3%	39.8%	83.6%
Turk	2,713	11	7	416	615,115	6	...
Percent	0.1%	0.0%	0.1%	1.8%	74.9%	0.0%	...
Jewish	4	...	1	2	2	28,002	15
Percent	0.0%	...	0.0%	0.0%	0.0%	57.8%	0.8%
Armenian	1,438	121	141	21,335	...	8	2
Percent	0.0%	0.3%	1.7%	90.9%	...	0.0%	0.1%
Gypsy	13,323	...	69	...	67,103	...	37
Percent	0.2%	...	0.8%	...	8.2%	...	2.0%
Russian	11,456	85	80	20	7	151	129
Percent	0.2%	0.2%	0.9%	0.1%	0.0%	0.3%	7.2%
Greek	9,578	10	8	1	...	1	3
Percent	0.2%	0.0%	0.1%	0.0%	...	0.0%	0.2%
Tatar	...	...	...	...	4,377	...	...
Percent	...	...	...	...	0.5%	...	...
German	317	2,185	1,045	3	...	600	21
Percent	0.0%	4.8%	12.5%	0.0%	...	1.2%	1.2%
Romanian	16,305	18	16	2	18	46	...
Percent	0.3%	0.0%	0.2%	0.0%	0.0%	0.1%	...
Other	1,148	2,595	2,021	8	551	321	88
Percent	0.0%	5.7%	24.1%	0.0%	0.1%	0.7%	4.9%
Unaccounted for	0	0	0	0	0	0	0
Percent	0%	0%	0%	0%	0%	0%	0%

Hungary, 1930

Native Tongue	Catholic	Uniate	Calvinist	Lutheran	Other Protestant[a]	Jewish	Orthodox	Other
TOTAL	5,634,003	201,093	1,813,162	534,165	18,152	444,567	39,839	3,338
Percent	100.0%	100.0%	100.0%	100.0%	100.0%	100.0%	100.0%	100.0%
Hungarian	5,132,523	194,770	1,805,033	401,644	16,402	432,759	15,554	2,423
Percent	91.1%	96.8%	99.5%	75.2%	90.4%	97.3%	39.0%	72.6%
German	392,255	164	7,201	67,891	894	9,893	112	220
Percent	7.0%	0.1%	0.4%	12.7%	5.0%	2.2%	0.3%	6.6%
Slovak	38,574	1,254	263	63,858	308	378	110	74
Percent	0.7%	0.6%	0.0%	12.0%	1.7%	0.1%	0.3%	2.2%
Romanian	592	2,034	67	32	359	77	13,043	17
Percent	0.0%	1.0%	0.0%	0.0%	2.0%	0.0%	32.7%	0.5%
Croat	27,221	63	23	43	5	158	131	39
Percent	0.5%	0.0%	0.0%	0.0%	0.0%	0.0%	0.3%	1.2%
Gypsy	7,387	20	109	5	41	2	280	1
Percent	0.1%	0.0%	0.0%	0.0%	0.2%	0.0%	0.7%	0.0%
Other	35,451	2,788	466	692	143	1,300	10,609	564
Percent	0.6%	1.4%	0.0%	0.1%	0.8%	0.3%	26.6%	16.9%
Unaccounted for	0	0	0	0	0	0	0	0
Percent	0%	0%	0%	0%	0%	0%	0%	0%

Czechoslovakia, 1930

Ethnic Affiliation	Catholic[b]	Uniate	Protestant, All Denom.	Czechoslovak Church	Orthodox	Jewish	Other Christian	Non-Christian	No Relig. or Unknow
TOTAL	10,854,408	585,041	1,129,758	793,385	145,598	356,830	7,890	362	856,264
Percent	100.0%	100.0%	100.0%	100.0%	100.0%	100.0%	100.0%	100.0%	100.0%
Czech & Slovak	7,266,142	114,602	713,094	792,068	13,069	87,489	4,358	16	765,766
Percent	66.9%	19.6%	63.1%	99.8%	9.0%	24.5%	55.2%	4.4%	89.4%
German	3,025,139	385	159,318	656	146	45,732	1,862	9	85,198
Percent	27.9%	0.1%	14.1%	0.1%	0.1%	12.8%	23.6%	2.5%	9.9%
Ruthenian & Russian	8,877	425,280	1,539	314	128,841	1,086	869	57	2,078
Percent	0.1%	72.7%	0.1%	0.0%	88.5%	0.3%	11.0%	15.7%	0.2%
Hungarian	454,913	27,194	219,265	21	64	16,807	118	...	1,187
Percent	4.2%	4.6%	19.4%	0.0%	0.0%	4.7%	1.5%	...	0.1%
Jewish	12	...	4	...	1	204,427	...	...	335
Percent	0.0%	...	0.0%	...	0.0%	57.3%	...	...	0.0%
Polish	62,313	1,819	33,814	238	125	818	355	1	839
Percent	0.6%	0.3%	3.0%	0.0%	0.1%	0.2%	4.5%	0.0%	0.1%
Romanian	356	12,786	41	3	510	171	96	...	207
Percent	0.0%	2.2%	0.0%	0.0%	0.3%	0.0%	1.2%	...	0.0%
Gypsy	28,855	2,355	1,577	...	45	...	...	...	2
Percent	0.3%	0.4%	0.1%	...	0.0%	...	...	...	0.0%
Other	7,801	620	1,106	85	2,797	300	232	279	62
Percent	0.1%	0.1%	0.1%	0.0%	1.9%	0.1%	2.9%	77.1%	0.1%
Unaccounted for	0	0	0	0	0	0	0	0	0
Percent	0%	0%	0%	0%	0%	0%	0%	0%	0%

Notes: a Includes Unitarians, Baptists, and Nazareens.   b Includes Old Catholic.

TABLE C-16   COMPARISON OF RELIGIOUS AFFILIATION AND LANGUAGE: POLAND, 1931

Native Tongue	Catholic	Uniate	Orthodox	Lutheran	Calvinist	Unitarian	Other Christian	Jewish	Other Non-Christian	Unknown or No Data
TOTAL	20,670,051	3,336,164	3,762,484	424,216	33,295	269,531	253,634	3,113,933	6,750	45,721
Percent	100.0%	100.0%	100.0%	100.0%	100.0%	100.0%	100.0%	100.0%	100.0%	100.0%
Polish	20,333,333	487,034	497,290	131,861	12,385	40,983	88,912	371,821	4,410	25,415
Percent	98.4%	14.6%	13.2%	31.1%	37.2%	15.2%	35.1%	11.9%	65.3%	55.6%
Ukrainian	12,617	1,676,763	1,501,308	1,294	935	135	27,582	255	31	1,055
Percent	0.1%	50.3%	39.9%	0.3%	2.8%	0.0%	10.9%	0.0%	0.4%	2.3%
Ruthenian	12,914	1,163,749	38,754	80	68	24	3,063	292	84	619
Percent	0.1%	34.9%	1.0%	0.0%	0.2%	0.0%	1.2%	0.0%	1.2%	1.3%
"Tutejszy"	1,477	524	696,397	146	124	24	8,170	75	42	109
Percent	0.0%	0.0%	18.5%	0.0%	0.4%	0.0%	3.2%	0.0%	0.6%	0.2%
Belorussian	77,790	2,303	903,557	64	73	19	4,516	200	1,020	310
Percent	0.4%	0.0%	24.0%	0.0%	0.2%	0.0%	1.9%	0.0%	15.1%	0.7%
Jewish	...	...	...	...	...	...	...	2,731,371	...	1,202
Percent	...	...	...	...	...	...	...	87.7%	...	2.6%
German	118,470	284	64	289,188	14,283	227,572	83,764	6,827	8	532
Percent	0.6%	0.0%	0.0%	68.2%	42.9%	84.4%	33.0%	0.2%	0.1%	1.2%
Lithuanian	82,723	5	105	87	13	91	20	18	1	53
Percent	0.4%	0.0%	0.0%	0.0%	0.0%	0.0%	0.0%	0.0%	0.0%	0.1%
Russian	1,877	908	99,636	351	91	39	35,135	444	105	127
Percent	0.0%	0.0%	2.6%	0.0%	0.3%	0.0%	13.8%	0.0%	1.6%	0.3%
Czech	8,984	251	21,672	213	5,017	356	1,420	95	2	87
Percent	0.0%	0.0%	0.6%	0.0%	15.1%	0.1%	0.6%	0.0%	0.0%	0.2%
Gypsy	...	...	...	...	...	...	...	...	...	...
Percent	...	...	...	...	...	...	...	...	...	...
Other	6,088	581	1,157	586	294	58	715	454	940	246
Percent	0.0%	0.0%	0.0%	0.1%	0.9%	0.0%	0.3%	0.0%	13.9%	0.5%
Indetermined	13,778	3,762	2,544	346	12	230	337	2,081	107	15,966
Percent	0.1%	0.1%	0.1%	0.0%	0.0%	0.1%	0.1%	0.1%	1.6%	34.9%
Unaccounted for	0	5	0	0	0	0	0	0	0	0
Percent	0%	0%	0%	0%	0%	0%	0%	0%	0%	0%

TABLE C-17   COMPARISON OF RELIGIOUS AFFILIATION AND ETHNIC AFFILIATION OR
LANGUAGE: YUGOSLAVIA, 1931-1953

1931

Native Tongue	Orthodox	Catholic	Moslem	Uniate	Protest.[a]	Jewish	Other[b]
TOTAL POPULATION	6,785,501	5,217,847	1,561,166	44,608	231,169	68,405	25,342
Percent	100.0%	100.0%	100.0%	100.0%	100.0%	100.0%	100.0%
Serbo-Croatian	6,577,398	3,186,295	908,167	13,944	4,224	26,896	13,899
Percent	96.9%	61.1%	58.2%	31.3%	1.8%	39.3%	54.8%
Slovenian	1,842	1,110,063	22	124	22,318	359	682
Percent	0.0%	21.3%	0.0%	0.0%	9.7%	0.5%	2.7%
Albanian	1,688	21,785	481,770	15	0	0	1
Percent	0.0%	0.4%	30.9%	0.0%	0.0%	0.0%	0.0%
Hungarian	2,271	410,350	34	347	39,996	11,170	4,017
Percent	0.0%	7.9%	0.0%	0.8%	17.3%	16.3%	15.9%
Turkish	102	28	132,781	0	0	11	0
Percent	0.0%	0.0%	8.5%	0.0%	0.0%	0.0%	0.0%
Romanian[c]	134,795	1,320	76	568	15	184	921
Percent	2.0%	0.0%	0.0%	1.3%	0.0%	0.3%	3.6%
Czech & Slovak	1,775	60,960	14	215	63,475	675	2,206
Percent	0.0%	1.2%	0.0%	0.5%	27.5%	1.0%	8.7%
German	3,220	383,674	36	115	100,806	10,026	2,092
Percent	0.0%	7.4%	0.0%	0.3%	43.6%	14.7%	8.3%
Russian & Ukrainian	34,680	1,957	44	26,685	103	228	317
Percent	0.5%	0.0%	0.0%	59.8%	0.0%	0.3%	1.3%
Jewish	28	16	0	0	0	17,998	2
Percent	0.0%	0.0%	0.0%	0.0%	0.0%	26.3%	0.0%
Gypsy	20,688	11,957	37,715	32	0	0	32
Percent	0.3%	0.2%	2.4%	0.1%	0.0%	0.0%	0.1%
Other Language	7,014	29,442	507	2,561	232	858	1,173
Percent	0.1%	0.6%	0%	5.7%	0.1%	1.3%	4.6%

1953

Ethnic Affiliation	Orthodox	Catholic	Moslem	Protest.	Jewish	Atheist[d]	Other
TOTAL POPULATION	6,984,686	5,370,760	2,090,380	157,702	2,565	2,137,971	192,509
Percent	100.0%	100.0%	100.0%	100.0%	100.0%	100.0%	100.0%
Serb	5,840,324	8,813	56,871	7,171	220	1,122,411	30,113
Percent	83.6%	0.2%	2.7%	4.5%	8.6%	52.5%	15.6%
Croat	9,215	3,487,773	19,986	7,904	693	409,858	40,121
Percent	0.1%	64.9%	1.0%	5.0%	27.0%	19.2%	20.8%
Slovene	3,010	1,236,813	186	20,494	53	154,983	71,561
Percent	0.0%	23.0%	0.0%	13.0%	2.1%	7.2%	37.2%
Macedonian	730,235	2,654	12,863	1,444	5	143,006	3,040
Percent	10.5%	0.0%	0.6%	0.9%	0.2%	6.7%	1.6%
Montenegrin	218,938	4,709	56,537	95	1	184,813	1,000
Percent	3.1%	0.1%	2.7%	0.1%	0.0%	8.6%	0.5%
Moslem	2,550	19,288	935,081	253	193	39,661	1,672
Percent	0.0%	0.4%	44.7%	0.2%	7.5%	1.9%	0.9%
Other Slavs	58,023	49,089	88	68,642	36	24,614	35,500
Percent	0.8%	0.9%	0.0%	43.5%	1.4%	1.2%	18.4%
Other Non-Slavs	122,391	561,621	1,008,768	51,699	1,364	58,625	9,502
Percent	1.8%	10.5%	48.3%	32.8%	53.2%	2.7%	4.9%

Notes: a Includes Lutherans and Reform Protestants. b Includes other Christians and
Others. c Includes Romanians and Vlachs. d Includes those without religion
and those "Undetermined, Indifferent."

166

SECTION D: EDUCATIONAL ATTAINMENT

Introduction

Table D-1   For Albania, the criteria for measuring illiteracy are not known. For Bulgaria, illiterates include, for 1956, those who can neither read nor write; those who can read but not write are included among the literate population. For all other years, illiterates are those who can neither read nor write, or read but not write. For comments on the reliability of the data on Albania, see the General Introduction.

Table D-2   Illiterates include those who can neither read nor write; those who can read but not write are included among the literate population. Those who can write but not read are considered illiterate.

Table D-3   See the remarks on Table D-2.

Table D-4   Illiterates include those who can neither read nor write; those who can read but not write are included among the literate population. Those who can write but not read are considered illiterate. For comments on the reliability of the data on Romania, see the General Introduction.

Table D-6   For 1931 and 1948, illiterates include those who can neither read nor write; those who can read but not write are included among the literate population. For all other years, illiterates include those who can read but not write, or write but not read. For comments on the reliability of the data on Yugoslavia, see the General Introduction.

Table D-8   Data for 1934 and 1946 exclude illiterates, who must be added to the totals for these years from Table D-1 in order to make the data comparable with those for later years. Data for Higher, Lower Level, Complete are for persons in the category "Semi-Higher" (see Appendix 4). Data on this group are given for 1956. For 1934, Series I; 1946, Series I; and for 1965 data on Higher, Lower Level, Complete are included with data on persons with a secondary education. For 1934 and 1946, Series II, it is not possible to determine in which group the data on persons with a semi-higher education were placed. Series I and Series II are comparable for 7-8 Year Basic Complete, Trade School, and Incomplete Secondary only.

Table D-9   For data on Czechoslovakia, see the remarks on Table D-14. For the GDR, see the remarks on Table D-16.

Table D-10   In the case of Hungary, data on Incomplete Higher for 1960 and 1970 include persons who did not receive a university diploma, including those who received only a university certificate (*Vegbizonyitvanyt*) and others who completed only several years of university education. For 1941 and 1949, data on Incomplete Higher refer only to those who received the university certificate but not the diploma, while those who began their university education, but ceased their studies after several years and received neither the certificate nor diploma, are included with lower levels of education.

Table D-11   For Poland, data for Higher, Lower Level, Complete are for persons with a post-secondary technical or *policealne* education. Data on this group are included with data on persons having a secondary education for 1960, and in the category of Higher, Lower Level Complete, for 1970. For the Soviet Union, those in the category Unaccounted for should have a level of education which is the same as the total of the categories for which no data are given (for 1959 and 1970, Without Schooling and 4 Year Elementary Incomplete). For an explanation of fn. *b*, see Appendix 11 and the General Introduction.

Table D-12   See the remarks on Table D-25.

Table D-13   Data for Higher, Lower Level, Complete are for persons in the category "Semi-Higher" (see Appendix 4).

Table D-14   It is assumed in this table that data on those with a basic education include persons with lower levels of education (7-8 Year Basic Incomplete, 4 Year Elementary Complete and Incomplete). Series I and Series II differ in the following respects: data on those with Trade School are shown in Series I but not in Series II; in Series II, a number of persons having a Specialized Secondary, Higher Level, education (*Vysshi odborna skola*) are classified as receiving a higher education.

Table D-16   Data for those with a Higher, Specialized Secondary Education are for those with *Fachschule* training. It is assumed here that persons graduating from lower level specialized secondary schools are not included in the data.

Table D-17 Data on Higher Education include those who received a university certificate but did not receive a university diploma, as well as those who received a diploma.

Table D-18 See the remarks for Table D-17.

Table D-19 Data on Incomplete Higher include persons receiving a university certificate.

Table D-20 *Policealne*, or post-secondary technical education, is here classified as Higher Education, Lower Level, Complete.

Table D-21 See the remarks for Table D-20.

Table D-24 See the remarks for Table D-11 on the Soviet Union.

Table D-25 Data on educational attainment for 1948 measure highest level of education taken but not necessarily completed, and with the exception of Higher Education, are not comparable with data for later years. Data on Higher Education for 1948 measure level of education completed, and can be compared, with caution, with the data for later years.

Table D-26 For 1971, those temporarily abroad are excluded.

TABLE D-1   NUMBER OF ILLITERATES IN POPULATION: ALBANIA AND BULGARIA

Albania

Age	1945 Total	1945 Female	1950 Total	1950 Female	1955 Total	1955 Female
TOTAL POPULATION						
9 & OVER[a]	...	...	[921,000]	[451,000]	[1,035,000]	[507,000]
Percent	100.0%	100.0%	100.0%	100.0%	100.0%	100.0%
No. Illiterate	...	...	[496,000]	[302,000]	[293,000]	[187,000]
Percent	75.4%	86.0%	53.8%	67.0%	28.3%	36.9%
Urban Population						
9 & over[a]	...	...	...	...	[291,000]	[131,000]
Percent	...	...	...	...	100.0%	100.0%
No. Illiterate	...	...	...	...	[49,500]	[34,000]
Percent	...	...	...	...	17.0%	25.6%
Rural Population						
9 & over[a]	...	...	...	...	[743,000]	[376,000]
Percent	...	...	...	...	100.0%	100.0%
No. Illiterate	...	...	...	...	[243,000]	[153,000]
Percent	...	...	...	...	32.7%	40.8%

Bulgaria

Age	1934 Total	1934 Female	1946 Total	1946 Female	1956 Total	1956 Female	1965 Total	1965 Female
TOTAL POPULATION								
8 & OVER	4,942,000	2,467,000	6,008,000	3,012,000	6,495,229	3,266,860	7,211,375	3,618,343
Percent	100.0%	100.0%	100.0%	100.0%	100.0%	100.0%	100.0%	100.0%
No. Illiterate	1,559,000	1,055,000	1,381,000	947,000	850,105	633,143	594,959[b]	449,890[b]
Percent	31.5%	42.8%	23.0%	31.4%	13.1%	19.4%	8.3%	12.4%
Urban Population								
8 & over	1,118,000	551,000	1,511,000	737,000	2,191,021	1,100,844	...	...
Percent	100.0%	100.0%	100.0%	100.0%	100.0%	100.0%	...	...
No. Illiterate	213,000	145,000	200,000	135,000	156,382	113,422	...	...
Percent	19.1%	26.3%	13.2%	18.3%	7.1%	10.3%	...	...
Rural Population								
8 & over	3,824,000	1,916,000	4,497,000	2,275,000	4,304,208	2,166,016	...	...
Percent	100.0%	100.0%	100.0%	100.0%	100.0%	100.0%	...	...
No. Illiterate	1,346,000	910,000	1,181,000	812,000	693,723	519,721	...	...
Percent	35.2%	47.5%	26.3%	35.7%	16.1%	24.0%	...	...
TOTAL POPULATION								
15 & OVER	3,918,997	1,966,332	5,070,067	2,552,509	5,591,453	2,822,465	6,115,502	3,081,918
Percent	100.0%	100.0%	100.0%	100.0%	100.0%	100.0%	100.0%	100.0%
No. Illiterate	1,377,246	963,725	1,229,064	870,906	822,056	618,819	584,863[b]	444,814[b]
Percent	35.1%	49.0%	24.2%	34.1%	14.7%	21.9%	9.6%	14.4%
Urban Population								
15 & over	...	...	...	...	1,896,880	954,947	...	...
Percent	...	...	...	...	100.0%	100.0%	100.0%	100.0%
No. Illiterate	...	...	...	...	147,080	108,570	153,571[c]	115,930[c]
Percent	...	...	...	...	7.8%	11.4%	5.2%	7.8%
Rural Population								
15 & over	...	...	...	...	3,694,573	1,867,518	...	...
Percent	...	...	...	...	100.0%	100.0%	100.0%	100.0%
No. Illiterate	...	...	...	...	674,976	510,249	460,372[c]	348,257[c]
Percent	...	...	...	...	18.3%	27.3%	13.8%	20.7%

Notes: For notes see next page.

TABLE D-1   (CONCLUDED)

Notes: <u>a</u> Estimate.   <u>b</u> Excludes semi-literates.   <u>c</u> Total of urban and rural illiterate exceeds total of all illiterate by 29,080; total of urban and rural female illiterate exceeds total of all female illiterate by 19,373.

Notes: <u>a</u> Estimate.   <u>b</u> Excludes semi-literates.   <u>c</u> Total of urban and rural illiterate exceeds total of all illiterate by 29,080; total of urban and rural female illiterate exceeds total of all female illiterate by 19,373.

e	1930 Total	1930 Female	1941 Total	1941 Female	1949 Total	1949 Female	1960 Total	1960 Female	1970[a] Total	1970[a] Female
AL POPULATION										
OVER	7,451,251	3,825,471	8,225,493	4,216,971	8,095,733	4,236,840	8,737,124	4,560,205	9,366,046	4,855,070
ercent	100.0%	100.0%	100.0%	100.0%	100.0%	100.0%	100.0%	100.0%	100.0%	100.0%
No. Illiterate	667,902	408,733	511,682	306,068	399,708	234,208	331,886	190,851	224,208	131,218
Percent	9.0%	10.7%	6.2%	7.3%	4.9%	5.5%	3.8%	4.2%	2.4%	2.7%
ban Population										
& over	...	...	...	...	2,991,498	1,609,758	3,535,889	1,867,138	4,272,471	2,258,492
ercent	...	...	...	...	100.0%	100.0%	100.0%	100.0%	100.0%	100.0%
No. Illiterate	...	...	...	...	88,548	57,152	82,273	49,250	62,766	38,064
Percent	...	...	...	...	3.0%	3.6%	2.3%	2.6%	1.5%	1.7%
ral Population										
& over	...	...	...	...	5,104,235	2,627,082	5,201,235	2,693,067	5,093,575	2,596,578
ercent	...	...	...	...	100.0%	100.0%	100.0%	100.0%	100.0%	100.0%
No. Illiterate	...	...	...	...	311,160	177,056	249,613	141,601	161,442	93,154
Percent	...	...	...	...	6.1%	6.7%	4.8%	5.3%	3.2%	3.6%
TAL POPULATION										
& OVER	6,292,864	3,253,320	6,895,673	3,557,358	6,914,709	3,652,570	7,431,591	3,918,517	8,145,592	4,261,343
ercent	100.0%	100.0%	100.0%	100.0%	100.0%	100.0%	100.0%	100.0%	100.0%	100.0%
No. Illiterate	630,276	389,798	437,356	269,720	322,342	197,361	231,910	142,867	163,768	102,603
Percent	10.0%	12.0%	6.3%	7.6%	4.7%	5.4%	3.1%	3.6%	2.0%	2.4%
ban Population										
& over	...	...	...	...	...	...	...	...	3,808,185	2,031,993
ercent	...	...	...	...	...	...	...	...	100.0%	100.0%
No. Illiterate	...	...	...	...	...	...	...	...	41,643	27,847
Percent	...	...	...	...	...	...	...	...	1.1%	1.4%
ral Population										
& over	...	...	...	...	...	...	...	...	4,337,407	2,229,350
ercent	...	...	...	...	...	...	...	...	100.0%	100.0%
No. Illiterate	...	...	...	...	...	...	...	...	122,125	74,756
Percent	...	...	...	...	...	...	...	...	2.8%	3.4%

te: a Those without schooling.

TABLE D-3   NUMBER OF ILLITERATES IN POPULATION: POLAND , 1931-1970

Age	1931 Total	1931 Female	1950[a] Total	1950[a] Female	1960[a] Total	1960[a] Female	1970 Total	1970 Female
TOTAL POPULATION								
10 & OVER	23,966,870	12,564,523	...	...	24,592,856	12,994,413	...	...
Percent	100.0%	100.0%	100.0%	100.0%	100.0%	100.0%	...	...
No. Illiterate	5,543,670	3,509,255	1,131,136	733,868	664,000	448,600	...	...
Percent	23.1%	28.0%	5.8%	6.9%	2.7%	3.5%	...	...
Urban Population								
10 & over	6,961,767	3,756,202	...	...	...	...	...	...
Percent	100.0%	100.0%	100.0%	100.0%	...	...	...	...
No. Illiterate	850,532	563,905	246,116	174,933	...	...	...	...
Percent	12.2%	15.0%	3.2%	4.1%	...	...	...	...
Rural Population								
10 & over	17,005,103	8,808,321	...	...	...	...	...	...
Percent	100.0%	100.0%	100.0%	100.0%	...	...	...	...
No. Illiterate	4,693,138	2,945,350	885,000	558,935	...	...	...	...
Percent	27.6%	33.4%	7.1%	8.6%	...	...	...	...
TOTAL POPULATION								
15 & OVER	21,189,685	11,192,123	17,789,603	9,702,055	23,756,000	12,421,000	23,994,081	12,559,889
Percent	100.0%	100.0%	100.0%	100.0%	100.0%	100.0%	100.0%	100.0%
No. Illiterate	5,360,313	3,407,362	1,110,423	723,864	656,405[b]	445,136[b]	414,677	287,965
Percent	25.3%	30.4%	6.2%	7.5%	2.8%	3.6%	1.7%	2.3%
Urban Population								
15 & over	...	...	6,704,900	[3,600,000][c]	11,503,000	...	13,069,559	...
Percent	...	...	100.0%	100.0%	100.0%	...	100.0%	...
No. Illiterate	835,151	...	241,402	172,593	172,564	...	117,796[d]	d
Percent	4.0%	...	3.6%	[4.8%][c]	1.5%	...	0.9%	d
Rural Population								
15 & over	...	...	10,823,900	[6,000,000][c]	11,883,000	...	10,945,235	...
Percent	...	...	100.0%	100.0%	100.0%	...	100.0%	...
No. Illiterate	4,525,162	...	869,021	551,271	483,841	...	296,881[d]	d
Percent	21.3%	...	8.0%	[9.2%][c]	4.1%	...	2.7%	d

Notes: a Data relate to population and to illiterates 10 and over and 14 and over. b Among those 15 and over, 536,708 were illiterate (2.2% of those 15 and over); among females 15 and over, 392,193 were illiterate (3.1% of those 15 and over). c Estimates. d Data conflict. UN sources give the number of urban illiterates 15 and over as 156,581; female urban illiterates 15 and over as 122,136; total rural illiterates, 15 and over as 380,568; and female rural illiterates 15 and over as 270,246.

TABLE D-4   NUMBER OF ILLITERATES IN POPULATION: ROMANIA, 1930-1956

Age	1930[a] Total	1930[a] Female	1930[b] Total	1930[b] Female	1948 Total	1948 Female	1956[c] Total	1956[c] Female	1956 Total	1956 Female
TOTAL POPULATION										
7 & OVER	14,524,878	7,419,715	...	...	13,862,816	7,236,014	14,566,957	7,554,798	...	...
Percent	100.0%	100.0%	100.0%	100.0%	100.0%	100.0%	100.0%	100.0%	...	...
No. Illiterate	6,200,568	4,023,438	...	...	3,197,278[d]	2,236,476[d]	1,472,082	1,089,803	...	...
Percent	42.9%	54.5%	38.9%	50.4%	23.1%	30.9%	10.1%	14.4%	...	...
Urban Population										
7 & over	3,161,992	1,593,362	...	...	...	...	4,735,165	2,428,311	...	...
Percent	100.0%	100.0%	100.0%	100.0%	100.0%	100.0%	100.0%	100.0%	...	...
No. Illiterate	710,518	469,851	...	...	...	...	309,061	235,508	...	...
Percent	22.6%	29.7%	20.5%	27.3%	10.7%	15.3%	6.5%	9.7%	...	...
Rural Population										
7 & over	11,362,886	5,826,353	...	...	...	...	9,831,792	5,126,187	...	...
Percent	100.0%	100.0%	100.0%	100.0%	100.0%	100.0%	100.0%	100.0%	...	...
No. Illiterate	5,490,050	3,553,587	...	...	...	...	1,163,021	854,295	...	...
Percent	48.5%	61.3%	44.4%	57.2%	27.0%	35.9%	11.8%	16.7%	...	...
TOTAL POPULATION										
15 & OVER	12,307,641	6,336,123	...	...	...	...	12,936,349	6,752,549	12,675,836	6,623,777
Percent	100.0%	100.0%	...	...	...	...	100.0%	100.0%	100.0%	100.0%
No. Illiterate	5,605,000	3,680,000	...	...	...	...	1,452,388	1,079,577	1,448,386	1,077,460
Percent	45.5%	58.1%	...	...	...	...	11.2%	16.0%	11.4%	16.3%
Urban Population										
15 & over	...	...	...	...	...	...	...	...	...	...
Percent	...	...	...	...	...	...	100.0%	100.0%	...	...
No. Illiterate	...	...	...	...	...	...	303,994	232,836	...	...
Percent	...	...	...	...	...	...	...	...	...	...
Rural Population										
15 & over	...	...	...	...	...	...	...	...	...	...
Percent	...	...	...	...	...	...	100.0%	100.0%	...	...
No. Illiterate	...	...	...	...	...	...	1,148,394	846,741	...	...
Percent	...	...	...	...	...	...	...	...	...	...

Notes: [a] Prewar boundaries. [b] Postwar boundaries. [c] Data relate to population and illiterates 8 and over and 14 and over. [d] Provisional data.

173

TABLE D-5 NUMBER OF ILLITERATES IN POPULATION, USSR, 1926-1979

Age	1926[a] Total	1926[a] Female	1939[b] Total	1939[b] Female	1939[c] Total	1939[c] Female	1959 Total	1959 Female	1970 Total	1970 Female	1979 Total	1979 Female
TOTAL POPULATION												
9 & OVER	111,621,633	58,377,276	...	...	...	...	...	...	...	...	...	...
Percent	100.0%	100.0%	100.0%	100.0%	100.0%	100.0%	...	...	...	...	...	...
No. Illiterate	54,517,644	36,709,288	...	...	...	...	...	...	...	...	...	...
Percent	48.8%	62.9%	18.8%	27.5%	12.6%	18.4%	...	...	...	...	...	...
Urban Population												
9 & over	21,423,720	10,986,573	...	...	...	...	...	...	...	...	...	...
Percent	100.0%	100.0%	100.0%	100.0%	100.0%	100.0%	...	...	...	...	...	...
No. Illiterate	5,003,504	3,557,313	...	...	...	...	...	...	...	...	...	...
Percent	23.3%	32.4%	10.5%	16.1%	6.2%	9.3%	...	...	...	...	...	...
Rural Population												
9 & over	90,197,913	47,390,703	...	...	...	...	...	...	...	...	...	...
Percent	100.0%	100.0%	100.0%	100.0%	100.0%	100.0%	...	...	...	...	...	...
No. Illiterate	49,514,140	33,151,975	...	...	...	...	...	...	...	...	...	...
Percent	54.9%	70.0%	23.3%	33.5%	16.0%	23.2%	...	...	...	...	...	...
TOTAL POPULATION												
9-49 YRS.	92,581,505	47,882,135	...	...	...	...	...	...	...	...	...	...
Percent	100.0%	100.0%	100.0%	100.0%	100.0%	100.0%	100.0%	100.0%	100.0%	100.0%	100.0%	100.0%
No. Illiterate	40,152,845	27,414,035	...	...	...	...	1,929,000	66,720	...	...	...	...
Percent	43.4%	57.3%	10.9%	16.6%	...	...	1.5%	2.2%	0.3%	0.3%	0.2%	0.2%
Urban Population												
9-49 Yrs.	18,267,398	9,173,323	...	...	...	...	...	...	...	...	...	...
Percent	100.0%	100.0%	100.0%	100.0%	100.0%	100.0%	100.0%	100.0%	100.0%	100.0%	100.0%	100.0%
No. Illiterate	3,488,310	2,395,321	...	...	...	...	...	...	...	...	...	...
Percent	19.1%	26.1%	5.8%	9.0%	...	...	1.3%	1.9%	0.2%	0.2%	0.1%	0.1%
Rural Population												
9-49 Yrs.	74,314,107	38,708,812	...	...	...	...	...	...	...	...	...	...
Percent	100.0%	100.0%	100.0%	100.0%	100.0%	100.0%	100.0%	100.0%	100.0%	100.0%	100.0%	100.0%
No. Illiterate	36,664,535	25,018,714	...	...	...	...	...	...	...	...	...	...
Percent	49.3%	64.6%	13.7%	20.8%	...	...	1.8%	2.5%	0.5%	0.6%	0.3%	0.3%

Notes: a Excludes those of unknown age. b 1939 boundaries. c Postwar boundaries.

TABLE D-6 NUMBER OF ILLITERATES IN POPULATION: YUGOSLAVIA, 1931–1971

Age	1931 Total	1931 Female	1948 Total	1948 Female	1953 Total	1953 Female	1961 Total	1961 Female	1971 Total	1971 Female
TOTAL POPULATION										
10 & OVER	9,882,547 [a]	5,053,803 [a]	12,438,502	6,554,121	13,381,106	6,991,793	14,611,391	7,581,144	16,895,893 [b]	8,674,877 [c]
Percent	100.0%	100.0%	100.0%	100.0%	100.0%	100.0%	100.0%	100.0%	100.0%	100.0%
No. Illiterate	4,408,471 [a]	2,850,540 [a]	3,162,941	2,256,279	3,404,429	2,506,475	3,066,165	2,292,980	2,549,571 [d]	1,929,710 [e]
Percent	44.6%	56.4%	25.4%	34.4%	25.4%	35.8%	21.0%	30.2%	15.1%	22.2%
Urban Population										
10 & over	...	...	...	...	...	...	...	...	5,853,784	3,021,149
Percent	...	...	100.0%	100.0%	...	...	...	...	100.0%	100.0%
No. Illiterate	...	...	211,091	156,168	...	...	...	...	405,128	314,302
Percent	...	...	9.9%	14.0%	...	...	...	...	6.8%	10.4%
Rural Population										
10 & over	...	...	...	...	...	...	...	...	10,889,992	5,548,559
Percent	...	...	100.0%	100.0%	...	...	...	...	100.0%	100.0%
No. Illiterate	...	...	2,951,850	2,100,111	...	...	...	...	2,147,486	1,610,630
Percent	...	...	28.6%	38.6%	...	...	...	...	19.7%	27.2%
TOTAL POPULATION										
15 & OVER	9,108,791	4,678,651	10,639,630	5,670,548	11,776,494	6,204,836	12,778,461	6,684,014	15,022,717	7,760,740
Percent	100.0%	100.0%	100.0%	100.0%	100.0%	100.0%	100.0%	100.0%	100.0%	100.0%
No. Illiterate	4,150,375	2,688,371	2,884,014	2,078,246	3,192,582	2,368,283	2,880,860	2,185,575	2,478,207	1,887,992
Percent	45.6%	57.5%	27.1%	36.6%	27.1%	38.2%	22.5%	32.7%	16.5%	24.3%
Urban Population										
15 & over	...	...	...	...	...	...	...	...	...	...
Percent	...	...	...	...	...	...	...	...	100.0%	100.0%
No. Illiterate	...	...	...	...	...	...	...	...	461,816	362,912
Percent	...	...	...	...	...	...	...	...	7.7%	11.6%
Rural Population										
15 & over	...	...	...	...	...	...	...	...	...	...
Percent	...	...	...	...	...	...	...	...	100.0%	100.0%
No. Illiterate	...	...	...	...	...	...	...	...	2,016,391	1,525,080
Percent	...	...	...	...	...	...	...	...	22.3%	32.8%

Notes: a 11 years and over. b Total of urban and rural population 10 and over 152,117 less than total population 10 and over. c Total of female urban and rural population 10 and over 105,169 less than total population 10 and over. d Total of urban and rural illiterate 10 and over exceed total illiterate 10 and over by 3,043. e Total of urban and rural female illiterate 10 and over 4,778 less than total female illiterate 10 and over.

TABLE D-7   LEVEL OF EDUCATION OF POPULATION 25 YEARS AND OVER IN CENSUS YEARS: EASTERN EUROPE AND THE USSR

Country, Census	Population 25 & Over	No Educ.	4 Yr. Inc.	4 Yr. Comp.	7-8 Yr. Inc.	7-8 Yr. Comp.	Inc. Second.	Gen. Second.	Special. Second.	Inc. High.	Comp. High.
1950s											
Bulgaria (1956)	4,369,429	770,219	456,176		1,722,012	942,219			337,258		141,545
Percent	100.0%	17.6%	10.4%		39.4%	21.6%			7.7%		3.2%
Hungary (1949)	5,355,014	304,807	387,783	1,113,882	2,647,559	517,703	96,398		183,298		103,584
Percent	100.0%	5.7%	7.2%	20.8%	49.4%	9.7%	1.8%		3.4%		1.9%
Romania (1956)	9,496,767	1,342,198	576,987		6,559,035	428,328			387,150		203,069
Percent	100.0%	14.1%	6.1%		69.1%	4.5%			4.1%		2.1%
Yugo. (1953)[a]	8,295,131	3,179,055	645,315	2,428,300	1,121,182	587,398	...	100,834	123,557	...	77,826
Percent	100.0%	38.3%	7.8%	29.3%	13.5%	7.1%		1.2%	1.5%		0.9%
USSR (1959)[b]	110,304,248	...	...		32,508,933	17,924,350	...	4,417,433	5,842,009	1,083,435	3,515,307
Percent	100.0%				29.5%	16.2%		4.0%	5.3%	1.0%	3.2%
1960s											
Bulgaria (1965)[c]	5,993,328	595,918	469,842		1,677,794	1,443,410		326,191	237,343	...	211,985
Percent	100.0%	9.9%	7.8%		28.0%	24.1%		5.4%	4.0%		3.5%
Czech. (1961)[d]	8,054,652	62,877			6,655,874			155,588	947,210	...	190,630
Percent	100.0%	0.8%			82.6%			1.9%	11.7%		2.4%
GDR (1964)	10,845,077	...	...		...	...	...	...	339,698[e]	...	201,956
Percent	100.0%								3.1%		1.9%
Hungary (1960)	5,998,432	223,725	375,263	983,782	2,941,503	883,096	127,127	...	294,810	...	169,126
Percent	100.0%	3.7%	6.3%	16.4%	49.0%	14.7%	2.1%		4.9%		2.8%
Poland (1960)[f]	15,594,000				8,073,000	5,570,000			1,548,000		398,000
Percent	100.0%				51.8%	35.7%			9.9%		2.6%
Romania (1966)	11,260,095				9,207,249	987,358		355,182	401,977		308,329
Percent	100.0%				81.8%	8.8%		3.2%	3.6%		2.7%
Yugo. (1961)[a]	9,801,179	3,123,418	656,374	3,228,913	1,132,143	1,131,029	...	96,017	233,728	...	186,018
Percent	100.0%	31.9%	6.7%	32.9%	11.5%	11.6%		1.0%	2.4%		1.9%
1970s											
Czech. (1970)[a]	8,530,683	37,132			6,448,664			216,276	1,384,813	11,846	344,787
Percent	100.0%	0.4%			75.6%			2.5%	16.2%	0.1%	4.0%
GDR (1971)	10,809,462	...	...		9,223,949[g]	...	144,651	34,625	1,067,316	...	338,921
Percent	100.0%				85.3%		1.3%	0.3%	9.9%		3.1%
Hungary (1970)	6,463,900	146,000	312,100	799,500	2,530,100	1,627,300	183,300	...	537,300	48,800	279,500
Percent	100.0%	2.3%	4.8%	12.4%	39.1%	25.2%	2.8%		8.3%	0.7%	4.3%
Poland (1970)[b]	17,559,467	912,667		4,436,379		8,794,464	514,885		1,830,014	149,724	791,571
Percent	100.0%	5.2%		25.3%		50.2%	3.6%		10.4%	0.8%	4.5%
Yugo. (1971)[a]	11,191,167	2,668,726	636,847	3,644,660	987,767	2,158,006	...	152,907	476,819	...	168,040
Percent	100.0%	23.8%	5.7%	32.6%	8.8%	19.2%		1.4%	4.3%		1.5%

Notes: [a] Persons of unknown age and unknown level of education excluded from columns on levels of education.   [b] Persons of unknown age and persons unaccounted for excluded from columns on levels of education.   [c] Persons unaccounted for excluded from columns on levels of education.   [d] Persons with unknown level of education excluded from columns on levels of education.   [e] Fachschule only.   [f] Data derived from percents.   [g] Of whom, 3,917,126 (36.2%) were graduates of trade schools.

TABLE D-8   LEVEL OF EDUCATION OF POPULATION OVER A GIVEN AGE IN CENSUS
            YEARS: BULGARIA, 1934-1965

Level of Education	1934[a] I	1934[a] II	1946[a] I	1946[a] II	1956	1965 I
POPULATION 8 & OVER	3,381,512	3,383,000	4,627,497	4,627,000	6,495,229	7,211,395
Percent	100.0%	100.0%	100.0%	100.0%	100.0%	100.0%
Without Schooling					850,105[b]	619,420[b]
Percent					13.1%	8.6%
4 Yr. Element. Inc.		1,020,000		956,000	973,184	
Percent		30.1%		20.7%	15.0%	
4 Yr. Element. Comp.	2,753,435		3,169,448			3,214,885
Percent	81.4%		68.5%			44.6%
7-8 Yr. Basic Inc.		1,139,000		2,203,000	2,367,812	
Percent		33.7%		47.6%	36.4%	
7-8 Yr. Basic Comp.						
Percent						
Trade School	443,113	867,000	1,125,410	1,125,000	1,616,225	2,311,137
Percent	13.1%	25.6%	24.3%	24.3%	24.9%	32.0%
Inc. Second.						
Percent						
General Second. Comp.						
Percent						
Specialized Second., Lower Level						
Percent						
Specialized Second., Higher Level	133,111	280,000	276,694	277,000	530,061	894,890
Percent	3.9%	8.3%	6.0%	6.0%	8.2%	12.5%
Inc. Higher						
Percent						
Higher, Lower Level, Comp.		...		...	45,336	
Percent		...		...	0.7%	
Higher, Faculty Level, Comp.	33,031	57,000	55,238	55,000	112,506	171,063
Percent	1.0%	1.7%	1.2%	1.2%	1.7%	2.4%
Unknown	...	20,000	...	9,000	...	...
Percent	...	0.6%	...	0.2%	...	...
Unaccounted for	18,822	0	707	2,000	0	0
Percent	0.5%	0%	0%	0%	0%	0%

Notes: a Excludes illiterates. b Illiterates and semi-literates.

TABLE D-9   LEVEL OF EDUCATION OF POPULATION IN CENSUS YEARS:
CZECHOSLOVAKIA AND GDR

Level of Education	Czechoslovakia - 15 Yrs. & Over			GDR - 25 Yrs. & Over	
	1950	1961	1970	1964	1971
POPULATION	9,204,900	10,002,500	11,030,375	10,845,077	10,809,462
Percent	100.0%	100.0%	100.0%	100.0%	100.0%
Without Schooling	63,000	68,540	41,571	...	
Percent	0.7%	0.7%	0.4%	...	
4 Yr. Element. Inc.				...	
Percent				...	
4 Yr. Element. Comp.				...	5,306,823
Percent				...	49.1%
7-8 Yr. Basic Inc.			6,166,175	...	
Percent			55.9%	...	
7-8 Yr. Basic Comp.	7,943,600	8,185,422		...	
Percent	86.3%	81.8%		...	
Trade School			2,227,920	...	3,917,126
Percent			20.2%	...	36.2%
Inc. Second.			...	...	144,651
Percent			...	...	1.3%
General Second. Comp.	172,700	280,732	393,610	...	34,625
Percent	1.9%	2.8%	3.6%	...	0.3%
Specialized Second., Lower Level	603,500	651,914	640,703	...	419,482
Percent	6.6%	6.5%	5.8%	...	3.9%
Specialized Second., Higher Level	238,300	560,069	1,068,801	339,698[a]	647,834
Percent	2.6%	5.6%	9.7%	3.1%	6.0%
Inc. Higher	...	...	11,998[c]	...	...
Percent	...	...	0.1%	...	...
Higher, Lower Level, Comp.	...	17,525[b]		...	...
Percent	...	0.2%		...	...
Higher, Faculty Level, Comp.	86,800	184,519	365,000	201,956	338,921
Percent	0.9%	1.8%	3.3%	1.9%	3.1%
Unknown	97,000	53,779	114,597	...	...
Percent	1.1%	0.5%	1.0%	...	...
Unaccounted for		0	0	10,303,423	0
Percent		0%	0%	95.0%	0%

Notes: a Fachschule only. b 3 year pedagogical colleges. c Courses in institutions of higher education and enterprise institutes.

TABLE D-10   LEVEL OF EDUCATION OF POPULATION OVER A GIVEN AGE IN CENSUS YEARS: HUNGARY AND ROMANIA

Level of Education	Hungary - 7 Yrs. & Over					Romania - 12 Yrs. & Over	
	1930	1941	1949	1960	1970	1956	1966
POPULATION	7,451,251	8,225,493	8,095,733	8,737,124	9,370,500	13,494,155	15,191,248
Percent	100.0%	100.0%	100.0%	100.0%	100.0%	100.0%	100.0%
Without Schooling	667,940	593,072	458,924	348,130	215,700	1,460,542[a]	
Percent	9.0%	7.2%	5.7%	4.0%	2.3%	10.8%	
4 Yr. Element. Inc.	1,156,556	1,023,964	974,364	950,017	761,500	747,232	
Percent	15.5%	12.4%	12.0%	10.9%	8.1%	5.5%	
4 Yr. Element. Comp.	1,934,149	1,963,146	1,608,481	1,440,439	1,140,100		11,441,062
Percent	26.0%	23.9%	19.9%	16.5%	12.2%	9,305,169	75.3%
7-8 Yr. Basic Inc.	2,866,493	3,590,798	3,598,114	3,489,551	2,935,100	68.9%	
Percent	38.5%	43.6%	44.4%	39.9%	31.3%		
7-8 Yr. Basic Comp.		609,797	923,209	1,609,408	2,709,000		1,680,443
Percent	469,842[b]	7.4%	11.4%	18.4%	28.9%		11.0%
Trade School	6.3%	...	...	...	...	1,139,234	729,477
Percent		...	...	...	...	8.4%	4.8%
Inc. Second.	81,473	178,348	176,063	283,952	424,700		...
Percent	1.1%	2.2%	2.2%	3.3%	4.5%		...
General Second. Comp.							559,380
Percent							3.7%
Specialized Second., Lower Level		163,525	249,320	389,250	786,500		
Percent		2.0%	3.1%	4.5%	8.4%		
Specialized Second., Higher Level	190,024	...	...	...	...	628,281	452,645
Percent	2.5%	...	...	...	...	4.7%	3.0%
Inc. Higher		15,754[c]	14,023[c]	56,732	94,900		
Percent		0.2%	0.2%	0.6%	1.0%		
Higher, Lower Level, Comp.	...	...	...	...	...	...	...
Percent	...	...	...	...	...	...	...
Higher, Faculty Level, Comp.	84,774	87,089	93,235	169,645	303,000	213,697	328,241
Percent	1.1%	1.1%	1.2%	1.9%	3.2%	1.6%	2.2%
Unknown	...	...	...	...	...	...	...
Percent	...	...	...	...	...	...	...
Unaccounted for	0	0	0	0	0	0	0
Percent	0%	0%	0%	0%	0%	0%	0%

Notes: a Illiterate. b First year of general secondary school included in total. c Vegbizonyitvanyt

TABLE D-11   LEVEL OF EDUCATION OF POPULATION OVER A GIVEN AGE IN CENSUS YEARS: POLAND AND USSR

Level of Education	Poland - 15 Yrs. & Over			USSR - 10 Yrs. & Over		
	1960[a]	1970	1974	1939[b]	1959	1970
POPULATION	20,004,000	24,014,794	25,476,530	147,202,000	162,464,288	196,604,461
Percent	100.0%	100.0%	100.0%	100.0%	100.0%	100.0%
Without Schooling		928,716		...	...	...
Percent		3.8%		...	...	...
4 Yr. Element. Inc.				...	...	...
Percent				...	...	...
4 Yr. Element. Comp.	9,040,000	4,899,283	4,806,380	...	50,307,568	57,647,088
Percent	45.2%	20.4%	18.9%	...	31.0%	29.3%
7-8 Yr. Basic Inc.				...		
Percent				...		
7-8 Yr. Basic Comp.	7,838,000	10,692,966	11,051,207		35,385,775	47,367,737
Percent	39.2%	44.5%	43.4%		21.8%	24.1%
Trade School	630,000	2,531,704	3,200,959			
Percent	3.1%	10.5%	12.6%			
Inc. Second.	...	926,500	1,306,678		c	c
Percent	...	3.9%	5.1%			
General Second. Comp.		945,003	1,236,206	[14,700,000]	9,935,630	23,390,868
Percent		3.9%	4.9%	10.0%	6.1%	11.9%
Specialized Second., Lower Level						
Percent		1,719,783	2,251,395		7,870,414	13,420,241
Specialized Second., Higher Level	2,046,000	7.2%	8.8%		4.8%	6.8%
Percent	10.2%					
Inc. Higher		269,793	354,791		1,737,839	2,605,683
Percent		1.1%	1.4%		1.1%	1.3%
Higher, Lower Level, Comp.		263,277	169,924	...	...	...
Percent		1.1%	0.7%	...	...	...
Higher, Faculty Level, Comp.	415,000	654,567	803,810	[1,200,000]	3,777,535	8,261,541
Percent	2.1%	2.7%	3.2%	0.8%	2.3%	4.2%
Unknown	...	183,202	295,180	...	...	...
Percent	...	0.8%	1.2%	...	...	...
Unaccounted for	35,000	0	0	131,302,000	53,449,527	43,911,303
Percent	0.2%	0%	0%	89.2%	32.9%	22.3%

Level of Education	USSR 10 Yrs. & Over 1979
POPULATION	[218,000,000]
Percent	100.0%
Without Schooling	...
Percent	...
4 Yr. Element. Inc.	...
Percent	...
4 Yr. Element. Comp.	...
Percent	...
7-8 Yr. Basic Inc.	...
Percent	...
7-8 Yr. Basic Comp.	
Percent	52,488,000
Trade School	24.1%
Percent	
Inc. Second.^c	
Percent	
General Second. Comp.	45,099,000
Percent	20.7%
Specialized Second., Lower Level	
Percent	23,439,000
Specialized Second., Higher Level	10.7%
Percent	
Inc. Higher	3,235,000
Percent	1.5%
Higher, Lower Level, Comp.	
Percent	14,826,000
Higher, Faculty Level, Comp.	6.8%
Percent	
Unknown	...
Percent	...
Unaccounted for	79,000,000
Percent	36.2%

Notes: a 14 years and over. b Postwar boundaries.
        c No equivalent Soviet category.

181

TABLE D-12   LEVEL OF EDUCATION OF POPULATION OVER A GIVEN AGE IN
              CENSUS YEARS: YUGOSLAVIA, 1948-1971

Level of Education	1948	1953	1961	1971 [a]
POPULATION 10 & OVER	12,437,671	13,381,106	14,611,385	16,895,893
Percent	100.0%	100.0%	100.0%	100.0%
Without Schooling	4,531,929	4,092,644	3,490,915	2,862,857
Percent	36.4%	30.6%	23.9%	16.9%
4 Yr. Element. Inc.		1,539,451	1,373,419	1,228,271
Percent	6,519,564	11.5%	9.4%	7.3%
4 Yr. Element. Comp.	52.4%	4,190,927	4,815,550	4,725,146
Percent		31.3%	32.9%	28.0%
7-8 Yr. Basic Inc.		1,969,936	2,277,268	2,421,045
Percent	964,536	14.7%	15.6%	14.3%
7-8 Yr. Basic Comp.	7.8%	555,984	1,068,543	2,547,789
Percent		4.1%	7.3%	15.1%
Trade School	...	531,030	877,761	1,515,259
Percent	...	4.0%	6.0%	9.0%
Inc. Second.		...	...	...
Percent		...	...	...
General Second. Comp.		154,258	175,915	333,597
Percent		1.2%	1.2%	2.0%
Specialized Second., Lower Level	360,787			
Percent	2.9%	191,325	311,612	726,513
Specialized Second., Higher Level		1.4%	2.1%	4.3%
Percent				
Inc. Higher		...	...	...
Percent		...	...	...
Higher, Lower Level, Comp.			64,214	195,453
Percent	59,480	80,605	0.4%	1.1%
Higher, Faculty Level, Comp.	0.5%	0.6%	132,454	278,128
Percent			0.9%	1.6%
Unknown	1,406	74,946	23,734	61,835
Percent	0%	0.6%	0.2%	0.4%
Unaccounted for	b	0	0	0
Percent		0%	0%	0%

Notes: a Excludes persons temporarily abroad. b Subtotals exceed
        total population by 31.

182

TABLE D-13   LEVEL OF EDUCATION OF POPULATION, ALTERNATIVE MINIMUM AGES: BULGARIA, 1956 AND 1965

Level of Education	1956						1965			
	8 Yrs. & Over[a]	10 Yrs. & Over[b]	15 Yrs. & Over[b]	20 Yrs. & Over[b]	25 Yrs. & Over[b]	Unknown Age	16 Yrs. & Over	20 Yrs. & Over	25 Yrs. & Over	Unknown Age
POPULATION	6,495,229	6,218,185	5,591,450	5,021,939	4,369,429	3	6,115,502	5,561,396	4,976,837	...
Percent	100.0%	100.0%	100.0%	100.0%	100.0%	100.0%	100.0%	100.0%	100.0%	...
Without Schooling[c]	850,105	837,992	822,053	801,543	770,219	3	612,599	605,836	595,918	...
Percent	13.1%	13.5%	14.7%	16.0%	17.6%	100.0%	10.0%	10.9%	12.0%	...
Pr. Element. Inc.	973,184	708,253	510,146	485,596	456,176	0	493,913	483,452	469,842	...
Percent	15.0%	11.4%	9.1%	9.6%	10.4%	0%	8.1%	8.7%	9.4%	...
Pr. Element. Comp.										...
Percent										
8 Yr. Basic Inc.	2,367,812	2,367,812	2,031,619	1,894,888	1,722,012	0	1,821,682	1,754,712	1,677,794	...
Percent	36.4%	38.1%	36.3%	37.7%	39.4%	0%	29.8%	31.6%	33.7%	...
8 Yr. Basic Comp.										...
Percent										...
Trade School	1,616,225	1,616,225	1,539,729	1,204,192	942,219	0	2,125,661	1,730,007	1,443,410	...
Percent	24.9%	26.0%	27.5%	24.0%	21.6%	0%	34.8%	31.1%	29.0%	...
Gen. Second.										...
Percent										...
General Second. Comp.							491,743	441,978	326,191	...
Percent							8.0%	7.9%	6.6%	...
Specialized Second., Lower Level										...
Percent										...
Specialized Second., Higher Level	530,061	530,061	530,061	478,124	337,258	0	328,590	304,164	237,343	...
Percent	8.2%	8.5%	9.5%	9.5%	7.7%	0%	5.4%	5.5%	4.8%	...
Ec. Higher							...	...	...	...
Percent							...	...	...	...
Higher, Lower Level, Comp.	45,336	45,336	45,336	45,090	34,823	0	67,995	67,928	57,856	...
Percent	0.7%	0.7%	0.8%	0.9%	0.8%	0%	1.1%	1.2%	1.2%	...
Higher, Faculty Level, Comp.	112,506	112,506	112,506	112,506	106,722	0	173,319	173,319	168,483	...
Percent	1.7%	1.8%	2.0%	2.2%	2.4%	0%	2.8%	3.1%	3.4%	...
Unknown	...	...	...	...	...	...	...	...	...	...
Percent	...	...	...	...	...	...	...	...	...	...
Not accounted for	0	0	0	0	0	0	0	0	0	...
Percent	0%	0%	0%	0%	0%	0%	0%	0%	0%	...

Notes: a Includes those of unknown age.   b Excludes those of unknown age.   c Illiterates and semiliterates.

TABLE D-14   LEVEL OF EDUCATION OF POPULATION, ALTERNATIVE MINIMUM AGES: CZECHOSLOVAKIA, 1950 AND 1961

Level of Education	1950 - 15 Yrs. & Over		1961			
	I	II	15 Yrs. & Over[a]	20 Yrs. & Over	25 Yrs. & Over	Unknown Age
POPULATION	9,204,606	9,204,900	10,002,500	8,929,622	8,054,652	11,248
Percent	100.0%	100.0%	100.0%	100.0%	100.0%	100.0%
Without Schooling	61,780	63,000	68,540	65,794	62,877	353
Percent	0.7%	0.7%	0.7%	0.7%	0.8%	3.1%
4 Yr. Element. Inc.						
Percent						
4 Yr. Element. Comp						
Percent						
7-8 Yr. Basic Inc.	7,797,023	7,943,600				
Percent	84.7%	86.3%				
7-8 Yr. Basic Comp.			8,185,422	7,274,584	6,655,874	6,876
Percent			81.8%	81.5%	82.6%	61.1%
Trade School	146,619					
Percent	1.6%					
Inc. Second.	...	...				
Percent	...	...				
General Second. Comp.	173,009	172,700	280,732	208,079	155,588	127
Percent	1.9%	1.9%	2.8%	2.3%	1.9%	1.1%
Specialized Second., Lower Level	603,470	603,500	651,914	622,033	556,813	218
Percent	6.6%	6.6%	6.5%	7.0%	6.9%	1.9%
Specialized Second., Higher Level	232,135[b]	238,300	560,069	511,692	390,397	250
Percent	2.5%	2.6%	5.6%	5.7%	4.8%	2.2%
Inc. Higher	...	...	...	...	...	...
Percent	...	...	...	...	...	...
Higher, Lower Level, Comp.	...	...	17,525	17,370	13,823	8
Percent	...	...	0.2%	0.2%	0.2%	0.1%
Higher, Faculty Level, Comp.	75,144	86,800	184,519	184,416	176,807	103
Percent	0.8%	0.9%	1.8%	2.1%	2.2%	0.9%
Unknown	97,896	97,000	53,779	45,654	42,473	3,313
Percent	1.1%	1.1%	0.5%	0.5%	0.5%	29.5%
Unaccounted for	17,530		0	0	0	0
Percent	0.2%		0%	0%	0%	0%

Notes: a Includes those of unknown age. b Includes 85,540 graduates of secondary teachers' schools.

TABLE D-15   LEVEL OF EDUCATION OF POPULATION, ALTERNATIVE MINIMUM
             AGES: CZECHOSLOVAKIA, 1970

Level of Education	All Age Groups	15 Yrs. & Over[a]	19 Yrs. & Over[b]	25 Yrs. & Over[b]	Unknown Age
POPULATION	14,361,557	11,030,375	10,046,852	8,530,683	7,086
Percent	100.0%	100.0%	100.0%	100.0%	100.0%
Without Schooling	3,372,753[c]	41,571	39,503	37,132	49
Percent	23.5%	0.4%	0.4%	0.4%	0.7%
4 Yr. Element. Inc.					
Percent					
4 Yr. Element. Comp.					
Percent					
7-8 Yr. Basic Inc.	6,166,175	6,166,175	5,323,868	4,848,469	2,253
Percent	42.9%	55.9%	53.0%	56.8%	31.8%
7-8 Yr. Basic Comp.					
Percent					
Trade School	2,227,920	2,227,920	2,131,628	1,595,795	401
Percent	15.5%	20.2%	21.2%	18.7%	5.7%
Inc. Second.	...	...	...	...	...
Percent	...	...	...	...	...
General Second. Comp.	393,610	393,610	373,539	216,276	101
Percent	2.7%	3.6%	3.7%	2.5%	1.4%
Specialized Second., Lower Level	640,703	640,703	629,969	583,843	97
Percent	4.5%	5.8%	6.3%	6.8%	1.4%
Specialized Second., Higher Level	1,068,801	1,068,801	1,068,420	800,970	36
Percent	7.4%	9.7%	10.6%	9.4%	0.5%
Inc. Higher					...
Percent					...
Higher, Lower Level, Comp.	11,998[d]	11,998[d]	11,998[d]	11,846[d]	...
Percent	0.1%	0.1%	0.2%	0.1%	...
Higher, Faculty Level, Comp.	365,000	365,000	364,904	344,787	96
Percent	2.5%	3.3%	3.6%	4.0%	1.4%
Unknown	114,597	114,597	103,023	91,565	4,053
Percent	0.8%	1.0%	1.0%	1.1%	57.2%
Unaccounted for	0	0	0	0	0
Percent	0%	0%	0%	0%	0%

Notes: [a] Includes those of unknown age. [b] Excludes those of unknown age.
  [c] Includes 41,571 persons without schooling and 3,331,182 children enrolled in elementary and basic schools at the time of the census.
  [d] Courses in institutions of higher learning and enterprise institutes.

TABLE D-16   LEVEL OF EDUCATION OF POPULATION, ALTERNATIVE MINIMUM AGES: GDR, 1964 AND 1971

Level of Education	1964			1971		
	All Age Groups	21 Yrs. & Over	25 Yrs. & Over	18 Yrs. & Over	20 Yrs. & Over	25 Yrs. & Over
POPULATION	17,003,646	11,862,779	10,845,077	12,304,193	11,780,069	10,809,462
Percent	100.0%	100.0%	100.0%	100.0%	100.0%	100.0%
Without Schooling	...	...	...			
Percent	...	...	...			
4 Yr. Element. Inc.	...	...	...			
Percent	...	...	...			
4 Yr. Element. Comp.	...	...	...	5,552,071[a]	5,456,206[a]	5,306,823[a]
Percent	...	...	...	45.1%	46.3%	49.1%
7-8 Yr. Basic Inc.	...	...	...			
Percent	...	...	...			
7-8 Yr. Basic Comp.	...	...	...			
Percent	...	...	...			
Trade School	...	...	...	4,260,656[b]	4,146,862[b]	3,917,126[b]
Percent	...	...	...	34.6%	35.2%	36.2%
Inc. Second.	...	...	...	312,114[c]	179,203[c]	144,651[c]
Percent	...	...	...	2.5%	1.5%	1.3%
General Second. Comp.	...	...	...	55,577[d]	49,132[d]	34,625[d]
Percent	...	...	...	0.5%	0.4%	0.3%
Specialized Second., Lower Level	...	...	...	949,079[e]	811,821[e]	419,482[e]
Percent	...	...	...	7.7%	6.9%	3.9%
Specialized Second., Higher Level	403,624[f]	393,630[f]	339,698[f]	823,338[g]	785,487[g]	647,834[g]
Percent	2.4%	3.3%	3.1%	6.7%	6.7%	6.0%
Inc. Higher	...	...	...	...	...	...
Percent	...	...	...	...	...	...
Higher, Lower Level, Comp.	...	...	...	...	...	...
Percent	...	...	...	...	...	...
Higher, Faculty Level, Comp.	214,158	214,126	201,956	351,358[h]	351,358[h]	338,921[h]
Percent	1.3%	1.8%	1.9%	2.9%	3.0%	3.1%
Unknown	...	...	...	...	...	...
Percent	...	...	...	...	...	...
Unaccounted for	16,385,864	11,255,023	10,303,423	0	0	0
Percent	96.4%	94.9%	95.0%	0%	0%	0%

Notes: <u>a</u> Persons not completing 10th year of basic school. <u>b</u> Persons with <u>Facharbeiter</u> or <u>Meisterabschluss</u> but not completing 10 grades of school, plus those given as "<u>Facharbeiter und Meisterabschluss</u>" in source. <u>c</u> Persons completing 10 years of basic school. <u>d</u> Persons with <u>Abitur</u>. <u>e</u> Persons with 10 year basic education and <u>Facharbeiter Abschluss</u> and those with 10 year basic education and <u>Meisterabschluss</u>. <u>f</u> <u>Fachschule</u>. <u>g</u> Includes following categories: (i) <u>Fachschulabschluss</u>, (ii) 10 year basic education and <u>Fachschulabschluss</u>, (iii) <u>Abitur</u> and <u>Facharbeiterabschluss</u>, (iv) <u>Abitur</u> and <u>Meisterabschluss</u>, (v) <u>Abitur</u> and <u>Fachschule</u>, (vi) <u>Facharbeiter</u> and <u>Fachschulabschluss</u>, (vii) <u>Meisterabschluss</u> and <u>Fachschulabschluss</u>. <u>h</u> All those with <u>Hochschulabschluss</u>.

TABLE D-17   LEVEL OF EDUCATION OF POPULATION, ALTERNATIVE MINIMUM AGES: HUNGARY, 1949

Level of Education	7 Yrs. & Over	12 Yrs. & Over	15 Yrs. & Over	18 Yrs. & Over	20 Yrs. & Over	25 Yrs. & Over	Unknown Age
POPULATION	8,095,733	7,355,322	6,914,438	6,455,350	6,138,004	5,355,014	271
Percent	100.0%	100.0%	100.0%	100.0%	100.0%	100.0%	100.0%
Without Schooling[a]	458,924	354,727	338,950	326,695	320,073	304,807	218
Percent	5.7%	4.8%	4.9%	5.1%	5.2%	5.7%	80.4%
4 Yr. Element. Inc.	974,364	486,686	432,358	414,208	406,661	387,783	10
Percent	12.0%	6.6%	6.3%	6.4%	6.6%	7.2%	3.7%
4 Yr. Element. Comp.[b]	1,608,481	1,466,303	1,318,466	1,241,906	1,209,392	1,113,882	8
Percent	19.9%	19.9%	19.1%	19.2%	19.7%	20.8%	3.0%
7-8 Yr. Basic Inc.[c]	3,598,114	3,591,761	3,399,697	3,204,461	3,075,755	2,647,559	30
Percent	44.4%	48.8%	49.2%	49.6%	50.1%	49.4%	11.1%
7-8 Yr. Basic Comp.[d]							
Percent	923,209	923,205	893,153	769,966	662,183	517,703	4
Trade School	11.4%	12.5%	12.9%	11.9%	10.8%	9.7%	1.5%
Percent							
Inc. Second.	176,063	176,063	175,237	141,646	119,629	96,398	...
Percent	2.2%	2.4%	2.5%	2.2%	1.9%	1.8%	...
General Second. Comp.							...
Percent							...
Specialized Second., Lower Level	249,320	249,320	249,320	249,211	237,054	183,298	...
Percent	3.1%	3.4%	3.6%	3.9%	3.9%	3.4%	...
Specialized Second., Higher Level							...
Percent							...
Inc. Higher							...
Percent							...
Higher, Lower Level, Comp.	...	...	...	...	...	...	...
Percent	...	...	...	...	...	...	...
Higher, Faculty Level, Comp.[e]	107,258[f]	107,257[f]	107,257[f]	107,257[f]	107,257[f]	103,584[g]	1
Percent	1.4%	1.5%	1.6%	1.7%	1.7%	1.9%	0.4%
Unknown	...	...	...	...	...	...	...
Percent	...	...	...	...	...	...	...
Unaccounted for	0	0	0	0	0	0	0
Percent	0%	0%	0%	0%	0%	0%	0%

Notes: a Includes those whose level of education not known. b Either 4 or 5 years of elementary education. c Either 6 or 7 years of basic education. d 8 years of basic education. e Includes those with a university certificate (Vegbizonyitvanyt) but no diploma. f Of whom, 93,235 received university diploma. g Of whom, 90,891 received university diploma.

TABLE D-18   LEVEL OF EDUCATION OF POPULATION, ALTERNATIVE MINIMUM AGES: HUNGARY, 1960

Level of Education	7 Yrs. & Over[a]	12 Yrs. & Over	15 Yrs. & Over	18 Yrs. & Over	20 Yrs. & Over	25 Yrs. & Over	Unknown Age
POPULATION	8,737,124	7,878,340	7,430,886	6,968,873	6,677,395	5,998,432	705
Percent	100.0%	100.0%	100.0%	100.0%	100.0%	100.0%	100.0%
Without Schooling	348,130	253,049	247,408	241,209	236,889	223,725	280
Percent	4.0%	3.2%	3.3%	3.5%	3.5%	3.7%	39.7%
4 Yr. Element. Inc.	950,017	420,893	403,904	396,934	392,722	375,263	41
Percent	10.9%	5.3%	5.4%	5.7%	5.9%	6.3%	5.8%
4 Yr. Element. Comp.[b]	1,440,439	1,206,185	1,103,396	1,072,302	1,052,417	983,782	59
Percent	16.5%	15.3%	14.8%	15.4%	15.8%	16.4%	8.4%
7-8 Yr. Basic Inc.[c]	3,489,551	3,489,376	3,237,079	3,159,373	3,100,991	2,941,503	175
Percent	39.9%	44.3%	43.6%	45.3%	46.4%	49.0%	24.8%
7-8 Yr. Basic Comp.[d]							
Percent	1,609,408	1,609,317	1,539,579	1,299,578	1,156,334	883,096	91
Trade School	18.4%	20.4%	20.7%	18.6%	17.3%	14.7%	12.9%
Percent							
Inc. Second.	283,952	283,940	283,940	184,037	163,546	127,127	12
Percent	3.3%	3.6%	3.8%	2.6%	2.5%	2.1%	1.7%
General Second. Comp.							
Percent							
Specialized Second., Lower Level	389,250	389,221	389,221	389,079	348,137		
Percent	4.4%	4.9%	5.2%	5.6%	5.2%		
Specialized Second., Higher Level	...	...	...	...	...	294,810	33
Percent	...	...	...	...	...	4.9%	4.7%
Inc. Higher	50,236	50,232	50,232	50,232	50,232		
Percent	0.6%	0.6%	0.7%	0.7%	0.8%		
Higher, Lower Level, Comp.	...	...	...	...	...	...	...
Percent	...	...	...	...	...	...	...
Higher, Faculty Level, Comp.[e]	176,141[f]	176,127[f]	176,127[f]	176,127[f]	176,127[f]	169,126[g]	14
Percent	2.0%	2.2%	2.4%	2.5%	2.6%	2.8%	2.0%
Unknown	...	...	...	...	...	...	...
Percent	...	...	...	...	...	...	...
Unaccounted for	0	0	0	0	0	0	0
Percent	0%	0%	0%	0%	0%	0%	0%

Notes: a Includes those whose level of education not known. b Either 4 or 5 years of elementary education. c Either 6 or 7 years of basic education. d 8 years of basic education. e Includes those with a university certificate (Vegbizonyitvanyt) but no diploma. f Of whom, 169,645 received university diploma. g Of whom, 163,005 received university diploma.

TABLE D-19   LEVEL OF EDUCATION OF POPULATION, ALTERNATIVE
MINIMUM AGES: HUNGARY, 1970

Level of Education	7 Yrs. & Over	10 Yrs. & Over	15 Yrs. & Over	20 Yrs. & Over	25 Yrs. & Over
POPULATION	9,370,500	8,967,800	8,148,600	7,248,900	6,463,900
Percent	100.0%	100.0%	100.0%	100.0%	100.0%
Without Schooling	215,700	164,600	158,100	152,100	146,000
Percent	2.3%	1.8%	1.9%	2.1%	2.3%
4 Yr. Element. Inc.	761,500	409,900	326,100	317,900	312,100
Percent	8.1%	4.6%	4.0%	4.4%	4.8%
4 Yr. Element. Comp.[a]	1,140,100	1,140,100	837,000	815,100	799,500
Percent	12.2%	12.7%	10.3%	11.2%	12.4%
7-8 Yr. Basic Inc.[b]	2,935,100	2,935,100	2,616,200	2,568,100	2,530,100
Percent	31.3%	32.8%	32.1%	35.4%	39.1%
7-8 Yr. Basic Comp.[c]					
Percent	2,709,000	2,709,000	2,602,100	2,054,400	1,627,300
Trade School	28.9%	30.2%	31.9%	28.3%	25.2%
Percent					
Inc. Second.	424,700	424,700	424,700	232,600	183,300
Percent	4.5%	4.7%	5.2%	3.2%	2.8%
General Second. Comp.					
Percent					
Specialized Second., Lower Level	786,500	786,500	786,500	715,800	537,300
Percent	8.4%	8.8%	9.7%	9.9%	8.3%
Specialized Second., Higher Level					
Percent [d]					
Inc. Higher	94,900	94,900	94,900	89,900	48,800
Percent	1.0%	1.1%	1.2%	1.2%	0.7%
Higher, Lower Level, Comp.	...	...	...	...	...
Percent	...	...	...	...	...
Higher, Faculty Level, Comp.	303,000[e]	303,000[e]	303,000[e]	303,000[e]	279,500[f]
Percent	3.2%	3.4%	3.7%	4.2%	4.3%
Unknown	...	...	...	...	...
Percent	...	...	...	...	...
Unaccounted for	0	0	0	0	0
Percent	0%	0%	0%	0%	0%

Notes: a 4-5 years of elementary education. b 6-7 years of basic school.
c 8 year basic. d Includes those with university certificate
(Vegbizonyitvanyt). e Of whom, 295,247 received university diploma.
f Of whom, 276,612 received university diploma.

TABLE D-20   LEVEL OF EDUCATION OF POPULATION, ALTERNATIVE
MINIMUM AGES: POLAND, 1960

Level of Education	14 Yrs. & Over		18 Yrs. & Over	25 Yrs. & Over
	I	II		
POPULATION	20,004,000	20,004,000	18,312,000	15,594,000
Percent	100.0%	100.0%	100.0%	100.0%
Without Schooling	...			
Percent	...			
4 Yr. Element. Inc.	...			
Percent	...			
4 Yr. Element. Comp.	...	[9,040,000]	[8,550,000]	[8,070,000]
Percent	...	45.2%	[46.7%]	[51.8%]
7-8 Yr. Basic Inc.	...			
Percent	...			
7-8 Yr. Basic Comp.	7,838,000	[7,860,000]	[6,682,000]	[5,149,000]
Percent	39.2%	39.3%	[36.5%]	[33.0%]
Trade School	630,000	[620,000]	[603,000]	[421,000]
Percent	3.1%	3.1%	[3.3%]	[2.7%]
Inc. Second.	...	...	...	...
Percent	...	...	...	...
General Second. Comp.				
Percent				
Specialized Second., Lower Level				
Percent				
Specialized Second., Higher Level	2,046,000	[2,060,000]	[2,050,000]	[1,550,000]
Percent	10.2%	10.3%	[11.2%]	[9.9%]
Inc. Higher				
Percent				
Higher, Lower Level, Comp.				
Percent				
Higher, Faculty Level, Comp.	415,000	[420,000]	[420,000]	[398,000]
Percent	2.1%	2.1%	[2.3%]	[2.6%]
Unknown	...	...	...	...
Percent	...	...	...	...
Unaccounted for	9,075,000	0	0	0
Percent	45.4%	0%	0%	0%

TABLE D-21 LEVEL OF EDUCATION OF POPULATION, ALTERNATIVE MINIMUM AGES: POLAND, 1970 AND 1974

Level of Education	1970				1974		
	15 Yrs. & Over[a]	18 Yrs. & Over	25 Yrs. & Over	Unknown Age	15 Yrs. & Over	18 Yrs. & Over	25 Yrs. & Over
POPULATION	24,014,794	21,882,437	17,559,467	20,713	25,476,530	23,289,000	18,602,000
Percent	100.0%	100.0%	100.0%	100.0%	100.0%	100.0%	100.0%
Without Schooling	928,716	923,597	912,667	545			
Percent	3.8%	4.2%	5.2%	2.6%			
4 Yr. Element. Inc.							
Percent							
4 Yr. Element. Comp.	4,899,283	4,548,416	4,436,379	4,977	4,806,380	4,481,000	4,398,000
Percent	20.4%	20.8%	25.3%	24.0%	18.9%	19.2%	23.6%
7-8 Yr. Basic Inc.							
Percent							
7-8 Yr. Basic Comp.	10,692,966	9,091,353	7,529,911	5,087	11,051,207	9,625,000	8,147,000
Percent	44.5%	41.5%	43.0%	24.5%	43.4%	41.3%	43.8%
Trade School	2,531,704	2,465,468	1,264,553	1,817	3,200,959	3,125,000	1,708,000
Percent	10.5%	11.3%	7.2%	8.8%	12.6%	13.4%	9.2%
Inc. Second.	926,500	837,567	514,885	327	1,306,678	1,062,000	551,000
Percent	3.9%	4.0%	3.0%	1.6%	5.1%	4.6%	3.0%
General Second. Comp.	945,003				1,236,206		
Percent	3.9%				4.9%		
Specialized Second., Lower Level	1,719,783	2,660,928	1,830,014	1,113	2,251,395	3,479,000	2,535,000
Percent	7.2%	12.1%	10.4%	5.4%	8.8%	14.9%	13.6%
Specialized Second., Higher Level							
Percent							
Inc. Higher	269,793	269,047	149,724	746	354,791	355,000	216,000
Percent	1.1%	1.2%	0.8%	3.6%	1.4%	1.5%	1.2%
Higher, Lower Level, Comp.[b]	263,277	262,857	175,166	420	169,924	170,000	133,000
Percent	1.1%	1.2%	1.0%	2.0%	0.7%	0.7%	0.7%
Higher, Faculty Level, Comp.	654,567	652,710	616,405	1,857	803,810	803,000	757,000
Percent	2.7%	3.0%	3.5%	9.0%	3.2%	3.4%	4.1%
Unknown	183,202	...	...	...	295,180	...	...
Percent	0.8%	...	...	...	1.2%	...	...
Unaccounted for	0	170,494	129,763	3,824	0	189,000	157,000
Percent	0%	0.8%	0.7%	18.5%	0%	0.8%	0.8%

Notes: a Includes those of unknown age. b Policealne.

TABLE D-22   LEVEL OF EDUCATION OF POPULATION, ALTERNATIVE MINIMUM AGES: ROMANIA, 1956

Level of Education	8 Yrs. & Over[a]	12 Yrs. & Over	15 Yrs. & Over	20 Yrs. & Over	25 Yrs. & Over	Unknown Age
POPULATION	14,566,957	13,494,155	12,674,361	11,092,146	9,496,767	1,475
Percent	100.0%	100.0%	100.0%	100.0%	100.0%	100.0%
Without Schooling	1,472,082	1,460,542	1,448,354	1,406,822	1,342,198	32
Percent	10.1%	10.8%	11.4%	12.7%	14.1%	2.2%
4 Yr. Element. Inc.	1,624,669	747,232	685,285	638,620	576,987	831
Percent	11.2%	5.5%	5.4%	5.8%	6.1%	56.3%
4 Yr. Element. Comp.						
Percent	9,488,801	9,305,169	8,634,907	7,659,809	6,559,035	419
7-8 Yr. Basic Inc.	65.1%	69.0%	68.1%	69.0%	69.1%	28.4%
Percent						
7-8 Yr. Basic Comp.						
Percent						
Trade School	1,139,299	1,139,234	1,063,837	630,349	428,328	65
Percent	7.8%	8.4%	8.4%	5.7%	4.5%	4.4%
Inc. Second.						
Percent						
General Second. Comp.						
Percent						
Specialized Second., Lower Level						
Percent						
Specialized Second., Higher Level	628,383	628,281	628,281	542,906	387,150	102
Percent	4.3%	4.7%	5.0%	4.9%	4.1%	6.9%
Inc. Higher						
Percent						
Higher, Lower Level, Comp.	...	...	...	...	...	...
Percent	...	...	...	...	...	...
Higher, Faculty Level, Comp.	213,723	213,679	213,679	213,640	203,069	26
Percent	1.5%	1.6%	1.7%	1.9%	2.1%	1.8%
Unknown	...	...	...	...	...	...
Percent	...	...	...	...	...	...
Unaccounted for	0	0	0	0	0	0
Percent	0%	0%	0%	0%	0%	0%

Notes: a Includes those of unknown age.

TABLE D-23   LEVEL OF EDUCATION OF POPULATION, ALTERNATIVE MINIMUM AGES:
ROMANIA, 1966

Level of Education	12 Yrs. & Over[a]	15 Yrs. & Over	16 Yrs. & Over	20 Yrs. & Over	25 Yrs. & Over	Unknown Age
POPULATION	15,191,248	14,118,067	13,758,327	12,527,896	11,260,095	16,572
Percent	100.0%	100.0%	100.0%	100.0%	100.0%	100.0%
Without Schooling						
Percent						
4 Yr. Element. Inc.						
Percent						
4 Yr. Element. Comp.	11,441,062	10,370,569	10,210,284	9,870,715	9,207,249	13,884
Percent	75.3%	73.5%	74.2%	78.8%	81.8%	83.8%
7-8 Yr. Basic Inc.						
Percent						
7-8 Yr. Basic Comp.	1,680,443	1,679,355	1,479,905	788,909	519,595	1,088
Percent	11.0%	11.9%	10.8%	6.3%	4.6%	6.6%
Trade School	729,477	728,947	728,947	612,998	467,763	530
Percent	4.8%	5.2%	5.3%	4.9%	4.2%	3.2%
Inc. Second.	...	...	...	...	...	...
Percent	...	...	...	...	...	...
General Second. Comp.	559,380	558,925	558,920	481,976	355,182	455
Percent	3.7%	4.0%	4.1%	3.8%	3.2%	2.7%
Specialized Second., Lower Level						
Percent	452,645	452,289	452,289	445,316	401,977	356
Specialized Second., Higher Level	3.0%	3.2%	3.3%	3.6%	3.6%	2.1%
Percent						
Inc. Higher	...	...	...	...	...	...
Percent	...	...	...	...	...	...
Higher, Lower Level, Comp.	...	...	...	...	...	...
Percent	...	...	...	...	...	...
Higher, Faculty Level, Comp.	328,241	327,982	327,982	327,982	308,329	259
Percent	2.2%	2.3%	2.4%	2.6%	2.7%	1.6%
Unknown	...	...	...	...	...	...
Percent	...	...	...	...	...	...
Unaccounted for	0	0	0	0	0	0
Percent	0%	0%	0%	0%	0%	0%

Notes: a Includes those of unknown age.

TABLE D-24   LEVEL OF EDUCATION OF POPULATION, ALTERNATIVE MINIMUM AGES: USSR, 1959-1979

Level of Education	1959				1970			
	10 Yrs. & Over[a]	20 Yrs. & Over	25 Yrs. & Over	Unknown Age	10 Yrs. & Over[a]	16 Yrs. & Over	20 Yrs. & Over	Unknown Age
POPULATION	162,464,288	130,647,276	110,304,248	8,362	196,604,461	166,741,127	149,478,148	138,711
Percent	100.0%	100.0%	100.0%	100.0%	100.0%	100.0%	100.0%	100.0%
Without Schooling	...	...	...	...	...	...	...	...
Percent	...	...	...	...	...	...	...	...
4 Yr. Element. Inc.	...	...	...	...	...	...	...	...
Percent	...	...	...	...	...	...	...	...
4 Yr. Element. Comp.	...	...	...	...	...	...	...	...
Percent	50,307,568	38,371,071	32,508,933	1,501	57,647,088	38,095,730	36,362,908	27,388
7-8 Yr. Basic Inc.	31.0%	29.4%	29.5%	18.0%	29.3%	22.8%	24.3%	19.7%
Percent								
7-8 Yr. Basic Comp.								
Percent	35,385,775	25,633,506	17,924,350	1,074	47,367,737	44,778,572	35,150,344	23,458
Trade School	21.8%	19.6%	16.2%	12.8%	24.1%	26.9%	23.5%	17.0%
Percent								
Inc. Second.[b]								
Percent								
General Second. Comp.	9,935,630	7,385,718	4,417,433	315	23,390,868	23,377,425	18,115,084	13,443
Percent	6.1%	5.7%	4.0%	3.8%	11.9%	14.0%	12.2%	9.7%
Specialized Second., Lower Level								
Percent	7,870,414	7,635,871	5,842,009	347	13,420,241	13,413,246	13,060,796	6,995
Specialized Second., Higher Level	4.8%	5.8%	5.3%	4.1%	6.8%	8.0%	8.7%	5.0%
Percent								
Inc. Higher	1,737,839	1,704,916	1,083,435	62	2,605,683	2,603,937	2,492,919	1,746
Percent	1.1%	1.3%	1.0%	0.7%	1.3%	1.6%	1.7%	1.3%
Higher, Lower Level, Comp.	...	...	...	...	...	...	...	...
Percent	...	...	...	...	...	...	...	...
Higher, Faculty Level, Comp.	3,777,535	3,777,313	3,515,307	170	8,261,541	8,256,774	8,256,774	4,767
Percent	2.3%	2.9%	3.2%	2.0%	4.2%	5.0%	5.5%	3.4%
Unknown	...	...	...	...	...	...	...	...
Percent	...	...	...	...	...	...	...	...
Unaccounted for	53,449,527	46,138,881	45,012,781	4,893	43,911,303	36,215,443	36,039,323	60,914
Percent	32.9%	35.3%	40.8%	58.5%	22.3%	21.7%	24.1%	44.0%

Level of Education	1979 10 Yrs. & Over
POPULATION	[218,000,000]
Percent	100.0%
Without Schooling	...
Percent	...
4 Yr. Element. Inc.	...
Percent	...
4 Yr. Element. Comp.	...
Percent	...
7-8 Yr. Basic Inc.	...
Percent	...
7-8 Yr. Basic Comp.	
Percent	52,488,000
Trade School	24.1%
Percent	
Inc. Second.b	
Percent	
General Second. Comp.	45,099,000
Percent	20.7%
Specialized Second., Lower Level	
Percent	23,439,000
Specialized Second., Higher Level	10.7%
Percent	
Inc. Higher	3,235,000
Percent	1.5%
Higher, Lower Level, Comp.	
Percent	14,826,000
Higher, Faculty Level, Comp.	6.8%
Percent	
Unknown	...
Percent	...
Unaccounted for	79,000,000
Percent	36.2%

Notes: a Includes persons of unknown age. b No
        equivalent Soviet category.

TABLE D-25 LEVEL OF EDUCATION OF POPULATION, ALTERNATIVE MINIMUM AGES: YUGOSLAVIA, 1948 AND 1953

Level of Education	1948					1953				
	10 Yrs. & Over[a]	15 Yrs. & Over[a]	20 Yrs. & Over[a]	25 Yrs. & Over[a]	Unknown Age	10 Yrs. & Over[b]	15 Yrs. & Over[a]	20 Yrs. & Over[a]	25 Yrs. & Over[a]	Unknown Age
POPULATION / Percent	12,437,671 / 100.0%	10,639,630 / 100.0%	8,916,725 / 100.0%	7,466,576 / 100.0%	831 / 100.0%	13,381,106 / 100.0%	11,775,381 / 100.0%	10,017,998 / 100.0%	8,295,131 / 100.0%	1,113 / 100.0%
Without Schooling / Percent	4,531,929 / 36.4%	3,890,375 / 36.6%	3,467,095 / 38.9%	3,121,272 / 41.8%	351 / 42.2%	4,092,644 / 30.6%	3,921,968 / 33.3%	3,585,753 / 35.8%	3,179,055 / 38.3%	400 / 35.9%
4 Yr. Element. Inc. / Percent	6,519,564 / 52.4%	5,548,651 / 52.1%	4,524,265 / 50.7%	3,636,971 / 48.7%	123 / 14.8%	1,539,451 / 11.5%	984,712 / 8.4%	824,215 / 8.2%	645,315 / 7.8%	44 / 4.0%
4 Yr. Element. Comp. / Percent	⎱	⎱	⎱	⎱	⎱	4,190,927 / 31.3%	3,652,851 / 31.0%	3,046,654 / 30.4%	2,428,300 / 29.3%	123 / 11.1%
7-8 Yr. Basic Inc. / Percent	964,505 / 7.8%	781,300 / 7.3%	593,162 / 6.7%	460,219 / 6.2%	31 / 3.7%	1,969,936 / 14.7%	1,675,106 / 14.2%	1,328,892 / 13.3%	1,121,182 / 13.5%	49 / 4.4%
7-8 Yr. Basic Comp. / Percent	⎱	⎱	⎱	⎱	⎱	555,984 / 4.1%	543,165 / 4.6%	330,532 / 3.3%	248,090 / 3.0%	21 / 1.9%
Trade School / Percent	...	...	...	...	...	531,030 / 4.0%	530,888 / 4.6%	458,260 / 4.6%	339,308 / 4.1%	7 / 0.6%
Inc. Second. / Percent	...	...	...	...	...	...	...	...	...	...
General Second. Comp. / Percent	360,787 / 2.9%	358,605 / 3.4%	271,669 / 3.0%	188,703 / 2.5%	16 / 1.9%	154,258 / 1.2%	154,250 / 1.4%	148,597 / 1.5%	100,834 / 1.2%	8 / 0.7%
Specialized Second. Lower Level / Percent	⎱	⎱	⎱	⎱	⎱	191,325 / 1.4%	191,321 / 1.6%	177,941 / 1.8%	123,557 / 1.5%	4 / 0.3%
Specialized Second. Higher Level / Percent	⎱	⎱	⎱	⎱	⎱	⎱	⎱	⎱	⎱	⎱
Inc. Higher / Percent	⎱	⎱	⎱	⎱	⎱	...	...	...	...	...
Higher, Lower Level, Comp. / Percent	59,480 / 0.5%	59,480 / 0.6%	59,475 / 0.7%	58,527 / 0.8%	15 / 1.8%	80,605 / 0.6%	80,599 / 0.7%	80,585 / 0.8%	77,826 / 0.9%	6 / 0.5%
Higher, Faculty Level, Comp. / Percent	⎱	⎱	⎱	⎱	⎱	⎱	⎱	⎱	⎱	⎱
Unknown / Percent	1,406 / 0.0%	1,219 / 0.0%	1,059 / 0.0%	884 / 0.0%	295 / 35.5%	74,946 / 0.6%	40,521 / 0.3%	36,574 / 0.4%	32,069 / 0.4%	451 / 40.5%
Unaccounted for / Percent	0 / 0%	0 / 0%	0 / 0%	0 / 0%	0 / 0%	0 / 0%	0 / 0%	0c / 0%	0d / 0%	0 / 0%

Notes: a Those of unknown age excluded. b Includes those of unknown age. c Total of subcategories exceeds population 20 and over by 5. d Total of subcategories exceeds population 25 and over by 405.

TABLE D-26   LEVEL OF EDUCATION OF POPULATION, ALTERNATIVE MINIMUM AGES: YUGOSLAVIA, 1961 AND 1971

Level of Education	1961					1971				
	10 Yrs. & Over[a]	15 Yrs. & Over	20 Yrs. & Over	25 Yrs. & Over	Unknown Age	10 Yrs. & Over[a]	15 Yrs. & Over	20 Yrs. & Over	25 Yrs. & Over	Unknown Age
POPULATION	14,611,385	12,760,810	11,382,715	9,801,179	17,651	16,895,893	14,930,438	12,945,494	11,191,167	92,279
Percent	100.0%	100.0%	100.0%	100.0%	100.0%	100.0%	100.0%	100.0%	100.0%	100.0%
Without Schooling	3,490,915	3,403,185	3,306,831	3,123,418	5,190	2,862,857	2,774,048	2,723,405	2,668,726	32,004
Percent	23.9%	26.7%	29.0%	31.9%	29.4%	16.9%	18.6%	21.0%	23.8%	34.7%
4 Yr. Element. Inc.	1,373,419	766,294	723,257	656,374	969	1,228,271	686,429	656,322	636,847	6,993
Percent	9.4%	6.0%	6.4%	6.7%	5.5%	7.3%	4.6%	5.1%	5.7%	7.6%
4 Yr. Element. Comp.	4,815,550	4,297,205	3,861,195	3,228,913	3,246	4,725,146	4,228,946	3,934,471	3,644,660	9,941
Percent	32.9%	33.7%	33.9%	32.9%	18.4%	28.0%	28.3%	30.4%	32.6%	10.8%
7-8 Yr. Basic Inc.	2,277,268	1,662,575	1,352,455	1,132,143	1,056	2,421,045	1,635,432	1,213,169	987,767	8,690
Percent	15.6%	13.0%	11.9%	11.5%	6.0%	14.3%	11.0%	9.4%	8.8%	9.4%
7-8 Yr. Basic Comp.	1,068,543	1,053,231	645,206	497,370	730	2,547,789	2,522,646	1,510,424	1,081,743	8,948
Percent	7.3%	8.2%	5.7%	5.1%	4.1%	15.1%	16.9%	11.7%	9.6%	9.7%
Trade School	877,761	877,050	817,659	633,659	711	1,515,259	1,511,878	1,400,036	1,076,263	3,381
Percent	6.0%	6.9%	7.2%	6.5%	4.0%	9.0%	10.1%	10.8%	9.6%	3.7%
Inc. Second.	...	...	...	...	...	...	...	...	...	...
Percent	...	...	...	...	...	...	...	...	...	...
General Second. Comp.	175,915	175,756	163,760	96,017	159	333,597	333,037	303,931	152,907	560
Percent	1.2%	1.4%	1.4%	1.0%	0.9%	2.0%	2.2%	2.3%	1.4%	0.6%
Specialized Second., Lower Level	...	...	...	...	...	...	...	...	...	...
Percent										
Specialized Second., Higher Level	311,612	311,333	300,459	233,728	279	726,513	725,008	696,880	476,819	1,505
Percent	2.1%	2.4%	2.6%	2.4%	1.6%	4.3%	4.8%	5.4%	4.3%	1.6%
Inc. Higher	...	...	...	...	...	...	...	...	...	...
Percent	...	...	...	...	...	...	...	...	...	...
Higher, Lower Level, Comp.	64,214	64,135	63,949	58,005	79	195,453	195,111	194,983	168,040	342
Percent	0.4%	0.5%	0.6%	0.6%	0.4%	1.1%	1.3%	1.5%	1.5%	0.4%
Higher, Faculty Level, Comp.	132,454	132,290	132,290	128,013	164	278,128	277,073	277,073	267,099	1,055
Percent	0.9%	1.0%	1.2%	1.3%	0.9%	1.6%	1.8%	2.1%	2.4%	1.1%
Unknown	23,734	17,756	15,654	13,539	5,068	61,835	40,830	34,800	30,296	18,860
Percent	0.2%	0.1%	0.1%	0.1%	28.7%	0.4%	0.3%	0.3%	0.3%	20.4%
Unaccounted for	0	0	0	0	0	0	0	0	0	0
Percent	0%	0%	0%	0%	0%	0%	0%	0%	0%	0%

Notes: a Includes those of unknown age.

TABLE D-27   LEVEL OF EDUCATION OF POPULATION IN CENSUS YEARS, INTERNATIONAL STANDARD
              CLASSIFICATION: EASTERN EUROPE AND THE USSR

	Total	No Schooling	First Level Incomplete	First Level Complete	Second Level Cycle 1	Second Level Cycle 2	Post Secondary
ALBANIA 1955							
All Ages							
Number	1,389,971	[762,000]	[498,000]	[93,000]	[11,000]	[13,000]	[6,000]
Percent	100.0%	54.8%	35.8%	6.7%	0.8%	0.9%	0.4%
BULGARIA 1946							
15 & Over							
Number	5,068,539	[1,230,000]	[1,170,000]	[1,970,000]	[576,000]		[125,000]
Percent	100.0%	24.3%	23.0%	38.8%	11.4%		2.5%
20 & Over							
Number	4,372,752	[1,150,000]	[1,020,000]	[1,710,000]	[375,000]		[118,000]
Percent	100.0%	26.4%	23.3%	39.0%	8.6%		2.7%
25 & Over							
Number	3,642,724	[1,080,000]	[860,000]	[1,360,000]	[266,000]		[84,000]
Percent	100.0%	29.6%	23.6%	37.2%	7.3%		2.3%
BULGARIA 1956							
15 & Over							
Number	5,591,450	[821,000]	[2,230,000]	[1,250,000]	[1,130,000]		[156,000]
Percent	100.0%	14.7%	39.9%	22.4%	20.1%		2.8%
20 & Over							
Number	5,021,939	[800,000]	[2,210,000]	[1,120,000]	[739,000]		[156,000]
Percent	100.0%	15.9%	44.0%	22.2%	14.7%		3.1%
25 & Over							
Number	4,369,429	[769,000]	[2,180,000]	[944,000]	[336,000]		[140,000]
Percent	100.0%	17.6%	49.9%	21.6%	7.7%		3.2%
BULGARIA 1965							
15 & Over							
Number	5,651,776	[2,350,000]		[2,230,000]	[822,000]		[243,000]
Percent	100.0%	41.6%		39.5%	14.6%		4.3%
20 & Over							
Number	4,955,560	[2,240,000]		[1,730,000]	[748,000]		[243,000]
Percent	100.0%	45.1%		34.9%	15.1%		4.9%
25 & Over							
Number	4,380,919	[2,150,000]		[1,440,000]	[565,000]		[228,000]
Percent	100.0%	49.0%		32.9%	12.9%		5.2%

	Total	No Schooling	First Level Incomplete	First Level Complete	Second Level Cycle 1	Second Level Cycle 2	Post Secondary
CZECHOSLOVAKIA 1961							
<u>15 & Over</u>							
Number	9,983,259	[69,000]	[8,220,000]		[1,490,000]		[205,000]
Percent	100.0%	0.7%	82.3%		14.9%		2.0%
<u>20 & Over</u>							
Number	8,926,441	[67,000]	[7,310,000]		[1,340,000]		[205,000]
Percent	100.0%	0.8%	81.9%		15.0%		2.3%
<u>25 & Over</u>							
Number	8,054,652	[64,400]	[6,690,000]		[1,100,000]		[193,000]
Percent	100.0%	0.8%	83.1%		13.7%		2.4%
CZECHOSLOVAKIA 1970							
<u>15 & Over</u>							
Number	10,873,716	[56,000]	[6,090,000]		[4,370,000]		[365,000]
Percent	100.0%	0.5%	56.0%		40.2%		3.4%
<u>20 & Over</u>							
Number	9,899,251	[53,400]	[5,250,000]		[4,240,000]		[365,000]
Percent	100.0%	0.5%	53.0%		42.8%		3.7%
<u>25 & Over</u>							
Number	8,390,982	[50,300]	[4,800,000]		[3,210,000]		[344,000]
Percent	100.0%	0.6%	57.2%		38.2%		4.1%
GDR 1971							
<u>25 & Over</u>							
Number	10,809,462		[5,310,000]		[4,580,000]		[919,000]
Percent	100.0%		49.1%		42.4%		8.5%
HUNGARY 1960							
<u>15 & Over</u>							
Number	7,430,886	[245,000]	[6,280,000]		[671,000]		[231,000]
Percent	100.0%	3.3%	84.6%		9.0%		3.1%
<u>20 & Over</u>							
Number	6,677,395	[235,000]	[5,700,000]		[513,000]		[228,000]
Percent	100.0%	3.5%	85.4%		7.7%		3.4%
<u>25 & Over</u>							
Number	5,998,432	[222,000]	[5,180,000]		[390,000]		[204,000]
Percent	100.0%	3.7%	86.4%		6.5%		3.4%

	Total	No Schooling	First Level Incomplete	First Level Complete	Second Level Cycle 1	Second Level Cycle 2	Post Secondary
HUNGARY 1970							
15 & Over							
Number	8,145,592	[167,000]	[1,160,000]	[5,220,000]	[1,200,000]		[399,000]
Percent	100.0%	2.0%	14.2%	64.0%	14.8%		4.9%
20 & Over							
Number	7,228,458	[161,000]	[1,130,000]	[4,620,000]	[924,000]		[394,000]
Percent	100.0%	2.2%	15.6%	63.9%	12.8%		5.4%
25 & Over							
Number	6,449,209	[155,000]	[1,100,000]	[4,170,000]	[697,000]		[329,000]
Percent	100.0%	2.4%	17.1%	64.6%	10.8%		5.1%
POLAND 1960							
18 & Over							
Number	17,840,420	[1,330,000]	[12,500,000]		[1,630,000]	1,790,000	[573,000]
Percent	100.0%	7.5%	70.2%		9.1%	10 0%	3.2%
25 & Over							
Number	15,342,360	[1,320,000]	[11,000,000]		[1,120,000]	[1,430,000]	[491,000]
Percent	100.0%	8.6%	71.7%		7.3%	9.3%	3.2%
POLAND 1970							
15 & Over							
Number	23,814,703	[922,000]	[4,900,000]	[10,700,000]	[6,120,000]		[1,190,000]
Percent	100.0%	3.9%	20.6%	44.9%	25.7%		5.0%
20 & Over							
Number	20,357,966	[915,000]	[4,510,000]	[8,570,000]	[5,190,000]		[1,180,000]
Percent	100.0%	4.5%	22.1%	42.1%	25.5%		5.8%
25 & Over							
Number	17,429,704	[906,000]	[4,440,000]	[7,530,000]	[3,610,000]		[941,000]
Percent	100.0%	5.2%	25.5%	43.2%	20.7%		5.4%
ROMANIA 1956							
15 & Over							
Number	12,674,361	[1,450,000]	[9,320,000]	[1,060,000]	[631,000]		[211,000]
Percent	100.0%	11.4%	73.5%	8.4%	5.0%		1.7%
20 & Over							
Number	11,092,146	[1,400,000]	[8,300,000]	[630,000]	[546,000]		[211,000]
Percent	100.0%	12.7%	74.8%	5.7%	4.9%		1.9%
25 & Over							
Number	9,496,767	[1,340,000]	[7,130,000]	[427,000]	[389,000]		[199,000]
Percent	100.0%	14.1%	75.1%	4.5%	4.1%		2.1%

TABLE D-27   (CONTINUED)

	Total	No Schooling	First Level Incomplete	First Level Complete	Second Level Cycle 1	Second Level Cycle 2	Post Secondary
ROMANIA 1966							
15 & Over							
Number	14,118,067		[10,400,000]		[3,420,000]		[324,000]
Percent	100.0%		73,5%		24.2%		2.3%
20 & Over							
Number	12,527,896		[9,870,000]		[2,330,000]		[324,000]
Percent	100.0%		78.8%		18.6%		2.6%
25 & Over							
Number	11,260,095		[9,210,000]		[1,750,000]		[304,000]
Percent	100.0%		81.8%		15.5%		2.7%
USSR 1959							
16 & Over							
Number	145,322,520		[88,500,000]		[51,400,000]		[5,540,000]
Percent	100.0%		60.9%		35.4%		3.8%
20 & Over							
Number	130,647,451		[84,500,000]		[40,700,000]		[5,510,000]
Percent	100.0%		64.7%		31.2%		4.2%
25 & Over							
Number	110,304,423		[77,500,000]		[28,200,000]		[4,630,000]
Percent	100.0%		70.3%		25.6%		4.2%
USSR 1970							
16 & Over							
Number	166,741,127		[74,300,000]		[81,600,000]		[10,900,000]
Percent	100.0%		44.5%		48.9%		6.5%
20 & Over							
Number	149,478,148		[72,300,000]		[66,400,000]		[10,760,000]
Percent	100.0%		48.4%		44.4%		7.2%
YUGOSLAVIA 1953							
15 & Over							
Number	11,748,000		[4,930,000]	[5,340,000]	[1,410,000]		[78,000]
Percent	100.0%		41.9%	45.4%	12.0%		0.7%
20 & Over							
Number	9,995,000		[4,440,000]	[4,380,000]	[1,110,000]		[78,000]
Percent	100.0%		44.4%	43.8%	11.0%		0.8%
25 & Over							
Number	8,272,000		[3,860,000]	[3,500,000]	[802,000]		[74,400]
Percent	100.0%		46.6%	42.8%	9.7%		0.9%

	Total	No Schooling	First Level Incomplete	First Level Complete	Second Level Cycle 1	Second Level Cycle 2	Post Secondary
YUGOSLAVIA 1961							
10 & Over							
Number	14,587,681	[3,060,000]	[8,900,000]	1,060,000		[1,370,000]	[190,000]
Percent	100.0%	21.0%	61.0%	7.3%		9.4%	1.3%
YUGOSLAVIA 1971							
15 & Over							
Number	14,889,608	[2,770,000]	[4,920,000]	[4,150,000]		[2,570,000]	[472,000]
Percent	100.0%	18.6%	33.0%	27.9%		17.3%	3.2%
20 & Over							
Number	12,910,694	[2,720,000]	[4,600,000]	[2,720,000]		[2,400,293]	[472,000]
Percent	100.0%	21.1%	35.6%	21.1%		18.6%	3.6%
25 & Over							
Number	11,160,871	[2,670,000]	[4,290,000]	[2,060,000]		[1,710,000]	[435,000]
Percent	100.0%	23.9%	38.4%	18.5%		15.3%	3.9%

SECTION E: CLASSES

Introduction

I.

Explanation of Column Headings

AE   *Active Earners.*   Scope of concept differs in the case of each individual country (see General Introduction for details). Includes all those with occupations (including independents in agriculture), excludes Other Earners and Dependents. In Tables E-2 through E-9, data on Active Earners appear as data on class divisions in column Total Population by Class, OE and D. In column Total Population by Class, OE, data on class divisions include Active Earners and Dependents.

AE & D   *Active Earners and Dependents.*   Includes all Active Earners and their dependents; excludes Other Earners and their dependents.

OE   *Other Earners.*   Includes all persons with independent sources of income, persons supported by the state, persons in state institutions, and students supported by state scholarships. Pensioners make up the bulk of this group. In Tables E-2 through E-9, data on Other Earners are presented independently of other groups in column Total Population by Class, OE & D. In column Total Population by Class, OE; Other Earners and their dependents are presented as one group.

D   *Dependents.*   Self-explanatory. Data on dependents in Tables E-2 through E-9 are presented independently of other groups in column Total Population by Class, OE & D. Elsewhere data on dependents are combined with data on other groups (Active Earners, Other Earners).

II.

Basic Class Divisions

Workers   Manual laborers employed in the socialist sector of the economy. Includes, where present, hired manual labor in the nonsocialist sector, and may include nonmanual labor employed in the socialist sector if directly engaged in production. Members of production cooperatives are excluded. Manual workers in defense industries may be excluded.

Other Employees   Nonmanual laborers employed in the socialist sector of the economy. Excludes members of collective farms but may include nonmanual workers employed by collective farms if such persons are not members. Excludes members of nonagricultural production cooperatives, as well as persons engaged in nonmanual occupations on own account. May include a certain number of manual workers employed in state institutions concerned with defense and security.

Collective Farm Members   Includes all members of production cooperatives in agriculture. Persons working in agricultural circles and other type of nonproduction cooperatives are excluded, as are persons working on collective farms who are not collective farm members.

Private Peasantry   Peasant proprietors and helping family members whose main source of income is from agriculture. Hired labor is excluded.

Members of Non-Agricultural Cooperatives   Members of production cooperatives not in agriculture. Hired labor is excluded. May in some cases include persons who are members of cooperatives other than those engaged in production.

Artisans on Own Account	Persons in the nonsocialist sector employed in handicrafts, or independents in the industrial branch of the economy. May include other independents not in agriculture.
Liberal Professions	Persons in creative occupations (artists, musicians, writers) and other professionals not receiving a salary or wage. Includes lawyers working on own account.
Capitalist Classes	Merchants, bankers, landowners, businessmen and related groups.
Helping Family Members	Persons not independently employed, contributing to the income of the household through assisting in the work of the head of the household. Relates primarily to individual peasant households, but may include persons employed in handicrafts or members of collective farms.

(For basic class divisions used in the census data for individual East European countries and the Soviet Union, see Appendix 13.)

III.

Introductory Notes to Tables

Table E-1 Data for 1950-1960 are census data. For remaining years, data are official estimates. Table assumes that data apply to the entire population.

Table E-2 All data are census data. Series I and II are comparable with the exception of Workers and Other Employees. Series II and III are comparable; differences between them are attributable to the preliminary nature of the results in Series II. Military are included in the data on Active Earners, distributed among other classes with the possible exception of professional military personnel, who may be included with Other Employees. Persons engaged in manual labor in defense and security establishments are included with Other Employees. Clergy are excluded from the category of Active Earners in 1956, but included in 1965. The position of apprentices in the class structure has not been established. Auxiliary personnel working on private plots are included among the Active Earners; for details on this group see Table E-10 on the class structure of Active Earners. Series I, 1956, does not distinguish between dependents and those receiving income in the category Other Earners. If the number of dependents in this category is estimated at 45,000, and this is added to the known number of dependents of Active Earners (3,232,977), then the number of dependents in column three would be 3,277,977, and the number of Other Earners in the same column would be 184,361.

Table E-3 All data are census data. Series I and II are not comparable, nor are differences between them consistent over time. Note the inclusion of apprentices and helping family members among Dependents in column three, 1961, Series II, in accordance with published results of the 1961 census.

Table E-4 All data are census data. Data for 1950 and 1964 are not comparable in absolute terms due to the exclusion of East Berlin from the data for 1950. Series I, 1964, includes the category of Independents but omits the distinction between Workers and Employees employed in 1950. Series II, 1964, omits Independents as a category, and identifies Intelligentsia as a class. Series I, 1964, does not include apprentices; Collective Farmers include all persons in production cooperatives in the agricultural branch of the economy. Series II, 1964, includes apprentices and gives data on the number of collective farmers in the population, regardless of branch.

Table E-5 All data are census data. In Series I, 1949, Workers include apprentices; shop foremen are included under Other Employees. Private Peasantry includes independents in agriculture, among whom are a small number of active earners and their dependents who are not peasant proprietors (2,654). Hired help on private holdings are excluded. Independents outside agriculture are divided among Artisans on Own Account (Independents in industry), Capitalist Classes (Independents in trade), and Other Active Earners. Identifying peasantry among Other Earners is not possible for column one; this group, very small in number, is included with Other Active Earners. Series II is comparable to Series I but excludes Apprentices. Series III differs from Series I and II by including foremen and related personnel directing the processes of production among the Workers, as well as including among Workers a certain percentage of persons included among the private pesantry in Series I.

Table E-6 All data are census data (1974—microcensus of that year). For 1931-1960, data are a series. Number of Active Earners is determined according to the concept of *Czynni zawodowo* (see the General Introduction for further details). Private Peasantry includes all independents in the agricultural branch; for more precise data on the number of private peasantry, see Table E-32. Data on Artisans on Own Account, Free Professions, and Capitalist Classes include all independents in nonagricultural branches of the economy. For 1970–1974, data are not a series, but columns on Total Population by Class, OE and Total Population by Class, OE & D are comparable. The comparability of the data in column Total Population by Class, 1970, with the remaining data for 1970 and 1974 is not firmly established. Data for Active Earners are defined in terms of "those supported from work" and are not comparable to data for *Czynni zawodowo* for the same years. Data on Private Peasantry in column Total Population by Class, OE and in column Total Population by Class, OE & D, include persons supported from peasant farming (*w gospodarstwie rolnym*) and are not comparable to data on Independents in Agriculture. Private Peasantry category also includes a small number of hired laborers working for private peasants who were not included in the column of Total Population by Class for 1970.

Table E-7   All data are census data. Data for 1956 and 1966 are comparable. Note the exclusion of over 600,000 collective farm members from among the active earners in 1966. A large number of these persons were probably engaged in part-time agricultural work.

Table E-8   Data for 1926, 1939, 1959, and 1970 are census data. Worker category includes workers in agriculture, but excludes hired labor employed by private peasantry. Service Personnel includes workers in agriculture, but excludes hired labor employed by private peasantry. Service personnel in the nonproductive sectors (guards, sanitary workers, and other manual laborers) are included with Other Employees (*Sluzhashchii*). Hired labor on peasant holdings is included with Private Peasantry. Series I and II are comparable except for workers and employees. Data for Series I, for 1959 and 1970, are presented in Soviet sources as though comparable, but no explanation is provided for the manner in which military personnel, shown as a separate category in 1959, are distributed among the other classes in 1970. Persons in auxiliary agricultural occupations (members of families of collective farmers, workers and employees who are tending private plots in agriculture) are not included among the Active Earners in the census, and this manner of presenting the data is adopted in Table E-8. See the remarks on Table E-34 for further information on the number of persons included among the Active Earners.

Table E-9   Data are census data. Apprentices are included with Workers and Employees in 1971.

Table E-10   Data are census data. Series I and II for 1956 are comparable except for the shift of approximately 50,000 persons from the category of Other Employees to the category of Workers in Series II. The existence of two sets of data for 1956 is the result of differences between the preliminary and final results of the census, and the inclusion of auxiliary agricultural workers with Other Classes in the preliminary results.

Table E-11   See the remarks on Table E-3. Data are census data.

Table E-12   Data are census data for 1946, 1950, and 1964. Data for remaining years are drawn from annual civilian labor force figures. Data for 1950 exclude East Berlin.

Table E-13   Data for Series I and II are census data. Data for Series III are drawn from annual civilian labor force figures. For differences among the three series, see the comments for Table E-5. Only in Series I, for 1949, are workers identified as a class in their own right. In all remaining cases, workers are those employees engaged in manual labor. Other Employees are those employees engaged in nonmanual labor. Data in the table on members of nonagricultural cooperatives are limited to production cooperatives only.

Table E-14   See the remarks on Table E-6. Data are census data; for 1974 the source is the microcensus of that year.

Table E-15   See the remarks on Table E-7. Data are census data.

Table E-16   See the remarks on Table E-8. Data are census data.

Table E-17   Data are census data. Subcategories under entry Workers and Employees have been arranged to reflect differences between manual and nonmanual occupations. For 1961 and 1971 subcategories are generally comparable. Nonmanual categories for 1953 are not comparable with data for later years because of the presence of unskilled workers (both manual and nonmanual) as a separate category in the data for 1953. See also the remarks on Table E-9.

Table E-18   Data are census data. Independents comprise those active earners not receiving a wage or a salary, the bulk of whom are private peasants.

Table E-19   Data are census data. Ind. Artisans—Independent Artisans (artisans on own account).

Table E-20   Data are census data. Data are generally comparable with that given for 1956 in Table E-19. The different composition of the working class in 1956 and 1966 should nevertheless be borne in mind (in the latter year, a greater percent was made up of agricultural workers).

Table E-21   Data are census data.

Table E-22   See the remarks on Table E-19.

Table E-23   See the remarks on Table E-19.

Table E-24   Data for 1939, 1959, and 1970 are census data. 1974 data are official estimates.

Table E-25   Data are census data. See comments on Table E-18 concerning Independents.

Table E-26   Data are on the civilian labor force, gathered periodically by cadre censuses. All persons in the private sector as well as in the military and in security-related occupations are excluded.

Table E-27   Data are census data.

Table E-28   Data are census data. Data on Agricultural Population by Age are for collective farmers and peasantry, and exclude agricultural workers.

Table E-29   Data are census data. Comparisons between years must be made with care because of varying approaches to the question of the inclusion or exclusion of apprentices and helping family members in the agricultural population.

Table E-30   Data for 1950 and 1964 are census data. For remaining years, data are civilian labor force figures for September 1 (December 13 for 1955).

Table E-31   Data are census data.

Table E-32   Data are census data; for 1974 the source is the microcensus of that year. Data on agricultural population by class are presented according to the concept of *Czynni zawodowo* and include all persons who receive income from work, as well as those other earners (primarily pensioners) who are employed part-time in agriculture. Data on the private peasantry relate only to peasant proprietors and their helping family members and dependents, and exclude hired labor working on private holdings.

Table E-33   Data are census data. The difference between the data on Population for 1956, and for AE & D for 1966, lies in the exclusion, from the latter, of Other Earners and Dependents in agriculture.

Table E-34   Data are census data. Differences between this table and Table H-11 concerning the total number in agriculture reflect the fact that Table H-11 includes members of families of collective farmers, workers, and employees working on private plots, while Table E-34 excludes this group.

Table E-35   Data are census data. Data on Agricultural Population Adjusted provide a figure for 1948 for the agricultural population comparable to data from subsequent censuses. Adjustments of the number in agriculture for 1948, and minor adjustments for 1953, are official estimates. In that part of the table dealing with the agricultural population by class, Independents (with and without hired labor) are private peasants.

Table E-36   Data are taken from national censuses, with the exception of the figures for Czechoslovakia for 1976 and the USSR for 1976, which are official estimates of the countries in question.

Table E-37   Data are census data. The standard of classification is that employed in the statistical annuals of the International Labour Organization and recommended (for the Not Economically Active) by the United Nations for the population censuses of 1970. In those cases indicated by fn. *a*, no ILO data exist, and national data have been adjusted, as closely as possible, to fit ILO and UN classifications. In those cases indicated by fn. *b*, ILO data are available and agree with data from national censuses. In the case of Yugoslavia, the agreement between national and ILO data is the result of the application of international standards to national data. In the remaining cases, the agreement between national and ILO data may reflect a failure to adjust national data to international standards. In those cases indicated by fn. *d*, ILO figures, which are the source of the data, differ from national data. Data on the Not Economically Active are taken solely from national sources, arranged as nearly as possible according to UN recommendations. Because of the different ways in which the data are obtained, comparisons among countries must be made with caution.

TABLE E-1   CLASS STRUCTURE OF POPULATION: ALBANIA, 1950-1973

Class	1950	1955	1960	1969	1973
POPULATION	1,218,943	1,391,499	1,626,315	2,079,800	2,296,800
Percent	100.0%	100.0%	100.0%	100.0%	100.0%
Workers	[136,000]	221,839	[481,000]	[684,000]	[831,000]
Percent	11.2%	15.9%	29.6%	32.9%	36.2%
Other Employees	[123,000]	164,080	[184,000]	[235,000]	[331,000]
Percent	10.1%	11.8%	11.3%	11.3%	14.4%
Private Peasants	[885,000]	877,803	[278,000]	[6,200]	0
Percent	72.6%	63.1%	17.1%	0.3%	0.0%
Collective Farmers	[19,500]	66,729	[676,000]	[1,152,000]	[1,135,000]
Percent	1.6%	4.8%	41.6%	55.4%	49.4%
Unaccounted for	[54,900]	61,048	[6,500]	[2,000]	0
Percent	4.5%	4.4%	0.4%	0.1%	0%

TABLE E-2   CLASS STRUCTURE OF POPULATION: BULGARIA, 1956-1965

Status & Class	1956 I Total Popul. by Class[a]	Total Popul. by Class, OE[b]	Total Popul. by Class, OE, & D[c]	1956 II Total Popul. by Class[a]	1965 II Total Popul. by Class[a]
POPULATION	7,613,709	7,613,709	7,613,709	7,613,709	8,226,564
Percent	100.0%	100.0%	100.0%	100.0%	100.0%
Class Divisions, Total	7,613,709	7,383,248	4,150,207	7,613,709	8,226,564
Percent	100.0%	97.0%	54.5%	100.0%	100.0%
Workers	2,112,395	2,051,486	970,988	2,219,809	3,468,906
Percent	27.7%	26.9%	12.8%	29.2%	42.2%
Other Employees	1,228,491	1,132,768	553,213	1,121,077	1,403,719
Percent	16.1%	14.9%	7.3%	14.7%	17.0%
Collective Farm Members	2,723,319	2,704,420	1,726,583	2,723,319	3,051,459
Percent	35.8%	35.5%	22.7%	35.8%	37.1%
Private Peasantry	1,209,934	1,200,535	771,875	...	...
Percent	15.9%	15.8%	10.1%	...	...
Mbrs. of Nonagric. Coop.	94,792	94,022	46,363	94,792	172,733
Percent	1.2%	1.2%	0.6%	1.2%	2.1%
Artisans on Own Account	167,455	165,702	68,413	...	...
Percent	2.2%	2.2%	0.9%	...	...
Liberal Professions	17,276	16,523	7,017	...	...
Percent	0.2%	0.2%	0.1%	...	...
"Capitalist Classes"[d]	15,595	14,483	5,730	...	...
Percent	0.2%	0.2%	0.1%	...	...
Military	....	...	...	...	...
Percent	....	...	...	...	...
Helping Family Members	....	...	...	...	...
Percent	....	...	...	...	...
Others	44,452[e]	3,309	25	1,447,408	129,747
Percent	0.6%	0.0%	0.0%	19.0%	1.6%
Other Earners		230,461	...		
Percent		3.1%	...		
Pensioners		162,970	...		
Percent		2.1%	...		
Scholarship Recipients		20,050	...		
Percent		0.3%	...		
Other Sources of Income		47,441[e]	...		
Percent		0.6%	...		
Dependents			...		
Percent			...		
Housewives			f		
Percent					
Students & Pupils			...		
Percent			...		
Others			...		
Percent			...		
Unaccounted for	0	0	3,463,502[g]	7,304	0
Percent	0%	0%	45.5%	0.1%	0%

Notes: a Data on Class Divisions include Other Earners and Dependents. b Dependents included with data on Class Divisions, Other Earners. c Data on class divisions apply to active earners only. d Private Traders. e Includes 37,148 "not working," of whom 9,521 were Clergy. f In 1956 the number of women not gainfully employed, age 25-60, was 519,714 (includes Other Earners and Dependents.) g Should equal the number of Dependents plus Other Earners. (cont'd.)

Status & Class	1965 Total Popul. by Class[a]	1965 Total Popul. by Class,OE[b]	1965 Total Popul. by Class, OE, & D[c]
POPULATION	8,227,866	8,227,866	8,227,866
Percent	100.0%	100.0%	100.0%
Class Divisions, Total	8,227,866	6,986,972	4,267,798
Percent	100.0%	84.9%	51.9%
Workers	3,433,244	3,097,650	1,755,014
Percent	41.7%	37.6%	21.3%
Other Employees	1,400,406	1,224,564	690,471
Percent	17.0%	14.9%	8.4%
Collective Farm Members	3,081,129	2,376,793	1,652,403
Percent	37.4%	28.9%	20.1%
Private Peasantry	42,767	32,856	21,465
Percent	0.5%	0.4%	0.3%
Mbrs. of Nonagric. Coop.	187,414	180,420	111,577
Percent	2.3%	2.2%	1.4%
Artisans on Own Account	59,863	56,203	27,688
Percent	0.7%	0.7%	0.3%
Liberal Professions	10,756	8,896	4,157
Percent	0.1%	0.1%	0.1%
"Capitalist Classes"[d]	6,324	4,603	2,177
Percent	0.1%	0.1%	0.0%
Military	...	...	...
Percent	...	...	...
Helping Family Members	...	...	...
Percent	...	...	...
Others	5,963[h]	4,987[h]	2,846[h]
Percent	0.1%	0.1%	0.0%
Other Earners		1,240,894	1,112,533
Percent		15.1%	13.5%
Pensioners		...	994,418
Percent		...	12.1%
Scholarship Recipients		...	20,296
Percent		...	0.2%
Other Sources of Income		3,829	97,819[i]
Percent		0.0%	1.2%
Dependents			2,847,535
Percent			34.6%
Housewives			j
Percent			
Students & Pupils			...
Percent			...
Others			...
Percent			...
Unaccounted for	0	0	0
Percent	0%	0%	0%

Notes (cont'd.): h Clergy. i Includes 1,350 persons supported by collective farms, 3,892 "not working," and 92,640 others. j In 1965 the number of female dependents, ages 16-60, was 474,878.

Status & Class	1930 I Total Popul. by Class[a]	1950 I Total Popul. by Class[a]	1950 II Total Popul. by Class[a]	1961 I Total Popul. by Class[a]
POPULATION	14,004,000	12,338,000	12,338,000	13,746,000
Percent	100.0%	100.0%	100.0%	100.0%
Class Divisions, Total	14,004,000	12,338,000	12,338,000	13,746,000
Percent	100.0%	100.0%	100.0%	100.0%
Workers	8,023,000	6,950,000	[5,680,000]	7,738,000
Percent	57.3%	56.4%	46.0%	56.3%
Other Employees	954,000	2,028,000	[2,790,000]	3,834,000
Percent	6.8%	16.4%	22.6%	27.9%
Collective Farm Members	...	2,000	0	1,466,000
Percent	...	0.0%	0.0%	10.6%
Private Peasantry	3,100,000	2,510,000	[2,710,000]	484,000
Percent	22.2%	20.3%	22.0%	3.5%
Mbrs. of Nonagric. Coop.	...	...	...	164,000
Percent	...	...	...	1.2%
Artisans on Own Account	1,153,000[b]	470,000[b]	[679,000][c]	51,000[b]
Percent	8.2%	3.8%	5.5%	0.4%
Liberal Professions	...	...	...	9,000
Percent	...	...	...	0.1%
"Capitalist Classes"	774,000	378,000	...	...
Percent	5.5%	3.1%	...	...
Military	...	...	...	...
Percent	...	...	...	...
Other	...	...	[481,000]	...
Percent	...	...	3.9%	...
Other Earners				
Percent				
Pensioners				
Percent				
Scholarship Recipients				
Percent				
Other Sources of Income				
Percent				
Dependents				
Percent				
Housewives				
Percent				
Students & Pupils				
Percent				
Apprentices				
Percent				
Helping FM in Agric.				
Percent.				
Others				
Percent				
Unaccounted for	0	0	0	0
Percent	0%	0%	0%	0%

Notes: a Data on Class Divisions include Other Earners and Dependents.   b Remaining
Small Entrepreneurs (Ostatni drobni podnikatele).   c Remaining Independents
(Ostatni samost. hospodarici, or ostatni soukrome hospodarici).   (cont'd.)

Status & Class	1961 II		
	Total Popul. by Class[a]	Total Popul. by Class,OE[d]	Total Popul. by Class, OE, & D[e]
POPULATION	13,745,577	13,745,577	13,745,577
Percent	100.0%	100.0%	100.0%
Class Divisions, Total	13,745,577	11,717,708	6,439,412
Percent	100.0%	85.2%[f]	46.8%
Workers	7,556,051	6,474,873[f]	3,361,392
Percent	55.0%	47.1%	24.4%
Other Employees	3,767,386	3,365,933[g]	1,869,780
Percent	27.4%	24.5%	13.6%
Collective Farm Members	1,443,360	1,376,795	930,471
Percent	10.5%	10.0%	6.8%
Private Peasantry	455,802	311,470	166,177
Percent	3.3%	2.3%	1.2%
Mbrs. of Nonagric. Coop.	162,624	158,943	95,839
Percent	1.2%	1.2%	0.7%
Artisans on Own Account	45,358[c]	10,821[c]	5,682[c]
Percent	0.3%	0.1%	0.0%
Liberal Professions	8,799	6,943	3,851
Percent	0.1%	0.1%	0.0%
"Capitalist Classes"	...	...	...
Percent	...	...	...
Military	...	...	...
Percent	...	...	...
Others	306,197	11,930	6,220
Percent	2.2%	0.1%	0.0%
Other Earners		2,027,869	1,585,294
Percent		14.8%	11.5%
Pensioners		1,922,466	1,515,238
Percent		14.0%	11.0%
Scholarship Recipients		38,291	38,291
Percent		0.3%	0.3%
Other Sources of Income		55,990	31,765
Percent		0.4%	0.2%
Dependents			5,720,871
Percent			41.6%
Housewives			1,425,557
Percent			10.4%
Students & Pupils			253,873
Percent			1.8%
Apprentices			243,832
Percent			1.8%
Helping FM in Agric.			43,252
Percent			0.3%
Others			3,754,357
Percent			27.3%
Unaccounted for	0	0	0
Percent	0%	0%	0%

Notes (cont'd.): d Dependents included with data on Class Divisions
and Other Earners. e Data on Class Divisions apply
to active earners only. f Includes 316,466 (cont'd.)

TABLE E-3   (CONCLUDED)

Status & Class	I 1970 Total Popul. by Class[a]	II 1970 Total Popul. by Class[a]	II 1970 Total Popul. by Class, OE[d]	II 1970 Total Popul. by Class, OE, & D[e]
POPULATION	14,366,000	14,362,000	14,362,000	14,362,000
Percent	100.0%	100.0%	100.0%	100.0%
Class Divisions, Total	14,366,000	14,362,000	11,648,000	6,989,000
Percent	100.0%	100.0%	81.1%	48.7%
Workers	8,329,000	8,388,000	6,874,000	4,019,000
Percent	58.0%	58.4%	47.9%	28.0%
Other Employees	4,304,000	4,072,000	3,635,000	2,237,000
Percent	30.0%	28.4%	25.3%	15.6%
Collective Farm Members	1,199,000	1,199,000	949,000	625,000
Percent	8.3%	8.3%	6.6%	4.4%
Private Peasantry	290,000	...	...	...
Percent	2.0%	...	...	...
Mbrs. of Nonagric. Coop.	177,000	...	...	...
Percent	1.2%	...	...	...
Artisans on Own Account	53,000	...	...	...
Percent	0.4%	...	...	...
Liberal Professions	14,000	...	...	...
Percent	0.1%	...	...	...
"Capitalist Classes"	...	...	...	...
Percent	...	...	...	...
Military	...	...	...	...
Percent	...	...	...	...
Others	...	703,000	190,000	108,000
Percent	...	4.9%	1.3%	0.8%
Other Earners			2,714,000	2,393,000
Percent			18.9%	16.7%
Pensioners			...	...
Percent			...	...
Scholarship Recipients			...	...
Percent			...	...
Other Sources of Income			...	...
Percent			...	...
Dependents				4,980,000
Percent				34.7%
Housewives				806,000
Percent				5.6%
Students & Pupils				497,000
Percent				3.5%
Apprentices				359,000
Percent				2.5%
Helping FM in Agric.				...
Percent				...
Others				3,318,000
Percent				23.1%
Unaccounted for	0	0	0	0
Percent	0%	0%	0%	0%

Notes (cont'd.): active workers with pensions and their dependents. g Includes
122,930 active Other Employees with pensions and their dependents.

TABLE E-4   CLASS STRUCTURE OF POPULATION: GDR, 1950-1964

Status & Class	1950[a] Total Popul. by Class, OE[b]	1950[a] Total Popul. by Class, OE, & D[c]	1964 I Total Popul. by Class, OE[b]	1964 I Total Popul. by Class, OE, & D[c]
POPULATION	17,199,098	17,199,098	17,003,611	17,003,611
Percent	100.0%	100.0%	100.0%	100.0%
Class Divisions, Total	13,778,209	7,923,222	13,491,122[d]	7,994,558[d]
Percent	80.1%	46.1%	79.3%	47.0%
Workers	7,544,927	4,125,519		
Percent	43.9%	24.0%		
Intelligentsia			11,156,476	6,631,281
Percent			65.6%	39.0%
Other Employees	3,120,882	1,687,277		
Percent	18.1%	9.8%		
Collective Farm Members	...	...	1,485,960[e]	856,840[e]
Percent	...	...	8.7%	5.0%
Private Peasantry				
Percent				
Mbrs. of Nonagric. Coop.	...	...	287,451[f]	148,822[f]
Percent	...	...	1.7%	0.9%
Artisans on Own Account & Small Producers				
Percent				
Independents	2,050,872	1,093,807	472,527	270,986
Percent	11.9%	6.4%	2.8%	1.6%
Helping Family Members	1,061,528	1,016,619	88,708	86,629
Percent	6.2%	5.9%	0.5%	0.5%
Others	...	...	...	...
Percent	...	...	...	...
Other Earners	3,420,889	2,413,534	...	...
Percent	19.9%	14.0%	...	...
Pensioners	2,198,280[g]	1,634,202[g]	...	...
Percent	12.8%	9.5%	...	...
Scholarship Recipients	...	...	...	...
Percent	...	...	...	...
Other Sources of Income	1,222,609	779,332	...	...
Percent	7.1%	4.5%	...	...
Dependents		6,862,342		...
Percent		40.0%		...
Housewives		2,704,644[h]		...
Percent		15.7%		...
Students & Pupils		...		...
Percent		...		...
Others		4,157,698		...
Percent		24.2%		...
Unaccounted for	0	0	3,512,489	9,009,053
Percent	0%	0%	20.7%	53.0%

213

Status & Class	1964 II		
	Total Popul. by Class[i]	Total Popul. by Class,OE[b]	Total Popul. by Class, OE, & D [c]
POPULATION	17,003,661	17,003,611	17,003,611
Percent	100.0%	100.0%	100.0%
Class Divisions, Total	16,504,097	13,842,367[j]	8,345,017[j]
Percent	97.1%	81.4%[k]	49.1%[k]
Workers	12,587,289	10,405,382[k]	6,410,989[k]
Percent	74.0%	61.2%	37.7%
Intelligentsia	1,150,387	1,103,382	544,318
Percent	6.8%	6.5%	3.2%
Other Employees	1	1	1
Percent			
Collective Farm Members	1,634,391	1,520,944	903,167
Percent	5.0%	8.9%	5.3%
Private Peasantry	...	...	...
Percent	...	...	...
Mbrs. of Nonagric. Coop.	292,415	282,955[m]	150,409[m]
Percent	1.7%	1.7%	0.9%
Artisans on Own Account			
& Small Producers	437,849	330,577	197,141
Percent	2.6%	1.9%	1.2%
Independents			
Percent			
Helping Family Members	...	...	...
Percent	...	...	...
Others	401,766[n]	199,127[n]	138,993[n]
Percent	2.4%	1.2%	0.8%
Other Earners		3,161,244	2,887,331
Percent		18.6%	17.0%
Pensioners		...	2,602,421
Percent		...	15.3%
Scholarship Recipients		...	122,490
Percent		...	0.7%
Other Sources of Income		...	162,420
Percent		...	1.0%
Dependents			5,771,263
Percent			33.9%
Housewives			...
Percent			...
Students & Pupils			...
Percent			...
Others			...
Percent			...
Unaccounted for	499,564[o]	0	0
Percent	2.9%	0%	0%

Notes: For notes, see next page.

TABLE E-4   (CONCLUDED)

Notes: a Excludes East Berlin. b Dependents included with data on Class Divisions and Other Earners. c Data on Class Divisions apply to active earners only. d Without Apprentices. e Members of cooperatives in the agricultural branch of the economy. f Members of cooperatives in nonagricultural branches of the economy. g Persons receiving social security and widows' benefits. h Wives listed as dependents. There were also 400,158 housewives and their dependents included among other earners with other sources of income. i Data on Class Divisions include Other Earners and Dependents. j With Apprentices. k Includes persons classifiable as Other Employees. l Included with workers. m Artisans belonging to cooperatives (Genossenschaftshandwerker). n Helping Family Members, Private Peasantry and others; data on total population by class include 111,244 Private Traders (Einzelhandler) and their dependents. o Not classifiable.

TABLE E-5 CLASS STRUCTURE OF POPULATION: HUNGARY, 1949-1973

Status & Class	1949 I Total Popul. by Class[a]	1949 I Total Popul. by Class,OE[b]	1949 I Total Popul. by Class, OE, & D[c]	1949 II Total Popul. by Class, OE, & D[c]	1949 III Total Popul. by Class[a]
POPULATION	9,204,799	9,204,799	9,204,799	9,204,799	9,204,799
Percent	100.0%	100.0%	100.0%	100.0%	100.0%
Class Divisions, Total	9,125,228	8,674,784	4,154,543	4,084,931	
Percent	99.1%	94.2%	45.1%	44.4%	
Workers	3,380,079[d]	3,125,964[d]	1,519,287[d]	1,449,675[e]	[3,790,000]
Percent	36.7%	34.0%	16.5%	15.7%	41.2%[f]
Other Employees	971,037	790,493	387,157	387,157[g]	[801,000]
Percent	10.5%	8.6%	4.2%	4.2%	8.7%[h]
Collective Farm Members	...	...	...	...	[28,000]
Percent	...	...	...	...	0.3%
Private Peasantry	3,073,719[i]	3,073,719[i]	1,131,825[i]	1,907,234[j]	[3,590,000]
Percent	33.4%	33.4%	12.3%	20.7%	39.0%[k]
Mbrs. of Nonagric. Coop.	...	...	...	...	...
Percent	...	...	...	...	...
Artisans on Own Account	548,828[l]	548,828[l]	200,387[l]	⎱	[838,000]
Percent	6.0%	6.0%	2.2%		9.1%
Liberal Professions	26,605	26,605	12,565	340,865[m]	...
Percent	0.3%	0.3%	0.1%	3.7%	...
"Capitalist Classes"	238,576[n]	222,791[n]	95,059[n]	⎰	[156,000]
Percent	2.6%	2.4%	1.0%		1.7%[o]
Military	...	...	...	...	...
Percent	...	...	...	...	...
Helping Family Members	867,304[p]	867,304[p]	800,813[q]	r	...
Percent	9.4%	9.4%	8.7%		...
Others	19,080[s]	19,080[s]	7,450	...	...
Percent	0.2%	0.2%	0.1%	...	...
Other Earners		450,444	254,756	...	
Percent		4.9%	2.8%	...	
Pensioners		434,659	244,150	...	
Percent		4.7%	2.7%	...	
Scholarship Recipients		...	...	...	
Percent		...	...	...	
Other Sources of Income		15,785	10,606	...	
Percent		0.2%	0.1%	...	
Dependents			4,795,500	...	
Percent			52.1%	...	
Housewives			...	...	
Percent			...	...	
Students & Pupils			...	...	
Percent			...	...	
Others			...	...	
Percent			...	...	
Others & Unknown	79,571	79,571	...	...	
Percent	0.9%	0.9%	...	...	
Unaccounted for	0	0	0	5,119,868	
Percent	0%	0%	0%	55.6%	

Notes: a Data on Class Divisions include Other Earners and Dependents. b Dependents included with data on Class Divisions, Other Earners. c Data on Class Divisions apply to active earners only. d Includes 69,618 Apprentices. e All Employees and Members of Cooperatives engaged in manual labor. f Includes workers engaged in manual labor (39.4%) and "workers directing the processing of production" (1.8%). g "Employees and Members of Cooperatives engaged in nonmanual occupations." h "Intelligentsia and other intellectuals--_Trudovaia intelligentsiia i prochie rabotniki umstvennogo truda_." i Excludes Helping Family Members. j Independents and Helping Family Members engaged in Agriculture. k Includes Helping Family Members. l Independents employed in industry. m Independents and Helping (cont'd.)

Status & Class	1960 III Total Popul. by Class[a]	1960 I Total Popul. by Class,OE[b]	1960 II Total Popul. by Class, OE, & D[c]	1963 I Total Popul. by Class, OE, & D[c]
POPULATION	9,961,044	9,961,044	9,961,044	10,072,000
Percent	100.0%	100.0%	100.0%	100.0%
Class Divisions, Total	9,961,044	9,280,000	4,759,616	8,923,000
Percent	100.0%	93.2%	47.8%	88.6%
Workers	[5,610,000]	4,703,000[u]	2,172,682	4,862,000
Percent	56.3%[t]	47.2%	21.8%	48.3%
Other Employees	[1,470,000]	1,387,000[v]	817,341	1,479,000
Percent	14.8%[h]	13.9%[k]	8.2%	14.7%[x]
Collective Farm Members	[1,200,000]	1,193,000[k]	580,664[w]	1,919,000[x]
Percent	12.1%	12.0%[k]	5.8%[k]	19.1%[k]
Private Peasantry	[1,390,000]	1,461,000[k]	943,865[k]	190,000[k]
Percent	13.9%[k]	14.7%	9.5%	1.9%
Mbrs. of Nonagric. Coop.	...	271,000	126,847	285,000
Percent	...	2.7%	1.3%	2.8%
Artisans on Own Account	[279,000]			
Percent	2.8%[y]			
Liberal Professions	...	265,000[m]	118,217[m]	188,000[m]
Percent	...	2.7%	1.2%	1.9%
"Capitalist Classes"	[10,000]			
Percent	0.1%[o]			
Military	...	...	...	...
Percent	...	...	...	...
Helping Family Members	...	...	z	aa
Percent	...	...		
Others	...	...	...	...
Percent	...	...	...	...
Other Earners		682,000	436,599[bb]	1,147,000[cc]
Percent		6.8%	4.4%	11.4%
Pensioners		614,000	...	...
Percent		6.2%	...	...
Scholarship Recipients				
Percent		68,000	...	...
Other Sources of Income		0.7%	...	...
Percent				
Dependents			dd	
Percent				
Housewives			...	
Percent			...	
Students & Pupils			...	
Percent			...	
Others			...	
Percent			...	
Others & Unknown			...	
Percent			...	
Unaccounted for			4,764,829	
Percent			47.8%	

Notes (cont'd.):   Family Members not engaged in agriculture. n Independents in Trade, Insurance, Banking, and with independent sources of income. o "Capitalists, Landowners." p 838,407 in agriculture. q 775,322 in agriculture. r Included with Private Peasantry. s Includes 439 Independents in Mining, 18,641 Independents in "other diverse occupations." t Includes workers engaged in manual occupations (54.9%) and "workers directing the processing of production" (1.4%). u Employees engaged in manual labor. v Employees engaged in nonmanual labor. (cont'd.)

Status & Class	1970 III Total Popul. by Class[a]	1970 III Total Popul. by Class, OE, & D[c]	1973 III Total Popul. by Class[a]	1973 III Total Popul. by Class, OE[b]	1973 III Total Popul. by Class, OE, & D[c]
POPULATION	10,322,099	10,322,099	10,416,387	10,416,387	10,416,387
Percent	100.0%	100.0%	100.0%	100.0%	100.0%
Class Divisions, Total	10,322,099	4,988,676	10,416,387	8,774,196	5,085,541
Percent	100.0%	48.3%	100.0%[ff]	84.2%[gg]	48.8%[hh]
Workers	[5,920,000][ee]	2,647,048	6,117,744	5,224,467	2,949,765
Percent	57.4%	25.6%	58.7%[h]	50.2%[h]	28.3%[h]
Other Employees	[2,000,000]	1,236,423	2,094,686[h]	1,819,023[h]	1,219,165[h]
Percent	19.5%[h]	12.0%	20.1%	17.5%	11.7%
Collective Farm Members	[2,100,000]	812,710[ii]	1,905,980	1,458,378	743,717
Percent	20.3%	7.9%[jj]	18.3%	14.0%	7.1%
Private Peasantry	[114,000]	58,800[jj]	111,795	108,773	87,397
Percent	1.1%	0.6%	1.1%	1.0%	0.8%
Mbrs. of Nonagric. Coop.	...	128,485	...	...	...
Percent	...	1.2%	...	...	...
Artisans on Own Account	[175,000]		186,182[y]	163,555[y]	85,497[y]
Percent	1.7%		1.8%	1.6%	0.8%
Liberal Professions	...	83,003[m]	...	...	...
Percent	...	0.8%	...	...	...
"Capitalist Classes"	0		...	...	...
Percent	0%		...	...	...
Military	...	...	...	...	...
Percent	...	...	...	...	...
Helping Family Members	...	...	...	...	...
Percent	...	...	...	...	...
Others	...	22,213	...	...	...
Percent	...	0.2%	...	...	...
Other Earners		1,395,490		1,642,191	1,642,191
Percent		13.5%		15.8%	15.8%
Pensioners		1,247,002		...	...
Percent		12.1%		...	...
Scholarship Recipients		...		...	...
Percent		...		...	...
Other Sources of Income		148,488		...	...
Percent		1.4%		...	...
Dependents		dd			3,688,655
Percent					35.4%
Housewives		...			...
Percent		...			...
Students & Pupils		...			...
Percent		...			...
Others		...			...
Percent		...			...
Others & Unknown		...			...
Percent		...			...
Unaccounted for	0	3,937,933	0	0	0
Percent	0%	38.2%	0%	0%	0%

Notes (cont'd.): w Members of cooperatives in agriculture. x Includes 227,000 Helping Family Members, of whom 81,000 were working private plots of members of cooperatives. y "Craftsmen, Retail Dealers, etc., and their Unpaid Family Members." z Helping Family Members included with other classes. There were 55,257 Helping Family Members among collective farmers. aa Helping Family Members included with other classes. bb Of whom, 327,429 were once manual workers, 109,170 nonmanual workers. cc Of whom, 894,000 were once manual workers, 192,000 nonmanual workers. dd Number of Dependents should equal number Unaccounted for. ee Includes workers engaged in   (cont'd.)

TABLE E-5   (CONCLUDED)

Manual occupations (54.9%) and "workers directing the processing of production" (2.5%). ff Includes workers engaged in manual occupations (5,806,536) and "workers directing the processing of production" (311,208). gg Includes workers engaged in manual occupations (4,942,349) and "workers directing the processing of production" (282,118). hh Includes workers engaged in manual occupations (2,796,404) and "workers directing the processing of production" (153,361). ii Includes 98,703 Helping Family Members. jj Includes 19,526 Helping Family Members.

TABLE E-6   CLASS STRUCTURE OF POPULATION: POLAND, 1931-1974

	1931		1950	
	Total Popul. by Class,OE[a]	Total Popul. by Class, OE, & D[b]	Total Popul. by Class,OE[a]	Total Popul. by Class, OE, & D[b]
POPULATION	32,107,300	32,107,300	25,008,200	25,008,200
Percent	100.0%	100.0%	100.0%	100.0%
Class Divisions, Total	29,048,900	13,622,200	23,618,200	12,404,200
Percent	90.5%	42.4%	94.4%	49.6%
Workers	7,505,500	3,488,700	11,771,600	5,444,800
Percent	23.4%	10.9%	47.1%	21.8%
Other Employees	1,224,600	563,000		
Percent	3.8%	1.8%		
Collective Farm Members	...	...	135,500	55,500
Percent	...	...	0.5%	0.2%
Private Peasantry[c]	11,601,200	3,321,900	6,604,600	2,698,300
Percent	36.1%	10.3%	26.4%	10.8%
Mbrs. of Nonagric. Coop.	...	...	338,400	160,400
Percent	...	...	1.4%	0.6%
Artisans on Own Account				
Percent				
Liberal Professions	3,256,900	1,069,100	448,700	169,800
Percent	10.1%	3.3%	1.8%	0.7%
"Capitalist Classes"				
Percent				
Military	d	...	e	...
Percent		...		...
Helping Family Members	5,170,600[f]	5,170,600[f]	3,972,700[g]	3,855,400[h]
Percent	16.1%	16.1%	15.9%	15.4%
Others	290,100	8,900	346,700	20,000
Percent	0.9%	0.0%	1.4%	0.1%
Other Earners	929,300	491,200	995,500	770,500
Percent	2.9%	1.5%	4.0%	3.1%
Pensioners	...	...	...	...
Percent	...	...	...	...
Scholarship Recipients	...	...	...	...
Percent	...	...	...	...
Other Sources of Income	...	...	...	...
Percent	...	...	...	...
Dependents		17,101,200		11,833,500
Percent		53.3%		47.3%
Housewives		...		...
Percent		...		...
Students & Pupils		...		...
Percent		...		...
Others		...		...
Percent		...		...
Others & Unknown	1,937,600[i]	892,700[j]	...	...
Percent	6.0%	2.8%	...	...
Unaccounted for	191,500	0	394,500	0
Percent	0.6%	0%	1.6%	0%

Notes: a Dependents included with data on Class Divisions, Other Earners. b Data on Class Divisions apply to active earners only. c Independents (persons working on own account) in agriculture. d Included among 191,500 Unaccounted for. e Included among 394,500 Unaccounted for. f 4,936,000 in agriculture. g 3,938,800 in agriculture. h 3,824,800 in agriculture. i Unemployed and their dependents. j Unemployed. (cont'd.)

	1960		1970	
	Total Popul. by Class,OE[a]	Total Popul. by Class, OE, & D[b]	Total Popul. by Class[k]	Total Popul. by Class,OE[a]
POPULATION	29,775,500	29,775,500	32,642,270	32,642,270
Percent	100.0%	100.0%	100.0%	100.0%
Class Divisions, Total	27,502,100	13,907,442	32,320,520	29,262,149
Percent	92.4%	46.7%	99.0%	89.6%
Workers	10,802,000	4,691,900	16,098,371	13,760,518
Percent	36.3%	15.8%	49.3%	42.2%
Other Employees	5,143,100	2,521,800	7,247,688	6,529,857
Percent	17.3%	8.5%	22.2%[1]	20.0%
Collective Farm Members	81,400	34,300	89,508[1]	88,592
Percent	0.3%	0.1%	0.3%	0.3%[m]
Private Peasantry	6,798,800	2,993,700	8,126,769[m]	8,070,976[m]
Percent	22.8%	10.1%	25.0%	24.7%
Mbrs. of Nonagric. Coop.	713,900	325,100		...
Percent	2.4%	1.1%		...
Artisans on Own Account				...
Percent				...
Liberal Professions	524,000	191,700	497,914	...
Percent	1.8%	0.6%	1.5%	...
"Capitalist Classes"				...
Percent				...
Military	n	...	...	...
Percent		...	...	...
Helping Family Members	3,303,500[o]	3,120,000[p]		
Percent	11.1%	10.5%		
Others	135,400	28,900	260,270	...
Percent	0.5%	0.1%	0.8%	...
Other Earners	1,903,600	1,433,500		3,380,121
Percent	6.4%	4.8%		10.4%
Pensioners	...	...		1,308,491
Percent	...	...		4.0%
Scholarship Recipients	...	...		59,310
Percent	...	...		0.2%
Other Sources of Income	...	...		2,012,320
Percent	...	...		6.2%
Dependents		14,434,600		
Percent		48.5%		
Housewives		...		
Percent		...		
Students & Pupils		...		
Percent		...		
Others		...		
Percent		...		
Others & Unknown	...	...	321,750[q]	...
Percent	...	...	1.0%	...
Unaccounted for	369,800	0	0	0
Percent	1.2%	0%	0%	0%

Notes (cont'd.):   k Data on Class Divisions include Other Earners and Dependents. l Includes approximately 1,000 persons employed in producers' cooperatives outside agriculture. m Persons supported from work in peasant farming. Helping Family (cont'd.)

	1970	1974	
	Total Popul. by Class, OE, & D [b]	Total Popul. by Class, OE [a]	Total Popul. by Class, OE, & D [b]
POPULATION	32,642,270	33,635,933	33,635,933
Percent	100.0%	100.0%	100.0%
Class Divisions, Total	16,429,101	29,525,388	17,089,452
Percent	50.3%	87.8%	50.8%
Workers	...	...	...
Percent	...	...	...
Other Employees	...	...	...
Percent	...	...	...
Collective Farm Members	41,254		
Percent	0.1%		
Private Peasantry [k]	5,400,460	7,420,750	4,901,132
Percent	16.5%	22.1%	14.6%
Mbrs. of Nonagric. Coop.	...	...	...
Percent	...	...	...
Artisans on Own Account	...	...	...
Percent	...	...	...
Liberal Professions	...	...	...
Percent	...	...	...
"Capitalist Classes"	...	...	...
Percent	...	...	...
Military	...	...	...
Percent	...	...	...
Helping Family Members	...	...	...
Percent	...	...	...
Others	...	...	...
Percent	...	...	...
Other Earners	2,452,445	4,110,545	3,110,614
Percent	7.5%	12.2%	9.2%
Pensioners	...	...	...
Percent	...	...	...
Scholarship Recipients	...	...	...
Percent	...	...	...
Other Sources of Income	...	...	...
Percent	...	...	...
Dependents	13,760,724		13,435,867
Percent	42.2%		39.9%
Housewives	...		...
Percent	...		...
Students & Pupils	...		...
Percent	...		...
Others	...		...
Percent	...		...
Others & Unknown	...	...	...
Percent	...	...	...
Unaccounted for	0	0	0
Percent	0%	0%	0%

Notes (cont'd.): Members included. n Included among 397,200 Unaccounted for. o 3,290,000 in agriculture.
p 3,108,000 in agriculture. q Social status not
established.

TABLE E-7   CLASS STRUCTURE OF POPULATION: ROMANIA, 1956-1966

Status & Class	1956 Total Popul. by Class[a]	1956 Total Popul. by Class, OE, & D[b]	1966 Total Popul. by class[a]	1966 Total Popul. by Class,OE[c]	1966 Total Popul. by Class, OE, & D[b]
POPULATION	17,489,450	17,489,450	19,103,163	19,103,163	19,103,163
Percent	100.0%	100.0%	100.0%	100.0%	100.0%
Class Divisions, Total	17,489,450	10,449,128	19,103,163	17,119,271	10,362,300
Percent	100.0%	59.7%	100.0%	89.6%	54.2%
Workers	4,142,932	2,093,989	7,624,981	6,855,046	3,380,953
Percent	23.7%	12.0%	39.9%	35.9%	17.7%
Other Employees	2,332,046	1,088,861	2,356,082	2,044,073	1,226,933
Percent	13.3%	6.2%	12.3%	10.7%	6.4%
Collective Farm Members	1,260,476	797,108	7,365,179	6,647,888	4,736,862
Percent	7.2%	4.6%	38.6%	34.8%	24.8%
Private Peasantry	8,945,889	6,151,973	996,600	972,411	699,884
Percent	51.1%	35.2%	5.2%	5.1%	3.7%
Mbrs. of Nonagric. Coop.	184,591	91,055	438,463	411,381	227,134
Percent	1.1%	0.5%	2.3%	2.2%	1.2%
Artisans on Own Account	447,254	196,736	176,196	169,272	83,984
Percent	2.6%	1.1%	0.9%	0.9%	0.4%
Liberal Professions	48,878	20,781	...	...	...
Percent	0.3%	0.1%	...	...	...
"Capitalist Classes"[d]	14,402	6,123	...	...	...
Percent	0.1%	0.0%	...	...	...
Military	...	...	...	...	...
Percent	...	...	...	...	...
Helping Family Members	...	...	...	...	...
Percent	...	...	...	...	...
Others	112,982	2,502	145,662	19,200	6,550
Percent	0.6%	0.0%	0.8%	0.1%	0.0%
Other Earners		412,659		1,983,892	1,623,763
Percent		2.4%		10.4%	8.5%
Pensioners		...		...	731,132
Percent		...		...	3.8%
Scholarship Recipients		...		...	230,014
Percent		...		...	1.2%
Other Sources of Income		...		...	662,617[e]
Percent		...		...	3.5%
Dependents		6,627,509			7,117,100
Percent		37.9%			37.3%
Housewives		f			...
Percent					...
Students & Pupils		...			...
Percent		...			...
Others		...			...
Percent		...			...
Unknown		154			...
Percent		0.0%			...
Unaccounted for	0	0	0	0	0
Percent	0%	0%	0%	0%	0%

Notes: a Data on Class Divisions include Other Earners and Dependents. b Data on Class Divisions apply to active earners only. c Dependents included with data on Class Divisions, Other Earners. d Commercial occupations. e Includes 569,155 supported by collective farms. f Of total number of Dependents, 995,775 were females ages 25-59.

TABLE E-8   CLASS STRUCTURE OF POPULATION: USSR, 1926-1979

Status & Class	1926 Total Popul. by Class,OE[a]	1926 Total Popul. by Class, OE, & D.[b]	1928 I Total Popul. by Class[c]	1939 I Total Popul. by Class[c]
POPULATION	147,027,915	147,027,915	152,300,000	170,557,093
Percent	100.0%	100.0%	100.0%	100.0%
Class Divisions, Total	144,378,035	84,357,715	152,300,000	170,557,093
Percent	98.2%	57.4%	100.0%	100.0%
Workers	12,771,977	5,602,512	[18,880,000]	[57,100,000]
Percent	8.7%	3.8%	12.4%	33.5%
Other Employees	9,165,263	3,980,705	[7,920,000]	[28,500,000]
Percent	6.2%	2.7%	5.2%	16.7%
Collective Farm Members	...	...	[4,420,000]	[80,500,000]
Percent	...	...	2.9%[d]	47.2%
Private Peasantry	63,813,682[e]	22,419,599[f]	[114,000,000]	[4,430,000]
Percent	43.4%	15.2%	74.9%[g]	2.6%
Mbrs. of Nonagric. Coop.	...	...	...	...
Percent	...	...	...	...
Artisans on Own Account	3,722,095[h]	1,316,703[h]	i	...
Percent	2.5%	0.9%		...
Liberal Professions	366,388	136,569	...	...
Percent	0.2%	0.1%	...	...
"Capitalist Classes"	102,099[j]	31,150[j]	[7,010,000]	...
Percent	0.1%	0.0%	4.6%[k]	...
Military	758,625	631,189	...	...
Percent	0.5%	0.4%	...	...
Helping Family Members	48,462,783[l]	48,462,783[l]	...	...
Percent	33.0%	33.0%	...	...
Others	5,215,123[m]	1,776,505[n]	...	...
Percent	3.5%	1.2%	...	...
Other Earners	2,649,880[o]	1,862,623[p]		
Percent	1.8%	1.3%		
Pensioners	...	...		
Percent	...	...		
Scholarship Recipients	...	...		
Percent	...	...		
Other Sources of Income	...	...		
Percent	...	...		
Dependents		60,807,568		
Percent		41.4%		
Mbrs. of Families of Coll. Farmers, Workers & Empl. Tending Private Plots in Agriculture		...		
Percent		...		
Housewives		...		
Percent		...		
Students & Pupils		...		
Percent		...		
Others		...		
Percent		...		
Unaccounted for	0	9	0	0
Percent	0%	0%	0%	0%

Notes: a Dependents included with data on Class Divisions, Other Earners. b Data on Class Divisions apply to active earners only. c Data on Class Divisions include Other Earners and Dependents. d Members of agricultural and handicraft cooperatives. e Persons in the agricultural branch of the economy and their dependents, of whom 56,812,094 were peasant proprietors and their helping family members, 2,040,372 were peasant proprietors working with hired labor, and 4,961,216 were peasant proprietors working without help. f Persons with occupations in the agricultural branch of the economy, (cont')

224

Status & Class	1939 II Total Popul. by Class[c]	1939 Total Popul. by Class, OE, & D[b]	1959 I Total Popul. by Class[c]	1959 II Total Popul. by Class[c]	1959 I Total Popul. by Class, OE, & D[b]
POPULATION	170,557,093	170,557,093	208,826,650	208,826,650	208,826,650
Percent	100.0%	100.0%	100.0%	100.0%	100.0%
Class Divisions, Total	170,557,093	[78,800,000]	208,826,650	208,826,650	99,130,212
Percent	100.0%	46.2%	100.0%	100.0%	47.5%
Workers	[55,400,000]	...	[103,000,000]	100,763,570	46,146,573
Percent	32.5%	...	49.5%	48.2%	22.1%
Other Employees	[30,200,000]	...	[39,300,000]	41,903,081	19,670,209
Percent	17.7%	...	18.8%	20.1%	9.4%
Collective Farm Members	[80,500,000]	...	[65,600,000]	65,548,826	33,047,126
Percent	47.2%	...	31.4%	31.4%	15.8%
Private Peasantry	[4,430,000]	...	[626,000]	557,998	266,304
Percent	2.6%	...	0.3%	0.3%	0.1%
Mbrs. of Nonagric. Coop.	...	...	...	...	...
Percent	...	...	...	...	...
Artisans on Own Account	...	...	...	i	i
Percent	...	...	...		
Liberal Professions	...	...	...	...	...
Percent	...	...	...	...	...
"Capitalist Classes"	...	...	...	...	...
Percent	...	...	...	...	...
Military	...	...	...	...	...
Percent	...	...	...	...	...
Helping Family Members	...	...	...	...	...
Percent	...	...	...	...	...
Others	...	...	...	53,175	...
Percent	...	...	...	0.0%	...
Other Earners		[5,120,000]			14,409,597
Percent		3.0%			6.9%
Pensioners		[2,220,000]			12,423,110
Percent		1.3%			5.9%
Scholarship Recipients		[1,710,000]			1,717,365
Percent		1.0%			0.8%
Other Sources of Income		[1,190,000]			269,122
Percent		0.7%			0.1%
Dependents		[86,600,000]			95,286,841
Percent		50.8%			45.6%
Mbrs. of Families of Coll. Farmers, Workers & Empl. Tending Private Plots in Agric.		[8,190,000]			9,864,801
Percent		4.8%			4.7%
Housewives					
Percent					
Students & Pupils		[78,500,000]			85,422,040
Percent		46.0%			40.9%
Others					
Percent					
Unaccounted for	0	0	0	0	0
Percent	0%	0%	0%	0%	0%

Notes (cont'd.): of whom 19,945,923 were peasant proprietors and their helping family members, 738,347 were peasant proprietors working with hired labor, and 1,735,329 were peasant proprietors working without help. g Includes Artisans on own Account. h Persons engaged in small and handicrafts industries. i Included with Private Peasantry. j All those working with hired labor, excluding those in agriculture and handicrafts. k Bourgeoisie, Landlords, Traders, and Kulaks. l 48,113,637 in agriculture. m Includes 2,413,318 persons working (cont'd.)

TABLE E-8 (CONTINUED)

Status & Class	1959 II Total Popul. by Class, OE, & D[b]	1970 I Total Popul. by Class[c]	Total Popul. by Class, OE[a]	Total Popul. by Class, OE, & D[b]
POPULATION	208,826,650	241,436,013	241,436,013	241,436,013
Percent	100.0%	100.0%	100.0%	100.0%
Class Divisions, Total	99,130,212	240,944,066	204,503,570	115,204,076
Percent	47.5%	99.8%	84.7%	47.7%
Workers	44,323,723	136,930,781	118,528,447	66,321,222
Percent	21.2%	56.7%	49.1%	27.5%
Other Employees	18,637,697	54,551,734	49,143,683	30,617,865
Percent	8.9%	22.6%	20.4%	12.7%
Collective Farm Members	32,279,727	49,461,551	36,831,440	17,899,838
Percent	15.5%	20.5%	15.3%	7.4%
Private Peasantry	266,065	...	...	...
Percent	0.1%	...	...	...
Mbrs. of Nonagric. Coop.	...	...	...	...
Percent	...	...	...	...
Artisans on Own Account	i	...	...	...
Percent		...	...	...
Liberal Professions	...	...	...	...
Percent	...	...	...	...
"Capitalist Classes"	...	...	...	...
Percent	...	...	...	...
Military	3,623,000	...	...	...
Percent	1.7%	...	...	...
Helping Family Members	...	...	...	...
Percent	...	...	...	...
Others	...	...	...	365,151[q]
Percent	...	...	...	0.2%
Other Earners	14,409,597		r	36,480,579
Percent	6.9%			15.1%
Pensioners	12,423,110			32,641,210
Percent	5.9%			13.5%
Scholarship Recipients	1,717,365			3,552,580
Percent	0.8%			1.5%
Other Sources of Income	269,122			286,789
Percent	0.1%			0.1%
Dependents	95,286,841			89,751,358
Percent	45.6%			37.2%
Mbrs. of Families of Coll. Farmers, Workers & Empl. Tending Private Plots in Agric.	9,864,801			1,823,499
Percent	4.7%			0.8%
Housewives				
Percent				
Students & Pupils	85,422,040			87,927,859
Percent	40.9%			36.4%
Others				
Percent				
Unaccounted for	0	491,947	36,932,443	0
Percent	0%	0.2%	15.3%	0%

Notes (cont'd.): with Helping Family Members or without help outside agriculture and handicrafts and 1,134,198 children under 10 years of age not listed elsewhere as Dependents. n Includes those working alone or only with Helping Family Members outside agriculture and handicrafts. o Includes 1,667,607 unemployed and 2,649,880 Pensioners and Other Earners. p Includes 1,014,431 (cont'd.)

TABLE E-8   (CONCLUDED)

1979

Status & Class	Total Popul. by Class, OE & D[b]
POPULATION	262,085,000
Percent	100.0%
Class Divisions, Total	134,860,000
Percent	51.5%
Workers	...
Percent	...
Other Employees	...
Percent	...
Collective Farm Members	...
Percent	...
Private Peasantry	...
Percent	...
Mbrs. of Nonagric. Coop.	...
Percent	...
Liberal Professions	...
Percent	...
"Capitalist Classes"	...
Percent	...
Military	...
Percent	...
Helping Family Members	...
Percent	...
Others	...
Percent	...
Others Earners	...
Percent	...
Pensioners	40,126,000
Percent	15.3%
Scholarship Recipients	6,633,000
Percent	2.5%
Other Sources of Income	...
Percent	...
Dependents	80,195,000
Percent	30.6%
Mbrs. of Families of Coll. Farmers, Workers & Empl. Tending Private Plots in Agric.	...
Percent	...
Housewives	...
Percent	...
Students & Pupils	...
Percent	...
Others	...
Percent	...
Unaccounted for	271,000
Percent	0.1%

Notes (cont'd.)   unemployed and 1,862,623 Other
                   Earners. q Unaccounted for. r
                   Other Earners and their dependents
                   included among those Unaccounted
                   for. s Includes Persons with
                   Other Sources of Income and Unknown.

TABLE E-9   CLASS STRUCTURE OF POPULATION: YUGOSLAVIA, 1953-1971

Status & Class	1953		1961	
	Total Popul. by Class,OE[a]	Total Popul by Class, OE, & D[b]	Total Popul. by Class,OE[a]	Total Popul. by Class, OE, & D[b]
POPULATION	16,936,573	16,936,573	18,549,291	18,549,291
Percent	100.0%	100.0%	100.0%	100.0%
Class Divisions, Total	16,030,891	7,848,857	17,399,942[c]	8,340,400[c]
Percent	94.7%	46.3%	93.8%	45.0%
Workers & Employees	5,453,471	2,352,143	8,236,527	3,529,847
Percent	32.2%	13.9%	44.4%	19.0%
Members of Cooperatives	1,271,318	593,063	27,847	11,418
Percent	7.5%	3.5%	0.2%	0.1%
Independents without Workers	5,708,100	1,912,284	5,934,327	2,189,840
Percent	33.7%	11.3%	32.0%	11.8%
Independents with Workers	155,320	57,050	79,703	29,924
Percent	0.9%	0.3%	0.4%	0.2%
Helping Family Members	3,311,034	2,803,832	2,984,014	2,442,106
Percent	19.5%	16.6%	15.9%	13.2%
Apprentices	130,970	130,167	113,292	111,293
Percent	0.8%	0.8%	0.6%	0.6%
Unknown Position in Occupation	678	318	60,432	25,927
Percent	0.0%	0.0%	0.3%	0.1%
Persons Temporarily Abroad	...	...	...	...
Percent	...	...	...	...
Other Earners	905,682	541,781	1,149,149	684,428
Percent	5.3%	3.2%	6.2%	3.7%
Pensioners	...	329,449	...	...
Percent	...	1.9%	...	...
Scholarship Recipients	...	8,661	...	...
Percent	...	0.1%	...	...
Other Sources of Income	...	203,671	...	...
Percent	...	1.2%	...	...
Dependents		8,545,935		9,524,414
Percent		50.5%		51.3%
Housewives		3,064,383		3,069,945
Percent		18.1%		16.6%
Students & Pupils		1,609,826		3,123,642
Percent		9.5%		16.8%
Others		3,871,726		3,330,828
Percent		22.9%		18.0%
Unaccounted for	0	0	200	49
Percent	0%	0%	0.0%	0.0%

Notes: a Dependents included with data on Class Divisions, Other Earners. b Data on Class Divisions apply to active earners only. c Subcategories of Class Divisions do not add up to totals. Errors in original. d Figure includes dependents living in Yugoslavia. The 1971 census recorded 82,322 dependents of persons temporarily abroad living abroad. e Does not include 2,959 Other Earners temporarily (cont'd.)

TABLE E-9   (CONCLUDED)

Status & Class	1971 Total Popul. by Class, OE[a]	1971 Total Popul. by Class, OE, & D[b]
POPULATION	20,522,972	20,522,972
Percent	100.0%	100.0%
Class Divisions, Total	18,314,621	8,889,816
Percent	89.2%	43.3%
Workers & Employees	...	4,399,006
Percent	...	21.4%
Members of Cooperatives	...	...
Percent	...	...
Independents without Workers	...	1,980,470
Percent	...	9.7%
Independents with Workers	...	31,826
Percent	...	0.2%
Helping Family Members	...	1,878,585
Percent	...	9.2%
Apprentices	...	...
Percent	...	...
Unknown Position in Occupation	...	10,761
Percent	...	0.1%
Persons Temporarily Abroad	1,131,180[d]	589,168[e]
Percent	5.5%	2.9%
Other Earners	2,208,351	1,241,498
Percent	10.8%	6.0%
Pensioners	...	1,118,157
Percent	...	5.4%
Scholarship Recipients	...	...
Percent	...	...
Other Sources of Income	...	123,341[f]
Percent	...	0.6%
Dependents		10,391,658
Percent		50.6%
Housewives		3,130,438
Percent		15.2%
Students & Pupils		3,909,681
Percent		19.1%
Others		3,351,539[g]
Percent		16.3%
Unaccounted for	0	0
Percent	0%	0%

Notes (cont'd.):   abroad. f Includes 2,959 Other Earners
temporarily abroad. g Includes 82,322
dependents of persons temporarily abroad
living abroad.

TABLE E-10   CLASS STRUCTURE OF ACTIVE EARNERS: BULGARIA,
             1956-1975

Class	1956	1956	1965[a]	1965	1975
ACTIVE EARNERS[b]	4,150,207	4,150,207	4,281,939	4,267,798	4,573,593
Percent	100.0%	100.0%	100.0%	100.0%	100.0%
Workers	970,988	1,022,240	1,788,328	1,736,243	...
Percent	23.4%	24.6%	41.8%	40.7%	...
Agricultural Occupations	116,941	...	256,132	...	...
Percent	2.8%	...	6.0%	...	...
Agric. Branches of Econ.	135,834	...	...	...	...
Percent	3.3%	...	...	...	...
Nonproductive Branches of Economy	...	...	...	...	...
Percent	...	...	...	...	...
Other Employees	553,213	501,961	693,614	689,007	...
Percent	13.3%	12.1%	16.2%	16.1%	...
Agricultural Occupations	2,710[c]	...	1,547	...	...
Percent	0.1%	...	0.0%	...	...
Agric. Branches of Econ.	27,258	...	...	...	...
Percent	0.7%	...	...	...	...
Productive Branches of Economy	239,438	...	...	...	...
Percent	5.8%	...	...	...	...
Collective Farm Members	1,726,583	1,726,583	1,635,121	1,570,211	...
Percent	41.6%	41.6%	38.2%	36.8%	...
Nonagricultural Occs.	137,720	...	200,997	...	...
Percent	3.3%	...	4.7%	...	...
Nonagricultural Branches of Economy	0.0	...	...	...	...
Percent	0%	...	...	...	...
Private Peasantry	771,875	...	...	21,465	...
Percent	18.6%	...	...	0.5%	...
Members of Nonagricultural Cooperatives	46,363	46,363	103,894	111,134	...
Percent	1.1%	1.1%	2.4%	2.6%	...
Artisans Working on Own Account	68,413	...	...	27,332	...
Percent	1.6%	...	...	0.6%	...
Liberal Professions	7,017	...	...	4,152	...
Percent	0.2%	...	...	0.1%	...
"Capitalist Classes"	5,730	...	...	2,168	...
Percent	0.1%	...	...	0.1%	...
Military	...	...	...	...	...
Percent	...	...	...	...	...
Auxiliary Agric. Personnel	...	...	...	103,331[d]	...
Percent	...	...	...	2.4%	...
Others	25	853,035	60,982	2,755[e]	...
Percent	0.0%	20.6%	1.4%	0.1%	...
Unaccounted for	0	25	0	0	...
Percent	0%	0.0%	0%	0%	...

Notes: For notes, see next page.

230

TABLE E-10   (CONCLUDED)

Notes: a Preliminary results of 1965 census. b Active (<u>Aktivni</u>). c Figure does not include collective
       farm members employed in leading positions, such as collective farm chairmen. Collective farm
       chairmen and their deputies numbered 3,966 in 1956. d Included among Active Earners in ori-
       ginal data, this category includes dependents of workers, Other Employees and Collective Farmers,
       and Other Earners. e Clergy.

TABLE E-11   CLASS STRUCTURE OF ACTIVE EARNERS:
CZECHOSLOVAKIA, 1950-1970

Class	1950	1961	1970
ACTIVE EARNERS[a]	5,811,724	6,439,412	6,989,000
Percent	100.0%	100.0%	100.0%
Workers	[2,371,000]	3,361,392	4,019,000
Percent	40.8%	52.2%	57.5%
Agricultural Occupations	...	...	...
Percent	...	...	...
Agric. Branches of Econ.	...	384,588	202,247
Percent	...	6.0%	2.9%
Nonproductive Branches of Economy	...	295,020[b]	...
Percent	...	4.6%	...
Other Employees	[1,232,000]	1,869,780	2,237,000
Percent	21.2%	29.0%	32.0%
Agricultural Occupations	...	...	...
Percent	...	...	...
Agric. Branches of Econ.	...	92,386	...
Percent	...	1.4%	...
Productive Branches of Economy	...	1,186,878[c]	...
Percent	...	18.4%	...
Collective Farm Members	[0]	930,471	625,000
Percent	0.0%	14.4%	8.9%
Nonagricultural Occup.	...	...	...
Percent	...	...	...
Nonagricultural Branches of Economy	...	0	...
Percent	...	0.0%	...
Private Peasantry	[1,947,000][d]	166,177	...
Percent	33.5%	2.6%	...
Members of Nonagricultural Cooperatives	...	95,839	...
Percent	...	1.5%	...
Artisans Working on Own Account	[262,000]	5,682	...
Percent	4.5%	0.1%	...
Liberal Professions	...	...	...
Percent	...	...	...
"Capitalist Classes"	...	...	...
Percent	...	...	...
Military	...	...	...
Percent	...	...	...
Others	...	6,220	108,000
Percent	...	0.1%	1.5%
Unaccounted for	0	3,851	0
Percent	0%	0.1%	0%

Notes: a Economically active individuals (Osoby ekonomicky aktivni). b Communal
services, health, science, education and related, administration and
related, others, branch not determined. c Industry, construction, agriculture, forestry, transport and communications, trade and communal catering. d Helping Family Members included.

TABLE E-12   CLASS STRUCTURE OF ACTIVE EARNERS: GDR, 1946-1975

Class	1946[a]	1950[b]	1955[c] I	1960[c] I	1964[d]
ACTIVE EARNERS	8,139,574	7,923,222	8,188,000	7,993,000	8,345,017
Percent	100.0%	100.0%	100.0%	100.0%	100.0%
Workers	4,410,508	4,125,519 ⌐		⌐	6,410,989
Percent	54.2%	52.1%			76.8%
Agricultural Occupations	...	...			...
Percent	...	...			...
Agric. Branches of Econ.	939,668	567,900			325,957
Percent	11.5%	7.2%			3.9%
Nonproductive Branches of Economy	...	316,886[e]			1,379,207[f]
Percent	...	4.0%			16.5%
Intelligentsia	...	...			544,318
Percent	...	...			6.5%
Other Employees	1,424,412	1,687,277	▸6,415,900	▸[6,470,000]	g
Percent	17.5%	21.3%	78.4%	81.0%	
Agric. Branches of Econ.	...	53,210			...
Percent	...	0.7%			...
Productive Branches of Economy	...	986,520[h]			...
Percent	...	12.5% ⌐		⌐	...
Collective Farm Members	...	...	190,200	[959,000]	903,167
Percent	...	...	2.3%	12.0%	10.8%
Nonagricultural Branches of Economy	...	...	...	...	21,068
Percent	...	...	...	...	0.2%
Helping Family Members					23,155
Percent					0.2%
Private Peasantry		i	1,028,900[j]	[32,000]	...
Percent			12.6%	0.4%	...
Members of Nonagricultural Cooperatives	...	...	2,400	[144,000]	150,409
Percent	...	...	0%	1.8%	1.8%
Artisans Working on Own Account			320,000	[224,000]	197,141
Percent			3.9%	2.8%	2.4%
Liberal Professions			33,900	[24,000]	...
Percent			0.4%	0.3%	...
"Capitalist Classes"			148,300[k]	[64,000]	138,993[l]
Percent			1.8%	0.8%[k]	1.7%
Helping Family Members	1,041,219	1,016,619		...	
Percent	12.8%	12.8%		...	
Independents	1,263,435	1,093,807			...
Percent	15.6%	13.8%			...
Unaccounted for			48,400	[72,000]	0
Percent			0.6%	0.9%	0%

Notes: a Earners (Erwerbspersonen). Census data. b Earners (Erwerbstatig). Excludes
East Berlin. c Employed (Berufstatig). Includes Apprentices. d Economically
Active (Wirtschaftlich Tatige). e Services and State Administration, including
Education, Culture and Health. f Includes that portion of Other Employees
not counted among Intelligentsia. g Included with Workers. (cont'd.)

Class	1965[c] I	1970[c] I	1975[c] I
ACTIVE EARNERS	8,071,700	8,218,100	8,401,100
Percent	100.0%	100.0%	100.0%
Workers			
Percent			
Agricultural Occupations			
Percent			
Agric. Branches of Econ.			
Percent			
Nonproductive Branches of Economy			
Percent			
Intelligentsia			
Percent			
Other Employees	▶[6,660,000]	▶6,942,100	▶7,419,800
Percent	82.5%	84.5%	88.3%
Agric. Branches of Econ.			
Percent			
Productive Branches of Economy			
Percent			
Collective Farm Members	[856,000]	711,000	612,900
Percent	10.6%	8.7%	7.3%
Nonagricultural Branches of Economy	...	...	...
Percent	...	...	...
Helping Family Members			
Percent			
Private Peasantry	[16,000]	9,300	7,200
Percent	0.2%	0.1%	0.1%
Members of Nonagricultural Cooperatives	[194,000]	251,600	142,000
Percent	2.4%	3.1%	1.7%
Artisans Working on Own Account	[202,000]	141,200	121,200
Percent	2.5%	1.7%	1.4%
Liberal Professions	[16,000]	15,600	10,700
Percent	0.2%	0.2%	0.1%
"Capitalist Classes"	[40,000]	63,400[m]	16,100
Percent	0.5%[k]	0.8%	0.2%
Helping Family Members	...	...	...
Percent	...	...	...
Independents			
Percent			
Unaccounted for	[89,000]	83,900	71,200
Percent	1.1%	1.0%	0.8%

Notes (cont'd.): h Agriculture, Mining, Industry, Construction, Communications, and Trade. (cont'd.)

TABLE E-12   (CONCLUDED)

<u>Notes</u> (cont'd.):   <u>i</u> In 1950, of a total of 2,058,536 Earners in the agricultural branch of the economy, 553,635 were classified as Independents. Helping Family Members were not included in this figure.   <u>j</u> Includes Helping Family Members.   <u>k</u> Retail Traders.   <u>l</u> Retail Traders and Other Independents.   <u>m</u> Retail and Other Traders.

TABLE E-13   CLASS STRUCTURE OF ACTIVE EARNERS: HUNGARY, 1930-1973

Class	1930 II	1949 II	1949 III	1960 II	1960 III
ACTIVE EARNERS [a]	3,737,456	4,154,543	4,084,931	4,084,931	4,759,616	4,759,616
Percent	100.0%	100.0%	100.0%	100.0%	100.0%	100.0%
Workers	1,880,512	1,519,287	1,449,675	[1,580,000]	2,172,682	[2,420,000]
Percent	50.3%	36.6%	35.5%	38.8%[b]	45.6%	50.8%[c]
Agricultural Occupations	...	...	...	...	...	...
Percent	...	...	...	...	...	...
Agric. Branches of Econ.	...	283,436	...	...	283,508	...
Percent	...	6.8%	...	...	6.0%	...
Nonproductive Branches of Economy	...	280,253[d]	...	...	325,502[e]	...
Percent	...	6.7%	...	...	6.8%	...
Other Employees [f]	252,986	387,157	387,157	[339,000]	817,341	[762,000]
Percent	6.8%	9.3%	9.5%	8.3%[g]	17.1%	16.0%[g]
Agricultural Occupations	...	...	...	...	...	...
Percent	...	...	...	...	...	...
Agric. Branches of Econ.	...	5,602	...	...	34,580	...
Percent	...	0.1%	...	...	0.7%	...
Productive Branches of Economy	...	121,429[h]	...	...	473,497[i]	...
Percent	...	2.9%	...	...	9.9%	...
Collective Farm Members	...	...	...	[12,000]	580,664	[571,000]
Percent	...	...	...	0.3%	12.2%	12.0%
Nonagricultural Occs.	...	...	...	...	...	...
Percent	...	...	...	...	...	...
Nonagricultural Branches of Economy						
Percent						
Helping Family Members	...	...	...	...	55,257	...
Percent	...	...	...	...	1.2%	...
Private Peasantry	1,236,922	1,907,147	1,907,234	[1,740,000]	943,865[j]	[890,000]
Percent	33.1%	45.9%	46.7%	42.6%[j]	19.8%	18.7%[j]
Helping Family Members	...	775,322	...	...	...	...
Percent	...	18.7%	...	...	...	...
Members of Nonagricultural Cooperatives	...	...	...	...	126,847	...
Percent	...	...	...	...	2.7%	...
Artisans Working on Own Account		200,387[k]		[331,000]		[114,000]
Percent		4.8%		8.1%[l]		2.4%[l]
			340,864		118,217[n]	
			8.3%		2.5%	
Liberal Professions & "Capitalist Classes"	367,036	107,624[m]		[78,000]		[5,000]
Percent	9.8%	2.6%		1.9%[o]		0.1%[o]
Others		32,941[p]	...	...	...	...
Percent		0.8%	...	...	...	...
Unaccounted for	0	0	0	0	0	0
Percent	0%	0%	0%	0%	0%	0%

Notes: a Active Earners (Aktiv keresok). b Includes employees engaged in manual occupations (36.7%) and "workers directing the processing of production" (1.2%). c Includes employees engaged in manual occupations (49.3%) and "workers directing the processing of production." d Banking and Insurance, Post, Public Services, Church Employees, and Others. e Workers employed in branches other than Industry, Construction, Agriculture, Transport, or Trade. f Employees engaged in nonmanual occupations. (cont'd.)

TABLE E-13   (CONTINUED)

Class	1970 II	1970 III	1973 III
ACTIVE EARNERS[a]	4,988,676	4,988,676	5,085,541
Percent	100.0%	100.0%	100.0%
Workers	2,647,048	[2,850,000]	2,949,765[r]
Percent	53.1%	57.1%[q]	58.0%
Agricultural Occupations	...	...	...
Percent	...	...	...
Agric. Branches of Econ.	318,616		247,457[s]
Percent	6.4%		4.9%
Nonproductive Branches of Economy	287,740[t]	...	...
Percent	5.8%	...	...
Other Employees[f]	1,236,423	[1,110,000]	1,219,165
Percent	24.8%	22.3%[g]	24.0%[g]
Agricultural Occupations	...	...	...
Percent	...	...	...
Agric. Branches of Econ.	69,972	...	...
Percent	1.4%	...	...
Productive Branches of Economy	785,150[u]	...	...
Percent	15.7%	...	...
Collective Farm Members	812,710	[868,000]	743,717
Percent	16.3%	17.4%	14.6%
Nonagricultural Occs.	v	...	...
Percent		...	...
Nonagricultural Branches of Economy		...	...
Percent		...	...
Helping Family Members	98,703	...	...
Percent	2.0%	...	...
Private Peasantry	58,800	[80,000]	87,397[j]
Percent	1.2%	1.6%[j]	1.7%
Helping Family Members	19,526	...	...
Percent	0.4%	...	...
Members of Nonagricultural Cooperatives	128,485	...	...
Percent	2.8%	...	...
Artisans Working on Own Account		[80,000]	85,497
Percent		1.6%[l]	1.7%[l]
	83,003[w]		
Liberal Professions & "Capitalist Classes"	1.7%		
Percent		...	...
		...	...
Others	22,213	...	...
Percent	0.4%	...	...
Unaccounted for	0	0	0
Percent	0%	0%	0%

Notes (cont'd.):   g "Intelligentsia and other intellectuals--
Trudovaia intelligentsiia i prochie rabotniki
umstvennogo truda." h Agriculture, Mining,
Industry, and Trade. (cont'd.)

TABLE E-13   (CONCLUDED)

Notes (cont'd.):   i Industry, Construction, Agriculture, Transport, and Trade.   j Includes Helping
Family Members.   k Independents employed in industry.   l "Craftsmen, Retail Dealers
etc. and their Unpaid Family Members."   m Includes Independents in Liberal Professions and Independents in Trade, Insurance, Banking, and with independent sources of
income.   n Independents Outside Agriculture.   o Capitalists, Landowners.   p Includes 25,491 Helping Family Members outside agriculture and 7,450 Others.
q Includes employees engaged in manual occupations (54.4%) and "workers directing
the processing of production" (2.0%).   r Includes employees engaged in manual
occupations and "workers directing the processing of production."   s Workers in
Agriculture, Forestry, Water Economy.   t Services, Health and Culture and Administration.   u Industry, Construction, Agriculture, Transport, and Trade.   v Of the
714,007 paid collective farmers, 678,522 were engaged in manual occupations,
35,485 in nonmanual occupations.   w Independents Outside Agriculture and their
Helping Family Members.

TABLE E-14   CLASS STRUCTURE OF ACTIVE EARNERS: POLAND, 1950-1974

Class	1950 Total	1960 Total	1970 Total	1970 Social.Sect.[a]	1974 Total	1974 Social.Sect.[a]
ACTIVE EARNERS[b]	12,404,200	13,907,442	16,943,848	10,781,064	17,506,555	11,906,608
Percent	100.0%	100.0%	100.0%	100.0%	100.0%	100.0%
Workers		4,691,900	6,945,425	6,754,981	7,565,749[c]	7,397,633[c]
Percent		33.7%	41.0%	62.7%	43.2%	62.1%
Agricultural Occupations			498,464	459,215	...	...
Percent			2.9%	4.3%	...	...
Agric. Branches of Econ.		327,800	...	...	528,607	492,607
Percent		2.4%	...	...	3.0%	4.1%
Nonproductive Branches of Economy		668,800[d]	822,610[e]	689,663[f]	...	...
Percent		4.8%	4.9%	6.4%	...	...
Other Employees	5,444,800	2,521,800	3,808,199	3,781,579	4,292,547[g]	4,292,547[g]
Percent	43.9%	18.1%	22.5%	35.1%	24.5%	36.1%
Agricultural Occupations			164,263	163,816	...	...
Percent			1.0%	1.5%	...	...
Agric. Branches of Econ.		54,600	...	...	168,993	168,993
Percent		0.4%	...	...	1.0%	1.4%
Productive Branches of Economy		1,345,600[h]	1,798,687[i]	1,754,484[j]	...	...
Percent		9.7%	10.6%	16.3%	...	...
Collective Farm Members	55,500	34,300	42,432	42,432	49,262	49,262
Percent	0.4%	0.2%	0.3%	0.4%	0.3%	0.4%
Nonagricultural Occs.	...	...	...	...	...	...
Percent	...	...	...	...	...	...
Nonagricultural Branches of Economy	...	...	...	...	...	...
Percent	...	...	...	...	...	...
Helping Family Members	...	...	...	...	...	...
Percent	...	...	...	...	...	...
Private Peasantry	6,523,100	6,102,000	5,714,190		5,193,302	
Percent	52.6%	43.9%	33.7%		29.7%	
Helping Family Members	3,824,800	3,108,300	2,828,935		...	
Percent	30.8%	22.3%	16.7%		...	
Members of Nonagricultural Cooperatives	160,400	325,100	955	955	k	k
Percent	1.3%	2.3%	0.0%	0.0%		
Independents Outside Agric. (Artisans, Liberal Professions "Capitalist" Classes)	200,400[l]	203,400[m]	223,249[n]		238,529	
Percent	1.6%	1.5%	1.3%		1.4%	
Others	...	...	201,290[o]	201,117[o]	167,166[o]	167,166[o]
Percent	...	...	1.2%	1.9%	1.0%	1.4%
Unknown	20,000	28,900	8,108		...	...
Percent	0.2%	0.1%	0.0%		...	...
Unaccounted for	0	0	0	0	0	0
Percent	0%	0%	0%	0%	0%	0%

Notes: a Socialist sector.   b Occupationally Active (Czynni zawodowo).   c Includes manual workers who are members of nonagricultural cooperatives.   d Education, Culture and Science, Health, and other nonproductive branches.   e Housing and Communal Services, Science, Education, Culture, and remaining nonproductive branches.   f Housing and Communal Services, Science, Education, Culture, Health, and other nonproductive branches.   g Includes nonmanual workers who are members of nonagricultural cooperatives.   h Industry, Agriculture, Construction, Transport and Communications, and Trade.   (cont'd.)

239

TABLE E-14   (CONCLUDED)

Notes (cont'd.):   i Industry, Agriculture, Forestry, Transport and Communications, and Trade.   j Indus-
                   try, Agriculture, Forestry, Transport and Communications, and Trade.   k Included under
                   Workers and Other Employees.   l Of whom, 30,600 were Helping Family Members.   m Of whom,
                   11,700 were Helping Family Members.   n Of whom, 15,310 were Helping Family Members.
                   o Those on commission, or in cottage work.

TABLE E-15   CLASS STRUCTURE OF ACTIVE EARNERS: ROMANIA, 1956-1966

Class	1956			1966		
	Total	Urban	Rural	Total	Urban	Rural
ACTIVE EARNERS[a]	10,449,128	2,719,096	7,730,032	10,362,300	3,626,655	6,735,645
Percent	100.0%	100.0%	100.0%	100.0%	100.0%	100.0%
Workers	2,093,989	1,313,541	780,448	3,380,953	2,071,437	1,309,516
Percent	20.0%	48.3%	10.1%	32.6%	57.1%	19.4%
Agricultural Occupations	...	...	...	...	...	...
Percent	...	...	...	...	...	...
Agric. Branches of Econ.	356,119	68,959	287,160	366,412	77,191	267,170
Percent	3.4%	2.5%	3.7%	3.5%	2.1%	4.0%
Nonproductive Branches of Economy	188,583[b]	147,806[b]	40,776[b]	381,629[c]	278,582[c]	103,047[c]
Percent	1.8%	5.4%	0.5%	3.7%	7.7%	1.5%
Other Employees	1,088,861	805,795	283,066	1,226,933	946,169	280,764
Percent	10.4%	29.6%	3.7%	11.8%	26.1%	4.2%
Agricultural Occupations	...	...	...	...	...	...
Percent	...	...	...	...	...	...
Agric. Branches of Econ.	61,851	24,391	37,460	97,672	34,631	63,041
Percent	0.6%	0.9%	0.5%	0.9%	1.0%	0.9%
Productive Branches of Economy	521,174[d]	407,603[d]	113,571[d]	566,163[e]	448,622[e]	117,541[e]
Percent	5.0%	15.0%	1.5%	5.5%	12.4%	1.7%
Collective Farm Members	797,108	44,592	752,516	4,736,862	404,448	4,332,414
Percent	7.6%	1.6%	9.7%	45.7%	11.2%	64.3%
Nonagricultural Occs.	...	...	...	...	...	...
Percent	...	...	...	...	...	...
Nonagricultural Branches of Economy	6,829	4,405	2,424	1,468	200	1,268
Percent	0.1%	0.2%	0.0%	0.0%	0.0%	0.0%
Private Peasantry	6,151,973	378,977	5,772,996	699,884	56,536	643,348
Percent	58.9%	13.9%	74.7%	6.7%	1.6%	9.6%
Members of Nonagricultural Cooperatives	91,055	80,252	10,803	227,134	116,585	110,549
Percent	0.9%	3.0%	0.1%	2.2%	3.2%	1.6%
Artisans Working on Own Account	196,736	76,319	120,417	83,984	28,238	55,746
Percent	1.9%	2.8%	1.6%	0.8%	0.8%	0.8%
Liberal Professions	20,781	12,431	8,350	...	...	...
Percent	0.2%	0.5%	0.1%	...	...	...
"Capitalist Classes"[f]	6,123	5,145	969	...	...	...
Percent	0.1%	0.2%	0.0%	...	...	...
Military	...	...	...	...	...	...
Percent	...	...	...	...	...	...
Helping Family Members	...	...	...	...	...	...
Percent	...	...	...	...	...	...
Others	2,502	2,035	467	6,550	3,242	3,308
Percent	0.0%	0.1%	0.0%	0.1%	0.1%	0.0%
Unaccounted for	0	9	0	0	0	0
Percent	0%	0%	0%	0%	0%	0%

Notes: For notes, see next page.

241

TABLE E-15   (CONCLUDED)

Notes: a Active Population (Populatia activa). b Communal Economy, Health, Education, Science and Culture, Finance, State Administration, Social and Political Organizations. c Communal Services, Education and Culture, Science, Health, Finance, Administration, Party and Mass Organizations, and Religion. d Industry, Agriculture, Construction, Transport and Communications, Commerce and Communal Catering. e Industry, Construction, Agriculture, Transport, Communications, and Trade. f Commercial Occupations.

TABLE E-16   CLASS STRUCTURE OF ACTIVE EARNERS: USSR, 1926-1970

Class	1926			1959		
	Total	Urban	Rural	Total	Urban	Rural
ACTIVE EARNERS[a]	84,357,724	10,718,525	73,639,199	99,130,212	46,810,706	52,319,506
Percent	100.0%	100.0%	100.0%	100.0%	100.0%	100.0%
Workers	5,602,512	3,283,967	2,318,545	44,323,723	30,008,153	14,315,570
Percent	6.6%	30.6%	3.1%	44.7%	64.1%	27.4%
Agricultural Occupations	1,041,797	55,573	986,224	...	...	...
Percent	1.2%	0.5%	1.3%	...	...	...
Agric. Branches of Econ.	1,103,065	70,609	1,032,456	5,918,418	810,197	5,108,221
Percent	1.3%	0.7%	1.4%	6.0%	1.7%	9.8%
Nonproductive Branches of Economy	1,052,300[b]	560,526[b]	491,774[b]	5,328,317[c]	3,721,332[c]	1,606,985[c]
Percent	1.2%	5.2%	0.7%	5.4%	7.9%	3.1%
Other Employees	3,980,705	3,010,295	970,410	18,637,697	13,756,888	4,880,809
Percent	4.7%	28.1%	1.3%	18.8%	29.4%	9.3%
Agricultural Occupations	0.0	0.0	0.0	...	...	...
Percent	0.0%	0.0%	0.0%	...	...	...
Agric. Branches of Econ.	98,587	38,059	60,528	693,044	200,138	492,906
Percent	0.1%	0.4%	0.1%	0.7%	0.4%	0.9%
Productive Branches of Economy	1,009,606[d]	789,004[d]	220,602[d]	9,514,284[e]	7,387,611[e]	2,126,673[e]
Percent	1.2%	7.4%	0.3%	9.6%	15.8%	4.1%
Collective Farm Members	...	...	...	32,279,727[f]	1,229,131[f]	31,050,596[f]
Percent	...	...	...	32.6%	2.6%	59.3%
Nonagricultural Occs.	...	...	...	...	...	...
Percent	...	...	...	...	...	...
Nonagricultural Branches of Economy	...	...	...	556,893	59,579	497,314
Percent	...	...	...	1.3%	0.1%	1.0%
Private Peasantry	22,419,599[g]	609,858[g]	21,809,741[g]	266,065[h]	75,128[h]	190,937[h]
Percent	26.6%	5.7%	29.6%	0.3%	0.2%	0.4%
Members of Nonagricultural Cooperatives	...	...	...	...	...	...
Percent	...	...	...	...	...	...
Artisans Working on Own Account	1,316,703[i]	695,156[i]	621,547[i]	...	...	...
Percent	1.6%	6.5%	0.8%	...	...	...
Liberal Professions	136,569	63,715	72,854	...	...	...
Percent	0.2%	0.6%	0.1%	...	...	...
"Capitalist Classes"	31,150[j]	24,988[j]	6,162[j]	...	...	...
Percent	0.0%	0.2%	0.0%	...	...	...
Helping Family Members	48,462,783	1,037,573	47,425,210	...	...	...
Percent	57.4%	9.7%	64.4%	...	...	...
Military	631,189	571,102	60,087	3,623,000	1,741,406	1,881,594
Percent	0.7%	5.3%	0.1%	3.7%	3.7%	3.6%
Others	1,772,514[k]	1,421,871[l]	350,643[m]	...	...	...
Percent	2.1%	13.3%	0.5%	...	...	...
Unaccounted for	3,991	0	4,000	0	0	0
Percent	0%	0%	0%	0%	0%	0%

TABLE E-16   (CONTINUED)

Class	1970 Total	Urban	Rural
ACTIVE EARNERS[a]	115,204,076	70,900,220	44,303,856
Percent	100.0%	100.0%	100.0%
Workers	66,321,222	45,911,714	20,409,508
Percent	57.6%	64.8%	46.1%
Agricultural Occupations	...	...	...
Percent	...	...	...
Agric. Branches of Econ.	9,991,768	1,020,823	8,970,945
Percent	8.7%	1.4%	20.2%
Nonproductive Branches			
of Economy[c]	8,521,902	6,140,665	2,381,237
Percent	7.4%	8.7%	5.4%
Other Employees	30,617,865	24,367,480	6,250,385
Percent	26.6%	34.4%	14.1%
Agricultural Occupations	...	...	...
Percent	...	...	...
Agric. Branches of Econ.	1,397,278	363,669	1,033,609
Percent	1.2%	0.5%	2.3%
Productive Branches			
of Economy[e]	14,573,688	11,999,308	2,574,380
Percent	12.7%	16.9%	5.8%
Collective Farm Members	17,899,838	502,440	17,397,398
Percent	15.5%	0.7%	39.3%
Nonagricultural Occs.	...	...	...
Percent	...	...	...
Nonagricultural Branches			
of Economy	669,534	71,979	597,555
Percent	0.6%	0.1%	1.3%
Private Peasantry	...	...	...
Percent	...	...	...
Members of Nonagricultural Cooperatives	...	...	...
Percent	...	...	...
Artisans Working on Own Account	...	...	...
Percent	...	...	...
Liberal Professions	...	...	...
Percent	...	...	...
"Capitalist Classes"	...	...	...
Percent	...	...	...
Helping Family Members	...	...	...
Percent	...	...	...
Military	...	...	...
Percent	...	...	...
Others	...	...	...
Percent	...	...	...
Unaccounted for	365,151	118,586	246,565
Percent	0.3%	0.2%	0.6%

Notes: For notes, see next page.

Notes: a Those with occupations (zanyato). b Trade and Credit, Institutions, and Other Branches (nature not indicated). c Education, Science, Arts, Health, Housing and Communal Economy, Personal Services, Administration, and Financial Credit System. d Agriculture, Industry, Construction, Railroad Transport and Other Forms of Transport. e Industry, Construction, Transport and Communications, Agriculture, Trade, Supply, and Communal Catering. f Probably includes members of handicraft cooperatives. See Table E-8, fn. i. g Private Peasants working with hired labor, Private Peasants working with Helping Family Members, Private Peasants working alone, and members of artels working in agricultural branch of the economy. h Should include Artisans on Own Account; see Table E-8, fn. i. i Persons engaged in small and handicraft industries. j Those working with hired labor, excluding those in agriculture and handicrafts. k Includes 1,014,431 Unemployed and 758,083 persons working alone or with Helping Family Members outside agriculture and handicrafts. l Includes 894,949 Unemployed and 526,922 persons working alone or with Helping Family Members outside agriculture and handicrafts. m Includes 119,482 Unemployed and 231,161 persons working alone or with Helping Family Members outside agriculture and handicrafts.

TABLE E-17   CLASS STRUCTURE OF ACTIVE EARNERS:
             YUGOSLAVIA, 1953-1971

Class	1953	1961	1971
ACTIVE EARNERS[a]	7,848,857	8,340,400	8,889,816
Percent	100.0%	100.0%	100.0%
Workers & Employees	2,352,143	3,529,847	4,399,006
Percent	30.0%	42.3%	49.5%
Agricultural Occs.	182,130	221,463	140,594
Percent	2.3%	2.7%	1.6%
Miners		104,582	64,019
Percent		1.3%	0.7%
Industrial & Handicraft Occs.	733,041	1,429,098	2,000,373
Percent	9.3%	17.1%	22.5%
Personnel in Occs. Related to Trade, Services, Communication & Protection	398,159	862,301	763,971
Percent	5.1%	10.3%	8.6%
Personnel in Occs. Related to Admin., Leadership & Professions	572,324	862,801	1,278,566
Percent	7.3%	10.3%	14.4%
Unskilled Workers	466,489		
Percent	5.9%		
Unknown	...	49,602[b]	151,483
Percent	...	0.6%	1.7%
Collective Farm Members[c]	547,000[d]	10,290	...
Percent	7.0%	0.1%	...
Private Peasantry[e]	4,444,000[d]	4,390,664	3,680,726
Percent	56.6%	52.6%	41.4%
Members of Nonagricultural Cooperatives	42,000[d]	1,128	...
Percent	0.5%	0.0%	...
Artisans Working on Own Account[f]	125,000[d]	106,388	153,934
Percent	1.6%	1.3%	1.7%
Liberal Professions			
Percent			
	187,000[d,g]	164,776[g]	56,221[g]
"Capitalist Classes"			
Percent	2.4%	2.0%	0.6%
Military	...	...	...
Percent	...	...	...
Others	138,000[d]	137,361	599,929[h]
Percent	1.8%	1.6%	6.7%
Unaccounted for	13,714[i]	[j]	0
Percent	0.2%		0%

Notes: For notes, see next page.

246

TABLE E-17   (CONCLUDED)

Notes: <u>a</u> Active (<u>Aktivno</u>). <u>b</u> Includes 68 unaccounted for. <u>c</u> Members of producers cooperatives in agricultural branch of the economy. <u>d</u> Preliminary results of the 1953 census. <u>e</u> Independents with and without workers and helping family members in agricultural branch of economy. <u>f</u> Independents with and without workers and helping family members in handicrafts branch of the economy. No independents recorded in industrial branch of the economy in Yugoslav data. <u>g</u> Independents with and without workers and helping family members in branches other than agriculture and handicrafts. <u>h</u> Includes 589,168 temporarily abroad. <u>i</u> Not accounted for due to combining of preliminary and final results of census in table. <u>j</u> Subcategories exceed total by 54.

TABLE E-18   MANUAL, NONMANUAL AND INDEPENDENT POPULATION: HUNGARY, 1949-1970

Status	1949 I Population[a]	1949 I Earners[b]	1960 I Population[a]	1960 I Earners[b]	1960 II Earners[b]	1970 II Population[a]	1970 II Earners[b]
TOTAL	9,204,799	4,409,299	9,961,044	5,312,831	5,196,215	10,322,099	6,384,166
Percent	100.0%	100.0%	100.0%	100.0%	100.0%	100.0%	100.0%
Active Earners	8,690,566	4,154,543	9,298,218	4,876,232	4,759,616	8,411,263	4,988,676
Percent	94.4%	94.2%	93.3%	91.8%	91.6%	81.5%	78.1%
Manual Workers	3,125,961	1,519,287	6,059,381	2,965,021	2,806,349	6,087,661	3,445,358
Percent	34.0%	34.5%	60.8%	55.8%	54.0%	59.0%	54.0%
Skilled		467,121	1,844,227	820,316		...	1,152,830
Percent	1,541,505	10.6%	18.5%	15.4%	1,505,534	...	18.0%
Semiskilled	16.7%	217,204	1,476,219	727,274	29.0%	...	983,591
Percent		4.9%	14.8%	13.7%		...	15.4%
Unskilled		765,350	2,622,186	1,300,815	1,300,815	...	1,265,309
Percent	1,584,456	17.4%	26.3%	24.5%	25.0%	...	19.8%
Industrial Apprentices	17.2%	69,612	116,749	116,616	...	...	43,628
Percent		1.6%	1.2%	2.2%	...	...	0.7%
Nonmanual Workers	790,493	387,157	1,434,945	793,872	835,928	1,958,347	1,280,605
Percent	8.6%	8.8%	14.4%	14.9%	16.1%	19.0%	20.1%
Leading Positions in Science, Culture and Related Occs.	...	...				...	221,525
Percent	...	...				...	3.5%
Leading Positions in State Administration, Economics	...	...	904,797	455,083	649,731	...	62,497
Percent	...	...	9.1%	8.6%	12.5%	...	1.0%
White Collar Employees	...	...				...	701,317
Percent	...	...				...	11.0%
Office Workers	...	...	530,148	338,789	186,197	...	295,266
Percent	...	...	5.3%	6.4%	3.6%	...	4.6%
Independents	3,906,808	1,447,286	1,289,486	627,270			117,416
Percent	42.4%	32.8%	12.9%	11.8%			1.8%
Helping Family Members	867,304	800,813	514,406	490,069	1,117,339	365,255	145,297
Percent	9.4%	18.2%	5.2%	9.2%	21.5%	3.5%	2.3%
Other Earners (Pensioners & Others)	434,659	254,756	614,019	436,599	436,599	1,910,836	1,395,490
Percent	4.7%	5.7%	6.1%	8.2%	8.4%	18.5%	21.9%
Manual Workers	254,115	141,736	466,326	312,457	...	1,267,633	...
Percent	2.8%	3.2%	4.7%	5.9%	...	12.3%	...
Nonmanual Workers	180,544	102,414	147,693	109,170	...	288,490	...
Percent	2.0%	2.3%	1.5%	2.1%	...	2.8%	...
Independents	...	10,606	...	14,972	...	17,211	...
Percent	...	0.2%	...	0.3%	...	0.2%	...
Others & Unknown	79,571	...	48,807	...	...	...	...
Percent	0.9%	...	0.5%	...	...	...	...

Notes: a Includes dependents.   b Excludes dependents.

TABLE E-19   CLASSES BY LEVEL OF EDUCATION: BULGARIA, 1956

Level of Education	All Classes	Workers	Other Employees	Coll. Farmers	Others in Coop.	Private Peasantry	Ind. Artisans	Others
ACTIVE EARNERS	4,150,207	970,988[a]	553,213	1,726,583	46,363	771,875	68,413	12,772
Percent	100.0%	100.0%	100.0%	100.0%	100.0%	100.0%	100.0%	100.0%
Without Schooling	468,578	66,408	1,121	205,853	544	181,280	12,129	1,243
Percent	11.3%	6.8%	0.2%	11.9%	1.2%	23.5%	17.7%	9.7%
4 Yr. Element. Inc.	393,978	63,799	4,575	214,796	1,181	103,251	5,436	940
Percent	9.5%	6.6%	0.8%	12.4%	2.5%	13.4%	7.9%	7.4%
4 Yr. Element. Comp.								
Percent	1,682,641	340,785	45,688	899,433	11,118	362,765	20,505	2,347
7-8 Yr. Basic Inc.	40.5%	35.1%	8.2%	52.1%	24.0%	47.0%	30.0%	18.4%
Percent								
7-8 Yr. Basic Comp.								
Percent								
Trade School	1,127,386	432,521	139,458	381,387	28,658	116,632	26,584	2,146
Percent	27.2%	44.5%	25.2%	22.1%	61.8%	15.1%	38.9%	16.8%
Inc. Second.								
Percent								
General Second. Comp.								
Percent								
Specialized Second., Lower Level								
Percent								
Specialized Second., Higher Level	343,239	63,655	239,342	23,905	4,275	7,367	3,477	1,218
Percent	8.3%	6.6%	43.3%	1.4%	9.2%	1.0%	5.1%	9.5%
Inc. Higher								
Percent								
Higher, Lower Level, Comp.	36,702	1,278	34,530	428	109	173	89	95
Percent	0.9%	0.1%	6.2%	0.0%	0.2%	0.0%	0.1%	0.7%
Higher, Faculty Level, Comp.	97,683	2,542	88,499	781	478	407	193	4,783[b]
Percent	2.4%	0.3%	16.0%	0.0%	1.0%	0.1%	0.3%	37.4%
Unaccounted for	0	0	0	0	0	0	0	0
Percent	0%	0%	0%	0%	0%	0%	0%	0%

Notes: a Of whom, 135,834 were in agricultural branch of the economy. Of this group, 15,131 were illiterate; 11,607 had incomplete 4 year education; 50,230 had completed elementary education; 54,895 had 7-8 year basic education, complete, trade school or incomplete secondary; 3,864 had general secondary complete, or incomplete higher; and 107 had some form of higher education. b Of whom 4,734 were in liberal professions.

Level of Education	All Classes	Workers	Other Employees	Coll. Farmers	Others in Coop.[a]	Others[b]
ACTIVE EARNERS	4,281,939	1,788,328	693,614	1,635,121	103,894	60,982
Percent	100.0%	100.0%	100.0%	100.0%	100.0%	100.0%
Without Schooling	227,286	69,991	263	146,934	855	9,243
Percent	5.3%	3.9%	0.0%	9.0%	0.8%	15.2%
4 Yr. Element. Inc.						
Percent						
4 Yr. Element. Comp.	1,626,901	592,890	15,537	970,159	19,866	28,449
Percent	38.0%	33.2%	2.2%	59.3%	19.1%	46.7%
7-8 Yr. Basic Inc.						
Percent						
7-8 Yr. Basic Comp.						
Percent						
Trade School	1,625,168	938,265	117,270	483,893	70,017	15,723
Percent	38.0%	52.5%	16.9%	29.6%	67.4%	25.8%
Inc. Second.						
Percent						
General Second. Comp.						
Percent						
Specialized Second., Lower Level						
Percent						
Specialized Second., Higher Level	652,107	184,531	421,664	29,729	12,728	3,455
Percent	15.2%	10.3%	60.8%	1.8%	12.3%	5.7%
Inc. Higher						
Percent						
Higher, Lower Level, Comp.						
Percent						
Higher, Faculty Level, Comp.	150,477	2,651	138,880	4,406	428	4,112
Percent	3.5%	0.1%	20.0%	0.3%	0.4%	6.7%
Unknown	...	...	...	...	...	...
Percent	...	...	...	...	...	...
Unaccounted for	0	0	0	0	0	0
Percent	0%	0%	0%	0%	0%	0%

Notes: a Handicraft cooperatives.   b Private peasantry and other independents.

TABLE E-21　　CLASSES BY LEVEL OF EDUCATION:　HUNGARY, 1949-1970

Level of Education	1949				1960		
	All Classes	Workers	Other Employees	Private Peasantry	All Classes	Workers	Other Employees
ACTIVE EARNERS	4,153,760	1,519,287	387,157	1,907,147	4,872,000	2,336,800	766,900
Percent	100.0%	100.0%	100.0%	100.0%	100.0%	100.0%	100.0%
Without Schooling	147,273	56,850	0	82,329	117,400	52,500	200
Percent	3.5%	3.7%	0.0%	4.3%	2.4%	2.2%	0.0%
4 Yr. Element. Inc.	238,549	81,369	531	147,769	226,900	96,500	1,600
Percent	5.7%	5.3%	0.1%	7.7%	4.6%	4.1%	0.2%
4 Yr. Element. Comp.	785,842	293,608	8,100	429,376	689,000	335,400	11,000
Percent	19.0%	19.3%	2.1%	22.5%	14.1%	14.3%	1.4%
7-8 Yr. Basic Inc.	2,120,814	791,085	50,934	1,101,358	2,043,400	995,500	80,400
Percent	51.1%	52.1%	13.1%	57.7%	41.9%	42.6%	10.5%
7-8 Yr. Basic Comp.	562,916	260,046	116,049	128,100	1,143,500	724,200	192,600
Percent	13.5%	17.1%	30.0%	6.7%	23.5%	31.0%	25.1%
Trade School	9,521	2,280	4,954	830	...	...	...
Percent	0.2%	0.1%	1.3%	0.0%	...	...	...
Inc. Second.	27,573	8,393	12,098	2,758	151,800	70,500	66,000
Percent	0.7%	0.5%	3.1%	0.1%	3.1%	3.0%	8.6%
General Second. Comp.							
Percent							
Specialized Second., Lower Level					316,000	52,000	247,900
Percent					6.5%	2.2%	32.3%
Specialized Second., Higher Level	166,505	19,601	126,189	6,844			
Percent	4.0%	1.3%	32.6%	0.4%			
Inc. Higher					34,400	4,800	26,600
Percent					0.7%	0.2%	3.5%
Higher, Lower Level, Comp.	...	...	...	...	...	...	...
Percent	...	...	...	...	...	...	...
Higher, Faculty Level, Comp.	86,342	2,964	68,197	3,195	149,300	5,200	140,500
Percent	2.1%	0.2%	17.6%	0.2%	3.1%	0.2%	18.3%
Unknown	...	...	...	4	300	200	100
Percent	...	...	...	0.0%	0.0%	0.0%	0.0%
Unaccounted for	8,425	3,091	105	4,584	0	0	0
Percent	0.2%	0.2%	0.0%	0.2%	0%	0%	0%

TABLE E-21   (CONCLUDED)

Level of Education	1960 In Agriculture[a]	1970 All Classes	Workers	Other Employees	Coll. Farmers-M[b]
ACTIVE EARNERS	1,500,900	4,988,676	2,647,048	1,236,423	777,225
Percent	100.0%	100.0%	100.0%	100.0%	100.0%
Without Schooling	59,600	48,208	27,059	18	17,353
Percent	4.0%	1.0%	1.0%	0.0%	2.2%
4 Yr. Element. Inc.	121,500				
Percent	8.1%	508,893	286,886	6,951	176,069
4 Yr. Element. Comp.	306,600	10.2%	10.8%	0.6%	22.7%
Percent	20.4%				
7-8 Yr. Basic Inc.	839,700	1,390,814	815,354	62,262	392,849
Percent	55.9%	27.9%	30.8%	5.0%	50.5%
7-8 Yr. Basic Comp.	159,400				
Percent	10.6%				
Trade School	...	2,088,860	1,399,836	369,979	186,787
Percent	...	41.9%	52.9%	29.9%	24.0%
Inc. Second.	7,100				
Percent	0.5%				
General Second. Comp.					
Percent					
Specialized Second., Lower Level	5,300				
Percent	0.4%				
Specialized Second., Higher Level		694,358	114,307	550,264	3,914
Percent		13.9%	4.3%	44.5%	0.5%
Inc. Higher	800				
Percent	0.1%				
Higher, Lower Level, Comp.	...	...	...	...	...
Percent	...	...	...	...	...
Higher, Faculty Level, Comp.	900	257,543	3,606	246,949	253
Percent	0.1%	5.2%	0.1%	20.0%	0.0%
Unknown	...	...	...	...	...
Percent	...	...	...	...	...
Unaccounted for	0	0	0	0	0
Percent	0%	0%	0%	0%	0%

Notes: a Private Peasantry and Collective Farmers. b Collective Farmers and manual workers in agriculture.

TABLE E-22   CLASSES BY LEVEL OF EDUCATION: POLAND, 1970

Level of Education	All Classes	Workers	Other Employees	Coll. Farmers	Private Peasantry	Ind. Artisans	Others
ACTIVE EARNERS 15 & OVER	16,943,848	6,945,425[a]	3,808,199[b]	42,432	5,714,190	223,249	210,353
Percent	100.0%	100.0%	100.0%	100.0%	100.0%	100.0%	100.0%
Without Schooling	474,908	58,973	731	983	410,061	2,796	1,364
Percent	2.8%	0.8%	0.0%	2.3%	7.2%	1.2%	0.6%
4 Yr. Element. Inc.							
Percent							
4 Yr. Element. Comp.	3,618,974	960,653	18,733	11,859	2,584,276	21,715	21,738
Percent	21.3%	13.8%	0.5%	28.0%	45.2%	9.7%	10.3%
7-8 Yr. Basic Inc.							
Percent							
7-8 Yr. Basic Comp.	6,978,146	3,806,467	523,233	24,218	2,398,330	103,439	122,459
Percent	41.2%	54.8%	13.7%	57.1%	42.0%	46.3%	58.2%
Trade School	2,168,156	1,588,281	324,234	2,977	177,035	48,780	26,849
Percent	12.8%	22.9%	8.5%	7.0%	3.1%	21.8%	12.8%
Inc. Second.	501,438	178,149	255,364	532	45,788	9,334	12,240
Percent	3.0%	2.6%	6.7%	1.2%	0.8%	4.2%	5.8%
General Second. Comp.	651,955	64,945	542,470	316	25,976	25,729	8,662
Percent	3.8%	0.9%	14.2%	0.7%	0.4%	11.5%	4.1%
Specialized Second., Lower Level							
Percent	1,460,572	209,332	1,179,665	1,093	42,606	1,970	9,795
Specialized Second., Higher Level	8.6%	3.0%	31.0%	2.6%	0.7%	0.9%	4.7%
Percent							
Inc. Higher	147,778	6,437	136,535	68	1,874	2,181	683
Percent	0.9%	0.1%	3.6%	0.1%	0.0%	1.0%	0.3%
Higher, Lower Level, Comp.	242,158	8,055	230,909	22	2,090	665	417
Percent	1.4%	0.1%	6.1%	0.0%	0.0%	0.3%	0.2%
Higher, Faculty Level, Comp.	601,101	5,088	585,913	167	3,220	5,787	926
Percent	3.5%	0.1%	15.4%	0.4%	0.0%	2.6%	0.4%
Unknown	98,662	59,075	10,414	197	22,934	853	5,189
Percent	0.5%	0.8%	0.3%	0.5%	0.4%	0.4%	2.5%
Unaccounted for	0	0	0	0	0	0	31
Percent	0%	0%	0%	0%	0%	0%	0%

Notes: a Subcategories exceed total by 30. b Subcategories exceed total by 2.

TABLE E-23   CLASSES BY LEVEL OF EDUCATION: ROMANIA, 1956

Level of Education	All Classes	Workers	Other Employees	Coll. Farmers	Coop. Members[a]	Private Peasantry	Ind. Artisans	Others[b]
ACTIVE EARNERS	10,449,128	2,093,989	1,088,861	797,108	91,055	6,151,973	196,736	29,406
Percent	100.0%	100.0%	100.0%	100.0%	100.0%	100.0%	100.0%	100.0%
Without Schooling	...	...	...	...	...	...	...	...
Percent	...	...	...	...	...	...	...	...
4 Yr. Element. Inc.	...	...	...	...	...	...	...	...
Percent	...	...	...	...	...	...	...	...
4 Yr. Element. Comp.	...	...	...	...	...	...	...	...
Percent	...	...	...	...	...	...	...	...
7-8 Yr. Basic Inc.	...	...	...	...	...	...	...	...
Percent	...	...	...	...	...	...	...	...
7-8 Yr. Basic Comp.	...	...	...	...	...	...	...	...
Percent	...	...	...	...	...	...	...	...
Trade School	...	...	...	...	...	...	...	...
Percent	...	...	...	...	...	...	...	...
Inc. Second.	...	...	...	...	...	...	...	...
Percent	...	...	...	...	...	...	...	...
General Second. Comp.								
Percent								
Specialized Second., Lower Level								
Percent								
Specialized Second., Higher Level	435,831	42,767	374,091	1,316	2,493	10,879	2,799	1,486
Percent	4.2%	2.0%	34.4%	0.2%	2.7%	0.2%	1.4%	5.1%
Inc. Higher								
Percent								
Higher, Lower Level, Comp.								
Percent	184,226	2,387	172,686	63	476	1,190	481	6,943
Higher, Faculty Level, Comp.	1.8%	0.1%	15.9%	0.0%	0.5%	0.0%	0.2%	23.6%
Percent								
Unknown	...	...	...	...	...	...	...	...
Percent	...	...	...	...	...	...	...	...
Unaccounted for	9,829,071	2,048,835	542,084	795,729	88,086	6,139,904	193,456	20,977
Percent	94.1%	97.8%	49.8%	99.8%	96.7%	99.8%	98.3%	71.3%

Notes: a Handicraft cooperatives. b Includes Liberal Professions, Commercial Classes, Others and Un-declared.

TABLE E-24   CLASSES BY LEVEL OF EDUCATION: USSR, 1939-1974

Level of Education	1939				1959			
	All Classes	Workers	Other Employees	Coll. Farmers	All Classes	Workers	Other Employees	Coll. Farmers
ACTIVE EARNERS[a]	78,810,976	...	...	...	99,130,212	46,146,573	19,670,209	33,047,126
Percent	100.0%	100.0%	100.0%	100.0%	100.0%	100.0%	100.0%	100.0%
Without Schooling	...	...	...	...	...	...	...	...
Percent	...	...	...	...	...	...	...	...
4 Yr. Element. Inc.	...	...	...	...	...	...	...	...
Percent	...	...	...	...	...	...	...	...
4 Yr. Element. Comp.	...	...	...	...	[32,800,000]	[19,300,000]	[1,810,000]	[11,700,000]
Percent	...	...	...	...	33.1%	41.8%	9.2%	35.5%
7-8 Yr. Basic Inc.	...	...	...	...				
Percent	...	...	...	...				
7-8 Yr. Basic Comp.					[25,800,000]	[14,200,000]	[5,070,000]	[6,410,000]
Percent					26.0%	30.7%	25.8%	19.4%
Trade School								
Percent								
Inc. Second.[b]								
Percent								
General Second. Comp.					[6,340,000]	[2,720,000]	[2,850,000]	[760,000]
Percent					6.4%	5.9%	14.5%	2.3%
Specialized Second., Lower Level	[8,670,000]		...					
Percent	11.0%		46.1%	...				
Specialized Second., Higher Level		...		1.8%	[7,530,000]		[6,180,000]	
Percent		8.4%			7.6%		31.4%	
Inc. Higher						[923,000]		[297,000]
Percent						2.0%		0.9%
Higher, Lower Level, Comp.	...		...		...		...	
Percent	...		...		...		...	
Higher, Faculty Level, Comp.	[1,020,000]		...		[3,270,000]		[3,460,000]	
Percent	1.3%		8.1%		3.3%		17.6%	
Unaccounted for	[69,100,000]	...	...	...	[23,400,000]	[9,040,000]	[295,000]	[13,800,000]
Percent	87.7%	91.6%	45.8%	98.2%	23.6%	19.6%	1.5%	41.9%

255

TABLE E-24   (CONCLUDED)

Level of Education	1970				1974			
	All Classes	Workers	Other Employees	Coll. Farmers	All Classes	Workers	Other Employees	Coll. Farmers
ACTIVE EARNERS[a]	115,204,076	66,321,222	30,617,865	17,899,838	...	...	...	...
Percent	100.0%	100.0%	100.0%	100.0%	100.0%	100.0%	100.0%	100.0%
Without Schooling	...	...	...	...	...	...	...	...
Percent	...	...	...	...	...	...	...	...
4 Yr. Element. Inc.	...	...	...	...	...	...	...	...
Percent	...	...	...	...	...	...	...	...
4 Yr. Element. Comp.					...	...	...	...
Percent					...	...	...	...
7-8 Yr. Basic Inc.	[28,600,000]	[20,400,000]	[1,190,000]	[7,030,000]	...	...	...	...
Percent	24.8%	30.8%	3.9%	39.3%	...	...	...	...
7-8 Yr. Basic Comp.								
Percent	[35,800,000]	[25,700,000]	[5,000,000]	[5,190,000]				
Trade School	31.1%	38.7%	16.4%	29.0%				
Percent								
Inc. Second.[b]								
Percent								
General Second. Comp.	[18,300,000]	[10,700,000]	[6,000,000]	[1,340,000]	65.9%		68.3%	
Percent	15.9%	16.2%	19.6%	7.5%				
Specialized Second., Lower Level								
Percent	[13,600,000]		[10,900,000]			67.9%		48.9%
Specialized Second., Higher Level	11.8%		35.5%					
Percent								
Inc. Higher		[2,450,000]		[501,000]				
Percent		3.7%		2.8%				
Higher, Lower Level, Comp.	...		...		...		...	
Percent	...		...		...		...	
Higher, Faculty Level, Comp.	[7,490,000]		[7,320,000]		...		...	
Percent	6.5%		23.9%		8.0%		28.2%	
Unaccounted for	[11,400,000]	[7,030,000]	[214,000]	[3,830,000]	...	...	...	...
Percent	9.9%	10.6%	0.7%	21.4%	26.1%	32.1%	3.5%	51.1%

Notes: a Persons with occupations. b No equivalent Soviet category.

TABLE E-25 MANUAL, NONMANUAL AND OTHER ACTIVE EARNERS, LEVEL OF EDUCATION: HUNGARY, 1949-1970

Level of Education	1949 I				1960 I			
	Total	Manual	Nonmanual	Ind. & HFM[a]	Total	Manual	Nonmanual	Ind. & HFM[a]
ACTIVE EARNERS	4,154,543	1,519,287	387,157	2,248,099	4,876,232	2,965,021	793,872	1,117,339
Percent	100.0%	100.0%	100.0%	100.0%	100.0%	100.0%	100.0%	100.0%
Without Schooling	155,737	59,941	104	95,692	113,032	70,810	368	41,854
Percent	3.7%	3.9%	0.0%	4.3%	2.3%	2.4%	0.0%	3.7%
4 Yr. Element. Inc.	238,566	81,369	531	156,666	227,961	139,749	1,896	86,316
Percent	5.7%	5.4%	0.1%	7.0%	4.7%	4.7%	0.2%	7.7%
4 Yr. Element. Comp.	799,413	300,499	8,949	489,965	681,154	440,781	12,996	227,377
Percent	19.2%	19.8%	2.3%	21.8%	14.0%	14.9%	1.6%	20.4%
7-8 Yr. Basic Inc.	2,079,301	775,290	36,918	1,267,093	2,070,405	1,379,910	92,832	597,663
Percent	50.1%	51.0%	9.5%	56.4%	42.5%	46.5%	11.7%	53.5%
7-8 Yr. Basic Comp.	553,374	256,749	112,413	184,212	1,143,021	793,830	201,844	147,347
Percent	13.3%	16.9%	29.0%	8.2%	23.4%	26.8%	25.4%	13.2%
Trade School	...	...	...	...	...	...	...	...
Percent	...	...	...	...	...	...	...	...
Inc. Second.	75,198	22,874	33,856	18,468	137,469	70,025	60,610	6,834
Percent	1.8%	1.5%	8.8%	0.8%	2.8%	2.4%	7.6%	0.6%
General Second. Comp.								
Percent								
Specialized Second., Lower Level					318,718	58,275	253,749	6,694
Percent					6.5%	2.0%	32.0%	0.6%
Specialized Second., Higher Level	176,156	20,753	132,966	22,437				
Percent	4.2%	1.4%	34.4%	1.0%				
Inc. Higher					33,338	5,300	27,055	983
Percent					0.7%	0.2%	3.4%	0.1%
Higher, Lower Level, Comp.	...	...	...	...	...	...	...	...
Percent	...	...	...	...	...	...	...	...
Higher, Faculty Level, Comp.	76,798	1,812	61,420	13,566	151,134	6,341	142,522	2,271
Percent	1.9%	0.1%	15.9%	0.6%	3.1%	0.2%	18.0%	0.2%
Unknown	...	...	...	...	...	...	...	...
Percent	...	...	...	...	...	...	...	...
Unaccounted for	0	0	0	0	0	0	0	0
Percent	0%	0%	0%	0%	0%	0%	0%	0%

TABLE E-25   (CONCLUDED)

Level of Education	1960				1970			
	Total	Manual	Nonmanual	Ind. & HFM[a]	Total	Manual	Nonmanual	Ind. & HFM[a]
ACTIVE EARNERS	4,759,616	2,903,662	793,872	1,062,082	5,001,200	3,556,100	1,284,400	160,700
Percent	100.0%	100.0%	100.0%	100.0%	100.0%	100.0%	100.0%	100.0%
Without Schooling	113,002	72,191	368	40,443	46,500	43,100	100	3,300
Percent	2.4%	2.5%	0.0%	3.8%	0.9%	1.2%	0.0%	2.1%
4 Yr. Element. Inc.								
Percent								
4 Yr. Element. Comp.	908,478	588,819	14,892	304,767	510,500	467,800	8,200	34,500
Percent	19.1%	20.3%	1.9%	28.7%	10.2%	13.2%	0.7%	21.5%
7-8 Yr. Basic Inc.	2,065,650	1,401,536	92,832	571,282	1,375,500	1,238,100	64,600	72,800
Percent	43.4%	48.3%	11.7%	53.8%	27.5%	34.8%	5.0%	45.3%
7-8 Yr. Basic Comp.								
Percent								
Trade School	1,175,377	777,138	262,454	135,785	2,112,600	1,686,400	382,900	43,300
Percent	24.7%	26.7%	33.1%	12.8%	42.3%	47.4%	29.8%	26.9%
Inc. Second.								
Percent								
General Second. Comp.								
Percent								
Specialized Second., Lower Level								
Percent								
Specialized Second., Higher Level	345,980	57,632	280,804	7,544	689,600	116,500	568,100	5,000
Percent	7.2%	2.0%	35.4%	0.7%	13.8%	3.3%	44.2%	3.1%
Inc. Higher								
Percent								
Higher, Lower Level, Comp.	...	...	...	...	...	...	...	...
Percent	...	...	...	...	...	...	...	...
Higher, Faculty Level, Comp.	151,129	6,346	142,522	2,261	266,500	4,200	260,500	1,800
Percent	3.2%	0.2%	17.9%	0.2%	5.3%	0.1%	20.3%	1.1%
Unknown	...	...	...	...	...	...	...	...
Percent	...	...	...	...	...	...	...	...
Unaccounted for	0	0	0	0	0	0	0	0
Percent	0%	0%	0%	0%	0%	0%	0%	0%

Note: a Ind. & HFM--Independents and Helping Family Members.

TABLE E-26   MANUAL AND NONMANUAL EMPLOYEES, LEVEL OF EDUCATION: POLAND, 1958-1973

Level of Education	1958			1964		
	Total	Manual	Nonmanual	Total	Manual	Nonmanual
TOTAL EMPLOYED IN SOCIALIST SECTOR[a]	6,350,816	4,370,697	1,980,119	7,137,279	4,781,112	2,356,167
Percent	100.0%	100.0%	100.0%	100.0%	100.0%	100.0%
Without Schooling						
Percent						
4 Yr. Element. Inc.						
Percent						
4 Yr. Element. Comp.	1,972,032	1,896,413	75,619	1,576,904	1,541,928	34,976
Percent	31.0%	43.4%	3.8%	22.1%	32.3%	1.5%
7-8 Yr. Basic Inc.						
Percent						
7-8 Yr. Basic Comp.	2,589,737	2,002,819	586,918	3,212,005	2,600,649	611,356
Percent	40.8%	45.8%	29.6%	45.0%	54.4%	25.9%
Trade School	522,016	358,983	163,033	798,476	535,685	262,791
Percent	8.2%	8.2%	8.2%	11.2%	11.2%	11.2%
Inc. Second.	312,831	67,333	245,498	327,462	62,131	265,331
Percent	4.9%	1.5%	12.4%	4.6%	1.3%	11.3%
General Second. Comp.	275,592	20,601	254,991	313,787	16,895	296,892
Percent	4.3%	0.5%	12.9%	4.4%	0.4%	12.6%
Specialized Second., Lower Level						
Percent	438,680	23,331	415,349	598,244	22,808	575,436
Specialized Second., Higher Level	6.9%	0.5%	21.0%	8.4%	0.5%	24.4%
Percent						
Inc. Higher	...	...	...	...	...	...
Percent	...	...	...	...	...	...
Higher, Lower Level, Comp.[b]	...	...	...	...	...	...
Percent	...	...	...	...	...	...
Higher, Faculty Level, Comp.	239,928	1,217	238,711	310,401	1,016	309,385
Percent	3.8%	0.0%	12.0%	4.3%	0.0%	13.1%
Unknown	...	...	...	...	...	...
Percent	...	...	...	...	...	...
Unaccounted for	0	0	0	0	0	0
Percent	0%	0%	0%	0%	0%	0%

Level of Education	1968			1973		
	Total	Manual	Nonmanual	Total	Manual	Nonmanual
TOTAL EMPLOYED IN SOCIALIST SECTOR[a]	8,527,852	5,611,635	2,916,217	10,558,470	6,904,855	3,653,615
Percent	100.0%	100.0%	100.0%	100.0%	100.0%	100.0%
Without Schooling						
Percent						
4 Yr. Element. Inc.						
Percent						
4 Yr. Element. Comp.	1,405,015	1,378,930	26,085	1,161,211	1,146,568	14,643
Percent	16.5%	24.6%	0.9%	11.0%	16.6%	0.4%
7-8 Yr. Basic Inc.						
Percent						
7-8 Yr. Basic Comp.	3,735,184	3,143,210	591,974	4,428,373	3,869,293	559,080
Percent	43.8%	56.0%	20.3%	41.9%	56.0%	15.3%
Trade School	1,306,217	949,403	356,814	1,991,809	1,621,845	369,964
Percent	15.3%	16.9%	12.2%	18.9%	23.5%	10.1%
Inc. Second.	325,750	71,833	253,917	175,021	47,104	127,917
Percent	3.8%	1.3%	8.7%	1.7%	0.7%	3.5%
General Second. Comp.	385,367	18,770	366,597	571,803	49,766	522,037
Percent	4.5%	0.3%	12.6%	5.4%	0.7%	14.3%
Specialized Second., Lower Level						
Percent	964,865	48,906	915,959	1,311,854	162,067	1,149,787
Specialized Second., Higher Level	11.3%	0.9%	31.4%	12.4%	2.3%	31.5%
Percent						
Inc. Higher	...	...	...	...	...	...
Percent	...	...	...	...	...	...
Higher, Lower Level, Comp.	b	b	b	307,270	6,610	300,660
Percent				2.9%	0.1%	8.2%
Higher, Faculty Level, Comp.	405,454	583	404,871	611,129	1,602	609,527
Percent	4.8%	0.0%	13.9%	5.8%	0.0%	16.7%
Unknown	...	...	...	...	...	...
Percent	...	...	...	...	...	...
Unaccounted for	0	0	0	0	0	0
Percent	0%	0%	0%	0%	0%	0%

Notes: a Total number employed in socialist sector on day of cadre census. Persons in military, ministries of interior and defense, political organizations, collective farms and agricultural circles excluded. b Included with those having specialized secondary education.

TABLE E-27 MANUAL AND NONMANUAL ACTIVE EARNERS, LEVEL OF EDUCATION: USSR, 1939-1970

Level of Education	1939			1959	
	Total	Manual	Nonmanual	Total	Manual
ACTIVE EARNERS	78,810,976	64,989,524	13,821,452	99,130,212	78,635,144
Percent	100.0%	100.0%	100.0%	100.0%	100.0%
Without Schooling	...	...	...	...	...
Percent	...	...	...	...	...
4 Yr. Element. Inc.	...	...	...	...	...
Percent	...	...	...	...	...
4 Yr. Element. Comp.	...	...	...	...	...
Percent	...	...	...	...	...
7-8 Yr. Basic Inc.	...	...	...	[32,800,000]	...
Percent	...	...	...	33.1%	...
7-8 Yr. Basic Comp.					
Percent				[25,800,000]	
Trade School				26.0%	
Percent					
Inc. Second. [a]					[23,700,000]
Percent					30.2%
General Second. Comp.				[6,340,000]	
Percent				6.4%	
Specialized Second., Lower Level	[9,690,000]	[2,860,000]	[7,080,000]		
Percent	12.3%	4.4%	51.2%		
Specialized Second., Higher Level				[7,530,000]	
Percent				7.6%	
Inc. Higher					[1,100,000]
Percent					1.4%
Higher, Lower Level, Comp.				...	
Percent				...	
Higher, Faculty Level, Comp.				[3,270,000]	
Percent				3.3%	
Unaccounted for	[69,100,000]	[62,100,000]	[6,740,000]	[23,400,000]	[53,800,000]
Percent	87.7%	95.6%	48.8%	23.6%	68.4%

261

TABLE E-27   (CONCLUDED)

Level of Education	1959 Nonmanual	1970 Total	1970 Manual	1970 Nonmanual
ACTIVE EARNERS	20,495,068	115,204,076	83,758,718	31,445,358
Percent	100.0%	100.0%	100.0%	100.0%
Without Schooling	...	...	...	...
Percent	...	...	...	...
4 Yr. Element. Inc.	...	...	...	...
Percent	...	...	...	...
4 Yr. Element. Comp.	...	...	...	...
Percent	...	...	...	...
7-8 Yr. Basic Inc.	...	...	...	...
Percent	...	...	...	...
7-8 Yr. Basic Comp.				
Percent			[30,700,000]	[5,280,000]
Trade School				
Percent			36.6%	16.8%
Inc. Second. [a]				
Percent				
General Second. Comp.	[8,360,000]	[54,100,000]	[12,000,000]	[6,130,000]
Percent	40.8%	47.0%	14.3%	19.5%
Specialized Second., Lower Level				
Percent				
Specialized Second., Higher Level		[13,600,000]	[2,510,000]	[11,130,000]
Percent		11.8%	3.0%	35.4%
Inc. Higher	[9,760,000]			
Percent	47.6%			
Higher, Lower Level, Comp.		...	...	...
Percent		...	...	...
Higher, Faculty Level, Comp.		[7,490,000]	[84,000]	[7,390,000]
Percent		6.5%	0.1%	23.5%
Unaccounted for	[2,380,000]	[40,000,000]	[38,500,000]	[1,510,000]
Percent	11.6%	34.7%	46.0%	4.8%

Notes: a   No equivalent Soviet category.

TABLE E-28   AGRICULTURAL POPULATION BY CLASS AND AGE:
             BULGARIA, 1956-1965

	1956		1965	
	Population	AE	AE & D [a]	AE
Agricultural Population by Class				
Total[b]	4,197,811	2,663,127	2,742,849	1,877,943
Percent	100.0%	100.0%	100.0%	100.0%
Agricultural Workers	249,423	135,834	442,316	...
Percent	5.9%	5.1%	16.1%	...
Collective Farmers	2,691,464	1,726,583	2,210,995	1,564,414
Percent	64.1%	64.8%	80.6%	83.3%
Private Peasantry			c	
Percent	1,199,712	771,875		21,835
Helping Family Members	28.6%	29.0%	...	1.2%
Percent			...	
Others	57,212[d]	28,835[e]	89,538[f]	291,694
Percent	1.4%	1.1%	3.3%	15.5%
Agricultural Population by Age				
Total[g]	3,933,253	2,498,458	3,123,896	1,673,868
Percent	100.0%	100.0%	100.0%	100.0%
0-14	916,680	39,076	614,864[h]	7,900[h]
Percent	23.3%	1.6%	19.7%	0.5%
15-19	303,839	155,321	180,972[i]	88,335[i]
Percent	7.7%	6.2%	5.8%	5.3%
20-29	545,825	488,563	311,741	272,214
Percent	13.9%	19.6%	10.0%	16.3%
30-39	533,647	514,267	386,067	373,304
Percent	13.6%	20.6%	12.4%	22.3%
40-49	574,966	542,071	398,667	380,809
Percent	14.6%	21.7%	12.8%	22.7%
50-54	287,715	254,938	235,908	213,572
Percent	7.3%	10.2%	7.6%	12.8%
55-59	229,017	189,938	267,607	170,140
Percent	5.8%	7.6%	8.6%	10.2%
60 & over	541,562	314,283	728,070	167,594
Percent	13.8%	12.6%	23.3%	10.0%
Unknown	0	0	0	0
Percent	0.0%	0.0%	0.0%	0.0%
Unaccounted for	2	1	0	0
Percent	0.0%	0.0%	0%	0%

Notes: a Preliminary results of 1965 census. b Agricultural population by
branch. c 42,767 in final results of 1965 census. d Of whom, 55,633
were employees. e Of whom, 27,258 were employees. f Includes 51,750
employees, 592 Artisans in Production Cooperatives, and 37,196 Others
(private peasantry). g Collective Farmers and Peasantry, including
collective farmers not in the agricultural branch of the economy.
Excludes agricultural workers. h For ages 0-15. i For ages 16-19.

TABLE E-29   AGRICULTURAL POPULATION BY CLASS AND AGE: CZECHOSLOVAKIA, 1950-1970

	1950		1961		1970	
	AE & D	AE	AE & D	AE	AE & D	AE
Agricultural Population **by Class**						
Total[a]	3,076,261	2,206,000	2,416,113[b]	1,462,370[c]	1,689,875	1,040,605
Percent	100.0%	100.0%	100.0%	100.0%	100.0%	100.0%
Agricultural Workers	...	...	450,572[d]	227,037[d]	...	...
Percent	...	...	18.6%	15.6%	...	...
Collective Farmers	...	...	1,493,656	994,716	...	...
Percent	...	...	61.8%	68.0%	...	...
Private Peasantry	...	...		167,007	...	...
Percent	...	...	309,382	11.4%	...	...
Helping Family Members	...	...	12.8%	e	...	...
Percent	...	...		...	...	...
Others	...	...	162,503[f]	73,610[f]	...	...
Percent	...	...	6.7%	5.0%	...	...
Agricultural Population **by Age**						
Total[g]	...	...	2,416,113	1,462,370	...	827,266
Percent	...	...	100.0%	100.0%	...	100.0%
0-14	...	...	623,675	2,703	...	...
Percent	...	...	25.8%	0.2%	...	...
15-19	...	...	144,876	71,438	...	36,674
Percent	...	...	6.0%	4.9%	...	4.4%
20-29	...	...	220,184	173,273	...	145,762
Percent	...	...	9.1%	11.8%	...	17.6%
30-39	...	...	339,187	289,998	...	148,995
Percent	...	...	14.0%	19.8%	...	18.0%
40-49	...	...	334,591	290,706	...	219,985
Percent	...	...	13.8%	19.9%	...	26.6%
50-54	...	...	237,626	204,055	...	75,640
Percent	...	...	9.8%	14.0%	...	9.1%
55-59	...	...	219,244	186,227	...	88,444
Percent	...	...	9.1%	12.7%	...	10.7%
60 & over	...	...	295,006	242,859	...	111,766
Percent	...	...	12.2%	16.6%	...	13.5%
Unknown	...	...	1,733	1,131	...	...
Percent	...	...	0.1%	0.1%	...	...
Unaccounted for	...	...	0	0	...	0
Percent	...	...	0%	0%	...	0%

Notes: a Agricultural branch of the economy. b Does not include persons in Forestry. c Excludes persons in Forestry, Helping Family Members, and Apprentices. d State Farmers. e 43,252 Helping Family Members included with Dependents. f MTS personnel. g For 1961, those in agricultural branch of the economy; for 1970, Workers in Agriculture and Collective Farmers including Collective Farmers not in the agricultural branch of the economy.

TABLE E-30   AGRICULTURAL POPULATION BY CLASS AND AGE: GDR, 1950-1964

	1950		1955	1960	1964
	AE & D	AE	I AE[a]	I AE[a]	AE & D
Agricultural Population by Class					
Total[b]	2,912,387	2,068,965	1,720,600	1,303,700	2,111,264
Percent	100.0%	100.0%	100.0%c	100.0%	100.0%
Agricultural Workers	907,356	575,922	500,900[c]	352,000[c]	579,404[c]
Percent	31.2%	27.8%	29.1%	27.0%	27.4%
Collective Farmers	...	...	190,200	916,900	1,485,960
Percent	...	...	11.1%	70.3%	70.4%
Private Peasantry	980,945	554,979			18,174
Percent	33.7%	26.8%		34,800	0.9%
Helping Family Members	926,285	884,282	1,029,500	2.7%	27,726
Percent	31.8%d	42.7%	59.8%		1.3%
Others	97,801[d]	53,782	...	...	...
Percent	3.4%	2.6%	...	...	...

	1964	1965	1970	1971	1975
	AE[a]	I AE[a]	I AE	I AE	I AE
Agricultural Population by Class (cont'd.)					
Total[b]	1,201,394	1,178,600	1,022,000	959,979	922,600
Percent	100.0%	100.0%	100.0%	100.0%	100.0%
Agricultural Workers	306,599	290,000[c]	232,200[c]	...	247,800[c]
Percent	25.5%	24.6%	22.7%	...	26.9%
Collective Farmers	856,840	874,500	755,700	...	639,500
Percent	71.3%	74.2%	73.9%	...	69.3%
Private Peasantry	10,919			...	
Percent	0.9%	14,200	9,300	...	
Helping Family Members	27,036	1.2%	0.9%	...	7,200
Percent	2.2%			...	0.8%
Others	...		24,900[e]	...	28,100[e]
Percent	...		2.4%	...	3.0%

| | 1964 | | |
	AE	Population	AE
Agricultural Population by Age			
Total	1,201,386[f]	1,634,401[g]	903,167[g]
Percent	100.0%	100.0%	100.0%
0-14	9,114[h]	544,838[i]	17,865[i]
Percent	0.8%	33.3%	2.0%
15-19			
Percent			
20-29	515,222[j]		
Percent	42.9%		
30-39			
Percent			
40-49	198,040	829,914[k]	729,571[k]
Percent	16.5%	50.8%	80.8%
50-54	135,026		
Percent	11.2%		
55-59	143,762		
Percent	12.0%		
60 & over	200,222	259,649	155,731
Percent	16.7%	15.9%	17.2%

Notes: a Without apprentices. b Agricultural branch of the economy. For 1950, Earners (Erwerbstatig); for 1964, Economically Active (Wirtschaftlich Tatige); for remaining years, Employed (Berufstatig). c Includes employees. d Employees. e Apprentices. f Agricultural branch of the economy. g Collective Farmers as a class, including those not in the agricultural branch of the economy. h For ages 0-16. i For ages 0-17 j For ages 17-39. k For ages 18-59.

TABLE E-31   AGRICULTURAL POPULATION BY CLASS, AGE, AND SIZE OF HOLDING:
             HUNGARY, 1949-1970

	1949		1960		1970	
	AE & D	AE	AE & D	AE	AE & D	AE
Agricultural Population by Class						
Total[a]	4,523,503	2,200,248	3,466,407[b]	1,842,617[b]	2,356,544	1,282,311
Percent	100.0%[c]	100.0%[c]	100.0%	100.0%	100.0%	100.0%
Workers	597,489[c]	286,574[c]	...	283,508	600,531	318,616
Percent	13.2%	13.0%	...	15.4%	25.5%	24.8%
Other Employees	13,888	6,440	...	34,580	119,540	69,972
Percent	0.3%	0.3%	...	1.9%	5.1%	5.5%
Collective Farm Members	...	...	...	580,664[d,e]	1,422,768	714,007
Percent	...	...	...	31.5%	60.4%	55.7%
Private Peasantry	3,073,719		...		69,071	39,274
Percent	67.9%	1,907,234	...	943,865	2.9%[f]	3.1%[g]
Helping Family Members	838,407	86.7%	...	51.2%	144,634	140,442
Percent	18.5%		...		6.1%	11.0%
Others	0	0	...	0	0	0
Percent	0.0%	0.0%	...	0.0%	0.0%	0.0%
Private Peasantry by Size of Holding						
Total	3,905,037	1,908,854	1,484,000	929,300	...	...
Percent	100.0%	100.0%	100.0%	100.0%	...	...
0-1 Square Hold[h]	164,243	85,206	69,500	47,800	...	...
Percent	4.2%	4.5%	4.7%	5.1%	...	...
1-3 Square Hold	610,652	303,337			...	...
Percent	15.6%	15.9%	559,800	347,600	...	...
3-5 Square Hold	765,688	363,976	37.7%	37.4%	...	...
Percent	19.6%	19.1%			...	...
5-10 Square Hold	1,421,129	674,855	580,100	357,000	...	...
Percent	36.4%	35.4%	39.1%	38.4%	...	...
10-25 Square Hold	815,988	409,056	270,000	173,600	...	...
Percent	20.9%	21.5%	18.2%	18.7%	...	...
25-50 Square Hold	101,449	54,135			...	...
Percent	2.6%	2.8%	4,600	3,300	...	...
Over 50 Square Hold	25,888	13,289	0.3%	0.4%	...	...
Percent	0.6%	0.7%			...	...

TABLE E-31   (CONCLUDED)

	1949		1960		1970	
	AE & D	AE	AE & D	AE	AE & D	AE
Agricultural Population by Age						
Total[a]	4,533,419	2,200,248	3,466,407[b]	1,842,617[b]	2,356,544	1,282,311
Percent	100.0%	100.0%	100.0%	100.0%	100.0%	100.0%
0-14	1,138,376	52,975	833,682	16,515	592,669	4,180
Percent	25.1%	2.4%	24.1%	0.9%	25.1%	0.3%
15-19	467,063	341,137	238,308	160,129	197,419	84,128
Percent	10.3%	15.5%	6.9%	8.7%	8.4%	6.6%
20-29	732,587	477,051	357,799	247,037	271,563	208,818
Percent	16.2%	21.7%	10.3%	13.4%	11.5%	16.3%
30-39	539,233	315,067	465,111	334,257	334,239	261,510
Percent	11.9%	14.3%	13.4%	18.1%	14.2%	20.4%
40-49 Percent	1,099,067	681,726	699,122	513,175	521,190	403,879
50-54 Percent	24.2%	31.0%	20.2%	27.9%	22.1%	31.5%
55-59			265,746	179,436	186,884	140,647
Percent			7.7%	9.7%	7.9%	11.0%
60 & over	557,093	332,292	606,639	392,068	252,580	179,149
Percent	12.3%	15.1%	17.5%	21.3%	10.7%	14.0%
Unknown	0	0	0	0	0	0
Percent	0.0%	0.0%	0.0%	0.0%	0.0%	0.0%

Notes: a Agricultural branch of the economy. b Active Earners as defined in 1970. c Includes 437,767 seasonal workers and their dependents. d Includes 55,257 Helping Family Members. e Of whom, 14,205 were in nonmanual occupations. f Of whom, 101,308 were members of collective farms, 20,685 were in private households, and 22,641 were Dual Helping Family Members. g Of whom, 98,703 were collective farm members, 19,526 were in private households, and 22,213 were Dual Helping Family Members. h One square hold equals .57 hectares.

AGRICULTURAL POPULATION BY CLASS, AGE, AND SIZE OF HOLDING: POLAND, 1950-1974

	1950		1960		1970		1974	
	AE & D	AE	AE & D	AE	AE & D	AE	AE & D	AE
icultural Population Class								
al[a]	11,597,500	7,016,100	11,243,600	6,545,800	10,233,321	6,420,968	9,561,437	5,940,486
rcent	100.0%	100.0%	100.0%	100.0%	100.0%	100.0%	100.0%	100.0%
kers			902,400	327,800	1,268,815[b]	498,470[c]	1,390,428[d]	528,607[e]
rcent	889,600	436,400[f]	8.0%	5.0%	12.4%	7.8%	14.5%	8.9%
er Employees	7.7%	6.2%	141,100	54,600	321,066	164,263	319,967	168,993[g]
rcent			1.3%	0.8%	3.1%	2.6%	3.3%	2.8%[h]
lective Farm Members	135,500	55,500	81,400	34,300	88,592	41,254	...	49,262[h]
rcent	1.2%	0.8%	0.7%	0.5%	0.9%	0.6%	...	0.8%
vate Peasantry	6,604,600	2,698,300	6,798,800	2,993,700	5,547,305	2,885,425		2,453,081
rcent	56.9%	38.5%	60.5%	45.7%	54.2%	44.9%	7,850,344	41.3%
ping Family Members	3,938,800	3,824,800	3,290,000	3,108,300	3,002,876	2,828,938	82.1%	2,739,980
rcent	34.0%	54.5%	29.3%.	47.5%.	29.3%.	44.1%[k]		46.1%
ers	...	...	27,400[i]	26,100[i]	4,331[j]	2,595[k]	698	563
rcent	...	...	0.2%	0.4%	0.0%	0.0%	0.0%	0.0%
nown	29,000	1,100	2,500	1,000	336	23	0	0
rcent	0.3%	0.0%	0.0%	0.0%	0.0%	0.0%	0.0%	0.0%
vate Peasantry by e of Holding								
al	10,357,500	6,349,400	10,081,161	6,098,530	7,893,683	5,400,277	...	4,901,047
rcent	100.0%	100.0%	100.0%	100.0%	100.0%	100.0%	...	100.0%
-1 hectare			435,442	317,278	348,060	303,693	...	
rcent	1,181,000	769,900	4.3%	5.2%	4.4%	5.6%	...	624,749
hectares	11.4%	12.1%	919,385	633,949	589,623	475,301	...	12.7%
rcent			9.1%	10.4%	7.5%	8.8%	...	
hectares			1,056,984	691,909	675,236	512,390	...	
rcent			10.4%	11.3%	8.6%	9.5%	...	
hectares	2,194,300	1,377,700	1,081,974	686,085	732,998	531,541	...	1,472,825
rcent	21.2%	21.7%	10.7%	11.2%	9.3%	9.8%	...	30.1%
hectares	1,074,900	664,200	1,025,111	633,352	760,322	532,231	...	
rcent	10.4%	10.5%	10.2%	10.4%	9.6%	9.9%	...	
hectares	1,934,600	1,174,900	1,776,640	1,060,157	1,388,318	934,929	...	867,378
rcent	18.7%	18.5%	17.6%	17.4%	17.6%	17.3%	...	17.7%
0 hectares	2,178,100	1,285,800	1,921,250	1,091,572	1,616,848	1,032,577	...	938,714
rcent	21.0%	20.3%	19.1%	17.9%	20.5%	19.1%	...	19.2%
15 hectares	1,138,600[l]	672,900[l]	1,297,465	710,827	1,244,609	755,698	...	686,095
rcent	11.0%	10.6%	12.9%	11.7%	15.8%	14.0%	...	14.0%
& over	621,000[m]	386,200[m]	478,192	268,191	525,397	313,792	...	279,748
rcent	6.0%	6.1%	4.7%	4.4%	6.7%	5.8%	...	5.7%
ers & Unknown	35,000	17,800	88,718	5,210	12,272	8,125	...	31,538
rcent	0.3%	0.3%	0.9%	0.0%	0.2%	0.2%	...	0.6%

	1950	1960		1970	
	AE	AE & D	AE	AE & D	AE
Agricultural Population by Age					
Total	7,016,100	11,150,775[n]	6,545,800	9,495,616	6,057,840
Percent	100.0%	100.0%	100.0%	100.0%	100.0%
0-14				2,471,419	0
Percent	[547,000]	4,198,070[o]	[242,000]	26.0%	0.0%
15-19	7.8%[p]	37.6%	3.7%[p]	869,911	380,938
Percent				9.2%	6.3%
20-29		1,398,633[q]		953,069	847,366
Percent		12.5%		10.0%	14.0%
30-39		1,486,374		1,091,505	1,032,382
Percent		13.3%		11.5%	17.0%
40-49	[5,697,000]	1,259,698	[5,224,000]	1,391,182	1,345,621
Percent	81.2%[r]	11.3%	79.8%	14.7%	22.2%
50-54		782,113		499,903	485,654
Percent		7.0%		5.3%	8.0%
55-59		680,423		587,020	567,332
Percent		6.1%		6.2%	9.4%
60 & over	[772,000]	1,335,977	[1,080,000]	1,624,734	1,392,522
Percent	11.0%	12.0%	16.5%	17.1%	23.0%
Unknown	...	9,487	...	6,862	6,005
Percent	...	0.1%	...	0.1%	0.1%
Private Peasantry					
Total	6,516,000	10,081,161	6,098,500	7,893,683	5,400,277
Percent	100.0%	100.0%	100.0%	100.0%	100.0%
0-14				1,839,726	...
Percent	[495,000]	3,669,038[q]	[226,000]	23.3%	...
15-19	7.6%[p]	36.4%	3.7%	693,106	327,476
Percent				8.8%	6.1%
20-29		1,200,538[q]		680,255	637,552
Percent		11.9%		8.6%	11.8%
30-39		1,334,568		859,484	849,943
Percent		13.2%		10.9%	15.7%
40-49	[5,284,000]	1,177,789	[4,818,000]	1,227,659	1,216,926
Percent	81.1%[s]	11.7%	79.0%	15.6%	22.5%
50-54		740,657		461,505	456,072
Percent		7.3%		5.8%	8.4%
55-59		649,767		549,324	538,920
Percent		6.4%		7.0%	10.0%
60 & over	[736,000]	1,300,047	[1,055,000]	1,576,387	1,367,792
Percent	11.3%	12.9%	17.3%	20.0%	25.3%
Unknown	...	8,757	...	6,236	5,596
Percent	...	0.1%	...	0.1%	0.1%

Notes: For notes, see next page.

TABLE E-32   (CONCLUDED)

Notes: a Agricultural branch of the economy; Active "Czynni zawodowo."   b Of whom, 60,443 hired laborers
working in private sector.   c Of whom, 39,249 hired laborers working in private sector.   d Includes
collective farm members and 51,433 hired laborers in private sector.   e Includes 35,957 hired laborers
working in private sector, 90,054 laborers working in agricultural circles, 95,521 working for trusts
and similar institutions, and 307,032 remaining manual laborers, presumably state farm employees.
f Of whom, 117,300 hired laborers working in private sector.   g Includes 4,537 working on collective
farms, 22,284 members of agricultural circles, 84,339 working in trusts and similar institutions, and
57,833 remaining nonmanual workers, presumably state farm employees.   h Includes unspecified number
working private plots.   i Persons working private plots.   j Includes 1,172 working private plots and
3,159 others.   k Includes 1,172 working private plots and 1,423 others.   l 10-14 hectares.   m 14 and
over.   n Excludes persons working in agricultural circles, hired labor in private sector.   o 0-17.
p 0-18 years.   q 18-29.   r Includes 18-24, 16.0%; 25-34, 18.5%; 35-59, 46.7%.   s Includes 18-24,
15.4%; 25-34, 18.3%; 35-59, 47.4%.

TABLE E-33   AGRICULTURAL POPULATION BY CLASS AND AGE: ROMANIA,
1956-1966

	1956		1966	
	Population	AE	AE & D	AE
Agricultural Population by Class				
Total[a]	11,085,000[b]	7,278,518	8,613,622	5,920,327
Percent	100.0%	100.0%	100.0%	100.0%
Agricultural Workers	778,000	356,119	774,322	366,412
Percent	7.0%	4.9%	9.0%	6.2%
Collective Farmers	1,250,000	790,279	6,646,069[c]	4,735,394
Percent	11.3%	10.9%	77.2%	80.0%
Private Peasantry				
Percent	8,946,000	6,069,701	972,411	699,884
Helping Family Members	80.7%	83.4%	11.3%	11.8%
Percent				
Others	111,000[d]	62,419[e]	220,820[f]	118,637[g]
Percent	1.0%	0.9%	2.6%	2.0%
Agricultural Population by Age				
Total	...	7,278,518	8,361,779[h]	5,436,746[h]
Percent	...	100.0%	100.0%	100.0%
0-14	...	0	1,847,925	13,854
Percent	...	0%	22.1%	0.3%
15-19	...	1,060,775[i]	712,373	446,251
Percent	...	14.6%	8.5%	8.2%
20-29	...	1,708,849	1,034,003	990,197
Percent	...	23.5%	12.4%	18.2%
30-39	...	1,236,989	1,255,015	1,225,993
Percent	...	17.0%	15.0%	22.6%
40-49	...	1,301,321	1,014,903	980,763
Percent	...	17.9%	12.1%	18.0%
50-54	...	574,765	551,188	517,490
Percent	...	7.9%	6.6%	9.5%
55-59	...	498,961	562,630	506,246
Percent	...	6.9%	6.7%	9.3%
60 & over	...		1,376,843	751,315
Percent	...	896,858	16.5%	13.8%
Unknown	...	12.3%	6,899	4,277
Percent	...		0.1%	0.1%
Unaccounted for	...	0	0	360
Percent	...	0%	0%	0.0%

Notes: a Agricultural branch of the economy. b Data on Agricultural Population by Class include estimates of number of Dependents and Other
Earners. c Does not include 569,155 persons supported by collective
farms. d Employees. e Includes 61,851 employees. f Includes 97,672
employees and 20,965 persons in handicraft cooperatives. g Includes
97,672 employees and 20,965 persons in handicraft cooperatives.
h Private Peasantry and Collective Farmers, including Collective
Farmers not in the agricultural branch of the economy. i For ages
14-19.

TABLE E-34   AGRICULTURAL POPULATION BY CLASS AND AGE: USSR, 1926-1970

	1926		1959		1970	
	AE & D	AE	Population	AE	Population	AE
Agricultural Population By Class						
Total[a]	114,055,516	71,734,888	75,293,000	38,425,967	...	28,937,593
Percent	100.0%	100.0%	100.0%	100.0%	...	100.0%
Agricultural Workers	1,858,320	1,103,065	11,836,000	5,918,418	...	9,991,768
Percent	1.6%	1.5%	15.7%	15.4%	...	34.5%
Collective Farmers	...	...	62,899,000	31,722,834	...	17,230,304
Percent	...[b]	...[b]	83.5%	82.6%	...	59.5%
Private Peasantry	63,813,682[b]	22,419,599[b]	558,000	91,671	...	...
Percent	55.9%	31.3%	0.7%	0.2%	...	...
Helping Family Members	48,113,637	48,113,637		c	...	d
Percent	42.2%	67.1%			...	
Others	269,877[e]	98,587[e]	...	693,044[e]	...	1,715,521[f]
Percent	0.2%	0.1%	...	1.8%	...	5.9%
Agricultural Population by Age						
Total	...	71,735,000	...	38,425,967	...	...
Percent	...	100.0%	...	100.0%	...	...
0-15	...	11,790,000	...	[423,000]	...	...
Percent	...	16.4%	...	1.1%	...	...
16-19	...	10,011,000	...	[4,150,000]	...	...
Percent	...	14.0%	...	10.8%	...	...
20-29	...	17,493,000	...	[10,500,000]	...	...
Percent	...	24.4%	...	27.3%	...	...
30-39	...	12,008,000	...	[8,110,000]	...	...
Percent	...	16.7%	...	21.1%	...	...
40-49	...	9,134,000	...	[6,880,000]	...	...
Percent	...	12.7%	...	17.9%	...	...
50-54	...	3,535,000	...	[3,230,000]	...	...
Percent	...	4.9%	...	8.4%	...	...
55-59	...	2,894,000	...	[2,230,000]	...	...
Percent	...	4.0%	...	5.8%	...	...
60 & over	...	4,870,000[g]	...	[2,920,000]	...	...
Percent	...	6.8%	...	7.6%	...	...

Notes: a Agricultural branch of the economy. b Approximately 800,000 in cooperatives (members of artels). c Active Earner population for 1959 excludes 9,864,801 members of families of Collective Farmers, Workers, and Other Employees tending private plots in agriculture. Census data do not indicate how many of these were Collective Farm Members. d In 1970, there were 1,823,499 members of families of Collective Farmers, Workers and Employees tending personal plots in agriculture, of whom 828,896 were Collective Farm Members. e Employees. f Of whom, 1,397,278 were Employees, 312,243 Others (Private Peasantry). g Of whom, 29,000 were of unknown age.

TABLE E-35　　AGRICULTURAL POPULATION BY CLASS, AGE, AND SIZE OF HOLDING:　YUGOSLAVIA, 1948-1971

	1948		1953		1961		1971	
	AE & D	AE	AE & D	AE	AE & D	AE	AE & D	AE
Total Agricultural Population, Adjusted[a]	10,606,000	5,627,000	10,315,834	5,360,026	9,197,597	4,691,679	7,843,986[b]	4,207,645[b]
Agricultural Population by Class[a]								
Total[c]	11,114,839	7,362,595	...	5,324,637	9,197,597	4,691,679	...	3,902,963
Percent	100.0%	100.0%	...	100.0%	100.0%	100.0%	...	100.0%
Workers-Employees	335,513[d]	214,115[d]	...	182,130			...	220,761
Percent	3.0%	2.9%	...	3.4%			...	5.7%
Apprentices	...	...	...	331	758,293	290,264	...	...
Percent	...	...	...	0.0%	8.2%	6.2%	...	...
Members of Cooperatives	220,182	129,498	...	549,894			...	...
Percent	2.0%	1.8%	...	10.3%			...	...
Independents[e]			...	1,808,117	5,597,886	2,057,672	...	1,820,930
Percent			...	34.0%	60.9%	43.9%	...	46.7%
Helping Family Members	10,559,144	7,018,982	...	2,784,071	2,830,383	2,338,858	...	1,859,796
Percent	95.0%	95.3%	...	52.3%	30.8%	49.9%	...	47.7%
Unknown	...	...	...	...	11,035	4,885	...	1,476
Percent	...	...	...	...	0.1%	0.1%	...	0.0%
Private Peasantry by Size of Holding								
Total[f]	10,559,144	7,018,982	8,685,557	4,592,976	8,428,269	4,396,530	7,749,823	3,680,726
Percent	100.0%	100.0%	100.0%	100.0%	100.0%	100.0%	100.0%	100.0%
Without Land	4,798	2,623	56,120	27,210	171,589	85,976	...	...
Percent	0.0%	0.0%	0.6%	0.6%	2.0%	2.0%	...	...
0-1 hectare	804,412	546,036	831,474	425,834	639,203	333,452	1,358,386	...
Percent	7.6%	7.8%	9.6%	9.3%	7.6%	7.6%	8.6%	...
1-3 hectares	3,270,203	2,169,536	2,775,479	1,445,683	2,429,564	1,275,016	2,116,415	...
Percent	31.0%	30.9%	32.0%	31.5%	28.8%	29.0%	28.0%	...
3-5 hectares	2,547,498	1,689,035	1,972,952	1,047,241	2,027,089	1,059,490	1,676,544	...
Percent	24.1%	24.1%	22.7%	22.8%	24.1%	24.1%	21.6%	...
5-10 hectares	2,625,379	1,745,949	1,994,037	1,074,437	2,402,669	1,253,087	1,997,804	...
Percent	24.9%	24.9%	23.0%	23.4%	28.5%	28.5%	25.8%	...
10 & over	1,301,466	864,882	954,491	519,074	758,155	389,509	550,674	...
Percent	12.3%	12.3%	11.0%	11.3%	9.0%	8.9%	7.1%	...
Unknown	5,388	921	101,004	53,497	0	0	0	...
Percent	0.1%	0.0%	1.2%	1.2%	0.0%	0.0%	0.0%	...

TABLE E-35   (CONCLUDED)

	1948		1953		1961		1971	
	AE & D	AE	AE & D	AE	AE & D	AE	AE & D	AE
Agricultural Population by Age								
Total[g]	11,114,839	7,362,595	...	5,324,637	9,197,597	4,691,679	7,843,986	3,902,963
Percent	100.0%	100.0%	...	100.0%	100.0%	100.0%	100.0%	100.0%
0-14	3,824,414	418,776	...	307,149	2,792,870	171,427	2,018,582	71,915
Percent	34.4%	5.7%	...	5.8%	30.4%	3.7%	25.7%[h]	1.8%
15-19	1,220,689	1,166,762	...	961,148			1,367,701[h]	482,882
Percent	11.0%	15.8%	...	18.0%			17.4%[i]	12.4%
20-29			...	1,421,644			853,813[i]	586,769
Percent			...	26.7%			10.9%	15.0%
30-39			...	694,716	4,188,912	3,169,107		705,620
Percent			...	13.0%	45.5%	67.5%		18.1%
40-49	4,638,473	4,578,944	...	853,369			1,604,245[j]	761,144
Percent	41.7%	62.2%	...	16.0%			20.5%	19.5%
50-54			...	357,031				227,400
Percent			...	6.7%				5.8%
55-59	418,395	400,768	...	247,839	1,535,590[k]	1,017,912[k]	1,187,775[k]	280,268
Percent	3.8%	5.4%	...	4.7%	16.7%	21.7%	15.1%	7.2%
60 & over	1,012,668	797,190	...	481,741	674,764[l]	330,456[l]	793,282[l]	781,980
Percent	9.1%	10.8%	...	9.0%	7.3%	7.0%	10.1%	20.0%
Unknown	200	155	...	...	5,461	2,777	18,588	4,985
Percent	0.0%	0.0%	...	...	0.0%	0.1%	0.2%	0.1%

Notes: a Agricultural Branch of the economy. Includes Active Earners and Dependents. Persons with pensions included among active earners if working full or part time on agricultural holdings. Also includes persons temporarily abroad. b Includes 328,000 Temporarily Abroad. c See fn. a. 1948 includes all Other Earners (pensioners) associated with agriculture, whether or not working on agricultural holdings, and a number of persons not employed in agriculture but residing in peasant households. For 1953, AE includes persons with agricultural occupations. For 1971, AE excludes those temporarily abroad. d Agricultural Workers only. e Includes Independents in agriculture with and without hired labor. f 1953, 1961, and 1971 include Independents with and without hired labor, and Helping Family Members. g For 1953 and 1971, AE includes persons with agricultural occupations. h For ages 15-24. i For ages 25-34. j For ages 35-49. k For ages 50-64. l For ages 65 & over.

TABLE E-36   CLASS STRUCTURE OF THE POPULATION OF EASTERN EUROPE AND
              THE USSR: CMEA DATA

Country, Date of Census	Total Population	Workers, Employees	Production Cooperatives	Peasants, Artisans	Liberal Professions	Others
Bulgaria						
1956	100.0%	43.9%	37.0%	18.1%	0.2%	0.8%
1965	100.0%	58.8%	39.7%	1.3%	0.1%	0.1%
1975	100.0%	83.8%	15.4%	0.4%	0.1%	0.3%
Czechoslovakia						
1961	100.0%	84.2%	11.9%	3.8%	0.1%	...
1970	100.0%	87.5%	11.1%	1.3%	0.1%	...
1976[a]	100.0%	89.2%	9.8%	0.9%	0.1%	...
Hungary						
1970	100.0%	75.5%	21.4%	2.8%	___ 0.3% ___	
GDR						
1964	100.0%	80.5%	11.5%	_____ 8.0% _____		
1971	100.0%	82.3%	11.7%	3.7%	0.3%	2.0%
Poland						
1960	100.0%	60.4%	2.7%	___ 36.8% ___		0.1%
1970	100.0%	69.4%	3.5%	___ 26.7% ___		0.4%
1974	100.0%	72.2%	3.7%	___ 23.6% ___		0.5%
Rumania						
1956	100.0%	37.0%	8.3%	53.7%	___ 1.0% ___	
1966	100.0%	52.2%	40.9%	6.1%	___ 0.8% ___	
USSR						
1959	100.0%	68.3%	31.4%	0.3%	...	...
1976[a]	100.0%	84.3%	15.7%	0.0%	...	...

Note: a End-of-Year estimate.

TABLE E-37 POPULATION BY TYPE OF ECONOMIC ACTIVITY ACCORDING TO INTERNATIONAL STANDARD CLASSIFICATION: EASTERN EUROPE AND USSR

	Bulgaria			Czechoslovakia			GDR		
	1956[a]	1965[b]	1975[a]	1950[b]	1961[b]	1970	1950[a]	1964[a]	1971[a]
TOTAL POPULATION	7,613,709	8,227,866	8,727,771	12,330,450	13,745,577	14,362,000	18,388,172	17,003,600	17,068,318
Percent	100.0%	100.0%	100.0%	100.0%	100.0%	100.0%	100.0%	100.0%	100.0%
Economically Active	4,150,207	4,267,798	4,573,593	5,811,724	6,482,000	6,989,000	8,477,159	8,345,000	8,214,251
Percent	54.5%	51.9%	52.4%	47.1%	47.2%	48.7%	46.1%	49.1%	48.1%
Salaried Workers & Employees	1,524,201	2,445,485	...	[3,603,000]	5,231,000	6,094,000	...	6,955,300	...
Percent	20.0%	29.7%	...	29.2%	38.1%	42.4%	...	40.9%	...
Employees & Workers on Own Account	853,035	55,487	...	[2,209,000]	176,000	64,000	...	336,100[c]	...
Percent	11.2%	0.7%	...	17.9%[c]	1.3%	0.4%	...	2.0%	...
Members of Producers' Cooperatives	1,772,946	1,763,980	...	0	1,026,000	625,000	...	1,053,500	...
Percent	23.3%	21.4%	...	0.0%	7.5%	4.4%	...	6.2%	...
Unpaid Family Workers	...	...	...	d	43,000	e	...	d	...
Percent	...	...	...		0.3%		...		...
Others	25	2,846	...	...	6,000	206,000	...	...	...
Percent	0.0%	0.0%	...	...	0.0%	1.4%	...	...	...
Not Economically Active	3,463,502	3,960,068	...	6,526,726	7,264,000	7,373,000	9,911,013	8,658,600	...
Percent	45.5%	48.1%	...	52.9%	52.8%	51.3%	53.9%	50.9%	...
Income Recipients	...	994,418	...	...	1,586,000	2,393,000	2,044,029	2,634,000	...
Percent	...	12.1%	...	...	11.5%	16.7%	11.1%	15.5%	...
Homemakers	...	...	...	...	1,426,000	806,000	413,067	...	...
Percent	...	...	...	...	10.4%	5.6%	2.2%	...	...
Students	...	2,965,650	...	...	254,000	497,000	7,453,917	6,024,600	...
Percent	...	36.0%	...	...	1.8%	3.5%	40.5%	35.4%	...
Others	...	...	...	...	3,998,000[f]	3,677,000[g]	...	...	...
Percent	...	...	...	...	29.1%	25.6%	...	...	...

(Bulgaria 1965: bracket joins Homemakers, Students and Others into the 2,965,650 / 36.0% figure. GDR 1950: bracket joins Students and Others into the 7,453,917 / 40.5% figure. GDR 1964: bracket joins Students and Others into the 6,024,600 / 35.4% figure.)

277

TABLE E-37   (CONTINUED)

	Hungary 1949[a]	Hungary 1960[d]	Hungary 1970[b]	Poland 1950[a]	Poland 1960[a]	Poland 1970[d]	Romania 1956[a]	Romania 1966[b]
TOTAL POPULATION	9,204,799	9,961,044	10,322,099	25,008,200	29,775,500	32,642,270	17,489,450	19,103,163
Percent	100.0%	100.0%	100.0%	100.0%	100.0%	100.0%	100.0%	100.0%
Economically Active	4,154,543	4,876,232	4,988,676	12,404,200	13,907,400	16,943,848	10,449,128	10,362,300
Percent	45.1%	49.0%	48.3%	49.6%	46.7%	51.9%	59.7%	54.2%
Salaried Workers & Employees	1,906,444	3,104,628	3,883,471	5,444,800	7,213,700	10,998,128	3,182,850	4,607,886
Percent	20.7%	31.2%	37.6%	21.8%	24.2%	33.7%	18.2%	24.1%
Employees & Workers on Own Account	1,439,836	627,270	141,803	2,868,100	3,185,400	5,937,612[c]	6,375,613	783,868
Percent	15.6%	6.3%	1.4%	11.5%	10.7%	18.2%	36.5%	4.1%
Members of Producers' Cooperatives	...	...	941,195	215,900	359,400	...	888,163	4,963,996
Percent			9.1%	0.9%	1.2%		5.1%	26.0%
Unpaid Family Workers	800,813	490,060	...	3,855,400	3,120,000	d	...	d
Percent	8.7%	4.9%		15.4%	10.5%			
Others	7,450	654,265	22,213	20,000	28,900	8,108	2,502	6,550
Percent	0.1%	6.6%	0.2%	0.1%	0.1%	0.0%	0.0%	0.0%
Not Economically Active	5,050,256	5,084,812	5,333,423	12,604,000	15,868,100	15,698,422	7,040,322	8,740,863
Percent	54.9%	51.0%	51.7%	50.4%	53.3%	48.1%	40.3%	45.8%[h]
Income Recipients	254,756	...	1,247,002	...	...	...	...	1,300,287
Percent	2.8%		12.1%					6.8%
Homemakers	...	...	...	...	...	...	...	...
Percent								
Students	4,795,500	...	4,086,421	...	...	...	...	7,440,576
Percent	52.1%		39.6%					38.9%
Others		...		...	...	...	...	

278

	USSR			Yugoslavia		
	1939[a]	1959[a]	1970[a]	1953[b]	1961[b]	1971[b]
TOTAL POPULATION	170,557,000	208,826,650	241,436,013	16,936,573	18,549,291	20,522,972
Percent	100.0%	100.0%	100.0%	100.0%	100.0%	100.0%
Economically Active	86,984,000	108,995,013	117,027,575	7,848,857	8,340,400	8,889,816
Percent	51.0%	52.2%	48.5%	46.3%	45.0%	43.3%
Salaried Workers & Employees	...	65,816,782	96,939,087	2,352,143	3,529,738	4,399,006
Percent	...	31.5%	40.2%	13.9%	19.0%	21.4%
Employees & Workers on Own Account	...	266,304	...	1,969,334	2,219,721	2,012,296
Percent	...	0.1%	...	11.6%	12.0%	9.8%
Members of Producers' Cooperatives	...	33,047,126	17,899,838	593,063	11,418	...
Percent	...	15.8%	7.4%	3.5%	0.1%	...
Unpaid Family Workers	8,187,000[i]	9,864,801[i]	1,823,499[i]	2,803,832	2,442,106	1,878,585
Percent	4.8%	4.7%	0.8%	16.6%	13.2%[k]	9.2%[l]
Others	...	...	365,151	130,485[j]	137,220[k]	599,929[l]
Percent	...	...	0.2%	0.8%	0.7%	2.9%
Not Economically Active	83,573,000	99,831,637	124,408,438	9,087,716	10,208,842	11,633,156
Percent	49.0%	47.8%	51.5%	53.7%	55.0%	56.7%
Income Recipients	2,217,000	12,423,110	32,641,210	533,120	684,428[m]	1,241,498
Percent	1.3%	5.9%	13.5%	3.1%	3.7%	6.0%
Homemakers				3,064,383	3,069,945	3,130,438
Percent				18.1%	16.6%	15.2%
Students	81,356,000	87,408,527	91,767,228	1,618,487	3,123,642	3,909,681
Percent	47.7%	41.9%	38.0%	9.6%	16.8%	19.1%
Others				3,871,726	3,330,828	3,351,539
Percent				22.9%	18.0%	16.3%

(Note: for USSR, the figures 81,356,000 / 87,408,527 / 91,767,228 and 47.7% / 41.9% / 38.0% are bracketed to cover Homemakers, Students, and Others combined.)

Notes: a Data from national censuses classified according to international standards used by International Labor Office statistical annuals. b Data from national censuses combined with data from International Labor Office statistical annuals. Two sources in agreement. c Includes Helping Family Members. d Data from International Labor Office statistical annuals. e Included, with Apprentices, among Not Economically Active. f Includes 201,000 apprentices (Helping Family Members included with Economically Active). g Includes 359,000 Apprentices and Helping Family Members. h Includes 569,155 persons supported by collective farms. i Members of families of collective farmers, workers, and employees tending private plots in agriculture. j Includes 130,167 Apprentices. k Includes 111,293 Apprentices. l Includes 589,168 temporarily abroad. m Includes scholarship recipients.

SECTION F: PARTY LEADERS

Introduction

Explanation of Column Headings, Tables F-1 Through F-10

Column 1: Birthdate	Self-explanatory.
Column 2: Birthplace	Rural, urban, or capital city (upper line). Place of birth in accordance with boundaries, either national or regional, in the period between the two World Wars. Urban includes all settlements over 5,000 persons.
Column 3: Ethnicity	Self-explanatory. In tables dealing with Eastern Europe, Jews are considered as members of a religious group; in the case of Tables F-8 and F-9, dealing with the Soviet Union, as a nationality.
Column 4: Social Origins	Profession or social status of father. In cases where the father changes position, the earlier position or occupation is normally shown in the table.
Column 5: Status Prior to Party Work	Occupation or position of the individual before becoming involved full-time in political work. Full-time political work is defined as follows: *a. Prior* to the seizure of power (World War I in the USSR, World War II in Eastern Europe), joining the party is considered evidence of entering into a revolutionary, or full-time political career. For persons joining the party prior to World War I (USSR) or World War II (Eastern Europe), the position or occupation recorded in Column 5 is that held when joining the party, or that position held when becoming involved in revolutionary activity as a member of a Communist youth organization, prior to joining the party. Joining a resistance movement during World War II is not, *per se*, considered proof of entering upon a revolutionary or full-time political career. *b. After* the seizure of power, full-time political work is defined as holding a job for at least one year, on a full-time basis, in one of the following organizations: (1) the party; (2) Communist trade unions; (3) Communist youth organizations; (4) the Main Political Administration, or its equivalent, in the military. Membership in the Central Committee or a party committee, if not accompanied by full-time responsibilities in the party apparatus, is not considered a full-time political career. Membership in the Executive Committee is considered a full-time political career, regardless of other posts and duties of the individual.
Column 6: Formal Education	Covers all educational institutions attended full-time, including military academies. Party schools are not included. "Prewar" and "Postwar" (top line) indicate whether the individual received the education in question before or after World War II (World War I in the case of Table F-8 on the Soviet Union). Institutions attended during World War II are considered "Prewar." *Elementary education* includes all persons with four years of elementary education or less. *Basic education* includes all those who completed five to eight years of compulsory education in accordance with the laws of the country in question at the time the individual attended school. *Secondary education* includes all those who completed a secondary education, and for whom no further details are available concerning the type of secondary school in question. *Gymnasium* includes all those who received a secondary education at a gymnasium. *Incomplete Gymnasium* includes those who, according to the sources used for this section, attended a gymnasium but did not complete it. This may include persons with five to eight years of education, the equivalent of a Basic education. The categories *Specialized Secondary* and *University* are self-explanatory. *Higher Education* refers to those who have completed a technical or military institute or other institute

at a higher level. This category also includes those who may have attended a university but are described by the sources used for this section as having a higher education. *Only institutions attended full-time are counted when determining the individual's level of education in Column 6.*

Column 7: Advanced Training	Indicates the type of training received in institutions of higher learning, party schools attended after completing formal education, and training received by correspondence or studying part-time. Specializations in the humanities and arts are excluded. Three dots (no information) are used in all cases where no specialization has been recorded, even if it is known that the individual in question had no advanced training in the sense used in this column.
Column 8: Party Membership	Self-explanatory. In the case of Social Democrats, the date given is that of the merger of the Social Democrats and the Communist Party.

Column 9:
Revolutionary
	Type of revolutionary, divided into two major categories and five subgroups:
	    a. Those who were raised and educated prior to World War II (World War I in the cases of Tables F-8 and F-9, dealing with the Soviet Union), who in turn are divided into five subgroups: (1) Worker Revolutionary, (2) Student Revolutionary, (3) No Revolutionary Experience, (4) Intellectual Revolutionary, and (5) Social Democrat.
	    b. Those who were raised and educated after World War II, all of whom fall into one subgroup, *Postwar. Worker Revolutionaries* (W-R) are those with a low level of education (Elementary or less) who came from lower-class backgrounds and were workers before becoming engaged in revolutionary activity. (In the case of the GDR, those with Basic education are included, and in the case of Czechoslovakia, those with Specialized Secondary education). *Student Revolutionaries* (St-R) are those, regardless of background, who became engaged in revolutionary activity (joined the party) while studying at an institution of higher learning or while at secondary school. (In the case of Czechoslovakia, the group is limited at the secondary level to those from nonworking class backgrounds.) *Intellectual Revolutionaries* (Int-R) are those who did not become involved in revolutionary activity while studying, but only after beginning a career in some profession. White-collar workers who joined the revolutionary movement after school are not included in this category, but are noted separately in the footnotes. Those with *No Revolutionary Experience* (NRE) were educated before the seizure of power, but did not engage in revolutionary activity (did not join the party) until World War II or after (1917 or after in the case of Tables F-8 and F-9 on the Soviet Union). *Social Democrats* are those who were members of the Social Democratic Party prior to its merger with the Communist Party after World War II. Those classified as *Postwar* include persons who were 18 or less in 1945 (born in 1927 or after) as well as those persons receiving a higher education, through full-time study, after World War II, if 18 or under in 1939 (born in 1921 or after). Persons who did not join the party until World War II or after, and obtained a higher education through part-time studies, are classified as having no revolutionary experience (NRE) if born before 1927. In the case of Tables F-8 and F-9 on the Soviet Union, *Postwar* is defined as all persons who were 18 or less in 1918 (born in 1899 or after), as well as those persons receiving a higher education through full-time study after World War I if 18 or under in 1914 (born in 1896 or after).

Column 10: World War II	*Home* indicates that the individual was in the country but did not take part in the resistance or illegal activity. *Illegal* indicates that the individual was involved in underground or other illegal work against the Germans or their allies, *Resistance* that the individual was active in some form of Partisan activity. *Military* is used in cases where the individual served in the armed forces of the country in question. All other entries are self-explanatory. The entry is considered inapplicable, and left blank, in the case of all those born in 1930 or after.
Column 11: Central Committee Membership	Self-explanatory. Date is that of first joining the Central Committee, either as a candidate or full member.

Column 12:   Date of first joining the ruling party body (Politburo, Presidium, Executive Committee).
Executive
Committee
Membership

Executive   Indicates ruling party bodies to which the individual belonged, as shown by the number at
Committee   the foot of the table; + indicates full member, x candidate member.
& Status:

Note: Persons not in the ruling party body on the dates indicated at the foot of the table are not included
         in the table. See Appendix 14 for a list of such persons, and their backgrounds, who were members
         of the Soviet Politburo from 1917 to 1945.

II.
Explanation of Tables F-11 Through F-17

Column headings (1., 2., 3., etc.) refer to the number of the Executive Committee given at the bottom of Tables F-1 through F-10. *All* refers to the total number of Executive Committee members. Levels of education are classified according to the system used in the remaining sections of the *Handbook*, expanded by the inclusion of several new categories of secondary and higher education. The result is a system employing ten categories:

1. *None or Elementary*. Self-explanatory.
2. *Basic or Secondary*. Self-explanatory. Includes Incomplete Secondary.
3. *Secondary Political*. Includes those with a secondary level education or less, plus a lower level party school or its equivalent. When the level of the party school cannot be determined, the individual will be shown in two series, once in level three, and once in level five.
4. *Specialized Secondary*. Self-explanatory. Persons with a lower level party education and Specialized Secondary Education are ranked as level four.
5. *Higher Political or Part-Time*. Those with a higher education obtained while employed full-time, as well as graduates of higher party schools and institutes associated with the party or clearly of a political character.
6. *Higher Military or Technical*. Those who have studied at a military or technical institute at the post-secondary level. Persons with an incomplete higher technical education are included in this group. In the case of Czechoslovakia, the category includes graduates of higher commercial academies.
7. *Incomplete University*. Includes all those who were enrolled at a university but did not graduate.
8. *University*. Completed higher education at a university.
9. *Professor or Advanced Degree*. Includes all persons who taught at an institution of higher learning (party schools excluded) or

who received an advanced degree. Persons who received their higher education part-time and then subsequently received an advanced degree, or taught at the university level, are included in this group.

10. *Unknown*.

Due to the varied types of education received by political leaders in Eastern Europe and the Soviet Union, and because essential data are sometimes lacking, the data in Tables F-11 through F-17 must be considered estimates only, based on the information given in Columns 6 and 7 and in the footnotes to Tables F-1 through F-10. In Tables F-11 through F-17, there are a greater number of persons classified as postwar, in terms of when they completed their education, than in Tables F-1 through F-10. This is because party schools are included in estimates of educational levels in the former set of tables, but not in latter.

III.
Introductory Notes to Tables

Table F-1   All persons born north of the river Shkumbi are considered Ghegs, all born south of the Shkumbi are considered Tosks. For further comments, see "General Remarks on Table" following tabular material in Table F-1.

Table F-2   For comments, see "General Remarks on Table" following tabular material in Table F-2.

Table F-3   For comments, see "General Remarks on Table" following tabular material in Table F-3.

Table F-4   Those attending a *Volksschule* prior to WWII are classified as having a basic education. For further comments, see "General Remarks on Table" following tabular material in Table F-4.

Table F-5   For comments, see "General Remarks on Table" following tabular material in Table F-5.

Table F-6   For comments, see "General Remarks on Table" following tabular material in Table F-6.

Table F-7   Data refer to politburo members up to June, 1960. After this date, data refer to the Executive Committee of the PCR. For further comments, see "General Remarks on Table" following tabular material in Table F-7.

Table F-8   For comments, see "General Remarks on Table" following tabular material in Table F-8.

Table F-9   For comments, see "General Remarks on Table" following tabular material in Table F-9.

Table F-10   For comments, see "General Remarks on Table" following tabular material in Table F-10.

Table F-12   In Series I, attendance at higher party schools (including the Marx-Lenin Institute, USSR) is classified as Higher Political or Part-Time. In Series II, attendance at higher party schools (in-cluding the Marx-Lenin Institute) is classified as Secondary Political.

Table F-14   In Series I, attendance at higher party schools (including the Marx-Lenin Institute, USSR) is classified as Higher Political or Part-Time. In Series II, attendance at higher party schools (including the Marx-Lenin Institute) is classified as Secondary Political. In Series I, a degree from the Institute of Social Sciences of the PUWP Central Committee is classified as either University, or as Professor or Advanced Degree. In Series II, this degree is classified as Higher Political or Part-Time.

Table F-15   In Series I, a degree from the Academy of Economic Studies is classified as Higher Political or Part-Time. In Series II, this degree is classified as Secondary Political.

TABLE F-1   BACKGROUND OF PARTY LEADERS: ALBANIA, 1948-1976

	1 Birth Date	2 Birth Place	3 Ethnicity	4 Status of Father	5 Status Prior to Party Work	6 Formal Educ.	7 Advanced Training	8 Party Mbr.	9 Revol. Type	10 WW II	11 CC Mbr.	12 EC Mbr.	Exec. Com. & Status
1. Beqir Balluku	1917	Urban Alb.	Gheg Alb.	...	Worker[a]	b	Military	1941	W-R	Resis.	1948	1948	123456 ++++++
2. Liri Belishova	1923[a]	Rural Alb.	Tosk Alb.	Upper Class[b]	Student[c]	Prewar SpecSec.[d]	Nursing[e]	f	St-R	Resis.	1948	1948	123 +++
3. Enver Hoxha	1908	Urban Alb.	Tosk Alb.	Middle Class	Teacher[a]	Prewar IncUniv.[b]	...	1941	Int-R	Resis.	1943	1943	1234567 ++++++
4. Tuk Jakova	1914	Urban Alb.	Alb.	...	Worker[a]	Prewar IncGym.	...	1941	St-R	Resis.	b	1948	1 +
5. Hysni Kapo	1915	Rural Alb.	Tosk Alb.	...	Nurse[a]	Prewar SpecSec.[b]	...	1941	c	Resis.	1943	1946	1234567 ++++++
6. Spiro Koleka	1908	Alb.	Tosk Alb.	Upper Class[a]	Engineer[b]	Prewar Univ.[c]	Engin.	d	Int-R	Resis.	1948	1948	1234567 ++++++
7. Gogo Nushi	1913	Rural Alb.	Tosk Alb.	...	Worker[a]	Prewar Elem.	...	1941	W-R	Resis.	1948	1948	12345 +++++
8. Mehmet Shehu*	1913	Rural Alb.	Tosk Alb.	Clergy[a]	Student	Prewar Elem.[b]	Military[c]	1942	St-R	Resis.	d	1948	234567 ++++++
9. Rita Marko	1920	Urban Alb.	Tosk Alb.	Peasant[a]	Student[b]	Prewar[c]	...	1942	St-R	Resis.	1950	1952	234567 x+++++
10. Manush Myftiu	1919	Urban Alb.	Tosk Alb.	a	Student[b]	Prewar IncUniv.[c]	Medicine	1941	St-R	Resis.	1948	1952	234567 x+++++
11. Pilo Peristeri	1909	Urban Alb.	Tosk Alb.	...	Worker[a]	Prewar Elem.	...	b	W-R	Resis.	1948	1952	234567 x+++++
12. Ramiz Alija	1925	Urban Alb.	Gheg Alb.	Lower Class	Student[a]	Prewar Second.	...	1943	NRE	Resis.	1948	1956	34567 xxxxxx
13. Adil Carcani	1922	Urban Alb.	Gheg Alb.	...	...	...	...	...	NRE	...	1948	1956	34567 x++++
14. Rrapo Dervishi	...	...	...	...	...	...	...	...	...	...	...	...	3 x
15. Koco Theodhosi	1913	Urban Alb.	Tosk Alb.	Middle Class	Engineer[a]	Prewar Univ.[b]	Engin.	1941	Int-R	Resis.	1952[c]	1956	3456 xxx+
16. Haki Toska	1920	Urban Alb.	Tosk Alb.	...	...	...	...	...	...	Resis.	1952	1956	34567 x++++
17. Petrit Dume	...	...	...	...	...	...	...	...	...	...	...	...	456 xxx
18. Kadri Hasbiu	1920	Rural Alb.	Tosk Alb.	...	...	Prewar SpecSec.[a]	...	1942	...	Resis.	1950	1961	4567 xx++
19. Abdyl Kellezi	1919	Urban Alb.	Gheg Alb.	a	b	c	...	d	NRE	Resis.	1961	1966	56 x+
20. Pirro Dodbiba	...	...	...	...	...	...	...	...	...	...	1956	1971	6 x
21. Xhafer Spahiu	...	...	...	...	...	...	...	...	...	...	1961	1971	6 x
22. Hekuran Isai	...	...	...	...	...	...	...	...	...	...	1966	1975	7 +

*Participant in Spanish Civil War
**Jewish Extraction

Exec. Com. Dates:
No. 1: Nov., 1948   No. 4: Feb., 1961
No. 2: April, 1952   No. 5: Nov., 1966
No. 3: June, 1956   No. 6: Nov., 1971   No. 7: Nov., 1976

+ Full Member
x Candidate Member

TABLE F-1   (CONTINUED)

		1 Birth Date	2 Birth Place	3 Ethnicity	4 Status of Father	5 Status Prior to Party Work	6 Formal Educ.	7 Advanced Training	8 Party Mbr.	9 Revol. Type	10 WW II	11 CC Mbr.	12 EC Mbr.	Exec. Com. & Status
23.	Pali Miska	...	...	...	...	...	...		...	...	...	1971	1975	?
24.	Lenka Cuko	...	...	...	...	...	...		...	...	...	...	1975	+
25.	Llambi Gegprifti	...	...	...	...	...	...		...	...	...	1971	1975	x
26.	Qirjako Mihali	...	...	...	...	...	...		...	...	...	1966	1975	x
27.	Simon Stefanovic	...	...	...	...	...	...		...	...	...	...	1975	x

*Participant in Spanish Civil War
**Jewish Extraction

Exec. Com. (or Presid.) Dates:
No.1: Nov., 1948
No.2: April, 1952
No.3: June, 1956
No.4: Feb., 1961
No.5: Nov., 1966
No.6: Nov., 1971
No.7: Nov., 1976

+ Full Member
x Candidate Member

General Remarks on Table: No list of 1948 politburo members elected at the first congress of the AWP could be found for this table. Thus only those politburo members who retained membership in 1952 and for whom proof exists of membership in 1948 are listed as members in 1948 in this table, and all these persons are listed as full members. The distinction between those with some type of revolutionary experience and those with no revolutionary experience (Column 9) is based on evidence of revolutionary activity in 1941 or earlier, and is more fully explained in footnotes for Column 9.

Abbreviations Used in This Table:

1. Alb.   Albania or Albanian
2. Elem.   Elementary
3. Engin.   Engineering
4. Gym.   Gymnasium

5. Inc.   Incomplete
6. Int-R   Intellectual Revolutionary
7. NRE   No Revolutionary Experience
8. Resis.   Resistance

9. Second.   Secondary
10. SpecSec. Specialized Secondary
11. St-R   Student Revolutionary
12. Univ.   University
13. W-R   Worker Revolutionary

For further explanation of these terms, see the introduction to this section.

Notes: Beqir Balluku: a. Metalworker before joining army, 1939; after demobilization, 1940, became active in Communist movement. b. Moroshilov Military Academy, 1952-1953. Prior to this, only elementary education. Liri Belishova: a. Conflicting data--date of birth also given as 1926. b. Daughter of member of prewar parliament. c. Helped organize Communist youth movement before joining resistance in 1941. d. Teacher's school. e. Studied nursing in Tirana; may also have attended party school when in Moscow, 1952-1954. f. Data lacking; probably joined party between 1941 and 1943. Enver Hoxha: a. Taught French in gymnasiums in Tirana and Korce between 1936 and 1939, then operated a tobacco store in Tirana, 1940-1941. b. Studied at University of Montpellier, France. Tuk Jakova: a. Carpenter, then jailed, 1938-1939. Active in organizing party, 1940-1942. b. Data lacking, but probably joined Central Committee in 1943. Hysni Kapo: a. Worked as bookkeeper, then nurse in state mental hospital. Helped form first resistance units in 1941. b. Commercial high school. c. Fits no revolutionary type, but could have been considered, at the time, an Intellectual Revolutionary (Int-R). Spiro Koleka: a. Father a minister in prewar government. b. Began to collaborate with Communists in 1940; position not known, but was trained as engineer. c. Degree in civil engineering, University of Pisa, 1934. d. Data lacking; probably joined party between 1941 and 1943. Gogo Nushi: a. Active as Communist in France before returning to Albania in 1940, at which time became engaged in illegal activity. Mehmet Shehu: a. Son of Moslem priest. b. Studied at American Vocational School in Tirana. c. Enrolled briefly in officers' training schools in Naples and Tirana; attended the Voroshilov Military Academy in the Soviet Union, 1945-1946. d. Joined the Central Committee between 1943 and 1945, expelled, late 1947, then reinstated, 1948. Rita Marko: a. Father a shepherd. b. Participated in pro-Communist political activity during or shortly after leaving school in 1936. c. Attended (cont'd.)

grammar school in Korce, number of years not known. Manush Myftiu: a. Data lacking, but probably of well-to-do parents. b. Member of Communist cell in 1939 in Vlore. c. Graduated from classical lycee in Rome and studied medicine one year at the University of Turin. Pilo Peristeri: a. Tinsmith, then active as labor organizer prior to WWII. b. Data lacking but probably joined the party in 1941. Ramiz Alija: a. Member of fascist youth organization before joining Communist youth group in 1942. Koco Theodhosi: a. Active in organizing Communist party in Korce, 1941; joined resistance in 1943. b. Graduated, University of Lyons, 1941. c. Conflicting data-- either 1952 or 1956. Kadri Hasbiu: a. Vlore Commercial High School; also studied in the Soviet Union, 1948-1950; subject not known. Abdyl Kellezi: a. Data lacking, but probably well-to-do parents. b. Engaged in anti-fascist activities, 1939, became associated with Communist resistance, 1942. Occupation or activity in intervening years not known. c. Conflicting data--either commercial studies, University of Florence, or military school in Rome. d. Sometime between 1941 and 1945.

TABLE F-2 BACKGROUND OF PARTY LEADERS: BULGARIA, 1945-1976

	1 Birth Date	2 Birth Place	3 Ethnicity	4 Status of Father	5 Status Prior to Party Work	6 Formal Educ.	7 Advanced Training	8 Party Mbr.	9 Revol. Type	10 WW II	11 CC Mbr.	12 EC Mbr.	Exec. Com. & Status
1. Georgi Chankov	1904	Rural Bulg.	Bulg.	Poor Peasant	Worker	Prewar Elem.	...	1932	W-R	Jail	1943	1944	123 +++
2. Vulko Chervenkov	1900	Rural Bulg.	Bulg.	Military	Student	Prewar Gym.	...	1919	St-R	USSR	1944	1944	1234 ++++
3. Georgi Damyanov *	1892	Rural Bulg.	Bulg.	Peasant	Teacher[a]	Prewar High.[b]	Military	1919	St-R[c]	USSR	1935	1945	1234 +++
4. Raiko Damyanov	1903	Rural Bulg.	Bulg.	Peasant	[a]	Prewar IncGym.	Party School[b]	1930	St-R	Jail	1935	1944	1234 ++++
5. Georgi Dimitrov	1882	Rural Bulg.	Bulg.	Artisan[a]	Trade Union[b]	Prewar Elem.	...	1919	W-R[c]	USSR	1919	1945	12 ++
6. Tsola Dragoicheva	1898[a]	Rural Bulg.	Bulg.	Peasant[b]	Student	Prewar SpecSec.[c]	Party School[d]	1919	St-R	Illeg.	1940	1940	1 678 + +++
7. Dimiter Ganev	1898	Rural Bulg.	Bulg.	Poor Peasant	Teacher[a]	Prewar Gym.	...	1921	Int-R	Illeg.	1929[b]	1942	1 45 + ++
8. Vasil Kolarov	1877	Urban Bulg.	Bulg.	Artisan[a]	Teacher	Prewar Univ.	Law	1919	Int-R[b]	USSR	1919	1945[c]	12 ++
9. Traicho Kostov	1897	Cap. Bulg.	Bulg.	Worker[a]	Gov. Employee[b]	Prewar High.[c]	Military	1920	Int-R[d]	Jail	1932	1945	12 ++
10. Petko Kunin	1900	Rural Bulg.	Bulg.	...	...	Prewar Univ.	Agric.[a]	1925	St-R	Resis.	1931	1936	1 +
11. Vladimir Poptomov	1890	Rural Bulg.	Maced.	...	Teacher	Prewar SpecSec.[a]	...	1919	Int-R	USSR	1944	1945	12 ++
12. Dobri Terpeshev	1884	Rural Bulg.	Bulg.	Peasant	Worker[a]	Prewar Elem.	...	1919	W-R[b]	Resis.[c]	1943	1943	12 ++
13. Anton Yugov	1904	Bulg.	Maced.	Poor Family	Worker[a]	Prewar Elem.	Party School[b]	1923	W-R	Resis.	1937	1937	1234 ++++
14. Dimiter Dimov	1903	Urban Bulg.	Bulg.	Worker	Teacher	Prewar SpecSec.[a]	...	1922	St-R	Resis.	1940	1945[b]	1 456 x xxx
15. Gocho Grozev	1900	Rural Bulg.	Bulg.	Peasant	Student	Prewar IncGym.	Military[a]	1920	St-R	Con.[b] Camp	...	1945	1 x
16. Titko Chernokolev	1910	Urban Bulg.	Bulg.	Gov. Official[a]	Student	Prewar Univ.	Agric.[b]	1930	St-R	Illeg.	[c]	1949	2 x
17. Mincho Neichev	1887	Urban Bulg.	Bulg.	Worker[a]	Lawyer	Prewar Univ.	Law	1919	Int-R	Illeg.[b]	1945	1948	2 x
18. Ivan Mihailov	1897	Rural Bulg.	Bulg.	Gov. Official[a]	Student	Prewar Univ.	Law[b] Military	1919	St-R	USSR	1954	1954	345678 +++++
19. Encho Staikov	1901	Rural Bulg.	Bulg.	Peasant	Student	Prewar Univ.	Law	1919	St-R	Con. Camp	1928	1936[a]	3 5 + +
20. Georgi Tsankov	1915	Rural Bulg.	Bulg.	Peasant	Worker	Prewar Elem.	...	1932	W-R	Resis.[a]	1945	1948	34 ++
21. Todor Zhivkov	1911	Rural Bulg.	Bulg.	Peasant	Worker[a]	Prewar Elem.	...	1932	W-R	Resis.	1945	1948	345678 ++++++
22. Petur Panchevski *	1902	Rural Bulg.	Bulg.	...	Student	Prewar High.[a]	Military	1924	St-R	USSR	1950	1954	3 x

*Participant in Spanish Civil War
**Jewish Extraction

Exec. Com. Dates:
No. 1: March, 1945 No. 4: June, 1958 No. 7: April, 1971
No. 2: Dec., 1948 No. 5: Nov., 1962 No. 8: April, 1976
No. 3: March, 1954 No. 6: Nov., 1966

+ Full Member
x Candidate Member

TABLE F-2 (CONTINUED)

	1 Birth Date	2 Birth Place	3 Ethnicity	4 Status of Father	5 Status Prior to Party Work	6 Formal Educ.	7 Advanced Training	8 Party Mbr.	9 Revol. Type	10 WW II	11 CC Mbr.	12 EC Mbr.	Exec. Com. & Status
23. Todor Prahov	1904	Rural Bulg.	Bulg.	...	...	Prewar Inc.Gym.	...	1929	St-R	Jail	1945	1954	34 xx
24. Boyan Balgaranov	1896	Urban Bulg.	Bulg.	Teacher	...	Prewar Gym.	Military[a]	1920	b	Illeg.	1937	1957	4567 ++++
25. Boris Taskov	1901	Rural Bulg.	Bulg.	Peasant	...	Prewar IncUniv.	...	1921	...	Resis.	1945	1957	4 +
26. Mladen Stoyanov	1896	Bulg.	Bulg.	Peasant	...	...	...	1921	...	...	1924	1957	4 x
27. Mitko Grigorov	1920	Rural Bulg.	Bulg.	Teacher	Student	Prewar Univ.	Law	1940	St-R	Jail	1954	1961	5 +
28. Stanko Todorov	1920	Rural Bulg.	Bulg.	Worker	Tailor[a]	Prewar Elem.	...	1943	NRE	Milit.[b]	1954	1959	5678 ++++
29. Pencho Kubadinski	1918	Rural Bulg.	Bulg.	...	Student	Prewar Gym.	Party School	1940	St-R	Resis.	1954	1962	5678 x+++
30. Tano Tsolov	1918	Rural Bulg.	Bulg.	...	...	Prewar Univ.	...	1940	...	Jail	1954	1962	5678 x+++
31. Todor Pavlov	1890	Urban Maced.	Bulg.	...	Teacher	Prewar Univ.	...	1919	Int-R	Con. Camp	1924	1966	67 ++
32. Ivan Popov	1907	Rural Bulg.	Bulg.	...	Engineer	Prewar Univ.	Engin.	1950[a]	Int-R	Hung.	1966	1966	67 ++
33. Boris Velchev	1914	Rural Bulg.	Bulg.	Artisan	...	Prewar[a]	...	1936	...	Jail	1954	1962	6 8 + +
34. Zhivko Zhivkov	1915	Rural Bulg.	Bulg.	Peasant[a]	Student	Prewar Univ.	Law	1935	St-R	Con. Camp	1948	1962	67 ++
35. Ivan Abadzhiev	1930	Rural Bulg.	Bulg.	Peasant	Student	Postwar Univ.	Law	1950	Po-W		1962	1966	67 xx
36. Lachezar Avramov	1922	Cap. Bulg.	Bulg.	Worker	Student	Prewar IncHigh[a]	Engin.	1945	St-R	Jail	1954	1966	6 x
37. Kostadin Gyaurov	1924	Rural Bulg.	Bulg.	...	Student	Prewar IncGym.	Party School[a]	1945	St-R	Resis.	1962	1966	67 xx
38. Peko Takov	1909	Rural Bulg.	Bulg.	...	Student	Prewar IncUniv.	Economics	1928	St-R	Resis.	1948	1966	678 xxx
39. Angel Tsanev	1912	Urban Bulg.	Bulg.	...	Student	Prewar IncHigh.	Military	1933	St-R	Jail	1958	1966	7 x
40. Venelin Kotsev	1926	Rural Bulg.	Bulg.	Teacher[a]	Student	Postwar High.[b]	...	1946	Po-W	Resis.	1962	1971	7 x
41. Krastya Trichkov	1923	Rural Bulg.	Maced.	Peasant	Worker	Prewar Second.	Party School	1942	W-R	Resis.	1958	1966	78 xx
42. Grisha Filipov	1919	Urban USSR[a]	Bulg.	...	Student	Prewar IncHigh[b]	Economics[c]	1940	St-R	Illeg.[d]	1962	1974	8 +
43. Aleksandur Lilov	1933	Rural Bulg.	Bulg.	Poor Peasant	...	Postwar IncHigh	...	1954	Po-W		1971	1976	8 +
44. Dobri Dzurov	1916	Rural Bulg.	Bulg.	...	...	High.[a]	Military	1938	St-R	Resis.	1958	1976	8 x

*Participant in Spanish Civil War

**Jewish Extraction

Exec. Com. Dates:

No. 1: March, 1945   No. 4: June, 1958   No. 7: April, 1971
No. 2: Dec., 1948   No. 5: Nov., 1962   No. 8: April, 1976
No. 3: March, 1954   No. 6: Nov., 1966

+ Full Member
x Candidate Member

289

TABLE F-2   (CONTINUED)

	1	2	3	4	5	6	7	8	9	10	11	12	
	Birth Date	Birth Place	Ethnic-ity	Status of Father	Status Prior to Party Work	Formal Educ.	Advanced Training	Party Mbr.	Revol. Type	WW II	CC Mbr.	EC Mbr.	Exec. Com. & Status
45. Petur Mladenov	1936	Rural Bulg.	Bulg.	Peasant^a	Student^b	Postwar Univ.	Foreign Relations^c Party School^a	...	Po-W	...	1971	1974	8 x
46. Todor Stoichev	1920	Rural Bulg.	Bulg.	Poor Peasant	...	...	...	1944	NRE	...	1958	1976	8 x
47. Drazha Vulcheva	1930	...	Bulg.	Peasant	State Official^a	Postwar Univ.^b	...	1954	Po-W	...	1966	1974	8 x

*Participant in Spanish Civil War
**Jewish Extraction

Exec. Com. Dates:

No.1: March, 1945   No.4: June, 1958   No.7: April, 1971
No.2: Dec., 1948   No.5: Nov., 1962   No.8: April, 1976
No.3: March, 1954   No.6: Nov., 1966

+ Full Member
x Candidate Member

General Remarks on Table: In coding revolutionary type, Column 9, membership in the Bulgarian Social Democratic Party prior to World War I has not been taken into account.

Abbreviations Used in This Table:

1. Agric.	Agriculture		17. Po-W	Postwar
2. Bulg.	Bulgaria, Bulgarian		18. Resis.	Resistance
3. Con. Camp	Concentration Camp		19. Second.	Secondary
4. Elem.	Elementary		20. SpecSec.	Specialized Secondary
5. Engin.	Engineering		21. St-R	Student Revolutionary
6. Gov.	Government		22. Univ.	University
7. Gym.	Gymnasium		23. W-R	Worker Revolutionary
8. High.	Higher			
9. Hung.	Hungarian			
10. Illeg.	Illegal			
11. IncHigh.	Incomplete Higher			
12. IncGym.	Incomplete Gymnasium			
13. IncUniv.	Incomplete University			
14. Int-R	Intellectual Revolutionary			
15. Maced.	Macedonian			
16. Milit.	Military			

For further explanation of these terms, see the introduction to this section.

Notes: Georgi Damyanov: a. Teacher, then served in military during WWI before joining party and becoming involved full-time in revolutionary activity. b. Completed gymnasium and military institute in Bulgaria prior to WWI as well as Frunze Military Academy, USSR, 1929. c. Coding does not take into account membership in Social Democratic Party prior to WWI. Raiko Damyanov: a. Data lacking; evidence suggests D. was working as shoemaker prior to 1923, date of becoming official in Communist youth organization. b. Completed Marx-Lenin Institute in USSR. Georgi Dimitrov: a. Father variously described as artisan, member of working class. b. Was active in printers' trade union prior to WWI. c. Coding does not take into account membership in the Social Democratic Party prior to WWI. Tsola Dragoicheva: a. Conflicting data - some sources give 1900 as date of birth. b. Father referred to as "middle peasant" in some sources. c. Teachers' institute. d. Comintern school, Moscow. Dimiter Ganev: a. Served in military, 1916-1918, then school teacher at time of becoming involved in revolutionary activity as a party member. b. Member of Bulgarian CP Central Committee, 1929-1934; Romanian CP Central Committee, 1934-1935; Bulgarian Central Committee 1944-1964. Vasil Kolarov: a. Father a shoemaker. b. Coding does not take into account membership in Social Democratic Party prior to WWI. c. In coding, brief membership in Central Committee Secretariat in 1920s not taken into account. Traicho Kostov: a. Father a railroad worker. b. Served in Bulgarian military in WWI, then as a local government official prior to joining party. c. First studied law, then received military training. d. Coding does not take into account membership in Social Democratic Party prior to WWI. Petko Kunin: a. Attended International Agrarian Institute, Moscow, 1934-1936. Vladimir Poptomov: a. Teachers' institute. Dobri Terpeshev: a. Conflicting data; said to be official of Social Democratic Party prior to WWI, unskilled agricultural laborer after WWI. b. Coding does not take into account membership in Social Democratic Party prior to WWI. c. Jail, 1940-1943; resistance, 1943-1944. Anton Yugov: a. Tobacco worker. b. Marx-Lenin Institute, USSR, dates not known. Dimiter Dimov: a. Teachers' institute. b. Candidate member, 1945-1948 and 1957-1968. Gocho Grozev: a. Incomplete military institute, USSR. b. 1941-1943. Titko Chernokolev: a. Father was government official, rank not known. b. Postgraduate degree in agronomy; professor of agronomy, 1956. c. Conflicting data - 1944 or 1945. Mincho Neichev: (cont'd.)

TABLE F-2 (CONCLUDED)

a. Artisan or metal worker. b. 1941-1943, concentration camp; 1943-1944, illegal underground activity. Ivan Mihailov: a. Father a government official, rank not known. b. Studied law, served as an attorney after WWI, then received military training in USSR. Encho Staikov: a. Politburo member, 1936-1945 and 1954-1966. Georgi Tsankov: a. 1941-1943, jail; 1943-1944, resistance. Todor Zhivkov: a. Worked as printer, 1925-1940. Petur Panchevski: a. Completed gymnasium in Bulgaria, then Frunze Military Academy, USSR, in 1936. Boyan Balgaranov: a. Attended general staff academy, Moscow, and Marx-Lenin Institute, Moscow. b. Data lacking; appears to be Student Revolutionary (S-R). Stanko Todorov: a. Worked as tailor, then served in Bulgarian army, 1940-1943, at which time became involved in revolutionary activity. b. Bulgarian army, jailed for revolutionary activity, 1944. Ivan Popov: a. Engaged in revolutionary activity as a youth, may have been a party member at the time; later (1945-1948), member of Hungarian CP. Boris Velchev: a. Conflicting data - incomplete gymnasium or complete secondary technical school. Zhivko Zhivkov: a. Father wealthy or middle peasant. Lachezar Avramov: a. Incomplete polytechnical education, USSR, 1938-1941. Kostadin Gyaurov: a. Attended party schools in Bulgaria, USSR. Venelin Kotsev: a. Parents described as "teacher-Communists." b. Higher education, character unknown. Appears to have completed higher education immediately after WWII. Grisha Filipov: a. Born in Kadievko, USSR; moved to Bulgaria in 1936. b. Sofia University, 1938. c. Studied economics in the USSR, 1948-1951. d. Arrested, 1944; presumably engaged in illegal activity. Aleksandur Lilov: a. 1966-1969, studied literature at the Academy of Social Sciences, Moscow. Dobri Dzurov: a. Gymnasium and training in military institute, date and place not known. Petur Mladenov: a. Parents were party members; father was killed in resistance struggle. b. Became active in politics full-time as member of youth organization after completing education. c. Studied at Institute for International Relations, Moscow. Todor Stoichev: a. Higher Party School of the BCP. Drazha Vulcheva: a. Was director of school in 1961 before becoming involved in full-time party work in 1962. b. Sofia University, dates not known.

TABLE F-3   BACKGROUND OF PARTY LEADERS: CZECHOSLOVAKIA, 1946-1976

	1 Birth Date	2 Birth Place	3 Ethnicity	4 Status of Father	5 Status Prior to Party Work	6 Formal Educ.	7 Advanced Training	8 Party Mbr.	9 Revol. Type	10 WW II	11 CC Mbr.	12 EC Mbr.	Exec. Com. & Status
1. Vaclav David	1910	Rural Czech.	Czech.	Worker	a	Prewar SpecSec[b]	...	1935	c	Resis.	1944	1946	12 / ++
2. Jaromir Dolansky	1895	Cap. Czech.	Czech.	Teacher	Lawyer	Prewar Univ.	Law	1922	Int-R[a]	Con. Camp	1939	1938	123456 / ++++++
3. Josef Frank	1909	Urban Czech.	Czech.	Worker	Small Merchant[a]	Prewar IncSec	...	1930	W-R[a]	Con. Camp	1946	1946	12 / ++
4. Klement Gottwald	1896	Rural Czech.	Czech.	Peasant	Worker	Prewar Elem.	...	1921	W-R[a]	USSR	1925	1926	12 / ++
5. Gustav Kliment	1889	Urban Czech.	Czech.	Worker	Worker[a]	Prewar Elem.	...	1921	W-R	Con. Camp	1946	1946	12 / ++
6. Vaclav Kopecky	1897	Rural Czech.	Czech.	Small Merchant	Student	Prewar IncUniv.	Law	1921	St-R	USSR	1929	1931	1234 / ++++
7. Ladislav Kopriva	1896	Rural Czech.	Czech.	...	...	...	...	1921	...	Con. Camp	...	1945	12 / ++
8. Josef Krosnar	1891	Cap. Czech.	Czech.	...	Worker	...	...	1921	...	USSR	1929	1945	12 / ++
9. Zdenek Nejedly	1878	Urban Czech.	Czech.	Middle Class	Professor	Prewar Univ.	...	1929	Int-R	USSR	1946	1946	12 / ++
10. Vaclav Nosek	1892	Urban Czech.	Czech.	Worker	Worker[a]	Prewar Elem.	...	1921	W-R	Eng.	1929	1945	12 / ++
11. Rudolf Slansky	1901	Rural Czech.	Czech.[**]	Middle Class	Student	Prewar SpecSec[a]	...	1921	St-R	USSR	1929	1929	12 / ++
12. Josef Smrkovsky	1911	Rural Czech.	Czech.	Peasant	Worker	Prewar Elem.	...	1933	W-R	Illeg.	1944	1945	12 / ++
13. Marie Svermova	1902	Urban Czech.	Germ.	Worker	Worker	Prewar Elem.	Party School[a]	1921	W-R	USSR	1945	1945	12 / ++
14. Antonin Zapotocky	1884	Rural Czech.	Czech.	Worker[a]	Trade Union Official[b]	Prewar Elem.	...	1921	W-R[c]	Con. Camp	1922	1929	123 / +++
15. Gustav Bares	1910	Rural Czech.	Czech.[**]	...	Student	Prewar SpecSec[a]	...	1930	St-R[a]	USSR	1946	1946	2 / +
16. Stefan Bastovansky	1910	Urban Hung.[a]	Slovak	...	b	Prewar Gym.	...	1939	c	Resis.	1949	1949	2 / +
17. Julius Duris	1904	Rural Slovak	Slovak	Teacher	Student	Prewar IncUniv.	Law	1927	St-R	Jail	1945	1949	2 / +
18. Evzen Erban	1912	Cap. Czech.	Czech.	...	NonCommunist Politician	Prewar Univ.	Law	1948	Social Dem.	Home	1948	1948	2 / +
19. Zdenek Fierlinger	1891	Urban Czech.	Czech.	Middle Class	NonCommunist Politician	Prewar SpecSec[a]	...	1948	Social Dem.	USSR	1948	1948	2345 / ++++
20. Ludmila Jankovcova	1897	Urban Czech.	Czech.	Middle Class	NonCommunist Politician	Prewar Higher[a]	...	...	...	Illeg.	1948	1948	2345 / +xxx
21. Oldrich John	...	...	...	...	NonCommunist Politician	Prewar Univ.	Law	1948	Social Dem.	...	...	1951	2 / +
22. Viliam Siroky	1902	Urban Slovak	Slovak	Worker	Worker	Prewar Gym.	...	1921	W-R	Jail	1929	1945	2345 / ++++

*Participant in Spanish Civil War
**Jewish Extraction

Exec. Com. Dates:

No. 1: March, 1946
No. 2: May, 1949
No. 3: July, 1954
No. 4: June, 1958
No. 5: Dec, 1962
No. 6: June, 1966
No. 7: March, 1968
No. 8: May, 1971
No. 9: April, 1976

+ Full Member
x Candidate Member

292

TABLE F-3 (CONTINUED)

	1 Birth Date	2 Birth Place	3 Ethnicity	4 Status of Father	5 Status Prior to Party Work	6 Formal Educ.	7 Advanced Training	8 Party Mbr.	9 Revol. Type	10 WW II	11 CC Mbr.	12 EC Mbr.	Exec. Com. & Status
23. Antonin Novotny	1904	Rural Czech.	Czech.	Worker	Worker[a]	Prewar Elem.	...	1921	W-R	Con. Camp	1946	1951	3456 ++++
24. Karol Bacilek	1896	Rural Slov.	Slovak	Worker	Worker[a]	Prewar Elem.	...	1921	W-R[b]	USSR	1949	c	345 +++
25. Rudolf Barak	1915	Rural Czech.	Czech.	...	Worker[a]	Prewar Elem.		1945	NRE	Home	1952	1954	34 ++
26. Alexej Cepicka	1910	Urban Czech.	Czech.	Worker[a]	Student	Prewar Univ.	Law	1929	St-R	Con. Camp	1949	1951	3 +
27. Otakar Simunek	1908	Urban Czech.	Czech.	Middle Class	...	Prewar Univ.	Engin.[a]	1934	...	Home	1954	1954	3456 x+++
28. Pavol David	1899	Rural Slov.	Slovak	Peasant	Worker	Prewar Univ.[a]	...	1921	W-R	USSR	1952	1958	4 +
29. Jiri Hendrych	1913	Rural Czech.	Czech.	Worker[a]	Student	Prewar IncUniv.	...	1931	St-R	Con. Camp	1946	1948	456 +++
30. Jan Hlina	1910	Rural Czech.	Czech.	...	[a]	Prewar SpecSec.[b]	Technical[c]	1945	NRE	Home	1958	1958	4 x
31. Rudolf Strechaj	1914	Rural Slov.	Slovak	Worker	Worker	Prewar SpecSec.[a]	Party School[b]	1935	W-R[c]	Resis.	1954	1958	4 x
32. Drahomir Kolder	1925	Urban Czech.	Czech.	Worker	Worker[a]	...	Party School[b]	1945	W-R	Illeg.	1958	1961	56 ++
33. Jozef Lenart	1923	Rural Slov.	Slovak	Worker	Plant Manager[a]	Prewar SpecSec.[b]	Party School	1943	W-R	Resis.	1958	1962	56 89 ++ ++
34. Alexander Dubcek	1921	Rural Slov.	Slovak	Worker	Worker	Prewar Second.[a]	Law[b]	1939	W-R	Resis.	1958	1962	56 x+
35. Antonin Kapek	1922	Urban Czech.	Czech.	...	Plant Manager[a]	Postwar High.[b]	Technical	1945	Po-W	Home	1958	1962	56 89 xx ++
36. Oldrich Cernik	1921	Urban Czech.	Czech.	Worker[a]	Worker[b]	Prewar High.[c]	Engin.	1945	NRE	Home	1958	1966	6 +
37. Michal Chudik	1914	Rural Slov.	Slovak	Worker	State Official[a]	Prewar Basic	...	1944	NRE	Resis.	1958	1964	6 +
38. Bohuslav Lastovicka *	1905	Rural Czech.	Czech.	...	Journalist	Prewar Gym.	Military	1931	St-R	Eng.	1946	1964	6 +
39. Miroslav Pastyrik	1912	Urban Czech.	Czech.	Worker	Worker	...	...	1933	W-R	...	1949	1966	6 x
40. Michal Sabolcik	1924	Rural Slov.	Slovak	Worker	...	Postwar Univ.[a]	Planning[b]	1945	Po-W	Resis.	1963	1966	6 x
41. Stefan Sadovsky	1928	Rural Slov.	Slovak	Worker	...	Prewar Elem.	Planning[a]	1948	Po-W	...	1966	1966	6 x
42. Martin Vaculik	1922	Rural Czech.	Czech.	Worker	Worker[a]	Prewar SpecSec.[b]	Technical[c]	1945	NRE	Home	1962	1963	6 x
43. Frantisek Barbirek	1927	Urban Slov.	Slovak	...	...	...	Planning[a]	1946	Po-W	...	1966	1968	7 +
44. Vasil Bilak	1917	Rural Slov.	Ruth.	Peasant	Worker[a]	Prewar Elem.	Party School[b]	1945	NRE	Resis.	1954	1968	789 +++

*Participant in Spanish Civil War
**Jewish Extraction

Exec. Com. (or Presid.) Dates:

No. 1: March, 1946
No. 2: May, 1949
No. 3: July, 1954
No. 4: June, 1958
No. 5: Dec., 1962
No. 6: June, 1966
No. 7: March, 1968
No. 8: May, 1971
No. 9: April, 1976

+ Full Member
x Candidate Member

	1 Birth Date	2 Birth Place	3 Ethnic- ity	4 Status of Father	5 Status Prior to Party Work	6 Formal Educ.	7 Advanced Training	8 Party Mbr.	9 Revol. Type	10 WW II	11 CC Mbr.	12 EC Mbr.	Exec. Com. & Status
45. Frantisek Kriegel	1908	a	Czech.**	...	Doctor	Prewar Univ.	Medicine	1935	Int-R	Eng.	1966	1968	7 +
46. Jan Piller	1922	Urban Czech.	Czech.	Worker	Worker[a]	Prewar Elem.	Party School[b]	1946	NRE	Home	1958	1958	7 +
47. Emil Rigo	1926	Rural Slov.	Gypsy	Worker	[a]	...	Party School[b]	1946	...	...	1966	1968	7 +
48. Josef Spacek	1927	Rural Czech.	Czech.	Peasant	Worker[a]	Prewar SpecSec.[b]	Party School[c]	1945	Po-W	Home	1962	1968	7 +
49. Oldrich Svestka	1922	Rural Czech.	Czech.	...	...	Prewar SpecSec.[a]	...	1945	NRE	...	1958	1967	7 +
50. Gustav Husak	1913	Urban Slov.	Slovak	Peasant	Student	Prewar Univ.	Law	1933	St-R	Resis.	1949	1968	89 ++
51. Peter Colotka	1925	Rural Slov.	Slovak	Peasant	Professor[a]	Postwar Univ.	Law	1947	Po-W	Home	1966	1969	89 ++
52. Karel Hoffman	1924	Rural Czech.	Czech.	...	...	Prewar High.	Party School[b]	1945	NRE	Home	1966	1969	89 ++
53. Alois Indra	1921	Rural Slov.	Czech.	Peasant	Worker[a]	Prewar Second.	Party School[b]	1945	NRE[c]	Illeg.	1962	1970	89 ++
54. Josef Kempny	1920	Rural Czech.	Czech.	...	Professor[a]	Postwar High.[b]	Archi- tecture	1945	NRE	Home	1969	1969	89 ++
55. Josef Korcak	1921	Rural Czech.	Czech.	...	Worker[a]	Prewar Elem.	Party School[b]	1945	NRE	Home	1958	1970	89 ++
56. Lubomir Strougal	1924	Rural Czech.	Czech.	Worker[a]	RR Official[a]	Postwar Univ.[b]	Law	1945	Po-W	...	1958	1968	89 ++
57. Ludvik Svoboda	1895	Rural Czech.	Czech.	Peasant[a]	State Official[b]	Prewar[c]	Military	1948	NRE	USSR	1968	1969	89 ++
58. Miloslav Hruskovic	1925	Rural Slov.	Slovak	...	[a]	High.	Technical	1948	Po-W	Home	1958	1971	89 xx
59. Vaclav Hula	1925	Rural Czech.	Czech.	...	...	Postwar High.[a]	Commerce	1945	NRE	...	1969	1970	89 xx

*Participant in Spanish Civil War

**Jewish Extraction

Exec. Com. (or Presid.) Dates:

No.1: March, 1946 No.4: June, 1958 No.7: March, 1968
No.2: May, 1949 No.5: Dec., 1962 No.8: May, 1971
No.3: July, 1954 No.6: June, 1966 No.9: April, 1976

+ Full Member

x Candidate Member

General Remarks on Table: In coding revolutionary type (Column 9), membership in Czech Social Democratic Party prior to 1938 has not been taken into account. See footnotes for details.

Abbreviations Used in This Table:

1. Con. Camp	Concentration Camp	7. Inc.	Incomplete
2. Czech.	Czech Lands	8. Int-R	Intellectual Revolutionary
3. Elem.	Elementary	9. NRE	No Revolutionary Experience
4. Engin.	Engineering	10. Resis.	Resistance
5. Gym.	Gymnasium	11. Ruth.	Ruthenia
6. Illeg.	Illegal	12. Slov.	Slovak

13. Soc. Dem.	Social Democrat
14. SpecSec.	Specialized Secondary
15. St-R	Student Revolutionary
16. Univ.	University
17. W-R	Worker Revolutionary

For further explanation of these terms, see the introduction to this section.

TABLE F-3 (CONCLUDED)

Notes: Vaclav David: a. Data lacking; probably white collar employee. b. Commercial academy. c. Fits no category; might be called "White Collar Revolutionary". Jaromir Dolansky: a. Coding does not take into account membership in Czech Social Democratic Party, 1918-1921. Josef Frank: a. Small rural shopowner, 1930. Klement Gottwald: a. Coding does not take into account membership in German Social Democratic Party, 1914-1921. Gustav Kliment: a. Worker prior to WWI, served in Austrian Army, 1914-1916, before joining party. Vaclav Nosek: a. Miner. Rudolf Slansky: a. Commercial academy. Marie Svermova: a. Marx-Lenin Institute, USSR, 1926-1928. Antonin Zapotocky: a. Father prominent Social Democrat who began career as worker. b. Trade union official and regional officer in the Social Democratic Party, 1907-1914; 1914-1918 in Austrian army. c. Coding does not take into account membership prewar in Social Democratic Party. Gustav Bares: a. Commercial academy. Stefan Bastovansky: a. Born in Budapest. b. Data lacking, but was railway supervisor in late 1920s. c. Data lacking; might have been "White Collar Revolutionary". Ludmila Jankovcova: a. Higher School of Commerce. Antonin Novotny: a. Trained as locksmith. Karol Bacilek: a. Worker prior to WWI, served in Austrian army, 1914-1918. b. Coding does not take into account membership in Czech Social Democratic Party, 1919-1921. c. Conflicting data. Was member of inner politburo by 1952. Rudolf Barak: a. Was worker before becoming engaged full-time in politics as local party official in 1945. Alexej Cepicka: a. Father a postman. Otakar Simunek: a. Chemistry engineer. Pavol David: a. Conflicting data. D. reportedly studied in the USSR, 1933-1941, but did not receive a higher education. Jiri Hendrych: a. Father a miner. Jan Hlina: a. Data lacking; was skilled worker, then plant technician, 1945. No record of full-time political activity until joining politburo in 1958. b. Completed polytechnical institute, 1935. c. Also completed Higher Party School, 1949. Rudolf Strechaj: a. Commercial academy. b. USSR, 1936. c. Coding does not take into account period of membership in Czech Social Democratic Party, 1932-1935. Drahomir Kolder: a. Miner before becoming engaged in full-time political activity as Communist youth organization official. b. Higher Party School, dates not known. Jozef Lenart: a. Was low-level plant manager before becoming involved full-time in politics, first in resistance, 1943-1945, then as local party official in Slovakia. b. Commercial academy. Alexander Dubcek: a. Also received degree in law from University of Bratislava after part-time studies. b. Also received diploma from Higher Party School, Moscow. Antonin Kapek: a. Was locksmith, skilled worker, plant technician and finally plant manager before becoming active full-time in politics in 1958 as a regional party secretary. b. Received Ph.D. Oldrich Cernik: a. Father a miner. b. Iron worker before becoming active full-time in politics in 1949 as Communist youth official. c. Degree from Higher Mining School, Ostrava. Michal Chudik: a. Member, Slovak Board of Commissioners, before becoming active full-time in politics as regional party secretary in 1946. Michal Sabolcik: a. Ph.D. in economics. b. Taught economics and planning, also attended party school, 1954-1958. Stefan Sadovsky: a. Undertook advanced studies in planning, 1950-1954, not clear whether full-time or part-time. Also attended party school, 1954-1957. Martin Vaculik: a. Iron worker, becoming active full-time in politics in 1947 as local party official. b. Graduate of industrial high school. c. Also attended party school, and Marx-Lenin Institute, USSR. Frantisek Barbirek: a. Also attended Higher Party School, 1955-1957. Vasil Bilak: a. Tailor before becoming active full-time in politics in 1945 as local party official. b. Higher Party School, completed around 1964. Frantisek Kriegel: a. Born in Galicia, in Austro-Hungarian Empire, then part of Poland between two World Wars. Jan Piller: a. Iron worker before becoming active full-time in politics in 1947 as local party official. b. Higher Party School, 1950-1952. Emil Rigo: a. Data lacking; became active in political life full-time in 1954 as official in party apparatus; between 1946 and 1949, worker. b. Higher Party School, graduated 1960. Josef Spacek: a. Was warehouse worker prior to WWII; became active full-time in party work shortly after joining party in 1945. b. Commercial academy. Oldrich Svestka: a. Commercial academy. c. Higher Party School, dates not known. Peter Colotka: a. University teacher and administrator prior to becoming engaged full-time in politics in 1962 as party official. Karel Hoffman: a. Higher School for Politics and Social Sciences, 1945-1950. Alois Indra: a. Was railway official before becoming active full-time in politics in 1948 as party official. b. Two year party school, 1950-1951. c. Coding based on assumption that I. not active in party during the war; was, however, member of Communist cell in 1939. Josef Kempny: a. Plant manager, then acquired university education, finally becoming a professor of engineering before entering full-time into politics in 1968 as member of central committee secretariat. b. Received Ph.D. in architecture. Josef Korcak: a. Iron worker, 1938-1948, before becoming active full-time in politics as a local party official. b. Prague Party College. Lubomir Strougal: a. Father, member of KPC, died in concentration camp during WWII. b. Received law degree from Charles University, Prague. Ludvik Svoboda: a. Wealthy peasant family. b. President of Czechoslovakia at time of entering politburo; before this time, held no party or mass organization post full-time. c. Attended agricultural school in early 1920s; apparently never received higher military training. Miloslav Hruskovic: a. Data lacking but appears to have been a worker, then plant technician before entering into political work full-time in 1956 as party official. Vaclav Hula: a. Higher Commercial academy.

TABLE F-4   BACKGROUND OF PARTY LEADERS: GDR, 1946-1976

	1 Birth Date	2 Birth Place	3 Ethnicity	4 Status of Father	5 Status Prior to Party Work	6 Formal Educ.	7 Advanced Training	8 Party Mbr.	9 Revol. Type	10 WW II	11 CC Mbr.	12 EC Mbr.	Exec. Com. & Status
1. Anton Ackermann *	1905	Rural Germ.	Germ.	a	Youth[b]	Prewar Basic	Party School[c]	1926	W-R	USSR	1935	1935	123 ++x
2. Franz Dahlem *	1892	Rural Germ.	Germ.	Worker[a]	White Collar[b]	Prewar Basic	...	1920	W-R	Con. Camp	1928	1946	123 +++
3. Max Fechner	1892	Germ.	Germ.	a	NonCommunist Politician	Prewar Basic	...	1946	Social Dem.	Jail	1950	1946	12 ++
4. Erich Gniffke	1895	Germ.	Germ.	Worker	NonCommunist Politician	...	...	1946	Social Dem.	Jail	a	1946	12 ++
5. Otto Grotewohl	1894	Urban Germ.	Germ.	Worker[a]	NonCommunist Politician	Prewar High.[b]	...	1946	Social Dem.	Home	1950[c]	1946	123456 ++++++
6. August Karsten	1888	Germ.	Germ.	a	NonCommunist Politician	...	...	1946	Social Dem.	Jail	b	1946	12 ++
7. Kathe Kern	1900	Urban Germ.	Germ.	Worker	NonCommunist Politician	Prewar Second.	...	1946	Social Dem.	Home	1950[a]	1946	12 ++
8. Helmut Lehmann	1882	Cap. Germ.	Germ.	Middle Class[a]	NonCommunist Politician	Prewar Basic	...	1946	Social Dem.	Jail	1950[b]	1946	12 ++
9. Hermann Matern	1893	Urban Germ.	Germ.	Worker	Worker	Prewar Basic	...	1919	W-R	USSR	1946	1946	1234567 +++++++
10. Otto Meier	1889	Urban Germ.	Germ.	...	NonCommunist Politician	...	...	1946	Social Dem.	Home	a	1946	12 ++
11. Paul Merker	1894	Urban Germ.	Germ.	a	Worker[b]	...	...	1920	W-R	France	1926	...	12 ++
12. Wilhelm Pieck	1876	Urban Germ.	Germ.	Worker	Worker[a]	Prewar Basic	...	1919	W-R[b]	USSR	1919	c	12345 +++++
13. Elli Schmidt	1908	Cap. Germ.	Germ.	a	Worker[b]	Prewar Basic	Party School[c]	1927	W-R	USSR	1950	1953	123 ++x
14. Walter Ulbricht	1893	Urban Germ.	Germ.	Worker[a]	Worker[b]	Prewar Basic	Party School[c]	1919	W-R[d]	USSR	1923	1946	12345678 ++++++++
15. Walter Beling	1899	...	Germ.	...	...	...	Military[c]	1924	Social Dem.	...	...	1947	2 +
16. Friedrich Ebert	1894	Urban Germ.	Germ.	Worker[a]	NonCommunist Politician	Prewar Second.	...	1946	Social Dem.	Home	1946	1947	23456789 ++++++++
17. Fred Oelssner	1903	Urban Germ.	Germ.	Trade Union[a]	...	Prewar Basic	b	1920	c	USSR	1947	1949	34 ++
18. Heinrich Rau *	1899	Urban Germ.	Germ.	Peasant[a]	Worker	Prewar Basic	...	1918	W-R	Con. Camp	1949	1949	345 +++
19. Wilhelm Zaisser *	1893	Urban Germ.	Germ.	a	Teacher	b	Military[c]	1920	Int-R	USSR	1950	1950	3 +
20. Rudolf Herrnstadt	1903	Urban Germ.	Germ.	Middle Class[a]	...	Prewar Gym.	...	1924	Int-R	USSR	1950	1950	3 x
21. Erich Honecker	1912	Urban Germ.	Germ.	Worker[a]	Worker	Prewar Basic	...	1929	W-R	Con. Camp	1946	1950	3456789 xx+++++
22. Hans Jendretzky	1897	Cap. Germ.	Germ.	Worker[a]	Worker	Prewar Trade	...	1920	W-R	Con. Camp	1950	1950	3 x

*Participant in Spanish Civil War
**Jewish Extraction

Exec. Com. Dates:
No. 1: April, 1946   No. 4: April, 1954   No. 7: April, 1967
No. 2: Sept., 1947   No. 5: July, 1958   No. 8: June, 1971
No. 3: July, 1950   No. 6: Jan., 1963   No. 9: May, 1976

+ Full Member
x Candidate Member

TABLE F-4 (CONTINUED)

	1 Birth Date	2 Birth Place	3 Ethnicity	4 Status of Father	5 Status Prior to Party Work	6 Formal Educ.	7 Advanced Training	8 Party Mbr.	9 Revol. Type	10 WW II	11 CC Mbr.	12 EC Mbr.	Exec. Com. & Status
23. Karl Schirdewan	1905	Urban Germ.	Germ.	Worker	...	Prewar Second.			...	Con. Camp	1953	1953	4 / +
24. Willi Stoph	1914	Cap. Germ.	Germ.	Worker	Worker[a]	Prewar Basic		1925	...	Milit.[b]	1950	1953	456789 / ++++++
25. Bruno Leuschner	1910	Cap. Germ.	Germ.	Worker[a]	White Collar[b]	Prewar Second.		1931	W-R	Con. Camp	1950	1953	456 / x++
26. Erich Muckenberger	1910	Urban Germ.	Germ.	Worker	Worker[a]	Prewar Basic	Party School[b]	1931	c	Con. Camp	1950	1954	456789 / x+++++
27. Alfred Neumann *	1909	Cap. Germ.	Germ.	Worker	Worker[a]	Prewar Basic		1927	W-R	Jail	1954	1954	456789 / x+++++
28. Herbert Warnke	1902	Urban Germ.	Germ.	Worker[a]	Worker[b]	Prewar Basic		1928	W-R	Jail[c]	1950	1953	45678 / x++++
29. Albert Norden	1904	Urban Pol.	Germ.**	Clergy[a]	Student[b]	Prewar Gym.		1923	W-R	USA	1955	1958	56789 / +++++
30. Edith Baumann	1909	Urban Germ.	Germ.	Worker	NonCommunist Politician	Prewar High.[a]	Party School[b]	1920	St-R	...	1955	1958	5 / x
31. Luise Ermisch	1916	Urban Germ.	Germ.	Worker[a]	Worker[b]	Prewar Basic		1946	Social Dem.	Home	1954	1958	5 / x
32. Paul Frohlich	1913	Germ.	Germ.	Worker[a]	Worker[b]	Prewar Basic		1950	NRE	Jail	1954	1954	567 / x++
33. Kurt Hager *	1912	Rural Germ.	Germ.	Worker[a]	Student	Prewar Second.		1930	W-R	Jail	1950	1958	56789 / x++++
34. Alfred Kurella	1895	Germ.	Germ.	Middle Class[a]	Student	Prewar High.[b]		1930	St-R	USSR	1958	1958	5 / x
35. Karl Mewis *	1907	Urban Germ.	Germ.	...	Worker[a]	Prewar Basic	Party School[b]	1954	St-R	Sw.	1939	1958	5 / x
36. Alois Pisnik	1908	Urban Pol.	Germ.	...	Technician[a]	Prewar SpecSec.	Engin.[b]	1924	W-R	Jail	1950	1958	5 / x
37. Paul Verner *	1911	Urban Germ.	Germ.	Worker[a]	Youth[b]	Prewar[c]		1945[c]	St-R	Sw.	1950	1958	56789 / x++++
38. Erich Apel	1917	Germ.	Germ.	Worker	State Official[a]	Prewar High.	Engin.	1929	d	Milit.	1958	1963	6 / x
39. Hermann Axen	1916	Urban Germ.	Germ.	Worker[a]	Student	Prewar Gym.	Military[b]	1952	NRE	Fran.	1950	1963	6789 / xx++
40. Karl Bartsch	1923	Urban Germ.	Germ.	Peasant	Government Employee[a]	Prewar Second.	Agric.[a]	1945	St-R	Milit.[b]	1963	1963	6 / x
41. Georg Ewald	1926	Germ.	Germ.	Peasant	Worker	Prewar Basic	Party School[b]	1949	NRE	Milit.	1963	1963	678 / xxx
42. Gerhard Gruneberg	1921	Rural Germ.	Germ.	Worker	Worker	Prewar Basic		1946	NRE	Milit.	1958	1959	6789 / x+++
43. Werner Jarowinsky	1927	Urban USSR	Germ.	Worker[a]	State Official[b]	Postwar Univ.	Econ.[c]	1945	Po-W	USSR	1963	1963	6789 / xxxx
44. Gunther Mittag	1926	Urban Germ.	Germ.	Worker	Worker[a]	Prewar Second.[b]	Econ.	1946	NRE	...	1958	1963	6789 / x+++

*Participant in Spanish Civil War
**Jewish Extraction

Exec. Com. Dates:

No. 1: April, 1946   No. 4: April, 1954   No. 7: April, 1967
No. 2: Sept., 1947   No. 5: July, 1958   No. 8: June, 1971
No. 3: July, 1950   No. 6: Jan., 1963   No. 9: May, 1976

+ Full Member
x Candidate Member

TABLE F-4 (CONTINUED)

	1 Birth Date	2 Birth Place	3 Ethnicity	4 Status of Father	5 Status Prior to Party Work	6 Formal Educ.	7 Advanced Training	8 Party Mbr.	9 Revol. Type	10 WW II	11 CC Mbr.	12 EC Mbr.	Exec. Com. & Status
45. Margarete Muller	1931	Urban Germ.	Germ.	...	Coll. Farm Chairman	Postwar Univ.a	Agric.	1951	Po-W	Home	1963	1963	6789 xxxx
46. Horst Sindermann	1915	Urban Germ.	Germ.	White Collara	Studentb	Prewar Gym.	...	1945	St-R	Con. Camp	1958	1963	6789 xxxx
47. Werner Krolikowski	1928	Rural Germ.	Germ.	Worker	Government Employeea	Prewar Basic	...	1946	Po-W	...	1963	1971	89 ++
48. Werner Lamberz	1929	Urban Germ.	Germ.	a	Workerb	Prewar Basic	Party Schoolc	1948	Po-W	...	1963	1970	89 ++
49. Walter Halbritter	1927	Rural Germ.	Germ.	a	State Officialb	Postwar IncSec.c	Econ.d	1946	Po-W	...	1967	1967	8 x
50. Gunther Kleiber	1931	Rural Germ.	Germ.	Worker	Professora	Postwar Univ.	Engin.	1949	Po-W	...	1967	1972	89 xx
51. Erich Mielke *	1907	Cap. Germ.	Germ.	...	Student	Prewar IncSec.	...	1925	St-R	USSR	1950	1971	89 xx
52. Harry Tisch	1927	Rural Germ.	Germ.	Worker	Workera	Prewar Basic	Party Schoolb	1946	Po-W	...	1963	1971	89 xx
53. Werner Felfe	1928	Rural Germ.	Germ.	Worker	...	Postwar Univ.a	Econ.	1945	Po-W	...	1954	1973	9 +
54. Heinz Hoffmann *	1910	Urban Germ.	Germ.	Workera	Student	Postwar High.a	Military	1931	W-R	USSR	1950	1973	9 +
55. Konrad Naumann	1928	Urban Germ.	Germ.	White Collara	Studentb	Prewar SpecSec.	Party Schoolc	1946	Po-W	...	1963	1976	9 +
56. Horst Dohlus	1925	Urban Germ.	Germ.	...	a	Postwar SpecSec.b	Party School	1946	Po-W	Milit.	1950	1976	9 x
57. Joachim Hermann	1928	Cap. Germ.	Germ.	Worker	Journalista	Prewar Second.	...	1946	Po-W	...	1967	1973	9 x
58. Egon Krenz	1937	Urban Germ.	Germ.	Workera	Studentb	Postwar SpecSec.c	Party Schoold	1955	Po-W	...	1971	1976	9 x
59. Ingeburg Lange	1927	Urban Germ.	Germ.	Worker	Workera	...	...	1945	Po-W	...	1963	1973	9 x
60. Gerhard Schurer	1921	Urban Germ.	Germ.	Worker	Government Employeea	Prewar Basic	Party Schoolb	1948	NRE	Milit.	1963	1973	9 x
61. Werner Walde	1928	Urban Germ.	Germ.	Worker	White Collara	Postwar Highb.	Econ.c	1946	Po-W	...	1971	1976	9 x

*Participant in Spanish Civil War
**Jewish Extraction

Exec. Com. Dates:

No. 1: April, 1946 No. 4: April, 1954 No. 7: April, 1967
No. 2: Sept., 1947 No. 5: July, 1958   No. 8: June, 1971
No. 3: July, 1950   No. 6: Jan, 1963   No. 9: May, 1976

+ Full Member
x Candidate Member

298

TABLE F-4 (CONTINUED)

General Remarks on Table: Between 1946 and 1949, the Politburo was known as the Central Secretariat and contained Social Democratic leaders who were not members of the Central Committee of the SED. Some of these persons subsequently became members of the SED Central Committee; they therefore are recorded as having joined the Politburo before becoming members of the Central Committee. In coding revolutionary types (Column 9), membership in the German Social Democratic Party prior to World War I has been disregarded. In coding levels of education (Column 6), those who attended a Volksschule prior to World War II are recorded as having received a basic education.

Abbreviations Used in This Table:

1.	Agric.	Agriculture	8. Germ.	Germany	15. Second.	Secondary
2.	Cap.	Capital	9. Gym.	Gymnasium	16. Social Dem.	Social Democrat
3.	Coll. Farm	Collective Farm	10. High.	Higher	17. SpecSec.	Specialized Secondary
4.	Con. Camp	Concentration Camp	11. Int-R	Intellectual Revolutionary	18. St-R	Student Revolutionary
5.	Econ.	Economics	12. Milit.	Military	19. Sw.	Sweden
6.	Engin.	Engineering	13. NRE	No Revolutionary Experience	20. Univ.	University
7.	Fran.	France	14. Po-W	Post War	21. W-R	Worker Revolutionary

For further explanation of these terms, see the introduction to this section.

Notes: Anton Ackermann: a. Data lacking but trained as a worker and appears to be of lower class origins. b. Was in socialist youth movement in 1919, at age 14, before becoming involved in revolutionary activity full-time. c. Lenin Party School, USSR, between 1928 and 1932. Franz Dahlem: a. Father a railroad worker. b. Salesman. Max Fechner: a. Data lacking, but trained as worker. Erich Gniffke: a. No evidence of being in SED Central Committee. b. Father a worker. Otto Grotewohl: a. Son of a tailor. b. Higher School for Politics, Berlin. c. Assumed date of joining SED Central Committee after serving in Central Secretariat. August Karsten: a. Data lacking, but worker upon leaving school. b. No evidence of membership in Central Committee of SED; served in Central Secretariat until 1949, when removed for pro-Titoist stand. Kathe Kern: a. Assumed date of joining SED Central Committee after serving in Central Secretariat. Helmut Lehmann: a. Father a writer. b. Assumed date of joining SED Central Committee after serving in Central Secretariat. Otto Meier: a. No evidence of membership in Central Committee of SED; served in Central Secretariat until 1949-1950. Paul Merker: a. Data lacking, but began career in lower class occupation. b. Waiter. Wilhelm Pieck: a. Was worker before joining Social Democratic Party in 1895. b. Coding disregards prior membership in Social Democratic Party. c. One of founders of KPD, chosen Secretary in 1935, exact date of joining Politburo not known. Elli Schmidt: a. Data lacking, but began career in lower class occupation (tailor). b. Trained as tailor. c. Lenin Party School, Moscow, 1932-1934. Walter Ulbricht: a. Father a tailor. b. Was apprentice furniture maker before WWI; joined Social Democratic Party in 1912, then served in German army, 1915-1918 before becoming involved in full-time political activity as a Communist in 1919. c. Attended party school in Moscow, 1926. d. Coding disregards earlier membership in Social Democratic Party. Friedrich Ebert: a. Son of Friedrich Ebert, originally a worker, later President of Germany. Fred Oelssner: a. Son of Alfred Oelssner, trade union functionary and later KPD leader. b. Studied political economy in Moscow, 1926-1932. c. Data lacking; probably Worker Revolutionary (W-R). Heinrich Rau: a. Father peasant, then KPD functionary in 1920s. Wilhelm Zaisser: a. Data lacking, but very likely of middle class origins. b. Probably specialized secondary education or higher in light of profession (teaching). c. Military training in USSR in early 1930s. Rudolf Herrnstadt: a. Father a lawyer. Erich Honecker: a. Father a miner. Hans Jendretzky: a. Father a printer. Willi Stoph: a. Mason. b. Served in German army, 1935-1945. Bruno Leuschner: a. Father a shoemaker. b. Salesman. c. Fits no category, was white collar employee for unknown period of time before joining party. Erich Muckenberger: a. Locksmith. b. Attended SED party school, 1946-1948. Alfred Neumann: a. Cabinet maker. Herbert Warnke: a. Father a mason. b. Employed as an apprentice riveter. c. Jailed in Sweden as a spy, 1939-1943. Albert Norden: a. Father a rabbi. b. Worked as a cabinet maker, but assumed here, in light of secondary education, to have been a student at time of joining party at age 16. Edith Baumann: a. Higher Commercial School. b. Moscow Higher Party School, 1960. Luise Ermisch: a. Father a butcher. b. Dressmaker. Paul Frohlich: a. Son of a miner. b. Miner, then industrial worker before joining the party and becoming involved in full-time revolutionary activity. Kurt Hager: a. Father a manservant. Alfred Kurella: a. Father a doctor. b. Received a doctorate from the University of Jena in 1968. Formal education included gymnasium and training in art. Karl Mewis: a. Locksmith, then briefly trade union steward before joining the party and becoming involved in full-time revolutionary activity. b. Lenin School, Moscow, 1932-1934. Alois Pisnik: a. Electrical technician before becoming party functionary in 1945. b. Studied electrical engineering through correspondence school. c. Date of joining SED. Joined Austrian CP in 1928. Paul Verner: a. Father a metal worker. b. Member of Communist youth group at age 14. c. Conflicting data--basic or (cont'd.)

TABLE F-4 (CONCLUDED)

secondary. d. Could be typed either as Student Revolutionary (St-R) or Worker Revolutionary (W-R). Erich Apel: a. Minister of Heavy Industry before entering into full-time party work in 1958. Hermann Axen: a. Father a worker, then a KPD functionary. b. Frunze Military Academy, USSR. Karl Bartsch: a. Professor of Agriculture, Humboldt University, 1949-1950, before becoming involved in full-time party work. b. SED Higher Party School, 1953-1954. Georg Ewald: a. Local government official, 1949-1950, before becoming involved in full-time party work. b. SED Higher Party School, 1953-1954. Werner Jarowinsky: a. Father a worker in USSR. b. Did not enter politics full-time until joining Politburo in 1963, at which time, Minister of State Supply. c. Assistant Professor, Faculty of Economics, Humboldt University, and PhD in economics. Gunther Mittag: a. State railway inspector before becoming involved in political activity full-time in trade union work. b. Completed commercial institute in 1958 while employed full-time; received doctorate in economics in 1961, also while employed full-time. Margarete Muller: a. Studied agronomy, University of Leningrad, 1950s; received degree in agronomy, 1960, in GDR. Horst Sindermann: a. Further information on father's position lacking. b. Involved in Communist youth activity while student in gymnasium in early 1930s. Werner Krolikowski: a. Served in local government post before becoming involved in full-time political work (in youth organization) around 1949. Werner Lamberz: a. Father party functionary before WWII. b. Employed as heating worker, or fitter, for several years before becoming involved in full-time party work. c. Komsomol Higher School, Moscow, 1952-1953. Walter Halbritter: a. Data lacking, but probably of peasant background. b. Official in Ministry of State Finance in 1955 at time of becoming involved in full-time party work. c. Received vocational training before 1945, attended Walter Ulbricht School of Government and Law after WWII. d. Advanced degree in economics received by correspondence. Gunther Kleiber: a. Served as Assistant Professor at Dresden Technical School, 1958-1962, before becoming involved in full-time political work. Harry Tisch: a. Trained as locksmith, then worker before becoming involved in politics full-time as a trade union functionary in 1948. b. Higher Party School, 1953-1955. Received degree from Dresden University in 1965 in "Engineering Economics" Heinz Hoffmann: a. Received degree in social sciences. Werner Felfe: a. Received degree trained in Soviet general staff academy, 1955-1957, where he received academic certificate in military sciences. Konrad Naumann: a. White Collar Employee, further information lacking. b. Engaged in full-time political work at age 18, shortly after finishing school; was also briefly a farm and construction worker. c. Komsomol University, Moscow. Horst Dohlus: a. Trained as a barber, served in German military briefly during WWII. Profession before becoming involved in full-time political work as a local party functionary not known. b. Attended "management" school in 1951. Joachim Hermann: a. Was journalist before becoming involved in full-time political activity in youth movement in 1949. Egon Krenz: a. Father a tailor. b. Was student before becoming involved in full-time political work in youth movement in 1959. c. Graduate of teachers' training institute, 1957. d. Degree in social sciences from "CPSU University" 1967. Ingeburg Lange: a. Dressmaker before becoming involved in full-time political activity in youth movement in 1946. Gerhard Schurer: a. Locksmith, 1945-1947, then employed by the government of Saxony, 1947, before becoming involved in full-time political activity as a party functionary in 1948. b. Received degree in the social sciences from CPSU "Party University" in 1958. Werner Walde: a. Worked as white collar employee in enterprise before becoming involved in full-time political activity as party functionary in 1951. b. Attended Berlin-Karlshorst University, 1964-1966, received degree in "economics and science." c. Also graduate of SED Higher Party School.

TABLE F-5   BACKGROUND OF PARTY LEADERS: HUNGARY, 1948-1975

	1 Birth Date	2 Birth Place	3 Ethnicity	4 Status of Father	5 Status Prior to Party Work	6 Formal Educ.	7 Advanced Training	8 Party Mbr.	9 Revol. Type	10 WW II	11 CC Mbr.	12 EC Mbr.	Exec. Com. & Status 123456789
1. Antal Apro	1913	Urban Hung.**	Hung.**	Worker	Worker[a]	Prewar ...	...	1931	W-R	USSR	1944	1946	123456789 +++++++++
2. Mihaly Farkas	1904	Rural Hung.	Hung.**	Worker	Worker	Prewar Elem.	...	a	W-R	USSR	1945	1945	123 +++
3. Erno Gero*	1898	Rural Hung.	Hung.**	Middle Class	Student	Prewar IncUniv.	Medicine	1919	St-R	USSR	1944	1944	1234 +++
4. Janos Kadar	1912	Urban Yugo.[a]	Hung.	Worker	Worker[b]	Prewar Second.	...	1932	W-R	Illeg.	1942	1945	123456789 +++++++++
5. Istvan Kossa	1904	Rural Hung.	Hung.	Peasant	Worker[a]	Prewar[b]	...	1940	W-R	USSR	1945	1946	1 +
6. Imre Nagy	1896	Urban Hung.	Hung.	Peasant	Apprentice	Prewar Basic	Agric.[a]	b	c	USSR	1944	1944	123 +++
7. Laszlo Rajk*	1909	Rural Hung.	Hung.	Worker	a	Prewar Univ.	...	1930	St-R	Jail	1945	1945	1 +
8. Matyas Rakosi	1892	Rural Hung.	Hung.**	Middle Class	Student	Prewar Univ.	...	1918	St-R	USSR	1918[a]	1918[a]	123 +++
9. Jozsef Revai	1898	Rural Hung.	Hung.**	Middle Class	Student	Prewar Second.	...	1919	Int-R	USSR	1944	1944	12 4 ++ +
10. Jozsef Harustyak	1894	...	...	...	...	...	...	1948	Social Dem.	...	1948	1948	12 ++
11. Gyorgy Marosan	1902	Urban Hung.	Hung.	...	NonCommunist Politician	...	...	1948	Social Dem.	Home	1948	1948	1 45 ++
12. Sandor Ronai	1892	Urban Hung.	Hung.	...	NonCommunist Politician	Prewar Elem.	...	1948	Social Dem.	Home	1948	1948	12 456 ++ x++
13. Arpad Szakasits	1888	Cap. Hung.	Hung.	Worker[a]	NonCommunist Politician	Prewar Univ.	...	1948	Social Dem.	Home	1948	1948	1 +
14. Imre Vajda	1900	...	Hung.**	...	NonCommunist Politician	Prewar Univ.	Econ.	1948	Social Dem.	...	1948	1948	1 +
15. Marton Horvath	1906	...	...	...	...	...	...			...	1945	1945	12 ++
16. Istvan Kovacs	1911	Cap. Hung.	Hung.	Middle Class	Youth[a]	Prewar Elem.	...	b	c	Jail	1948	1948	12 4 x+ +
17. Zoltan Vas	1900	Cap. Hung.	Hung.	Middle Class[a]	...	Prewar IncSec.	b	1919	c	USSR	1945	1948	12 x+
18. Andras Hegedus	1919	Rural Hung.	Hung.	Peasant	Student[a]	Prewar Univ.[b]	Party School[c]	1945	NRE	Home	1953	1953	234 +++
19. Karoly Kiss	1903	Rural Hung.	Hung.	Worker[a]	Worker	Prewar Elem.	...	1922	W-R	USSR	1956	1956	2 45 + ++
20. Istvan Szabo	1924	...	...	...	...	...	...			...	1951	...	2 +
21. Sandor Zold	1913	...	Hung.	Worker	Student	Prewar Univ.	Medicine	1932	St-R	...	1951	...	2 +
22. Mihaly Zsofinyecz	1906	...	Hung.	Worker	...	...	...	a	Social Dem.	...	1951	1951	2 +

*Participant in Spanish Civil War
**Jewish Extraction

Exec. Com. Dates:

No. 1: June, 1948	No. 4: Aug., 1956	No. 7: Dec., 1966
No. 2: March, 1951	No. 5: Dec., 1959	No. 8: Nov., 1970
No. 3: May, 1954	No. 6: Nov., 1962	No. 9: Nov., 1975

+ Full Member
x Candidate Member

TABLE F-5   (CONTINUED)

	1 Birth Date	2 Birth Place	3 Ethnicity	4 Status of Father	5 Status Prior to Party Work	6 Formal Educ.	7 Advanced Training	8 Party Mbr.	9 Revol. Type	10 WW II	11 CC Mbr.	12 EC Mbr.	Exec. Com. & Status
23. Istvan Denes	...	...	...	...	...	...		...		...		1951	2 / x
24. Istvan Hidas	1918	Cap. Hung.	Hung.	Worker	Worker			1943	Social Dem.	Illeg.	1951	1951	234 / x++
25. Istvan Kristof	1912	...	...	...	Worker	...			W-R	...	1951	1951	2 / x
26. Laszlo Piros	1917	Hung.	Hung.	...	Worker[a]	Prewar High.[b]	Military	1934	W-R	USSR	1951	1951	2 4 / x x
27. Lajos Acs	1915	...	Hung.	...	...		Party School[a]	1944			1951	1953	34 / ++
28. Bela Szalai	1922	...	Hung.	...	...		Party School	...		Illeg.	1954	1954	34 / ++
29. Istvan Bata	1910	...	Hung.	Worker	Worker[a]	High.[b]	Military	1930	W-R	Home	1954	1954	34 / xx
30. Jozsef Mekis	...	...	...	...	...	...		...		Illeg.	1948	1954	34 / x+
31. Sandor Gaspar	1917	Rural Hung.	Hung.	Peasant	Worker	...		1936	W-R	Illeg.	1946	1956	456789 / xx+++++
32. Bela Biszku	1921	Rural Hung.	Hung.	Peasant	Worker[a]	Prewar Second.		1944	W-R	Illeg.	1957	1957	56789 / +++++
33. Lajos Feher	1917	Rural Hung.	Hung.	Peasant	Journalist	Prewar Univ.		1942	Int-R	Illeg.	1954	1957	5678 / ++++
34. Jeno Fock	1916	Urban Hung.	Hung.	Worker	Worker[a]	Prewar Univ.		1932	W-R	Jail	1956	1957	56789 / +++++
35. Gyula Kallai	1910	Urban Hung.	Hung.	Worker	Journalist	Prewar Univ.		1931	St-R	Home	1956	1956	5678 / ++++
36. Ferenc Munnich*	1886	Rural Hung.	Hung.	Middle Class	Writer	Prewar Univ.	Law	1918	Int-R	USSR	1956	1957	56 / ++
37. Dezso Nemes	1908	Urban Czech.	Hung.**	...	Worker[a]	Prewar Univ.[b]	Party School[c]	1926	W-R	USSR	1957	1957	56789 / +++++
38. Miklos Somogyi	1896	Urban Hung.	Hung.**	Poor Family	Trade Union				W-R	Illeg.	1956	1956	56 / ++
39. Zoltan Komocsin	1923	Urban Hung.	Hung.	Worker	Worker			1938	W-R	Home	1957	1957	5678 / x+++
40. Istvan Szirmai	1906	Rum.	Hung.**	Middle Class	Journalist	Second.		1943[a]	Int-R	Illeg.	1946	1959	567 / x++
41. Miklos Ajtai	1914	Rural Hung.	Hung.	Middle Class	Engineer	Prewar Univ.[a]	Chem.	1943	NRE	Illeg.	1961	1962	67 / xx
42. Janos Brutyo	1911	Urban Hung.	Hung.	...	Worker			1934	W-R	Home	1957	1962	6 / x
43. Lajos Czinege	1924	Urban Hung.	Hung.	Peasant	Agric. Laborer	Postwar[a]	Military	1945	Po-W	Home	1959	1961	67 / xx
44. Lajos Cseterki	1921	...	Hung.	...	Worker	... SpecSec.[b]	Party School[b]	...	...	...	1959	1962	6 / x

*Participant in Spanish Civil War
**Jewish Extraction

Exec. Com. Dates:

No. 1: June, 1948   No. 4: Aug., 1956   No. 7: Dec., 1966
No. 2: March, 1951   No. 5: Dec., 1959   No. 8: Nov., 1970
No. 3: May, 1954   No. 6: Nov., 1962   No. 9: Nov., 1975

+ Full Member
x Candidate Member

TABLE F-5 (CONTINUED)

	1 Birth Date	2 Birth Place	3 Ethnic- ity	4 Status of Father	5 Status Prior to Party Work	6 Formal Educ.	7 Advanced Training	8 Party Mbr.	9 Revol. Type	10 WW II	11 CC Mbr.	12 EC Mbr.	Exec. Com. & Status
45. Pal Ilku	1912	Czech.	Hung.	Peasant	Teacher	Prewar SpecSec[a]	...	1937	Int-R	Home	1959	1962	67 / xx
46. Rezso Nyers	1923	Cap. Hung.	Hung.	Worker	State Official[a]	Postwar Univ.[b]	Econ.	1948	Social Dem.	Home	1954	1962	678 / x++
47. Karoly Nemeth	1922	Rural Hung.	Hung.	[a]	Worker[b]	...	Party School[c]	1945	NRE[d]	...	1956	1966	789 / x++
48. Valeria Benke	1920	Rural Hung.	Hung.	Peasant	Teacher	Prewar SpecSec[a]	[b]	1941	NRE	Home	1957	1970	89 / ++
49. Gyorgy Aczel	1917	Cap. Hung.	Hung.	...	Actor	...	...	1935	W-R	Home	1956	1970	9 / +
50. Gyorgy Lazar	1924	Urban Hung.	Hung.	Worker	State Official[a]	Prewar SpecSec[b]	...	1945	NRE	Home	1970	1970	9 / +
51. Laszlo Marothy	1942	Hung.	Hung.	Peasant	Student[a]	Postwar Univ.[b]	Agric.	1965	Po-W		1965	1975	9 / +
52. Miklos Ovari	1925	Cap. Hung.	Hung.	...	Student[a]	Postwar Univ.	Party School[b]	1946	Po-W	Home	1962	1975	9 / +
53. Istvan Sarlos	1921	Cap. Hung.	Hung.	Worker	NonCommunist† Politician	Prewar Univ.	...	1948	Social Dem.	...	1966	1975	9 / +

*Participant in Spanish Civil War
**Jewish Extraction

Exec. Com. Dates:
No.1: June, 1948   No.4: Aug., 1956   No.7: Dec., 1966
No.2: March, 1951   No.5: Dec., 1959   No.8: Nov., 1970
No.3: May, 1954   No.6: Nov., 1962   No.9: Nov., 1975

+ Full Member
x Candidate Member

General Remarks on Table: Persons described in Hungarian sources as in resistance movement during World War II coded as engaged in illegal activity (Illeg.). All persons shown as born outside the borders of Hungary as they existed between the two World Wars were born prior to World War I, on what was then Hungarian territory.

Abbreviations Used in This Table:

1. Cap. Capital
2. Chem. Chemistry
3. Czech. Czechoslovakia
4. Elem. Elementary
5. Econ. Economics
6. High. Higher
7. Hung. Hungarian
8. IncSec. Incomplete Secondary
9. Int-R Intellectual Revolutionary
10. Illeg. Illegal
11. NRE No Revolutionary Experience
12. Second. Secondary
13. Social Dem. Social Democrat
14. SpecSec. Specialized Secondary
15. St-R Student Revolutionary
16. Univ. University
17. W-R Worker Revolutionary
18. Yugo. Yugoslavia

For further explanation of these terms, see the introduction to this section.

Notes: Antal Apro: a. Housepainter. Mihaly Farkas: a. 1920s, exact date not known. Janos Kadar: a. Fiume, now Rijeka. b. Construction worker. Istvan Kossa: a. Streetcar conductor. b. Conflicting data--either Elementary or Incomplete Basic education. Imre Nagy: a. Member of the Agricultural Institute, Moscow. b. Joined Bolshevik party in 1917, and Hungarian Communist Party upon return to Hungary. c. Does not fit any type, might be called "Peasant Revolutionary." Laszlo Rajk: a. Conflicting data--either teacher or worker (bricklayer). Matyas Rakosi: a. Assumption, based on fact that Rakosi was one of founders of Hungarian Communist Party. Arpad Szakasits: a. Shoemaker. Istvan Kovacs: a. Active in Communist underground as youth, arrested, 1931, not released until end of WWII. b. Late 1920s, early 1930s, exact date not known. c. Fits no revolutionary type, most resembles a Student Revolutionary (St-R). Zoltan Vas: a. "Lower Middle Class" according to source. b. Probably received military or police training while in USSR. c. Fits no revolutionary type, might simply be called "Professional Revolutionary." Andras Hegedus: a. Was student before becoming involved full-time in politics as party functionary after (cont'd.)

TABLE F-5 (CONCLUDED)

WWII. b. Gyorffy College, Budapest; graduated in 1944. c. CPSU Higher Party School, 1948. Karoly Kiss: a. Son of cobbler. Mihaly Zsofinyecz: a. Joined "workers movement" in 1923. Laszlo Piros: a. Shoemaker. b. Military academy, USSR. Lajos Acs: a. Higher Party School of CPSU, 1950s. Istvan Bata: a. Tram conductor. b. Frunze Military Academy, USSR. Bela Biszku: a. Locksmith. Jeno Fock: a. Mechanic. Dezso Nemes: a. Upholsterer's assistant. b. Studied in USSR, 1939-1942. c. USSR, 1931-1933. Istvan Szirmai: a. Member of the Romanian CP, 1929. Miklos Ajtai: a. PhD in Chemistry, Budapest University. Lajos Czinege: a. Graduated from Petofi Academy, a training school for political officers. Could be ranked as either Higher or Specialized Secondary. Lajos Cseterki: a. Teacher's training college, here ranked as Specialized Secondary education. b. Attended party school in USSR in period 1946-1947. Pal Ilku: a. Finished teacher's college, here ranked as Specialized Secondary education. Rezso Nyers: a. Minister of Finance, 1962, at time of becoming involved in full-time political activity as member of Central Committee Secretariat. b. Karl Marx University of Economic Sciences, 1956. Karoly Nemeth: a. Conflicting data--father either worker or peasant. b. Butcher. c. Party Academy, 1952-1954. d. Coding based on assumption that no postwar higher education. Valeria Benke: a. Teacher's college, here ranked as Specialized Secondary education. b. No record of having attended party school, but taught at Party Academy, 1945-1946. Gyorgy Lazar: a. Permanent representative to COMECON, 1973-1975, before becoming involved in full-time political activity as a member of the politburo. b. Industrial high school. Laszlo Marothy: a. Student before becoming involved in politics full-time as youth leader. b. Graduate of Godollo Agricultural University, 1965. Miklos Ovari: a. Student before becoming involved full-time in politics as instructor at party school, then Central Committee functionary. b. Also taught at party academy, 1949-1958.

304

TABLE F-6   BACKGROUND OF PARTY LEADERS: POLAND, 1945-1975

	1 Birth Date	2 Birth Place	3 Ethnicity	4 Status of Father	5 Status Prior to Party Work	6 Formal Educ.	7 Advanced Training	8 Party Mbr.	9 Revol. Type	10 WW II	11 CC Mbr.	12 EC Mbr.	Exec. Com. & Status
1. Jakub Berman	1901	Cap. Pol.	Pol.**	Middle Class	Student	Prewar Univ.	Law Military[a]	1928	St-R	USSR	1945	1945	123 +++
2. Boleslaw Bierut	1892	Rural Pol.	Pol.	Peasant	Worker[a]	Prewar IncSec	Party School[b]	1919	W-R	USSR	1925[c]	1945	123 ++
3. Wladyslaw Gomulka	1905	Urban Pol.	Pol.	Worker	Worker	Prewar Elem.	Party School[a]	1927	W-R	Resis.	1942	1945[b]	1 456 + +++
4. Hilary Minc	1905	Rural Pol.	Pol.**	Middle Class	Student	Prewar IncUniv.	Econ.	1928	St-R	USSR	1945	1945	123 +++
5. Stanislaw Radkiewicz	1903	Rural Pol.	Pol.	Poor Peasant	Student	Prewar Gym.	Party School[a]	1930	St-R	USSR	1945	1945	123 +++
6. Marian Spychalski	1906	Urban Pol.	Pol.	Worker	Student	Prewar Univ.	Arch.	1931	St-R	Resis.	1945	1945	12 456 ++ +++
7. Roman Zambrowski	1909	Cap. Pol.	Pol.**	Clergy[a]	Student	Prewar Second.	Party School[b]	1925[c]	St-R	USSR	1945	1945	1234 ++++
8. Aleksander Zawadzki	1899	Urban Pol.	Pol.	Worker	Worker[a]	Prewar Elem.	...	1923	W-R	USSR	1936	1944	12345 +++++
9. Hilary Chelchowski	1908	Rural Pol.	Pol.	Peasant	Trade Union Official	Prewar IncElem.	...	1932	W-R	Resis.	1943	1945	123 xxx
10. Jozef Cyrankiewicz	1911	Urban Pol.	Pol.	Middle Class	NonCommunist Politician	Prewar IncHigh[a]	Law Military	1948	Social Dem.	Con. Camp	1948	1948	23456 +++++
11. Franciszek Jozwiak	1895	Rural Pol.	Pol.	Peasant	Peasant[a]	NFE	Party School[b]	1921	c	Resis.	1931	1948	23 ++
12. Adam Rapacki	1909	Urban Pol.	Pol.	Middle Class[a]	NonCommunist Politician	Prewar Univ.	Commerce	1948	Social Dem.	Con. Camp	1948	1948	2345 +x++
13. Henryk Swiatkowski	1895	Rural Pol.	Pol.	Peasant	NonCommunist Politician	Prewar Univ.	Law	1948	Social Dem.	Resis.	1948	1948	2 +
14. Franciszek Mazur	1895	...	a	Poor Peasant	Worker[b]	Prewar Trade	...	1919	W-R	USSR	1930	1948	23 x+
15. Stefan Matuszewski	1905	Pol.	Pol.	...	NonCommunist Politician	Prewar Second[a]	...	1946[b]	Social Dem.	USSR	1948[c]	1948	2 x
16. Edward Ochab	1906	Urban Pol.	Pol.	Gov. Official[a]	Student	Prewar High.	Commerce[b] Military	1929	St-R	USSR	1944	1948	2345 x+++
17. Wladyslaw Dworakowski	1908	...	...	...	...	...	...	1942	NRE	Resis.	1945	1952	3 +
18. Zenon Nowak	1905	Urban Pol.	Pol.	Worker	Worker	NFE	...	1924	W-R	Con. Camp	1932	1950	3 +
19. Konstanty Rokossowski	1897	Cap. Pol.	Pol.[a]	Worker[b]	Worker	Prewar High.[c]	Military	1919	W-R	USSR	1949	1950	3 +
20. Edward Gierek	1913	Urban Pol.	Pol.	Worker[a]	Worker[b]	...	Engin.[c]	1946[d]	W-R	Belg.	1954	1956	45678 +++++
21. Stefan Jedrychowski	1910	Cap. Pol.	Pol.	Middle Class[a]	Student	Prewar Univ.[b]	Econ.	1935	St-R	USSR	1945	1956	456 +++
22. Zenon Kliszko	1908	Urban Pol.	Pol.	Worker	Trade Union Official	Prewar IncUniv.	Law	1931	St-R	Resis.	1945	1959	456 +++

*Participant in Spanish Civil War
**Jewish Extraction

Exec. Com. Dates:
No. 1: Dec., 1945   No. 4: March, 1959   No. 7: Dec., 1971
No. 2: Dec., 1948   No. 5: June, 1964   No. 8: Dec., 1975
No. 3: March, 1954 No. 6: Nov., 1968

+ Full Member
x Candidate Member

TABLE F-6 (CONTINUED)

	1 Birth Date	2 Birth Place	3 Ethnicity	4 Status of Father	5 Status Prior to Party Work	6 Formal Educ.	7 Advanced Training	8 Party Mbr.	9 Revol. Type	10 WW II	11 CC Mbr.	12 EC Mbr.	Exec. Com. & Status
23. Ignacy Loga-Sowinski	1914	Rural Pol.	Pol.	Poor Peasant	Worker		Party School	1935	W-R	Resis.	1942	1956	456 +++
24. Jerzy Morawski	1918	Cap. Pol.	Pol.	Middle Class	Teacher	Prewar IncUniv.	...	1942	St-R	Resis.	1948	1956	4 x
25. Eugeniusz Szyr*	1915	Rural Pol.	Pol.**	Worker	Youth[a]	Prewar IncUniv.	...	1934	St-R	Con. Camp	1948	1964	5 +
26. Franciszek Waniolka	1912	Urban Pol.	Pol.	...	[a]	Postwar High.[b]	Engin.	1946	NRE	c	1959	1964	5 +
27. Mieczyslaw Jagielski	1924	Urban Pol.	Pol.**	Peasant	...	Prewar Second.	Planning[a]	1945	NRE	...	1954	1964	5678 xx++
28. Piotr Jaroszewicz	1909	Rural Pol.	Pol.	Middle Class[a]	State Official[b]	Prewar High.[c]	Military[d]	1944	NRE	USSR	1948	1964	5678 xx++
29. Ryszard Strzelecki	1907	Cap. Pol.	Pol.	Worker	Student	Prewar Univ.	Engin.	1937	St-R	Resis.	1944	1964	56 x+
30. Boleslaw Jaszczuk	1913	Cap. Pol.	Pol.	Middle Class[a]	Engineer	Prewar High.	Engin.	1942	St-R	Resis.	1948	1968	6 +
31. Stanislaw Kociolek	1933	Cap. Pol.	Pol.	...	Student[a]	Postwar IncUniv.	...	1955	Po-W	...	1964	1968	6 +
32. Wladyslaw Kruczek	1916	Urban Pol.	Pol.	Worker	Youth[a]	...	Party School[b]	1932	W-R	Resis.	1954	1968	678 +++
33. Jozef Tejchma	1927	Rural Pol.	Pol.	Poor Peasant	Student[a]	Postwar High.[b]	Party School[c]	1952	Po-W	Home	1959	1968	678 +++
34. Mieczyslaw Moczar	1913	Urban Pol.	Pol.	Worker	...			1937	W-R	Resis.	1945	1968	6 x
35. Jan Szydlak	1925	Urban Pol.	Pol.	Worker[a]	Worker[b]	Postwar Univ.[c]	Party School[c]	1945	NRE[d]	Home	1959	1968	678 x+
36. Edward Babiuch	1927	Urban Pol.	Pol.	Worker[a]	Student[b]	Postwar SpecSec	Party School[c]	1948	Po-W	Home	1964	1970	78 ++
37. Henryk Jablonski	1909	Rural Pol.	Pol.	Worker[a]	State Official[b]	Prewar Univ.[c]	...	1948	Social Dem.	Resis.	1948	1970	78 ++
38. Wojciech Jaruzelski	1923	Rural Pol.	Pol.	Middle Class[a]	State Official[b]	Postwar High.[c]	Military	1947	Po-W	USSR[d]	1964	1970	78 ++
39. Stefan Olszowski	1931	Pol.	Pol.	Middle Class[a]	Student[b]	Postwar Univ.[c]	...	1951	Po-W	...	1964	1970	78 ++
40. Franciszek Szlachcic	1920	Urban Pol.	Pol.	Worker[a]	State Official[b]	Postwar Univ.[c]	Engin.	1943	NRE	Resis.	1964	1970	7
41. Kazimierz Barcikowski	1927	Rural Pol.	Pol.	Peasant	Student[a]	Postwar High.[b]	Agric.	1953	Po-W	Home	1964	1971	78 xx
42. Zdzislaw Grudzien	1924	Rural Fran.	Pol.	Worker[a]	Worker[b]	Prewar Elem.	Engin.[c]	1946	W-R	Resis.[d]	1964	1971	78 xx
43. Stanislaw Kania	1927	Rural Pol.	Pol.	Peasant	...	Postwar High.	Engin.[a]	1945	Po-W	Home	1964	1971	78 x+
44. Jozef Kepa	1928	Rural Pol.	Pol.	Peasant	Peasant[a]	Postwar High.[b]	...	1948	Po-W	...	1968	1970	78 x+

*Participant in Spanish Civil War
**Jewish Extraction

Exec. Com. Dates:

No. 1: Dec., 1945   No. 4: March, 1959   No. 7: Dec., 1971
No. 2: Dec., 1948   No. 5: June, 1964   No. 8: Dec., 1975
No. 3: March, 1954   No. 6: Nov., 1968

+ Full Member
x Candidate Member

TABLE F-6   (CONTINUED)

	1 Birth Date	2 Birth Place	3 Ethnic-ity	4 Status of Father	5 Status Prior to Party Work	6 Formal Educ.	7 Advanced Training	8 Party Mbr.	9 Revol. Type	10 WW II	11 CC Mbr.	12 EC Mbr.	Exec. Com. & Status
45. Stanislaw Kowalczyk	1924	Pol.	Pol.	Worker	a	Postwar High.b	Engin.	1948	Po-W^c	Home	1948	1973	8 +
46. Jerzy Lukaszewicz	1931	Cap. Pol.	Pol.	a	Student^b	Postwar High.c	...	1951	Po-W		1964	1975	8 x
47. Tadeusz Wrzaszczyk	1932	Pol.	Pol.	Worker	State Official^a	Postwar Univ.b	Engin.	...	Po-W		1971	1975	8 x

* Participant in Spanish Civil War
** Jewish Extraction

Exec. Com. Dates:
No.1: Dec., 1945   No.4: March, 1959   No.7: Dec., 1971
No.2: Dec., 1948   No.5: June, 1964   No.8: Dec., 1975
No.3: March, 1954   No.6: Nov., 1968

+ Full Member
x Candidate Member

General Remarks on Table: None

Abbreviations Used in This Table:

1. Arch.	Architecture	8. Gym.	Gymnasium	15. Po-W	Postwar
2. Cap.	Capital	9. High.	Higher	16. Second.	Secondary
3. Econ.	Economics	10. Inc.	Incomplete	17. Social Dem.	Social Democrat
4. Elem.	Elementary	11. IncSec.	Incomplete Secondary	18. SpecSec.	Specialized Secondary
5. Engin.	Engineering	12. NFE	No Formal Education	19. St-R	Student Revolutionary
6. Fran.	France	13. NRE	No Revolutionary Experience	20. Univ.	University
7. Gov. Official	Government Official	14. Pol.	Poland, Polish	21. W-R	Worker Revolutionary

For further explanation of these terms, see the introduction to this section.

Notes: Jakob Berman: a. Trained in Soviet military academy. Boleslaw Bierut: a. Skilled worker in printing industry. b. Marx-Lenin Institute, USSR, 1950. c. In Central Committee 1925-1927 and 1943-1956. Wladyslaw Gomulka: a. Marx-Lenin Institute, USSR, b. 1945-1948 and 1956-1970. Stanislaw Radkiewicz: a. USSR, 1940-1941. Roman Zambrowski: a. Father a rabbi. b. Marx-Lenin Institute, USSR, 1930-1931. c. Joined party at age of 16. Aleksander Zawadzki: a. Miner. Jozef Cyrankiewicz: a. Incomplete law; completed military institute, 1935. Franciszek Jozwiak: a. Peasant, then soldier in WWI before joining party. b. Party school, USSR. c. Does not fit any category; might be considered "Peasant Revolutionary." Adam Rapacki: a. Father a professor. Franciszek Mazur: a. Real name believed to be Karpienka, and thought to be of either Russian or Ukrainian origin. b. Worker then soldier in WWI before joining party. Stefan Matuszewski: a. Completed Catholic seminary and ordained a priest. b. Date of expulsion from Socialist Party; was considered an active Communist before this time. c. Assumed on basis of membership in Politburo in same year. Edward Ochab: a. Father a policeman. b. Completed Higher School of Business, Warsaw, then military training, 1928-1928. Kostanty Rokossowski: a. Also a Soviet citizen. b. Father a railroad worker. c. Frunze Military Academy, USSR. Edward Gierek: a. Father a miner. b. Active as worker in revolutionary movement as member of French CP prior to WWII. c. Received a degree in mining engineering in 1954 after part-time study. d. French CP, 1931. Stefan Jedrychowski: a. Father a teacher. b. Conflicting data - university complete or incomplete. Eugeniusz Szyr: a. Member of CP youth organization at age 14, CP at age 19. Franciszek Waniolka: a. Data lacking; locksmith, then skilled worker, 1946. In 1952 became engaged full-time in political activity as party official. b. Received diploma after two year course in mining engineering. c. Prisoner of War in Germany. Mieczyslaw Jagielski: a. Graduate degree in planning received while working full-time. Also attended party school. Piotr Jaroszewicz: a. Father a teacher. b. Was Deputy Prime Minister and permanent representative to CMEA in 1964 at time of becoming engaged full-time in political work as Politburo member. c. Completed teachers' institute before the war, then continued pedagogical studies part-time after WWII. d. Completed Soviet military academy in 1943. Boleslaw Jaszczuk: a. Father a teacher. Stanislaw Kociolek: a. Was university student before becoming engaged full-time in political activity as local party official in 1957. Wladyslaw Kruczek: a. Communist youth movement at age 14, joined party at age 16. b. Higher Party School, dates not known. Jozef Tejchma: a. Engaged in full-time political activity as official in Communist youth organization, 1948-1954, while still a student. b. Degree in history, Central Committee Higher School of Social Sciences, full-time study, 1955-1958. c. Central Committee Higher School of Social Sciences. Jan Szydlak: a. Father a miner. b. Was locksmith in 1945 before (cont'd.)

307

TABLE F-6 (CONCLUDED)

becoming engaged in full time political activity as official in Communist youth organization. c. Central Committee Party School, dates not known. d. Coding assumes no postwar higher education. Edward Babiuch: a. Father a miner. b. After finishing studies became involved full-time in political activity as official in Communist youth organization in Silesia. c. Two year party school, graduated, 1955. Henryk Jablonski: a. Conflicting data - official biography says worker's family, other sources that father middle-class government employee. b. Was Minister of Education before becoming active full-time in politics in 1970 as member of Politburo. c. PhD in history, 1934. Wojciech Jaruzelski: a. Parents described as members of intelligentsia. b. Did not enter full-time political work until joining the Politburo in 1970, at which time Minister of Defense. c. Completed Soviet military academy, 1955, as well as being educated in Polish military schools after WWII. d. Served in Soviet army. Stefan Olszowski: a. Teacher's family. b. Became engaged in full-time political activity, after finishing studies, as official in Communist youth organization. c. University of Lodz, degree in philology Franciszek Szlachcic: a. Father a miner. b. Did not enter full-time political activity until joining the Politburo in 1971, when Minister of the Interior. c. Degree from Mining and Metallurgy Academy, Moscow, 1960. Kazimierz Barcikowski: a. Became engaged in full-time political activity after finishing studies, as official of Communist youth organization. b. Received a degree in agronomy in 1950, and a PhD in economics from the Higher School of Social Sciences of the Central Committee, 1965. Zdzislaw Grudzien: a. Father a miner. b. Active as a worker in revolutionary movement in France prior to WWII. c. Degree in mining obtained after WWII while engaged full-time in youth work. d. Participated in resistance in France. Stanislaw Kania: a. Also attended two year party school. Jozef Kepa: a. Became involved in politics full-time while still a peasant working for peasant youth organization, and in 1948, for Communist youth organization. b. Studied history at the Institute for Social Sciences, Warsaw, 1954-1958. Stanislaw Kowalczyk: a. Was locksmith, then trained as engineer; full-time political activity began with work in the trade unions, 1949 - whether before or after receiving training as engineer not known. b. Degree in metallurgical engineering from Mining Academy, Cracow. Assumed to be postwar. c. Membership in Social Democratic Party, 1949, not taken into account in coding. Jerzy Lukaszewicz: a. Parents called members of "working intelligentsia." b. Became engaged full-time in politics as official in Communist youth organization after completing secondary school education in late 1940s. c. Graduated from Higher School for the Social Sciences, date not known. Tadeusz Wrzaszczyk: a. Did not become engaged in full-time political activity until joining politburo in 1971, when Minister of Engineering. b. Studied metallurgical engineering at Warsaw University.

TABLE F-7   BACKGROUND OF PARTY LEADERS: ROMANIA, 1948-1974

	1 Birth Date	2 Birth Place	3 Ethnicity	4 Status of Father	5 Status Prior to Party Work	6 Formal Educ.	7 Advanced Training	8 Party Mbr.	9 Revol. Type	10 WW II	11 CC Mbr.	12 EC Mbr.	Exec. Com. & Status
1. Gheorghe Apostol	1913	Rural Mold.	Rom.	Worker	Worker	Prewar Trade[a]	...	1934	W-R	Jail	1945	1948	1234 +++
2. Emil Bodnaras	1904	Rural Bukov.	Ukr.	Worker	Military	Prewar High.	Law Military[a]	1940	b	USSR	1945	1945	123456 +++++
3. Iosif Chisinevschi	1905	Rural Bess.	Russ.**	Poor Family	Journalist	Prewar IncGym.	...	1928	Int-R	Jail	1940	1948	12 ++
4. Miron Constantinescu	1917	Urban Trans.	Rom.	Middle Class	Student	Prewar Univ.[a]	Econ.	1936	St-R	Jail	1945	1945	12 ++
5. Teohari Georgescu	1908	Cap. Wall.	Rom.**	Small Merchant[a]	Worker[b]	Prewar Elem.	...	1929	W-R	Jail[c]	1944	...	1 +
6. Cheorghe Gheorghiu Dej	1901	Urban Mold.	Rom.	Worker	Worker[a]	Prewar Elem.	...	1930	W-R	Jail[b]	1932	1945	123 +++
7. Theodor Iordachescu	a	...	...	...	...	Prewar Univ.	...	...	Int-R	...	...	...	1 +
8. Vasile Luca	1898	Rural Trans.	Hung.**	Peasant	Worker[a]	b	...	1921	W-R[c]	USSR	1945	1948	1234 ++++
9. Alexandru Moghioros	1914	Urban Trans.	Hung.**	Peasant	Worker[a]	Prewar Gym.[b]	...	1929	St-R	Jail	1948	1948	1234 ++++
10. Ana Pauker	1893	Rural Mold.	Rom.**	Clergy[a]	Teacher	Prewar IncUniv.	Medicine[b]	1921	St-R[c]	USSR	1945	1945	1 +
11. Lothar Radaceanu	1899	Urban Bukov.	Germ.**	...	NonCommunist Politician	Prewar Univ.	...	1948	Social Dem.	Home	1948	1948	1 +
12. Gheorghe Vasilichi*	1902	Wall.	Rom.**	Peasant	Worker[a]	...	...	1933	W-R	Fran.	1945	1945	1 +
13. Stefan Voitec	1900	...	Rom.	...	NonCommunist Politician	Prewar Univ.	Engin.	1948	Social Dem.	Home	1948	1948	123456 +xx+++
14. Mihai Moraru	...	...	...	...	...	...	...	...	...	...	...	...	1 x
15. Iosif Ranghet	1904	Banat	Hung.**	...	...	...	...	1930	...	...	1945	1948	1 x
16. Chivu Stoica	1900	Rural Wall.	Rom.	Peasant	Worker[a]	Prewar Elem.	Party School	1931	W-R	Jail	1945	1948	12345 x++++
17. Vasile Vaida	...	Urban Mold.	...	...	...	...	...	...	...	...	1948	1948	1 x
18. Tanase Zaharia	1891	Urban Mold.	Rom.	...	Worker	...	...	a	W-R	...	1948	1948	1 x
19. Petre Borila*	1906	Rural Bess.	Bulg.	Worker	Worker	Prewar High.	Military	1924	W-R	USSR	1948	1952	234 +++
20. Nicolae Ceausescu	1918	Rural Wall.	Rom.	Peasant	Worker[a]	...	Party School[b]	1936	W-R	Jail	1945	1954	23456 +++++
21. Alexandru Draghici	1913	Urban Mold.	Rom.	Peasant	Worker[a]	Prewar Elem.	...	1934	W-R	Jail	1954	1954	234 +++

*Participant in Spanish Civil War
**Jewish Extraction

Exec. Com. (or Presid.) Dates:

No. 1: Feb., 1948   No. 4: July, 1965
No. 2: Dec., 1955   No. 5: Aug., 1969
No. 3: June, 1960   No. 6: Dec., 1974

+ Full Member
x Candidate Member

TABLE F-7 (CONTINUED)

	1 Birth Date	2 Birth Place	3 Ethnicity	4 Status of Father	5 Status Prior to Party Work	6 Formal Educ.	7 Advanced Training	8 Party Mbr.	9 Revol. Type	10 WW II	11 CC Mbr.	12 EC Mbr.	Exec. Com. & Status
22. Constantin Pirvulescu	1895	Rural Wall.	Rom.	Worker	Worker[a]	Prewar IncGym.	...	1921	W-R	USSR	1929[b]	1952	23 ++
23. Dumitru Coliu	1907	Dobr.	Bulg.	...	...	Prewar Trade[a]	...	1930	b	Jail	1945	1952	234 xxx
24. Leonte Rautu	1910	Rural Bess.	Russ.**	Middle Class	Student[a]	Prewar Univ.	...	1931	St-R[b]	Illeg.	1948	1955	23456 xx+++
25. Leontin Salajan	1913	Urban Banat	Hung.	...	Worker[a]	...	Military[b]	c	W-R	USSR	1945	1955	234 xx+
26. Ion Maurer	1902	Cap. Wall.	a	Middle Class[b]	Middle Class[c]	Prewar Univ.	Law	1936	Int-R	Illeg.	1945	1960	345 +++
27. Alexandru Birladeanu	1911	Urban Mold.	...**	Middle Class[a]	...	Prewar Univ.[b]	Engin.	1938	c	USSR	1955	1962	4 +
28. Constantin Dragan	1922	Rural Mold.	Rom.[a]	...	...	...	Party School[b]	1945	NRE[c]	...	1960	1965	45 ++
29. Paul Niculescu-Mizel	1923	Urban Wall.	Rom.	Worker[a]	Student	Prewar High.[b]	Commerce	1945	NRE	Home	1955	1965	456 +++
30. Gheorghe Radulescu	1914	Cap. Wall.	Rom.	Small Merchant[a]	Student	Prewar High.[b]	Military Planning[c]	1933	St-R	USSR	1960	1965	456 +++
31. Maxim Berghianu	1925	Urban Wall.	...	...	...	a	...	...	...	...	1955	1965	45 x+
32. Petre Blajovici	1922	Rural Trans.	Serb	...	...	...	Party School[a]	1947	NRE[b]	...	1960	1965	45 xx
33. Iosif Banc	a	...	b	...	...	...	...	...	...	...	1955	1965	456 xxx
34. Florian Danalache	1915	Cap. Wall.	a	Worker	...	Prewar Elem.	Party School[b]	1944	NRE	...	1955	1965	45 x+
35. Janos Fazekas	1926	Urban Trans.	Hung.**	...	...	...	...	1946	...	...	1954	1965	456 x++
36. Mihai Gere	1919	Urban Banat	Hung.**	Worker	...	Prewar Gym.	Party School	1940	...	...	1965	1965	456 xxx
37. Petre Lupu	1920	Urban Mold.	Rom.**	...	...	...	Party School[a]	1936	...	Jail	1952	1965	456 x++
38. Manea Manescu	1916	Urban Wall.	Rom.	a	State Official[b]	Prewar Univ.	Party School[c]	1945	NRE	...	1960	1965	456 x++
39. Ilie Verdet	1925	Rural Mold.	Rom.	...	...	...	Party School[a]	1945	NRE[b]	Jail	1955	1965	456 x++
40. Vasile Vilcu	1910	Rural Dobr.	Bulg.	...	...	...	Party School[a]	1929	...	Jail	1958	1965	456 x++
41. Emil Draganescu	1919	Urban Mold.	Rom.	...	State Official[a]	Prewar Univ.[b]	Engin.	1946	NRE	...	1965	1969	56 ++
42. Gheorghe Pana	1927	Rural Wall.	Rom.	...	Worker	...	Party School[a]	1947	Po-W	...	1969	1969	56 ++

*Participant in Spanish Civil War
**Jewish Extraction

Exec. Com. (or Presid.) Dates:

No. 1: Feb., 1948
No. 2: Dec., 1955
No. 3: June, 1960
No. 4: July, 1965
No. 5: Aug., 1969
No. 6: Dec., 1974

+ Full Member
x Candidate Member

TABLE F-7 (CONTINUED)

	1 Birth Date	2 Birth Place	3 Ethnicity	4 Status of Father	5 Status Prior to Party Work	6 Formal Educ.	7 Advanced Training	8 Party Mbr.	9 Revol. Type	10 WW II	11 CC Mbr.	12 EC Mbr.	Exec. Com. & Status
43. Dumitru Petrescu	1906	Cap. Wall.	Rom.	Worker	Worker[a]	...	...	1921	W-R	USSR	1945	...	5 +
44. Dumitru Popescu	1928	Urban Wall.	Rom.	Peasant	...	...	Party School[a]	1953	Po-W	...	1965	1968	56 ++
45. Virgil Trofin	1926	Rural Mold.	Russ.[a]	...	...	...	Party School[b]	1945	...	...	1955	1967	56 ++
46. Miu Dobrescu	...	Mold.	Rom.	...	...	...	...	...	...	...	1965	1969	56 xx
47. Aurel Duca	1920	...	Rom.	...	...	...	...	1960	...	...	1960	1969	5 x
48. Ion Iliescu	1930	Wall.	Rom.	Worker	Student	High.[a]	Engin.	1953	Po-W	...	1965	1969	56 xx
49. Ion Ionita	1924	Rural Wall.	Rom.	...	State Official[a]	Postwar High.[b]	Military	1945	Po-W	...	1955	1969	56 xx
50. Carol Kiraly	...	...	Hung.	...	...	...	...	...	...	...	1969	1969	5 x
51. Vasile Patilinet	...	Trans.	Rom.	Worker[a]	Worker[b]	...	...	...	...	...	1955	1969	56 xx
52. Dumitru Popa	1925	Cap. Wall.	Rom.	...	...	...	Party School[a]	...	...	...	1965	1966	5 x
53. Ion Stanescu	1929	Cap. Wall.	Rom.	...	...	...	...	...	Po-W	...	1965	1969	5 x
54. Stefan Andrei	1931	Wall.	Rom.	...	...	...	Engin.	...	...	...	1969	1974	6 +
55. Gheorghe Oprea	...	...	Rom.	...	...	...	...	...	...	...	1965	1974	6 +
56. Ion Patan	1926	Rural Wall.	Rom.	Peasant	...	a	Party School[b]	...	Po-W	...	1965	1972	6 +
57. Emil Bobu	...	...	Rom.	...	...	...	...	...	...	...	1960	1974	6 +
58. Cornel Burtica	1931	...	Rom.	...	...	Postwar Univ.[a]	...	...	Po-W	...	1969	1972	6 +
59. Elena Ceausescu	...	...	Rom.	Small Merchant[a]	...	Postwar Univ.[b]	Chem.	...	...	...	1972	1973	6 +
60. Gheorghe Cioara	1924	...	Rom.	...	...	High.[a]	Engin.	...	...	...	1960	1972	6 +
61. Lina Ciobanu	1929	...	Rom.	...	...	...	...	...	...	...	1965	1974	6 +
62. Iosif Uglar	...	...	Rom.	...	...	...	...	...	...	...	1965	1971	6 +
63. Mihai Dalea	1917	...	Rom.	...	...	...	...	...	...	...	...	1970	6 x

*Participant in Spanish Civil War
**Jewish Extraction

Exec Com. (or Presid.) Dates:
No. 1: Feb., 1948   No. 4: July, 1965
No. 2: Dec., 1955   No. 5: Aug., 1969
No. 3: June, 1960   No. 6: Dec., 1974

+ Full Member
x Candidate Member

TABLE F-7 (CONTINUED)

	1 Birth Date	2 Birth Place	3 Ethnicity	4 Status of Father	5 Status Prior to Party Work	6 Formal Educ.	7 Advanced Training	8 Party Mbr.	9 Revol. Type	10 WW II	11 CC Mbr.	12 EC Mbr.	Exec. Com. & Status
64. Nicolae Giosan	1921	...	Rom.	...	...	Prewar Univ.	Agric.	...	...	...	1955	1974	6 x
65. Mihai Telescu	...	...	Rom.	...	...	...	...	...	...	...	1969	1971	6 x
66. Ion Ursu	...	...	Rom.	...	...	...	...	...	...	...	1969	1974	6 x
67. Richard Winter	...	...	Germ.	...	...	...	...	...	...	...	1965	1971	6 x

*Participant in Spanish Civil War

**Jewish Extraction

Exec. Com. (or Presid.) Dates:

No. 1: Feb., 1948
No. 2: Dec., 1955
No. 3: June, 1960
No. 4: July, 1965
No. 5: Aug., 1969
No. 6: Dec., 1974

+ Full Member
x Candidate Member

General Remarks on Table: Executive Committee members included in politburos from December, 1964 to December, 1974. In coding revolutionary type (Column 9), membership in the Rumanian Social Democratic Party prior to 1921 has been disregarded.

Abbreviations Used in This Table:

1. Ban. — Banat
2. Bess. — Bessarabia
3. Bukov. — Bukovina
4. Bulg. — Bulgarian
5. Cap. — Capital
6. Chem. — Chemistry
7. Dobr. — Dobrudja
8. Econ. — Economics
9. Elem. — Elementary
10. Engin. — Engineering
11. Germ. — German
12. Gym. — Gymnasium
13. Hung. — Hungarian
14. Illeg. — Illegal
15. Inc. — Incomplete
16. Int-R — Intellectual Revolutionary
17. Mold. — Moldavia
18. NRE — No Revolutionary Experience
19. Po-W — Postwar
20. Rom. — Romanian
21. Russ. — Russian
22. Social Dem. — Social Democrat
23. St-R — Student Revolutionary
24. Trans. — Transylvania
25. Wall. — Wallachia
26. W-R — Worker Revolutionary
27. Ukr. — Ukrainian
28. Univ. — University

For further explanation of these terms, see the introduction to this section.

Notes: Gheorghe Apostol: a. Railway vocational school in Galati. Emil Bodnaras: a. Studied law at the University of Iasi, then completed military institute, 1930. b. Fits none of revolutionary types; might be called "Military Revolutionary." Miron Constantinescu: a. PhD in economics, University of Bucharest. Teohari Georgescu: a. Poor tradesman. b. Printer. c. Jail, 1933-1944. Theodor Iordachescu: a. 1890s. Gheorghe Gheorghiu Dej: a. Railway worker. b. Jail, 1933-1944. Vasile Luca: a. Locksmith. b. Data lacking but probably not above elementary level; was apprentice locksmith after leaving school. c. Coding disregards membership in Social Democratic Party prior to 1921. Alexandru Moghioros: a. Locksmith. b. Conflicting data--gymnasium complete or incomplete. Ana Pauker: a. Father a rabbi. b. Studied medicine for two years. c. Coding disregards membership in Social Democratic Party prior to 1921. Gheorghe Vasilichi: a. Railway worker. Chivu Stoica: a. Railway worker. Tanase Zaharia: a. Joined party prior to WWII. Petre Borila: a. No formal education until receiving military training at the Frunze Military Academy, USSR. Nicolae Ceausescu: a. Railway worker. b. Academy of Economic Studies, Bucharest. Alexandru Draghici: (cont'd.)

312

TABLE F-7 (CONCLUDED)

a. Railway worker. Constantin Pirvulescu: a. Iron worker. b. Member of Central Committee, 1929-1934 and 1945-1960. Dumitru Coliu: a. Attended trade school for saddle makers. b. Insufficient data to determine revolutionary type, but probably Worker Revolutionary (W-R). Leonte Rautu: a. Based on assumption that R. studied at a university in the early 1930's. b. Based on assumption that R. was a student when joining party. Leontin Salajan: a. Locksmith. b. USSR, military institute incomplete. c. Conflicting data: 1930, 1938 or 1939. Ion Maurer: a. Of mixed national origin; mother a Jew from Alsace, nationality of father not known. b. Teacher. c. Lawyer. Alexandru Birladeanu: a. Teacher. b. Degree in electrical engineering at Iasi University, completed commercial academy in USSR, 1944. c. Either Student Revolutionary (St-R) or Intellectual-Revolutionary (Int-R). Constantin Dragan: a. Gypsy. b. Academy of Economic Studies, Bucharest. c. Coding based on assumption that no postwar higher education. Paul Niculescu-Mizel: a. Parents were workers, helped found Romanian CP. b. Graduate of Academy of Higher Commercial and Industrial Sciences, Bucharest, 1944. Gheorghe Radulescu: a. Father owned small restaurant. b. Graduate of Academy of Higher Commercial and Industrial Sciences, Bucharest. c. Completed military institute, USSR, 1941, and received PhD in economics, Tashkent Planning Institute, prior to end of WWII. Maxim Berghianu: a. Studied at Economic Sciences and Planning Institute, Bucharest, dates and level of education completed not known. Petre Blajovici: a. Academy of Economic Studies, Bucharest. b. Coding based on assumption that no postwar higher education. Iosif Banc: a. Around 1921. b. Believed to be of Romanian nationality, notwithstanding German-sounding name. Florian Danalache: a. Nationality not established; believed to be Romanian, also part Gypsy. b. Academy of Economic Studies, Bucharest. Petre Lupu: a. Studied at Academy of Political and Social Sciences, date and level of education received not known. Manea Manescu: a. Father was member of Executive Committee of RCP in 1965. b. Minister of Finance before becoming involved in politics full-time as member of Executive Committee of RCP. c. Studied economics in party schools after war, then professor of economics. Ilie Verdet: a. Academy of Economic Studies. b. Coding based on assumption that no postwar higher education. Vasile Vilcu: a. Attended Stefan Gheorghiu Academy--date, level of education received not known. Emil Draganescu: a. Deputy Prime Minister before becoming involved in politics full-time in 1969 as member of the Executive Committee of the RCP. b. Polytechnical institute, Bucharest. Gheorghe Pana: a. Academy of Economic Studies, Bucharest. Dumitru Petrescu: a. Locksmith. Dumitru Popescu: a. Academy of Economic Studies, Bucharest. Virgil Trofin: a. Lippovan. b. Academy of Economic Studies, Bucharest. Ion Iliescu: a. Studied at polytechnical institute, Bucharest, and polytechnical institute, Moscow. No information on dates or whether studies completed at either institution. Ion Ionita: a. Minister of Defense in 1969 at time of becoming involved in full-time political activity as member of the Executive Committee of the RCP. b. Romanian military academy and war college, no dates available but assumed postwar. Vasile Patilinet: a. Father a miner. b. Miner. Dumitru Popa: a. Academy of Economic Studies, Bucharest. Ion Patan: a. Said to have received university education before or during WWII. b. Academy of Economic Studies, Bucharest. Elena Ceausescu: a. Father an innkeeper. Gheorghe Cioara: a Electrical engineer; from 1950 to 1956, university lecturer. b. Degree in chemistry from the University of Iasi. Date and place of receiving higher education not known.

TABLE F-8   BACKGROUND OF PARTY LEADERS: USSR, 1917-1939

	1 Birth Date	2 Birth Place	3 Ethnicity	4 Status of Father	5 Status Prior to Party Work	6 Formal Educ.	7 Advanced Training	8 Party Mbr.	9 Revol. Type	10 WW II	11 CC Mbr.	12 EC Mbr.	Exec. Com. & Status
1. A. S. Bubnov	1883	Urban RSFSR	Russ.	...	Student	Prewar IncHigh[a]	...	1903	St-R		1917	1917	1 +
2. L. B. Kamenev	1883	Cap. RSFSR	Jew	Middle Class	Student	Prewar IncUniv.	...	1903	St-R		1917	1917	1234 +++x
3. V. I. Lenin	1870	Urban RSFSR	Russ.	Middle Class	Student	Prewar IncUniv.	Law	1903	St-R		1912	1917	123 +++
4. G. Y. Sokolnikov	1888	Urban Ukr.	Jew	Middle Class	Student	Prewar Univ.	Law	1905	St-R		1917	1917	1 +
5. J. V. Stalin	1879	Rural Georg.	Georg.	Worker[a]	Student	Prewar IncSec[b]	...	1903	St-R		1912	1912	12345678 ++++++++
6. L. D. Trotsky	1879	Rural Ukr.	Jew	Peasant[a]	Student	Prewar IncHigh	...	1917	St-R		1917	1917	1234 +++
7. G. Y. Zinoviev	1883	Urban Ukr.	Russ.	Farmer[a]	Student	Prewar IncUniv.	...	1903	St-R		1912	1917	1234 +xx+
8. N. N. Krestinsky	1883	Urban BeloR.	Russ.	Teacher	Student	Prewar Univ.	Law	1905	St-R		1917	1919	2 +
9. N. I. Bukharin	1888	Cap. RSFSR	Russ.	Teacher	Student	Prewar IncUniv.	...	1906	St-R		1917	1918	2345 x+++
10. M. I. Kalinin	1875	Rural RSFSR	Russ.	Peasant	Worker	Prewar Elem.	...	1906	W-R		1919	1919	2345678 xx+++++
11. Y. A. Preobrazhensky	1886	Urban RSFSR	Russ.	Clergy	Student	Prewar Gym.	...	1905	St-R		1917	1920	3 +
12. L. P. Serebryakov	1890	Urban RSFSR	Russ.	Worker	Worker	Prewar Elem.	...	1905	W-R		1919	1920	3 +
13. V. M. Molotov	1890	Rural RSFSR	Russ.	Small Merchant	Student	Prewar IncHigh[a]	Technical	1906	St-R		1920	1921	45678 +++++
14. A. I. Rykov	1881	Urban RSFSR	Russ.	Peasant	Student	Prewar IncUniv.[a]	...	1903	St-R		1917	b	456 +++
15. M. P. Tomsky	1880	Urban RSFSR[a]	Russ.	Worker	Worker	Prewar Elem.	...	1904	W-R		1919	1922	45 ++
16. K. Y. Voroshilov	1881	Rural Ukr.	Russ.	Worker	Worker	Prewar Elem.	...	1903	W-R		1921	1925	45678 +++++
17. F. E. Dzerzhinsky	1877	Rural Pol.	Pole	Landowner	Student	Prewar Gym.	...	1917	St-R		1917	1924	4 x
18. G. I. Petrovsky	1878	Urban Ukr.	Russ.	Worker	Worker		...	1903[a]	W-R		1920	1925	4567 xxxx
19. Y. E. Rudzutak	1887	Rural Lat.	Latvian	Poor Peasant	Worker		...	1905	W-R		1920	1923	4567 x+++x
20. N. A. Uglanov	1886	Urban RSFSR	Russ.	Peasant	Worker		...	1907	W-R		1921	1925	45 xx
21. V. V. Kuybyshev	1888	Urban RSFSR	Russ.	Military[a]	Student	Prewar IncHigh[b]	c	1904	St-R		1921	1925	567 +++
22. A. A. Andreyev	1895	Rural BeloR.	Russ.	Worker	Worker	Prewar Elem.	...	1914	W-R		1920	1926	5678 xx++

Exec. Com. Dates:

No. 1: Oct., 1917
No. 2: March, 1919
No. 3: March, 1920
No. 4: Dec., 1925
No. 5: Dec., 1927
No. 6: July, 1930
No. 7: Jan., 1934
No. 8: March, 1939

+ Full Member
x Candidate Member

TABLE F-8 (CONTINUED)

	1 Birth Date	2 Birth Place	3 Ethnicity	4 Status of Father	5 Status Prior to Party Work	6 Formal Educ.	7 Advanced Training	8 Party Mbr.	9 Revol. Type	10 WW II	11 CC Mbr.	12 EC Mbr.	Exec. Com. & Status
23. V. Y. Chubar	1891	Rural Ukr.	Ukr.	Poor Peasant	Student	Prewar High.[a]	Technical	1907	St-R		1921	1927	567 xxx
24. L. M. Kaganovich	1893	Rural Ukr.	Jew	Poor Family	Worker	Prewar Elem.	...	1911	W-R		1923	1926	5678 x+++
25. S. M. Kirov	1886	Rural RSFSR	Russ.	Poor Family[a]	Student	Prewar High.[b]	Engin.	1905	St-R		1921	1926	567 x++
26. S. V. Kossior	1889	Rural Pol.	Pol.[a]	Worker	Worker	Prewar Elem.		1907	W-R		1923	1927	567 x++
27. A. I. Mikoyan	1895	Rural Georg.	Arm.	Worker	Student	Prewar Second.[a]	...	1915	St-R		1922	1926	5678 xxx+
28. S. I. Syrtsov	1893	Rural Ukr.	Russ.	White Collar[a]	Student	Prewar High.[b]	Technical	1913	St-R		1924	1929	6 x
29. G. K. Ordzhonikidze	1886	Rural Georg.	Georg.	Upper Class[c]	Student	Prewar Second.[b]	...	1903	St-R		1912	1926	7 +
30. P. P. Postyshev	1888	Ukr.	Ukr.	Worker	Worker	[a]	...	1904	W-R		1925	1934	7 x
31. N. S. Khrushchev	1894	Rural RSFSR	Russ.	Peasant[a]	Worker	Postwar Basic[b]	Technical[c]	1918	W-R		1934	1938	8 +
32. A. A. Zhdanov	1896	Urban Ukr.	Russ.	Teacher[a]	...	...	...	1913	...		1924	1935	8 +
33. L. P. Beria	1899	Rural Georg.	Georg.	Peasant	Student	Postwar High.[a]	Technical	1917	St-R[b]		1934	1939	8 x
34. N. M. Shvernik	1888	Urban RSFSR[a]	Russ.	Worker	Worker	Prewar Elem.	...	1905	W-R		1925	1939	8 x

Exec. Com. Dates:

No.1: Oct., 1917	No.4: Dec., 1917	No.7: Jan., 1934
No.2: March, 1919	No.5: Dec., 1927	No.8: March, 1939
No.3: March, 1920	No.6: Dec., 1930	

+ Full Member
x Candidate Member

General Remarks on Table: In Column 2, "Capital" (Cap.) refers only to Moscow; republic and state boundaries are those of the interwar period. "Prewar" in Column 6 refers to pre-World War I, and includes all persons born in 1899 (18 in 1917) or younger, and all persons born between 1896 and 1898 if receiving a higher education after World War I. (For further explanation of Column 9, see introductory remarks to this section.) Party membership in Column 8 is given as 1903 for those persons associated with the Bolsheviks at the time of the split of the RSDLP into Bolshevik and Menshavik factions. In Column 6, the following rules are adhered to in respect to levels of education: (i) seminaries are classified as secondary education; (ii) the following institutions are classified as higher education—Moscow Agricultural Institute; Medical Academy, St. Petersburg; Kazan Mechanical Engineering College; Petrograd Polytechnical Institute; "Technical School" (Beria); and "Technical College" (Chubar).

Abbreviations Used in This Table:

1. Arm.	Armenian	8. High.	Higher	14. Russ.	Russian
2. BeloR.	Belorussia	9. IncGym.	Incomplete Gymnasium	15. Second.	Secondary
3. Cap.	Capital	10. IncHigh.	Incomplete Higher	16. SpecSec.	Specialized Secondary
4. Elem.	Elementary	11. IncSec.	Incomplete Secondary	17. St-R	Student Revolutionary
5. Engin.	Engineering	12. Lat.	Latvia	18. Ukr.	Ukraine
6. Georg.	Georgia	13. Pol.	Poland	19. Univ.	University
7. Gym.	Gymnasium			20. W-R	Worker Revolutionary

For further explanation of these terms, see the introduction to this section.

TABLE F-8   (CONCLUDED)

Notes: A.S. Bubnov: a. Expelled from Moscow Agricultural Institute for revolutionary activities.   J. V. Stalin:
a. Father a cobbler.   b. Expelled from Tiflis Orthodox Theological Seminary.   L. D. Trotsky: a. Father
a well-to-do farmer.   G. Y. Zinoviev: a. Father owned dairy farm.   V. M. Molotov: a. Studied briefly at St.
Petersburg Polytechnic Institute.   A. I. Rykov: a. Studied law before being expelled from Kazan University.
b. Date of joining Politburo usually given as 1919, but not included in lists of Politburo members published
for that date.   M. P. Tomsky: a. Born, St. Petersburg.   G. I. Petrovsky: a. Date of joining party assumed
on basis of early association with Bolsheviks.   V. V. Kuybyshev: a. Father an officer.   b. Medical Academy,
St. Petersburg.   c. Commenced but did not complete military training.   V. Y. Chubar: a. Graduate of technical
college.   S. M. Kirov: a. Raised in orphanage.   b. Graduated from Kazan Mechanical Engineering College.
S. V. Kossior: a. Father was Polish laborer.   A. I. Mikoyan: a. Completed theological seminary.   S. I. Syrtsov:
a. Father a clerical worker.   b. Studied at Petrograd Polytechnical Institute, 1912-1916.   G.K. Ordzonikidze:
a. Father a minor nobleman.   b. Studied at Medical Orderlies' School.   P. P. Postyshev: a. Data lacking, but
probably not educated above the trade school level.   N. S. Khrushchev: a. Father a wealthy peasant and blacksmith.   b. Completed workers' university, here considered equivalent of 7-8 year basic education.   c. Studied
at Moscow Industrial Academy, part-time, never completed studies.   A. A. Zhdanov: a. School inspector.   L. P.
Beria: a. Completed technical college, 1919.   b. Could also be classified postwar.   N. M. Shvernik: a. Born,
St. Petersburg.

316

TABLE F-9 BACKGROUND OF PARTY LEADERS: USSR AFTER WORLD WAR II

	1 Birth Date	2 Birth Place	3 Ethnicity	4 Status of Father	5 Status Prior to Party Work	6 Formal Educ.	7 Advanced Training	8 Party Mbr.	9 Revol. Type	10 WW II	11 CC Mbr.	12 EC Mbr.	Exec. Com. & Status
1. L. P. Beria	1899	Rural Georg.	Georg.	Peasant	Student	Prewar High.	Technical	1917	St-R		1934	1939	12 ++
2. N. A. Bulganin	1895	Urban RSFSR	Russ.	White Collar[a]	Student	Prewar SpecSec.	...	1917	St-R		1934	1946	1234 ++++
3. L. M. Kaganovich	1893	Urban Ukr.	Jew	Poor Family	Worker	Prewar Elem.	...	1911	W-R		1923	1926	123 +++
4. N. S. Khrushchev	1894	Rural RSFSR	Russ.	Peasant[a]	Worker	Prewar Basic[c]	Technical[c]	1918	W-R		1934	1938	12345 +++++
5. G. M. Malenkov	1902	Urban RSFSR	Russ.	Middle Class[a]	Military[b]	Prewar High.	Technical	1920	Po-W		1939	1941	123 +++
6. A. I. Mikoyan	1895	Rural Georg.	Arm.	Worker	Student	Prewar Second[a]	...	1915	St-R		1922	1926	1234 ++++
7. L. G. Melnikov	1906	...	Russ.	Worker	Worker[a]	Prewar High.[b]	Technical	c	Po-W		1952	1952	12 +x
8. V. M. Molotov	1890	Rural RSFSR	Russ.	Small Merchant	Student	Prewar IncHigh.[a]	Technical	1906	St-R		1916	1921	123 +++
9. M. G. Pervukhin	1904	RSFSR	Russ.	Worker[a]	State Official[b]	Prewar High.[c]	Engin.	1919	Po-W		1939	1952	1234 +++x
10. P. K. Ponomarenko	1902	RSFSR	Ukr.	Peasant	Worker[a]	Prewar High.[b]	Engin.	1925	Po-W		1939	1952	12 +x
11. M. Z. Saburov	1900	Urban Ukr.	Russ.	Worker	Worker[a]	Prewar High.[b]	Engin.[c]	1920	Po-W		1952	1952	123 +++
12. N. M. Shvernik	1888	Urban RSFSR[a]	Russ.	Worker	Worker	Prewar Elem.	...	1905	W-R		1925	1939	12345 +xx++
13. J. V. Stalin	1879	Rural Georg.	Georg.	Worker[a]	Student	Prewar IncSec.[b]	...	1903	St-R		1912	1917	1 +
14. K. Y. Voroshilov	1881	Rural Ukr.	Russ.	...	Worker	Prewar Elem.	...	1903	W-R		1921	1925	234 +++
15. M. D. Bagirov	1896	Urban Azer.	Azer.	...	Teacher	Prewar[a]	...	1917	Int-R		1934	1953	2 x
16. M. A. Suslov	1902	Rural RSFSR	Russ.	Peasant	Professor[a]	Prewar High.	Party School[b]	1921	Po-W		1941	1952	345678 +++++
17. A. I. Kirichenko	1908	Rural Ukr.	Ukr.	Worker[a]	State Official[b]	Prewar High.[c]	Engin.	1930	Po-W		1952	1955	34 ++
18. L. I. Brezhnev	1906	Urban Ukr.	Russ.	Worker	State Official[a]	Prewar High.[b]	Engin.	1931	Po-W		1952	1952	345678 x++++
19. Y. A. Furtseva	1910	Rural RSFSR	Russ.	Worker	Worker[a]	Prewar High.[b]	Engin.[c]	1930	Po-W		1952	1956	34 x+
20. N. A. Mukhitdinov	1917	Urban Uzbek.	Uzbek.	Peasant	Student[a]	Prewar SpecSec.	Admin.[b]	1942	Po-W		1952	1956	3 x
21. D. T. Shepilov	1905	Urban Turk.	Russ.	...	Professor[a]	Prewar Univ.[b]	Agric.	1926	Po-W		1952	1956	3 x

Exec. Com. (or Presid.) Dates:

No. 1: Oct., 1952   No. 4: Feb., 1957   No. 7: April, 1971
No. 2: 7 March, 1953   No. 5: Oct., 1961   No. 8: March, 1976
No. 3: Feb., 1956   No. 6: March, 1966

+ Full Member
x Candidate Member

317

TABLE F-9 (CONTINUED)

	1 Birth Date	2 Birth Place	3 Ethnicity	4 Status of Father	5 Status Prior to Party Work	6 Formal Educ.	7 Advanced Training	8 Party Mbr.	9 Revol. Type	10 WW II	11 CC Mbr.	12 EC Mbr.	Exec. Com. & Status
22. G. K. Zhukov	1896	Rural RSFSR	Russ.	Peasant	State Official[a]	Prewar High.[b]	Military	1919	Po-W		1952	1956	34 x+
23. A. B. Aristov	1903	Rural RSFSR	Russ.	a	Worker[b]	Prewar High.[c]	Technical	1921	Po-W		1952	1957	4 +
24. N. I. Belyayev	1903	Rural RSFSR	Russ.	Peasant	Student[a]	Prewar High.[b]	Agric.	1921	Po-W		1952	1957	4 +
25. N. G. Ignatov	1901	Rural RSFSR	Russ.	Worker	Security Official[a]	...	...	1924	Po-W		1939	1952	4 +
26. F. R. Kozlov	1908	Rural RSFSR	Russ.	Peasant	Engineer[a]	Prewar High.[b]	Technical	1926	Po-W		1952	1957	45 ++
27. O. V. Kuusinen	1881	...	Finnish	Worker	Student	Prewar Univ.	Party School[a]	1905	St-R		1941	1952	45 ++
28. Y. E. Kalnberzin	1893	Urban Lat.	Latvian	Worker	Worker	...	Party School[a]	1917	W-R		1941	1957	4 x
29. A. P. Kirilenko	1906	Rural RSFSR	Russ.	Worker	Engineer[a]	Prewar High.[b]	Technical	1931	Po-W		1956	1957	4 678 x xxx
30. D. S. Korotchenko	1894	Rural Ukr.	Ukr.	Peasant	Worker	...	...	1918	W-R		1939	1952	4 x
31. A. N. Kosygin	1904	Urban RSFSR[a]	Russ.	Worker	State Official[b]	Prewar High.[c]	Technical	1927	Po-W		1939	1957 d	45678 x++++
32. K. T. Mazurov	1914	Rural BeloR.	BeloR.	Peasant	State Official[a]	Prewar SpecSec[c]	Party School[c]	1940	Po-W		1956	1957	45678 x++++
33. V. P. Mzhavanadze	1902	Urban Georg.	Georg.	Worker	Military[a]	Prewar High.[b]	Military	1927	Po-W		1956	1957	4567 x++++
34. P. N. Pospelov	1898	Rural RSFSR	Russ.	...	Student	Prewar SpecSec[a]	Party School[b]	1916	St-R		1939	1957	4 x
35. V. V. Grishin	1914	Urban RSFSR	Russ.	Worker	State Official[a]	Prewar SpecSec[b]	...	1938	Po-W		1952	1961	5678 xx++
36. D. A. Kunaev	1912	Urban Kazakh.	Kazakh.	White Collar[a]	State Official[b]	Prewar High.[c]	Engin.	1939	Po-W		1956	1959	5678 xx++
37. N. V. Podgorny	1903	Rural Ukr.	Ukr.	Worker	State Official[a]	Prewar High.[b]	Technical	1930	Po-W		1956	1958	5678 ++++
38. D. S. Polyansky	1917	Rural Ukr.	Ukr.	Peasant	Student[a]	Prewar High.[b]	Agric.[c]	1939	Po-W		1956	1958	567 +++
39. G. I. Voronov	1912	Rural RSFSR	Russ.	Teacher	...	Prewar High.[a]	Technical[b]	1931	Po-W		1952	1961	567 +++
40. S. R. Rashidov	1917	Rural Uzbek.	Uzbek.	Peasant	Newspaper Editor[a]	Prewar Univ.[b]	Party School[c]	1939	Po-W		1956	1961	5678 xxxx
41. V. V. Shcherbitsky	1918	Rural Ukr.	Ukr.	Worker	Military[a]	Prewar High.[b]	Technical	1941	Po-W		1961	1961	5678 xx++
42. A. Y. Pelshe	1899	Rural Lat.	Latvian	Peasant	...	...	Party School[a]	1915	W-R		1961	1966	678 +++
43. A. N. Shelepin	1918	Urban RSFSR	Russ.	a	Student[b]	Prewar High.[c]	...	1940	Po-W		1952	1964	67 ++

Exec. Com. (or Presid.) Dates:

No. 1: Oct., 1952   No. 4: Feb., 1957   No. 7: April, 1971
No. 2: 7 March, 1953   No. 5: Oct., 1961   No. 8: March, 1976
No. 3: Feb., 1956   No. 6: March, 1966

+ Full Member
x Candidate Member

318

TABLE F-9 (CONTINUED)

	1 Birth Date	2 Birth Place	3 Ethnicity	4 Status of Father	5 Status Prior to Party Work	6 Formal Educ.	7 Advanced Training	8 Party Mbr.	9 Revol. Type	10 WW II	11 CC Mbr.	12 EC Mbr.	Exec. Com. & Status
44. P. Y. Shelest	1908	Rural Ukr.	Ukr.	Peasant	Engineer[a]	...	Engin.[b]	1928	Po-W		1961	1963	67 ++
45. P. N. Demichev	1918	Rural RSFSR	Russ.	Worker	Teacher[a]	Prewar High.[b]	Technical[c]	1939	Po-W		1961	1964	678 xxx
46. P. M. Masherov	1918	Rural BeloR.	BeloR.	Peasant	Partisan[a]	Prewar SpecSec.[b]	...	1943	Po-W		1961	1966	678 xxx
47. D. F. Ustinov	1908	Urban RSFSR	Russ.	Worker	State Official[a]	Prewar High.[b]	Technical	1927	Po-W		1952	1965	678 xxx
48. F. D. Kulakov	1918	...	Russ.	Peasant	Manager[a]	...	Agric.[b]	1940	Po-W		1965	1971	78 ++
49. Y. V. Andropov	1914	RSFSR	Russ.	...	Student[a]	IncUniv.[b]	Party School[c]	1939	Po-W		1961	1967	78 x+
50. M. S. Solomentsev	1913	RSFSR	Russ.	Peasant	Director[a]	Prewar High.[b]	Technical	1940	Po-W		1961	1971	78 xx
51. A. A. Grechko	1903	Rural Ukr.	Ukr.	Peasant	Military[a]	Prewar High.[b]	Military	1928	Po-W		1961	1976	8 +
52. A. A. Gromyko	1909	Rural RSFSR	Russ.	Peasant	State Official[a]	Prewar High.[b]	...	1931	Po-W		1956	1976	8 +
53. G. V. Romanov	1923	RSFSR	Russ.	Peasant	State Official[a]	Postwar High.[a]	Engin.	1944	Po-W		1966	1973	8 +
54. G. A. Aliyev	1923	Azer.	Azer.	...	State Official[a]	Postwar Univ.	...	1945	Po-W		1971	1976	8 x
55. B. N. Ponomarev	1905	Rural RSFSR	Russ.	...	[a]	Prewar Univ.[b]	Party School[c]	1919	Po-W		1952	1972	8 x

Exec. Com. (or Presid.) Dates:

No.1: Oct., 1952   No.4: Feb., 1957   No.7: April, 1971
No.2: 7 March 1953   No.5: Oct., 1961   No.8: March, 1976
No.3: Feb., 1956   No.6: March, 1966

+ Full Member
x Candidate Member

General Remarks on Table: In Column 2, "Cap."(Capital) refers only to Moscow. State and republic boundaries are those of the inter-war period. "Prewar" in Column 6 refers to World War II. "Post-War" (Po-W) in Column 9 refers to World War I. (For explanation of term "Post-War" in Column 9, see general remarks following Table F-8.) In Column 6, technical institutes are classified as higher education if attended full-time (see notes for further details); pedagogical institutes are classified as specialized secondary education.

Abbreviations Used in This Table:

1. Admin.   Administration
2. Agric.   Agriculture
3. Arm.   Armenian
4. Azer.   Azerbaidzani
5. BeloR.   Belorussia, Belorussian
6. Elem.   Elementary
7. Engin.   Engineering
8. Georg.   Georgia, Georgian
9. High.   Higher
10. IncGym.   Incomplete Gymnasium
11. IncSec.   Incomplete Secondary
12. IncUniv.   Incomplete University
13. Lat.   Latvia
14. Po-W   Postwar
15. Russ.   Russia, Russian
16. Second.   Secondary
17. SpecSec.   Specialized Secondary
18. Ukr.   Ukraine, Ukrainian
19. Univ.   University
20. Uzbek.   Uzbekistan
21. W-R   Worker Revolutionary

For further explanation of these terms, see introduction to this section.

TABLE F-9   (CONTINUED)

Notes: N.A. Bulganin: a. Father an office worker. N.S. Khrushchev: a. Father wealthy peasant and blacksmith. b. Completed worker's university, here considered equivalent of 7-8 year basic education. c. Attended Moscow Industrial Academy part-time, never completed studies. G.M. Malenkov: a. Son of government official. b. Served in Red Army during civil war, then completed education after joining party. A.I. Mikoyan: a. Completed theological seminary. L.G. Melnikov: a. Was worker before becoming active full-time in politics in 1920 as local party official. b. Graduated Donetsk Industrial Institute, date not known. c. Date of joining party given as 1928 in several sources, but M. a party official by 1927. V.M. Molotov: a. Incomplete gymnasium, then studied briefly at St. Petersburg Polytechnical Institute. M.G. Pervukhin: a. Father a blacksmith. b. No full-time party or mass organization posts before joining Politburo in 1952; prior to this, Deputy Prime Minister. c. Degree in electrical engineering, 1929. P.K. Ponomarenko: a. Was a worker before becoming a party and Komsomol official for a brief period in the 1920s, then left party work until 1938, at which time, an engineer. b. Graduated, Moscow Institute of Transport Engineers, 1938. M.Z. Saburov: a. Foundry worker before becoming politically active full-time in early 1920s as Komsomol official. b. Graduated, Machine Building Institute 1931. c. Also attended party school (Sverdlov Communist University). N.M. Shvernik: a. Born, St. Petersburg. J.V. Stalin: a. Father a cobbler. b. Expelled from Tiflis Orthodox Theological Seminary. M.D. Bagirov: a. Completed pedagogical program for teachers in village schools. M.A. Suslov: a. No party or mass organization posts before becoming full-time Central Committee official in 1931; prior to this, professor at Moscow University. b. Institute of Red Professors. A.I. Kirichenko: a. Father a railroad worker. b. Director of studies at an agricultural technical school prior to becoming involved full-time in political activity in 1938 as party official in Ukrainian party apparatus. c. Graduated, Institute for Engineers and Mechanics of Socialist Agriculture, 1926. L.I. Brezhnev: a. Director of technical school and local government official in Dnepropetrovsk, 1938, at the time of becoming involved in full-time party work as oblast party official. b. Metallurgical Institute, 1935. Y.A. Furtseva: a. Worked as weaver before becoming involved full-time in political activity in 1930 as local party official. b. Institute of Fine Chemical Technology, 1942. c. Also graduate of Higher Party School. N.A. Mukhitdinov: a. Student, 1938, then military service, 1939-1946, at which time became involved in full-time political activity in Komsomol. b. Graduate of All Union Cooperative Institute by correspondence, 1938, while serving in military. D.T. Shepilov: a. Taught political economy at the Institute of Red Professors prior to becoming involved full-time in political work as head of the agricultural department of the CC. b. Law faculty, Moscow University and Agricultural Division of Institute of Red Professors, 1931-1933. G.K. Zhukov: a. Was Minister of Defense, 1956, prior to becoming involved in full-time political activity as politburo member. b. Frunze Military Academy, 1931. A.B. Aristov: a. Son of fisherman. b. Worker in fishing trade before becoming involved full-time in political activity as Komsomol official. c. Kalinin Polytechnical Institute, 1932. N.I. Belyayev: a. Student prior to becoming involved full-time in political activity in 1919 as Komsomol official. b. Moscow Agricultural Institute, 1925. N.G. Ignatov: a. Worked for secret police before becoming involved full-time in political activity in 1934 as local party official. F.R. Kozlov: a. Engineer in metallurgical plant before becoming involved full-time in political activity as party official in 1940. b. Graduated from industrial institute, 1936. Y.E. Kalnberzin: a. Institute of Red Professors. A.P. Kirilenko: a. Was design engineer in airplane factory before becoming involved full-time in political activity in 1938 as local party official. b. Aviation Institute, 1936. A.N. Kosygin: a. St. Petersburg. b. No full-time post in party or mass organizations before joining Politburo in 1946; prior to this, Deputy Chairman, Council of Ministers. c. Leningrad Textile Institute, 1936. d. Candidate Politburo member, 1946-1948, full member, 1948-1952. K.T. Mazurov: a. Was railway official before becoming involved full-time in political activity, 1939-1940, as local party functionary. b. Highway technicum graduate, 1933. c. Higher Party School, 1947. V.P. Mzhavanadze: a. Was in military before becoming involved full-time in political activity as political officer in army, 1933. b. Lenin Military Academy, 1937. P.N. Pospelov: a. Moscow Agricultural Academy, 1916. b. Institute of Red Professors, 1930. V.V. Grishin: a. Railroad official prior to becoming involved full-time in political activity in 1942 as party official. b. Moscow Technicum of Locomotive Traction, 1937. D.A. Kunaev: a. Father a clerical worker. b. No fulltime party or mass-organization posts before becoming First Party Secretary of Kazakh CP; prior to this, Chairman, Kazak Council of Ministers. c. Institute of Non-Ferrous Metals, 1936. N.V. Podgorny : a. No full-time party or mass organization post before becoming First Secretary of Kharkhov Oblast Committee; prior to this, member of Council of Ministers of Ukraine. b. Institute of Food Industry, 1931. D.S. Polyansky : a. Was student before becoming involved full-time in political activity in 1939 as Komsomol official in Ukraine. b. Graduate   (cont'd.)

320

of Kharkov Agricultural Institute, 1939. <u>c</u>. Also graduate of Higher Party School, 1942. <u>G.I. Voronov</u>: <u>a</u>. Kirov Industrial Institute, 1932-1936. <u>b</u>. Also graduate of Novosibirsk Institute of Marxism-Leninism, 1937. <u>S.R. Rashidov</u>: <u>a</u>. Editor of newspaper before becoming involved full-time in political activity as oblast party official. <u>b</u>. Graduate of Uzbek University, Samarkand, 1941. <u>c</u>. Higher Party School, dates not known. <u>V.V. Shcherbitsky</u> : <u>a</u>. Was student, then served in military, 1941-1946, before becoming involved in full-time political activity in period 1946-1948 as party official. <u>b</u>. Dnepropetrovsk Chemical Technical Institute, 1941. <u>A.Y. Pelshe</u>: <u>a</u>. Moscow Institute of Red Professors, 1931. <u>A.N. Shelepin</u>: <u>a</u>. Father a railway employee; sources disagree over whether worker or middle class. <u>b</u>. Was student before becoming involved full-time in political activity as political offier in the Soviet army in 1939. <u>c</u>. Moscow Institute of History, Philosophy and Literature, 1941. <u>P.Y. Shelest</u>: <u>a</u>. Engineer prior to becoming involved full-time in political activity in 1940 as party official. <u>b</u>. Graduated Mariupol Metallurgical Institute, 1935 (studied part-time). <u>P.N. Demichev</u>: <u>a</u>. Assistant at Mendeleev Institute of Chemical Technology prior to becoming engaged in full-time party work in 1945. <u>b</u>. Graduated from Mendeleev Institute of Chemical Technology, Moscow, 1944. <u>c</u>. Also graduate of Higher Party School, 1953. <u>P.M. Masherov</u>: <u>a</u>. Secondary school teacher, 1935-1941; joined resistance movement in Belorussia, 1941; engaged in full-time party work after WWII. <u>b</u>. Vitebsk Pedagogical Institute, 1939. <u>D.F. Ustinov</u>: <u>a</u>. No full-time party or mass organization work before entering Politburo in 1965; prior to this, First Deputy Chairman of the Council of Ministers. <u>b</u>. Leningrad Military Mechanical Institute, 1934. <u>F.D. Kulakov</u>: <u>a</u>. Section Manager, sugar refinery, before becoming involved full-time in party work in 1941. <u>b</u>. All-Union Agricultural Institute, degree by correspondence, 1957. <u>Y.V. Andropov</u>: <u>a</u>. Was student prior to becoming involved full-time in political activity in 1936 as Komsomol official. <u>b</u>. Petrozavodsk University, dates not known. <u>c</u>. Higher Party School. <u>M.S. Solomentsev</u>: <u>a</u>. Chief engineer, then director of factory before entering into full-time party work in 1954 as oblast party official. <u>b</u>. Graduated, Leningrad Polytechnical Institute, 1940. <u>A.A. Grechko</u>: <u>a</u>. No full-time party or mass organization work before joining Politburo in 1976; prior to this, Minister of Defense. <u>b</u>. Graduated, Frunze Military Academy, 1936. <u>A.A. Gromyko</u>: <u>a</u>. No full-time party or mass organization work before joining Politburo in 1976; prior to this, Minister of Foreign Affairs. <u>b</u>. Graduated, Minsk Institute of Agriculture, 1934, and Lenin Institute of Economy. <u>G.V. Romanov</u>: <u>a</u>. Graduated, Leningrad Shipbuilding Institute, 1953. <u>G.A. Aliyev</u>: <u>a</u>. No full-time party or mass organization work before joining the Politburo in 1976; prior to this, Chairman of the Council of Ministers, Azerbaidjan. <u>B.N. Ponomarev</u>: <u>a</u>. If official biography correct, entered party at age 14 and began full-time Komsomol and party work at age 15. <u>b</u>. Graduate of Moscow University, 1926. <u>c</u>. Graduate of Moscow Institute of Red Professors, 1932.

TABLE F-10 BACKGROUND OF PARTY LEADERS: YUGOSLAVIA, 1948-1974

	1 Birth Date	2 Birth Place	3 Ethnicity	4 Status of Father	5 Status Prior to Party Work	6 Formal Educ.	7 Advanced Training	8 Party Mbr.	9 Revol. Type	10 WW II	11 CC Mbr.	12 EC Mbr.	Politburo & Status
1. Josip Broz Tito	1892	Rural Croat.	Croat.	Poor Peasant	Skilled Worker	Prewar Elem.	...	1920	W-R	Resis.	1934	1934	123456 / +++++
2. Milovan Djilas	1911	Rural Mont.	Mont.	Peasant	Student	Prewar IncUniv.	...	1932	St-R	Resis.	1938	1940	12 / ++
3. Ivan Gosnjak*	1909	Rural Croat.	Croat.	Artisan[a]	Worker[b]	[c]	Military[d]	1933	W-R	Resis.	1945	1948	12345 / +++++
4. Edvard Kardelj	1910	Urban Slov.	Slovene	Worker[a]	Student	Prewar SpecSec.	[b]	1928	St-R	Resis.	1937	1938	1234567 9 / ++++++ +
5. Boris Kidric	1912	Urban Austr.	Slovene	Middle Class[a]	Student	Prewar IncUniv.	Science[b]	1928	St-R	Resis.	1935	1952	123 / +++
6. Franc Leskosek	1897	Urban Slov.	Slovene	Worker[a]	Skilled Worker[b]	Prewar Basic	...	1926	W-R	Resis.	...	1936	123 / +++
7. Blagoje Neskovic*	1907	Urban Serb.	Serb	...	Doctor	Prewar Univ.	Medicine	1935	Int-R	Resis.	1948	1948	12 / ++
8. Mosa Pijade	1890	Cap. Serb.	Serb**	...	Journalist	Prewar Univ.	...	1920	Int-R	Resis.	1940	1948	12 / ++
9. Aleksandar Rankovic	1909	Rural Serb.	Serb	Poor Peasant	Worker[a]	Prewar Elem.	...	1928	W-R	Resis.	1937	1937	1234 / +++
10. Vladimir Bakaric	1912	Rural Croat.	Croat	...	Student	Prewar Univ.	Law	1935	St-R	Resis.	1948	1952	1234567 9 / x+++++ +
11. Lazar Kolisevski	1914	Rural Maced.	Maced.	Poor Peasant	Skilled Worker[a]	Prewar Trade	...	1935	W-R	Resis.	1948	1952	12345 7 9 / +++++ + +
12. Djuro Pucar	1899	Rural B-H	Serb	Poor Peasant	Trade Union	Prewar Elem.	...	1922	W-R	Resis.	1940	1952	12345 / +++++
13. Svetozar Vukmanovic	1912	Rural Mont.	Mont.	...	Student	Prewar Univ.	Law	1935	St-R	Resis.	1948	1952	12345 / x++++
14. Djuro Salai	1889	Rural Croat.	Croat	...	Worker[a]	[b]	...	1919	W-R	Resis.	1948	1952	23 / ++
15. Blazo Jovanovic	1907	Rural Mont.	Mont.	...	Lawyer	Prewar Univ.	Law	1924	St-R	Resis.	1948	1954	345 / +++
16. Miha Marinko	1900	Urban Slov.	Slovene	Worker[a]	Worker[b]	...	Party School[c]	1924	W-R	Resis.	1948	1958	345 / +++
17. Petar Stambolic	1912	Rural Serb.	Serb.	...	Student	Prewar IncUniv.	Agric.	1935	St-R	Resis.	1948	1954	345 7 9 / +++ + +
18. Jovan Veselinov	1906	Rural Serb.	Serb	Poor Peasant	Worker[a]	Prewar Elem.	...	1926	W-R	Resis.	1948	1958	345 / +++
19. Veljko Vlahovic*	1914	Rural Mont.	Mont.	...	Student	Prewar Univ.	Engin.	1935	St-R	USSR	1948	1958	34567 9 / +++++ +
20. Krste Crvenkovski	1921	Urban Maced.	Maced.	...	Student	Prewar IncUniv.	Party School[a]	1939	St-R	Resis.	1952	1964	4567 / ++++
21. Boris Krajger	1914	Urban Slov.	Slovene	Middle Class[a]	Student	Prewar Univ.	Engin.	1934	St-R	Resis.	1948	1964	45 / ++
22. Cvijetin Mijatovic	1913	Rural B-H	Serb	Poor Peasant	Student	Prewar IncUniv.	...	1933	St-R	Resis.	1948	1964	4567 9 / +++ +

*Participant in Spanish Civil War
**Jewish Extraction

Exec. Com. (or Presid.) Dates:

No. 1: July, 1948   No. 4: Dec., 1964   No. 7: Mar., 1969
No. 2: Dec., 1952   No. 5: Oct., 1966   No. 8: May, 1974
No. 3: Apr., 1958   No. 6: Mar., 1969   No. 9: May, 1974

_____ Indicates Presidium

+ Full Member
x Candidate Mbr.

TABLE F-10 (CONTINUED)

	1 Birth Date	2 Birth Place	3 Ethnicity	4 Status of Father	5 Status Prior to Party Work	6 Formal Educ.	7 Advanced Training	8 Party Mbr.	9 Revol. Type	10 WW II	11 CC Mbr.	12 EC Mbr.	Exec. Com. & Status
23. Djoko Pajkovic	1917	Rural Mont.	Mont.	...	Student	Prewar Basic	...	1936	St-R	Resis.	1948	1964	45 ++
24. Mika Spiljak	1916	Rural Croat.	Croat.	...	Worker	...	...	1938	W-R	Resis.	1952	1964	45 9 ++ +
25. Mijalko Todorovic	1913	Rural Serb.	Serb	...	Student	Prewar Univ.[a]	Engin.[b]	1938	St-R	Resis.	1952	1964	4 67 + ++
26. Jakov Blazevic	1912	Rural Croat.	Croat	...	Student	Prewar Univ.	Law	1928	St-R	Resis.	1940	1966	5 7 + +
27. Savka Dabcevic	1923	Rural Croat.	Croat.	...	Professor	Postwar Univ.	Economics	1943	Po-W	Resis.	1964	1966	5 +
28. Ratomir Dugonjic	1916	Rural B-H	Serb	...	Student	Prewar Univ.	Law	1937	St-R	Resis.	1948	1966	5 7 9 ++ +
29. Fadilj Hodza	1916	Urban Kos.	Alb.	...	Student[a]	Prewar Second.[b]	Party School[c]	1941	St-R	Resis.	1958	1966	56789 ++++
30. Avdo Humo	1914	Urban B-H	Serb	...	Student	Prewar Univ.	...	1935	St-R	Resis.	1948	1966	5 +
31. Osman Kara-begovic	1911	Urban B-H	Moslem	...	Student	Prewar Univ.	Medicine	1932	St-R	Resis.	1948	1966	5 +
32. Rudi Kolak	1918	Rural B-H	Croat	...	Student	Prewar Univ.	Law	1940	St-R	Resis.	1964	1966	5 +
33. Ivan Macek	1908	Urban Slov.	Slovene	Worker[a]	Worker[b]	Prewar Elem.	...	1930	W-R	Resis.	1964	1966	5 +
34. Milentije Popovic	1913	Rural Serb.	Serb	Merchant	Engineer	Prewar Univ.	Engin.	1939	a	Resis.	1948	1966	5 7 ++ +
35. Vladimir Popovic*	1914	Rural Mont.	Mont.	Peasant	Student	Prewar Univ.	Medicine	1932	St-R	Resis.	1940	1966	5 +
36. Dusan Petrovic	1914	Urban Serb.	Serb	Artisan[a]	Trade Union	Prewar Basic[b]	...	1935	W-R	Resis.	1948	1966	5 9 + +
37. Koca Popovic*	1908	Cap. Serb.	Serb	Upper Class	Journalist	Prewar Univ.	...	1933	Int-R	Resis.	1952	1966	5 +
38. Dobri. Rad-osavljevic[a]	1915	Rural Serb.	Serb	...	Student	Prewar Univ.	...	1933	St-R	Resis.	1948	1966	5 +
39. Nikola Sekulic	1911	Urban Croat.	Serb	Worker[a]	Lawyer	Prewar Univ.	Law	1931	Int-R	Resis.	1952	1966	5 +
40. Vidoje Smilevski	1915	Rural Maced.	Maced.	Small Merchant	Bank Clerk	Prewar Second.	b	1940	c	Resis.	1948	1966	5 +
41. Lidija Senturc	1911	Urban Slov.	Slovene	Small Merchant[a]	Student	Prewar Univ.[b]	...	1932	St-R	Resis.	1952	1966	5 +
42. Pal Soti	1916	Urban Voj.	Hung.	...	Trade Union	...	...	1939	W-R	Resis.	1952	1966	5 +
43. Borko Temelkovski	1919	Urban Maced.	Maced.	Poor Peasant	Worker[a]	Prewar Elem.	...	1939	W-R	Resis.	1948	1966	5 +

*Participant in Spanish Civil War
**Jewish Extraction

Exec. Com. (or Presid.) Dates:

No. 1: July, 1948
No. 2: Dec., 1952
No. 3: Apr, 1958
No. 4: Dec., 1964
No. 5: Oct., 1966
No. 6: Mar., 1969
No. 7: Mar., 1969
No. 8: May, 1974
No. 9: May, 1974

___ Indicates Presidium
+ Full Member
x Candidate Member

TABLE F-10   (CONTINUED)

	1 Birth Date	2 Birth Place	3 Ethnicity	4 Status of Father	5 Status Prior to Party Work	6 Formal Educ.	7 Advanced Training	8 Party Mbr.	9 Revol. Type	10 WW II	11 CC Mbr.	12 EC Mbr.	Exec. Com. & Status
44. Nijaz Dizdarevic	1920	Rural B-H	Moslem	...	Student[a]	Prewar Univ.	...	1942	St-R	Resis.	1966	1966	6
45. Stane Dolanc	1925	Urban Slov.	Slovene	...	Military[a]	Postwar Univ.	Law	1944	Po-W	[b]	1974	1969	6789 ++++
46. Stevan Doronjski	1919	Rural Voj.	Serb	...	Student[a]	Prewar IncUniv.	[a]	1939	St-R	Resis.	1952	1969	6 9 +
47. Kiro Gligorov	1917	Urban Maced.	Maced.	...	State Official[a]	Prewar Univ.	Law	1944	NRE	Resis.[b]	1964	1969	6 9 +
48. Miroslav Pecujlic	1929	Urban Croat.	Serb	...	[a]	Postwar Univ.	Law	1945	Po-W	Resis.	1964	1966	6
49. Budislav Soskic	1925	Urban Serb.	Mont.	...	Student[a]	Postwar Univ.	...	1943	Po-W	Resis.	1964	1966	6 +
50. Miko Tripalo	1926	Rural Croat.	Croat	...	Partisan[a]	Postwar Univ.	Law	1943	Po-W	Resis.	1958	1969	6 +
51. Krsta Avramovic	1928	Rural Serb.	Serb	...	...	Postwar Univ.	Economics	1946	Po-W	Home	None	1969	7 +
52. Dimce Belovski	1923	Urban Maced.	Maced.	...	Partisan[a]	...[b] Univ.	Party School[c]	1943	...	Resis.	1974	1969	7 +
53. Srecko Bijelic	1930	Rural Croat.	Serb	...	Director[a]	Postwar Univ.	Economics[b]	1948	Po-W	Resis.	1964	1966	7 +
54. Branko Borojevic	1919	Rural Croat.	...	...	Student[a]	Prewar Univ.	Military Academy[b]	1941	St-R	Resis.	1974	1969	7 +
55. Angel Cemerski	1923	Rural Maced.	Maced.	...	[a]	Postwar Univ.	Economics	1942	Po-W	Resis.	1974	1969	7 9 ++
56. Dobroslav Culafic	1926	Rural Mont.	Mont.	...	Student[a]	Postwar Univ.	Party School[b]	1944	Po-W	Resis.	1964	1969	7 +
57. Emin Dobardjic	1930	Rural Mont.	Mont.	...	[a]	Postwar Univ.	Economics	1952	Po-W	Resis.	None	1969	7 +
58. Ivan Dolnicar	1921	Rural Slov.	Slovene	...	Partisan[a]	Prewar Trade	Party School[b]	1941	NRE	Resis.	1964	1969	7 +
59. Veselin Djuranovic	1925	Rural Mont.	Mont.	...	Student[a]	Prewar IncGym	Party School[b]	1944	St-R	Resis.	1964	1969	7 9 ++
60. Pavle Gazi	1927	Rural Croat.	Croat.	...	...	Postwar Univ.	Agric.	1945	Po-W	Home	None	1969	7 +
61. Stane Kavcic	1919	Urban Slov.	Slovene	...	Worker[a]	Prewar IncUniv.	...	1941	W-R	Resis.	1952	1969	7 +
62. Sergej Krajger	1914	Rural Slov.	Slovene	...	Student	Prewar IncUniv.	Medicine	1934	St-R	Resis.	1964	1969	7 +
63. Stane Kranjc	1929	Rural Slov.	Slovene	...	Student[a]	...	Party School[b]	1948	Po-W	Home	None	1969	7 +

*Participant in Spanish Civil War
**Jewish Extraction

Exec. Com. (or Presid.) Dates:
No.1: July, 1948   No.4: Dec., 1964   No.7: Mar., 1969
No.2: Dec., 1952   No.5: Oct., 1966   No.8: May, 1974
No.3: Apr., 1958   No.6: Mar., 1969   No.9: May, 1974

___ Indicates Presidium
+ Full Member   x Candidate Member

324

TABLE F-10 (CONTINUED)

	1 Birth Date	2 Birth Place	3 Ethnicity	4 Status of Father	5 Status Prior to Party Work	6 Formal Educ.	7 Advanced Training	8 Party Mbr.	9 Revol. Type	10 WW II	11 CC Mbr.	12 EC Mbr.	Exec. Com. & Status
64. Zvonko Liker	1929	Urban Croat.	Croat	...	Worker^a	Prewar Basic	...	1948	Po-W	Home	None	1969	7 +
65. Nikola Ljubicic	1916	Rural Serb.	Serb	Poor Peasant	Military^a	Prewar Second.^b	Military^c	1941	NRE	Resis.	1964	1969	7 9 + +
66. Slavko Milosavlevski	1928	Rural Maced.	Maced.	...	Student^a	Postwar Univ.	Law & Pol. Sc.^b	1943	Po-W	Resis.	1964	1969	7 +
67. Branko Mikulic	1928	Rural B-H	Croat	...	Student^a	Postwar SpecSec^b	Economics	1945	NRE	Home	1974	1969	7 9 + +
68. Jozef Nagy	1921	Urban Voj.	Hung.	...	a	Prewar Second.	...	...	NRE	Home	None	1969	7 +
69. Marko Nikezic	1921	Cap. Serb.	Serb	Middle Class	Student	Prewar IncUniv.	Engin.	1940	St-R	Resis.	1958	1969	7 +
70. Jovan Pecenovic	1933	Urban Kos.	...	...	a	Postwar Univ.	Political Science^b	1952	Po-W		None	1969	7 +
71. Latinka Perovic	1933	Urban Serb.	Serb	...	Student^a	Postwar Univ.	Political Science^b	1951	Po-W		None	1969	7 +
72. Franz Popit	1921	Rural Slov.	Slovene	...	...	Prewar Gym.	...	1940	St-R	Resis.	1964	1969	7 9 + +
73. Hamdija Pozderac	1923	Rural B-H	Moslem	...	Student^a	Postwar Univ.	Party School^b	1943	Po-W	Resis.	1974	1969	7 +
74. Mitja Ribicic	1919	Urban Italy	Slovene	...	Student^a	Prewar IncUniv.	Law	1941	St-R	Resis.	1964	1966	7 +
75. Milorad Stanojevic	1931	Cap. Serb.	Mont.	...	...	Postwar Univ.	Economics	1948	Po-W	Resis.	...	1969	7 +
76. Bosko Siljegovic	1915	Rural B-H	Serb	...	Student	Prewar IncUniv.	...	1940	St-R	Resis.	1958	1969	7 +
77. Kolj Siroka	1922	Urban Kos.	Alb.	...	Student^a	Prewar IncGym.	Party School^b	1941	St-R	Resis.	None	1969	7 +
78. Mirko Tepavac	1922	Urban Voj.	Serb	...	Student^a	Prewar Gym.	Party School^b	1942	St-R	Resis.	...	1969	7 +
79. Stanko Tomic	1926	Rural B-H	Serb	...	...	...	Party School	1942	...	Resis.	1974	1969	7 +
80. Vidoje Zarkovic	1927	Rural Mont.	Mont.	...	Partisan	Postwar High.^a	Political Science^b	1943	Po-W	Resis.	1974	1969	7 9 + +
81. Azem Zulficari	1925	Rural Maced.	Alb.	...	a	Prewar ...	Political Science^b	1948	NRE	Home	1964	1969	7 +
82. Jure Bilic	1922	Rural Croat.	Croat	...	a	Prewar Basic	Party School^b	1941	NRE	Resis.	1974	1972	8 9 + +
83. Aleksandar Grlickov	1923	Urban Maced.	Maced.	...	Planner^a	Postwar Univ.	Economics	1943	Po-W	Resis.	1964	1974	8 9 + +

*Participant in Spanish Civil War
**Jewish Extraction

Exec. Com. (or Presid.) Dates:

No.1: July, 1948	No.4: Dec., 1964	No.7: Mar., 1969
No.2: Dec., 1952	No.5: Oct., 1966	No.8: May, 1974
No.3: Apr., 1958	No.6: Mar., 1969	No.9: May, 1974

———— Indicates Presidium

+ Full Member
x Candidate Member

325

TABLE F-10 (CONTINUED)

	1 Birth Date	2 Birth Place	3 Ethnic-ity	4 Status of Father	5 Status Prior to Party Work	6 Formal Educ.	7 Advanced Training	8 Party Mbr.	9 Revol. Type	10 WW II	11 CC Mbr.	12 EC Mbr.	Exec. Com. & Status
84. Ivan Kukoc	1918	Urban Croat.	Croat	...	Worker	...	...	1935	W-R	Resis.	1974	1974	8 +
85. Todo Kurtovic	1919	Rural B-H	Serb	...	...	Prewar Gym.	Party School[a]	1941	NRE	Resis.	1964	1972	89 ++
86. Munir Mesihovic	1928	Rural B-H	Moslem	...	...	...	Political Science[a]	1946	NRE	Home	1974	1974	8 +
87. Dusan Popovic	1921	Urban Voj.	Serb	...	Diplomat[a]	...	Party School[b]	1944	NRE	Resis.	1974	1974	8 +·
88. Mirko Popovic	1923	Rural Serb.	Serb	...	Partisan[a]	...	Party School[b]	1941	NRE	Resis.	1974	1974	89 ++
89. Vojo Srzentic	1934	Rural Mont.	Mont.	...	Student[a]	Postwar Univ.	Economics	1952	Po-W		1974	1974	89 ++
90. Dragoljub Stavrev	1932	Urban Maced.	Maced.	...	Student[a]	Postwar Univ.	Law	1950	Po-W		1974	1974	8 +
91. Ali Sukrija	1919	Urban Kos.	Alb.	...	Student	Prewar IncUniv.[a]	Party School[b]	1939	St-R	Resis.	1964	1974	8 +
92. Dobrivoje Vidic	1918	Urban Serb.	Serb	...	Student	Prewar IncUniv.	...	1939	St-R	Resis.	1958	1974	8 +
93. Roman Albreht	1921	Rural Slov.	Slovene	...	...	Prewar Gym.	Party School[a]	1945	NRE	Resis.	1964	b	9 +
94. Dusan Alimpic	1921	Rural Voj.	Serb	...	Security Official[a]	Prewar Basic	...	1941	NRE	Resis.	1974	1974	9 +
95. Mahmut Bakali	1936	Urban Kos.	Alb.	...	Student[a]	...	Political Science[b]	1957	Po-W		1974	1974	9 +
96. Imre Balint	1930	Rural Voj.	Hung.	...	...	Postwar SpecSec.	...	...	Po-W		1974	1974	9 +
97. Dzemal Bijedic	1917	Urban B-H	Moslem	...	Student	Prewar IncUniv.	a	1939	St-R	Resis.	1974	1974	9 +
98. Krste Markovski	1925	Rural Maced.	Maced.	...	Student[a]	Prewar Gym.[b]	...	1941	NRE	Resis.	1974	1974	9 +
99. Milos Minic	1914	Rural Serb.	Serb	...	Student	Prewar Univ.	Law	1936	St-R	Resis.	1948	1974	9 +
100. Milka Planinc	1924	Rural Croat.	Croat	...	a	Postwar High[b]	Public Admin.	1944	Po-W	Resis.	1974	1974	9 +
101. Dusan Ristic	1907	Urban Serb.	Serb	...	Student[a]	Prewar Univ.	Law	1940	St-R	Resis.	1974	1974	9 +
102. Dzemail Sarac	1921	Urban B-H	Moslem	...	Partisan[a]	Prewar IncUniv.	Military Academy[b]	1941	NRE	Resis.	1974	1974	9 +
103. Joze Smole	1927	Urban Slov.	Slovene	...	...	...	Party School[a]	1943	NRE	Resis.	1974	1974	9 +

*Participant in Spanish Civil War
**Jewish Extraction

Exec. Com. (or Presid.) Dates:

No.1: July, 1948   No.4: Dec., 1964   No.7: Mar., 1969
No.2: Dec., 1952   No.5: Oct., 1966   No.8: May, 1974
No.3: Apr., 1958   No.6: Mar., 1969   No.9: May, 1974

___ Indicates Presidium

+ Full Member
x Candidate Member

326

TABLE F-10 (CONTINUED)

	1 Birth Date	2 Birth Place	3 Ethnicity	4 Status of Father	5 Status Prior to Party Work	6 Formal Educ.	7 Advanced Training	8 Party Mbr.	9 Revol. Type	10 WW II	11 CC Mbr.	12 EC Mbr.	Exec. Com. & Status
104. Tihomir Vlaskalic	1923	Rural Serb.	Serb	...	Professor^a	Postwar Univ.	Economics	1945	Po-W	b	1974	1974	9 +
105. Josip Vrhovec	1926	Urban Croat.	Croat	Worker	Newspaper Editor^a	Postwar Univ.	Economics	1945	Po-W	Resis.	1974	1974	9 +
106. Jovan Vujadinovic	1921	Rural Mont.	Mont.	...	...	Postwar Univ.^a	Economics	1943	Po-W	Resis.	1974	1974	9 +

*Participant in Spanish Civil War

**Jewish Extraction

Exec. Com. (or Presid.) Dates:

No.1: July, 1948   No.4: Dec., 1964   No.7: Mar., 1969
No.2: Dec., 1952   No.5: Oct., 1966   No.8: May, 1974
No.3: Apr., 1953   No.6: Mar., 1969   No.9: May, 1974

——— Indicates Presidium

+ Full Member
x Candidate Member

Note on Yugoslav Leadership Bodies: The leading party body of the League of Communists was first known as the Politburo. In 1952, it became known as the Executive Committee. In October, 1966, the Executive Committee was reorganized and the Presidium created, with leading party figures giving up membership in the Executive Committee and becoming members of the Presidium. In 1969 the Central Committee was eliminated and the Presidium expanded in size, while an Executive Bureau, with leading party figures, was created. In 1972 the Executive Bureau was reorganized, many leading party figures leaving the body while retaining membership in the Presidium. In 1974 the Central Committee was reintroduced, the Executive Bureau renamed the Executive Committee and its role strengthened, while the Presidium was retained, but in a subordinate role. Because of these changes, it is not possible to assign the role of leading party body to the Executive Committee in certain periods. Because of these changes, it is also possible for an individual to become a member of the Executive Committee before becoming a member of the Central Committee.

Abbreviations Used in This Table:

1. Admin.	Administration	11. High.	High.	18. PolSc.	Political Science
2. Agric.	Agriculture	12. Hung.	Hungarian	19. Po-W	Postwar
3. Alb.	Albania	13. Inc.	Incomplete	20. Resis.	Resistance
4. Austr.	Austria	14. Kos.	Kosovo	21. Second.	Secondary
5. B-H	Bosnia-Hercegovina	15. Maced.	Macedonia, Macedonian	22. Serb.	Serbia
6. Cap.	Capital	16. Mont.	Montenegro, Montenegrin	23. Slov.	Slovenia
7. Croat.	Croatia	17. NRE	No Revolutionary Experience	24. St-R	Student Revolutionary
8. Elem.	Elementary			25. Univ.	University
9. Engin.	Engineering			26. Voj.	Vojvodina
10. Gym.	Gymnasium			27. W-R	Worker Revolutionary

For further explanation of these terms, see the introduction to this section.

Notes: Ivan Gosnjak: a. Father a tinsmith. b. Carpenter. c. No information on education, but probably not above elementary level. d. Attended party schools in the Soviet Union and took part in officers' training program while in the USSR. No record of having attended a military academy or other institution at the advanced level. Edvard Kardelji: a. Parents described as part of the revolutionary working class; mother was trade union official. b. Received teachers' training at secondary level and political training in the USSR. Boris Kidric: a. Father a professor. b. Chemistry. Franc Leskosek: a. Father a manual laborer. b. Metal worker. Aleksandar Rankovic: a. Tailor. Lazar Kolisevski: a. Metal worker. Djuro Salaj: a. Trained as tailor, became trade union official in mid-1920s. b. Data lacking, but probably not above elementary level. Miha Marinko: a. Miners' family. b. Miner. c. Communist University of National Minorities of the West, Moscow. Jovan Veselinov: a. Locksmith. Krste Crvenkovski: a. Higher Party School Djuro Djakovic in Belgrade. Boris Krajger: a. Father a doctor. Mijalko Todorovic: a. Unclear whether complete or incomplete. b. Was enrolled in Technical Faculty, Belgrade University. Fadilj Hodza: a. Joined workers' movement in Albania in 1936, assumed to have been a student prior to that time. b. Graduated from teachers' school in Albania. c. Higher Political School Djuro

Djakovic in Belgrade. <u>Ivan Macek</u>: <u>a</u>. Father a manual laborer. <u>b</u>. Stonecutter. <u>Milentije Popovic</u>: <u>a</u>. Data lacking; probably belongs in group "Student Revolutionary." <u>Dusan Petrovic</u>: <u>a</u>. Father a stonecutter. <u>b</u>. Two years of gymnasiu<u>m</u> <u>Dobri. Radosavljevic</u>: <u>a</u>. Full first name: Dobrivoje. <u>Nikola Sekulic</u>: <u>a</u>. Father poor worker. <u>Vidoje Smilevsky</u>: <u>a</u>. Father cafe owner. <u>b</u>. Completed commercial academy in Belgrade. <u>c</u>. Does not fit any revolutionary type; might be called "White Collar Revolutionary" by virtue of participation in revolutionary activity while bank clerk. <u>Lidija Sentur</u> <u>a</u>. Father killed in WWI; mother owned small cafe. <u>b</u>. Unclear whether complete or incomplete. <u>Borko Temelkovski</u>: <u>a</u>. W worker. <u>Nijaz Dizdarevic</u>: <u>a</u>. Member of Communist youth organization, 1940. <u>Stane Dolanc</u>: <u>a</u>. Served in military unti<u>l</u> 1960; subsequently party functionary in CC of LC Slovenia. <u>b</u>. Joined resistance in 1944; prior to this time, member of Hitler Youth. <u>Stevan Doronjski</u>: <u>a</u>. Studied veterinary medicine for unspecified time. <u>Kiro Gligorov</u>: <u>a</u>. Was Feder Secretary for Finance prior to becoming member of EC in 1969; no record of full-time party or mass organization posts up to this time. <u>Miroslav Pecujlic</u>: <u>a</u>. Was professor of law at Belgrade University prior to joining the EC in 1966; also served in secretariat of city party committee in 1960s (exact dates not known). <u>Budislav Soskic</u>: <u>a</u>. Member of Communis<u>t</u> youth organization, 1940, prior to joining resistance. <u>Miko Tripalo</u>: <u>a</u>. Began full-time political work in Communist yo organization during WWII. <u>Dimce Belovski</u>: <u>a</u>. Political commisar during WWII; status prior to joining resistance not kn <u>b</u>. Not clear whether prewar or postwar. Studied law. <u>c</u>. Higher Political School Djuro Djakovic in Belgrade. <u>Srecko</u> <u>Bijelic</u>: <u>a</u>. Date of beginning full-time party work not known; was director of enterprise Jamko Grdelj, 1962-1966, prior to entering EC in 1966. <u>b</u>. Graduated in law, postgraduate work in economics. <u>Branko Borojevic</u>: <u>a</u>. In "progressive student movement" prior to WWII; political commisar during WWII. <u>b</u>. Studied law before WWII, attended Higher Military Academy of Yugoslav Army after WWII. <u>Angel Cemerski</u>: <u>a</u>. Member of Secretariat of LC Macedonia in early 1960s; also held posts in Macedonian government. Exact date of entering full-time political work not known. <u>Dobroslav Culafic</u>: <u>a</u>. Employed in youth work after finishing university, then district party secretary in Ivangrad. <u>b</u>. Graduated in law, then received training at Higher Party School Djuro Djakovic in Belgrade. <u>Emin Dobardjic</u>: <u>a</u>. Data lacking; was enterprise director, may have moved from that post to full-time party work. <u>Ivan Dolnicar</u>: <u>a</u>. Was political commissar durin and after WWII. <u>b</u>. Completed Higher Political School Djuro Djakovic in Belgrade. <u>Veselin Djuranovic</u>: <u>a</u>. Expelled from teachers' school in 1941 for Communist activity; active in Communist youth movement during WWII. <u>b</u>. 1947-1948, plac type of party school not known. Stane Kavcic: a. Worker in lumbermill at time of becoming active in revolutionary movement prior to WWII. <u>Stane Kranjc</u>: <u>a</u>. Date of entering full-time political work not known; appears to have become involved in party work shortly after finishing party school. <u>b</u>. Higher Political School Djuro Djakovic in Belgrade. <u>Zvonko Liker</u>: <u>a</u>. Steel worker at time of becoming presidium member. <u>Nikola Ljubicic</u>: <u>a</u>. No full-time party or mass organization work before joining presidium in 1969, at which time Minister of Defense. <u>b</u>. Completed Middle Agricultural School in Valjevo. <u>c</u>. Higher Military Academy in Belgrade after WWII. <u>Slavko Milosavlevski</u>: <u>a</u>. Date of beginning full-time political work not known; appears to have become involved in party work shortly after completing education. <u>b</u>. Doctorate in political science. <u>Branko Mikulic</u>: <u>a</u>. Date of entering full-time political work not known; appears to have become involved in party work shortly after completing education. <u>b</u>. Higher Economic School. <u>Jozef Nagy</u>: <u>a</u>. Dat lacking, but was school teacher 1942-1944 before becoming involved in party work after WWII. <u>Jovan Pecenovic</u>: <u>a</u>. Date of entering full-time political work not known; appears to have become involved in youth work shortly after completing education. <u>b</u>. Higher School of Political Science, Belgrade. <u>Latinka Perovic</u>: <u>a</u>. Commenced full-time political work a youth organization official after completing education. <u>b</u>. Higher School of Political Science, Belgrade. <u>Hamdija</u> <u>Pozderac</u>: <u>a</u>. Commenced full-time political work as local party functionary after completing education. <u>b</u>. Higher Party School, Moscow. <u>Mitja Ribicic</u>: <u>a</u>. Involved in revolutionary activity prior to WWII as student. <u>Kolj Siroka</u>: <u>a</u>. Memb of Communist youth organization prior to WWII. <u>b</u>. Higher Political School Djuro Djakovic in Belgrade. <u>Mirko Tepavac</u>: <u>a</u>. A member of "progressive student movement" prior to WWII. <u>b</u>. Higher Political School Djuro Djakovic, Belgrade. <u>Vidoje Zarkovic</u>: <u>a</u>. Naval Military Academy. <u>b</u>. Higher School of Political Science, Belgrade. <u>Azem Zulficari</u>: <u>a</u>. Data lacking; was teacher, school inspector and then president of local government in Gostivar around time of becoming involved in full-time party work as local party official. <u>b</u>. Higher School of Political Science, Belgrade. <u>Jure Bilic</u>: <u>a</u>. Date of entering full-time political work not known; appears to have become involved in party work shortly after completing party school. <u>b</u>. Higher Political School Djuro Djakovic, Belgrade. <u>Aleksandar Grlickov</u>: <u>a</u>. First known pa post that of member of EC of LC Macedonia, 1955, at which time director of Institute for Economic Planning, Skoplje. <u>Tod</u> <u>Kurtovic</u>: <u>a</u>. Higher Political School Djuro Djakovic, Belgrade. <u>Munir Mesihovic</u>: <u>a</u>. Higher School of Political Scien Belgrade. <u>Dusan Popovic</u>: <u>a</u>. Ambassador to Sweden before becoming involved in full-time political work as CC functionar then secretary of party committee for Novi Sad. <u>b</u>. Higher Political School Djuro Djakovic, Belgrade. <u>Mirko Popovic</u>: <u>a</u>. Involved in full-time political activity as political commissar at end of WWII. <u>b</u>. Higher Political School Djuro Djakovic, Belgrade. <u>Vojo Srzentic</u>: <u>a</u>. Began full-time political work as youth organization official after completing education. <u>Dragoljub Stavrev</u>: <u>a</u>. Law student at University of Skoplje before becoming involved in full-time party and youth work. <u>Ali Sukrija</u>: <u>a</u>. Studied medicine at the University of Belgrade. <u>b</u>. Higher Political School Djuro Djakovic, Belgrade. <u>Roman Albreht</u>: <u>a</u>. Higher Political School Djuro Djakovic, Belgrade. <u>b</u>. EC, 1966-1969 and 1974-1978. <u>Dusan Alimpic</u>: <u>a</u>. Active in youth work during WWII, then in security organs, 1945-1963, before becoming involved full-time in political activity as party secretary for Novi Sad. <u>Mahmut Bakali</u>: <u>a</u>. Began full-time political work as party and youth organization official after completing party school in early 1960s. <u>b</u>. Higher School of Political Science, Belgrade. <u>Dzemail Bijedic</u>: <u>a</u>. Studied law briefly at Belgrade University. <u>Krste Markovski</u>: <u>a</u>. Involved in full-time party and youth work after completing party school. <u>b</u>. Unclear whether complete or incomplete. <u>Milka Planinc</u>: <u>a</u>. Worked in enterprise in Zagreb before beginning full-time political activity in 1949. <u>b</u>. Higher School of Administration, Zagreb. <u>Dusan Ristic</u>: <u>a</u>. Based on assumption that still a student, or just completed studies, when joining party in 1940 at age 23. <u>Dzemail Sarac</u>: <u>a</u>. Political commissar during WWII; prior to that time studied medicine. <u>b</u>. Higher Military Academy of the Yugoslav National Army (postwar). <u>Joze Smole</u>: <u>a</u>. Higher Political School Djuro Djakovic, Belgrade. <u>Tihomir Vlaskalic</u>: <u>a</u>. No record of full-time political work until appointed President of LC Serbic in 1971. <u>b</u>. Resistance in 1944. <u>Josip Vrhovec</u>: <u>a</u>. Chief editor of newspaper Vjesnik before becoming party secretary of Croatia in 1971. <u>Jovan Vujadinovic</u>: <u>a</u>. Dates of attending university not known; "Postwar" based on assumption that V. could not have completed university by 1941.

TABLE F-11 ESTIMATED LEVEL OF EDUCATION OF PARTY LEADERS: ALBANIA AND BULGARIA

Executive Committees: Albania

Level of Education	1.	2.	3.	4.	5.	6.	7.	All	Prewar Educ.	Postwar Educ.
TOTAL	7	10	15	15	16	17	17	27	14	0
Percent	100%	100%	100%	100%	100%	100%	100%	100%	100%	100%
None or Elementary	1	4	4	4	4	3	3	4	4	0
Percent	14%	40%	27%	27%	25%	18%	18%	15%	29%	0%
Basic or Secondary	1	0	1	2	2	2	2	3	3	0
Percent	14%	0%	7%	13%	13%	12%	12%	11%	21%	0%
Secondary Political	0	0	0	0	0	0	0	0	0	0
Percent	0%	0%	0%	0%	0%	0%	0%	0%	0%	0%
Secialized Secondary	3	3	4	2	2	2	1	3	3	0
Percent	43%	30%	27%	13%	13%	12%	6%	11%	21%	0%
Higher Political or Part-Time	0	0	0	0	0	0	0	0	0	0
Percent	0%	0%	0%	0%	0%	0%	0%	0%	0%	0%
Higher Military or Technical	0	0	0	0	0	0	0	0	0	0
Percent	0%	0%	0%	0%	0%	0%	0%	0%	0%	0%
Incomplete University	1	2	2	2	2	2	2	2	2	0
Percent	14%	20%	13%	13%	13%	12%	12%	7%	14%	0%
University	1	1	1	2	2	2	1	2	2	0
Percent	14%	10%	7%	13%	13%	12%	6%	7%	14%	0%
Professor or Advanced Degree	0	0	0	0	0	0	0	0	0	0
Percent	0%	0%	0%	0%	0%	0%	0%	0%	0%	0%
Unknown	0	0	3	3	4	6	8	13		
Percent	0%	0%	20%	20%	25%	35%	47%	48%		

Executive Committees: Bulgaria

Level of Education	1.	2.	3.	4.	5.	6.	7.	8.	All	Prewar Educ.	Postwar Educ.
TOTAL	15	12	11	13	10	16	16	15	47	39	6
Percent	100%	100%	100%	100%	100%	100%	100%	100%	100%	100%	100%
None or Elementary	2	2	3	2	2	2	2	2	5	5	0
Percent	13%	17%	27%	15%	20%	13%	13%	13%	11%	13%	0%
Basic or Secondary	4	2	2	3	2	1	1	1	6	6	0
Percent	27%	17%	18%	23%	20%	6%	6%	7%	13%	15%	0%
Secondary Political	0	0	0	0	0	0	0	0	0	0	0
Percent	0%	0%	0%	0%	0%	0%	0%	0%	0%	0%	0%
Specialized Secondary	3	1	0	1	1	3	1	2	4	4	0
Percent	20%	8%	0%	8%	10%	19%	6%	13%	9%	10%	0%
Higher Political or Part-Time	2	2	2	2	0	1	2	2	5	4	1
Percent	13%	17%	18%	15%	0%	6%	13%	13%	11%	10%	17%
Higher Military or Technical	1	1	2	2	1	1	2	1	5	5	0
Percent	7%	8%	18%	15%	10%	6%	13%	7%	11%	13%	0%
Incomplete University	0	0	0	1	0	2	1	3	5	4	1
Percent	0%	0%	0%	8%	0%	13%	6%	20%	11%	10%	17%
University	3	3	2	1	3	5	6	3	14	10	4
Percent	20%	25%	18%	8%	30%	31%	38%	20%	30%	26%	67%
Professor of Advanced Degree	0	1	0	0	0	0	0	0	1	1	0
Percent	0%	8%	0%	0%	0%	0%	0%	0%	2%	3%	0%
Unknown	0	0	0	1	1	1	1	1	2		
Percent	0%	0%	0%	8%	10%	6%	6%	7%	4%		

TABLE F-12 ESTIMATED LEVEL OF EDUCATION OF PARTY LEADERS: CZECHOSLOVAKIA

Executive Committees

Level of Education	1.	2. I	2. II	3.	4.	5. I	5. II	6. I	6. II	7. I	7. II
TOTAL	14	22	22	11	13	12	12	15	15	7	7
Percent	100%	100%	100%	100%	100%	100%	100%	100%	100%	100%	100%
None or Elementary	5	5	5	4	3	2	2	1	1	0	0
Percent	36%	23%	23%	36%	23%	17%	17%	7%	7%	0%	0%
Basic or Secondary	1	3	3	1	1	1	1	2	2	0	0
Percent	7%	14%	14%	9%	8%	8%	8%	13%	13%	0%	0%
Secondary Political	0	0	1	0	0	0	1	0	1	0	3
Percent	0%	0%	4%	0%	0%	0%	8%	0%	7%	0%	43%
Specialized Secondary	2	4	4	1	2	1	2	0	2	1	2
Percent	14%	18%	18%	9%	15%	8%	17%	0%	13%	14%	29%
Higher Political or Part-Time	1	1	0	0	1	3	1	5	2	5	1
Percent	7%	4%	0%	0%	8%	25%	8%	33%	13%	71%	14%
Higher Military or Technical	0	1	1	1	1	1	1	1	1	0	0
Percent	0%	4%	4%	9%	8%	8%	8%	7%	7%	0%	0%
Incomplete University	1	2	2	1	2	1	1	1	1	0	0
Percent	7%	9%	9%	9%	15%	8%	8%	7%	7%	0%	0%
University	2	4	4	3	2	2	2	2	2	1	1
Percent	14%	18%	18%	27%	15%	17%	17%	13%	13%	14%	14%
Professor or Advanced Degree	0	0	0	0	0	1	1	2	2	0	0
Percent	0%	0%	0%	0%	0%	8%	8%	13%	13%	0%	0%
Unknown	2	2	2	0	1	0	0	1	1	0	0
Percent	14%	9%	9%	0%	8%	0%	0%	7%	7%	0%	0%

Executive Committees

Level of Education	8. I	8. II	9. I	9. II	All I	All II	Prewar Educ. I	Prewar Educ. II	Postwar Educ. I	Postwar Educ. II
TOTAL	13	13	13	13	59	59	35	35	20	20
Percent	100%	100%	100%	100%	100%	100%	100%	100%	100%	100%
None or Elementary	0	0	0	0	8	8	8	8	0	0
Percent	0%	0%	0%	0%	14%	14%	23%	23%	0%	0%
Basic or Secondary	0	0	0	0	5	5	5	5	0	0
Percent	0%	0%	0%	0%	8%	8%	14%	14%	0%	0%
Secondary Political	1	3	1	3	1	7	0	1	1	6
Percent	8%	23%	8%	23%	2%	12%	0%	3%	5%	30%
Specialized Secondary	0	1	0	1	6	9	6	7	0	2
Percent	0%	8%	0%	8%	10%	15%	17%	20%	0%	10%
Higher Political or Part-Time	4	1	4	1	14	5	2	0	12	5
Percent	31%	8%	31%	8%	24%	8%	6%	0%	60%	25%
Higher Military or Technical	3	3	3	3	5	5	3	3	2	2
Percent	23%	23%	23%	23%	8%	8%	9%	9%	10%	10%
Incomplete University	0	0	0	0	3	3	3	3	0	0
Percent	0%	0%	0%	0%	5%	5%	9%	9%	0%	0%
University	3	3	3	3	10	10	8	8	2	2
Percent	23%	23%	23%	23%	17%	17%	23%	23%	10%	10%
Professor or Advanced Degree	2	2	2	2	3	3	0	0	3	3
Percent	15%	15%	15%	15%	5%	5%	0%	0%	15%	15%
Unknown[a]	0	0	0	0	4	4				
Percent	0%	0%	0%	0%	7%	7%				

Note: a Includes two workers – Miroslav Pastyrik and Josef Krosnar – who probably did not receive more than a basic education.

TABLE F-13   ESTIMATED LEVEL OF EDUCATION OF PARTY LEADERS: GDR AND HUNGARY

Executive Committees: GDR

Level of Education	1.	2.	3.	4.	5.	6.	7.	8.	9.	All	Prewar Educ.	Postwar Educ.
TOTAL	14	16	14	14	21	23	19	23	28	61	47	9
Percent	100%	100%	100%	100%	100%	100%	100%	100%	100%	100%	100%	100%
None or Elementary	0	0	0	0	0	0	0	0	0	0	0	0
Percent	0%	0%	0%	0%	0%	0%	0%	0%	0%	0%	0%	0%
Basic or Secondary[a]	10	11	12	13	17	18	16	18	17	39	39	0
Percent	71%	69%	86%	93%	81%	78%	84%	78%	61%	64%	83%	0%
Secondary Political	0	0	0	0	0	0	0	0	0	0	0	0
Percent	0%	0%	0%	0%	0%	0%	0%	0%	0%	0%	0%	0%
Specialized Secondary	0	0	1	0	0	0	0	0	2	3	2	1
Percent	0%	0%	7%	0%	0%	0%	0%	0%	7%	5%	4%	11%
Higher Political or Part-Time	0	0	0	0	0	0	0	1	1	2	0	2
Percent	0%	0%	0%	0%	0%	0%	0%	4%	4%	3%	0%	22%
Higher Military or Technical	0	0	0	0	2	0	0	0	1	3	2	1
Percent	0%	0%	0%	0%	10%	0%	0%	0%	4%	5%	4%	11%
Incomplete University	0	0	0	0	0	1	1	1	2	2	0	2
Percent	0%	0%	0%	0%	0%	4%	5%	4%	7%	3%	0%	22%
University	1	1	1	1	1	2	0	1	2	4	2	2
Percent	7%	6%	7%	7%	5%	9%	0%	4%	7%	7%	4%	22%
Professor or Advanced Degree	0	0	0	0	1	2	2	2	2	3	2	1
Percent	0%	0%	0%	0%	5%	9%	11%	10%	7%	5%	4%	11%
Unknown	3	4	0	0	0	0	0	0	1	5		
Percent	21%	25%	0%	0%	0%	0%	0%	0%	4%	8%		

Executive Committees: Hungary

Level of Education	1.	2.	3.	4.	5.	6.	7.	8.	9.	All	Prewar Educ.	Postwar Educ.
TOTAL	17	21	12	16	15	19	15	12	13	53	29	6
Percent	100%	100%	100%	100%	100%	100%	100%	100%	100%	100%	100%	100%
None or Elementary[b]	4	4	1	3	2	1	0	0	0	5	5	0
Percent	24%	19%	8%	19%	13%	5%	0%	0%	0%	9%	17%	0%
Basic or Secondary	3	3	1	2	3	3	3	2	2	5	5	0
Percent	18%	14%	8%	13%	20%	16%	20%	17%	15%	9%	17%	0%
Secondary Political	0	0	0	0	0	0	0	0	0	0	0	0
Percent	0%	0%	0%	0%	0%	0%	0%	0%	0%	0%	0%	0%
Specialized Secondary	0	0	0	0	0	2	0	0	1	3	3	0
Percent	0%	0%	0%	0%	0%	11%	0%	0%	8%	6%	10%	0%
Higher Political or Part-Time	0	0	0	0	0	0	0	0	0	0	0	0
Percent	0%	0%	0%	0%	0%	0%	0%	0%	0%	0%	0%	0%
Higher Military or Technical	1	2	3	3	1	2	4	3	2	8	5	3
Percent	6%	10%	25%	19%	7%	11%	27%	25%	15%	15%	17%	50%
Incomplete University	1	1	1	1	0	0	0	0	0	1	1	0
Percent	6%	5%	8%	6%	0%	0%	0%	0%	0%	2%	3%	0%
University	3	3	2	1	3	4	3	2	3	12	9	3
Percent	18%	14%	17%	6%	20%	21%	20%	17%	23%	23%	31%	50%
Professor or Advanced Degree	0	0	0	0	0	1	1	0	0	1	1	0
Percent	0%	0%	0%	0%	0%	5%	7%	0%	0%	2%	3%	0%
Unknown[c]	5	8	4	6	6	6	4	5	5	18		
Percent	29%	38%	33%	38%	40%	32%	27%	42%	38%	34%		

Notes: a Education not known, but assumed to be basic: Paul Merker. b Education not known, but assumed to be none or elementary: Istvan Kossa. c Of total of 18 unknown, 10 are of working class background. It can be assumed that the majority of these had no more than an elementary education.

332

TABLE F-14   ESTIMATED LEVEL OF EDUCATION OF PARTY LEADERS: POLAND

Executive Committees

Level of Education	1.	2. I	2. II	3. I	3. II	4. I	4. II	5. I	5. II	6. I	6. II
TOTAL	9	15	15	15	15	12	12	15	15	16	16
Percent	100%	100%	100%	100%	100%	100%	100%	100%	100%	100%	100%
None or Elementary	2	2	2	3	3	1	1	1	1	0	0
Percent	22%	13%	13%	20%	20%	8%	8%	7%	7%	0%	0%
Basic or Secondary	0	2	2	1	1	0	0	0	0	0	0
Percent	0%	13%	13%	7%	7%	0%	0%	0%	0%	0%	0%
Secondary Political	0	0	4	0	4	1	3	1	2	1	4
Percent	0%	0%	27%	0%	27%	8%	25%	7%	13%	6%	25%
Specialized Secondary	0	0	0	0	0	0	0	0	0	0	0
Percent	0%	0%	0%	0%	0%	0%	0%	0%	0%	0%	0%
Higher Political or Part-Time	4	4	0	4	0	3	1	3	2	4	2
Percent	44%	27%	0%	27%	0%	25%	8%	20%	13%	25%	13%
Higher Military or Technical	0	1	1	2	2	1	1	2	2	2	2
Percent	0%	7%	7%	13%	13%	8%	8%	13%	13%	13%	13%
Incomplete University	1	2	2	2	2	3	3	3	3	3	3
Percent	11%	13%	13%	13%	13%	25%	25%	20%	20%	19%	19%
University	2	4	4	2	2	3	3	4	4	4	3
Percent	22%	27%	27%	13%	13%	25%	25%	27%	27%	25%	19%
Professor or Advanced Degree	0	0	0	0	0	0	0	1	1	1	1
Percent	0%	0%	0%	0%	0%	0%	0%	7%	7%	6%	6%
Unknown	0	0	0	1	1	0	0	0	0	1	1
Percent	0%	0%	0%	7%	7%	0%	0%	0%	0%	6%	6%

Executive Committees

Level of Education	7. I	7. II	8. I	8. II	All I	All II	Prewar Educ. I	Prewar Educ. II	Postwar Educ. I	Postwar Educ. II
TOTAL	15	15	17	17	47	47	28	28	17	17
Percent	100%	100%	100%	100%	100%	100%	100%	100%	100%	100%
None or Elementary	0	0	0	0	4	4	4	4	0	0
Percent	0%	0%	0%	0%	9%	9%	14%	14%	0%	0%
Basic or Secondary	0	0	0	0	2	2	2	2	0	0
Percent	0%	0%	0%	0%	4%	4%	7%	7%	0%	0%
Secondary Political	0	2	0	2	1	8	1	6	0	2
Percent	0%	13%	0%	12%	2%	17%	4%	21%	0%	12%
Specialized Secondary	1	1	1	1	1	1	0	0	1	1
Percent	7%	7%	6%	6%	2%	2%	0%	0%	6%	6%
Higher Political or Part-Time	4	4	4	5	11	5	6	1	5	4
Percent	27%	27%	24%	29%	23%	11%	21%	4%	29%	24%
Higher Military or Technical	4	4	4	4	8	8	4	4	4	4
Percent	27%	27%	24%	24%	17%	17%	14%	14%	24%	24%
Incomplete University	0	0	0	0	6	6	5	5	1	1
Percent	0%	0%	0%	0%	13%	13%	18%	18%	6%	6%
University	3	2	5	3	9	9	5	5	4	4
Percent	20%	13%	29%	18%	19%	19%	18%	18%	24%	24%
Professor or Advanced Degree	3	2	3	2	3	2	1	1	2	1
Percent	20%	13%	18%	12%	6%	4%	4%	4%	12%	6%
Unknown	0	0	0	0	2	2				
Percent	0%	0%	0%	0%	4%	4%				

TABLE F-15   ESTIMATED LEVEL OF EDUCATION OF PARTY LEADERS: ROMANIA

Executive Committees

Level of Education	1.	2. I	2. II	3. I	3. II	4. I	4. II	5. I	5. II
TOTAL	18	15	15	14	14	26	26	32	32
Percent	100%	100%	100%	100%	100%	100%	100%	100%	100%
None or Elementary[a]	6	3	3	3	3	2	2	2	2
Percent	33%	20%	20%	21%	21%	8%	8%	6%	6%
Basic or Secondary	3	5	5	4	4	4	4	1	1
Percent	17%	33%	33%	29%	29%	15%	15%	3%	3%
Secondary Political	0	0	1	0	1	0	6	0	10
Percent	0%	0%	7%	0%	7%	0%	23%	0%	31%
Specialized Secondary	0	0	0	0	0	0	0	0	0
Percent	0%	0%	0%	0%	0%	0%	0%	0%	0%
Higher Political or Part-Time	0	1	0	1	0	7	1	11	1
Percent	0%	7%	0%	7%	0%	27%	4%	34%	3%
Higher Military or Technical[b]	1	2	2	2	2	4	4	5	5
Percent	6%	13%	13%	14%	14%	15%	15%	16%	16%
Incomplete University	1	0	0	0	0	0	0	0	0
Percent	6%	0%	0%	0%	0%	0%	0%	0%	0%
University	3	2	2	3	3	5	5	5	5
Percent	17%	13%	13%	21%	21%	19%	19%	16%	16%
Professor or Advanced Degree	1	1	1	0	0	0	0	0	0
Percent	6%	7%	7%	0%	0%	0%	0%	0%	0%
Unknown	3	1	1	1	1	4	4	8	8
Percent	17%	7%	7%	7%	7%	15%	15%	25%	25%

Executive Committees

Level of Education	6. I	6. II	All I	All II	Prewar Educ.	Postwar Educ. I	Postwar Educ. II
TOTAL	35	35	67	67	29	17	17
Percent	100%	100%	100%	100%	100%	100%	100%
None or Elementary[a]	0	0	7	7	7	0	0
Percent	0%	0%	10%	10%	24%	0%	0%
Basic or Secondary	1	1	6	6	6	0	0
Percent	3%	3%	9%	9%	21%	0%	0%
Secondary Political	0	6	0	10	0	0	10
Percent	0%	17%	0%	15%	0%	0%	59%
Specialized Secondary	0	0	0	0	0	0	0
Percent	0%	0%	0%	0%	0%	0%	0%
Higher Political or Part-Time	7	1	11	1	0	11	1
Percent	20%	3%	16%	1%	0%	65%	6%
Higher Military or Technical[b]	6	6	7	7	4	3	3
Percent	17%	17%	10%	10%	14%	18%	18%
Incomplete University	0	0	1	1	1	0	0
Percent	0%	0%	1%	1%	3%	0%	0%
University	8	8	12	12	9	3	3
Percent	23%	23%	18%	18%	31%	18%	18%
Professor or Advanced Degree	1	1	2	2	2	0	0
Percent	3%	3%	3%	3%	7%	0%	0%
Unknown	12	12	21	21			
Percent	34%	34%	31%	31%			

Notes: a Education not known, but assumed to be none or elementary: Vasile Luca, Gheorge Vasilichi, Tanase Zaharia, Dumitru Petrescu. b Education not known, but assumed to be higher, technical: Stefan Andrei.

TABLE F-16   ESTIMATED LEVEL OF EDUCATION OF PARTY LEADERS: USSR, 1917-1939 AND
             USSR AFTER WORLD WAR II

Executive Committee: USSR, 1917-1939

Level of Education	1.	2.	3.	4.	5.	6.	7.	8.	All	Prewar[a] Educ.	Postwar Educ.
TOTAL	7	8	9	14	17	15	15	11	34	31	2
Percent	100%	100%	100%	100%	100%	100%	100%	100%	100%	100%	100%
None or Elementary[b]	0	1	2	6	9	7	7	5	11	11	0
Percent	0%	13%	22%	43%	53%	47%	47%	45%	32%	35%	0%
Basic or Secondary	1	1	2	2	2	2	4	2	6	6	0
Percent	13%	13%	22%	14%	12%	13%	27%	18%	18%	19%	0%
Secondary Political	0	0	0	0	0	0	0	0	0	0	0
Percent	0%	0%	0%	0%	0%	0%	0%	0%	0%	0%	0%
Specialized Secondary	0	0	0	0	0	0	0	0	0	0	0
Percent	0%	0%	0%	0%	0%	0%	0%	0%	0%	0%	0%
Higher Political or Part-Time	0	0	0	1	1	1	1	2	2	1	1
Percent	0%	0%	0%	7%	6%	7%	7%	18%	6%	3%	50%
Higher Military or Technical	0	0	0	0	3	4	3	1	5	4	1
Percent	0%	0%	0%	0%	18%	27%	20%	9%	14%	13%	50%
Incomplete University	5	5	5	5	2	1	0	0	7	7	0
Percent	62%	62%	56%	36%	12%	7%	0%	0%	21%	23%	0%
University	1	1	0	0	0	0	0	0	2	2	0
Percent	13%	13%	0%	0%	0%	0%	0%	0%	6%	6%	0%
Professor or Advanced Degree	0	0	0	0	0	0	0	0	0	0	0
Percent	0%	0%	0%	0%	0%	0%	0%	0%	0%	0%	0%
Unknown	0	0	0	0	0	0	0	1	1		
Percent	0%	0%	0%	0%	0%	0%	0%	9%	3%		

Executive Committees: USSR After World War II

Level of Education	1.	2.	3.	4.	5.	6.	7.	8.	All	Prewar[c] Educ.	Postwar Educ.
TOTAL	13	14	17	23	16	19	22	22	55	53	2
Percent	100%	100%	100%	100%	100%	100%	100%	100%	100%	100%	100%
None or Elementary[d]	2	3	3	4	1	0	0	0	5	5	0
Percent	15%	21%	18%	17%	6%	0%	0%	0%	9%	9%	0%
Basic or Secondary	2	1	1	1	0	0	0	0	2	2	0
Percent	15%	7%	6%	4%	0%	0%	0%	0%	4%	4%	0%
Secondary Political	0	0	0	0	0	0	0	0	0	0	0
Percent	0%	0%	0%	0%	0%	0%	0%	0%	0%	0%	0%
Specialized Secondary	1	2	2	1	1	2	2	2	5	5	0
Percent	8%	14%	12%	4%	6%	11%	9%	9%	9%	9%	0%
Higher Political or Part-Time	2	2	2	5	3	5	6	3	10	10	0
Percent	15%	14%	12%	22%	19%	26%	27%	14%	18%	19%	0%
Higher Military or Technical	6	6	7	10	8	10	11	12	26	25	1
Percent	46%	43%	41%	43%	50%	53%	50%	55%	47%	47%	50%
Incomplete University	0	0	0	0	0	0	1	1	1	1	0
Percent	0%	0%	0%	0%	0%	0%	5%	5%	2%	2%	0%
University	0	0	0	1	2	1	1	3	3	2	1
Percent	0%	0%	0%	4%	13%	5%	5%	14%	5%	4%	50%
Professor or Advanced Degree	0	0	2	1	1	1	1	1	3	3	0
Percent	0%	0%	12%	4%	6%	5%	5%	5%	5%	6%	0%
Unknown	0	0	0	0	0	0	0	0	0		
Percent	0%	0%	0%	0%	0%	0%	0%	0%	0%		

Notes: a Pre-World War I. b Education not known, but assumed to be none or elementary: L.P. Serebryakov, M.P. Tomsky, G.I. Petrovsky, Y.E. Rudzutak, I.M. Kaganovic, S.V. Kossior, P.P. Postyshev. c Pre-World War II. d Education not known, but assumed to be none or elementary: M. Shkiryatov and D.S. Korotchenko.

335

TABLE F-17 ESTIMATED LEVEL OF EDUCATION OF PARTY LEADERS: YUGOSLAVIA

Executive Committees

Level of Education	1.	2.	3.	4.	5.	6.	7.	8.	9.	All	Prewar Educ.	Postwar Educ.
TOTAL	13	14	16	19	35	15	44	13	38	106	57	44
Percent	100%	100%	100%	100%	100%	100%	100%	100%	100%	100%	100%	100%
None or Elementary	4	4	5	5	6	1	2	0	0	10	10	0
Percent	31%	29%	31%	26%	17%	7%	5%	0%	0%	9%	17%	0%
Basic or Secondary	2	2	2	2	4	0	4	0	5	9	9	0
Percent	15%	14%	13%	11%	11%	0%	9%	0%	13%	8%	16%	0%
Secondary Political	0	0	0	0	0	0	5	4	6	11	0	11
Percent	0%	0%	0%	0%	0%	0%	11%	31%	16%	10%	0%	25%
Specialized Secondary[a]	1	1	1	1	2	2	4	2	5	7	1	6
Percent	8%	7%	6%	5%	6%	13%	9%	15%	13%	7%	2%	14%
Higher Political or Part-Time	0	0	0	0	0	0	0	0	0	0	0	0
Percent	0%	0%	0%	0%	0%	0%	0%	0%	0%	0%	0%	0%
Higher Military or Technical	0	0	0	0	0	0	2	0	3	3	0	3
Percent	0%	0%	0%	0%	0%	0%	5%	0%	8%	3%	0%	7%
Incomplete University	1	1	1	3	4	3	6	2	4	12	12	0
Percent	8%	7%	6%	16%	11%	20%	14%	15%	11%	11%	21%	0%
University	5	5	5	6	15	8	20	4	13	45	25	20
Percent	38%	36%	31%	32%	43%	53%	45%	31%	34%	42%	44%	45%
Professor or Advanced Degree	0	0	0	0	1	1	1	0	1	4	0	4
Percent	0%	0%	0%	0%	3%	7%	2%	0%	3%	4%	0%	9%
Unknown	0	1	2	2	3	0	0	1	1	5		
Percent	0%	7%	13%	11%	9%	0%	0%	8%	3%	5%		

Note: a Includes three persons - Azem Zulficari, Munir Mesihovic and Mahmut Bakali - who graduated from Higher School of Political Science, Belgrade.

336

SECTION G: OCCUPATIONS

Introduction

I.
General Remarks

All entries refer to occupations. Data relating to agriculture; mining; manufacturing; construction; transport and communication; and trade, services and supply cover similar types of occupations and are not branch data, with the exception of Table G-5 (Poland). Reference to "Workers" indicates that the occupation was considered manual in the original source. Reference to "Personnel" indicates that the occupation was considered nonmanual.

II.
Introductory Notes to Tables

Table G-1   Data are census data. Data for 1956 and 1965 appear broadly comparable for most categories; note, however, the expansion of the category "Other Manual Workers" in 1965 to include occupations previously listed as technical, or belonging to the group of those in economic services. Within the major category of Trade, Services and Supply, manual and nonmanual occupations have been reclassified in 1965. Postmen have been transferred in 1965 from nonmanual to manual status and a certain number of laboratory assistants transferred from nonmanual to manual.

Table G-2   Data are census data. Apprentices are excluded.

Table G-3   Data are census data. The original data for 1950 were given in terms of eight categories: (1) Agricultural occupations, (2) Raw materials production and processing occupations, (3) Technical occupations, (4) Occupations in trade and communications, (5) Health and communal service occupations, (6) Occupations in administration and justice, (7) Occupations in religion and culture, (8) Undetermined. Only categories (1), (2), and (3) are compatible with the 13 major classifications used in this section. With the possible exception of agricultural occupations, the comparability of 1950 and 1964 data is limited due to the exclusion of East Berlin from the data for 1950. In the data for 1964, Engineers include ship captains (1,846) and Economic Engineers (*Wirtschaftsingenieur*) (8,398). Under Personnel in Administration, Fi-

nance, and Office Work, Commercial Occupations include Persons in Trade (322,698), Bank Clerks (29,698), Insurance Salesmen (14,392), and Others.

Table G-4   Data are census data. The comparability of the data for 1960 and 1970 is limited by the inclusion in the 1970 data of Sales Personnel in the category of Persons in Administration, Finance, and Office Work. The decline in the number of leaders from 1960 to 1970 is in part due to exclusion of Head Bookkeepers and Party Leaders from the 1970 data. Data for Agricultural Occupations, Education and Culture, and Health are broadly comparable between the two censuses. See especially Footnotes *b*, *c*, *d*, and *e* in the table for the classification of service, trade, and communications personnel and how data for these categories should be redistributed to be made more comparable among the different censuses as well as with other tables in this section.

Table G-5   Data are census data. Series I and II are based on a classification of occupations developed for the 1970 census and are broadly comparable in cases where basic categories correspond; note, however, the large number of Unknown or undeclared (14.1 percent) in the data for 1960. Data in the table are presented in terms of the categories, Those Supported Mainly From Work (*Utrzymujacy sie głownie z pracy*) for 1970, and Occupationally Active (*Czynni zawodowo*) for 1974. For 1960, data are for the Occupationally Active, military excluded, but the number of persons with supplementary incomes is small, and the total can be compared to the data for 1970. For further comments on Polish labor force concepts, see the General Introduction.

Table G-6   Data are census data. Data for 1956 include technicians under other major classifications (agriculture, industry, etc); see Table G-9 for the total number of technicians in 1956. Data are broadly comparable in respect to occupations in education and culture, and in health. Other major categories are not comparable in the two censuses; as noted, technicians are included with other categories for 1956, and the 1956 data include a large residual category of Other Functionaries (184,466) distributed among other occupational groups in 1966.

Table G-7   Data are census data. Data are comparable within each series. The primary differences between Series I and Series II are the result of the reclassification of persons with Unknown Occupations in Series I to other categories in Series II, and transfer of Sales Clerks from nonmanual to manual status in Series II.

Table G-8   Data are census data. Additional data for 1970 provided in the footnotes are census data on employees (Workers and White Collar Employees) which differ from data on Active Earners insofar as (1) those employed in the private sector are excluded; (2) those looking for work are excluded. Data on agricultural occupations are comparable in both censuses if account is taken of the failure to include unskilled agricultural workers in the 1953 data (this group probably did not number over 50,000). In other productive occupations, data for 1953 and 1961 are not comparable, due to exclusion of unskilled workers from these categories in 1953. Data on Leaders, Health Personnel, and Personnel in Education and Culture are broadly comparable between 1953 and 1961 (but not the subcategories in these groups). Data for 1953 and 1961 on technical occupations, and on administrative personnel, are comparable at the level of subcategories, as indicated in the table. For 1961 and 1971, data for leaders are not comparable. Data on technical personnel are not comparable due to the placement of communication personnel in this group in 1971 and to an unexplained increase in the number of engineers in 1971. Categories of Agricultural Occupations, Manufacturing, Mining, Construction, Health, and Education and Culture are broadly comparable in 1961 and 1971.

Table G-9   Data are census data.

Table G-10   Data are census data.

Table G-11   Data are census data.

Table G-12   Data are census data.

Table G-13   Data are census data.

Table G-14   Data are census data.

Table G-15   Data are census data.

Table G-16   Data are census data.

Table G-17   Data are census data.

Table G-18   Data are census data.

Table G-19   Data are census data. Private Peasantry and Other Active not earning a wage or salary are excluded as are the military and persons in security-related occupations.

Table G-20   Data are census data, as reported by the International Labour Organization. No effort has been made in this table, as in E-37, to arrange data originating in national sources according to The International Standard Classification of Occupations. While national data in this table have been modified by the ILO to accord with international classifications, comparability of the data among countries cannot be assumed. The classification of occupations used in this table corresponds to that utilized by the ILO prior to 1968; data presented according to the post-1968 system of classifying occupations are given in such a way as to correspond as closely as possible to the pre-1968 classification system, but are not necessarily comparable. See the General Introduction for a further discussion of the problem of comparing occupational data presented according to the International Standard Classification of Occupations.

TABLE G-1   MAJOR OCCUPATIONS: BULGARIA, 1956-1965

	1956			1965		
	Total	Male	Female	Total	Male[a]	Female
ACTIVE EARNERS, TOTAL	4,150,206	2,405,344	1,744,863	4,267,798	2,389,674	1,878,124
Percent	100.0%	100.0%	100.0%	100.0%	100.0%	100.0%
Agriculture & Forestry	2,511,881	1,178,155	1,333,726	1,746,504	731,739	1,014,765
Percent	60.5%	49.0%	76.4%	40.9%	30.6%	54.0%
Agricultural Workers	2,481,962	1,150,998	1,330,964	1,714,233	706,569	1,007,664
Percent	59.8%	47.8%	76.3%	40.2%	29.6%	53.6%
Forestry Workers	26,382	23,629	2,753	32,271	25,170	7,101
Percent	0.6%	1.0%	0.2%	0.8%	1.0%	0.4%
Fishing & Animal Breeding	3,537	3,528	9			
Percent	0.1%	0.1%	0.0%			
Mining	54,133	52,307	1,826	48,396	44,359	4,037
Percent	1.3%	2.2%	0.1%	1.1%	1.9%	0.2%
Manufacturing	450,976	321,511	129,465	772,162	482,345	289,817
Percent	10.9%	13.4%	7.4%	18.1%	20.2%	15.4%
Construction	108,311	106,358	1,953	198,235	190,803	7,432
Percent	2.6%	4.4%	0.1%	4.6%	8.0%	0.4%
Transport & Communications	175,468	163,299	12,169	305,472	280,468	25,004
Percent	4.2%	6.8%	0.7%	7.2%	11.7%	1.3%
Railroad Workers	27,287	26,965	322	36,155	34,335	1,820
Percent	0.6%	1.1%	0.0%	0.8%	1.4%	0.1%
Water Transport Workers	1,401	1,394	7	3,700	3,686	14
Percent	0.0%	0.0%	0.0%	0.1%	0.1%	0.0%
Auto Transport Workers	34,056	33,010	1,046	109,775	103,609	6,166
Percent	0.8%	1.4%	0.1%	2.6%	4.3%	0.3%
Air Transport Workers	85	81	4	440	400	40
Percent	0.0%	0.0%	0.0%	0.0%	0.0%	0.0%
Other Workers in Transport	95,368	93,168	2,200	136,888	131,541	5,347
Percent	2.3%	3.9%	0.1%	3.2%	5.5%	0.3%
Communications Personnel	9,958	2,793	7,165	10,799	1,538	9,261
Percent	0.2%	0.1%	0.4%	0.2%	0.0%	0.5%
Postal Workers	7,313	5,888	1,425	7,715	5,359	2,356
Percent	0.2%	0.2%	0.1%	0.2%	0.2%	0.1%
Trade, Services & Protection	218,619	154,279	64,340	305,295	128,453	176,842
Percent	5.3%	6.4%	3.7%	7.1%	5.4%	9.4%
Protective Service Personnel	42,837	40,692	2,145	15,518	15,205	313
Percent	1.0%	1.7%	0.1%	0.3%	0.6%	0.0%
Economic Service Workers[b]	66,516	39,149	27,367			
Percent	1.6%	1.6%	1.6%			
Personal Service Workers	21,245	15,048	6,197			
Percent	0.5%	0.6%	0.3%			
Workers in Communal Catering	32,083	15,608	16,475			
Percent	0.8%	0.6%	0.9%			
Communal & Personal Service Workers				147,149	54,457	92,692
Percent				3.4%	2.3%	4.9%
Workers in Trade	55,938	43,782	12,156	142,628	58,791	83,837
Percent	1.3%	1.8%	0.7%	3.3%	2.5%	4.4%

TABLE G-1   (CONCLUDED)

	1956			1965		
	Total	Male	Female	Total	Male[a]	Female
Leading & Supervisory Personnel	56,321	52,153	4,168	58,142	53,055	5,087
Percent	1.4%	2.2%	0.2%	1.4%	2.2%	0.3%
Leaders of Party Organs, State, Cooperative & Social Insts. & Enterprises	56,321	52,153	4,168			
Percent	1.4%	2.2%	0.2%			
Leaders of State & Cooperative Inst. & Enterprises				49,004	45,300	3,704
Percent				1.1%	1.9%	0.2%
Leaders of Party & Social Org.				9,138	7,755	1,383
Percent				0.2%	0.3%	0.1%
Technical Personnel	88,196	73,392	14,804	172,005	130,035	41,970
Percent	2.1%	3.0%	0.8%	4.0%	5.4%	2.2%
Engineers & Technical Personnel	88,196	73,392	14,804	151,568	113,930	37,638
Percent	2.1%	3.0%	0.8%	3.5%	4.8%	2.0%
Other Technical Personnel[c]				20,437	16,105	4,332
Percent				0.5%	0.7%	0.2%
Educational, Scientific & Cultural Personnel	91,550	43,372	48,178	143,626	64,128	79,498
Percent	2.2%	1.8%	2.8%	3.4%	2.7%	4.2%
Personnel in Culture, Education, & Propaganda	79,792	34,546	45,246			
Percent	1.9%	1.4%	2.6%			
Personnel in Science & Research				5,628	3,823	1,805
Percent				0.1%	0.2%	0.0%
Personnel in Education				109,289	42,507	66,782
Percent				2.6%	1.8%	3.5%
Personnel in Religion				2,521	2,368	153
Percent				0.1%	0.1%	0.0%
Personnel in the Arts	11,758	8,826	2,932	26,188	15,430	10,758
Percent	0.3%	0.4%	0.2%	0.6%	0.6%	0.6%
Health Personnel	49,215	16,911	32,304	54,177	15,399	38,778
Percent	1.2%	0.7%	1.8%	1.3%	0.6%	2.1%
Personnel in Administration, Finance & Office Work	169,270	100,863	68,407	208,695	91,402	117,293
Percent	4.1%	4.2%	3.9%	4.9%	3.8%	6.2%
Legal Personnel	4,947	4,471	476	5,763	4,884	879
Percent	0.1%	0.2%	0.0%	0.1%	0.2%	0.0%
Bookkeepers	111,874	66,725	45,149	150,329	65,383	84,946
Percent	2.7%	2.8%	2.6%	3.5%	2.7%	4.5%
Clerks & Secretaries	29,493	10,947	18,546	27,025	4,928	22,097
Percent	0.7%	0.4%	1.1%	0.6%	0.2%	1.2%
Planning Personnel	22,956	18,720	4,236	25,578	16,207	9,371
Percent	0.5%	0.8%	0.2%	0.6%	0.7%	0.5%
Other Occupations	176,241	142,721	33,520	254,534	177,204	77,330
Percent	4.2%	5.9%	1.9%	6.0%	7.4%	4.1%
Other Manual Workers	97,119[d]	69,718	27,401	179,914[e]	110,686	69,228
Percent	2.3%	3.0%	1.6%	4.2%	4.6%	3.7%
Other Nonmanual Personnel	79,122	73,003	6,119	74,620	66,518	8,102
Percent	1.9%	3.0%	0.3%	1.7%	2.8%	0.4%
Unknown or Undeclared	25	22	3	555	284	271
Percent	0.0%	0.0%	0.0%	0.0%	0.0%	0.0%

Notes: a Difference between total and number of females.   b Porters, Messengers, and related.
c Agronomists, Veterinarians, Forestry Specialists, and related.   d Includes Operators of
Lifting Mechanisms and Related Power Equipment (25,904), and Other Workers in Productive
Occupations including Packers and Sorters (6,385) and General Workers (46,489).   e In-
cludes 51,746 Operators of Lifting Mechanisms and Related Equipment, and 128,168 Others
(Stock Clerks, Sorters, and related).

TABLE G-2   MAJOR OCCUPATIONS: CZECHOSLOVAKIA, 1961

Occupation	Total	Male	Female	Occupation	Total	Male	Female
ACTIVE EARNERS, TOTAL	6,439,412	3,811,207	2,628,205				
Percent	100.0%	100.0%	100.0%				
Agriculture & Forestry	1,281,337	548,774	732,563	Technical Personnel	543,065	478,019	65,046
Percent	19.9%	14.4%	27.9%	Percent	8.4%	12.5%	2.5%
Agricultural Workers	1,212,550	507,723	704,827	Engineering-Technical			
Percent	18.8%	13.3%	26.8%	Personnel	456,228	396,568	59,660
Forestry Workers	68,787	41,051	27,736	Percent	7.1%	10.4%	2.3%
Percent	1.1%	1.1%	1.1%	Technical Personnel			
				in Agriculture[c]	86,837	81,451	5,386
Mining	145,018	134,122	10,896	Percent	1.3%	2.1%	0.2%
Percent	2.2%	3.5%	0.4%				
				Educational, Scientif-			
Manufacturing	1,649,161	1,056,606	592,555	ic & Cultural Personnel	252,845	126,492	126,353
Percent	25.6%	27.7%	22.5%	Percent	3.9%	3.3%	4.8%
				Personnel in Educ.	205,164	91,409	113,755
Construction	403,683	384,930	18,753	Percent	3.2%	2.4%	4.3%
Percent	6.3%	10.1%	0.7%	Personnel in Culture	22,978	15,595	7,383
				Percent	0.4%	0.4%	0.3%
Transport &				Personnel in Arts	19,432	14,403	5,029
Communication	450,403	373,561	76,842	Percent	0.3%	0.4%	0.2%
Percent	7.0%	9.8%	2.9%	Clergy	5,271	5,085	186
Transport Workers	387,101	349,930	37,171	Percent	0.1%	0.1%	0.0%
Percent	6.0%	9.2%	1.4%				
Communic. Personnel	42,842	13,505	29,337	Health Personnel	116,182	29,216	86,966
Percent	0.7%	0.3%	1.1%	Percent	1.8%	0.8%	3.3%
Aux. Workers in							
Transp. & Communic.	20,460	10,126	10,334	Personnel in Admin.,			
Percent	0.3%	0.3%	0.4%	Finance & Office Work	589,532	251,126	338,406
				Percent	9.1%	6.6%	12.9%
Trade, Services &				Economists	334,019	151,728	182,291
Protection	896,928	342,791	554,137	Percent	5.2%	4.0%	6.9%
Percent	13.9%	9.0%	21.1%	Legal Personnel	9,601	8,343	1,258
Security Personnel[a]	6,953	6,648	305	Percent	0.1%	0.2%	0.0%
Percent	0.1%	0.2%	0.0%	Office Personnel	245,912	91,055	154,857
Trade, Supply &				Percent	3.8%	2.4%	5.9%
Warehouse Workers	358,119	156,255	201,864				
Percent	5.6%	4.1%	7.7%	Other Occupations	67,881	48,123	19,758
Communal Services				Percent	1.0%	1.3%	0.7%
Personnel	10,905	7,305	3,600				
Percent	0.2%	0.2%	0.1%	Unknown or Undeclared	11,467	7,575	3,892
Workers in Communal				Percent	0.2%	0.2%	0.1%
Catering	103,802	20,317	83,485				
Percent	1,6%	0.5%	3.2%				
Service Workers[b]	417,149	152,266	264,883				
Percent	6.5%	4.0%	10.1%				
Leading & Supervisory							
Personnel	31,910	29,872	2,038				
Percent	0.5%	0.8%	0.1%				
Leaders in State							
Admin. & Social Orgs.	31,910	29,872	2,038				
Percent	0.5%	0.8%	0.1%				

Notes: [a] Persons in nonmanual occupations concerned with the preservation of public order. [b] Includes 32,785 guards and firemen concerned with protective services. [c] Agronomists, Veterinarians and other Specialists and Technicians in agriculture.

TABLE G-3   MAJOR OCCUPATIONS: GDR, 1950-1964

Occupation	1950[a]			1964		
	Total	Male[b]	Female	Total	Male[b]	Female
ACTIVE EARNERS, TOTAL	7,923,222	4,767,624	3,155,598	7,994,526[c]	4,459,689[c]	3,534,837[c]
Percent	100.0%	100.0%	100.0%	100.0%	100.0%	100.0%
Agriculture & Forestry	2,040,009	944,467	1,095,542	993,501	522,102	471,399
Percent	25.7%	19.8%	34.7%	12.4%	11.7%	13.3%
Workers in Farming & Animal Husbandry	2,040,009	944,467	1,095,542			
Percent	25.7%	19.8%	34.7%			
Agricultural Workers				710,472	373,561	336,911
Percent				8.9%	8.4%	9.5%
Gardeners				69,082	30,076	39,006
Percent				0.9%	0.7%	1.1%
Workers in Animal Husbandry				178,914	94,338	84,576
Percent				2.2%	2.1%	2.4%
Fresh Water Fishermen				1,336	1,271	65
Percent				0.0%	0.0%	0.0%
Forestry Workers				33,697	22,856	10,841
Percent				0.4%	0.5%	0.3%
Mining				57,452	54,349	3,103
Percent				0.7%	1.2%	0.1%
Manufacturing	3,151,444	2,285,114	866,330	2,018,751	1,313,197	705,554
Percent	39.8%	47.9%	27.4%	25.2%	29.4%	20.0%
Construction				419,005	409,320	9,685
Percent				5.2%	9.2%	0.3%
Transport & Communications	1,156,794	791,410	365,384	640,783	505,691	135,092
Percent	14.6%	16.6%	11.6%	8.0%	11.3%	3.8%
Land Transport Occs.				399,482	354,373	45,109
Percent				5.0%	7.9%	1.3%
Water Transport Occs.				7,870	7,010	860
Percent				0.1%	0.1%	0.0%
Air Transport Occs.				448	314	134
Percent				0.0%	0.0%	0.0%
Information Dissemination				92,000	20,942	71,058
Percent				1.1%	0.5%	2.0%
Other Occs. Related to Transport & Communications				140,983	123,052	17,931
Percent				1.8%	2.7%	0.5%
Trade,Services, & Protection	436,337[d]	82,447[d]	353,890[d]	1,356,088	377,137	978,951
Percent	5.5%	1.7%	11.2%	17.0%	8.4%	27.7%
Buyers, Sellers, Dealers, & Traders				368,629	87,354	281,275
Percent				4.6%[c]	1.9%	7.9%[c]
Innkeepers, Hotel & Restaurant Workers				227,539	34,071	193,468
Percent				2.8%	0.8%	5.5%
Testers, Sorters, Warehouse Personnel,& Shippers				260,898	121,132	139,766
Percent				3.3%	2.7%	3.9%
Guards & Security Personnel				104,615	89,504	15,111
Percent				1.3%	2.0%	0.4%
Cleaning Workers				307,653	25,462	282,191
Percent				3.8%	0.6%	8.0%
Other Service Personnel				86,754	19,614	67,140
Percent				1.1%	0.4%	1.9%

342

Occupation	1950			1964		
	Total	Male [b]	Female	Total	Male [b]	Female
Leading & Supervisory Personnel						
Percent						
Technical Personnel	209,833	197,390	12,443	386,966	304,592	82,374
Percent	2.6%	4.1%	0.4%	4.8%	6.8%	2.3%
Engineers				159,921	148,005	11,916
Percent				2.0%	3.3%	0.3%
Technicians				151,716	128,546	23,170
Percent				1.9%	2.9%	0.6%
Specialists				67,171	22,159	45,012
Percent				0.8%	0.5%	1.3%
Agric. Technicians [e]				8,158	5,882	2,276
Percent				0.1%	0.1%	0.1%
Educational, Scientific & Cultural Personnel	179,279 [f]	97,323 [f]	81,956 [f]	370,858	173,014	197,844
Percent	2.3%	2.0%	2.6%	4.6%	3.9%	5.6%
Personnel in Education				310,077	131,105	178,972
Percent				3.9%	2.9%	5.1%
Writers, Artists, & Musicians				29,549	20,669	8,880
Percent				0.4%	0.5%	0.2%
Scientists				6,811	5,546	1,265
Percent				0.1%	0.1%	0.0%
Social Scientists				6,145	4,979	1,166
Percent				0.1%	0.1%	0.0%
Personnel in Religion				18,276	10,715	7,561
Percent				0.2%	•0.2%	0.2%
Health Personnel				205,233	37,118	168,115
Percent				2.6%	0.8%	4.7%
Personnel in Administration, Finance & Office Work	592,761 [g]	353,675 [g]	239,086 [g]	989,136	359,008	630,128
Percent	7.5%	7.4%	7.6%	12.4%	8.0%	17.8%
Commercial Occs.				385,361	185,996	199,365
Percent				4.8%	4.2%	5.6%
Planning & Accounting				285,664	88,596	197,068
Percent				3.6%	2.0%	5.6%
Office Workers				183,732	11,766	171,966
Percent				2.3%	0.3%	4.9%
Government Officials				120,728	63,213	57,515
Percent				1.5%	1.4%	1.6%
Other Related Occs.				13,651	9,437	4,214
Percent				0.2%	0.2%	0.1%
Other Occupations				556,754	404,162	152,592
Percent				7.0%	9.1%	4.3%
Power Machine Operators				207,511	181,926	25,585
Percent				2.6%	4.1%	0.7%
Others				349,243	222,236	127,007
Percent				4.4%	5.0%	3.6%
Unknown or Undeclared	156,765	15,798	140,967			
Percent	2.0%	0.3%	4.5%			

Notes: a Excludes East Berlin. b Difference between total and number of females. c Economically Active, apprentices not included. d Health and Communal Services. e Veterinarians and Botanists. Agronomists not listed. f Religion and Cultural Affairs. g Administration and Justice.

TABLE G-4   MAJOR OCCUPATIONS: HUNGARY, 1960-1970

Occupation	1960			1970		
	Total	Male	Female	Total	Male	Female
TOTAL ACTIVE EARNERS[a]	4,875,361	3,164,405	1,710,956	4,988,676	2,933,484	2,055,192
Percent	100.0%	100.0%	100.0%	100.0%	100.0%	100.0%
Agriculture & Forestry	1,642,975	957,999	684,976	922,212	510,673	411,539
Percent	33.7%	30.3%	40.0%	18.5%	17.4%	20.0%
Agricultural Workers	1,288,792	748,511	540,281	537,148	197,562	339,586
Percent	26.4%	23.6%	31.6%	10.8%	6.7%	16.5%
Animal Husbandry Workers	90,365	81,911	8,454	132,519	105,443	27,076
Percent	1.8%	2.6%	0.5%	2.6%	3.6%	1.3%
Day Laborers	47,924	33,378	14,546	8,131	4,268	3,863
Percent	1.0%	1.0%	0.8%	0.2%	0.1%	0.2%
Forestry Workers	31,704	22,793	8,911	20,384	14,166	6,218
Percent	0.6%	0.7%	0.5%	0.4%	0.5%	0.3%
Gardeners	21,404	14,694	6,710	59,325	30,564	28,761
Percent	0.4%	0.5%	0.4%	1.2%	1.0%	1.4%
Mining	100,425	97,353	3,072	71,845	68,006	3,839
Percent	2.1%	3.1%	0.2%	1.4%	2.3%	0.2%
Manufacturing	916,089	621,104	294,985	1,156,340	715,349	440,991
Percent	18.8%	19.6%	17.2%	23.2%	24.4%	21.4%
Construction	238,374	233,475	4,899	341,300	330,948	10,352
Percent	4.9%	7.4%	0.3%	6.8%	11.3%	0.5%
Transport & Communications	275,687[b]	262,541	13,146	247,023[c]	224,445	22,578
Percent	5.6%	8.3%	0.8%	4.9%	7.6%	1.1%
Auto, Bus & Tram Drivers	63,492	62,578	914	121,364	120,545	819
Percent	1.3%	2.0%	0.0%	2.4%	4.1%	0.0%
Post & Telecommunications Workers	13,946[d]	10,201	3,745	15,349[c]	8,477	6,872
Percent	0.3%	0.3%	0.2%	0.3%	0.3%	0.3%
Haulers & Related Workers	85,769	85,475	294	9,321	9,050	271
Percent	1.7%	2.7%	0.0%	0.2%	0.3%	0.0%
Trade, Services & Protection	199,488	87,461	112,027	274,428[e]	94,423	180,005
Percent	4.1%	2.8%	6.5%	5.5%	3.2%	8.7%
Catering Workers	51,859	17,708	34,151			
Percent	1.1%	0.6%	2.0%			
Trade Workers	112,376	51,475	60,901			
Percent	2.3%	1.6%	3.6%			
Trade & Catering Workers				145,060	39,620	105,440
Percent				2.9%	1.3%	5.1%
Service Workers	35,253	18,278	16,975	31,185	12,556	18,629
Percent	0.7%	0.6%	1.0%	0.6%	0.4%	0.9%
Stock Clerks & Related Workers				98,183	42,247	55,936
Percent				2.0%	1.4%	2.7%
Protective Service Personnel	...	...	...	...	...	...
Percent	...	...	...	...	...	...

TABLE G-4   (CONTINUED)

Occupation	1960			1970		
	Total	Male	Female	Total	Male	Female
Leading & Supervisory Personnel	40,625	35,349	5,276	29,961	25,260	4,701
Percent	0.8%	1.1%	0.3%	0.6%	0.9%	0.2%
Administrative Leaders	2,146	1,973	173			
Percent	0.0%	0.1%	0.0%			
Leaders of Executive Bodies & Courts				10,733	9,220	1,513
Percent				0.2%	0.3%	0.1%
Local Leaders	8,910	7,800	1,110			
Percent	0.2%	0.2%	0.1%			
Enterprise Directors	9,242	8,604	638	6,049	5,637	412
Percent	0.2%	0.3%	0.0%	0.1%	0.2%	0.0%
Collective Farm Chairmen	4,519	4,489	30	5,166	5,014	152
Percent	0.1%	0.1%	0.0%	0.1%	0.2%	0.0%
Transport & Communic. Ldrs.				8,013	5,389	2,624
Percent				0.2%	0.2%	0.1%
Head Bookkeepers	8,412	6,643	1,769			
Percent	0.2%	0.2%	0.1%			
Party & Mass Organ. Ldrs.	7,396	5,840	1,556			
Percent	0.1%	0.2%	0.1%			
Technical Personnel	183,900	154,862	29,038	301,427	239,137	62,290
Percent	3.8%	4.9%	1.7%	6.0%	8.2%	3.0%
Engineers, Designers & Related Personnel f	134,128	112,987	21,141			
Percent	2.7%	3.6%	1.2%			
Agronomists, Foresters & Related Personnel f	22,263	21,173	1,090			
Percent	0.4%	0.7%	0.1%			
Transportation & Communic. Specialists f	27,509	20,702	6,807			
Percent	0.6%	0.6%	0.4%			
Agric. Managers, Technical Directors of Enterprises & Related				33,026	31,092	1,934
Percent				0.7%	0.8%	0.1%
Engineers, Designers, Veterinarians & Related				68,939	59,846	9,093
Percent				1.4%	2.0%	0.4%
Skilled Personnel				199,462	148,199	51,263
Percent				4.0%	5.0%	2.5%
Educational, Scientific & Cultural Personnel	133,862	68,687	65,175	167,438	76,035	91,403
Percent	2.7%	2.2%	3.8%	3.3%	2.6%	4.4%
Educational Personnel	91,477	36,792	54,685	119,349	44,356	74,993
Percent	1.9%	1.2%	3.2%	2.4%	1.5%	3.6%
Actors, Writers & Artists	12,774	8,377	4,397			
Percent	0.3%	0.3%	0.2%			
Professionals in the Arts				17,673	11,162	6,511
Percent				0.3%	0.4%	0.3%
Skilled Personnel in Culture	11,257	9,456	1,801			
Percent	0.2%	0.3%	0.1%			
Entertainers				7,993	6,668	1,325
Percent				0.2%	0.2%	0.1%
Other Intellectual Occs.	14,317	12,191	2,126	22,423	13,849	8,574
Percent	0.3%	0.4%	0.1%	0.4%	0.5%	0.4%

Occupation	1960			1970		
	Total	Male	Female	Total	Male	Female
Health Personnel	70,921	20,954	49,967	99,806	20,201	79,605
Percent	1.4%	0.7%	2.9%	2.0%	0.7%	3.9%
Doctors & Pharmacists	18,514	13,454	5,060	23,113	14,333	8,780
Percent	0.4%	0.4%	0.3%	0.5%	0.5%	0.4%
Veterinarians	2,226	2,169	57			
Percent	0.0%	0.1%	0.0%			
Nurses, Midwives & Medical Assistants				47,943	3,071	44,872
Percent				1.0%	0.1%	2.2%
Skilled Health Personnel	50,181	5,331	44,850			
Percent	1.0%	0.2%	2.6%			
Other Health Occs.				28,750	2,797	25,953
Percent				0.6%	0.1%	1.3%
Personnel in Administration, Finance & Office Work	368,256	157,544	210,712	684,243	246,313	437,930
Percent	7.5%	5.0%	12.3%	13.7%	8.4%	21.3%
Legal Personnel	7,118	6,460	658	9,220	7,509	1,711
Percent	0.1%	0.2%	0.0%	0.2%	0.2%	0.1%
Bookkeepers	82,154	28,469	53,685			
Percent	1.7%	0.9%	3.1%			
Chief Accountants & Economists				23,413	15,407	8,006
Percent				0.5%	0.5%	0.4%
Town Council Mbrs. & Related				27,888	16,813	11,075
Percent				0.6%	0.6%	0.5%
Post & Communication Personnel	12,965	3,687	9,278			
Percent	0.3%	0.1%	0.5%			
Commercial & Accounting Personnel[c, e]				328,388	129,698	198,690
Percent				6.6%	4.4%	9.7%
Office Workers	230,959	92,191	138,768	295,334	76,886	218,448
Percent	4.7%	2.9%	8.1%	5.9%	2.6%	10.6%
Other Occupations	704,759	467,076	237,683	692,653	382,694	309,959
Percent	14.4%	14.8%	13.9%	13.9%	13.0%	15.1%
Other Manual Occs. [g]	704,759	467,076	237,683	692,653	382,694	309,959
Percent	14.4%	14.8%	13.9%	13.9%	13.0%	15.1%
Unknown or Undeclared	0	0	0	0	0	0
Percent	0%	0%	0%	0%	0%	0%

Notes: a Active Earners (Aktiv keresok). b Note 11,136 Skilled Employees in Transport and Communication included in data for Transport and Communication Specialists under category of Technical Personnel. c Note 31,140 Skilled Employees in Communications and Transport, and 9,845 Telephone and Telegraph Operators included in data for Commercial and Accounting Personnel under category of Persons in Administration, Finance and Office Work. d Note 12,965 Skilled Personnel in Post and Communications included under Personnel in Administration, Finance and Office Work. e Note 72,795 Persons in Goods Circulation and Sales, and 55,879 Managers of Trade and Eating Establishments included in figure for Commercial and Accounting Personnel under category of Persons in Administration, Finance and Office Work. f Includes Engineers, Technicians and Skilled Employees (Szakalkalmazott). g Includes Street Cleaners, Loaders and Haulers, Office Assistants, Odd-Job Workers, Janitors and Unskilled laborers.

TABLE G-5   MAJOR OCCUPATIONS: POLAND, 1960-1974

Occupation	1960[a] I	1970 II Total	Male	Female	1974 II Total	Male	Female
ACTIVE EARNERS, TOTAL[b]	13,907,442	16,429,101	8,828,853	7,600,248	17,506,555	9,424,317	8,082,238
Percent	100.0%	100.0%	100.0%	100.0%	100.0%	100.0%	100.0%
Agriculture & Forestry		5,882,543	2,491,091	3,391,452	5,694,630	2,573,853	3,120,777
Percent		35.8%	28.2%	44.6%	32.5%	27.3%	38.6%
Agric. & Forestry Workers	[264,000]	368,860	265,509	103,351	371,702	255,743	115,959
Percent	1.9%	2.2%	3.0%	1.3%	2.1%	2.7%	1.4%
Fishermen		9,730	9,636	94	14,185	14,033	152
Percent		0.1%	0.1%	0.0%	0.1%	0.1%	0.0%
Collective Farmers	[28,000]	27,274	15,139	12,135	33,441	18,830	14,611
Percent	0.2%	0.2%	0.2%	0.2%	0.2%	0.2%	0.2%
Private Peasantry		2,626,493	1,525,548	1,100,945	2,441,998	1,632,716	809,282
Percent	[6,175,000]	16.0%	17.3%	14.5%	13.9%	17.3%	10.0%
Helping Family Mbrs.	44.4%	2,758,451	613,341	2,145,110	2,733,116	582,761	2,150,355
Percent		16.8%	6.9%	28.2%	15.6%	6.2%	26.6%
Self-Employed & HFM in Agric. Services		16,610	8,949	7,661	18,526	10,060	8,466
Percent		0.1%	0.1%	0.1%	0.1%	0.1%	0.1%
Self-Employed in Other Agric. Occs.		75,125	52,969	22,156	81,662	59,710	21,952
Percent		0.4%	0.6%	0.3%	0.5%	0.6%	0.3%
Workers in Industrial, Construction & Related Occupations	[2,017,000]	4,299,667	3,217,797	1,081,870	4,994,512	3,655,074	1,339,438
Percent	14.5%	26.2%	36.4%	14.2%	28.5%	38.8%	16.6%
Industrial Branch		3,090,359	2,082,321	1,008,038	3,592,473	2,355,133	1,237,340
Percent		18.8%	23.6%	13.3%	20.5%	25.0%	15.3%
Construction Branch		642,153	623,331	18,822	710,665	684,892	25,773
Percent		3.9%	7.1%	0.2%	4.1%	7.3%	0.3%
Agric. Branch		112,077	108,216	3,861	146,681	140,111	6,570
Percent		0.7%	1.2%	0.0%	1.0%	1.5%	0.1%
Other Branches		455,078	403,929	51,149	544,693	474,938	69,755
Percent		2.8%	4.6%	0.7%	3.1%	5.0%	0.9%
Unskilled Personnel in Services	[376,000]						
Percent	2.7%						
Persons in Service Occs. Related to Transport & Communic.		719,248	621,643	97,605	891,173	766,270	124,903
Percent		4.4%	7.0%	1.3%	5.1%	8.1%	1.5%
Persons in Service Occs. Related to Trade & Non-Ind.Services		979,543	356,716	622,827	1,125,199	356,340	768,859
Percent		6.0%	4.0%	8.2%	6.4%	3.8%	9.5%

TABLE G-5   (CONCLUDED)

Occupation	1960[a] I	1970 II Total	Male	Female	1974 II Total	Male	Female
Leading & Supervisory Personnel		299,045	247,015	52,030	312,174	255,464	56,710
Percent		1.8%	2.8%	0.7%	1.8%	2.7%	0.7%
Leaders & Direct. in Technical Sphere[c]		152,854	142,469	10,385	175,242	159,517	15,725
Percent		0.9%	1.6%	0.1%	1.0%	1.7%	0.2%
Personnel in State & Admin. Occs., Higher Level[d]		146,191	104,546	41,645	136,932	95,947	40,985
Percent		0.9%	1.2%	0.5%	0.8%	1.0%	0.5%
Personnel in Admin., Finance & Office Work	[918,000]						
Percent	6.6%						
Administrative, State & Office Personnel							
Percent							
Personnel in State & Admin. Occs., Lower Level[e]		1,271,314	405,808	865,506	1,541,797	430,274	1,111,523
Percent		7.7%	4.6%	11.4%	8.8%	4.6%	13.7%
Technical & Professional Personnel		1,352,339	685,615	666,724	1,655,350	832,880	822,470
Percent		8.2%	7.8%	8.8%	9.4%	8.8%	10.2%
Specialized Pers. in Service Occs.	[793,000]						
Percent	5.7%						
Specialists in Technical Occs.f	[417,000]	508,849	392,515	116,334	681,608	500,797	180,811
Percent	3.0%	3.1%	4.4%	1.5%	3.9%	5.3%	2.2%
Specialists in Non-Technical Occs.g	[459,000]	763,055	227,213	535,842	886,764	266,134	620,630
Percent	3.3%	4.6%	2.6%	7.1%	5.1%	2.8%	7.7%
Agric. Specialists[h]		80,435	65,887	14,548	86,978	65,949	21,029
Percent		0.5%	0.7%	0.2%	0.5%	0.7%	0.3%
Other Occupations		1,625,351	803,125	822,226	1,291,720	554,162	737,558
Percent		9.9%	9.1%	10.8%	7.4%	5.9%	9.1%
Unskilled Workers & Personnel Without Established Occs.	[195,000]	1,436,196	773,476	662,720	1,124,102	527,724	596,378
Percent	1.4%i	8.7%	8.8%	8.7%	6.4%	5.6%	7.4%
Persons Working on Commission & Cottage Laborers		188,233	28,780	159,453	167,146	26,038	141,108
Percent		1.1%	0.3%	2.1%	0.9%	0.3%	1.7%
Remaining Occs.	[167,000]	922	869	53	472	400	72
Percent	1.2%	0.0%	0.0%	0.0%	0.0%	0.0%	0.0%
Unknown or Undeclared	[1,962,000]	51	43	8	0	0	0
Percent	14.1%	0.0%	0.0%	0.0%	0%	0%	0%

Notes: a Data based on 5 percent sample of 1960 census. b See introduction for explanation of AE totals. c Directors and Deputy Directors of Enterprises (technical directors excluded). d Heads of Government Departments and Leading Personnel in State Administration at the Central, Regional, and District Levels; Political Leaders and Leaders of Mass Organizations. e Supervisors in Places of Work (with the exception of technical and production supervisors), Bookkeepers, Inspectors, Economists and other personnel in state administration; Secretaries and Other Office Personnel. f Technical Directors, Technical and Production Supervisors, Engineers and Technical Personnel. g Doctors and Other Health Specialists, Teachers, Scientists, Librarians Artists and Writers, Clergy, and other non-technical specialists. h Veterinarians, Agronomists and Other agricultural specialists. i Unskilled Workers only.

TABLE G-6   MAJOR OCCUPATIONS: ROMANIA, 1956-1966

Occupation	1956			1966		
	Total	Male	Female	Total	Male[a]	Female
ACTIVE EARNERS, TOTAL	10,449,128	5,714,181	4,734,947	10,362,300	5,675,176	4,687,124
Percent	100.0%	100.0%	100.0%	100.0%	100.0%	100.0%
Agriculture & Forestry	7,211,614[b]	3,320,500	3,891,114	5,744,647	2,377,450	3,367,197
Percent	69.0%	58.1%	82.2%	55.4%	41.9%	71.8%
Agricultural Workers	7,193,088	3,302,775	3,890,313	5,718,257	2,353,767	3,364,490
Percent	68.9%	57.8%	82.2%	55.2%	41.5%	71.8%
Forestry Workers	18,526	17,725	801	23,394	20,948	2,446
Percent	0.2%	0.3%	0.0%	0.2%	0.4%	0.1%
Veterinarians				2,996	2,735	261
Percent				0.0%	0.0%	0.0%
Mining	69,599[c]	66,036	3,563	102,039	99,193	2,846
Percent	0.7%	1.1%	0.1%	1.0%	1.7%	0.1%
Manufacturing	1,254,792[d]	999,266	255,526	1,596,763	1,223,402	373,361
Percent	12.0%	17.5%	5.4%	15.4%	21.6%	8.0%
Construction	222,983[e]	210,416	12,567	431,325	411,048	20,277
Percent	2.1%	3.7%	0.3%	4.2%	7.2%	0.4%
Transport & Communications	250,618[f]	223,534	27,084	465,712	419,027	46,685
Percent	2.4%	3.9%	0.6%	4.5%	7.4%	1.0%
Transportation Workers	206,430[f]	196,962	9,468	409,041	388,556	20,485
Percen	2.0%	3.4%	0.2%	3.9%	6.8%	0.4%
Postal, Telecommunications & Related Personnel	44,188	26,572	17,616	56,671	30,471	26,200
Percent	0.4%	0.5%	0.4%	0.5%	0.5%	0.6%
Trade, Services & Protection	485,135[g]	282,783	202,352	608,603	316,577	292,026
Percent	4.6%	4.9%	4.3%	5.9%	5.6%	6.2%
Occs. Relating to Trade, Catering & Supply	197,269	131,129	66,140	250,739	129,477	121,262
Percent	1.9%	2.3%	1.4%	2.4%	2.3%	2.6%
Service Occupations	204,840	71,760	133,080	247,045	77,676	169,369
Percent	2.0%	1.3%	2.8%	2.4%	1.4%	3.6%
Protective Services Occs.	83,026	79,894	3,132	110,819	109,424	1,395
Percent	0.8%	1.4%	0.1%	1.1%	1.9%	0.0%
Leading & Supervisory Personnel	146,498	130,681	15,817	127,169	112,680	14,489
Percent	1.4%	2.3%	0.3%	1.2%	2.0%	0.3%
Leading Personnel	41,382	39,012	2,370	41,819	37,982	3,837
Percent	0.4%	0.7%	0.0%	0.4%	0.7%	0.1%
Lower Level Supervisory Personnel	77,867	68,635	9,232	68,530	59,737	8,793
Percent	0.7%	1.2%	0.2%	0.7%	1.0%	0.2%
Party Activists & Organizers	27,249	23,034	4,215	16,820	14,961	1,859
Percent	0.3%	0.4%	0.1%	0.2%	0.3%	0.0%

TABLE G-6   (CONCLUDED)

Occupation	1956			1966		
	Total	Male	Female	Total	Male[a]	Female
Technical Personnel	36,551[h]	32,524	4,027	220,704	178,800	41,904
Percent	0.3%	0.6%	0.1%	2.1%	3.2%	0.9%
Engineers	36,551	32,524	4,027			
Percent	0.3%	0.6%	0.1%			
Engineers & Architects				69,134	56,695	12,439
Percent				0.7%	1.0%	0.3%
Technicians	h			151,570	122,105	29,465
Percent				1.5%	2.1%	0.6%
Educational, Scientific & Cultural Personnel	181,246	100,377	80,869	254,302	116,430	137,872
Percent	1.7%	1.8%	1.7%	2.4%	2.0%	2.9%
Personnel in Art & Culture	37,273	28,272	9,001	42,191	24,740	17,451
Percent	0.3%	0.5%	0.2%	0.4%	0.4%	0.4%
Personnel in Religion	14,388	14,127	261	14,875	13,380	1,495
Percent	0.1%	0.2%	0.0%	0.1%	0.2%	0.0%
Personnel in Publishing & Journalism	4,550	3,113	1,437			
Percent	0.0%	0.1%	0.0%			
Scientific Personnel[i]				4,171	1,722	2,449
Percent				0.0%	0.0%	0.1%
Research Personnel				5,262	3,045	2,217
Percent				0.1%	0.0%	0.0%
Personnel in Education	123,038	53,019	70,019	187,803	73,543	114,260
Percent	1.2%	0.9%	1.5%	1.8%	1.3%	2.4%
Health Personnel	85,230	29,697	55,533	156,283	42,305	113,978
Percent	0.8%	0.5%	1.2%	1.5%	0.7%	2.4%
Personnel in Administration Finance, and Office Work	242,124	149,478	92,646	510,635	266,675	243,960
Percent	2.3%	2.6%	1.9%	4.9%	4.7%	5.2%
Economic & Planning Personnel	21,685	14,911	6,774			
Percent	0.2%	0.3%	0.1%			
Finance & Accounting Personnel	204,726	121,153	83,573	340,491	194,280	146,211
Percent	1.9%	2.1%	1.8%	3.3%	3.4%	3.1%
Legal Personnel	15,713	13,414	2,299	12,369	10,355	2,013
Percent	0.1%	0.2%	0.0%	0.1%	0.2%	0.0%
Secretaries & Administrators Service Personnel				157,776	62,040	95,736
Percent				1.5%	1.1%	2.0%
Other Occupations	260,287	167,687	92,600	139,872	109,150	30,722
Percent	2.5%	2.9%	2.0%	1.3%	1.9%	0.7%
Mastercraftsmen				59,106	57,020	2,086
Percent				0.6%	1.0%	0.0%
Other Occupations	260,287[j]	167,687	92,600	80,766	52,130	28,636
Percent	2.5%	2.9%	2.0%	0.8%	0.9%	0.6%
Unknown or Undeclared	2,451	1,202	1,249	4,245	2,438	1,807
Percent	0.0%	0.0%	0.0%	0.0%	0.0%	0.0%

Notes: a Difference between total and number of females. b Includes 21,589 technicians working in agriculture. c Includes 2,755 technicians working in mining. d Includes 46,788 technicians working in manufacturing. e Includes 16,745 technicians working in construction. f Includes 19,261 technicians working in transport. g Includes 5,369 technicians working in trade. h Excludes 130,009 technicians included in other occupational categories. i Physicists, Mathematicians, Chemists, Biologists, Botanists, Geologists. j Includes 184,466 "Other Functionaries."

TABLE G-7   MAJOR OCCUPATIONS: USSR, 1926-1970 (in Thousands)

Occupation	1926 I	1939 I Total	1939 I Female	1959 I Total	1959 I Female	1959 II Total	1959 II Female	1970 II Total	1970 II Female
ACTIVE EARNERS, TOTAL	78,751	78,811	34,102	99,130	47,605	99,130	47,605	115,204	57,376
Percent	100.0%	100.0%	100.0%	100.0%	100.0%	100.0%	100.0%	100.0%	100.0%
Agriculture & Forestry		35,955	20,199	35,036	19,828	34,838	19,786	23,335	12,633
Percent		45.6%	59.2%	35.3%	41.7%	35.1%	41.6%	20.3%	22.0%
Agricultural Workers	71,305	34,764	20,159	33,893	19,743	33,950	...	22,724	...
Percent	90.5%	44.1%	59.1%	34.2%	41.5%	34.2%	...	19.7%	...
Forestry Workers		923	11	981	66	727	...	520	...
Percent		1.2%	0.0%	1.0%	0.1%	0.7%	...	0.4%	...
Fishing Workers		185	...	128	...		...		...
Percent		0.2%	...	0.1%	...	161	...	91	...
Hunters		83	...	34	...	0.2%	...	0.1%	...
Percent		0.1%	...	0.0%	...		...		...
Mining	181	589	...	1,187	...	1,187	...	1,004	...
Percent	0.2%	0.7%	...	1.2%	...	1.2%	...	0.9%	...
Manufacturing	3,478	9,171	2,759	15,658	5,256	15,658	5,107	22,887	7,290
Percent	4.4%	11.6%	8.1%	15.8%	11.0%	15.8%	10.7%	19.9%	12.7%
Construction	516	2,479	120	5,094	905	5,094	905	5,432	1,482
Percent	0.6%	3.1%	0.3%	5.1%	1.9%	5.1%	1.9%	4.7%	2.6%
Transport & Communications	474	5,062	510	8,745	1,296	8,802	1,258	10,302	1,531
Percent	0.6%	6.4%	1.5%	8.8%	2.7%	8.9%	2.6%	8.9%	2.7%
Railroad Workers	321	939	175	1,664	519	1,664	519	1,380	474
Percent	0.4%	1.2%	0.5%	1.7%	1.1%	1.7%	1.1%	1.2%	0.8%
Workers in Sea Transp.	61	160	12	244	39	244	...	225	...
Percent	0.1%	0.2%	0.0%	0.2%	0.1%	0.2%	...	0.2%	...
Auto, Truck Drivers	18								
Percent	0.0%								
Tram, Subway Drivers	8								
Percent	0.0%								
Conductors	12								
Percent	0.0%								
Workers in Auto & City Transport		801	69	3,395	189	3,395	189	6,244	261
Percent		1.0%	0.2%	3.4%	0.4%	3.4%	0.4%	5.4%	0.4%
Other Workers in Transp.		2,715	...	2,722	...	2,780	...	1,501	...
Percent		3.4%	...	2.7%	...	2.8%	...	1.3%	...
Postal Workers		181	75	243	177	243	177	354	298
Percent		0.2%	0.2%	0.2%	0.4%	0.2%	0.4%	0.3%	0.5%
Radio, Telegraph, & Telephone Operators	55								
Percent	0.1%								
Communications Personnel		265	180	476	372	476	372	598	498
Percent		0.3%	0.5%	0.5%	0.8%	0.5%	0.8%	0.5%	0.9%
Trade, Services,& Protection	859	7,568	3,760	9,395	6,497	9,621	6,722	12,394	10,160
Percent	1.1%	9.6%	11.0%	9.5%	13.6%	9.7%	14.1%	10.8%	17.7%
Cooks	69								
Percent	0.1%								
Waiters	26								
Percent	0.0%								
Shopkeepers & Related	666								
Percent	0.8%								
Personnel in Communal & Personal Services[a]		202	65	277	147	100	...	161	...
Percent		0.2%	0.2%	0.3%	0.3%	0.1%	...	0.1%	...
Workers in Communal & Personal Services		2,258[b]	...	2,858[b]	...	3,261[c]	...	3,730[c]	...
Percent		2.9%	...	2.9%	...	3.3%	...	3.2%	...

Occupation	1926 I	1939 I Total	1939 I Female	1959 I Total	1959 I Female	1959 II Total	1959 II Female	1970 II Total	1970 II Female
Workers in Communal Catering		578	474	784	703				
Percent		0.7%	1.4%	0.8%	1.5%				
Workers in Trade & Communal Catering						1,900	1,656	3,576	3,269
Percent						1.9%	3.5%	3.1%	5.7%
Personnel in Trade, Communal Catering, Supply & Related		1,626	507	2,268	1,380	1,152	428	1,440	806
Percent		2.1%	1.5%	2.3%	2.9%	1.2%	9.0%	1.2%	1.4%
Workers in Protective Services[d]		2,298	...	2,167	...	2,167	...	1,713	...
Percent		2.9%	...	2.2%	...	2.2%	...	1.5%	...
Agents & Expeditors		176	23	146	54	146	54	169	91
Percent		0.2%	0.1%	0.1%	0.1%	0.1%	0.1%	0.1%	0.2%
Sanitary Workers, Governesses & Related	98	429	410	895	869	895	869	1,605	1,569
Percent	0.1%	0.5%	1.2%	0.9%	1.8%	0.9%	1.8%	1.4%	2.7%
Leading & Supervisory Personnel		1,202	101	1,347	219	1,490	241	1,976	384
Percent		1.5%	0.3%	1.4%	0.5%	1.5%	0.5%	1.7%	0.7%
Leaders of Enterprises, Coop. & State Farms, & Admin. Orgs.	365								
Percent	0.5%								
Leaders of Government & Social Orgs.		445	54	392	100		100		128
Percent		0.6%	0.2%	0.4%	0.2%		0.2%		0.2%
Leaders of Party & Other Social Orgs.						146	...	195	...
Percent						1.5%	...	0.2%	...
Leaders of Enterprises		757	46	955	118	1,098	141	1,570	256
Percent		1.0%	0.1%	1.0%	0.2%	1.1%	0.3%	1.4%	0.4%
Leaders of Government Orgs.						246	...	210	...
Percent						0.2%	...	0.2%	...
Technical Personnel	267	1,951	401	4,683	1,815	4,522	1,795	9,075	3,979
Percent	0.3%	2.5%	1.2%	4.7%	3.8%	4.6%	3.8%	7.9%	6.9%
Engineers & Technical Pers. (Including Tech. Pers. in Agric.)	267								
Percent	0.3%								
Engineers & Technical Pers.		1,656	360	4,206	1,650	4,045	1,630	8,450	3,754
Percent		2.1%	1.1%	4.2%	3.5%	4.1%	3.4%	7.3%	6.5%
Agronomists, Zoologists,& Veterinarians		295	40	477	165	477	165	625	225
Percent		0.4%	0.1%	0.5%	0.3%	0.5%	0.3%	0.5%	0.4%
Educational, Scientific & Cultural Personnel	500	2,039	1,029	3,593	2,328	3,753	2,348	6,181	4,095
Percent	0.6%	2.6%	3.0%	3.6%	4.9%	3.8%	4.9%	5.4%	7.1%
Scientific Pers. & Teachers in Tech. Schools	14								
Percent	0.0%								
Scientific Personnel & Teachers		1,553	830	2,836	1,904	2,836	1,904	4,951	3,403
Percent		2.0%	2.4%	2.9%	4.0%	2.9%	4.0%	4.3%	5.9%

Occupation	1926 I	1939 I Total	1939 I Female	1959 I Total	1959 I Female	1959 II Total	1959 II Female	1970 II Total	1970 II Female
Teachers & Personnel in Culture	486								
Percent	0.6%								
Writers & Newspapermen		58	17	104	47	104	47	143	76
Percent		0.1%	0.0%	0.1%	0.1%	0.1%	0.1%	0.1%	0.1%
Artists		143	41	190	59	190	59	275	89
Percent		0.2%	0.1%	0.2%	0.1%	0.2%	0.1%	0.2%	0.1%
Health Personnel	199	680	549	1,702	1,517	1,702	1,517	2,744	2,429
Percent	0.2%	0.9%	1.6%	1.7%	3.2%	1.7%	3.2%	2.4%	4.2%
Leading Health Personnel		17	6	44	23	39	21	60	32
Percent		0.0%	0.0%	0.0%	0.0%	0.0%	0.0%	0.0%	0.0%
Doctors & Dentists		136	86	369	292	370	292	628	465
Percent		0.2%	0.3%	0.4%	0.6%	0.4%	0.6%	0.5%	0.8%
Nurses		180	178	693	689	693	689	1,287	1,275
Percent		0.2%	0.5%	0.7%	1.4%	0.7%	1.4%	1.1%	2.2%
Personnel in Administration, Finance & Office Work	481	3,654	1,632	4,117	3,023	4,099	3,009	6,037	5,086
Percent	0.6%	4.6%	4.8%	4.1%	6.3%	4.1%	6.3%	5.2%	8.9%
Legal Personnel	27	62	8	79	25	79	25	108	41
Percent	0.0%	0.1%	0.0%	0.1%	0.0%	0.1%	0.1%	0.1%	0.1%
Accountants & Bookkeepers	376								
Percent	0.5%								
Cashiers	78								
Percent	0.1%								
Planning & Accounting Personnel		3,102	1,246	3,502	2,499	3,502	2,499	5,074	4,223
Percent		3.9%	3.6%	3.5%	5.2%	3.5%	5.2%	4.4%	7.4%
Office Personnel		489	378	535	497				
Percent		0.6%	1.1%	0.5%	1.0%				
Typists & Stenographers						130	129	246	243
Percent						0.1%	0.3%	0.2%	0.4%
Secretaries & Other Office Personnel						388	354	609	580
Percent						0.4%	0.7%	0.5%	1.0%
Other Occupations	127	2,355	135	5,088	557	5,944	1,029	7,028	1,959
Percent	0.2%	3.0%	0.4%	5.1%	1.2%	6.0%	2.2%	6.1%	3.4%
Warehouse Workers, Sorters, Operators of Power Equipment, & Related Workers	127	2,354	...	5,088	...	5,871	...	6,693	...
Percent	0.2%	2.9%	...	5.1%	...	5.9%	...	5.6%	...
Laboratory Workers						73	68	335	303
Percent						0.1%	0.1%	0.3%	0.5%
Unknown or Undeclared		6,107	2,907	3,486	4,364	2,420	3,888	6,808	6,347
Percent		7.7%	8.5%	3.5%	9.2%	2.4%	8.2%	5.9%	11.1%

Notes: a Includes Leaders of Enterprises in Communal Catering, Managers of Communal Centers, Barbers and Hairdressers, Photographers, and others in related nonmanual service occupations. b Janitors, Laundrywomen, Messengers, and others in related manual service occupations. c Janitors, Messengers, and others in related manual service occupations, as well as Hairdressers, Barbers, and Photographers formerly classified as nonmanual service personnel. d Firemen and Guards.

TABLE G-8   MAJOR OCCUPATIONS: YUGOSLAVIA, 1953-1971

Occupation	1953 Total	1953 Male[a]	1953 Female	1961 Total	1961 Male	1961 Female[b]	1971 Total	1971 Male	1971 Female[b]
ACTIVE EARNERS, TOTAL	7,848,857	5,168,592	2,680,265	8,340,343	5,387,200	2,953,143	8,889,816	5,686,332	3,203,484
Percent	100.0%	100.0%	100.0%	100.0%	100.0%	100.0%	100.0%	100.0%	100.0%
Agriculture & Forestry	5,324,637	3,172,889	2,151,748	4,731,222	2,723,383	2,007,839	3,820,227	2,149,033	1,671,194
Percent	67.8%	61.4%	80.3%	56.7%	50.5%	68.0%	43.0%	37.8%	52.2%
Agricultural Workers	5,277,712	3,127,032	2,150,680	4,631,671	2,636,216	1,995,455	3,770,675	2,100,676	1,669,999
Percent	67.2%	60.5%	80.2%	55.5%	48.9%	67.6%	42.4%	36.9%	52.1%
Forestry Workers	31,576	31,182	394	43,414	42,239	1,175	43,917	42,916	1,001
Percent	0.4%	0.6%	0.0%	0.5%	0.8%	0.0%	0.5%	0.7%	0.0%
Unskilled Agric., Forestry, & Fishing Workers				30,715	22,330	8,385			
Percent				0.4%	0.4%	0.3%			
Hunters & Fishermen							5,635	5,441	194
Percent							0.1%	0.1%	0.0%
Mining	57,629	57,102	527	107,051	104,216	2,835	64,262	63,342	920
Percent	0.7%	1.1%	0.0%	1.3%	1.9%	0.1%	0.7%	1.1%	0.0%
Manufacturing	866,062	734,357	131,705	1,435,814	1,142,341	293,473	1,621,218	1,239,054	382,164
Percent	11.0%	14.2%	4.9%	17.2%	21.2%	9.9%	18.2%	21.8%	11.9%
Unskilled Workers				231,213	176,811	54,402			
Percent				2.8%	3.3%	1.8%			
Construction	94,070	93,587	483	190,785	187,443	3,342	317,320	313,221	4,099
Percent	1.2%	1.8%	0.0%	2.3%	3.5%	0.1%	3.6%	5.5%	0.1%
Transport & Communications	107,578	107,113	465	209,216	198,928	10,288	219,833[c]	218,062[c]	1,771[c]
Percent	1.4%	2.1%	0.0%	2.5%	3.7%	0.3%	2.5%	3.8%	0.0%
Drivers of Highway Vehicles	53,305	53,138	167	96,219	95,389	830	d	...	...
Percent	0.7%	1.0%	0.0%	1.1%	1.8%	0.0%		...	...
Railroad Engineers, Firemen, & Related	20,901	20,874	27	27,706	27,149	557	e	...	...
Percent	0.3%	0.4%	0.0%	0.3%	0.5%	0.0%		...	...
Sailors & Ship Machinists	10,320	10,312	8	11,651	11,503	148			
Percent	0.1%	0.2%	0.0%	0.1%	0.2%	0.0%			
Telephone Operators				9,371	4,913	4,458			
Percent				0.1%	0.1%	0.1%			
Unskilled Workers in Transp.				7,666	418	7,248			
Percent				0.1%	0.0%	0.2%			
Trade, Services, & Protection	335,109	259,614	75,495	714,364	475,886	238,478	797,228	438,264	358,964
Percent	4.3%	5.0%	2.8%	8.6%	8.8%	8.1%	9.0%	7.7%	11.2%
Occupations in Trade	100,114	75,148	24,966	225,511	170,326	55,185	281,810	178,789	103,021
Percent	1.3%	1.4%	0.9%	2.7%	3.2%	1.9%	3.2%	3.1%	3.2%
Occupations in Services	109,908	60,431	49,477	352,873	171,212	181,661	367,695	114,639	253,056
Percent	1.4%	1.2%	1.8%	4.2%	3.2%	6.1%	4.1%	2.0%	7.9%
Occupations in Protection	125,087	124,035	1,052	135,980	134,348	1,632	147,723	144,836	2,887
Percent	1.6%	2.4%	0.0%	1.6%	2.5%	0.1%	1.7%	2.5%	0.1%

354

TABLE G-8 (CONTINUED)

Occupation	1953 Total	Male[a]	Female	1961 Total	Male	Female[b]	1971 Total	Male	Female[b]
Leading & Supervisory Personnel	51,869	47,120	4,749	93,972	82,848	11,124	92,136[f]	84,004	8,132
Percent	0.7%	0.9%	0.2%	1.1%	1.5%	0.4%	1.0%	1.5%	0.2%
Mbrs. of Reprs. Bodies	4,770	4,737	33	2,213	2,107	106	8,887[g]	7,923	964
Percent	0.1%	0.1%	0.0%	0.0%	0.0%	0.0%	0.1%	0.1%	0.0%
Administrative Leaders[h]	20,138	17,396	2,742	39,232	32,973	6,259			
Percent	0.2%	0.3%	0.1%	0.5%	0.6%	0.2%			
Enterprise Directors	26,961	24,987	1,974	27,223	25,539	1,684		...	...
Percent	0.3%	0.5%	0.1%	0.3%	0.5%	0.1%	i	...	...
Technical Directors				9,014	8,581	433			
Percent				0.1%	0.1%	0.0%			
Commercial & Financial Directors				2,682	2,553	129			
Percent				0.0%	0.0%	0.0%			
Organizers of Work & Production in Enterprises							78,731[j]	72,160	6,571
Percent							0.9%	1.3%	0.2%
Technical Personnel	46,925	41,876	5,049	91,656	76,881	14,775	289,683	178,879	110,804
Percent	0.6%	0.8%	0.2%	1.1%	1.4%	0.5%	3.2%	3.1%	3.4%
Engineers				15,523	13,413	2,110		...	...
Percent	38,527	34,328	4,199	0.2%	0.2%	0.1%	k	...	...
Technical Personnel	0.5%	0.7%	0.1%	47,663	41,540	6,123			
Percent				0.6%	0.8%	0.2%			
Veterinarians & Agronomists	8,398	7,548	850	7,977	6,904	1,073		...	...
Percent	0.1%	0.1%	0.0%	0.1%	0.1%	0.0%	k	...	...
Agrotechnicians				9,932	9,06 3	869			
Percent				0.1%	0.2%	0.0%			
Draftsmen, Lab. Assistants, & Related				10,561	5,961	4,600			
Percent				0.1%	0.1%	0.1%			
Experts in Technical Fields							129,448[l]	103,092	26,356
Percent							1.4%	1.8%	0.8%
Communications Experts							7,758	7,407	351
Percent							0.1%	0.1%	0.0%
Other Specialists							152,477[m]	68,380	84,097
Percent							1.7%	1.2%	2.6%
Educational, Scientific & Cultural Personnel	110,615	64,932	45,683	155,715	82,180	73,535	261,184	142,309	118,875
Percent	1.4%	1.2%	1.7%	1.9%	1.5%	2.5%	2.9%	2.5%	3.7%
Physicists, Chemists, & Mathematicians	3,874	2,833	1,041	2,572	1,786	786	11,936	6,301	5,635
Percent	0.0%	0.0%	0.0%	0.0%	0.0%	0.0%	0.1%	0.1%	0.2%
Educational & Cultural Pers.	75,700	37,435	38,265						
Percent	1.0%	0.7%	1.4%						
Teachers				118,820	55,706	63,114	195,093	92,338	102,755
Percent				1.4%	1.0%	2.1%	2.2%	1.6%	3.2%
Artists	21,973	17,223	4,752	19,713	15,702	4,011	23,888	18,298	5,590
Percent	0.3%	0.3%	0.2%	0.2%	0.3%	0.1%	0.3%	0.3%	0.2%
Experts in Natural Sciences							28,560	23,770	4,790
Percent							0.3%	0.4%	0.1%

Occupation	1953			1961			1971		
	Total	Male[a]	Female	Total	Male	Female[b]	Total	Male	Female[b]
Health Personnel	44,909	19,503	25,406	72,299	27,643	44,656	118,382	37,729	.80,653
Percent	0.6%	0.4%	0.9%	0.9%	0.5%	1.5%	1.3%	0.7%	2.5%
Doctors, Dentists, & Pharmacists	7,123[n]	5,399[n]	1,724[n]	19,550	12,614	6,936		...	...
Percent	0.1%	0.1%	0.1%	0.2%	0.2%	0.2%	p	...	...
Nurses	20,031	4,717	15,314	25,482[o]	7,453[o]	18,029[o]		...	...
Percent	0.2%	0.1%	0.6%	0.3%	0.1%	0.6%	p	...	...
Health Technicians				27,267	7,576	19,691			
Percent				0.3%	0.1%	0.7%			
Specialists in Medical Sciences							118,382[q]	37,729	80,653
Percent							1.3%	0.7%	2.5%
Personnel in Administration, Finance, & Office Work	331,796	216,210	115,586	459,186	228,169	231,017	531,884	269,481	262,403
Percent	4.2%	4.2%	4.3%	5.5%	4.2%	7.8%	6.0%	4.7%	8.2%
"Officials"[r]	312,207	201,548	110,659						
Percent	4.0%	3.9%	4.1%						
Office Personnel				221,244	108,418	112,826			
Percent				2.6%	2.0%	3.8%			
Financial & Accounting Personnel				96,024	44,616	164,233	214,967	103,895	111,072
Percent				1.1%	0.8%	5.6%	2.4%	1.8%	3.5%
Economists				119,236	55,395	63,841		...	...
Percent				1.4%	1.0%	2.2%	s	...	...
Legal Personnel	19,547[t]	14,628[t]	4,919[t]	22,682	19,739	2,943		...	...
Percent	0.2%	0.3%	0.2%	0.3%	0.4%	0.1%	s	...	...
Workers in Manipulative Tasks in Communic. & Transp.							69,312	56,123	13,189
Percent							0.8%	1.0%	0.4%
Other Occupations	477,700	354,323	123,377	7,138	5,242	1,896	600,279	449,194	151,085
Percent	6.1%	6.8%	4.6%	0.1%	0.1%	0.1%	6.8%	7.9%	4.7%
Unskilled Workers	475,218	352,088	123,130						
Percent	6.0%	6.8%	4.6%						
Political Workers	2,482	2,235	247	2,824	2,455	369			
Percent	0.0%	0.0%	0.0%	0.0%	0.0%	0.0%			
Clergy	8,756	7,142	1,614	8,566	6,376	2,190	11,111	7,438	3,673
Percent	0.1%	0.1%	0.1%	0.1%	0.1%	0.1%	0.1%	0.1%	0.1%
Persons Abroad							589,168	441,756	147,412
Percent							6.6%	7.8%	4.6%
Unknown or Undeclared				71,925	52,040	19,885	156,180	103,760	52,420
Percent				0.9%	1.0%	0.7%	1.7%	1.8%	1.6%

Notes: For notes, see next page.

TABLE G-8 (CONCLUDED)

Notes: <u>a</u> Difference between total and number of females. <u>b</u> Difference between total and number of males. <u>c</u> Transport Workers only, Communications Personnel included with Technicians. <u>d</u> Number 144,227 in census data on the employed (<u>Zaposleno</u>), of whom, 143,421 were male and 806, female. <u>e</u> Numbered 16,277 in census data on the employed (<u>Zaposleno</u>), of whom, 16,103 were male, 174 were female. <u>f</u> Subcategories do not include Political Workers or Heads of Economic Associations. There was a total of 2,788 employed as Political Leaders and Political Functionaries according to the 1971 census. <u>g</u> Numbered 8,856 among those employed (<u>Zaposleno</u>) according to the census data, of whom 1,675 were Members of Representative Bodies, 1,581 were Elected Functionaries, and 4,507 were Other Leading Functionaries. <u>h</u> Includes State Functionaries and Heads of State Institutions (<u>Ustanova</u>). <u>i</u> See following fn. <u>j</u> Numbered 78,393 among those employed (<u>Zaposleno</u>) according to the census data. Includes 68,888 Directors and Other Leaders of Economic Organizations, 7,321 Leaders of Economic Organizations, 7,321 Leaders of Educational, Cultural, Health, Research, and related institutions, and 2,184 Leaders of other institutions. <u>k</u> See following fn. <u>l</u> Among those employed (<u>Zaposleno</u>), census data showed 41,772 Engineers, and 10,521 Biologists, Agronomists, and related specialists. <u>m</u> Among those employed (<u>Zaposleno</u>), census data showed 85,012 Economists and Financial Experts, 11,786 Economic and Financial Specialists, and 16,869 Legal Personnel. <u>n</u> Doctors only. <u>o</u> Nurses and Therapists. <u>p</u> See following fn. <u>q</u> Among those employed (<u>Zaposleno</u>), census data showed 25,651 Doctors, 1,872 Dentists, 3,894 Pharmacists, 22,021 Nurses and remaining auxilliary health personnel, and 59,232 Dental Technicians. <u>r</u> <u>Sluzbenici</u> <u>s</u> Included with Technical Personnel. <u>t</u> Lawyers, Economists, Economic Technicians, and Statisticians.

TABLE G-9   OCCUPATION AND EDUCATION: BULGARIA, 1956

Major Occupational Categories[a]

Level of Education	Total AE	Agric.	Mining	Manu.	Constr.	Transp.[b]	Trade[c]	Leaders	Technical	Education[d]	Health	Office Admin.
TOTAL	4,150,207	2,511,881	54,133	450,976	108,311	175,468	218,619	56,321	88,196	91,550	49,215	169,27
Percent	100.0%	100.0%	100.0%	100.0%	100.0%	100.0%	100.0%	100.0%	100.0%	100.0%	100.0%	100.0
Elem. or Less Percent Inc. Basic Percent	2,545,197	1,980,469	30,255	175,061	64,852	84,526	114,452	6,207	4,832	2,670	9,907	4,66
	61.3%	78.8%	55.9%	38.8%	59.9%	48.2%	52.3%	11.0%	5.5%	2.9%	20.1%	2.7
Basic Percent Inc. Second. Percent	1,127,386	503,301	21,019	237,387	38,254	76,438	85,537	21,518	19,288	7,466	9,202	42,71
	27.2%	20.0%	38.8%	52.6%	35.3%	43.6%	39.1%	38.2%	21.9%	8.1%	18.7%	25.2
Secondary Percent Inc. Higher Percent	343,239	26,884	2,734	36,741	4,678	13,589	16,451	17,284	41,662	39,861	13,019	95,07
	8.3%	1.1%	5.0%	8.1%	4.3%	7.7%	7.5%	30.7%	47.2%	43.5%	26.4%	56.2
Higher	134,385	1,227	125	1,787	527	915	2,179	11,312	22,414	41,553	17,087	26,81
Percent	3.2%	0.0%	0.2%	0.4%	0.5%	0.5%	1.0%	20.1%	25.4%	45.4%	34.7%	15.8

Selected Nonmanual Occupations

Level of Education	Central Leaders[f]	Local Leaders[g]	Leaders in Cells[h]	Directors[i]	Coll.Farm Chrmn.	Engrs.	Planning Pers.	Teachers	Doctors[j]	Health Pers.	Techni-cians	Office Pers.[k]
TOTAL	2,526	13,569	2,477	6,000	3,966	8,318	22,956	62,671	15,729	33,486	65,518	141,36
Percent	100.0%	100.0%	100.0%	100.0%	100.0%	100.0%	100.0%	100.0%	100.0%	100.0%	100.0%	100.0
Elem. or Less Percent Inc. Basic Percent	16	583	262	269	1,242	45	474	91	0	9,907	4,774	4,18
	0.6%	4.3%	10.6%	4.5%	31.3%	0.5%	2.1%	0.1%	0.0%	29.6%	7.3%	2.9
Basic Percent Inc. Second. Percent	273	5,176	1,541	1,561	2,107	323	4,645	2,028	0	9,202	18,845	38,03
	11.0%	38.1%	62.2%	26.0%	53.1%	3.9%	20.2%	3.2%	0.0%	27.5%	28.8%	26.9
Secondary Percent Inc. Higher Percent	817	5,559	585	2,986	444	1,151	11,385	28,049	908	12,111	36,405	83,61
	32.3%	41.0%	23.6%	49.8%	11.2%	13.8%	49.6%	44.7%	5.8%	36.2%	55.6%	59.1
Higher	1,420	2,251	89	1,184	173	6,799	6,452	32,503	14,821	2,266	5,494	15,53
Percent	56.2%	16.6%	3.6%	19.7%	4.4%	81.7%	28.1%	51.9%	94.2%	6.8%	8.4%	11.0

Notes: a Does not include persons with occupations classified as Other or Unknown. b Includes Transport Workers and Communications Personnel. c Trade, Services, and Supply. d Education, Culture, and the Arts. e Legal Personnel; Personnel in Finance, Planning and Accounting; Clerks and Secretaries. f Leading Personnel of Party, State (cont'd.)

TABLE G-9   (CONCLUDED)

<u>Notes</u> (cont'd.):   Cooperative and Social Institutions at the national level. <u>g</u> Leading Personnel of Party,
State, Cooperative and Social Institutions at the Regional and Local Level. <u>h</u> Leaders in Basic
Party Organizations, Youth Organizations, Trade Unions, and Other Social Organizations. <u>i</u> Leaders
in Enterprises. Does not include management or supervisory personnel in agriculture, trade,
services, or state institutions, nor supervisory personnel in subdivisions of the enterprise.
<u>j</u> Doctors, Dentists, and Pharmacists. <u>k</u> Financial And Accounting Personnel, Office Clerks,
and Secretaries.

TABLE G-10   OCCUPATION AND EDUCATION: BULGARIA, 1965

Major Occupational Categories[a]

Level of Education	Total AE	Agric.	Mining	Manu.	Constr.	Transp.[b]	Trade[c]	Leaders	Technical[d]	Education[e]	Health	Office Admin.[f]
TOTAL	4,281,939	1,716,569	53,173	794,863	188,234	294,601	306,420	54,484	170,599	141,678	54,777	208,390
Percent	100.0%	100.0%	100.0%	100.0%	100.0%	100.0%	100.0%	100.0%	100.0%	100.0%	100.0%	100.0%
Elem. or Less Percent — Inc. Basic Percent	1,854,187	1,221,036	23,809	203,833	94,435	107,151	129,899	1,646	3,060	1,019	427	2,598
	43.3%	71.1%	44.8%	25.6%	50.2%	36.4%	42.4%	3.0%	1.8%	0.7%	0.8%	1.2%
Basic Percent — Inc. Second. Percent	1,625,168	476,837	24,752	492,610	86,300	163,272	144,360	14,045	30,298	6,844	2,072	38,395
	38.0%	27.8%	46.5%	62.0%	45.8%	55.4%	47.1%	25.8%	17.8%	4.8%	3.9%	18.4%
Secondary Percent — Inc. Higher Percent	652,107	18,035	4,578	97,191	7,188	23,812	31,862	24,872	105,017	94,163	33,030	140,557
	15.2%	1.1%	8.6%	12.2%	3.8%	8.1%	10.4%	45.7%	61.6%	66.5%	60.3%	67.4%
Higher	150,477	661	34	1,229	311	366	299	13,921	32,224	39,652	19,248	26,840
Percent	3.5%	0.0%	0.0%	0.2%	0.2%	0.1%	0.1%	25.6%	18.9%	28.0%	35.1%	12.9%

Notes: a Does not include occupations classified as Other or Unknown. b Includes Transport Workers and Communications Personnel; excludes Postal Workers. c Includes Trade, Services, and Protection. d Includes Engineering-Technical Personnel, Agronomists, Veterinarians, Foresters, and related. e Includes Science, Education, Cultural and the Arts. f Personnel in Planning, Finance and Accounting, and Office Personnel.

Major Occupational Categories[a]

Level of Education	Total AE	Agric.	Mining	Manu.	Constr.	Transp.	Trade	Leaders	Technical	Educ.	Health	Office & Admin.[b]
TOTAL	4,875,361	1,642,975	100,425	916,089	238,374	275,687	199,488	40,625	183,900	133,862	70,921	361,138
Percent	100.0%	100.0%	100.0%	100.0%	100.0%	100.0%	100.0%	100.0%	100.0%	100.0%	100.0%	100.0%
Elem. or Less	1,021,744	553,384	21,562	115,170	45,054	57,559	20,917	1,262	3,651	3,316	1,620	5,557
Percent	20.9%	33.7%	21.5%	12.6%	18.9%	20.9%	10.5%	3.1%	2.0%	2.5%	2.3%	1.5%
Inc. Basic	2,070,193	886,404	52,892	384,024	109,136	142,753	80,353	10,319	25,453	5,917	11,900	39,441
Percent	42.5%	53.9%	52.7%	41.9%	45.8%	51.8%	40.3%	25.4%	13.8%	4.4%	16.8%	10.9%
Basic	1,142,837	190,400	22,853	348,180	73,602	65,349	79,765	9,392	36,555	7,810	21,452	127,369
Percent	23.4%	11.6%	22.7%	38.0%	30.9%	23.7%	40.0%	23.1%	19.9%	5.8%	30.2%	35.3%
Inc. Second.	137,437	6,646	1,584	32,835	5,270	4,811	8,826	2,713	11,883	4,021	4,546	37,793
Percent	2.8%	0.4%	1.6%	3.6%	2.2%	1.7%	4.4%	6.7%	6.5%	3.0%	6.4%	10.5%
Secondary	318,671	4,560	1,240	30,835	4,337	4,566	8,361	9,235	63,554	52,339	9,991	119,189
Percent	6.5%	0.3%	1.2%	3.4%	1.8%	1.6%	4.2%	22.7%	34.5%	39.1%	14.1%	33.0%
Inc. Higher	33,333	541	170	2,622	492	371	568	2,116	8,277	5,357	1,137	10,291
Percent	0.7%	0.0%	0.2%	0.3%	0.2%	0.1%	0.3%	5.2%	4.5%	4.0%	1.6%	2.8%
Higher	151,116	1,040	124	2,423	483	278	698	5,588	34,527	55,102	20,275	21,498
Percent	3.1%	0.1%	0.1%	0.3%	0.2%	0.1%	0.3%	13.7%	18.8%	41.2%	28.6%	5.9%

Selected Nonmanual Occupations

Level of Education	Central Admin.[c]	Local Admin.	Directors	Coll.Farm Chrmn.	Engineers	Teachers	Party Workers	Doctors	Health Personnel	Office Workers	Technicians
TOTAL	2,146	8,910	9,242	4,519	...	91,477	7,396	14,748	50,181	230,959	...
Percent	100.0%	100.0%	100.0%	100.0%	...	100.0%	100.0%	100.0%	100.0%	100.0%	...
Elem. or Less	14	215	275	579	...	197	163	0	1,620	4,362	...
Percent	0.6%	2.4%	3.0%	12.8%	...	0.2%	2.2%	0.0%	3.2%	1.9%	...
Inc. Basic	90	2,744	2,529	3,016	...	1,414	1,705	0	11,900	29,383	...
Percent	4.2%	30.8%	27.4%	66.7%	...	1.5%	23.0%	0.0%	23.7%	12.7%	...
Basic	205	2,570	2,293	542	...	2,106	2,674	0	21,452	89,564	...
Percent	9.5%	28.8%	24.8%	12.0%	...	2.3%	36.1%	0.0%	42.7%	38.8%	...
Inc. Second.	73	724	628	84	...	1,647	695	0	4,546	24,910	...
Percent	3.4%	8.1%	6.8%	1.8%	...	1.8%	9.4%	0.0%	9.0%	10.8%	...
Secondary	441	1,601	1,677	147	...	45,015	991	8	9,889	67,430	...
Percent	20.5%	18.0%	18.1%	3.2%	...	49.2%	13.4%	0.0%	19.7%	29.2%	...
Inc. Higher	207	445	431	35	...	2,525	375	455	492	5,805	...
Percent	9.6%	5.0%	4.7%	0.8%	...	2.8%	5.1%	3.1%	1.0%	2.5%	...
Higher	1,116	611	1,409	116	...	38,573	793	14,285	282	9,505	...
Percent	52.0%	6.8%	15.2%	2.6%	...	42.2%	10.7%	96.9%	0.6%	4.1%	...

Notes: a Does not include persons in category Other Manual Occupations.   b Legal personnel not included. c Administrative Leaders.

Major Occupational Categories[a]

Level of Education	Total AE	Agric.	Mining	Manu.	Constr.	Transp.	Trade	Leaders	Technical	Educ.	Health	Off: Adr
TOTAL	4,988,676	922,212	71,845	1,156,340	341,300	247,023	274,428	29,961	301,427	167,438	99,806	684
Percent	100.0%	100.0%	100.0%	100.0%	100.0%	100.0%	100.0%	100.0%	100.0%	100.0%	100.0%	100
Elem. or Less	557,101	243,175	9,236	74,473	42,215	19,043	16,759	176	1,848	1,356	618	3
Percent	11.2%	26.4%	12.8%	6.4%	12.3%	7.7%	6.1%	0.6%	0.6%	0.8%	0.6%	0
Inc. Basic	1,390,814	461,845	30,651	305,497	96,710	76,232	77,042	1,786	18,061	3,207	6,164	40
Percent	27.9%	50.1%	42.7%	26.4%	28.3%	30.9%	28.1%	6.0%	6.0%	1.9%	6.2%	6
Basic Percent	2,088,860	211,570	29,798	699,774	192,314	143,193	159,250	7,917	57,556	12,611	37,965	270
Inc. Second. Percent	41.9%	22.9%	41.5%	60.5%	56.4%	58.0%	58.0%	26.4%	19.1%	7.5%	38.0%	3
Secondary Percent	694,358	5,054	2,065	74,589	9,729	8,250	20,748	11,966	150,719	56,869	30,898	314
Inc. Higher Percent	13.9%	0.5%	2.9%	6.5%	2.9%	3.3%	7.6%	39.9%	50.0%	34.0%	31.0%	46
Higher	257,543	568	95	2,007	332	305	629	8,116	73,243	93,395	24,161	53
Percent	5.2%	0.1%	0.1%	0.2%	0.1%	0.1%	0.2%	27.1%	24.3%	55.8%	24.2%	7

Selected Nonmanual Occupations

Level of Education	Admin. Leaders[b]	Party Workers	Directors[c]	Coll. Farm Chrmn.	Engineers[d]	Teachers	Doctors[e]	Health Personnel	Techni- cians	Office Workers
TOTAL	10,733	...	6,049	5,166	21,029	119,349	19,281	76,693	199,462	295,334
Percent	100.0%	...	100.0%	100.0%	100.0%	100.0%	100.0%	100.0%	100.0%	100.0%
Elem. or Less	37	...	20	74	0	0	0	618	1,599	1,635
Percent	0.3%	...	0.3%	1.4%	0.0%	0.0%	0.0%	0.8%	0.8%	0.6%
Inc. Basic	370	...	224	889	0	956	0	6,164	15,275	15,027
Percent	3.4%	...	3.7%	17.2%	0.0%	0.8%	0.0%	8.0%	7.6%	5.1%
Basic Percent	2,316	...	779	1,985	0	5,982	0	37,965	49,189	135,885
Inc. Second. Percent	21.6%	...	12.9%	38.4%	0.0%	5.0%	0.0%	49.5%	24.7%	46.0%
Secondary Percent	3,970	...	2,193	1,472	98	42,563	39	30,833	118,261	127,107
Inc. Higher Percent	37.0%	...	36.2%	28.5%	0.5%	35.7%	0.2%	40.2%	59.3%	43.0%
Higher	4,040	...	2,833	746	20,931	69,848	19,242	1,113	15,138	15,680
Percent	37.6%	...	46.8%	14.4%	99.5%	58.5%	99.8%	1.5%	7.6%	5.3%

Notes: a Does not include persons in category Other Manual Occupations.   b Leaders of Executive Agencies and Courts. c Does not include production managers or technical directors. d Does not include agricultural engineers. e Does not include dentists or pharmacists.

BLE G-13   OCCUPATION AND EDUCATION: ROMANIA, 1956

Major Occupational Categories[a]

Level of education	Total AE	Agric.	Mining	Manu.	Constr.	Transp.[b]	Trade[c]	Leaders	Technical	Education	Health	Office& Admin.[d]
TOTAL	10,449,128	7,190,025	66,844	1,208,004	206,238	231,357	479,766	146,498	166,560	181,246	85,230	453,659
percent	100.0%	100.0%	100.0%	100.0%	100.0%	100.0%	100.0%	100.0%	100.0%	100.0%	100.0%	100.0%
Elem. or Less	9,045,233	6,941,193	60,083	926,140	175,657	186,482	430,833	59,505	38,772	25,067	28,803	143,672
Inc. Basic percent	86.6%	96.5%	90.0%	76.7%	85.2%	80.6%	89.8%	40.6%	23.3%	13.8%	33.8%	31.7%
Basic	783,838	228,082	5,479	251,385	27,140	33,381	37,932	27,690	27,495	12,410	22,861	107,338
Inc. Second. percent	7.5%	3.2%	8.2%	20.8%	13.2%	14.4%	7.9%	18.9%	16.5%	6.8%	26.8%	23.7%
Secondary	435,831	17,362	1,227	28,834	3,173	11,074	10,004	41,327	59,178	94,108	9,666	158,695
Inc. Higher percent	4.2%	0.2%	1.8%	2.4%	1.5%	4.8%	2.1%	28.2%	35.5%	51.9%	11.3%	35.0%
Higher	184,226	3,388	55	1,645	268	420	997	17,976	41,115	49,661	23,900	43,954
percent	1.8%	0.0%	0.1%	0.1%	0.1%	0.2%	0.2%	12,3%	24.7%	27.4%	28.0%	9.7%

Selected Nonmanual Occupations

Level of education	Admin. Leaders[e]	Inst. Leaders[f]	Political Workers[g]	Directors[h]	Engineers	Economists & Planners	Teachers	Doctors	Health Personnel[i]	Techni- cians	Office Workers[j]
TOTAL	19,020	3,507	27,249	17,292	36,551	21,685	123,038	23,346	61,884[k]	130,009	416,261
percent	100.0%	100.0%	100.0%	100.0%	100.0%	100.0%	100.0%	100.0%	100.0%	100.0%	100.0%
Elem. or Less	9,769	692	16,302	9,950	108	2,194	2,198	0	28,417	38,664	139,674
Inc. Basic percent	51.4%	19.7%	59.8%	57.5%	0.3%	10.1%	1.8%	0.0%	45.9%	29.7%	33.5%
Basic	2,998	362	5,300	3,008	276	4,200	5,926	0	22,861	27,219	101,744
Inc. Second. percent	15.8%	10.3%	19.5%	17.4%	0.7%	19.4%	4.8%	0.0%	36.9%	20.9%	24.4%
Secondary	4,038	1,003	4,635	3,379	1,694	10,259	82,758	0	9,666	57,484	146,841
Inc. Higher percent	21.2%	28.6%	17.0%	19.5%	4.6%	47.3%	67.3%	0.0%	15.6%	44.2%	35.3%
Higher	2,215	1,450	1,012	955	34,473	5,032	32,156	23,346	554	6,642	28,002
percent	11.6%	41.3%	3.7%	5.5%	94.3%	23.2%	26.1%	100.0%	0.9%	5.1%	6.7%

Notes: a Table does not include persons in categories Other Occupations and Occupations Unknown.   b Occupations related to Transportation, Post, and Telecommunications.   c Commerce, Catering, Supply, and Services.   d Includes (cont'd.)

TABLE G-13   (CONCLUDED)

Notes (cont'd.):   Economic and Planning Occupations, Financial and Accounting Occupations, Legal Personnel, Typists
and Stenographers and Other Functionaries. e Leaders of Central and Local Administration
and Cooperatives. f Leaders of Education, Health, Cultural, and Related Institutions. g
Party Activists and Organizers. h Leaders and Organizers of the Economy. i Health Technicians
and Other Personnel in Health. j Financial and Accounting Personnel, Typists and Stenographers,
and Other Functionaries. k Includes 386 unaccounted for.

Major Occupational Categories[a]

el of cation	Total AE	Agric.	Mining	Manu.	Constr.	Transp.[b]	Trade[c]	Leaders	Technical	Educ.[d]	Health	Office& Admin.[e]
AL	10,362,300	5,744,647[f]	102,039	1,596,763	431,325	465,712	608,603	127,169	220,704	254,302	156,283	510,636
rcent	100.0%	100.0%	100.0%	100.0%	100.0%	100.0%	100.0%	100.0%	100.0%	100.0%	100.0%	100.0%
m. or Less rcent	7,735,600	5,257,143	85,734	1,019,929	321,784	285,463	491,919	21,528	9,183	11,352	47,672	121,711
. Basic rcent	74.6%	91.5%	84.0%	63.9%	74.6%	61.3%	80.8%	16.9%	4.2%	4.5%	30.5%	23.8%
ic rcent	969,106	404,578	8,685	214,959	61,406	94,529	67,211	6,925	5,516	7,822	9,272	74,272
	9.3%	7.0%	8.5%	13.5%	14.2%	20.3%	11.0%	5.4%	2.5%	3.1%	5.9%	14.5%
de School rcent	632,832	70,224	6,214	312,475	42,379	53,852	34,133	9,649	15,238	5,761	23,338	35,131
	6.1%	1.2%	6.1%	19.6%	9.8%	11.6%	5.6%	7.6%	6.9%	2.3%	14.9%	6.9%
. Second.[g] rcent	...	...	...	...	...	...	...	...	...	...	...	...
ondary rcent	...	...	...	...	...	...	...	...	...	...	...	...
. Higher rcent	734,808	9,303	1,365	48,274	5,541	31,372	14,781	52,248	118,407	134,785	42,782	233,284
	7.1%	0.2%	1.3%	3.0%	1.3%	6.7%	2.4%	41.1%	53.6%	53.0%	27.4%	45.7%
her rcent	289,954	3,489[h]	41	1,126	215	496	559	36,818	72,360	94,582	33,219	46,238
	2.8%	0.1%	0.0%	0.1%	0.0%	0.1%	0.1%	28.9%	32.8%	37.2%	21.3%	9.1%

Selected Nonmanual Occupations

el of cation	Admin. Leaders[i]	Inst. Leaders[j]	Political Workers[k]	Direc-tors	Coll.Farm Chrmn.	Engineers[l]	Econs. & Planners	Teachers	Doctors[m]	Health Personnel	Techni-cians	Office Workers[n]
AL	12,783	10,882	16,820	5,897	6,054[o]	69,134	72,583	187,803	32,007	122,559	151,570	425,684
rcent	100.0%	100.0%	100.0%	100.0%	100.0%	100.0%	100.0%	100.0%	100.0%	100.0%	100.0%	100.0%
m. or Less rcent	4,526	202	2,194	805	4,945	54	2,982	10	0	47,509	9,129	118,729
. Basic rcent	35.4%	1.8%	13.0%	13.6%	81.7%	0.1%	4.1%	0.0%	0.0%	38.8%	6.0%	27.9%
ic	996	137	1,966	228	441	29	3,035	3,261	0	9,148	5,487	71,237
rcent	7.8%	1.2%	11.7%	3.9%	7.3%	0.0%	4.2%	1.7%	0.0%	7.5%	3.6%	16.7%
de School	628	141	3,347	371	187	133	1,979	3,172	0	23,220	15,105	33,152
rcent	4.9%	1.3%	19.9%	6.3%	3.1%	0.2%	2.7%	1.7%	0.0%	18.9%	10.0%	7.8%
. Second.[g] rcent	...	...	...	...	...	...	...	...	...	...	...	...
ondary rcent	...	...	...	...	...	...	...	...	...	...	...	...
. Higher rcent	2,787	5,937	6,850	2,071	401	1,260	42,680	116,386	0	41,842	117,147	190,482
	21.8%	54.5%	40.7%	35.1%	6.6%	1.8%	58.8%	62.0%	0.0%	34.1%	77.3%	44.7%
her	3,846	4,465	2,463	2,422	180	67,658	21,907	64,974	32,007	840	4,702	12,084
rcent	30.1%	41.0%	14.6%	41.1%	3.0%	97.9%	30.2%	34.6%	100.0%	0.7%	3.1%	2.8%

es: For notes, see next page.

TABLE G-14   (CONCLUDED)

Notes: a Does not include persons in categories Other Occupations or Unknown Occupations.   b Transport and
         Communications.   c Trade, Services, and Protection.   d Education, Culture, Publishing, and Journalism, Religion
         Physical Culture, Science, and Research.   e Economic, Planning, Accounting, Secretarial and Administrative Services
         Personnel.   f Subtotals exceed total in agriculture by 90.   g Included with basic and vocational education.   h
         Includes 2,996 Veterinarians with higher education.   i Includes Leaders in Administration, in Financial and Insurance
         Institutions, and Presidents and Secretaries of Executive Committees of Communal Councils.   j Leaders in Socio-
         cultural units.   k Activists - Organizers of Party and Masses.   l Engineers and Architects.   m Doctors and Pharmacists
         n Personnel in Finance and Accounting, Secretarial and Administrative Services.   o Subtotals exceed total by 100.

TABLE G-15　　OCCUPATION AND EDUCATION, MAJOR NONMANUAL OCCUPATIONS:　USSR, 1939-1970 (in Thousands)

Level of Education	1939					1959				
	I & II Total AE[a]	I Leaders[b]	I Technical[c]	I Education[d]	I Health	I Total AE[a]	I Leaders[b]	I Technical[c]	I Education[d]	I Health
TOTAL	78,811	1,202	1,951	2,039	680	99,130	1,347	4,683	3,593	1,702
Percent	100.0%	100.0%	100.0%	100.0%	100.0%	100.0%	100.0%	100.0%	100.0%	100.0%
Elem. or Less Percent	[69,200]	[765]	[724]	[345]	[222]	[56,200]	[178]	[400]	[66]	[53]
Inc. Basic Percent	87.8%	[63.6%]	[37.1%]	[16.9%]	32.6%	56.7%	[13.2%]	[8.6%]	[1.8%]	3.1%
Basic Percent										
Inc. Second. Percent										
Secondary Percent	[8,670]	[437]	[1,230]	[1,690]	[458]	[42,900]	[1,170]	[4,280]	[3,530]	[1,650]
Inc. Higher Percent	11.0%	[36.4%]	[62.9%]	[83.1%]	[67.4%]	43.3%	[86.9%]	[91.4%]	[98.1%]	96.9%
Higher Percent	[1,020] 1.3%									

Level of Education	1959					1970				
	II Total AE[a]	II Leaders[b]	II Technical[c]	II Education[d]	II Health	II Total AE[a]	II Leaders[b]	II Technical[c]	II Education[d]	II Health
TOTAL	99,130	1,490	4,522	3,753	1,702	115,204	1,976	9,075	6,181	2,744
Percent	100.0%	100.0%	100.0%	100.0%	100.0%	100.0%	100.0%	100.0%	100.0%	100.0%
Elem. or Less Percent	[23,400] 23.6%	[271]	[370]	[66]	[53]	[11,400] 9.9%	[110]	[301]	[88]	[60]
Inc. Basic Percent	[32,800] 33.1%	[18.2%]	[8.2%]	[1.8%]	3.1%	[28,600] 24.8%	[5.6%]	[3.3%]	[1.4%]	2.2%
Basic Percent	[25,800]					[35,800]	[243]	[1,030]	[386]	[200]
Inc. Second. Percent	26.0%					31.1%	[12.3%]	[11.4%]	[6.2%]	7.3%
Secondary Percent	[13,000] 13.1%	[1,220] [81.8%]	[4,150] [91.8%]	[3,690] [98.2%]	[1,650] 96.9%	[30,400] 26.4%	[941] [47.6%]	[5,460] [60.2%]	[3,020] [48.9%]	[1,870] [68.3%]
Inc. Higher Percent	[892] 0.9%					[1,500] 1.3%				
Higher Percent	[3,270] 3.3%					[7,500] 6.5%	[682] [34.5%]	[2,280] [25.1%]	[2,680] 43.4%	[609] 22.2%

Notes:　a Persons with Occupations.　b Includes Leaders of Organs of State Administration, Social Organizations (including party), Enterprises and Collective Farms, and their structural subdivisions.　c Includes Engineers, Technical Personnel and Agricultural Specialists (Agronomists, Zootechnicians, Veterinarians and Foresters). d Includes Scientific Workers and Teachers, Personnel in Culture, Writers, Newspapermen and Artists.

TABLE G-16   OCCUPATION AND EDUCATION, SELECTED NONMANUAL OCCUPATIONS: USSR, 1959-1970
(in Thousands)

	1939					1959				
	I Admin. & Political Ldrs.[a]	I Economic Leaders Total[b]	Direc-tors[c]	Coll.Farm Chrmn.[d]	I Teachers & Scientists[e]	I Admin. & Political Ldrs.[a]	I Economic Leaders Total[b]	Direc-tors[c]	Coll.Farm Chrmn.[d]	I Teachers & Scientists[e]
Level of Education										
TOTAL	445	757	231	279	1,553	392	955	292	103	2,836
Percent	100.0%	100.0%	100.0%	100.0%	100.0%	100.0%	100.0%	100.0%	100.0%	100.0%
Elem. or Less										
Percent	[223]	[541]	[149]	[272]	[168]	[37]	[140]	[39]	[30]	[26]
Inc. Basic	50.2%	71.5%	64.5%	97.7%	10.8%	9.2%	14.7%	13.4%	29.6%	0.9%
Percent										
Basic										
Percent										
Inc. Second.	[222]	[216]	[82]	[6]	[1,390]	[355]	[815]	[253]	[72]	[2,810]
Percent	49.8%	28.5%	35.5%	2.3%	89.2%	90.8%	85.3%	86.6%	70.4%	99.1%
Secondary										
Percent										
Inc. Higher										
Percent										
Higher										
Percent										

	1959					1970				
	II Admin. & Political Ldrs.[a]	II Economic Leaders Total[b]	Direc-tors[f]	Coll.Farm Chrmn.[g]	II Teachers & Scientists[h]	II Admin. & Political Ldrs.[a]	II Economic Leaders Total[b]	Direc-tors[f]	Coll.Farm Chrmn.[g]	II Teachers & Scientists[h]
Level of Education										
TOTAL	392	1,098	283	103	2,836	406	1,570	301	51	4,951
Percent	100.0%	100.0%	100.0%	100.0%	100.0%	100.0%	100.0%	100.0%	100.0%	100.0%
Elem. or Less										
Percent	[36]	[235]	[38]	[30]	[26]	[9]	[100]	[11]	[3]	[40]
Inc. Basic	[9.2%]	21.4%	13.4%	29.6%	0.9%	[2.3%]	6.4%	3.8%	6.7%	0.8%
Percent										
Basic										
Percent						[51]	[192]	[32]	[6]	[153]
Inc. Second.						[12.6%]	12.2%	10.6%	11.3%	3.1%
Percent										
Secondary	[356]	[863]	[245]	[72]	[2,810]	[199]	[743]	[139]	[26]	[2,310]
Percent	[90.8%]	78.6%	86.6%	70.4%	99.1%	[48.9%]	47.3%	46.3%	52.7%	46.7%
Inc. Higher										
Percent										
Higher						[147]	[535]	[118]	[15]	[2,450]
Percent						[36.2%]	34.1%	39.3%	29.3%	49.4%

Notes: For notes, see next page.

TABLE G-16   (CONCLUDED)

Notes: a Leaders of Organs of State Administration and of Social Organizations (including party) and their
Structural Subdivisions. b Includes Directors and Heads of Subdivisions of Enterprises, Chairmen and
Heads of Subdivisions of Collective and State Farms, and Captains and Navigators of ships. c Directors and
Heads of Enterprise Subdivisions. d Collective Farm Chairmen and their Deputies. e Scientific Workers,
Educators and Teachers, including Physical Culture and Kindergarten Teachers. f Heads of
Enterprise Subdivisions not included. g Deputy Chairmen and Heads of Subdivisions of Collective Farms not
included. h Includes Leaders of Scientific Research Organizations, Researchers and Teachers, including
Physical Education and Kindergarten Teachers.

TABLE G-17   OCCUPATION AND EDUCATION: YUGOSLAVIA, 1953

Major Occupational Groups[a]

Level of Education	Total AE	Agric.	Mining	Manu.[b]	Constr.[c]	Transp.	Trade	Leaders	Technical	Education	Health	Office Admin
TOTAL	7,848,857	5,324,637	57,629	960,132	...	107,578	335,109	51,911	46,925	101,818	44,909	312,1
Percent	100.0%	100.0%	100.0%	100.0%	...	100.0%	100.0%	100.0%	100.0%	100.0%	100.0%	100.
Elem. or Less	5,726,807	4,600,958	44,547	404,831	...	64,138	128,580	12,248	1,473	7,126	8,074	76,2
Percent	73.0%	86.4%	77.3%	42.2%	...	59.6%	38.4%	23.6%	3.1%	7.0%	18.0%	24.
Inc. Basic	1,104,390	626,288	9,429	222,870	...	20,316	69,519	8,298	1,701	5,153	6,009	56,8
Percent	14.1%	11.8%	16.4%	23.2%	...	18.9%	20.7%	16.0%	3.6%	5.1%	13.4%	18.
Basic	265,234	41,205	528	49,383	...	5,793	45,641	8,748	3,649	9,209	3,924	84,3
Percent	3.4%	0.8%	0.9%	5.1%	...	5.4%	13.6%	16.8%	7.8%	9.0%	8.7%	27.
Trade School	445,172	38,808	2,709	272,035	...	13,273	50,307	6,896	3,247	4,871	7,434	30,0
Percent	5.7%	0.7%	4.7%	28.3%	...	12.3%	15.0%	13.3%	6.9%	4.8%	16.5%	9.
Inc. Second.	...	...	...	...	...	...	...	...	...	...	...	..
Percent	...	...	...	...	...	...	...	...	...	...	...	..
Secondary					...							
Percent	219,554	3,130	259	9,131	...	3,715	36,094	11,017	27,024	54,521	8,398	59,4
Inc. Higher	2.8%	0.1%	0.4%	0.9%	...	3.4%	10.8%	21.2%	57.6%	53.5%	18.7%	19.
Percent					...							
Higher	68,573	235	1	161	...	120	4,048	4,637	9,780	20,794	11,019	4,7
Percent	0.9%	0.0%	0.0%	0.0%	...	0.1%	1.2%	8.9%	20.8%	20.4%	24.5%	1.

Selected Nonmanual Occupations

Level of Education	Admin. Leaders[e]	Inst. Leaders[f]	Political Workers	Directors	Engineers[g]	Economists & Lawyers	Teachers[h]	Doctors	Health Personnel	Techni- cians	Office Workers
TOTAL	9,489	10,649	2,482	26,961	38,527	19,547	75,700	...	...	...	...
Percent	100.0%	100.0%	100.0%	100.0%	100.0%	100.0%	100.0%	...	...	...	...
Elem. or Less	2,305	848	288	6,304	1,248	894	1,088	...	...	...	...
Percent	24.3%	8.0%	11.6%	23.4%	3.2%	4.6%	1.4%	...	...	...	...
Inc. Basic	1,707	994	446	4,694	1,502	1,501	2,059	...	...	...	...
Percent	18.0%	9.3%	18.0%	17.4%	3.9%	7.7%	2.7%	...	...	...	...
Basic	1,865	1,647	514	4,829	3,430	3,683	5,106	...	...	...	...
Percent	19.6%	15.5%	20.7%	17.9%	8.9%	18.8%	6.7%	...	...	...	...
Trade School	825	811	382	4,921	2,350	763	1,701	...	...	...	...
Percent	8.7%	7.6%	15.4%	18.2%	6.1%	3.9%	2.2%	...	...	...	...
Inc. Second.	...	...	...	...	...	...	...	...	...	...	...
Percent	...	...	...	...	...	...	...	...	...	...	...
Secondary								...	...	...	...
Percent	1,950	4,187	556	4,611	23,157	3,557	47,761	...	...	...	...
Inc. Higher	20.5%	39.3%	22.4%	17.1%	60.1%	18.2%	63.1%	...	...	...	...
Percent								...	...	...	...
Higher	828	2,148	295	1,561	6,796	9,143	17,900	...	...	...	...
Percent	8.7%	20.2%	11.9%	5.8%	17.6%	46.8%	23.6%	...	...	...	...

Notes: For notes, see next page.

TABLE G-17   (CONCLUDED)

Notes: a Does not include persons in category Other Occupations. b Includes Construction. c Included with Manufac-
        turing. d Officials (sluzbenici) only. e Functionaries in State Administration. f Heads of Institutions
        (schools, cultural and research institutions, and related). g Engineers and Technicians. h Cultural and
        Educational Workers.

TABLE G-18   OCCUPATION AND EDUCATION: YUGOSLAVIA, 1961

Major Occupational Categories[a]

Level of Education	Total AE	Agric.	Mining	Manu.[b]	Constr.[c]	Transp.	Trade	Leaders	Technical	Education	Health	Office Admin.
TOTAL	8,340,344	4,731,359	106,860	1,626,583	...	209,216	714,394	93,972	91,656	147,149	72,299	459,24
Percent	100.0%	100.0%	100.0%	100.0%	...	100.0%	100.0%	100.0%	100.0%	100.0%	100.0%	100.0
Elem. or Less	5,430,658	3,999,273	86,984	761,184	...	110,005	361,834	7,429				
Percent	65.1%	84.5%	81.4%	46.8%	...	52.6%	50.6%	7.9%				
Inc. Basic	1,035,729	549,728	10,476	246,658	...	37,068	109,783	7,393	12,473	15,042	19,596	276,03
Percent	12.4%	11.6%	9.8%	15.2%	...	17.7%	15.4%	7.9%	13.6%	10.2%	27.1%	60.1
Basic	603,749	140,621	3,294	134,495	...	23,858	77,604	17,313				
Percent	7.2%	3.0%	3.1%	8.3%	...	11.4%	10.9%	18.4%				
Trade School	750,212	35,871	5,068	462,457	...	30,682	113,300	13,766	8,932	5,654	17,067	50,58
Percent	9.0%	0.7%	4.7%	28.4%	...	14.7%	15.8%	14.6%	9.7%	3.8%	23.6%	11.0
Inc. Second.	...	...	...	...	...	...	...	...	...	...	...	...
Percent	...	...	...	...	...	...	...	...	...	...	...	...
Secondary Percent	328,368	3,153	818	18,645	...	6,229	24,773	27,272	44,394	77,850	16,097	104,18
Inc. Higher	3.9%	0.1%	0.8%	1.1%	...	3.0%	3.5%	29.0%	48.4%	52.9%	22.2%	22.7
Percent												
Higher	177,176	442	77	1,353	...	1,104	26,235	20,669	25,857	48,603	19,639	28,08
Percent	2.1%	0.0%	0.1%	0.1%	...	0.5%	3.7%	22.0%	28.2%	33.0%	27.2%	6.1

Selected Nonmanual Occupations

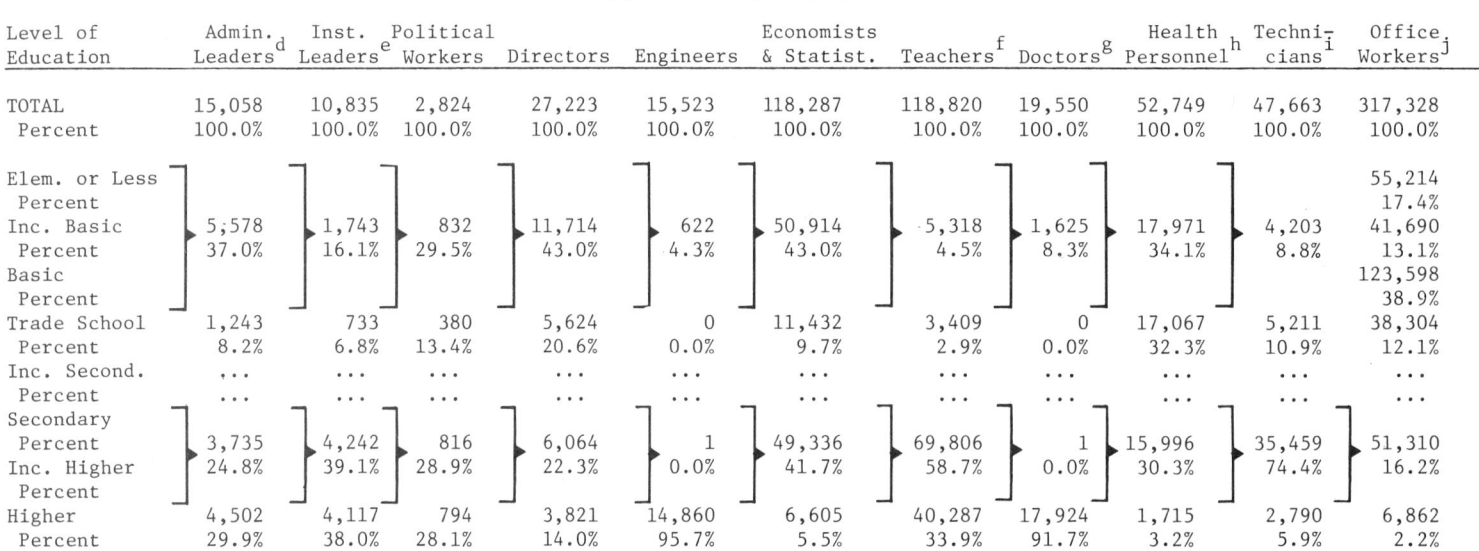

Level of Education	Admin. Leaders[d]	Inst. Leaders[e]	Political Workers	Directors	Engineers	Economists & Statist.	Teachers[f]	Doctors[g]	Health Personnel[h]	Technicians[i]	Office Workers[j]
TOTAL	15,058	10,835	2,824	27,223	15,523	118,287	118,820	19,550	52,749	47,663	317,328
Percent	100.0%	100.0%	100.0%	100.0%	100.0%	100.0%	100.0%	100.0%	100.0%	100.0%	100.0%
Elem. or Less											55,214
Percent											17.4%
Inc. Basic	5,578	1,743	832	11,714	622	50,914	5,318	1,625	17,971	4,203	41,690
Percent	37.0%	16.1%	29.5%	43.0%	4.3%	43.0%	4.5%	8.3%	34.1%	8.8%	13.1%
Basic											123,598
Percent											38.9%
Trade School	1,243	733	380	5,624	0	11,432	3,409	0	17,067	5,211	38,304
Percent	8.2%	6.8%	13.4%	20.6%	0.0%	9.7%	2.9%	0.0%	32.3%	10.9%	12.1%
Inc. Second.	...	...	...	...	...	...	...	...	...	...	...
Percent	...	...	...	...	...	...	...	...	...	...	...
Secondary Percent	3,735	4,242	816	6,064	1	49,336	69,806	1	15,996	35,459	51,310
Inc. Higher	24.8%	39.1%	28.9%	22.3%	0.0%	41.7%	58.7%	0.0%	30.3%	74.4%	16.2%
Percent											
Higher	4,502	4,117	794	3,821	14,860	6,605	40,287	17,924	1,715	2,790	6,862
Percent	29.9%	38.0%	28.1%	14.0%	95.7%	5.5%	33.9%	91.7%	3.2%	5.9%	2.2%

Notes: For notes, see next page.

372

TABLE G-18   (CONCLUDED)

Notes: a Does not include persons in category Other Occupations. b Includes Construction. c Included with Manufac-
turing. d Functionaries in State Administration, Heads of Subdivisions of State Administration (Nacelnici),
and State Inspectors. e Heads of Institutions (schools, cultural institutions, and related). f Professors,
Teachers, and Educators. g Doctors, Dentists, and Pharmacists. h Nurses, Therapists, Medical and Health
Technicians. i Excludes Agrotechnicians, Technical Draftsmen, and Laboratory Assistants. j Financial
Personnel and Office Employees.

TABLE G-19   OCCUPATION AND EDUCATION: YUGOSLAVIA, 1971 (EMPLOYEES)

Major Occupational Categories

Level of Education	Total Employed	Agric.[a]	Mining	Manu.	Constr.	Transp.	Trade	Leaders	Technical[b]	Education[c]	Health	Office Admin.
TOTAL	4,134,240	62,119	1,407,465	272,464	196,357	741,376	91,734	263,099	236,141	112,715	523,244
Percent	100.0%	100.0%	100.0%	100.0%	100.0%	100.0%	100.0%	100.0%	100.0%	100.0%	100.0%
Elem. or Less	1,180,457	41,276	427,876	163,340	76,445	264,076	2,045	3,796	3,152	5,130	63,841
Percent	28.5%	66.4%	30.4%	59.9%	38.9%	35.6%	2.2%	1.4%	1.3%	4.5%	12.2%
Inc. Basic	350,707	7,169	159,066	34,985	25,197	63,356	1,063	3,142	1,304	1,909	25,506
Percent	8.5%	11.5%	11.3%	12.8%	12.8%	8.5%	1.1%	1.2%	0.5%	1.7%	4.9%
Basic	652,471	6,392	237,226	33,809	48,926	111,376	4,353	21,472	4,108	6,718	144,001
Percent	15.8%	10.3%	16.8%	12.4%	24.9%	15.0%	4.7%	8.2%	1.7%	6.0%	27.5%
Trade School	947,965	5,743	541,711	36,565	42,043	194,527	9,156	13,286	6,995	15,076	67,018
Percent	22.9%	9.2%	38.5%	13.4%	21.4%	26.2%	10.0%	5.0%	3.0%	13.4%	12.8%
Inc. Second.	...	...	...	...	...	...	...	...	...	...	...
Percent	...	...	...	...	...	...	...	...	...	...	...
Secondary Percent / Inc. Higher Percent	602,745	1,196	33,644	2,638	2,866	69,286	25,707	131,846	99,498	47,981	175,784
	14.6%	1.9%	2.4%	1.0%	1.4%	9.3%	28.0%	50.1%	42.1%	42.6%	33.6%
Higher	386,982	88	4,201	274	505	36,475	48,938	88,544	120,130	35,541	45,582
Percent	9.4%	0.1%	0.3%	0.1%	0.2%	4.9%	53.3%	33.6%	50.9%	31.5%	8.7%

Selected Nonmanual Occupations

Level of Education	Admin. Leaders	Inst. Leaders	Political Workers	Directors	Engineers	Economists & Statist.	Teachers	Doctors	Health Personnel	Technicians[e]	Office Workers[f]
TOTAL	...	...	...	...	...	...	185,736	...	...	114,544	455,097
Percent	...	...	...	...	...	...	100.0%	...	...	100.0%	100.0%
Elem. or Less	...	...	...	...	...	...	621	...	...	707	49,456
Percent	...	...	...	...	...	...	0.3%	...	...	0.6%	10.9%
Inc. Basic	...	...	...	...	...	...	283	...	...	419	20,093
Percent	...	...	...	...	...	...	0.1%	...	...	0.4%	4.4%
Basic	...	...	...	...	...	...	1,276	...	...	4,026	120,614
Percent	...	...	...	...	...	...	0.7%	...	...	3.5%	26.5%
Trade School	...	...	...	...	...	...	3,805	...	...	6,228	57,036
Percent	...	...	...	...	...	...	2.0%	...	...	5.4%	12.5%
Inc. Second.	...	...	...	...	...	...	...	...	...	...	...
Percent	...	...	...	...	...	...	...	...	...	...	...
Secondary Percent / Inc. Higher Percent	...	...	...	...	...	...	78,058	...	...	64,453	163,407
	...	...	...	...	...	...	42.0%	...	...	56.3%	35.9%
Higher	...	...	...	...	...	...	100,977	...	...	38,246	43,155
Percent	...	...	...	...	...	...	54.4%	...	...	33.4%	9.5%

Notes: For notes, see next page.

TABLE G-19   (CONCLUDED)

Notes: a Data omitted; relates only to those with status of Employees (employed in state farms). b Includes Experts in Technical Fields, Communications Specialists and Other Specialists. c Includes Specialists in the Natural Sciences, Chemists, Physicists, and Related Specialties; also includes Artists and Physical Culture Personnel and Teachers. d Workers in Administration, Financial Work and Manipulative Work in Communications and Transport. e Experts in Technical Fields and Technology. f Workers in Administration and Finance.

TABLE G-20   OCCUPATIONS ACCORDING TO INTERNATIONAL STANDARD CLASSIFICATION OF OCCUPATIONS:
EASTERN EUROPE, 1961-1971

	Bulgaria 1965[a]		Czechoslovakia 1961[a]		Czechoslovakia 1970[b]		Hungary 1960[a]	
Occupation	Total	Female	Total	Female	Total	Female	Total	Female
TOTAL ACTIVE	4,267,798	1,878,124	6,482,664	2,659,956	6,982,502	3,112,526	4,876,232	1,711,287
Percent	100.0%	100.0%	100.0%	100.0%	100.0%	100.0%	100.0%	100.0%
Professional & Technical Personnel	354,299	149,679	906,331	313,988	1,356,120	563,624	351,081	137,477
Percent	8.3%	8.0%	14.0%	11.8%	19.4%	18.1%	7.2%	8.0%
Administrative, Executive, & Managerial Personnel	324,096	129,507	110,318	5,047	165,363	22,801	67,273	11,830
Percent	7.6%	6.9%	1.7%	0.2%	2.4%	0.7%	1.4%	0.7%
Clerical Workers			425,716	292,938	519,122	431,267	318,697	196,112
Percent			6.6%	11.0%	7.4%	13.9%	6.5%	11.5%
Sales Workers	142,628	83,837	358,119	201,864	490,617	342,765	112,376	60,901
Percent	3.3%	4.5%	5.5%	7.6%	7.0%	11.0%	2.3%	3.6%
Service Workers	176,663	104,078	531,856	351,968	590,888	433,891	300,403	176,510
Percent	4.1%	5.5%	8.2%	13.2%	8.5%	13.9%	6.2%	10.3%
Farmers, Forestry Workers, & Fishermen	1,748,025	1,014,787	1,381,343	767,878	837,479	441,913	1,654,741	685,495
Percent	41.0%	54.0%	21.3%	28.9%	12.0%	14.2%	33.9%	40.1%
Miners	65,295	5,177	189,230	19,117			103,025	3,075
Percent	1.5%	0.3%	2.9%	0.7%			2.1%	0.2%
Workers in Transport & Communication	306,307	25,007	491,771	80,419	2,980,716	864,726	336,421	40,678
Percent	7.2%	1.3%	7.6%	3.0%	42.7%	27.8%	6.9%	2.4%
Craftsmen, Production Workers,& Other Laborers	805,488	297,084	2,076,513	622,845			1,631,344	398,878
Percent	18.9%	15.8%	32.0%	23.4%			33.5%	23.3%
Workers not Classifiable by Occupation	344,997	68,968	11,467	3,892	42,197	11,539	871	331
Percent	8.1%	3.7%	0.2%	0.1%	0.6%	0.4%	0.0%	0.0%

Occupation	Hungary 1970[b]		Poland 1970[b]		Romania 1966[c]	
	Total	Female	Total	Female	Total	Female
TOTAL ACTIVE	4,988,676	2,055,192	16,943,848	7,795,038	10,362,300	4,687,124
Percent	100.0%	100.0%	100.0%	100.0%	100.0%	100.0%
Professional & Technical Personnel	544,797	256,923	1,325,900	659,995	949,845	422,113
Percent	10.9%	12.5%	7.8%	8.5%	9.2%	9.0%
Administrative, Executive, & Managerial Personnel	28,491	4,364	163,135	44,152	322,245	130,351
Percent	0.6%	0.2%	1.0%	0.6%	3.1%	2.8%
Clerical Workers	542,659	363,320	1,500,054	904,007		
Percent	10.9%	17.7%	8.9%	11.6%		
Sales Workers	174,018	106,595	331,204	280,747	181,078	73,785
Percent	3.5%	5.2%	2.0%	3.6%	1.7%	1.6%
Service Workers	287,578	203,001	951,725	723,541	508,438	246,880
Percent	5.8%	9.9%	5.6%	9.3%	4.9%	5.3%
Farmers, Forestry Workers, & Fishermen	900,660	412,686	6,191,811	3,506,094	5,744,819	3,367,282
Percent	18.0%	20.1%	36.5%	45.0%	55.4%	71.8%
Miners					164,768	4,619
Percent					1.6%	0.1%
Workers in Transport & Communication	2,510,473	708,303	5,558,240	1,373,552	467,364	46,690
Percent	50.3%	34.5%	32.8%	17.6%	4.5%	1.0%
Craftsmen, Production Workers, & Other Laborers					2,019,498	393,597
Percent					19.5%	8.4%
Workers not Classifiable by Occupation	...	...	921,779	302,950	4,245	1,807
Percent	...	...	5.4%	3.9%	0.1%	0.0%

TABLE G-20   (CONCLUDED)

| | Yugoslavia | | | |
| | 1961[a] | | 1971[c] | |
Occupation	Total	Female	Total	Female
TOTAL ACTIVE	8,340,400	2,953,165	8,889,816	3,203,484
Percent	100.0%	100.0%	100.0%	100.0%
Professional & Technical Personnel	468,726	201,646	678,653	313,900
Percent	5.6%	6.8%	7.6%	9.8%
Administrative, Executive, & Managerial Personnel	93,972	11,124	92,136	8,132
Percent	1.1%	0.4%	1.0%	0.3%
Clerical Workers	317,268	164,233	531,884	262,403
Percent	3.8%	5.6%	6.0%	8.2%
Sales Workers	225,511	55,185	281,810	103,021
Percent	2.7%	1.9%	3.2%	3.2%
Service Workers	488,853[d]	183,293[d]	517,125	256,048
Percent	5.9%	6.2%	5.8%	8.0%
Farmers, Forestry Workers, & Fishermen	4,731,222	2,007,839	3,820,227	1,671,194
Percent	56.7%	68.0%	43.0%	52.2%
Miners	107,051	2,835	64,262	920
Percent	1.3%	0.1%	0.7%	0.0%
Workers in Transport & Communication	209,216	10,288		
Percent	2.5%	0.3%	2,158,371	388,034
Craftsmen, Production Workers, & Other Laborers	1,626,599	296,815	24.3%	12.1%
Percent	19.5%	10.1%		
Workers not Classifiable by Occupation	71,982	19,907	745,348	199,832
Percent	0.9%	0.7%	8.4%	6.2%

Notes: a International standard classification of occupations in effect
prior to 1968. b International standard classification of occupations in effect after 1968. c Classification of occupations modified version of post-1968 international standard classification. d
Includes armed forces.

SECTION H: DEVELOPMENTAL INDICATORS AND THE STANDARD OF LIVING

Introduction

Table H-1 Data are drawn from other tables in Section H, supplemented by League of Nations data on infant mortality prior to World War II, and data on higher education taken from Table D-7. Data on the percent of population in agriculture are extrapolated from data for census years; see the General Introduction for further comments on how the agricultural population is measured vis-à-vis the remainder of the population. GNP per capita are estimates based on data published by the CIA National Foreign Assessment Center and the Research Project on National Income in East Central Europe (see Table H-4).

Table H-2 NMP indexes, with the exception of Yugoslavia, are drawn from CMEA handbooks, adjusted to 1965 = 100. Yugoslav NMP data are official Yugoslav estimates. GNP indexes for Eastern Europe, with the exception of Yugoslavia, are those published by the Research Project on National Income in East Central Europe; GNP is measured at factor cost by sector of origin. Indexes combine two series, for 1950–1960 and for 1970–1975, each with different sectoral weights. The GNP index for Yugoslavia is derived from Series I data on GNP given in Table H-3. The Soviet GNP index is CIA data; GNP is measured by sector of origin at factor cost.

Table H-3 Series I data are estimates based on Gross Domestic Product for 1965, moved to 1976 by means of indices of real GNP and the weighted average GNP deflator for the European market economies. For additional comments on the physical indicators approach used to calculate data for GNP in 1965, see the General Introduction. Data for Romania are based on estimates which understate national income; see the General Introduction for further comments. Estimates of GNP for Yugoslavia in Series II do not use the physical indicators approach, but are based on United Nations Standard National Account procedures for calculating GNP. Series II data for Eastern Europe are estimates published by the CIA National Foreign Assessment Center, based on data published by the Research Project on National Income in East Central Europe; estimates are in billions of 1977 dollars, and are arrived at by converting estimates of GNP in domestic prices to dollars at U.S. purchasing power equivalents, the result then extended to 1977 by means of the U.S. official deflator for GNP. Data on Yugoslavia, Series II, are CIA estimates. Data on Soviet GNP are calculated by the CIA by end use in U.S. 1977 dollars, converted to U.S. dollars by the average purchasing power ratio of the dollar and the ruble.

Table H-4 Data are derived from midyear population estimates given in Section A and data on GNP in Table H-3.

Table H-5 1965 data are taken from preliminary results of 1965 census; for final results, see footnote *c*.

Table H-6 Data on Active Earners include helping family members. Apprentices are included in the data on Active Earners in agriculture for 1961 but not for 1970; apprentices are included in the data for the total number of Active Earners in all branches for both 1961 and 1970. 1950 data on Active Earners are taken from a different source than data on Active Earners and Dependents; the two figures may not be comparable. For 1961, estimates of the total male and female population in agriculture are made separately from the estimate of the total population in agriculture.

Table H-7 Series I is civilian labor force data; apprentices are excluded. For 1964, estimates of the total male and female population in agriculture are made separately from the estimate of the total population in agriculture.

Table H-8 Series I is census data. Series II is data on the civilian labor force and includes Active Earners in agriculture, forestry, and water economy, calculated for January 1. Census data on Active Earners in agriculture are based on 1970 definitions of Active Earners. For 1970, estimates of the total male and female population in agriculture are made separately from the estimate of the total population in agriculture.

Table H-9 Data for Active Earners, and for Active Earners and Dependents, are based on the concept of Supported from Work (*Utrzymujacy sie z pracy*), and exlude Other Earners with supplementary incomes in agriculture (see the General Introduction for comments on Polish labor force terminology). The number of persons in agriculture in Table H-9 is less than the number in agriculture in Table E-32, which utilizes data on those Occupationally Active (*Czynni zawodowo*).

Table H-10   For 1956, estimates of the total male and female population in agriculture are made separately from the estimate of the total population in agriculture.

Table H-12   1948 census data have been adjusted to make them comparable with data for later years. The 1976 figure for Active Earners and Dependents in Agriculture is an official estimate.

Table H-13   Urban settlements are localities of over 400 persons legally defined as urban. Data on the total number in urban settlements for 1945, 1950, 1955, and 1960 are census data; data for 1970 and 1973 are official estimates. Boundaries of urban settlements are those of the year for which the data are given. Data for 1965 and preceding years on urban settlements by size are based on retrospective data on the size of urban settlements given in the 1966 Albanian statistical annual.

Table H-14   Urban settlements are those legally recognized as urban. Boundaries of urban settlements are those of the year for which the data are given. Data for 1934, 1946, 1965, and 1975 are census data; for the remaining years, data are official estimates.

Table H-15   For the years 1930–1955, urban settlements are defined as settlements of 2,000 persons or more. For 1961, urban settlements are defined as all settlements of 2,000 and over (see footnote *d*), or as settlements meeting certain criteria of urbanization, namely, large towns usually of 5,000 or more inhabitants having a density of over 100 persons per hectare, as well as meeting other criteria. For a complete list of these requirements, see the *United Nations Demographic Yearbook 1977*, pp. 184–85, or Czechoslovakia, Ústřední Komise Lidové Kontroly, *Vývoj společnosti ČSSR v Číslech*, pp. 51–52. Data are for urban settlements in the boundaries of the years for which the data are given. Data for 1921, 1930, 1946–1947, 1950, 1961, and 1970 are census data; for the remaining years, data are official estimates. For 1970, official sources do not give data on the total number of persons in urban settlements; data for the total population in urban settlements for that year are for all settlements of 2,000 and over, or for urban settlements as given in *United Nations Demographic Yearbooks*.

Table H-16   Urban settlements include all settlements of 2,000 and over. Boundaries of urban set-

tlements are those of the year in question or as close to that year as possible. Data for 1939, 1946, 1964, and 1971 are census data; for the remaining years, data are official estimates.

Table H-17   Urban settlements are those legally recognized as urban. Boundaries of urban settlements are those of the year for which the data are given. Data for 1930, 1941, 1949, 1960, and 1970 are census data; for remaining years, data are estimates.

Table H-18   Urban settlements are those legally recognized as urban. Boundaries of urban settlements are those of the year for which the data are given. Data for 1946 include persons living temporarily in urban areas. Data for 1946, 1950, 1960, and 1970 are census data; for remaining years, data are official estimates.

Table H-19   Urban settlements are those legally recognized as urban. Boundaries of urban settlements are those of the year for which the data are given. Data for 1930, 1948, 1956, 1966, and 1977 are census data. For remaining years, data are official estimates. In Series I, assimilated urban settlements are included with the data on other urban areas. In Series II, data on assimilated urban settlements are presented independently of the data on other urban areas.

Table H-20   Urban settlements are localities officially designated as cities, with a predominantly nonagricultural population and a minimum size of 500 to 2,000 persons, depending on the occupational structure of the settlement. Boundaries of urban settlements are those of the year for which data are given. Data for 1926, 1939, 1959, and 1970 are census data. For remaining years, data are official estimates. Figures for the total urban population are not strictly comparable between censuses because of changes in the criteria by which settlements are defined as urban.

Table H-21   Data for urban settlements for 1921 and 1931 are for localities legally designated as urban, and include rural areas surrounding urban settlements. For 1948, urban settlements are defined as all settlements with a city committee (*gradski odbor*). For subsequent years, urban settlements are defined as those of 2,000 persons or over with 90 percent or more nonfarm population; 10,000 persons or over with 40 percent or more nonfarm population; and 15,000 persons or over with 30 percent or more nonfarm population. Boundaries of urban settlements are those of the year for which the data are given.

Tables H-22 through H-28   Data refer to conventional occupied dwellings unless otherwise specified, that is, housing units (excluding hotels, institutions, camps, and other types of living quarters) of a permanent character. For the number of different types of housing units in Eastern Europe, see Table X in the General Introduction.

Table H-29 Data are national data and are not comparable. See the General Introduction for further comments.

Table H-30 Data are based on food balance sheets published by the FAO; see the General Introduction for further comments.

Table H-31 Data for radios and TV sets are for the number of licenses issued. Data for telephones include both public and private telephones in use. Data for autos relate to passenger vehicles only, and to autos in use.

TABLE H-1   SELECTED INDICATORS OF DEVELOPMENT: EASTERN EUROPE AND THE USSR, PREWAR AND 1950-1975

	Prewar	1950	1955	1960	1965	1970	1975
Illiterates (Percent of Total Population)							
Albania[a]	...	53.8%	28.3%	...	...	...	...
Bulgaria[b]	31.5% (1934)	...	13.1%[c]	...	8.3%	...	...
Czechoslovakia	4.1% (1930)	...	...	...	...	...	...
GDR	...	...	...	...	...	...	...
Hungary[d]	9.0% (1930)	...	...	3.8%	...	2.4%	...
Poland[e]	23.1% (1931)	5.8%	...	2.7%	...	...	...
Romania[d]	42.9% (1930)	23.1%[j]	10.1%[g]	...	...	...	...
USSR[h]	43.4% (1926)	...	...	1.5%[i]	...	0.3%	...
Yugoslavia[e]	44.6% (1931)	25.4%[j]	25.4%[k]	21.0%[l]	...	15.1%[m]	...
Infant Mortality (Rates per Thousand Live Births)							
Albania	...	...	103.9	83.0	86.8	...	...
Bulgaria	147 (1935)	94.5	82.4	45.1	30.8	27.3	23.1
Czechoslovakia	130 (1935)	77.7	34.1	23.5	25.5	22.1	20.9
GDR	...	72.0	48.8	38.8	24.8	18.5	15.9
Hungary	157 (1935)	85.7	60.0	47.6	38.8	35.9	32.8
Poland	137 (1935)	111.2	82.2	54.8	41.4	33.4	25.1
Romania	182 (1935)	116.7	78.2	74.6	44.1	49.4	...
USSR	181 (1926)	80.7	59.6	35.3	27.2	24.7	...
Yugoslavia	153 (1935)	118.4	112.8	87.7	71.8	55.5	39.9
Agricultural Population (Active Earners and Dependents in Agriculture as Percent of Total Population)							
Albania	...	...	...	...	...	...	...
Bulgaria	73.2% (1934)	...	54.8%[g]	45.2%	33.3%	...	...
Czechoslovakia	34.7% (1930)	24.9%	22.1%	19.3%[l]	16.1%	13.2%	...
GDR	...	15.8%	14.6%	13.7%	12.4%[n]	...	...
Hungary	51.9% (1930)	49.3%[p]	40.5%	34.8%	28.7%	22.8%	...
Poland	60.0% (1931)	46.4%	42.3%	37.8%	33.7%	29.8%	27.1%[o]
Romania	72.3% (1930)	...	...	...	45.1%[r]	...	...
USSR	77.5% (1926)	...	...	...	...	22.8%	...
Yugoslavia	76.6% (1931)	...	57.7%	49.6%[l]	...	38.2%[m]	33.2%
GNP per Capita (in Dollars)							
Albania	...	...	...	...	...	...	...
Bulgaria	...	...	...	1,200	1,600	2,000	2,400
Czechoslovakia	...	...	...	2,900	3,000	3,600	4,000
GDR	...	...	...	2,500	2,900	3,400	4,000
Hungary	...	...	...	1,700	2,000	2,300	2,600
Poland	...	...	...	1,500	1,800	2,100	2,700
Romania	...	...	...	1,100	1,500	1,900	2,500
USSR	...	...	...	2,200	2,700	3,300	3,800
Yugoslavia	...	...	...	1,000	1,300	1,600	2,000
Urbanization (Population in Urban Areas 20,000 and over as Percent of Total Population)							
Albania	6.9% (1938)	...	18.4%	20.3%	22.1%	...	...
Bulgaria	12.1% (1934)	...	24.3%[g]	...	33.9%	39.7%	41.1%
Czechoslovakia	16.6% (1930)	23.6%	24.8%	25.3%[l]	28.6%	31.1%	34.1%
GDR	43.4% (1939)	39.1%	...	40.4%	42.5%[n]	44.1%	46.5%
Hungary	29.1% (1930)	34.3%[p]	...	37.0%	...	...	46.8%[q]
Poland	17.0% (1931)	25.6%	...	31.8%	34.0%	37.3%	42.7%
Romania	13.4% (1930)	17.1%[j]	...	19.6%	26.3%[r]	28.4%	37.2%[s]
USSR	12.0% (1926)	...	...	35.6%[i]	...	44.3%	...
Yugoslavia	...	...	15.7%[k]	18.8%[l]	...	26.0%[m]	...

TABLE H-1   (CONCLUDED)

	Prewar	1950	1955	1960	1965	1970	1975
Number of Hospital							
Beds per Person							
Albania	...	...	4.2	4.9	5.9	6.7	...
Bulgaria	...	...	5.0	5.7	7.1	7.7	8.3
Czechoslovakia	...	...	8.7	9.5	10.0	10.0	10.0
GDR	...	10	10.8	11.1	11.1	11.1	11.1
Hungary	...	5.6	6.1	6.7	7.7	8.3	8.3
Poland	...	...	6.3	6.7	7.7	7.7	7.7
Romania	...	4.2	5.9	7.4	7.7	8.3	9.1
USSR	...	5.3	6.3	8.3	10.0	11.1	12.5
Yugoslavia	...	...	3.8	4.8	5.4	5.9	5.9
Number of Dwellings							
with Under Two							
Persons per Room							
(Percent of Total No.							
of Dwellings)							
Albania	...	...	...	...	...	...	...
Bulgaria	...	...	...	...	76.7%	...	87.6%
Czechoslovakia	...	...	...	77.8%[l]	...	89.6%	...
GDR	...	...	...	...	...	...	...
Hungary	...	...	...	76.2%	...	91.5%	...
Poland	...	...	...	56.8%	...	72.4%	...
Romania	...	...	...	...	72.2%[r]	...	...
USSR	...	...	...	...	...	...	...
Yugoslavia	...	...	...	63.0%[l]	...	69.2%[m]	...
Number of TV Sets							
(per Thousand Inhabitants)							
Albania		...	...	0.5	1	1.8	1.8
Bulgaria		...	0.3	0.6	23	121	173
Czechoslovakia		...	2	58	149	214	249
GDR		...	0.8	60	177	261	307
Hungary		...	0.1	10	82	171	223
Poland		...	0.0	14	66	129	190
Romania		...	0.0	2	26	73	127
USSR		...	4	22	68	143	217
Yugoslavia		...	...	1	30	88	144
Population 25 and over							
with Higher Education							
(Percent of Total Population)							
Albania	...	...	...	...	...	...	...
Bulgaria	...	...	3.2%[g]	...	3.5%	...	...
Czechoslovakia	...	...	...	2.4%[l]	...	4.0%	...
GDR	...	...	...	...	1.9%[j]	3.1%[m]	...
Hungary	...	1.9%[p]	...	2.8%	...	4.3%	...
Poland	...	...	...	2.6%	...	4.5%	...
Romania	...	...	2.1%[g]	...	2.7%[r]	...	...
USSR	...	...	...	3.2%[i]	...	...	...
Yugoslavia	...	...	0.9%[k]	1.9%[l]	...	1.5%[m]	...

Notes: a 9 and over. b 8 and over. c 1956. d 7 and over. e 10 and over. f 1950.
g 1956. h 9-49 years. i 1959. j 1948. k 1953. l 1961. m 1971. n 1964.
o 1974. p 1949. q 1976. r 1966 s 1977

TABLE H-2   INDEXES OF GROWTH IN NATIONAL INCOME: EASTERN EUROPE AND THE USSR,
              1950-1977 (in Constant Prices; Index: 1965=100)

Country	1950	1955	1960	1965	1970	1971	1972	1973	1974	1975	1976	1977
Albania												
NMP	...	...	66.3	100.0	139.3	...	...	...	...	...	...	...
GNP	...	...	...	...	...	...	...	...	...	...	...	...
Bulgaria												
NMP	25.6	45.6	72.5	100.0	152.2	162.4	174.9	189.1	203.5	221.7	236.2	...
GNP	36.7	49.9	73.2	100.0	128.9	133.3	139.7	145.4	150.2	162.0	167.9	168.6
Czechoslovakia												
NMP	43.9	64.9	90.9	100.0	140.0	146.4	154.6	161.8	171.8	182.7	190.0	...
GNP	55.3	65.4	88.9	100.0	118.4	122.4	126.8	131.0	135.7	139.7	141.9	146.7
GDR												
NMP	32.3	59.7	84.7	100.0	129.7	135.6	143.2	151.7	161.0	168.6	175.4	...
GNP	45.5	68.0	86.5	100.0	116.7	119.3	123.4	127.2	133.3	138.3	141.6	147.2
Hungary												
NMP	46.3	61.1	82.0	100.0	139.3	148.4	155.7	167.2	178.7	188.5	194.3	...
GNP	52.5	68.3	82.5	100.0	116.2	121.8	124.7	130.9	134.1	137.7	138.4	145.1
Poland												
NMP	35.7	53.9	74.1	100.0	133.3	144.4	159.2	177.7	198.5	212.6	227.4	...
GNP	51.0	64.2	80.3	100.0	121.6	130.2	139.5	150.0	158.9	166.2	174.0	182.8
Romania												
NMP	24.2	47.0	64.5	100.0	143.9	162.6	179.4	198.7	223.9	246.4	272.3	
GNP	42.3	59.7	77.0	100.0	127.4	145.4	154.6	159.7	168.7	176.2	196.2	203.2
USSR												
NMP	27.5	47.0	73.0	100.0	145.3	153.3	159.9	173.7	183.2	191.2	201.4	...
GNP	44.9	59.5	78.8	100.0	129.4	134.4	136.4	146.7	152.1	155.2	...	...
Yugoslavia												
NMP	38.4	49.2	71.8	100.0	132.4	143.0	149.1	156.5	169.9	176.1	183.3	...
GNP	...	...	74.9	100.0	137.1	...	...	...	...	192.3	206.0	220.2

TABLE H-3   ESTIMATES OF GROSS NATIONAL PRODUCT: EASTERN EUROPE AND THE USSR, 1960-1977
(in Billions of U.S. Dollars)

Country	1960 I^a	1960 II^b	1965 I^a	1965 II^b	1970 I^a	1970 II^b	1975 I^a	1975 II^b	1976 I^a	1976 II^b	1977 I^a	1977 II^b
Albania	0.5	...	0.7	...	1.0	...	1.4	...	1.5	...	1.5	...
Bulgaria	9.3	9.5	12.8	13.1	16.6	16.9	20.8	21.2	21.6	22.0	21.7	22.1
Czechoslovakia	35.5	39.0	39.8	43.1	47.2	51.0	55.7	60.2	56.5	61.2	58.5	63.2
GDR	46.9	43.0	53.5	49.6	62.5	58.0	74.1	68.6	75.8	70.3	78.8	73.1
Hungary	14.6	17.0	17.9	20.3	20.9	23.5	24.8	27.9	24.8	28.0	26.0	29.4
Poland	45.7	45.3	56.9	55.0	69.2	66.8	94.6	91.4	99.1	95.6	104.1	100.5
Romania[c]	6.8	21.1	10.7	29.6	15.8	37.8	27.0	52.2	30.0	58.1	32.5	60.2
USSR	340.3	473.1	435.2	614.5	568.1	806.7	685.7	972.6	717.5	1013.5	742.5	1047.9
Yugoslavia	13.7	19.0	18.3	25.5	25.1	32.9	35.2	43.8	37.7	45.5	40.3	48.6

Notes: a World Bank estimates. For methodology, see introduction to this section. b Estimates of the CIA National Foreign Assessment Center. For methodology, see introduction to this section. c Series I understates GNP. For further comments, see introduction to this section.

TABLE H-4 ESTIMATES OF GROSS NATIONAL PRODUCT PER CAPITA: EASTERN EUROPE AND THE USSR, 1960-1977
(in U.S. Dollars)

Country	1960 I[a]	1960 II[b]	1965 I[a]	1965 II[b]	1970 I[a]	1970 II[b]	1975 I[a]	1975 II[b]	1976 I[a]	1976 II[b]	1977 I[a]	1977 II[b]
Albania	300	...	400	...	500	...	600	...	600	...	600	...
Bulgaria	1,200	1,200	1,600	1,600	2,000	2,000	2,400	2,400	2,500	2,500	2,500	2,500
Czechoslovakia	2,600	2,900	2,800	3,000	3,300	3,600	3,800	4,000	3,800	4,100	3,900	4,200
GDR	2,700	2,500	3,100	2,900	3,700	3,400	4,400	4,000	4,500	4,200	4,700	4,400
Hungary	1,500	1,700	1,800	2,000	2,000	2,300	2,400	2,600	2,300	2,600	2,400	2,800
Poland	1,500	1,500	1,800	1,800	2,100	2,100	2,800	2,700	2,900	2,800	3,000	2,900
Romania[c]	400	1,100	600	1,500	800	1,900	1,300	2,500	1,400	2,700	1,500	2,800
USSR	1,600	2,200	1,900	2,700	2,300	3,300	2,700	3,800	2,800	3,900	2,900	4,000
Yugoslavia	700	1,000	900	1,300	1,200	1,600	1,600	2,000	1,700	2,100	1,900	2,200

Notes: a Based on World Bank estimates. b Based on estimates of CIA National Foreign Assessment Center. c Series I under-states per capita GNP. For further comments, see introduction to this section.

TABLE H-5   NUMBER OF PERSONS IN AGRICULTURE: BULGARIA, 1934-1965

Measures of Agric. Popul.	1934			1946		
	Total	Male	Female	Total	Male	Female
TOTAL POPULATION	6,077,939	3,053,893	3,024,046	7,029,349	3,516,774	3,512,575
Percent	100.0%	100.0%	100.0%	100.0%	100.0%	100.0%
Popul. in Agric.	...	...	...	...	...	...
Percent	...	...	...	...	...	...
ACTIVE EARNERS & DEPENDENTS, TOTAL	5,858,491	2,948,533	2,909,958	...	...	...
Percent	100.0%	100.0%	100.0%	...	...	...
AE & D in Agric.	4,446,784	2,175,727	2,271,057	...	...	...
Percent	75.9%	73.8%	78.0%	...	...	...
ACTIVE EARNERS, TOTAL	3,346,161	1,841,606	1,504,555	4,093,000	2,292,000	1,800,000
Percent	100.0%	100.0%	100.0%	100.0%	100.0%	100.0%
AE in Agric.	2,744,927	1,347,902	1,397,025	3,160,000	1,541,000	1,619,000
Percent	82.0%	73.2%	92.8%	77.2%	67.2%	89.9%

Measures of Agric. Popul.	1956			1965		
	Total	Male	Female	Total	Male	Female
TOTAL POPULATION	7,613,709	3,799,356	3,814,353	8,226,564[a]	4,111,236[a]	4,115,328[a]
Percent	100.0%	100.0%	100.0%	100.0%	100.0%	100.0%
Popul. in Agric.	4,197,811	1,975,588	2,222,223	3,400,000[b]	...	...
Percent	55.1%	52.0%	58.3%	41.3%	...	...
ACTIVE EARNERS & DEPENDENTS, TOTAL	7,383,248	3,691,237	3,692,011	6,933,654	3,618,383	3,375,271
Percent	100.0%	100.0%	100.0%	100.0%	100.0%	100.0%
AE & D in Agric.	4,169,513	1,961,925	2,207,588	2,743,445	1,268,984	1,474,461
Percent	56.5%	53.2%	59.8%	39.2%	35.1%	43.7%
ACTIVE EARNERS, TOTAL	4,150,207	2,405,344	1,744,863	4,280,426[c]	2,395,821[c]	1,884,605[c]
Percent	100.0%	100.0%	100.0%	100.0%	100.0%	100.0%
AE in Agric.	2,663,127	1,317,169	1,345,958	1,899,180	862,425	1,036,755
Percent	64.2%	54.8%	77.1%	44.4%	36.0%	55.0%

Notes: a Preliminary census results. b Estimate. c Final results of 1965 census gave total Active Earners as 4,260,412, of whom 1,891,398 (44.4%) were in agriculture and forestry; total male Active Earners as 2,385,723, of whom 857,080 (35.9%) were in agriculture and forestry; and total female Active Earners as 1,874,689, of whom 1,034,318 (55.2%) were in agriculture and forestry.

TABLE H-6   NUMBER OF PERSONS IN AGRICULTURE: CZECHOSLOVAKIA, 1930-1970

Measures of Agric. Popul.	1930[a] Total	1930[a] Male	1930[a] Female	1930[b] Total	1930[b] Male	1930[b] Female	1946-1947 Total	1946-1947 Male	1946-1947 Female
TOTAL POPULATION	14,729,536	7,143,116	7,586,420	14,004,179	6,788,098	7,216,081	12,165,000	5,909,000	6,256,000
Percent	100.0%	100.0%	100.0%	100.0%	100.0%	100.0%	100.0%	100.0%	100.0%
Popul. in Agric.	...	...	...	...	...	...	...	...	...
Percent	...	...	...	...	...	...	...	...	...
ACTIVE EARNERS & DEPENDENTS, TOTAL	13,264,367	6,569,511	6,694,856	12,680,862	...	...	...	...	...
Percent	100.0%	100.0%	100.0%	100.0%	...	...	...	...	...
AE & D in Agric.	5,117,386	2,418,235	2,699,151	4,605,684	...	...	...	...	...
Percent	38.6%	36.8%	40.3%	36.3%	...	...	...	...	...
ACTIVE EARNERS, TOTAL	6,865,710[c]	4,610,424	2,255,286	...	...	...	5,852,000	3,793,000	2,059,000
Percent	100.0%	100.0%	100.0%	...	...	...	100.0%	100.0%	100.0%
AE in Agric.	2,695,329[c]	1,583,692	1,111,637	...	...	...	2,207,000	1,123,000	1,084,000
Percent	39.3%	34.4%	49.3%	...	...	...	37.7%	29.6%	52.6%

Measures of Agric. Popul.	1950 Total	1950 Male	1950 Female	1961 Total	1961 Male	1961 Female	1970 Total	1970 Male	1970 Female
TOTAL POPULATION	12,338,450	5,996,783	6,341,667	13,745,577	6,704,674	7,040,903	14,361,557	6,989,486	7,372,071
Percent	100.0%	100.0%	100.0%	100.0%	100.0%	100.0%	100.0%	100.0%	100.0%
Popul. in Agric.	...	...	...	3,000,000[d]	1,400,000[d]	1,600,000[d]	...	...	...
Percent	...	...	...	21.8%	20.9%	22.7%	...	...	...
ACTIVE EARNERS & DEPENDENTS, TOTAL	10,448,341	...	...	11,759,205	5,954,754	5,804,451	11,671,656	...	...
Percent	100.0%	...	...	100.0%	100.0%	100.0%	100.0%	...	...
AE & D in Agric.	3,076,261	...	...	2,653,300	1,219,023	1,434,277	1,896,480	...	...
Percent	29.4%	...	...	22.6%	20.5%	24.7%	16.2%	...	...
ACTIVE EARNERS, TOTAL	5,811,724	...	...	6,726,496	4,007,484	2,719,012	7,348,000	4,117,000	3,231,000
Percent	100.0%	...	...	100.0%	100.0%	100.0%	100.0%	100.0%	100.0%
AE in Agric.	2,206,000	...	...	1,643,065	839,825	803,240	1,141,303	635,172	506,131
Percent	38.0%	...	...	24.4%	21.0%	29.5%	15.5%	15.4%	15.7%

Notes: a Prewar boundaries. b Postwar boundaries. c By postwar definitions, 7,091,000 were Active Earners with 2,802,000 (39.5%) in Agriculture. d Estimate.

388

TABLE H-7 NUMBER OF PERSONS IN AGRICULTURE: GDR, 1950-1975

Measures of Agric. Popul.	1950[a] I			1950[b]			1955[a] I		
	Total	Male	Female	Total	Male	Female	Total	Male	Female
TOTAL POPULATION	18,388,000	8,161,000	10,227,000	18,388,172	8,161,189	10,226,983	17,718,000	7,923,000	9,795,000
Percent	100.0%	100.0%	100.0%	100.0%	100.0%	100.0%	100.0%	100.0%	100.0%
Popul. in Agric.	...	...	...	...	...	...	...	...	...
Percent	...	...	...	...	...	...	...	...	...
ACTIVE EARNERS & DEPENDENTS, TOTAL	...	...	...	14,713,950	6,955,051	7,758,899	...	...	...
Percent	...	...	...	100.0%	100.0%	100.0%	...	...	...
AE & D in Agric.	...	...	...	2,912,387	1,318,163	1,594,224	...	...	...
Percent	...	...	...	19.8%	19.0%	20.5%	...	...	...
ACTIVE EARNERS, TOTAL	7,196,000	4,316,000	2,880,000	8,477,159	5,090,321	3,386,838	7,722,000	4,326,000	3,396,000
Percent	100.0%	100.0%	100.0%	100.0%	100.0%	100.0%	100.0%	100.0%	100.0%
AE in Agric.	2,005,000	928,000	1,077,000	2,068,965	966,069	1,102,896	1,721,000	838,000	883,000
Percent	27.9%	21.5%	37.4%	24.4%	19.0%	32.6%	22.3%	19.4%	26.0%

Measures of Agric. Popul.	1960[a] I			1964			1965[a] I		
	Total	Male	Female	Total	Male	Female	Total	Male	Female
TOTAL POPULATION	17,134,000	7,725,000	9,409,000	17,003,661	7,748,142	9,255,519	17,056,000	7,794,000	9,262,000
Percent	100.0%	100.0%	100.0%	100.0%	100.0%	100.0%	100.0%	100.0%	100.0%
Popul. in Agric.	...	...	...	2,300,000[c]	1,100,000[c]	1,200,000[c]	...	...	...
Percent	...	...	...	13.5%	14.2%	13.0%	...	...	...
ACTIVE EARNERS & DEPENDENTS, TOTAL	...	...	...	13,491,122	6,576,011	6,915,111	...	...	...
Percent	...	...	...	100.0%	100.0%	100.0%	...	...	...
AE & D in Agric.	...	...	...	2,111,264	1,049,823	1,061,441	...	...	...
Percent	...	...	...	15.6%	16.0%	15.3%	...	...	...
ACTIVE EARNERS, TOTAL	7,686,000	4,230,000	3,456,000	7,994,558	4,459,702	3,534,856	7,676,000	4,095,000	3,581,000
Percent	100.0%	100.0%	100.0%	100.0%	100.0%	100.0%	100.0%	100.0%	100.0%
AE in Agric.	1,304,000	708,000	596,000	1,201,394	670,417	530,977	1,179,000	616,000	563,000
Percent	17.0%	16.7%	17.2%	15.0%	15.0%	15.0%	15.4%	15.0%	15.7%

TABLE H-7   (CONCLUDED)

Measures of Agric. Popul.	1970[a] I			1975[a] I		
	Total	Male	Female	Total	Male	Female
TOTAL POPULATION	17,061,000	7,869,000	9,192,000	16,850,000	7,823,000	9,027,000
Percent	100.0%	100.0%	100.0%	100.0%	100.0%	100.0%
Popul. in Agric.	...	...	...	...	...	...
Percent	...	...	...	...	...	...
ACTIVE EARNERS & DEPENDENTS, TOTAL	...	...	...	...	...	...
Percent	...	...	...	...	...	...
AE & D in Agric.	...	...	...	...	...	...
Percent	...	...	...	...	...	...
ACTIVE EARNERS, TOTAL	7,769,000	4,019,000	3,750,000	7,948,000	4,002,000	3,946,000
Percent	100.0%	100.0%	100.0%	100.0%	100.0%	100.0%
AE in Agric.	997,000	540,000	457,000	895,000	511,000	384,000
Percent	12.8%	13.4%	12.2%	11.3%	12.8%	9.7%

Notes: a July 1. Does not include apprentices. b Includes East Berlin. c Estimate.

Measures of Agric. Popul.	1930 I			1949 I			1960 I		
	Total	Male	Female	Total	Male	Female	Total	Male	Female
TOTAL POPULATION	8,685,109	4,248,452	4,436,657	9,204,799	4,423,420	4,781,379	9,961,044	4,804,043	5,157,001
Percent	100.0%	100.0%	100.0%	100.0%	100.0%	100.0%	100.0%	100.0%	100.0%
Popul. in Agric.	...	...	...	...	...	...	...	...	...
Percent	...	...	...	...	...	...	...	...	...
ACTIVE EARNERS & DEPENDENTS, TOTAL	8,251,873	4,075,779	4,176,094	8,691,446	4,224,878	4,466,568	9,281,951	4,537,744	4,744,207
Percent	100.0%	100.0%	100.0%	100.0%	100.0%	100.0%	100.0%	100.0%	100.0%
AE & D in Agric.	4,511,310	2,263,410	2,247,900	4,533,419	2,210,441	2,322,978	3,466,407	1,603,152	1,863,255
Percent	54.7%	55.5%	53.8%	52.2%	52.3%	52.0%	37.3%	35.3%	39.3%
ACTIVE EARNERS, TOTAL	3,737,456	2,760,772	976,684	4,084,931	2,892,072	1,192,859	4,759,616	3,068,489	1,691,127
Percent	100.0%	100.0%	100.0%	100.0%	100.0%	100.0%	100.0%	100.0%	100.0%
AE in Agric.	2,035,597	1,563,865	471,732	2,200,248	1,547,718	652,530	1,842,617	1,139,900	702,717
Percent	54.5%	56.6%	48.3%	53.9%	53.5%	54.7%	38.7%	37.1%	41.6%

Measures of Agric. Popul.	1960[a] II			1965[a] II			1970 I		
	Total	Male	Female	Total	Male	Female	Total	Male	Female
TOTAL POPULATION	9,961,000	4,804,000	5,157,000	10,140,000	4,904,000	5,236,000	10,322,099	5,003,651	5,318,448
Percent	100.0%	100.0%	100.0%	100.0%	100.0%	100.0%	100.0%	100.0%	100.0%
Popul. in Agric.	...	...	...	...	...	...	2,988,000[b]	1,422,000[b]	1,567,000[b]
Percent	...	...	...	...	...	...	29.0%	28.4%	29.5%
ACTIVE EARNERS & DEPENDENTS, TOTAL	...	...	...	...	...	...	8,411,263	4,281,925	4,129,338
Percent	...	...	...	...	...	...	100.0%	100.0%	100.0%
AE & D in Agric.	...	...	...	...	...	...	2,356,544	1,177,667	1,178,877
Percent	...	...	...	...	...	...	28.0%	27.5%	28.5%
ACTIVE EARNERS, TOTAL	4,735,000	...	...	4,649,200	...	...	4,988,676	2,933,484	2,055,192
Percent	100.0%	...	...	100.0%	...	...	100.0%	100.0%	100.0%
AE in Agric.	1,842,600	...	...	1,382,100	...	...	1,282,311	799,549	482,762
Percent	38.9%	...	...	29.7%	...	...	25.7%	27.3%	23.5%

TABLE H-8 (CONCLUDED)

Measures of Agric. Popul.	1970[a] II			1975[a] II		
	Total	Male	Female	Total	Male	Female
TOTAL POPULATION	10,322,000	5,004,000	5,318,000	10,509,000	5,097,000	5,412,000
Percent	100.0%	100.0%	100.0%	100.0%	100.0%	100.0%
Popul. in Agric.	...	...	...	...	...	...
Percent	...	...	...	...	...	...
ACTIVE EARNERS & DEPENDENTS, TOTAL	...	...	...	...	...	...
Percent	...	...	...	...	...	...
AE & D in Agric.	...	...	...	...	...	...
Percent	...	...	...	...	...	...
ACTIVE EARNERS, TOTAL	4,980,200	...	...	5,085,500	2,850,100	2,235,400
Percent	100.0%	...	...	100.0%	100.0%	100.0%
AE in Agric.	1,313,300	...	...	1,156,800	703,800	453,000
Percent	26.4%	...	...	22.7%	24.7%	20.3%

Notes: a Jan. 1. b Estimate.

TABLE H-9   NUMBER OF PERSONS IN AGRICULTURE: POLAND, 1931-1974

Measures of Agric. Popul.	1931[a]			1950[a]			1960[a]		
	Total	Male	Female	Total	Male	Female	Total	Male	Female
TOTAL POPULATION	31,915,779	15,427,502	16,488,277	25,008,179	11,927,988	13,080,191	29,775,508	14,404,218	15,371,290
Percent	100.0%	100.0%	100.0%	100.0%	100.0%	100.0%	100.0%[b]	100.0%	100.0%
Popul. in Agric.	...	...	...	...	...	...		...	...
Percent	...	...	...	...	...	...		...	...
ACTIVE EARNERS & DEPENDENTS, TOTAL	29,048,900	...	...	23,618,200	...	...	27,502,138	13,316,366	14,185,772
Percent	100.0%	...	...	100.0%	...	...	100.0%	100.0%	100.0%
AE & D in Agric.	19,134,300	...	...	11,597,500	...	...	11,243,651	5,075,985	6,167,666
Percent	65.9%	...	...	49.1%	...	...	40.9%	38.1%	43.5%
ACTIVE EARNERS, TOTAL	13,622,200	...	...	12,404,200	...	...	13,907,442	7,752,731	6,154,711
Percent	100.0%	...	...	100.0%	...	...	100.0%	100.0%	100.0%
AE in Agric.	9,576,800	...	...	7,016,100	...	...	6,545,855	2,929,004	3,616,851
Percent	70.3%	...	...	56.6%	...	...	47.1%	37.8%	58.8%

Measures of Agric. Popul.	1970			1974		
	Total	Male	Female	Total	Male	Female
TOTAL POPULATION	32,642,270	15,853,618	16,788,652	33,635,933	16,312,730	17,323,203
Percent	100.0%	100.0%	100.0%	100.0%	100.0%	100.0%
Popul. in Agric.	[c]	...	...	[d]	...	...
Percent		...	...		...	...
ACTIVE EARNERS & DEPENDENTS, TOTAL	29,262,149	14,455,883	14,806,266	29,525,388	14,616,553	14,908,835
Percent	100.0%	100.0%	100.0%	100.0%	100.0%	100.0%
AE & D in Agric.	9,732,331	4,335,171	5,397,160	9,118,885	4,149,491	4,969,394
Percent	33.3%	30.0%	36.5%	30.9%	28.4%	33.3%
ACTIVE EARNERS, TOTAL	16,429,101	8,828,853	7,600,248	17,089,452	9,153,136	7,936,316
Percent	100.0%	100.0%	100.0%	100.0%	100.0%	100.0%
AE in Agric.	6,096,533	2,655,393	3,441,140	5,641,968	2,570,553	3,071,415
Percent	37.1%	30.1%	45.3%	33.0%	28.1%	38.7%

Notes: a   Military excluded from data on Active Earners and Dependents, and on Active Earners--both for total population and for persons in agriculture. 1931 data exclude unemployed.   b   Czynni zawodowo in agriculture, including Active Earners and their Dependents, and pensioners with supplementary incomes in agriculture and their dependents: 11,382,000 (38.2%).   c   Czynni zawodowo in agriculture, including Active Earners and their Dependents, and pensioners with supplementary incomes in agriculture and their dependents: 10,234,000 (31.6%).   d   Czynni zawodowo in agriculture, including Active Earners and their Dependents, and pensioners with supplementary incomes in agriculture and their dependents: 9,561,437 (28.4%).

393

TABLE H-10   NUMBER OF PERSONS IN AGRICULTURE: ROMANIA, 1930-1966

Measures of Agric. Popul.	1930			1956			1966		
	Total	Male	Female	Total	Male	Female	Total	Male	Female
TOTAL POPULATION	18,057,028	8,886,883	9,170,195	17,489,450	8,503,420	8,986,030	19,103,163	9,351,075	9,752,088
Percent	100.0%	100.0%	100.0%	100.0%	100.0%	100.0%	100.0%	100.0%	100.0%
Popul. in Agric.	...	...	...	11,000,000[a]	5,000,000[a]	6,000,000[a]	9,500,000[a]	...	...
Percent	...	...	...	62.9%	58.8%	66.8%	49.7%	...	...
ACTIVE EARNERS & DEPENDENTS, TOTAL	...	...	...	...	...	...	17,119,271	8,494,651	8,624,620
Percent	100.0%	100.0%	100.0%	...	...	...	100.0%	100.0%	100.0%
AE & D in Agric.	13,063,213	6,358,511	6,704,702	...	...	...	8,613,622	3,788,223	4,825,399
Percent	...	...	...	...	...	...	50.3%	44.6%	55.9%
ACTIVE EARNERS, TOTAL	10,542,900	5,745,900	4,797,000	10,449,128	5,714,181	4,734,947	10,362,300	5,675,176	4,687,124
Percent	100.0%	100.0%	100.0%	100.0%	100.0%	100.0%	100.0%	100.0%	100.0%
AE in Agric.	8,244,500	4,063,600	4,180,900	7,278,518	3,380,263	3,898,255	5,920,327	2,530,823	3,389,504
Percent	78.2%	70.7%	87.2%	69.7%	59.2%	82.3%	57.1%	44.6%	72.3%

Notes: a Estimates.

TABLE H-11   NUMBER OF PERSONS IN AGRICULTURE: USSR, 1926-1970

Measures of Agric. Popul.	1926[a]			1959[a]		
	Total	Male	Female	Total	Male	Female
TOTAL POPULATION	147,027,915	71,043,357	75,984,558	208,826,650	94,050,303	114,776,347
Percent	100.0%	100.0%	100.0%	100.0%	100.0%	100.0%
Popul. in Agric.	115,000,000[b]	55,085,000[b]	59,915,000[b]	79,000,000[b]	33,000,000[b]	46,000,000[b]
Percent	78.2%	77.5%	78.9%	37.8%	35.1%	40.1%
ACTIVE EARNERS & DEPENDENTS, TOTAL	144,378,035	69,770,730	74,607,305	...	...	...
Percent	100.0%	100.0%	100.0%	...	...	...
AE & D in Agric.	114,055,516	54,667,715	59,387,801	...	...	...
Percent	79.0%	78.4%	79.6%	...	...	...
ACTIVE EARNERS, TOTAL	84,357,724	45,217,928	39,139,796	108,995,013[c]	52,439,504[d]	56,555,538[e]
Percent	100.0%	100.0%	100.0%	100.0%	100.0%	100.0%
AE in Agric.	71,734,888	36,169,978	35,564,910	48,290,768[c]	18,575,560[d]	29,715,208[e]
Percent	85.0%	80.0%	90.9%	44.3%	35.4%	52.5%

Measures of Agric. Popul.	1959[f]			1970[f]		
	Total	Male	Female	Total	Male	Female
TOTAL POPULATION	208,826,650	94,050,303	114,776,347	241,436,013	111,182,265	130,253,748
Percent	100.0%	100.0%	100.0%	100.0%	100.0%	100.0%
Popul. in Agric.	81,000,000[b]	35,000,000[b]	46,000,000[b]	71,000,000[b]	31,000,000[b]	40,000,000[b]
Percent	38.8%	37.2%	40.1%	29.4%	27.9%	30.7%
ACTIVE EARNERS & DEPENDENTS, TOTAL	...	...	...	203,131,935	98,273,764	104,858,171
Percent	...	...	...	100.0%	100.0%	100.0%
AE & D in Agric.	...	...	...	55,000,000[b]	27,000,000[b]	28,000,000[b]
Percent	...	...	...	27.1%	27.5%	26.7%
ACTIVE EARNERS, TOTAL	108,995,013[c]	52,439,504[d]	56,555,538[e]	117,027,575[g]	57,990,328[h]	59,037,247[i]
Percent	100.0%	100.0%	100.0%	100.0%	100.0%	100.0%
AE in Agric.	49,333,000[b]	20,000,000[b]	29,715,208[e]	30,761,092[g]	14,652,202[h]	16,108,890[i]
Percent	45.3%	38.1%	52.5%	26.3%	25.3%	27.3%

Notes: a Military excluded from data on persons in agriculture. b Estimate. c Includes 9,864,801 Members of Families of Collective Farmers, Workers and Employees tending private plots in agriculture. d Includes 913,903 Members of Families of Collective Farmers, Workers and Employees tending private plots in agriculture. e Includes 8,950,898 Members of Families of Collective Farmers, Workers and Employees tending private plots in agriculture. f Military included in data on persons in agriculture. g Includes 1,823,499 Members of Families of Collective Farmers, Workers and Employees tending private plots in agriculture. h Includes 161,874 Members of Families of Collective Farmers, Workers and Employees tending private plots in agriculture. i Includes 1,661,625 Members of Families of Collective Farmers, Workers and Employees tending private plots in agriculture.

TABLE H-12   NUMBER OF PERSONS IN AGRICULTURE: YUGOSLAVIA, 1931-1976

Measures of Agric. Popul.	1931			1948			1953		
	Total	Male	Female	Total	Male	Female	Total	Male	Female
TOTAL POPULATION	13,934,038	6,891,627	7,042,411	15,772,098	7,582,461	8,189,637	16,936,573	8,204,595	8,731,978
Percent	100.0%	100.0%	100.0%	100.0%	100.0%	100.0%	100.0%	100.0%	100.0%
Popul. in Agric.	...	...	...	...	...	...	...	...	...
Percent	...	...	...	...	...	...	...	...	...
ACTIVE EARNERS & DEPENDENTS, TOTAL	13,575,714	6,770,100	6,805,614	...	...	...	16,030,801	7,857,870	8,173,021
Percent	100.0%	100.0%	100.0%	100.0%	100.0%	100.0%	100.0%	100.0%	100.0%
AE & D in Agric.	10,670,565	5,181,725	5,488,840	10,606,000	5,000,000	5,606,000	10,315,834	4,832,745	5,483,089
Percent	78.6%	76.5%	80.7%	72.7%	...	...	64.4%	61.5%	67.1%
ACTIVE EARNERS, TOTAL	6,458,276	4,332,026	2,126,250	[7,740,000]	[4,865,000]	[2,877,000]	7,848,857	5,168,592	2,680,265
Percent	100.0%	100.0%	100.0%	100.0%	100.0%	100.0%	100.0%	100.0%	100.0%
AE in Agric.	5,098,888	3,234,295	1,864,593	5,627,000	3,357,000	2,270,000	5,360,026	3,197,808	2,162,218
Percent	79.0%	74.7%	87.7%	72.7%	69.0%	78.9%	68.3%	61.9%	80.7%

Measures of Agric. Popul.	1961			1971			1976		
	Total	Male	Female	Total	Male	Female	Total	Male	Female
TOTAL POPULATION	18,549,291	9,043,424	9,505,867	20,522,972	10,077,282	10,445,690	21,560,000	...	...
Percent	100.0%	100.0%	100.0%	100.0%	100.0%	100.0%	100.0%	...	...
Popul. in Agric.	...	...	...	...	...	...	...	...	...
Percent	...	...	...	...	...	...	...	...	...
ACTIVE EARNERS & DEPENDENTS, TOTAL	17,399,942	8,568,031	8,831,911	18,314,621	9,141,162	9,173,459	...	...	...
Percent	100.0%	100.0%	100.0%	100.0%	100.0%	100.0%	100.0%a	...	...
AE & D in Agric.	9,197,597	4,231,958	4,965,639	7,843,986	...	...	7,150,000a	...	...
Percent	52.9%	49.4%	56.2%	42.8%	...	...	...	...	...
ACTIVE EARNERS, TOTAL	8,340,400	5,387,201	2,953,144	8,889,816	5,686,332	3,203,484	...	...	...
Percent	100.0%	100.0%	100.0%	100.0%	100.0%	100.0%	...	...	...
AE in Agric.	4,691,679	2,676,062	2,015,617	4,207,645	2,433,289	1,774,356	...	...	...
Percent	56.3%	49.7%	68.3%	47.3%	42.8%	55.4%	...	...	...

Note: a Estimate.

TABLE H-13   URBAN POPULATION: ALBANIA, 1923-1973

Measures of Urbanization	1923	1938	1945	1950	1955	1960	1965	1970	1973
TOTAL POPULATION	803,959	1,040,353	1,122,044	1,218,943	1,391,499	1,626,315	1,865,300	2,135,600	2,296,800
Percent	100.0%	100.0%	100.0%	100.0%	100.0%	100.0%	100.0%	100.0%	100.0%
In Urban Settlements Under 5,000	...	...	...	...	51,204	62,891	69,025	...	...
Percent	...	...	...	...	3.7%	3.9%	3.7%	...	...
In Urban Settlements of 5,000 & over	...	...	...	...	331,965	439,565	550,930	...	...
Percent	...	...	...	...	23.9%	27.0%	29.5%	...	...
In Urban Settlements of 10,000 & over	68,431	94,817	172,398	...	295,440	414,351	492,935	...	...
Percent	8.5%	9.1%	15.4%	...	21.2%	25.5%	26.4%	...	...
In Urban Settlements of 20,000 & over	47,178	71,593	118,887	...	255,987	330,109	411,650	...	...
Percent	5.9%	6.9%	10.6%	...	18.4%	20.3%	22.1%	...	...
In Urban Settlements of 50,000 & over	0	0	59,950	...	108,183	136,295	161,330	...	...
Percent	0.0%	0.0%	5.3%	...	7.8%	8.4%	8.6%	...	...
In Urban Settlements of 100,000 & over	0	0	0	...	108,183	136,295	161,330	...	...
Percent	0.0%	0.0%	0.0%	...	7.8%	8.4%	8.6%	...	...
In All Urban Settlements	127,595	160,000	238,812	249,783	383,169	502,456	619,955	719,000	777,900
Percent	15.9%	15.4%	21.3%	20.5%	27.5%	30.9%	33.2%	33.7%	33.9%

TABLE H-14 URBAN POPULATION: BULGARIA, 1934-1975

Measures of Urbanization	1934[a]	1946	1956	1960[b]	1965	1970[b]	1975
TOTAL POPULATION	6,077,939	7,029,349	7,613,709	7,905,500	8,227,866	8,514,900	8,729,720
Percent	100.0%	100.0%	100.0%	100.0%	100.0%	100.0%	100.0%
In Urban Settlements Under 5,000	106,418	97,746	68,703	...	131,458	...	178,162
Percent	1.8%	1.4%	0.9%	...	1.6%	...	2.0%
In Urban Settlements of 5,000 & over	1,196,680	1,638,442	2,487,368	...	3,691,366	...	4,883,273
Percent	19.7%	23.3%	32.7%	...	44.9%	...	55.9%
In Urban Settlements of 10,000 & over	973,696	1,396,783	2,219,885	...	3,190,816	...	4,370,460
Percent	16.0%	19.9%	29.2%	...	38.8%	...	50.1%
In Urban Settlements of 20,000 & over	737,303	1,067,876	1,846,465	...	2,792,119	3,376,959	3,589,937[c]
Percent	12.1%	15.2%	24.3%	...	33.9%	39.7%	41.1%
In Urban Settlements of 50,000 & over	...	d	1,255,466	...	2,094,067	2,504,402	3,023,684
Percent	...		16.5%	...	25.5%	29.4%	34.6%
In Urban Settlements of 100,000 & over	287,095	563,186	926,908	...	1,438,732	1,771,120	2,052,191
Percent	4.7%	8.0%	12.2%	...	17.5%	20.8%	23.5%
In all Urban Settlements	1,303,098	1,735,188	2,556,071	3,005,000	3,822,824	4,509,800	5,061,435
Percent	21.4%	24.7%	33.6%	38,0%	46.5%	53.0%	58.0%

Notes: a Prewar boundaries. b Dec. 31. c 25,000 and over. d 691,540 (9.8%) according to preliminary results of 1946 census.

TABLE H-15   URBAN POPULATION: CZECHOSLOVAKIA, 1921-1975

Measures of Urbanization	1921[a]	1921[b]	1930[a]	1930[b]	1946-47	1950	1955[c]
TOTAL POPULATION	13,613,172	13,008,000	14,729,536	14,004,000	12,164,095	12,338,450	13,093,000
Percent	100.0%	100.0%	100.0%	100.0%	100.0%	100.0%	100.0%
In Settlements from 2,000 to 5,000	2,244,261	2,088,000	2,605,390	2,369,000	...	1,749,543	1,945,000
Percent	16.5%	16.1%	19.7%	16.9%	...	14.2%	14.9%
In Settlements of 5,000 & over	3,637,568	3,518,000	4,436,282	4,266,000	...	4,572,302	5,033,000
Percent	26.7%	27.0%	30.1%	30.5%	...	37.1%	38.4%
In Settlements of 10,000 & over	2,572,800	2,506,000	3,331,362	3,220,000	...	3,654,598	4,019,000
Percent	18.9%	19.3%	22.6%	23.0%	...	29.6%	30.7%
In Settlements of 20,000 & over	1,773,562	1,732,000	2,441,484	2,389,000	2,548,880	2,906,073	3,252,000
Percent	13.0%	13.3%	16.6%	17.1%	21.0%	23.6%	24.8%
In Settlements of 50,000 & over	1,190,124	1,190,000	1,614,157	1,614,000	...	2,080,685	2,300,000
Percent	8.7%	9.1%	11.0%	11.5%	...	16.9%	17.6%
In Settlements of 100,000 & over	1,120,153	1,044,000	1,477,600	1,478,000	1,666,849	1,722,433	...
Percent	8.2%	8.0%	10.0%	10.6%	13.7%	14.0%	...
In all Urban Settlements[d]	5,881,829	5,606,000	7,041,672	6,635,000	5,935,433	6,321,845	6,978,000
Percent	43.2%	43.1%	47.8%	47.4%	48.8%	51.2%	53.3%

TABLE H-15 (CONCLUDED)

Measures of Urbanization	1961	1961[e]	1965[f]	1970	1970[e]	1974[c]	1975[f]
TOTAL POPULATION	13,745,577	13,745,577	14,194,055	14,357,557	14,344,986	14,685,775	14,857,145
Percent	100.0%	100.0%	100.0%	100.0%	100.0%	100.0%	100.0%
In Settlements from 2,000 to 5,000	2,253,212	972,460[g]	...	2,147,498	...	...	...
Percent	16.4%	7.1%	...	15.0%	...	...	...
In Settlements of 5,000 & over	5,651,482	5,567,998	...	6,804,532	...	...	...
Percent	41.1%	40.5%	...	47.4%	...	...	...
In Settlements of 10,000 & over	4,469,425	4,458,603	5,094,311	5,610,560	...	6,216,577[h]	6,481,213
Percent	32.5%	32.4%	35.9%	39.1%	...	42.3%	43.6%
In Settlements of 20,000 & over	3,477,444	3,477,444	4,057,286	4,459,311	...	4,857,174[h]	5,064,951
Percent	25.3%	25.3%	28.6%	31.1%	...	33.1%	34.1%
In Settlements of 50,000 & over	2,487,773	2,487,773	2,922,995	3,201,781	...	3,537,798	3,710,870
Percent	18.1%	18.1%	20.6%	22.3%	...	24.1%	25.0%
In Settlements of 100,000 & over	1,932,841	1,932,841	2,138,824	2,269,349	...	2,412,639[h]	2,501,803
Percent	14.1%	14.1%	15.1%	15.8%	...	16.4%	16.8%
In all Urban Settlements	7,904,694[d]	6,540,458[e]	...	8,952,030[d]	7,964,266[e]	9,795,000[h]	...
Percent	57.5%	47.6%	...	62.4%	55.5%	66.7%	...

Notes: [a] Prewar boundaries. [b] Postwar boundaries. [c] 1 July. [d] All settlements 2,000 and over. [e] Urban settlements only. [f] Dec. 31. [g] Urban type settlements under 5,000. [h] Criteria for urban not specified; probably all settlements 2,000 and over.

TABLE H-16 URBAN POPULATION: GDR, 1939-1975

Measures of Urbanization	1939	1946	1950[a]	1960[a]	1964	1971	1975
TOTAL POPULATION	16,745,300	18,355,000	18,388,200	17,188,500	17,003,600	17,068,300	16,820,200
Percent	100.0%	100.0%	100.0%	100.0%	100.0%	100.0%	100.0%
Settlements from 2,000 to 5,000	2,047,600	2,414,900	2,516,900	2,203,200	2,037,200	2,013,600	2,018,200
Percent	12.2%	13.2%	13.7%	12.8%	12.0%	11.8%	12.0%
Settlements of 5,000 & over	10,044,400	9,990,100	10,523,600	10,164,500	10,360,000	10,578,700	10,670,000
Percent	60.0%	54.4%	57.2%	59.1%	60.9%	62.0%	63.4%
Settlements of 10,000 & over	8,625,500	8,158,400	8,837,700	8,620,300	8,807,000	9,139,200	9,301,500
Percent	51.5%	44.4%	48.1%	50.1%	51.8%	53.5%	55.3%
Settlements of 20,000 & over	7,265,100	6,616,000	7,190,900	6,951,800	7,231,400	7,519,300	7,819,400
Percent	43.4%	36.0%	39.1%	40.4%	42.5%	44.1%	46.5%
Settlements of 50,000 & over	5,378,200	4,508,800	4,685,000	4,559,100	4,726,800	4,904,600	5,224,800
Percent	32.1%	24.6%	25.5%	26.5%	27.8%	28.7%	31.1%
Settlements of 100,000 & over	4,474,100	3,485,200	3,810,800	3,671,400	3,716,200	3,746,600	4,077,100
Percent	26.7%	19.0%	20.7%	21.4%	21.9%	22.0%	24.2%
All Urban Settlements[b]	12,092,000	12,405,000	13,040,500	12,367,700	12,397,200	12,592,300	12,688,200
Percent	72.2%	67.6%	70.9%	72.0%	72.9%	73.8%	75.4%

Notes: [a] Dec. 31. [b] All settlements of 2,000 and over.

TABLE H-17   URBAN POPULATION: HUNGARY, 1920-1975

Measures of Urbanization	1920[a]	1930[a]	1941[a]	1949[a]	1955[a]	1960[a]	1966[a]	1970[a]	1976
TOTAL POPULATION	7,990,202	8,688,319	9,316,074	9,204,799	9,749,000	9,961,044	10,160,380	10,300,996	10,572,0
Percent	100.0%	100.0%	100.0%	100.0%	100.0%	100.0%	100.0%	100.0%	100.
In Urban Settlements Under 5,000									
Percent									
In Urban Settlements of 5,000 & Over	2,476,759	2,881,251	3,243,940	3,389,935	3,910,000	3,958,407		4,785,208	5,325,6
Percent	31.0%	33.2%	34.8%	36.8%	40.1%	39.7%		46.5%	50.
In Urban Settlements of 10,000 & Over	2,449,327	2,837,807	3,225,423	3,363,663	3,895,000	3,938,759	4,377,465	4,775,488	5,315,6
Percent	30.7%	32.7%	34.6%	36.5%	40.0%	39.5%	43.1%	46.4%	50.
In Urban Settlements of 20,000 & Over	2,221,687	2,524,952	3,044,461	3,161,503	3,634,000	3,688,905	4,185,147	4,445,521	4,944,3
Percent	27.8%	29.1%	32.7%	34.3%	37.3%	37.0%	41.2%	43.2%	46.
In Urban Settlements of 50,000 & Over	1,499,893	1,761,906	2,113,830	2,279,216	2,667,000	2,752,487	3,147,138	3,317,256	3,759,7
Percent	18.8%	20.3%	22.7%	24.8%	27.4%	27.6%	31.0%	32.2%	35.
In Urban Settlements of 100,000 & Over	1,151,291	1,258,530	1,427,648	1,944,985	2,227,000	2,192,998	2,522,080	2,719,713	2,910,2
Percent	14.4%	14.5%	15.3%	21.1%	22.8%	22.0%	24.8%	26.4%	27.
In All Urban Settlements	2,476,759	2,881,251	3,243,940	3,389,935	3,910,000	3,958,407	4,377,465	4,785,208	5,325,6
Percent	31.0%	33.2%	34.8%	36.8%	40.1%	39.7%	43.1%	46.5%	50.

Note: a Jan. 1.

TABLE H-18 URBAN POPULATION: POLAND, 1931-1975

Measures of Urbanization	1931[a]	1946[b]	1950	1960[c]	1965[c]	1970[c]	1975[c]
TOTAL POPULATION	31,915,779	23,929,800	25,008,179	29,775,508	31,551,000	32,642,270	34,184,800
Percent	100.0%	100.0%	100.0%	100.0%	100.0%	100.0%	100.0%
In Urban Settlements Under 5,000	926,875	1,103,843	1,066,300	1,208,400	1,122,700	1,099,300	879,400
Percent	2.9%	4.6%	4.3%	4.1%	3.6%	3.4%	2.6%
In Urban Settlements of 5,000 & over	7,753,104	6,368,568	8,539,000	12,997,700	14,558,000	15,988,700	18,150,600
Percent	24.3%	26.6%	34.1%	43.7%	46.1%	49.0%	53.1%
In Urban Settlements of 10,000 & over	6,522,401	5,418,465	7,426,100	11,346,100	12,817,300	14,417,900	16,783,700
Percent	20.4%	22.6%	29.7%	38.1%	40.6%	44.2%	49.1%
In Urban Settlements of 20,000 & over	5,427,383	4,436,263	6,392,000	9,466,000	10,728,200	12,174,800	14,595,400
Percent	17.0%	18.5%	25.6%	31.8%	34.0%	37.3%	42.7%
In Urban Settlements of 50,000 & over	...	3,195,081	4,868,800	7,384,700	8,398,500	9,259,000	11,253,300
Percent	...	13.3%	19.5%	24.8%	26.6%	28.4%	32.9%
In Urban Settlements of 100,000 & over	3,348,317	2,410,626	4,036,900	6,112,200	6,765,200	7,388,100	8,777,900
Percent	10.5%	10.1%	16.1%	20.5%	21.4%	22.6%	25.7%
In All Urban Settlements	8,686,284[d]	7,472,411	9,605,300	14,206,100	15,680,700	17,088,000	19,030,000
Percent	27.2%	31.2%	38.4%	47.7%	49.7%	52.3%	55.7%

Notes: a Prewar boundaries. The estimated urban population, 1931, within postwar boundaries was 37%. b See introduction to this section for comments on the reliability of the 1946 data. c Dec. 31. d The figure for all urban settlements is 6,305 more than the total of urban settlements under 5,000 and urban settlements over 5,000.

TABLE H-19   URBAN POPULATION: ROMANIA, 1930-1977

Measures of Urbanization	1930[a] I	1930[b] I	1948 I	1956 II	1960[c] I	1966 II
TOTAL POPULATION	18,057,028	14,280,729	15,872,624	17,489,450	18,403,414	19,103,163
Percent	100.0%	100.0%	100.0%	100.0%	100.0%	100.0%
In Urban Settlements Under 5,000	110,482	93,843	121,817	70,998	459,813	69,089
Percent	0.6%	0.7%	0.8%	0.4%	2.5%	0.4%
In Urban Settlements of 5,000 & over	3,540,557	2,957,410	3,591,322	4,675,674	5,452,198	6,674,798
Percent	19.6%	20.7%	22.6%	26.7%	29.6%	34.9%
In Urban Settlements of 10,000 & over	3,129,107	2,608,964	3,263,593	4,303,242	4,805,091	6,107,427
Percent	17.3%	18.3%	20.6%	24.6%	26.1%	32.0%
In Urban Settlements of 20,000 & over	2,424,370	2,045,504	2,720,825	3,425,676	3,609,434[d]	5,023,523
Percent	13.4%	14.3%	17.1%	19.6%	19.6%	26.3%
In Urban Settlements of 50,000 & over	1,802,740	1,575,417	2,113,660	2,688,028	2,904,721	3,750,726
Percent	10.0%	11.0%	13.3%	15.4%	15.8%	19.6%
In Urban Settlements of 100,000 & over	1,170,690	943,367	1,271,709	2,034,956	2,566,529	3,149,212
Percent	6.5%	6.6%	8.0%	11.6%	13.9%	16.5%
In Assimilated Urban Settlements	e	e	e	727,592	e	561,827
Percent				4.2%		2.9%
In All Urban Settlements	3,651,039	3,051,253	3,713,139	5,474,264	5,912,011	7,305,714
Percent	20.2%	21.4%	23.4%	31.3%	32.1%	38.2%

TABLE H-19   (CONCLUDED)

Measures of Urbanization	1970[c] II	1970 I	1975 II	1977[f]	1977[c] II
TOTAL POPULATION	20,252,541	20,252,541	21,245,103	21,559,416	21,657,569
Percent	100.0%	100.0%	100.0%	100.0%	100.0%
In Urban Settlements Under 5,000	...	...	...	...	52,575
Percent	...	...	...	...	0.2%
In Urban Settlements of 5,000 & over	...	...	...	...	9,465,744
Percent	...	...	...	...	43.7%
In Urban Settlements of 10,000 & over	...	...	...	...	9,006,683
Percent	...	...	...	...	41.6%
In Urban Settlements of 20,000 & over	5,750,154	6,569,043	...	...	8,046,937
Percent	28.4%	32.4%	...	...	37.2%
In Urban Settlements of 50,000 & over	4,322,938	5,252,086	...	...	6,330,786
Percent	21.3%	25.9%	...	...	29.2%
In Urban Settlements of 100,000 & over	3,472,930	4,165,214	...	...	5,115,588
Percent	17.1%	20.6%	...	...	23.6%
In Assimilated Urban Settlements	...	e	843,234	...	843,964
Percent	...		4.0%	...	3.9%
In All Urban Settlements	8,258,138	8,258,138	9,182,463	10,236,846	10,362,283
Percent	40.8%	40.8%	43.2%	47.5%	47.8%

Notes: a Prewar boundaries.   b Postwar boundaries.   c July 1.   d 25,000 and over.
e Assimilated Urban Settlements included with other urban settlements.   f Census
results of Jan. 5, 1977.

TABLE H-20   URBAN POPULATION: USSR, 1926-1979 (in Thousands)

Measures of Urbanization	1926[a]	1939[a]	1951[b]	1956[b]	1959	1966[b]	1970	1976[b]	1979
TOTAL POPULATION	146,975	170,557	181,603	197,902	208,827	232,243	241,720	255,500	262,436
Percent	100.0%	100.0%	100.0%	100.0%	100.0%	100.0%	100.0%	100.0%	100.0%
In Urban Settlements Under 5,000	2,463	2,350	...	...	5,207	...	6,150	...	...
Percent	1.7%	1.4%	...	...	2.5%	...	2.5%	...	...
In Urban Settlements of 5,000 & over	23,853	53,775	...	...	94,770	...	129,842	...	...
Percent	16.2%	31.5%	...	...	45.4%	...	53.7%	...	...
In Urban Settlements of 10,000 & over	21,165	49,027	...	...	85,557	...	119,772	...	...
Percent	14.4%	28.7%	...	...	41.0%	...	49.5%	...	...
In Urban Settlements of 20,000 & over	17,642	42,573	...	...	74,407	...	107,050	...	...
Percent	12.0%	25.0%	...	...	35.6%	...	44.3%	...	...
In Urban Settlements of 50,000 & over	...	33,805	...	...	59,578	...	88,581	...	...
Percent	...	19.8%	...	...	28.5%	...	36.6%	...	...
In Urban Settlements of 100,000 & over	9,551	26,997	...	...	48,589	...	75,526	...	98,853
Percent	6.5%	15.8%	...	...	23.3%	...	31.2%	...	37.7%
In All Urban Settlements	26,316	56,125	73,000	88,200	99,978	123,700	135,992	156,600	163,586
Percent	17.9%	32.9%	40.2%	44.6%	47.9%	53.3%	56.3%	61.3%	62.3%

Notes: a Prewar boundaries. b Jan. 1.

TABLE H-21   URBAN POPULATION: YUGOSLAVIA, 1921-1971

Measures of Urbanization	1921[a]	1931[a]	1948[a]	1953[b]	1961[b]	1971[b]
TOTAL POPULATION	11,984,911	13,934,038	15,772,098	16,936,573	18,549,291	20,522,972
Percent	100.0%	100.0%	100.0%	100.0%	100.0%	100.0%
In Urban Settlements Under 5,000	142,000	77,400	4,200	223,000	450,846	733,985
Percent	1.2%	0.5%	0.0%	1.3%	2.4%	3.6%
In Urban Settlements of 5,000 & over	1,001,400	1,627,000	2,553,600	3,465,000	4,815,206	7,185,541
Percent	8.4%	11.7%	16.2%	20.5%	26.0%	35.0%
In Urban Settlements of 10,000 & over	881,400	1,462,100	2,396,000	3,153,000	4,185,115	6,258,350
Percent	7.3%	10.5%	15.2%	18.6%	22.6%	30.5%
In Urban Settlements of 20,000 & over	696,100	1,216,100	1,907,800	2,659,000	3,478,743	5,335,400
Percent	5.8%	8.7%	12.1%	15.7%	18.8%	26.0%
In Urban Settlements of 50,000 & over	449,500	822,800	1,284,700	1,695,000	2,177,336	...
Percent	3.7%	5.9%	8.1%	10.0%	11.7%	...
In Urban Settlements of 100,000 & over	238,900	552,500	988,500	...	1,662,309	2,597,298
Percent	2.0%	4.0%	6.3%	...	9.0%	12.7%
In All Urban Settlements	1,143,400	1,704,400	2,557,700	3,688,000	5,266,052	7,919,526
Percent	9.5%	12.2%	16.2%	21.8%	28.4%	38.6%

Notes: a Settlements defined as urban at time of census. b Urban settlements defined by size and percent of population engaged in agriculture. See introduction to this section for further details.

TABLE H-22 HOUSING: BULGARIA, 1956-1975 (in Thousands)

	Distribution by Number of Persons							Distribution by Number of Dwellings						
	1956	1965			1975			1956	1965			1975		
		Total	Urban	Rural	Total	Urban	Rural		Total	Urban	Rural	Total	Urban	Rural
No. of Households Per Dwelling														
Total	7,557	8,065	3,701	4,364	8,557	4,934	3,623	1,688	2,019	874	1,145	2,339	1,288	1,051
Percent	100.0%	100.0%	100.0%	100.0%	100.0%	100.0%	100.0%	100.0%	100.0%	100.0%	100.0%	100.0%	100.0%	100.0%
1 Household	...	6,199	2,312	3,887	7,147	3,765	3,382	...	1,710	642	1,068	2,090	1,077	1,013
Percent	...	76.9%	62.4%	89.1%	83.5%	76.3%	93.3%	...	84.7%	73.4%	93.3%	89.3%	83.6%	96.4%
Over 1 Household	...	1,866	1,389	477	1,410	1,169	241	...	309	232	77	249	211	38
Percent	...	23.1%	37.5%	10.9%	16.5%	23.7%	6.7%	...	15.3%	26.6%	6.7%	10.6%	16.4%	3.6%
Persons per Room														
Total[a]	...	8,145	3,745	4,400	8,557	4,934	3,623	...	2,022	875	1,147	2,339	1,288	1,051
Percent	...	100.0%	100.0%	100.0%	100.0%	100.0%	100.0%	...	100.0%	100.0%	100.0%	100.0%	100.0%	100.0%
Under 1 Person	...	...	...	...	...	...	...	...	...	...	...	...	...	...
Percent	...	16.2%	9.3%	22.0%	27.0%	19.6%	37.0%	...	25.2%	13.9%	33.9%	39.8%	28.7%	53.5%
1 to 2 Persons	...	...	...	...	...	...	...	...	...	...	...	...	...	...
Percent	...	53.2%	55.9%	51.0%	55.5%	60.5%	48.7%	...	51.5%	57.0%	47.2%	47.8%	55.7%	38.0%
2 or More Persons	...	...	...	...	...	...	...	...	...	...	...	...	...	...
Percent	...	30.6%	34.8%	27.0%	17.5%	19.9%	14.3%	...	23.3%	29.1%	18.9%	12.4%	15.6%	8.5%
Facilities														
Total[a]	...	8,145	...	...	8,653	...	...	...	2,022	...	...	2,343	...	...
Percent	...	100.0%	...	...	100.0%	...	...	...	100.0%	...	...	100.0%	...	...
Piped Water	...	2,501	...	...	5,870	...	...	...	571	...	...	1,548	...	...
Percent	...	30.7%	...	...	67.8%	...	...	...	28.2%	...	...	66.1%	...	...
Central Heating	...	111	...	...	660	...	...	...	25	...	...	175	...	...
Percent	...	1.4%	...	...	7.6%	...	...	...	1.2%	...	...	7.5%	...	...
Electricity	...	7,721	...	...	8,632	...	...	...	1,916	...	...	2,338	...	...
Percent	...	94.8%	...	...	99.8%	...	...	...	94.8%	...	...	99.8%	...	...
Toilet in Dwelling	...	1,109	...	...	2,522	...	...	...	248	...	...	656	...	...
Percent	...	13.6%	...	...	29.1%	...	...	...	12.3%	...	...	28.0%	...	...
Age of Dwellings														
Total[b]	1,688	...	...	...	...	...	...	1,688	2,020	875	1,145	2,491	1,337	1,154
Percent	...	...	...	...	...	...	...	...	100.0%	100.0%	100.0%	100.0%	100.0%	100.0%
Built Before 1920	...	...	...	...	...	...	...	...	288	128	160	201	88	113
Percent	...	...	...	...	...	...	...	...	14.3%	14.6%	14.0%	8.1%	6.6%	9.8%
Built 1920-1944	...	...	...	...	...	...	...	...	612	260	352	537	231	306
Percent	...	...	...	...	...	...	...	...	30.3%	29.7%	30.7%	21.6%	17.3%	26.5%
Built After 1944	...	...	...	...	...	...	...	...	1,120	487	633	1,753	1,018	735
Percent	...	...	...	...	...	...	...	...	55.4%	55.7%	55.3%	70.4%	76.1%	63.7%
Built 1945-1960	...	...	...	...	...	...	...	...	800	315	485	773	335	438
Percent	...	...	...	...	...	...	...	...	39.6%	36.0%	42.4%	31.0%	25.1%	38.0%

Notes: a Includes all occupied living quarters, excluding semipermanent buildings. b For 1965, includes occupied conventional dwellings in residential buildings, including vacant villas. For 1975, includes conventional dwellings, occupied or not, in residential buildings only.

TABLE H-23 HOUSING: CZECHOSLOVAKIA, 1950-1970 (in Thousands)

	Distribution by Number of Persons							Distribution by Number of Dwellings						
	1950	1961			1970			1950	1961			1970		
		Total	Urban	Rural	Total	Urban	Rural		Total	Urban	Rural	Total	Urban	Rural
No. of Households Per Dwelling														
Total	...	13,666	6,491	7,175	14,252	7,920	6,332	3,613	3,820	1,954	1,866	4,239	2,504	1,735
Percent	...	100.0%	100.0%	100.0%	100.0%	100.0%	100.0%	100.0%	100.0%	100.0%	100.0%	100.0%	100.0%	100.0%
1 Household	...	...	...	...	12,467	7,053	5,414	...	...	...	...	3,892	2,320	1,572
Percent	...	...	...	...	87.5%	89.1%	85.5%	...	...	...	...	91.8%	92.7%	90.6%
Over 1 Household	...	...	...	...	1,785	867	918	...	...	...	...	347	184	163
Percent	...	...	...	...	12.5%	10.9%	14.5%	...	...	...	...	8.2%	7.3%	9.4%
Persons per Room														
Total	...	13,666	...	...	14,252	...	...	3,613	3,829	...	...	4,239[a]	...	...
Percent	...	100.0%	...	...	100.0%	...	...	100.0%	100.0%	...	...	100.0%	...	...
Under 1 Person	...	...	...	...	...	...	...	...	...	...	...	...	...	...
Percent	...	...	...	...	...	...	...	...	19.3%	...	...	32.1%	...	...
1 to 2 Persons	...	...	...	...	...	...	...	...	...	...	...	...	...	...
Percent	...	...	...	...	...	...	...	...	58.5%	...	...	57.5%	...	...
2 or More Persons	...	...	...	...	...	...	...	...	...	...	...	...	...	...
Percent	...	...	...	...	...	...	...	...	22.2%	...	...	10.4%	...	...
Facilities														
Total	...	...	...	...	14,252	...	...	2,113[b]	3,820	...	...	4,239[a]	...	...
Percent	...	...	...	...	100.0%	...	...	100.0%	100.0%	...	...	100.0%	...	...
Piped Water	...	...	...	...	10,885	...	...	...	1,876	...	...	3,194	...	...
Percent	...	...	...	...	76.4%	...	...	...	49.1%	...	...	75.3%	...	...
Central Heating	...	1,117	...	...	4,631	...	...	27	311	...	...	1,309	...	...
Percent	...	...	...	...	32.5%	...	...	1.3%	8.1%	...	...	30.9%	...	...
Electricity	...	...	...	...	14,216	...	...	1,749	3,716	...	...	4,226	...	...
Percent	...	...	...	...	99.7%	...	...	82.8%	97.3%	...	...	99.7%	...	...
Toilet in Dwelling	...	...	...	...	7,649	...	...	...	1,109	...	...	2,220	...	...
Percent	...	...	...	...	53.7%	...	...	...	29.0%	...	...	52.4%	...	...
Age of Dwellings														
Total	...	...	...	...	...	...	...	3,613	3,820[c]	1,954	1,866	4,239[a]	2,504[d]	1,735
Percent	...	...	...	...	...	...	...	100.0%	100.0%	100.0%	100.0%	100.0%	100.0%	100.0%
Built Before 1920	...	...	...	...	...	...	...	...	1,700	804	896	1,382	718	664
Percent	...	...	...	...	...	...	...	...	44.5%	41.1%	48.0%	32.6%	28.7%	38.3%
Built 1920-1945	...	...	...	...	...	...	...	...	1,278	704	574	1,174	701	473
Percent	...	...	...	...	...	...	...	...	33.5%	36.0%	30.8%	27.7%	28.0%	27.3%
Built After 1945	...	...	...	...	...	...	...	...	751	398	353	1,622	1,043	579
Percent	...	...	...	...	...	...	...	...	19.7%	20.4%	18.9%	38.3%	41.7%	33.4%
Built 1946-1960	...	...	...	...	...	...	...	...	...	...	...	757	437	320
Percent	...	...	...	...	...	...	...	...	...	...	...	17.9%	17.5%	18.4%

Notes: a Includes approximately 9,000 housing units in semi-permanent buildings. b Data refer to residential buildings. c Includes 91,000 dwellings for which period of construction unknown. d Includes 61,000 dwellings for which period of construction unknown.

409

TABLE H-24 HOUSING: GDR, 1961-1971 (in Thousands)

| | Distribution by Number of Persons | | | | | | Distribution by Number of Dwellings | | | | | |
| | 1961 | | | 1971 | | | 1961 | | | 1971 | | |
	Total	Urban	Rural	Total	Urban	Rural	Total	Urban	Rural	Total	Urban	Rural
No. of Households per Dwelling												
Total	...	...	...	16,876	...	...	5,427	...	...	5,933	...	...
Percent	...	...	...	100.0%	...	...	100.0%	...	...	100.0%	...	...
1 Household	...	...	...	...	...	...	...	...	...	...	...	...
Percent	...	...	...	...	...	...	...	...	...	...	...	...
Over 1 Household	...	...	...	...	...	...	...	...	...	...	...	...
Percent	...	...	...	...	...	...	...	...	...	...	...	...
Persons per Room[a]												
Total	...	...	...	...	...	...	5,507[b]	...	...	5,938[c]	...	...
Percent	...	...	...	...	...	...	100.0%	...	...	100.0%	...	...
Under 1 Person	...	...	...	...	...	...	...	...	...		...	...
Percent	...	...	...	...	...	...	...	...	...		...	...
1 to 2 Persons	...	...	...	...	...	...	...	...	...	1.1[d]	...	...
Percent	...	...	...	...	...	...	...	...	...		...	...
2 or More Persons	...	...	...	...	...	...	...	...	...		...	...
Percent	...	...	...	...	...	...	...	...	...		...	...
Facilities												
Total	...	...	...	...	...	...	5,447	...	...	5,933	...	...
Percent	...	...	...	...	...	...	100.0%	...	...	100.0%	...	...
Piped Water	...	...	...	...	...	...	3,579	...	...	4,871	...	...
Percent	...	...	...	...	...	...	65.7%	...	...	82.1%	...	...
Central Heating	...	...	...	...	...	...	...	...	...	...	...	...
Percent	...	...	...	...	...	...	...	...	...	...	...	...
Electricity	...	...	...	...	...	...	...	...	...	5,933	...	...
Percent	...	...	...	...	...	...	...	...	...	100.0%	...	...
Toilet in Dwelling	...	...	...	...	...	...	1,781	...	...	2,575	...	...
Percent	...	...	...	...	...	...	32.7%	...	...	43.4%	...	...
Age of Dwellings												
Total	...	...	...	...	...	...	5,447	...	...	5,971	...	...
Percent	...	...	...	...	...	...	100.0%	...	...	100.0%	...	...
Built Before 1920	...	...	...	...	...	...	3,524	...	...	3,391	...	...
Percent	...	...	...	...	...	...	64.7%	...	...	56.8%	...	...
Built 1920-1945	...	...	...	...	...	...	1,351	...	...	1,341	...	...
Percent	...	...	...	...	...	...	24.8%	...	...	22.5%	...	...
Built After 1945	...	...	...	...	...	...	572	...	...	1,239	...	...
Percent	...	...	...	...	...	...	10.5%	...	...	20.8%	...	...
Built 1946-1960	...	...	...	...	...	...	...	...	...	602	...	...
Percent	...	...	...	...	...	...	...	...	...	10.1%	...	...

Notes: a Kitchen not counted as room. b Includes 80,000 rustic and improved housing units. c Includes 5,000 living quarters other than housing units. d Average number of persons per room.

TABLE H-25 HOUSING: HUNGARY, 1949-1970 (in Thousands)

	Distribution by Number of Persons							Distribution by Number of Dwellings						
	1949	1960			1970[a]			1949	1960			1970[a]		
	Total	Total	Urban	Rural	Total	Urban	Rural	Total	Total	Urban	Rural	Total	Urban	Rural
No. of Households per Dwelling														
Total	9,021	9,456	3,919	5,537	9,926	4,511	5,415	2,425	2,711	1,169	1,542	3,034	1,423	1,611
Percent	100.0%	100.0%	100.0%	100.0%	100.0%	100.0%	100.0%	100.0%	100.0%	100.0%	100.0%	100.0%	100.0%	100.0%
1 Household	...	...	...	...	8,631	3,706	4,925	...	2,428	...	...	2,743	1,237	1,506
Percent	...	...	...	...	87.0%	82.2%	91.0%	...	89.6%	...	...	90.4%	86.9%	93.5%
Over 1 Household	...	...	...	...	1,295	805	490	...	283	...	...	291	186	105
Percent	...	...	...	...	13.0%	17.8%	9.0%	...	10.4%	...	...	9.6%	13.1%	6.5%
Persons per Room														
Total	9,021	9,456	3,919	5,537	9,926	4,511	5,415	2,425	2,711	1,169	1,542	3,034	1,423	1,611
Percent	100.0%	100.0%	100.0%	100.0%	100.0%	100.0%	100.0%	100.0%	100.0%	100.0%	100.0%	100.0%	100.0%	100.0%
Under 1 Person	...	...	...	...	...	...	...	...	...	...	...	...	...	...
Percent	...	16.0%	...	...	18.3%	19.5%	17.3%	...	32.1%	...	...	35.6%	36.8%	34.4%
1 to 2 Persons	...	...	...	...	...	...	...	...	...	...	...	...	...	...
Percent	...	43.7%	...	...	64.3%	65.4%	63.2%	...	44.1%	...	...	55.9%	56.2%	55.8%
2 or More Persons	...	...	...	...	...	...	...	...	...	...	...	...	...	...
Percent	...	40.3%	...	...	17.4%	15.1%	19.5%	...	23.8%	...	...	8.5%	7.0%	9.8%
Facilities														
Total	...	9,456	...	...	9,926	...	...	2,425	2,711	...	...	3,034	...	...
Percent	...	100.0%	...	...	100.0%	...	...	100.0%	100.0%	...	...	100.0%	...	...
Piped Water	...	2,106	...	...	3,568	...	...	...	615	...	...	1,096	...	...
Percent	...	22.3%	...	...	35.9%	...	...	...	22.7%	...	...	36.1%	...	...
Central Heating	...	...	...	...	...	...	...	...	...	...	...	...	...	...
Percent	...	...	...	...	...	...	...	...	...	...	...	...	...	...
Electricity	...	7,030	...	...	9,157	...	...	...	2,021	...	...	2,782	...	...
Percent	...	74.3%	...	...	92.2%	...	...	...	74.5%	...	...	91.7%	...	...
Toilet in Dwelling	...	...	...	...	...	...	...	...	...	...	...	...	...	...
Percent	...	...	...	...	...	...	...	...	...	...	...	...	...	...
Age of Dwellings														
Total	...	...	...	...	...	...	...	2,425	2,711	...	...	3,034	1,423	1,611
Percent	...	...	...	...	...	...	...	100.0%	100.0%	...	...	100.0%	100.0%	100.0%
Built Before 1920	...	...	...	...	...	...	...	...	...	...	...	1,085	533	552
Percent	...	...	...	...	...	...	...	...	...	...	...	35.8%	37.5%	34.3%
Built 1919-1944	...	...	...	...	...	...	...	...	...	...	...	812	400	412
Percent	...	...	...	...	...	...	...	...	...	...	...	26.8%	28.1%	25.6%
Built After 1944	...	...	...	...	...	...	...	...	...	...	...	1,137	490	647
Percent	...	...	...	...	...	...	...	...	...	...	...	37.5%	34.4%	40.2%
Built 1945-1959	...	...	...	...	...	...	...	...	...	...	...	537	185	352
Percent	...	...	...	...	...	...	...	...	...	...	...	17.7%	13.0%	21.8%

Note: [a] Data based on sample census returns.

TABLE H-26   HOUSING: POLAND, 1950-1970 (in Thousands)

| | Distribution by Number of Persons ||||||| Distribution by Number of Dwellings |||||||
| | 1950 | 1960 ||| 1970 ||| 1950 | 1960 ||| 1970 |||
	Total	Total	Urban	Rural	Total	Urban	Rural	Total	Total	Urban	Rural	Total	Urban	Rural
No. of Households Per Dwelling														
Total	23,996	28,695	13,628	15,067	31,859	16,418	15,441	5,851	7,026	3,560	3,465	8,081	4,507	3,574
Percent	100.0%	100.0%	100.0%	100.0%	100.0%	100.0%	100.0%	100.0%	100.0%	100.0%	100.0%	100.0%	100.0%	100.0%
1 Household	...	...	...	...	25,949	12,744	13,205	...	...	...	...	7,036	3,828	3,208
Percent	...	...	...	...	81.4%	77.6%	85.5%	...	...	...	...	87.1%	84.9%	89.8%
Over 1 Household	...	...	...	...	5,910	3,674	2,236	...	...	...	...	1,045	679	366
Percent	...	...	...	...	18.6%	22.4%	14.5%	...	...	...	...	12.9%	15.1%	10.2%
Persons per Room														
Total	...	28,710	13,563	15,147	31,859	16,418	15,441	...	7,024	3,546	3,478	8,081	4,507	3,574
Percent	...	100.0%	100.0%	100.0%	100.0%	100.0%	100.0%	...	100.0%	100.0%	100.0%	100.0%	100.0%	100.0%
Under 1 Person	...	...	...	...	...	...	...	...	...	...	...	...	...	...
Percent	...	4.9%	5.2%	4.5%	9.8%	9.4%	10.1%	...	9.6%	10.1%	9.2%	17.0%	16.3%	18.0%
1 to 2 Persons	...	...	...	...	...	...	...	...	...	...	...	...	...	...
Percent	...	41.2%	50.5%	33.0%	53.7%	60.6%	46.4%	...	47.2%	54.7%	39.4%	55.4%	60.6%	48.7%
2 or More Persons	...	...	...	...	...	...	...	...	...	...	...	...	...	...
Percent	...	53.9%	44.3%	62.5%	36.5%	30.0%	43.5%	...	43.2%	35.2%	51.4%	27.6%	23.1%	33.3%
Facilities														
Total	5,851	28,695	...	...	31,859	...	...	5,851	7,026	...	...	8,081	...	...
Percent	100.0%	100.0%	...	...	100.0%	...	...	100.0%	100.0%	...	...	100.0%	...	...
Piped Water	...	8,572	...	...	14,502	...	...	...	2,099	...	...	3,821	...	...
Percent	...	29.9%	...	...	45.5%	...	...	...	29.9%	...	...	47.3%	...	...
Central Heating	...	1,898	...	...	6,613	...	...	...	489	...	...	1,796	...	...
Percent	...	6.6%	...	...	20.8%	...	...	...	7.0%	...	...	22.2%	...	...
Electricity	...	22,639	...	...	30,621	...	...	...	5,625	...	...	7,774	...	...
Percent	...	78.9%	...	...	96.1%	...	...	...	80.0%	...	...	96.2%	...	...
Toilet in Dwelling	...	5,589	...	...	10,343	...	...	...	1,329	...	...	2,701	...	...
Percent	...	19.5%	...	...	32.5%	...	...	...	18.9%	...	...	33.4%	...	...
Age of Dwellings[a]														
Total	...	...	...	...	...	...	...	...	6,934	3,501	3,433	8,003	4,465	3,538
Percent	...	...	...	...	...	...	...	...	100.0%	100.0%	100.0%	100.0%	100.0%	100.0%
Built Before 1920	...	...	...	...	...	...	...	...	2,747	1,515	1,232	2,425	1,400	1,025
Percent	...	...	...	...	...	...	...	...	39.6%	43.3%	35.9%	30.3%	31.3%	29.0%
Built 1920-1945	...	...	...	...	...	...	...	...	2,638	1,300	1,338	2,118	1,107	1,011
Percent	...	...	...	...	...	...	...	...	38.0%	37.1%	39.0%	26.5%	24.8%	28.6%
Built After 1945	...	...	...	...	...	...	...	...	1,549	686	863	3,460	1,958	1,502
Percent	...	...	...	...	...	...	...	...	22.3%	19.6%	25.1%	43.2%	43.9%	42.5%
Built 1945-1960	...	...	...	...	...	...	...	...	...	...	...	1,667	774	893
Percent	...	...	...	...	...	...	...	...	...	...	...	20.8%	17.3%	25.2%

Note: a   Data apply to dwellings in residential buildings only.

TABLE H- 27 HOUSING: ROMANIA, 1966 (in Thousands)

	Distribution by No. of Persons			Distribution by No. of Dwellings		
	Total	Urban	Rural	Total	Urban	Rural
No. of Households						
per Dwelling						
Total	18,774	6,737	12,037	5,250	1,956	3,293
Percent	100.0%	100.0%	100.0%	100.0%	100.0%	100.0%
1 Household	...	...	...	...	...	...
Percent	...	...	...	...	...	...
Over 1 Household	...	...	...	...	...	...
Percent	...	...	...	...	...	...
Persons per Room						
Total	18,774	6,737	12,037	5,250	1,956	3,293
Percent	100.0%	100.0%	100.0%	100.0%	100.0%	100.0%
Under 1 Person	...	...	...	...	...	...
Percent	...	...	...	18.5%	17.1%	19.4%
1 to 2 Persons	...	...	...	...	...	...
Percent	...	...	...	53.7%	59.6%	50.1%
2 or More Persons	...	...	...	...	...	...
Percent	...	...	...	27.8%	23.3%	30.5%
Facilities						
Total	...	...	...	5,380[a]	...	...
Percent	...	...	...	100.0%	...	...
Piped Water	...	...	...	664	...	...
Percent	...	...	...	12.3%	...	...
Central Heating	...	...	...	...	...	...
Percent	...	...	...	...	...	...
Electricity	...	...	...	2,613	...	...
Percent	...	...	...	48.6%	...	...
Toilet in Dwelling	...	...	...	...	...	...
Percent	...	...	...	...	...	...
Age of Dwellings						
Total	...	...	...	5,250	...	...
Percent	...	...	...	100.0%	...	...
Built Before 1920	...	...	...	...	...	...
Percent	...	...	...	...	...	...
Built 1920-1945	...	...	...	...	...	...
Percent	...	...	...	...	...	...
Built After 1945	...	...	...	...	...	...
Percent	...	...	...	...	...	...
Built 1945-1960	...	...	...	...	...	...
Percent	...	...	...	...	...	...

Note: a Includes vacant dwellings.

TABLE H-28   HOUSING: YUGOSLAVIA, 1951-1971   (in Thousands)

	Persons 1951	Persons 1961 Total	Persons 1961 Urban	Persons 1961 Rural	Persons 1971 Total	Persons 1971 Urban	Persons 1971 Rural	Dwellings 1951	Dwellings 1961 Total	Dwellings 1961 Urban	Dwellings 1961 Rural	Dwellings 1971 Total	Dwellings 1971 Urban	Dwellings 1971 Rural
No. of Households Per Dwelling														
Total	...	17,984	5,692	12,292	20,086	7,667	12,419	...	4,082	1,328	2,754	4,935	2,098	2,837
Percent	...	100.0%	100.0%	100.0%	100.0%	100.0%	100.0%	...	100.0%	100.0%	100.0%	100.0%	100.0%	100.0%
1 Household	...	...	...	...	18,419	6,525	11,894	...	...	1,058	...	4,586[a]	1,889[a]	2,697[a]
Percent	...	...	...	...	91.7%	85.1%	95.8%	...	...	79.7%	...	92.9%	90.0%	95.1%
Over 1 Household	...	...	...	...	1,667	1,142	525	...	...	269	...	281	201	80
Percent	...	...	...	...	8.3%	14.9%	4.2%	...	...	20.3%	...	5.7%	9.6%	2.8%
Persons per Room														
Total	...	17,984	5,692	12,292	20,086	7,667	12,419	...	4,082	1,328	2,754	4,935	2,098	2,837
Percent	...	100.0%	100.0%	100.0%	100.0%	100.0%	100.0%	...	100.0%	100.0%	100.0%	100.0%	100.0%	100.0%
Under 1 Person														
Percent	...	4.5%	5.1%	4.2%	8.1%	10.5%	6.7%	...	10.2%	10.5%	10.0%	16.9%	18.8%	15.6%
1 to 2 Persons														
Percent	...	43.0%	61.2%	34.7%	48.0%	56.8%	42.6%	...	52.8%	67.5%	45.8%	52.3%	57.8%	48.2%
2 or More Persons														
Percent	...	52.5%	33.7%	61.1%	43.9%	32.7%	50.7%	...	37.0%	22.0%	44.2%	30.8%	23.4%	36.2%
Facilities														
Total	3,490	17,984	...	...	20,086	...	...	3,490	...	...	...	4,935	...	...
Percent	100.0%	100.0%	...	...	100.0%	...	...	100.0%	...	...	...	100.0%	...	...
Piped Water	...	...	...	...	6,305	...	...	...	...	...	...	1,656	...	...
Percent	...	...	...	...	31.4%	...	...	...	...	...	...	33.6%	...	...
Central Heating	...	...	...	...	760	...	...	...	...	...	...	222	...	...
Percent	...	...	...	...	3.8%	...	...	...	...	...	...	4.5%	...	...
Electricity	1,246	...	...	...	17,763	...	...	1,246	2,225	...	...	4,336	...	...
Percent	35.7%	...	...	...	88.4%	...	...	35.7%	54.5%	...	...	87.9%	...	...
Toilet in Dwelling	...	...	...	...	5,487	...	...	...	...	...	...	1,441	...	...
Percent	...	...	...	...	27.3%	...	...	...	...	...	...	29.2%	...	...
Age of Dwellings														
Total	3,490	...	...	...	...	...	...	3,490[b]	4,082[b]	1,328[b]	2,754[b]	4,935[c]	2,098[c]	2,837[c]
Percent	100.0%	...	...	...	...	...	...	100.0%	100.0%	100.0%	100.0%	100.0%	100.0%	100.0%
Built Before 1920	...	...	...	...	...	...	...	...	1,330	460	870	884	344	540
Percent	...	...	...	...	...	...	...	...	32.6%	34.6%	31.6%	17.9%	16.4%	19.0%
Built 1920-1945	...	...	...	...	...	...	...	...	1,270	396	874	1,002	367	635
Percent	...	...	...	...	...	...	...	...	31.1%	29.8%	31.7%	20.3%	17.5%	22.4%
Built After 1945	...	...	...	...	...	...	...	...	1,364	433	931	2,917	1,330	1,587
Percent	...	...	...	...	...	...	...	...	33.4%	32.6%	33.8%	59.1%	63.4%	55.9%
Built 1945-1960	...	...	...	...	...	...	...	...	...	...	...	1,214	441	773
Percent	...	...	...	...	...	...	...	...	...	...	...	24.6%	21.0%	27.2%

Notes: a Data refer to dwellings for which member of households was stated. b Includes 118,000 (2.9%) dwellings for which period of construction is unknown, of which 39,000 (2.9%) were in urban areas and 79,000 (2.9%) were in rural areas. c Includes 132,000 (2.7%) dwellings for which period of construction is unknown, of which 57,000 (2.7%) were in urban areas and 75,000 (2.6%) were in rural areas.

TABLE H-29   PER CAPITA CONSUMPTION OF SELECTED FOODS, EASTERN
              EUROPE AND THE USSR, 1950-1975 (in Kilograms)

Type of Food	1950	1955	1960	1965	1970	1975
Cereals						
Albania	...	...	...	...	...	...
Bulgaria[a]	...	...	261.4	265.4	238.8	217.8
Czechoslovakia[b]	...	129.1	119.0	122.6	119.8	112.3
GDR[c]	...	126.1	101.6	100.2	97.0	94.8
Hungary[d]	142.1	151.7	136.2	139.2	128.2	122.2
Poland[e]	166	171	145	141	131	120
Romania	...	...	...	...	...	...
USSR[f]	172	...	164	156	149	141
Yugoslavia[g]	...	184.8	186.0	194.1	184.4	183
Potatoes						
Albania	...	...	...	...	...	...
Bulgaria	...	...	...	...	...	...
Czechoslovakia	...	121.2	100.3	93.2	103.4	95.8
GDR	...	174.6	173.9	156.5	153.5	142.1
Hungary	108.7	119.9	97.6	84.3	75.0	66.8
Poland	...	229	223	215	197	173
Romania	...	...	...	...	...	...
USSR	241	...	143	141	130	120
Yugoslavia	...	60.3	69.7	63.0	...	65.5
Sugar						
Albania	...	...	...	...	...	...
Bulgaria[h]	...	...	17.7	22.3	32.9	32.5
Czechoslovakia	...	33.7	36.3	37.5	37.7	38.0
GDR[i]	...	27.4	29.3	30.1	34.5	36.8
Hungary	16.3	24.4	26.6	30.1	33.5	39.4
Poland	21.0	24.0	27.9	32.6	38.9	43.2
Romania	...	...	...	...	...	...
USSR	11.6	...	28.0	34.2	39.1	40.8
Yugoslavia	...	10.8	14.9	23.8	27.9	32.8
Vegetables						
Albania	...	...	...	...	...	...
Bulgaria[j]	...	...	97.2	88.8	88.9	90.1
Czechoslovakia	...	85.2	87.3	76.7	76.3	73.7
GDR	...	...	60.7	63.8	84.8	90.0
Hungary	...	...	84.1	76.7	84.0	85.2
Poland	...	...	...	...	...	...
Romania	...	...	...	...	...	...
USSR[k]	51	...	70	73	82	87
Yugoslavia	...	38.8	56.6	51.5	74	79.1

Notes: a Bread and bakery articles measured in terms of whole grain,
        including corn. b In terms of wheat and rye flower only.
        c In terms of flour; includes wheat, rye and milled rice.
        d In terms of flour; includes wheat, rye and rice. e In terms
        of flour; includes all types of cereal grain, but exludes rice. (cont'd.)

TABLE H-29 (CONCLUDED)

Type of Food	1950	1955	1960	1965	1970	1975
Fruit						
Albania	...	...	...	...	...	...
Bulgaria[1]	...	...	95.3	131.4	148.2	118.6
Czechoslovakia	...	43.8	70.4	34.2	46.6	47.7
GDR[m]	...	...	80.1	46.5	55.5	66.6
Hungary	...	...	55.3	52.8	72.5	74.0
Poland	...	...	...	...	...	...
Romania	...	...	...	...	...	...
USSR	...	...	22	28	35	37
Yugoslavia	...	57.9	39.1	48.7	59.9	62.1
Meat and Meat Products						
Albania	...	...	...	...	...	...
Bulgaria	...	...	29.1	39.6	41.4	58.0
Czechoslovakia	...	44.8	56.8	61.7	71.9	81.1
GDR	...	45.0	55.0	58.7	66.0	77.8
Hungary[n]	34.3	36.9	47.6	51.6	58.0	68.5
Poland	36.5	37.7	42.5	49.2	53.0	70.0
Romania	...	...	...	...	...	...
USSR[o]	26	...	40	41	48	57.0
Yugoslavia[p]	...	23.5	29.8	29.4	35.6	48.3
Fish						
Albania	...	...	...	...	...	...
Bulgaria	...	...	...	...	...	...
Czechoslovakia	...	3.7	4.7	4.9	5.2	5.8
GDR	...	12.2	12.8	9.1[q]	7.9[q]	8.5[q]
Hungary	...	...	1.5	1.6	2.3	2.7
Poland	1.7	2.7	4.5	5.0	6.3	7.2
Romania	...	...	...	...	...	...
USSR	7.0	...	9.9	12.6	15.4	16.8
Yugoslavia	...	1.3	1.4	1.5	2.5	3.0
Milk[r]						
Albania	...	...	...	...	...	...
Bulgaria[s]	...	...	92.3	103.6	116.6	142.8
Czechoslovakia	...	145.3	108.6	106.5	119.2	117.5
GDR	...	90.7	94.5	94.1	98.5	100.8
Hungary	111.9	86.7	114.0	97.1	109.6	126.6
Poland	206	204	227	233	262	264
Romania	...	...	...	...	...	...
USSR[t]	172	...	240	252	307	315
Yugoslavia	...	65.0	78.0	68.0	76.2	90.1

Notes (cont'd.): f In terms of flour and other milling equivalents. g In terms of flour; includes all types of cereal grains. h Sugar and sugar preparations. i Includes sugar products. j Vegetables, fresh and canned. k Vegetables and melons. l Fruit, fresh and canned. m Fruits and nuts. n Includes meat products converted to raw meat basis. o Meats and fats, including poultry and edible offals. p Includes beef, pork, mutton, game and horse meat. q Product weight (new series). r Liters. s Milk and dairy products. Excludes butter. t Milk and dairy products in terms of milk.

TABLE H-30: CALORIES, PROTEINS AND FATS AVAILABLE
PER CAPITA: EASTERN EUROPE AND THE
USSR, 1961-1974 (Calories-Number per
day; Proteins and Fats-Grams per day)

Country	1961-63	1965	1970	1974	1972-74
Albania					
Calories	2,340	2,380	2,540	2,523	2,503
Proteins	70.1	70.1	72.9	73.0	71.8
Fats	45.8	45.5	47.6	48.4	48.2
Bulgaria					
Calories	3,181	3,374	3,391	3,453	3,461
Proteins	94.9	99.8	97.5	101.7	101.1
Fats	77.5	83.4	87.7	99.7	97.5
Czechoslovakia					
Calories	3,371	3,415	3,462	3,492	3,489
Proteins	90.9	93.8	95.7	97.4	96.5
Fats	111.6	113.4	119.5	127.1	125.6
GDR					
Calories	3,217	3,292	3,428	3,482	3,463
Proteins	83.5	86.7	92.1	95.8	94.7
Fats	133.9	138.5	142.4	144.7	144.0
Hungary					
Calories	3,243	3,296	3,461	3,581	3,548
Proteins	82.7	84.5	87.4	90.0	89.0
Fats	110.4	111.0	127.8	137.8	135.6
Poland					
Calories	3,234	3,318	3,345	3,505	3,474
Proteins	97.5	100.9	100.5	105.4	104.4
Fats	89.3	96.5	98.3	114.0	110.5
Romania					
Calories	2,878	2,953	3,057	3,300	3,262
Proteins	84.9	86.2	90.2	98.0	96.7
Fats	65.8	68.7	74.2	85.1	82.8
USSR					
Calories	3,268	3,295	3,475	3,530	3,475
Proteins	95.7	94.6	104.6	107.0	104.3
Fats	80.8	85.3	96.3	106.2	101.5
Yugoslavia					
Calories	3,131	3,311	3,309	3,458	3,380
Proteins	92.0	94.3	92.2	97.2	94.3
Fats	66.7	75.8	85.8	96.7	92.3

TABLE H-31   INDICATORS OF DEVELOPMENT IN THE FIELDS OF COMMUNICATIONS
AND TRANSPORT: EASTERN EUROPE AND THE USSR, 1950-1975
(per Thousand Persons)

Indicator	1950	1955	1960	1965	1970	1975
Radio Receivers						
Albania	7	13	33	70	74	71
Bulgaria	31	84	182	251	270	288
Czechoslovakia	195	220	259	263	267	265
GDR	190	279	323	337	351	356[a]
Hungary	66	146	222	245	245	241
Poland	59	112	177	179	173	239
Romania	19	67	109	147	152	145
USSR	61	128	205	320	390	481
Yugoslavia	21	34	84	143	163	196
TV Sets						
Albania	...	...	0.5	1	1.8	1.8
Bulgaria	...	0.3	0.6	23	121	173
Czechoslovakia	...	2	58	149	214	249
GDR	...	0.8	60	177	261	307
Hungary	...	0.1	10	82	171	223
Poland	...	0.0	14	66	129	190
Romania	...	0.0	2	26	73	127
USSR	...	4	22	68	143	217
Yugoslavia	...	...	1	30	88	144
Telephones						
Albania	...	...	...	...	...	...
Bulgaria	...	...	...	34	56	89
Czechoslovakia	...	...	74	105	140	177
GDR	...	...	76	97	122	153
Hungary	16	19	24	56	80	99
Poland	9	9	30	41	57	76
Romania	...	...	...	25	32	...
USSR	...	...	...	...	45	67
Yugoslavia	7	9	14	21	36	61
Passenger Autos						
Albania	...	...	...	...	...	...
Bulgaria	...	...	...	...	...	...
Czechoslovakia	...	...	...	...	58	102
GDR	...	...	18	39	68	112
Hungary	...	...	3	10	23	55
Poland	...	1	4	8	15	32
Romania	...	...	...	...	...	...
USSR	...	...	...	...	7	...
Yugoslavia	...	1	3	10	35	72

Note: a   1974.

TABLE H-32   INDICATORS OF DEVELOPMENT IN THE FIELDS OF HEALTH AND CULTURE: EASTERN EUROPE AND THE USSR, 1950-1975

Indicator	1950	1955	1960	1965	1970	1975
Number of Physicians per Thousand Persons						
Albania	...	...	0.3	0.5	0.5	...
Bulgaria	0.2[a]	...	1.3[b]	1.7	1.9[c]	2.2
Czechoslovakia	...	1.4	1.8	1.9	2.0[d]	2.4
GDR	...	...[f]	...[b]	1.3[e]	1.6[d]	1.9
Hungary	...	1.4[f]	1.5[b]	1.6	1.9[d]	2.0
Poland	...	0.6[f]	0.9	1.3	1.5	1.7
Romania	...	1.0[c,f]	1.4[c]	1.3	1.4[g]	1.2[h]
USSR	1.5	1.7[f]	1.8	2.1	2.3[d]	2.9
Yugoslavia	0.3	0.4[i]	0.7	0.8	1.0	1.2
Number of Hospital Beds per Thousand Persons						
Albania	...	4.2	4.9	5.9	6.7	...
Bulgaria	...	5.0	5.7	7.1	7.7	8.3
Czechoslovakia	...	8.7	9.5	10.0	10.0	10.0
GDR	10.0	10.8	11.1	11.1	11.1	11.1
Hungary	5.6	6.1	6.7	7.7	8.3	8.3
Poland	...	6.3	6.7	7.7	7.7	7.7
Romania	4.2	5.9	7.4	7.7	8.3	9.1
USSR	5.3	6.3	8.3	10.0	11.1	12.5
Yugoslavia	...	3.8	4.8	5.4	5.9	5.9
Number of Visits to Cinemas per Person						
Albania	...	...	4	4	...	...
Bulgaria	...	7.3	14	15[e]	13	13.1
Czechoslovakia	...	12.4	13	9	8	5.8
GDR	5.3	...	14	7	5	4.6
Hungary	...	11.8[f]	14	10[e]	8	7.0
Poland	...	6.4[f]	6	5[e]	4	4.1
Romania	...	...	9	11[e]	10	8.7
USSR	...	12.6	17.7	18[e]	19	17.7
Yugoslavia	...	5.5	7.0	6[e]	4	3.8
Number of Titles of Books Published per Year						
Albania	125	...	422	502	...	...
Bulgaria	2,155	2,883	3,369	3,634	3,799	3,669
Czechoslovakia	4,990	4,399[f]	7,930	9,043	9,041	10,372
GDR	2,142	5,359	6,103	5,374	5,234	5,800
Hungary	4,219	5,206	5,205	4,525	5,238	8,603
Poland	5,218	7,199	7,305	8,509	10,038	10,277
Romania	...	5,182	6,335	6,090[j]	7,681	7,860
USSR	43,060	54,732	76,064	76,101	78,899	78,697
Yugoslavia	4,371	5,105	5,355	7,980	8,119	11,239

Notes: a 1951.   b 1959.   c Includes dentists.   d 1969.   e 1966.   f 1954.
g 1968.   h 1973.   i 1953.   j 1964.

APPENDIX 1

DATES OF CENSUSES, EASTERN EUROPE AND THE USSR

	1920s		1930s		1940s		1950s		1960s	1970s
Albania			May 1930		Sept. 1945		Sept. 1950	Oct. 1955	Oct. 1960	Jan. 1979
	Sept. 1923									
Bulgaria	Dec. 1920	Dec. 1926	Dec. 1934		Dec. 1946		Dec. 1956		Dec. 1965	Dec. 1975
Czechoslovakia		Feb. 1921	Dec. 1930		Oct. 1946[a]	May 1947[b]	March 1950		March 1961	Dec. 1970
GDR		June 1925	June 1933	May 1939	Oct. 1946		Aug. 1950		Dec. 1964	Jan. 1971
Hungary		Dec. 1920	Dec. 1930		Jan. 1941	Jan. 1949			Jan. 1960	Jan. 1970
Poland		Sept. 1921	Dec. 1931		Feb. 1946		Dec. 1950		Dec. 1960	Dec. 1970
Romania			Dec. 1930		April 1941	Jan. 1948	Feb. 1956		March 1966	Jan. 1977
USSR	Aug. 1920	Dec. 1926	Jan. 1939				Jan. 1959			Jan. 1970 Jan. 1979
Yugoslavia		Jan. 1921	March 1931		March 1948		March 1953		March 1961	March 1971

Notes: a Slovakia. b Czech lands.

APPENDIX 2

DIVISIONS UTILIZED IN CLASSIFYING LEVELS OF
EDUCATION IN APPENDICES 3 THROUGH 9

I. No Schooling and Incomplete Elementary (less than 4 years of schooling).

II. Elementary and Incomplete Basic (from 4 years to 6-7 years of schooling).

III. Basic School, Trade School, and Incomplete Secondary (from 7-8 years of schooling to the level of Incomplete Secondary).

IV. Secondary, Specialized Secondary, and Incomplete Higher Education (self-explanatory).

V. Higher Education (self-explanatory).

APPENDIX 3

CLASSIFICATION OF LEVELS OF EDUCATION: BULGARIA AND USSR

	USSR 1959 & 1970	Standard Form	Bulgaria 1956	Bulgaria 1965
I		Without Schooling	Illiterate (Negramotni)	Illiterate (Negramotni)
				Semi-literate (Malo gramotni)
		4 Year Elementary Incomplete	Incomplete Elementary (Nachalno-nezavursheno)	Incomplete Elementary (Nezavursheno nachalno)
II	Primary (Nachalnoe)	4 Year Elementary Complete / 7-8 Year Basic Incomplete	Elementary (Nachalno zavursheno)	Elementary (Nachalno)
III	Incomplete Secondary (Nepolnoe srednee)	7-8 Year Basic Complete / Trade School	Basic (Osnovno)	Basic (Osnovno)
	No Equivalent	Incomplete Secondary		
IV	Completed General Secondary (Srednee obshchee)	General Secondary Complete		General Secondary (Sredno obshto)
	Specialized Secondary (Srednee spetsial'noe	Specialized Secondary Lower Level / Specialized Secondary Higher Level	General Secondary (Sredno)	Specialized Secondary (Sredno spetsialno)
	Higher Incomplete (Vysshee nezakonchennoe)	Higher Education Incomplete		[See either General Secondary or Specialized Secondary]
		Higher Education Lower Level Complete	Semi-Higher (Poluvisshe)	Semi-Higher (Poluvisshe)
V	Higher Complete (Vysshee zakonchennoe)	Higher Education Faculty Level Complete	Higher (Visshe)	Higher (Visshe)

APPENDIX 4

CLASSIFICATION OF LEVELS OF EDUCATION: CZECHOSLOVAKIA

	Czechoslovakia 1950	Standard Form	Czechoslovakia 1961	Czechoslovakia 1970
I	Persons without Schooling (Osoby bez skolniho vzdelani)	Without Schooling 4 Year Elementary Incomplete	Persons without Schooling (Osoby bez skolniho vzdelani)	Persons without Schooling (Osoby bez skolniho vzdelani)
II	National School (Narodni skola)	4 Year Elementary Complete 7-8 Year Basic Incomplete		
III	Basic School Education (Stredni skola) Basic Specialists Education (Zakladni odborna skola [See either Basic School Education or Basic Special. Educ.]	7-8 Year Basic Complete Trade School Incomplete Secondary	Basic School Education (Zakladni vzdelani)	Basic School Education (Zakladni vzdelani) Trade School (Ucnovska skola) [See either Basic School Education or Trade School]
IV	Gymnasium and Secondary Teachers' Education (Gymnasium and Pedagogicke gymnasium) Specialists' Education, Lower Level (Nizsi odborna skola) Specialists' Education, Higher Level (Vyssi odborna skola [See either Comp. General Second. or Specialists' Educ. Higher Level]	General Secondary, Complete Specialized Secondary, Lower Level Specialized Secondary, Higher Level Higher Education, Incomplete	Completed General Secondary School (Uplne stredoskolske vzdelani) Specialists' Education, Lower Level (Odborne vzdelani, nizsi) Specialists' Education, Higher Level (Odborne vzdelani, vyssi) [See either Comp. General Second. or Specialists' Educ. Higher Level]	Completed General Secondary (Stredni vseobecne vzdelavaci skoly) Specialists' Education (Odborne skoly) Specialists' Education, Secondary Level (Stredni odborne skoly) [See either Comp. General Second. or Specialists' Educ. Second. Level]
V		Higher Education, Lower Level, Complete	Completed Pedagogical Education (Vysokoskolske vzdelani, pedagogicke)	Enterprise Institutes and Courses in Inst. of Higher Learning (Podnikove instituty a kursy na VS)
	Higher Education (Vysoka skola)	Higher Education Faculty Level, Complete	Higher Education (Vysokoskolske vzdelani)	Higher Education (Vysoke skoly)

424

APPENDIX 5

CLASSIFICATION OF LEVELS OF EDUCATION: GDR

GDR 1971

Standard Form	
Without Schooling	
I 4 Year Elementary Incomplete	
4 Year Elementary Complete	▶ Less than 10 Years of Schooling (<u>Abschluss niedriger als 10. Klasse</u>)
7-8 Year Basic Incomplete	
7-8 Year Basic Complete	

II Trade School	Completion of Skilled Worker Training (<u>Facharbeiterabschluss</u>) Completion of Training as "Meister" (<u>Meisterabschluss</u>) Completion of Training as Skilled Worker and "Meister" (<u>Facharbeiter- und Meisterabschluss</u>)
Incomplete Secondary	Completion of 10th Grade (<u>Abschluss 10. Klasse</u>)
General Secondary Complete	"Abitur" (<u>Abitur</u>)

Specialized Secondary Lower Level	Completion of 10th Grade and Skilled Worker Training (<u>Abschluss 10. Klasse und Facharbeiterabschluss</u>) Completion of 10th Grade and "Meister" Training (<u>Abschluss 10. Klasse und Meisterabschluss</u>)
III Specialized Secondary, Higher Level	Completion of Technical School (<u>Fachschulabschluss</u>) "Abitur" and Skilled Worker Training (<u>Abitur und Facharbeiter Abschluss</u>) "Abitur" and "Meister" Training (<u>Abitur und Meisterabschluss</u>) "Abitur" and Technical School (<u>Abitur und Fachschulabschluss</u>) Skilled Worker Training and Technical School (<u>Facharbeiter- und Fachschul- abschluss</u>) "Meister" Training and Technical School (<u>Meister und Fachschulabschluss</u>)
Higher Education Incomplete	[Included in General Secondary, Complete or Specialized Secondary, or in subcategories of these categories.]
Higher Education, Lower Level	

IV Higher Education, Faculty Level, Complete	Completion of Higher Education (<u>Hochschulabschluss</u>) Completion of 10th Grade and Higher Education (<u>Abschluss 10. Klasse und Hochschulabschluss</u>) "Abitur" and Higher Education (<u>Abitur und Hochschulabschluss</u>) Skilled Worker Training and Higher Education (<u>Facharbeiter und Hochschulabschluss</u>) "Meister" Training and Higher Education (<u>Meister- und Hochschulabschluss</u>) Technical School and Higher Education (<u>Fachschul- und Hochschulabschluss</u>)

APPENDIX 6

CLASSIFICATION OF LEVELS OF EDUCATION: HUNGARY

	Hungary 1949	Hungary 1960	Standard Form	Hungary 1970	
I	Unknown (Ismeretlen vegzettsegu) Unable to Write or Read, or only Able to Read (Csak olvas, nem ir, nem olvas)	Unable to Write or Read, or only Able to Read (Nem ir nem olvas, ill csak olvas)[a]	Without Schooling	0 Years of Schooling (0)	
		1-3 Years of Primary School (Az altalanos: 1-3)	4 Year Elementary Incomplete	1-3 Years of Primary School (Altalanos iskola 1-3)	
	Primary or Elementary School (Altalanos, vagy elemi iskola): a) Less than 4 Years (4-nel kevesebb)	4-5 Years of Primary School (Az altalanos: 4-5)	4 Year Elementary Complete	4-5 Years of Primary School (Altalanos iskola 4-5)	
II	b) 4 Years c) 6 Years	6-7 Years of Primary School (Az altalanos: 6-7)	7-8 Year Basic Incomplete	6-7 Years of Primary School (Altalanos iskola 6-7)	
	d) 8 Years	8 Years of Primary School (Az altalanos: 8)	7-8 Year Basic Complete	8 Years of Primary School (Altalanos iskola 8)	
	Vocational or Technical School (Kozepfoku szakiskola): a) Less than 4 Years (4-nel kevesebb)[b] b) 4 Years		Trade Schools		
III	Secondary (Specialized Secondary) (Kozep-[Kozepfoku] iskola): a) Less than 4 Years[b] (4-nel kevesebb) b) 4 Years[c] c) 6 Years d) 8 Years	1-4 Years of Middle School (A kozepiskola 1-4)	Incomplete Secondary	1-4 Years of Middle School (Kozepiskola 1-4)	III
IV	Certificate of Maturity (Qualifying) Acquired (Erettsegi [kepesito] bizonyitvanyt szerzett)	Middle School Matriculated (Erettsegi bizonyitvanyt szerzett)	General Secondary Complete / Specialized Secondary, Lower Level, Complete / Specialized Secondary, Higher Level, Complete	General Secondary Complete (Erettsegi)	IV
		University Certificate, Diploma, not Received (Vegbizonyitvanyt, oklevet nem szerzett)	Incomplete Higher	Higher Education, Degree not Received (Felsofoku tanintezet oklevel nelkul)	
V	University Qualified (Diploma or Leaving Certificate Acquired) (Foiskolat vegzett [Oklevelet ill. vegbizonyitvanyt szerzett])		Higher Education Lower Level Complete		
		Diploma Received (Oklevelet szerzett)	Higher Education Faculty Level Complete	Higher Education, Degree Received (Felsofoku tanintezet, oklevellel)	V

a Includes "Able to read and write without schooling (Ir, olvas iskolai vegzettseg nelkul)." b 7-8 Year Basic Incomplete. c 7-8 Year Basic Complete.

APPENDIX 7

CLASSIFICATION OF LEVELS OF EDUCATION: POLAND

Poland 1960	Standard Form	Poland 1960 and 1970[a]	

Unknown:
  (i) Lack of Information (Brak informacji)(26)*
  (ii) Incomplete Primary, Class Completed not Known (Podstawowe nie ukonczone, nieustalone) (22)*
  (iii) Vocational School Incomplete, Whether Primary or Secondary not Determined (Nie ukonczone zawodowe, nie ustalono srednie czy zasadnicze)(13)*
	Without Schooling
	
	4 Year Elementary Incomplete
		Not Able to Write or Read (Nie umiejacy pisac ani czytac)	I

(iv) Vocational School Complete, Whether Primary or Secondary not Determined (Ukonczone zawodowe nie ustalono srednie czy zasadnicze) (8)* I (v) Completed Secondary, Whether General or Vocational Secondary not Determined (Ukonczone srednie, nie ustalono ogolnoksztalcace czy zawodowe (6)*	4 Year Elementary Complete	Incomplete Primary (Niepelne podstawowe)	II
Unable to Write and Read (Nie umiejacy pisac ani czytac (25)* Not Able to Write (Nie umiejacy pisac (24)* Self-taught (Samoucy (23)*			

Incomplete Primary, Class Completed (Podstawowe nie ukonczone, ukonczona klasa):
    1. (16)*
    2. (17)*
II   3. (18)*
    4. (19)*
    5. (20)*
    6. (21)*
			III

Completed Primary (Podstawowe ukonczone) (14)* Vocational School Incomplete (Nie ukonczone zasadnicze zawodowe) (12)*	7-8 Year Basic Complete	Primary (Podstawowe)	
Completed Vocational School (Ukonczone zasadnicze zawodowe) (7)*	Trade School	Vocational School	
Incomplete Secondary, Whether General or Specialized Secondary not Determined (Nieukonczone, nie ustalono ogolnoksztalcace czy zawodowe srednie) (11)*	Incomplete Secondary	Incomplete Secondary (Niepelne srednie)	
Incomplete Specialized Secondary (Srednie zawodowe nie ukonczone) (10)* Incomplete General Secondary (Srednie ogolnoksztalcace nie ukonczone) (9)*	General Secondary Complete	Secondary (Srednie)	
Completed General Secondary (Ukonczone srednie ogolnoksztalcace) (4)*	Specialized Secondary Lower Level		IV
IV Completed Vocational Secondary (Ukonczone srednie zawodowe) (5)*	Specialized Secondary Higher Level	Specialized Secondary (Srednie zawodowe)	
Higher Incomplete (Wyzsze nie ukonczone) (3)*	Higher Education Incomplete	Incomplete Higher (Niepelne wyzsze)	
	Higher Education Lower Level Complete	Post-lycee (Policealne)	
V Higher Complete (Wyzsze ukonczone) (2)*	Higher Education Faculty Level Complete	Higher (Wyzsze)	V

( )* Number of category as presented in original table. a Form appearing in statistical annuals and other publications (censuses excluded) of the statistical office.

427

APPENDIX 8

CLASSIFICATION OF LEVELS OF EDUCATION: ROMANIA

	Romania 1956	Standard Form	Romania 1966 and General
	Illiterate (Nestiutori de carte)	Without Schooling	Illiterate (Nestiutori de carte)
I	4 Year School Incomplete or School not Reported (Scoala de 4 ani neterminata si Sc. nedeclarata)	4 Year Elementary Incomplete	4 Year School Incomplete or School not Reported (Scoala de 4 ani neterminata si Sc. nedeclarata)
II	4 Year School (Scoala de 4 ani)	4 Year Elementary Complete	4 Year School (Scoala de 4 ani)
	[Included with 4 Year School]	7–8 Year Basic Incomplete	[Included with 4 Year School]
III	7 Year Schools (Scoala de 7 ani)	7–8 Year Basic Complete	General 8 Year School (Scoala generala de 8 [7] ani)
		Trade School	Professional and Trade Schools (Scoli profesionale si de meserii)
		Incomplete Secondary	[Included with General 8 Year Schools]
IV	Middle Schools (Scoala medie)	General Secondary Complete	Middle Schools of General Culture – Lycee (Scoli medii de cultura generala – licee)
		Specialized Secondary Lower Level	Middle Technical Schools (Scoli medii tehnice si de specialitate)
		Specialized Secondary Higher Level	
		Higher Education Incomplete	[Included with Middle Schools of General Culture or Middle Technical Schools]
V		Higher Education Lower Level Complete	
	Schools of Higher Learning (Scoala superiora)	Higher Education Faculty Level Complete	Institutions of Higher Learning (Institutii de invatamint superior)

428

APPENDIX 9

CLASSIFICATION OF LEVELS OF EDUCATION: YUGOSLAVIA

	Yugoslavia 1948	Yugoslavia 1953	Standard Form	Yugoslavia 1961	Yugoslavia 1971
I	Without Schooling (Did not Finish 1 Yr. of Basic) (Bez skole)	Without Schooling (Bez skole) Incomplete Basic (Nezavrsena osnovna)	Without Schooling 4 Year Elementary Incomplete	Without Schooling (Bez skolske spreme) 1-3 Years of Basic School (1-3 razreda osnovne skole)	Without Schooling (Bez skolske spreme) 1-3 Years of Basic School (1-3 razreda osnovne skole)
II	Basic School (Osnovna skola)	4 Year Basic (4 razreda osnovne) Over 4 Yrs. of Basic (Vise od 4 razreda osnovne)	4 Year Elementary Complete 7-8 Year Basic Incomplete	4 Years of Basic School (4 razreda osnovne skole) Over 4 Yrs. of Basic School (Vise od 4 razreda osnovne skole)	4 Years of Basic School (4 razreda osnovne skole) 5-7 Years of Basic School (5-7 razreda osnovne skole)
III	Lower Middle School (Niza srednja skola)	8 Year School and Lower Middle School[a] Lower Expert School (Niza strucna skola) [See 8 Year School]	7-8 Year Basic Complete Trade School Incomplete Secondary	Basic School (Osnovna skola) Schools for Qualified Workers and Remaining Expert Cadre[b] Schools for Highly Qualified Workers and Remaining Expert Cadre[c] [See Basic School]	Basic School (Osnovna skola) Schools for Qualified Workers and Remaining Expert Cadre[b] Schools for Highly Qualified Workers and Remaining Expert Cadre[c] [See Basic School]
IV	Higher Middle School (Visa srednja skola)	Gymnasium, Complete (Potpuna gimnazija) Middle Expert School (Srednja strucna skola) [See Completed Gymn. and Middle Expert School]	General Secondary Complete Specialized Secondary Lower Level Specialized Secondary Higher Level Higher Educ. Incomplete	Gymnasium (Gimnazija) Schools for Middle Expert Cadre (Srednje skole za struc. kadar) [See Gymnasium and Schools for Middle Expert Cadre]	Gymnasium (Gimnazija) Schools for Middle Expert Cadre (Srednje skole za struc. kadar)
V	Faculty, High and Higher Schools (Fakulteti, visoke i vise skole)	Faculty, High and Higher Schools (Fakulteti, visoke i vise skole)	Higher Educ. Lower Level Complete Higher Educ. Faculty Level Complete	Higher Schools (Vise skole) Faculties and High Schools (Fakulteti i visoke skole)	Higher Schools (Vise skole) Faculties and High Schools (Fakulteti i visoke skole)

a Osmogodisnja i niza srednja skola za opste obrazovanje. b Skole za kvalifikovane radnike i ostali strucni kadar. c Skole za visokokvalifikovane radnike. d For Incomplete Secondary, see Basic School.

COMPARISON OF INTERNATIONAL STANDARD CLASSIFICATION OF EDUCATION
WITH STANDARD CLASSIFICATION USED IN THE HANDBOOK

	First Level		Second Level		Post Secondary
	Incomplete	Complete	Cycle 1	Cycle 2	
Albania					
Criteria Reported to UNESCO	...	8 yrs., ages 6-14	4 yrs., ages 14-18	...	...
Closest Equiv. in Handbook	...	7-8 Yr. Basic Complete	...	...	...
Bulgaria					
Criteria Reported to UNESCO	...	8 yrs., ages 7-15	4 yrs., ages 15-19	...	...
Closest Equiv. in Handbook:					
1956	...	7-8 Yr. Basic Complete	...	...	Higher (both levels)
1965	...	7-8 Yr. Basic Complete	...	Gen. Sec. & Spec. Sec.	Higher (both levels)
Czechoslovakia					
Criteria Reported to UNESCO	...	9 yrs., ages 6-15	4 yrs., ages 15-19	...	...
Closest Equiv. in Handbook:					
1961	...	Inc. Second.	...	Gen. Sec. & Spec. Sec.	Higher (both levels)
1970	...	7-8 Yr. Basic Complete	...	Trade Sch. & Spec. Sec.*	Higher (both levels)
GDR					
Criteria Reported to UNESCO	...	10 yrs., ages 7-17	2 yrs., ages 17-19	...	...
Closest Equiv. in Handbook:					
1971	...	7-8 Yr. Basic Complete*	...	Trade Sch. to Spec. Sec., Lower Level	Spec. Second., Higher Level, & Higher, Fac. Level
Hungary					
Criteria Reported to UNESCO	...	8 yrs., ages 6-14	4 yrs., ages 14-18	...	...
Closest Equiv. in Handbook:					
1960	...	7-8 Yr. Basic & Trade Sch.*	...	Inc. Sec. & Sec. Complete	Inc. Higher & Higher Fac. Level
1970	...	7-8 Yr. Basic & Trade Sch.*	...	Inc. Sec. & Spec. Sec.	Inc. Higher & Higher Fac. Level

	First Level		Second Level		Post Secondary
	Incomplete	Complete	Cycle 1	Cycle 2	
Poland					
Criteria Reported to UNESCO	...	8 yrs., ages 7-15	4 yrs., ages 15-19	...	...
Closest Equiv. in Handbook:					
1960	...	7-8 Yr. Basic Complete*	...	Inc. Sec. to Spec. Sec.	Higher Fac. Level
1970	...	7-8 Yr. Basic Complete*	...	Trade Sch. to Spec. Sec.	...
Romania					
Criteria Reported to UNESCO	...	8 or 10 yrs., ages 6-14 or 6-16	4 yrs., ages 14-18	...	...
Closest Equiv. in Handbook:					
1956	...	7-8 Yr. Basic & Inc. Sec.*	...	Sec. & Inc. Higher*	Higher Fac. Level
1966	...	7-8 Yr. Basic Incomplete*	...	7-8 Yr. Basic to Spec. Sec.	Higher Fac. Level
USSR					
Criteria Reported to UNESCO	...	8 yrs., ages 7-15	2 to 4 yrs., ages 15-17 or 15-19	...	...
Closest Equiv. in Handbook:					
1959	...	...	...	...	...
1970	...	...	...	...	...
Yugoslavia					
Criteria Reported to UNESCO	...	8 yrs., ages 7-15	4 yrs., ages 15-19	...	...
Closest Equiv. in Handbook:					
1953	...	7-8 Yr. Basic Incomplete	...	7-8 Yr. Basic to Spec. Sec.	Higher Fac. Level
1961	...	7-8 Yr. Basic & Trade Sch.	...	...	...
1971	...	...	...	...	...

*Number of persons with given level of education identical (or differences minimal) in data given according to standard form and data provided by UNESCO.

APPENDIX 11

LEVELS OF EDUCATIONAL ATTAINMENT IN THE SOVIET UNION
AND THEIR RELATIONSHIP TO THE STANDARD FORM USED IN *THE HANDBOOK*

The Standard Form used in the tables showing levels of educational attainment in the Soviet Union and Eastern Europe is based on Eastern European practice. However, measures of education attainment in the Soviet Union differ from those in Eastern Europe in a number of important ways, and allowance must be made for these differences.

The Standard Form differs from the measures of educational attainment used in the Soviet Union, first, in respect to the manner in which levels of education are designated. Soviet statistics do not use the term "basic" to refer to the 7–8 year school common to both Eastern Europe and the Soviet Union. Rather, it is called Incomplete Secondary Education (*nepolnoe srednee*). In Eastern Europe, those with 7 to 8 years of education are considered to have completed a basic school. The category Incomplete Secondary is reserved for those who have completed 8, 9, or 10 years of secondary school, or who have completed secondary school but have not received a certificate of maturity. This level is one step beyond the Soviet Incomplete Secondary or 7–8 year school.

Secondly, secondary education is completed sooner in the Soviet Union than in Eastern Europe. In both Eastern Europe and the Soviet Union education begins at age 7, and the 7–8 year school is completed by age 13 or 14. At this point, the Soviet system diverges from that in Eastern Europe. Secondary education is in effect completed in the Soviet Union after 10 years (although secondary education extends to 11 years in certain republics). In Eastern Europe secondary education normally lasts 11 or 12 years. In the Soviet Union, the student enters the university at age 17, compared to ages 18 or 19 in Eastern Europe. While differences of a year in length of schooling at any given level can also be found among Eastern European countries, none has reduced secondary education intended to prepare the pupil for the university to only 2 years following only 7 or 8 years of basic education. Viewed solely in terms of grades completed, the closest equivalent in Eastern Europe to the Soviet level of Completed Secondary Education (again, the 10 year school) would be Incomplete Secondary.

Reconciling these differences in such a way as to maintain the closest possible equivalence between the Soviet system and that of Eastern Europe may be done either by establishing equivalent levels of education on the basis of the number of years of education completed, or by matching levels of education, in the formal sense, as closely as possible. Under the first approach, the Soviet Completed Secondary (10 year school) would be, in the standard form, Incomplete Secondary. Under the second approach an effort would be made to match formal levels of education. Thus, higher education in the Soviet Union and Eastern Europe would be considered equivalent. Correcting for misleading terminology, the Soviet level of Incomplete Secondary (7–8 year school) would be considered 7–8 Year Basic Complete in the standard form, since both refer to the same type of schooling.

The *Handbook* follows the second approach since it facilitates comparisons between levels of educational attainment of groups covered in the tables in Sections of the *Handbook* dealing with classes, occupations, party members, and party leaders. The level of educational attainment of an individual with a higher education in the Soviet Union is therefore considered the same as that of a person with higher education in Eastern Europe. Completion of a secondary education in the Soviet Union is considered the equivalent of completion of a secondary education in Eastern Europe. Thus, the Soviet level of Completed Secondary (*srednee obshchee*) is rendered as Completed General Secondary in the standard form, notwithstanding the fact that this level in the Soviet Union in most cases represents only 10 years of education. Following the same procedure, the Soviet level of Incomplete Higher Education is shown as Incomplete Higher in the Standard Form.

At the lower end of the scale, the Soviet level of Primary Education (*nachalnoe*) is rendered as 4 Year Elementary Complete in the Standard Form, and Incomplete Secondary (*nepolnoe srednee*) as 7–8 Year Basic Complete. These adjustments to the standard form do not go beyond changes in terminology; in other words, the levels of education being compared are exactly equivalent. (It is true that there is no term used in Soviet statistics to describe persons having completed 5 to 6 years of education, the group in Eastern Europe which would be considered to have attained the level of 7–8 Year Basic Incomplete. Such a category, if it existed in the Soviet system, would have to be called "Incomplete Incomplete Secondary." Persons in this group are included with those having a Primary Education in the Soviet Union, and therefore appear in the tables in *The Handbook* with those having completed an elementary education.)

Beginning with the lower levels of education and working upward, the category of Incomplete Secondary in the Standard Form should designate the next stage of educational attainment beyond 7–8 Year Basic Complete, or in the Soviet case, the next stage after Incomplete Secondary. This, in the Soviet case, is Completed General Secondary (*srednee obshchee*). To make these two levels of education in the Soviet and Standard Form equivalent nevertheless runs counter to the decision, noted above, that Completed General Secondary in the Soviet and Standard Forms are considered equivalent. At this point it becomes clear that it is not possible to match formal levels of educational attainment in the two systems without encountering a basic problem, namely, that the Soviet system does not provide the number of distinctions between levels of education common in Eastern Europe and incorporated into the Standard Form.

The solution adopted by the *Handbook* is to designate the level of Incomplete Secondary in the Standard Form as one for which there is no exact equivalent in the Soviet system of measuring levels of educational attainment. This is indicated in tables on educational attainment by a footnote; in this manner the reader is alerted to the discontinuity that results from comparing formal levels of educational attainment in the Soviet Union with the Standard Form derived from Eastern European practice. The reader should bear in mind that under a different approach, an equivalent could be found for the level of Incomplete Secondary in the Standard Form (those who, in the Soviet system, had a General Secondary level of education). The method chosen here seems, nevertheless, to best facilitate comparisons between levels of educational attainment in Eastern Europe and the Soviet Union.

APPENDIX 12

GUIDE TO NUMBER OF ACTIVE
(Active Earners and Economically Active)

BULGARIA

Tables in which Number Appears as Economically Active

	1956	1965	1975
E-37	4,150,207*	4,267,798**	4,573,593*
G-20	...	4,267,798**	...

Tables in which Number Appears as Active Earners

	1956	1965	1975
E-2	4,150,207*	4,267,798**	4,573,593*
E-10	4,150,207*	4,267,798**	4,573,593*
G-1	4,150,206*	4,267,798**	...
H-5	4,150,207*	4,280,426**	...

CZECHOSLOVAKIA

Tables in which Number Appears as Economically Active

	1950	1961	1970
E-37	5,811,724**	6,482,000[xxx]	6,989,000**
G-20	...	6,482,664***	6,989,000**

Tables in which Number Appears as Active Earners

	1950	1961	1970
E-3	5,811,724**	6,439,412[xx]	6,989,000**
E-11	5,811,724**	6,439,412[xx]	6,989,000**
G-2	...	6,439,412[xx]	...
H-6	5,811,724**	6,726,496[a]	7,348,000[a]

GDR

Tables in which Number Appears as Economically Active

	1950	1964	1971
E-37	8,477,159*	8,345,017*	8,214,251*
G-20	...	...	...

Tables in which Number Appears as Active Earners

	1950	1964	1971
E-4	7,923,222[xx]	7,994,558[xx] and 8,345,017*	...
E-12	7,923,222[xx]	8,345,017*	8,214,251*
G-3	7,923,222[xx]	7,994,526[xx]	...
H-7	8,477,159*	7,994,558[xx]	...

HUNGARY

<u>Tables in which Number Appears as Economically Active</u>

	<u>1949</u>	<u>1960</u>	<u>1970</u>
E-37	4,154,543*	4,876,232***	4,988,676**
G-20	...	4,876,232***	4,988,676**

<u>Tables in which Number Appears as Active Earners</u>

	1949	1960	1970
E-5	4,154,543*	4,759,616[x]	4,988,676**
E-13	4,154,543*	4,759,616[x]	4,988,676**
G-4	...	4,875,361[x]	4,988,676**
H-8	4,084,931[b]	4,759,616[x]	4,988,676**

POLAND

<u>Tables in which Number Appears as Economically Active</u>

	<u>1950</u>	<u>1960</u>	<u>1970</u>
E-37	12,404,200*	13,907,442*	16,943,848**
G-20	...	...	16,943,848**

<u>Tables in which Number Appears as Active Earners</u>

	1950	1960	1970
E-6	12,404,200*	13,907,442*	16,429,101[x]
E-14	12,404,200*	13,907,442*	16,943,848**
G-5	...	13,907,442*	16,429,101[x]
H-9	12,404,200*	13,907,442*	16,429,101[x]

ROMANIA

<u>Tables in which Number Appears as Economically Active</u>

	<u>1956</u>	<u>1966</u>
E-37	10,449,128*	10,362,300**
G-20	...	10,362,300**

<u>Tables in which Number Appears as Active Earners</u>

	1956	1966
E-7	10,449,128*	10,363,300**
E-15	10,449,128*	10,362,300**
G-6	10,449,128*	10,362,300**
H-10	10,449,128*	10,362,300**

USSR

Tables in which Number Appears as Economically Active

	1939	1959	1970
E-37	86,984,000[c]	108,995,013[c]	117,027,575[c]
G-20	...	...	...

Tables in which Number Appears as Active Earners

E-8	78,800,000[xx]	99,130,212[xx]	115,204,076[xx]
E-16	...	99,130,212[xx]	115,204,076[xx]
G-7	78,811,000[xx]	99,130,000[xx]	115,204,000[xx]
H-11	...	108,995,013[c]	117,027,575[c]

YUGOSLAVIA

Tables in which Number Appears as Economically Active

	1953	1961	1971
E-37	7,848,857*	8,340,400**	8,889,816**
G-20	7,848,857*	8,340,400**	8,889,816**

Tables in which Number Appears as Active Earners

E-9	7,848,857*	8,340,400**	8,889,816**
E-17	7,848,857*	8,340,400**	8,889,816**
G-8	7,848,857*	8,340,400**	8,889,816**
H-12	7,848,857*	8,340,400**	8,889,816**

   * Figure taken from national census; used in tables employing international system of classification of labor force in lieu of other data.

  ** Figure taken from national census; also appears in International Labor Office annual.

 *** Figure taken from International Labor Office annual; does not appear in national census data.

   x Figure taken from national census; does not correspond to figure appearing in International Labor Office annual.

  xx Figure taken from national census; considered incomplete (lacks portion of active population; does not cover entire territory of country in question; or is the preliminary result of the census).

 xxx Figure taken from national census and adjusted to approximate figure appearing in International Labor Office annual.

   a Figure based on national census; includes apprentices and helping family members.

   b Number active in 1949 according to definition of active adopted in 1970.

   c Figure based on national census; includes persons tending private plots in agriculture.

APPENDIX 13

CLASSIFICATION OF SOCIAL CLASSES

I.
ALBANIA (1950-1973)

Standard Form	Albanian Classification
Workers	Workers (Punetore)
Other Employees	Employees (Nepunes)
Collective Farm Members	Cooperative Peasant (Fshatare-Kooperativiste)
Private Peasantry	Private Peasant (Fshatare - Individuale)
Members of Nonagricultural Cooperatives	-----
Artisans on Own Account	
Liberal Professions	Private Handicrafts and Merchants (Zanatcinj e tregtare private)
Capitalist Classes	
Military	-----
Helping Family Members	-----

II.
BULGARIA (1965)

Standard Form	Bulgarian Classification
Workers	Worker (Rabotnik)
Other Employees	White Collar Employee (Sluzhesht)
Collective Farm Members	Collective Farm Members (Chlen na TKZS)
Private Peasantry	Private Agriculturalist (Chasten zemedelski stopanin)
Member of Nonagricultural Cooperatives	Member of Handicraft Cooperative (Kooperiran zaniiatchiia)
Artisans on Own Account	Artisan not a Member of a Handicraft Cooperative (Nekooperiran zaniiatchiia)
Liberal Professions	Free Professions (Litse sus svobodna profesiia)
Capitalist Classes	Private Trader (Chasten turgovets)
Military	-----
Helping Family Members	-----
-----	Religious Functionary (Sluzhitel na religiiata)

III.
CZECHOSLOVAKIA (1961)

Standard Form	Czechoslovak Classification
Workers	Workers (Delnici)
Other Employees	Remaining Employees (Ostatni zamestnanci)
Collective Farm Members	Collective Farmers (Druzstevni rolnici)
Private Peasantry	Independent Peasantry (Jednotlivi hospodarici rolnici)
Members of Nonagricultural Cooperatives	Remaining Socialist Producers - Members of Production Cooperatives (Ostatni druzstevni vyrobci - clenove lidovych vyrobnich druzstev)
Artisans on Own Account	Private Artisans and Tradesmen (Soukromni remeslnici a zivnostnici)
Liberal Professions	Free Professions (Osoby svobodnych povolani)
Capitalist Classes	-----
Military	-----
Helping Family Members	-----

IV.
GDR (1964)

Standard Form	GDR Classification
Workers	Workers (Arbeiterklasse)
Other Employees	
-----	Intelligentsia (Intelligenz)
Collective Farm Members	Collective Farmers (Klasse der Genossenschaftsbauern)
Private Peasantry	-----
Members of Nonagricultural Cooperatives	Artisans, Members of Producers Cooperatives (Genossenschaftshandwerker)
Artisans on Own Account	Private Artisans and Small Cottage Industries (Privat Handwerker und Kleingewerbetreibende))
Liberal Professions	-----
Capitalist Classes	-----
Military	-----
Helping Family Members	-----

V.

GDR (Civilian Labor Force)

Standard Form	GDR Classification
Workers	⎤ Workers and Employees (Arbeiter und Angestellte)
Other Employees	⎦
Collective Farm Members	Members of Agricultural Production Cooperatives (Mitgleider von LPG)
Private Peasantry	Individual Peasants and Persons Tending Private Plots (Einzelbauern und private Gartner)
Members of Nonagricultural Cooperatives	Members of Handicraft Production Cooperatives (Mitgleider von PGH)
Artisans on Own Account	Private Artisans (Private Handwerker)
Liberal Professions	Free Professions (Freiberufliche Tatige)
Capitalist Classes	Retail and Wholesale Trade (Privat Gross und Einzelhandler)
Military	-----
Helping Family Members	-----

VI.

HUNGARY (1970)

Standard Form	Hungarian Classification
Workers	Employees – Physical Workers (Alkalmazasban allok, fizikai dolgozok)
Other Employees	Employees, Mental Workers (Alkalmazasban allok, szellemi dolgozok)
Collective Farm Members	Members of Production Cooperatives (Termeloszovet-kezeti tag – mezogazdasag)
Private Peasantry	Independents – Agriculture (Onallo – mezogazdasag)
Members of Nonagricultural Cooperatives	Members of Production Cooperatives – Nonagricultural Branches (Termeloszovetkezeti tag . . . .)
Artisans on Own Account	Independents – Industry (Onallo – ipar)
Liberal Professions	-----
Capitalist Classes	-----
Military	-----
Helping Family Members	Helping Family Members (Segito csaladtag)

439

Standard Form   Polish Classification

Workers   Physical Workers (Pracownicy fizyczni)

Other Employees   Mental Workers (Pracownicy umyslowi)

Collective Farm Members   Members of Work Cooperatives in Agriculture
                                                (Czlonkowie spoldzielni pracy w rolnictwie)

Private Peasantry   Working on Own Account in Agriculture (Pracujacy
                                                na rachunek wlasny w rolnictwie)

Members of Nonagricultural Cooperatives   Members of Work Cooperatives Outside Agriculture
                                                (Czlonkowie spoldzielni pracy poza rolnictwem)

Artisans on Own Account   Working on Own Account Outside Agriculture
                                                (Pracujacy na rachunek wlasny poza rolnictwem)

Liberal Professions   -----

Capitalist Classes   -----

Military   -----

Helping Family Members   Helping Family Members (Pomagajacy czlonkowie
                                                rodziny)

Standard Form   Polish Classification

Workers   Physical Workers (Pracownicy fizyczni)

Other Employees   Mental Workers (Pracownicy umyslowi)

Collective Farm Members   Members of Agricultural Production Cooperatives
                                                and Workers on Private Plots (Czlonkowie
                                                spoldzielni produkcynych i pracujacy na dzialkach
                                                przyzagrodowych)

Private Peasantry   Peasant Proprietors (Gospodarujacy w swoim
                                                gospodarstwie rolnym)

Members of Nonagricultural Cooperatives   Members of Producers Cooperatives Outside Agricul-
                                                ture (Czlonkowie spoldzielni produkcyjnych poza
                                                rolnictwem)

Artisans on Own Account   Workers on Own Account in Nonsocialist Sector
                                                Outside Agriculture (Pracujacy na rachunek wlasny
                                                i pomagajacy poza rolnictwem, w godpodarce nie
                                                uspolecznionej)

Liberal Professions   -----

Capitalists   -----

Military   -----

Helping Family Members   Helpers of Peasant Proprietors (Pomagajacy
                                                gospodarujacym w rolnictwie, w gospadarce nie
                                                uspolecznionej)

          -----   Working Under Commission in the Socialist Sector
                                                (Pracujacy w oparciu o umowe agencyjna, w
                                                gospodarce uspolecznionej)

Standard Form	Rumanian Classification
Workers	Workers (Muncitori)
Other Employees	Intellectuals-Functionaries (Intelectuali-Functionari)
Collective Farm Members	Cooperative Peasants (Tarani cooperatori)
Private Peasantry	Independent Peasantry (Tarani cu gospodarii individuale)
Members of Nonagricultural Cooperatives	Cooperative Handicrafts (Meseriasi cooperatori)
Artisans on Own Account	Private Handicrafts (Meseriasi particulari)
Liberal Professions	-----
Capitalists	-----
Military	-----
Helping Family Members	-----

X.
USSR (1926)

Standard Form	USSR Classification
Workers	Workers (Rabochie)
Other Employees	White Collar Employees (Sluzhashchie)
Collective Farm Members	-----
Private Peasantry	Employers with Hired Labor, Employers Working Only with Helping Family Members and Members of Cooperatives, Independents - Those in Agriculture (Khozyaeva s naemnymi rabochimi, khozyaeva, rabotayushchie tolko s chlenami semi i chleny arteli . . .)
Members of Nonagricultural Cooperatives	-----
Artisans on Own Account	Employers with Hired Labor, Employers Working Only with Helping Family Members and Members of Cooperatives, Independents - Those Outside Agriculture (Khozyaeva s naemnymi rabochimi, khozyaeva, rabotayushchie tolko s chlenami semi i chleny arteli . . .)
Liberal Professions	Free Professions (Litsa svobodnykh professiy)
Capitalists	-----
Military	Those Serving in Military (Voennosluzhashchiye)
-----	Unemployed (Bezrabotnye)

441

XI

USSR (1959)

Standard Form	USSR Classification
Workers	Workers (Rabochie)
Other Employees	White Collar Employees (Sluzhashchie)
Collective Farm Members	Collective Farmers (Kolkhozniki)
Private Peasantry	Individual Peasants (Krestyanine- edinolichniki)
Members of Nonagricultural Cooperatives	Members of Handicraft Cooperatives (Kooper- irovannye kustari)
Artisans on Own Account	Artisans, not Members of a Cooperative (Nekooperirovannye kustari)
Liberal Professions	Free Professions (Litsa svobodnykh professiy)
Capitalists	----
Military	----
Helping Family Members	----
-----	Religious Functionaries (Sluzhiteli kulta)

XII

YUGOSLAVIA (1960)

Standard Form	Yugoslav Classification
Workers	
Other Employees	Worker-Employee (Radnik-Sluzbenik)
Collective Farm Members	Members of Work Cooperative - Agriculture (Clan radne zadruga . . . .)
Private Peasantry	Independent with Workers, Independent without Workers - Agriculture (Samostalan bez radnika, Poslodavac . . . .)
Members of Nonagricultural Cooperatives	Members of Work Cooperatives - Outside Agriculture (Clan radne zadruga . . . .)
Artisans on Own Account	Independents with Workers, Independent without Workers - Outside Agriculture (Samostalan bez radnika, Poslodavac . . . .)
Helping Family Members	Helping Family Members (Pomazuci clan porodice)
-----	Apprentices (Ucenik u privredi)

APPENDIX 14

POLITBURO MEMBERS NOT ELECTED AT PARTY CONGRESSES: USSR, 1917-1945

	1 Birth Date	2 Birth Place	3 Ethnicity	4 Social Origins	5 Status Prior to Party Work	6 Formal Educ.	7 Advanced Training	8 Party Memb.	9 Revol. Type	10 WW II	11 CC Memb.	12 EC Memb.	Exec. Com. & Status
1. M. V. Frunze	1885	...	Russ.	...	...	...	...	1904	...	...	...	1924 1925	Candidate
2. K. Y. Bauman	1892	...	Lat.	Peasant	...	...	...	1907	...	...	...	1929 1930	Candidate
3. N. I. Ezhov	1901	...	...	...	...	...	...	1917	...	...	...	1934 1938	Candidate
4. R. I. Eikhe	1890	...	Lat.	Peasant	...	...	...	1905	...	...	...	1935 1938	Candidate
5. A. S. Shcherbakov	1901	...	Russ.	Worker	...	...	...	...	...	...	...	1941 1945	Candidate
6. N. A. Vosnesenskiy	1903	...	Russ.	Peasant	...	...	...	1919	...	...	...	1947 1949	Full
7. L. N. Efremov	1912	...	Russ.	...	...	...	...	1941	...	...	...	1962 1966	Candidate

443

APPENDIX 15

ALPHABETICAL LISTING OF POLITICAL LEADERS INCLUDED IN SECTION F

I.
Albania

Name	Entry No., Table F-1	Name	Entry No., Table F-1
Alija, Ramiz	12	Këllezi, Abdyl	19
Balluku, Bequir	1	Koleka, Spiro	6
Belishova, Liri	2	Marko, Rita	9
Çarçani, Adil	13	Mihali, Qirjako	26
Cuko, Lenka	24	Miska, Pali	23
Dervishi, Rrapo	14	Myftiu, Manush	10
Dodbiba, Pirro	20	Nushi, Gogo	7
Dume, Petrit	17	Peristeri, Pilo	11
Gegprifti, Llambi	25	Shehu, Mehmet	8
Hasbiu, Kadri	18	Spahiu, Xhafer	21
Hoxha, Enver	3	Stefanovic, Simon	27
Isai, Hekuran	22	Theodhosi, Koço	15
Jakova, Tuk	4	Toska, Haki	16
Kapo, Hysni	5		

II.
Bulgaria

Name	Entry No., Table F-2	Name	Entry No., Table F-2
Abadzhiev, Ivan	35	Mladenov, Petur	45
Avramov, Lachezar	36	Neichev, Mincho	17
Balgaranov, Boyan	24	Panchevski, Petur	22
Chankov, Georgi	1	Pavlov, Todor	31
Chernokolev, Titko	16	Popov, Ivan	32
Chervenkov, Vulko	2	Poptomov, Vladimir	11
Damyanov, Georgi	3	Prahov, Todor	23
Damyanov, Raiko	4	Staikov, Encho	19
Dimitrov, Georgi	5	Stoichev, Todor	46
Dimov, Dimiter	14	Stoyanov, Mladen	26
Dragoicheva, Tsola	6	Takov, Peko	38
Dzurov, Dobri	44	Taskov, Boris	25
Filipov, Grisha	42	Terpeshev, Dobri	12
Ganev, Dimiter	7	Todorov, Stanko	28
Grigorov, Mitko	27	Trichkov, Krastya	41
Grozev, Gocho	15	Tsanev, Angel	39
Gyaurov, Kostadin	37	Tsankov, Georgi	20
Kolarov, Vasil	8	Tsolov, Tano	30
Kostov, Traicho	9	Velchev, Boris	33
Kotsev, Venelin	40	Vulcheva, Drazha	47
Kubadinski, Pencho	29	Yugov, Anton	13
Kunin, Petko	10	Zhivkov, Todor	21
Lilov, Aleksandur	43	Zhivkov, Zhivko	34
Mihailov, Ivan	18		

III.
Czechoslovakia

Name	Entry No., Table F-3	Name	Entry No., Table F-3
Bacílek, Karol	24	Kliment, Gustav	5
Barák, Rudolf	25	Kolder, Drahomír	32
Barbírek, František	43	Kopecký, Václav	6
Bareš, Gustav	15	Kopřiva, Ladislav	7
Baštovanský, Štefan	16	Korčák, Josef	55
Bilák, Vasil	44	Kriegel, František	45
Čepička, Alexej	26	Krosnar, Josef	8
Černík, Oldřich	36	Laštovička, Bohuslav	38
Chudík, Michal	37	Lenárt, Jozef	33
Čolotka, Peter	51	Nejedlý, Zdeněk	9
David, Pavol	28	Nosek, Václav	10
David, Václav	1	Novotný, Antonín	23
Dolanský, Jaromír	2	Pastyřík, Miroslav	39
Dubček, Alexander	34	Piller, Jan	46
Ďuriš, Julius	17	Rigo, Emil	47
Erban, Evžen	18	Sabolčik, Michal	40
Fierlinger, Zdeněk	19	Sadovský, Štefan	41
Frank, Josef	3	Šimůnek, Otakar	27
Gottwald, Klement	4	Široký, Viliam	22
Hendrych, Jiří	29	Slánský, Rudolf	11
Hlína, Jan	30	Smrkovský, Josef	12
Hoffman, Karel	52	Špaček, Josef	48
Hruškovič, Miloslav	58	Strechaj, Rudolf	31
Hůla, Václav	59	Strougal, Lubomír	56
Husák, Gustav	50	Švermová, Marie	13
Indra, Alois	53	Švestka, Oldřich	49
Jankovcová, Ludmila	20	Svoboda, Ludvík	57
John, Oldřich	21	Vaculík, Martin	42
Kapek, Antonín	35	Zápotocký, Antonín	14
Kempný, Josef	54		

IV.
GDR

Name	Entry No., Table F-4	Name	Entry No., Table F-4
Ackermann, Anton	1	Gruneberg, Gerhard	42
Apel, Erich	38	Hager, Kurt	33
Axen, Hermann	39	Halbritter, Walter	49
Bartsch, Karl	40	Hermann, Joachim	57
Baumann, Edith	30	Hernstadt, Rudolf	20
Beling, Walter	15	Hoffman, Heinz	54
Dahlem, Franz	2	Honecker, Erich	21
Dohlus, Horst	56	Jarowinsky, Werner	43
Ebert, Friedric	16	Jendretzky, Hans	22
Ermisch, Luise	31	Karsten, August	6
Ewald, Georg	41	Kern, Käthe	7
Fechner, Max	3	Kleiber, Günther	50
Felfe, Werner	53	Krenz, Egon	58
Fröhlich, Paul	32	Krolikowski, Werner	47
Gniffke, Erich	4	Kurella, Alfred	34
Grotewohl, Otto	5	Lamberz, Werner	48

Name	Entry No., Table F-2	Name	Entry No., Table F-2
Lange, Ingeburg	59	Pieck, Wilhelm	12
Lehmann, Helmut	8	Pisnik, Alois	36
Leuschner, Bruno	25	Rau, Heinrich	18
Matern, Hermann	9	Schirdewann, Karl	23
Meier, Otto	10	Schmidt, Elli	13
Mielke, Erich	51	Schürer, Gerhard	60
Merker, Paul	11	Sindermann, Horst	46
Mewis, Karl	35	Stoph, Willi	24
Mittag, Günther	44	Tisch, Harry	52
Muckenberger, Erich	26	Ulbricht, Walter	14
Müller, Margarete	45	Verner, Paul	37
Naumann, Konrad	55	Walde, Werner	61
Neumann, Alfred	27	Warnke, Herbert	28
Norden, Albert	29	Zaisser, Wilhelm	19
Oelssner, Fred	17		

V.
Hungary

Name	Entry No., Table F-5	Name	Entry No., Table F-5
Ais, Lajos	27	Kristóf, István	25
Aczél, György	49	Lázár, György	50
Ajtai, Miklós	41	Marosán, György	11
Apró, Antal	1	Marothy, László	51
Bata, István	29	Mekis, József	30
Benke, Valéria	48	Münnich, Ferenc	36
Biszku, Béla	32	Nagy, Imre	6
Brutyó, János	42	Nemes, Dezső	37
Cseterki, Lajos	44	Németh, Károly	47
Czinege, Lajos	43	Nyers, Rezső	46
Dénes, István	23	Óvári, Miklós	52
Farkas, Mihály	2	Piros, László	26
Fehér, Lajos	33	Rajk, László	7
Fock, Jenő	34	Rákosi, Mátyás	8
Gáspár, Sándor	31	Révai, József	9
Gerő, Ernő	3	Rónai, Sándor	12
Harustyák, József	10	Sarlós, István	53
Hegedüs, András	18	Somogyi, Miklós	38
Hidas, István	24	Szabó, István	20
Horváth, Márton	15	Szakasits, Árpád	13
Ilku, Pál	45	Szalai, Béla	28
Kádar, János	4	Szirmai, István	40
Kállai, Gyula	35	Vajda, Imre	14
Kiss, Károly	19	Vas, Zoltán	17
Komócsin, Zoltán	39	Zöld, Sándor	21
Kossa, István	5	Zsofinyecz, Mihály	22
Kovács, István	16		

VI.
Poland

Name	Entry No., Table F-6	Name	Entry No., Table F-6
Babiuch, Edward	36	Bierut, Bolesław	2
Barcikowski, Kazimierz	41	Chelchowski, Hilary	9
Berman, Jakób	1	Cyrankiewicz, Józef	10

Name	Entry No., Table F-6	Name	Entry No., Table F-6
Dworakowski, Władysław	17	Minc, Hilary	4
Gierek, Edward	20	Moczar, Mieczysław	34
Gomulka, Władysław	3	Morawski, Jerzy	24
Grudzień, Zdzisław	42	Nowak, Zenon	18
Jabłoński, Henryk	37	Ochab, Edward	16
Jagielski, Mieczysław	27	Olszowski, Stefan	39
Jaroszewicz, Piotr	28	Radkiewicz, Stanisław	5
Jaruzelski, Wojciech	38	Rapacki, Adam	12
Jaszczuk, Bolesław	30	Rokossowski, Konstanty	19
Jędrychowski, Stefan	21	Spychalski, Marian	6
Jóźwiak, Franciszek	11	Strzelecki, Ryszard	29
Kania, Stanisław	43	Światkowski, Henryk	13
Kępa, Józef	44	Szlachcic, Franciszek	40
Kliszko, Zenon	22	Szydlak, Jan	35
Kociołek, Stanisław	31	Szyr, Eugeniusz	25
Kowalczyk, Stanisław	45	Tejchma, Józef	33
Kruczek, Władysław	32	Waniołka, Franciszek	26
Loga-Sowiński, Ignacy	23	Wrzaszczyk, Tadeusz	47
Łukaszewicz, Jerzy	46	Zambrowski, Roman	7
Matuszewski, Stefan	15	Zawadzki, Aleksander	8
Mazur, Franciszek	14		

VII.
Romania

Name	Entry No., Table F-7	Name	Entry No., Table F-7
Andrei, Ştefan	54	Ioniţă, Ion	49
Apostol, Gheorghe	1	Iordachescu, Theodor	7
Banc, Josif	33	Kiraly, Carol	50
Berghianu, Maxim	31	Luca, Vasile	8
Birladeanu, Alexandru	27	Lupu, Petre	37
Blajovici, Petre	32	Mănescu, Manea	38
Bobu, Emil	57	Maurer, Ion	26
Bodnăraş, Emil	2	Moghioros, Alexandru	9
Borilă, Petre	19	Moraru, Mihai	14
Burtică, Cornel	58	Niculescu-Mizel, Paul	29
Ceauşescu, Elena	59	Oprea, Gheorghe	55
Ceauşescu, Nicolae	20	Pana, Gheorghe	42
Chişinevschi, Iosif	3	Păţan, Ion	56
Cioară, Gheorghe	60	Patilineţ, Vasile	51
Ciobanu, Lina	61	Pauker, Ana	10
Coliu, Dumitru	23	Petrescu, Dumitru	43
Constantinescu, Miron	4	Pîrvulescu, Constantin	22
Dalea, Mihai	63	Popa, Dumitru	52
Dănălache, Florian	34	Popescu, Dumitru	44
Dej, Gheorghe Gheorghiu	6	Radaceanu, Lothar	11
Dobrescu, Miu	46	Rădulescu, Gheorghe	30
Drăgan, Constantin	28	Ranghet, Iosif	15
Drăgănescu, Emil	41	Răutu, Leonte	24
Drăghici, Alexandru	21	Sălăjan, Leontin	25
Duca, Aurel	47	Stănescu, Ion	53
Fazekaş, Jánoş	35	Stoica, Chivu	16
Georgescu, Teohari	5	Telescu, Mihai	65
Gere, Mihai	36	Trofin, Virgil	45
Giosan, Nicolae	64	Uglar, Iosif	62
Iliescu, Ion	48	Ursu, Ioan	66

Name	Entry No., Table F-7	Name	Entry No., Table F-7
Vaida, Vasile	17	Voitec, Ştefan	13
Vasilichi, Gheorghe	12	Winter, Richard	67
Verdet, Ilie	39	Zaharia, Tanase	18
Vîlcu, Vasile	40		

VIII.
USSR-Prewar

Name	Entry No., Table F-8	Name	Entry No., Table F-8
Andreyev, A. A.	22	Ordzhonikidze, G. K.	29
Beria, L. P.	33	Petrovsky, G. I.	18
Bubnov, A. S.	1	Postyshev, P. P.	30
Bukharin, N. I.	9	Preobrazhensky, Y. A.	11
Chubar, V. Y.	23	Rudzutak, Y. E.	19
Dzerzhinsky, F. E.	17	Rykov, A. I.	14
Kaganovich, M.	24	Serebryakov, L. P.	12
Kalinin, M. I.	10	Shvernik, N. M.	34
Kamenev, L. B.	2	Sokolnikov, G. Y.	4
Khrushchev, N. S.	31	Stalin, J. V.	5
Kirov, S. M.	25	Syrtsov, S. I.	28
Kossior, S. V.	26	Tomsky, M. P.	15
Krestinsky, N. N.	8	Trotsky, L. D.	6
Kuybyshev, V. V.	21	Uglanov, N. A.	20
Lenin, V. I.	3	Voroshilov, K. Y.	16
Mikoyan, A. I.	27	Zhdanov, A. A.	32
Molotov, V. M.	13	Zinoviev, G. Y.	7

IX.
USSR-Postwar

Name	Entry No., Table F-9	Name	Entry No., Table F-9
Aliyev, G. A.	55	Kuusinen, O. V.	28
Andropov, Y. V.	50	Malenkov, G. M.	5
Aristov, A. B.	24	Masherov, P. M.	47
Bagirov, M. D.	17	Mazurov, K. T.	33
Belyayev, N. I.	25	Melnikov, L. G.	13
Beria, L. P.	1	Mikoyan, A. I.	6
Brezhnev, L. I.	19	Molotov, V. M.	7
Bulganin, N. A.	2	Mukhitdinov, N. A.	21
Demichev, P. N.	46	Mzhavanadze, V. P.	34
Furtseva, Y. A.	20	Pelshe, A. Y.	43
Grechko, A. A.	52	Pervukhin, M. G.	8
Grishin, V. V.	36	Podgorny, N. V.	38
Gromyko, A. A.	53	Polyansky, D. S.	39
Ignatov, N. G.	26	Ponomarenko, P. K.	14
Kaganovich, L. M.	3	Ponomarev, B. N.	56
Kalnberzin, Y. E.	29	Pospelov, P. N.	35
Khrushchev, N. S.	4	Rashidov, S. R.	41
Kirichenko, A. I.	18	Romanov, G. V.	54
Kirilenko, A. P.	30	Saburov, M. Z.	9
Korotchenko, D. S.	31	Shcherbitsky, V. V.	42
Kosygin, A. N.	32	Shelepin, A. N.	44
Kozlov, F. R.	27	Shelest, P. Y.	45
Kulakov, F. D.	49	Shepilov, D. T.	22
Kunayev, D. A.	37	Shkiryatov, M. F.	15

Name	Entry No., Table F-9	Name	Entry No., Table F-9
Shvernik, N. M.	10	Ustinov, D. F.	48
Solomentsev, M. S.	51	Voronov, G. I.	40
Stalin, J. V.	11	Voroshilov, K. Y.	12
Suslov, M. A.	16	Zhukov, G. K.	23

X.
Yugoslavia

Name	Entry No., Table F-10	Name	Entry No., Table F-10
Albreht, Roman	93	Markovski, Krste	98
Alimpić, Dušan	94	Mesihović, Munir	86
Avramović, Krsta	51	Mijatović, Cvijetin	22
Bakali, Mahmut	95	Mikulić, Branko	67
Bakarić, Vladimir	10	Milosavlevski, Slavko	66
Balint, Imre	96	Minić, Miloš	99
Belovski, Dimče	52	Nagy, Jozef	68
Bijedić, Dzemal	53	Nešković, Blagoje	7
Bijelić, Srećko	97	Nikezić, Marko	69
Bilić, Jure	82	Pajković, Djoko	23
Blažević, Jakov	26	Pečenović, Jovan	70
Borojević, Branko	54	Pečujlić, Miroslav	48
Čemerski, Angel	55	Perović, Latinka	71
Crvenkovski, Krste	20	Petrović, Dušan	36
Ćulafić, Dobroslav	56	Pijade, Moša	8
Dabčević-Kucar, Savka	27	Popit, Franc	72
Djilas, Milovan	2	Popović, Dušan	87
Djuranović, Veselin	59	Popović, Koča	37
Dizdarević, Nijaz	44	Popović, Milentije	34
Dobardjić, Emin	57	Popović, Mirko	88
Dolanc, Stane	45	Popović, Vladimir	35
Dolničar, Ivan	58	Pozderac, Hamdija	73
Doronjski, Stevan	46	Pucar-Stari, Djuro	12
Dugonjić, Ratomir	28	Radosavljević, Dobrivoje	38
Gazi, Pavle	60	Ranković, Aleksandar	9
Gligorov, Kiro	47	Ribičić, Mitja	74
Gošnjak, Ivan	3	Ristić, Dušan	101
Grličkov, Aleksandar	83	Salaj, Djure	14
Hodza, Fadilj	29	Šarac, Dzemal	102
Humo, Avdo	30	Sekulić, Nikola	39
Jovanović, Blažo	15	Šenturc, Lidija	41
Karabegović, Osman	31	Šiljegović, Boško	76
Kardelj, Edvard	4	Široka, Kolj	77
Kavčić, Stane	61	Smilevski, Vidoje	40
Kidrič, Boris	5	Šoškić, Budislav	49
Kolak, Rudi	32	Šoti, Pal	42
Koliševski, Lazar	11	Špiljak, Mika	24
Krajger, Boris	21	Srzentić, Vojislav	89
Krajger, Sergej	62	Stambolić, Petar	17
Kranjc, Stane	63	Stanojević, Milorad	75
Kukoč, Ivan	84	Stavrev, Dragoljub	90
Kurtović, Todo	85	Šukrija, Ali	91
Leskošek, Franc	6	Temelkovski, Borko	43
Liker, Zvonko	64	Tepavac, Mirko	78
Ljubičić, Nikola	65	Tito, Josip-Broz	1
Maček, Ivan	33	Todorović, Mijalko	25
Marinko, Miha	16	Tomić, Stanko	79

Name	Entry No., Table F-10	Name	Entry No., Table F-10
Tripalo, Miko	50	Vrhovec, Josip	105
Veselinov, Jovan	18	Vujadinović, Jovan	106
Vidić, Dobrivoje	92	Vukmanović-Tempo, Svetozar	13
Vlahović, Veljko	19	Žarković, Vidoje	80
Vlaškalić, Tihomir	104	Zulfićari, Azem	81

APPENDIX 16

DATES OF PARTY CONGRESSES CHOOSING POLITBUROS INCLUDED IN SECTION F

Albania: 1st Congress, November, 1948; 2nd Congress, April, 1952; 3rd Congress, May, 1956; 4th Congress, February, 1961; 5th Congress, November, 1966; 6th Congress, November, 1971; 7th Congress, November, 1976.

Bulgaria: No congress, March, 1945; 5th Congress, December, 1948; 6th Congress, March, 1954; 7th Congress, June, 1958; 8th Congress, November, 1962; 9th Congress, November, 1966; 10th Congress, April, 1971; 11th Congress, April, 1976.

Czechoslovakia: 8th Congress, March, 1946; 9th Congress, May, 1949; 10th Congress, July, 1954; 11th Congress, June, 1958; 12th Congress, December, 1962; 13th Congress, June–July, 1966; no congress, March–April, 1968; 14th Congress, May, 1971; 15th Congress, April, 1976.

GDR: 1st Congress, April, 1946; 2nd Congress, September, 1947; 3rd Congress, July, 1950; 4th Congress, April, 1954; 5th Congress, July, 1958; 6th Congress, January, 1963; 7th Congress, April, 1967; 8th Congress, June, 1971; 9th Congress, May, 1976.

Hungary: 1st (HWP) Congress, June, 1948; 2nd Congress, March, 1951; 3rd Congress, May, 1954; no congress, August, 1956; 7th (HSWP) Congress, December, 1959; 8th Congress, November, 1962; 9th Congress, December, 1966; 10th Congress, November, 1970; 11th Congress, March, 1975.

Poland: 1st (PWP) Congress, December, 1945; 1st (PUWP) Congress, December, 1948; 2nd Congress, March, 1954; 3rd Congress, March, 1959; 4th Congress, June, 1964; 5th Congress, November, 1968; 6th Congress, December, 1971; 7th Congress, December, 1975.

Romania: 1st (RWP) Congress, February 1948; 2nd Congress, December, 1955; 3rd Congress, June, 1960; 9th (RCP) Congress, July, 1965; 10th Congress, August, 1969; 11th Congress, December, 1974.

USSR 1917-1939: No congress, October, 1917; 8th Congress, March, 1919; 9th Congress, March, 1920; 14th Congress, December, 1925; 15th Congress, December, 1927; 16th Congress, December, 1930; 17th Congress, January, 1934; 18th Congress, March, 1939.

USSR After World War II: 19th Congress, October, 1952; no congress, March, 1953; 20th Congress, February, 1956; 22nd Congress, October, 1961; 23rd Congress, March, 1966; 24th Congress, April, 1971; 25th Congress, March, 1976.

Yugoslavia: 5th Congress, July, 1948; 6th Congress, December, 1952; 7th Congress, April, 1958; 8th Congress, December, 1964; no congress, March, 1969; 10th Congress, May, 1974.

APPENDIX 17

ABBREVIATIONS

Admin.	Administration, Administrative	Georg.	Georgia, Georgian
AE	Active Earners	Gov.	Government
AE	Agricultural Branch of Economy	Gov. Official	Government Official
		Gym.	Gymnasium
Affil.	Affiliation	High.	Higher
Agric.	Agriculture, Agricultural	HFM	Helping Family Members
Alb.	Albania, Albanian	Hung.	Hungarian
Arch.	Architect		
Arm.	Armenian	Illeg.	Illegal
Austr.	Austria	Inc.	Incomplete
Auxiliary	Auxiliary	Inc. Gym.	Incomplete Gymnasium
Azer.	Azerbaidzani	Inc. High.	Incomplete Higher
		Inc. Sec.	Incomplete Secondary
Ban.	Banat	Inc. Univ.	Incomplete University
Belor.	Belorussia, Belorussian	Ind.	Independent
Bess.	Bessarabia	Inst.	Institutional
B-H	Bosnia–Hercegovina	Insts.	Institutions
Bukov.	Bukovina	Int-R	Intellectual Revolutionary
Bulg.	Bulgaria		
		Kos.	Kosovo
Cap.	Capital	Kazakh.	Kazakhstan
CC	Central Committee		
Chem.	Chemistry	Lab.	Laboratory
Coll. Farm	Collective Farm	Lat.	Latvia
Coll. Farm. Chrmn.	Collective Farm Chairmen	Ldrs.	Leaders
Communic.	Communication	Maced.	Macedonia
Comp.	Complete	Manu.	Manual
Con. Camp	Concentration Camp	Mbrs.	Members
Constr.	Construction	Mbrship.	Membership
Coop.	Cooperatives	Milit.	Military
Croat.	Croatia	Mold.	Moldavia
Czech.	Czechoslovakia, Czech Lands	Mont.	Montenegro, Montenegrin
Denom.	Denominations	Nat. Increase	Natural Increase
Depts.	Departments	NFE	No Formal Education
D	Dependents	No.	Number
Direct.	Directors	Nonagric.	Nonagricultural
Dobr.	Dobrudja	NRE	No Revolutionary Experience
Econ.	Economy	Occs.	Occupations
Econs.	Economists	OE	Other Earners
Ed.		Org.	Organizations
Educ.	Education, Educational	Org.	Organ
Element.	Elementary	Organ. Ldrs.	Organizational Leaders
Empl.	Employees	Orgs.	Organs
Engin.	Engineering		
Engrs.	Engineers	Pers.	Personnel
Enterpr.	Enterprises	Pol.	Poland, Polish
Exec. Com.	Executive Committee	Pol. Sc.	Political Science
		Popul.	Population
Fran.	France	Presid.	Presidium
		Protest.	Protestant
Gen. Second.	General Secondary	Po-W	Postwar
Germ.	Germany		

Relig.	Religion	St.-R	Student Revolutionary
Reprs.	Representative	Sw.	Sweden
Resis.	Resistance		
Rev.	Revolutionary	Trans.	Transylvania
Rom.	Romanian	Transp.	Transport
Russ.	Russia, Russian	Turk.	Turkestan
Ruth.	Ruthenia		
		Ukr.	Ukraine, Ukrainian
		Univ.	University
		Uzbek.	Uzbekistan
Second.	Secondary		
Serb.	Serbia	Voj.	Vojvodina
Slov.	Slovak		
Slov.	Slovenia	Wall.	Wallachia
Soc. Dem.	Social Democrat	W-R	Worker Revolutionary
Social. Sect.	Socialist Sector	Yugo.	Yugoslavia
Special.	Specialized	Yr.	Year
Spec. Sec.	Specialized Secondary	Yrs.	Years

BIBLIOGRAPHY

The sources cited below are restricted to those from which data were taken for *The Handbook*, and do not include all works consulted in the preparation of the volume, or containing data relating to the subjects treated therein. In the case of statistical annuals and newspapers used more than once, dates refer to the first and last year from which data were taken. Earlier and later years were also consulted in most cases in the preparation of *The Handbook*.

A Magyar Dolgozók Pártja [Hungarian Workers' Party]. *II. kongresszusának anyagából* [Material of the IId Congress]. Budapest: Szikra, 1951.

A Magyar Szocialista Munkáspárt [Hungarian Socialist Workers' Party]. *VII kongresszusának jegyzőkönyve 1959* [Minutes of the VIIth Congress of 1959]. Budapest: Kossuth Könyvkiadó, 1960.

_____ *VIII kongresszusának jegyzőkönyve 1962* [Minutes of the VIIIth Congress of 1962]. Budapest: Kossuth Könyvkiadó, 1963.

_____ *IX kongresszusának jegyzőkönyve* [Minutes of the IXth Congress]. Budapest: Kossuth Könyvkiadó, 1967.

_____ *X kongresszusának jegyzőkönyve 1970* [Minutes of the Xth Congress of 1970]. Budapest: Kossuth Könyvkiadó, 1971.

Academia Republici Populare Romîne [The Academy of the Peoples Republic of Romania]. *Dictionar enciclopedic romîn* [Encyclopedic Dictionary of Romania]. Bucharest: Editura Politica, 1962-1966.

Albania. Drejtoria e Statistikës [Statistical Office]. *Anuari statistikor i R.P.SH.* [Statistical Annual of the Peoples Republic of Albania]. Tirana: 1958-1961.

_____ _____ *30 vjet Shqipëri socialiste: shifra dhe fakte mbi zhvillimin e ekonomisë dhe kultures* [Thirty Years of Socialist Albania: Figures and Facts on Economic and Social Development]. Tirana: Drejtoria e Përgjithshme e Statistikës, 1974.

_____ _____ *Vjetari statistikor i RP SH* [Statistical Yearbook of the PRA]. Tirana: Drejtoria e Statistikës, 1962-1970.

Alster, A. and Andrzejewski, J. "W sprawie składu socjalnego PZPR [On the Question of the Social Composition of the PUWP]." *Nowe drogi*, vol. 5, no. 1 (Jan.-Feb., 1951), pp. 234-54.

Alton, Thad et al. *Economic Growth in Eastern Europe, 1965-1977*. Occasional Papers of the Research Project on National Income in Eastern Europe, no. 53. New York: Economic Studies, L.W. International Financial Research, Inc., 1978.

Archive on Political Elites in Eastern Europe. University of Pittsburgh Project on Elites in Eastern Europe. "BKP v t͡sifri [The BCP in Figures]." *Partien zhivot*, vol. 18, no. 10 (1974), p. 37.

Balevski, Dano. *Prebroi͡avane 1975. Rezultati. Perspektivi* [The Census of 1975. Results. Perspectives]. Sofia: Partizdat, 1976.

Bol'sha͡ia sovetska͡ia entsiklopedi͡ia [The Great Soviet Encyclopedia]. 1st ed. Moscow: Sovetska͡ia entsiklopedi͡ia, 1926-1947.

Bol'shevik No. 15-16, 1939, p. 113.

Borba, Jan. 24, 1970, Supplement, pp. 22-27.

Breyer, Richard. "Minderheiten im heutigen Polen," *Ostbrief*, vol. 4, no. 6 (Feb., 1958), pp. 265-74.

British Broadcasting System. *Summary of World Broadcasts*. Part 2, *Eastern Europe*. May 3, 1979.

"Brojno stanje i struktura članstva SKJ [The Situation in Respect to the Number and Structure of the Membership of the LCY], *Jugoslovenski pregled*, vol. 11, no. 6 (June, 1967), pp. 19-22.

Buch, Günther. *Namen and Daten: Biographien wichtiger Personen der DDR*. Berlin: J.H.W. Dietz, 1973.

Bulgaria. Glavna Direkt͡si͡ia na Statistikata [Main Directorate of Statistics]. *Obshti rezultati ot prebroi͡avane na naselenieto vu T͡sarstvo Bŭlgari͡ia na 31 dekembrii 1926 god.* [General Results of the Census of the Population of the Kingdom of Bulgaria on 31 December 1926]. Volume 1: *Plan i organizat͡si͡ia na prebroi͡avaneto domakinstva* [Plan and Organizaion of the Census of Households]. Sofia: Dŭrzhavna Pechatnit͡sa, 1931. Volume 2: *Vuzrast, semeĭno polozhenie i gramotnost' na nalichnoto naselenie* [Age, Family Position and Literacy of the Resident Population]. Sofia: Dŭrzhavna Pechatnit͡sa, 1931.

_____ _____ *Prebroi͡avane na naselenieto na 31 dekembriĭ 1934* [Census of the Population of 1934]. Volume 1: *Obshti rezultati: Pol', mi͡estorozhdenie, podanstvo, vi͡eroizpovidanie, govorim' ezik', gramotnost i obrazovanie* [General Results: Sex, Place of Birth, Citizenship, Religion, Spoken Language, Literacy and Education]. Sofia: Dŭrzhavna Pechatnit͡sa, 1938. Volume 2: *Obshti rezultati: Vŭzrast', semeĭno polozhenie i vĭeroizpovĭedanie naselenie* [General Results: Age, Family Status and Religion of the Population] . Sofia: Dŭrzhavna Pechatnifsa, 1937.

_____ _____ *Predvaritelni rezultati prebroĭavane na naselenieto na 31 dekembri 1946: Broi na naselenieto po naseleni mesta* [Preliminary Results of the Population Census of 31 December 1946: The Size of the Population by Settlements] . Sofia: Dŭrzhavna Pechatnifsa, 1947.

_____ _____ *Statisticheski godishnik na Tsarstvo Bŭlgariĭa* [Statistical Annual of the Kingdom of Bulgaria] . Sofia: Glavna Direkfsiĭa na Statistikata, 1936-1940.

_____ Ministerstvo na Informafsiĭata i Suobshteniĭata [Ministry of Information and Communications]. *Naselenie*. Sofia: 1969-1974.

_____ _____ *Statisticheski godishnik na Narodna Republika Bŭlgariĭa* [Statistical Yearbook of the Peoples' Republic of Bulgaria] . Sofia: Ministerstvo na Informatsiĭata i Suobshcheniĭata, 1975-1977.

_____ Tsentralno Statistichesko Upravlenie pri Ministerskiĭa Suvet [Central Statistical Administration of the Council of Ministers] . *Demografska statistika* [Demographic Statistics] . Sofia: 1960-1967.

_____ _____ *Prebroĭavane na naselenieto v Narodna Republika Bŭlgariĭa na 1 XII. 1956 godina* [The Census of the Population in the Peoples' Republic of Bulgaria on 1 XII 1956]. Volume 2: *Obshti rezultati (semeĭstva, kategorii naselenie, nafsionalnost i ravnishte na obrazovanie)* [General Results (Households, Categories of the Population, Nationality and Levels of Education)]. Sofia: Nauka i Izkustvo, 1960. Volume 3: *Obshti rezultati (zanĭatie, obshtestveni i vuzrastovi grupi i ravnishte na obrazovanie)* [General Results (Occupations, Social and Age Groups and Levels of Education)]. Sofia: Nauka i Izkustvo, 1960.

_____ _____ *Rezultati ot prebroĭavaneto na naselenieto na 1 dekembri 1965 godina (tri profsentova reprezentativna razrabotka)* [Results of the Census of the Population of 1 December 1965 (Three Percent Representative Sample)] . Sofia: Ts. St. Upr., 1966.

_____ _____ *Rezultati ot prebroĭavane na naselenieto na 1.XII.1965 g.*. Volume 1: *Chast Purva: Obshto za NR Bŭlgariĭa* [First Part: General for the PR of Bulgaria] . Sofia: Ts. St. Upr., 1968.

_____ _____ *Returns of the 1 December 1965 Population Census in the Peoples Republic of Bulgaria (Three Percent Advanced Sample Tabulation)*. Sofia: Central Statistical Office, 1966.

_____ _____ *Statisticheskiĭ ezhegodnik–Statistical Yearbook*. Sofia: Tsentral'noe Statisticheskoe Upravlenie, 1968-76.

Bŭlgarska Komunisticheska Partiĭa [Bulgarian Communist Party]. *Deseti kongres na Bŭlgarskata Komunisticheska Partiĭa* [Tenth Congress of the Bulgarian Communist Party] . Sofia: Partizdat, 1971.

_____ *IX Kongres na Bŭlgarskata Komunisticheska Partiĭa* [IXth Congress of the Bulgarian Communist Party] . Sofia: BKP, 1967.

_____ *Osmi kongres na Bŭlgarskata Komunisticheska Part ĭa* [Eighth Congress of the Bulgarian Communist Party] . Sofia: BKP, 1963.

_____ *Peti kongres na Bŭlgarskata Komunisticheska Partiĭa 18-25 dekembri 1948. Stenografski protokol* [Fifth Congress of the Bulgarian Communist Party 18-25 December 1948. Stenographic Record] . Sofia: BKP, 1949.

_____ *Shesti kongres na Bŭlgarskata Komunisticheska Partiĭa 25 februari 3 mart 1954. Stenografski protokol* [The Sixth Congress of the Bulgarian Communist Party 25 February to 3 March 1954. Stenographic Record] . Sofia: BKP, 1954.

Bukowski, Ludwik. "Portret partii [Portrait of the Party] ." *Życie partii* no. 12 (Dec. 8-12, 1975), pp. 3-5.

Burks, R. V. *The Dynamics of Communism in Eastern Europe*. Princeton: Princeton University Press, 1961.

Busek, Vratislav, and Spulber, Nicolas, eds. *East Central Europe Under the Communists: Czechoslovakia*. New York: Praeger, 1957.

Byrnes, Robert F., ed. *East Central Europe Under the Communists: Yugoslavia*. New York: Praeger, 1957.

Central Intelligence Agency. National Foreign Assessment Center. *Handbook of Economic Statistics 1978*. Washington, D.C.: GPO, 1978.

"Cikánské obyvatelstvo v ČSSR [Gypsy Population in the Czechoslovak Socialist Republic] ." *Demografie*, vol. 9, no. 3 (1967), pp. 276-79.

Cingo, Nikola. "The Macedonians and the First Population Census in Post-War Bulgaria." *Socialist Thought and Practice*, vol. 16, no. 2 (Feb., 1976), pp. 56-76.

"Članstvo Saveza Komunista Jugoslavije [Membership of the League of Communists of Yugoslavia] ." *Jugoslovenski pregled*, vol. 3, no. 7-8 (July-Aug., 1964), pp. 293-95.

_____ *Jugoslovenski pregled*, vol. 20, no. 12 (Dec., 1976), pp. 453-58.

"The CPSU in Figures." *Soviet Law and Government*, vol. 15, no. 3 (Winter, 1976-77), pp. 3-23.

Czechoslovakia. Federální Statistický Úřad. *Předběžné výsledky sčítání lidu, domů, a bytů k 1.prosinci 1970 v ČSSR* [Preliminary Results of the Census of the Population, Households and Dwellings of 1 December 1970 in the CSR]. Volume 1: *1. Díl* [Part 1]. Prague: Federální Statistický Úřad, 1971. Volume 2: *2. Díl—2% výběrové šetření* [Part 2—2% Selected Sample]. Prague: Federální Statistický Úřad, 1971. Volume 3: *Mikrocensus 1970. 2% výběrové šetření—príjmová část. 3. díl.* [Microcensus of 1970. 2% Selected Sample]. Prague: Federální Statistický Úřad, 1972.

———— ———— *Statistická ročenka ČSSR* [Statistical Annual of the CSR]. Prague: SNTL, 1957-1976.

———— Státí Úřad Statistický. *Volkszählung in der Tschechoslovakischen Republik vom 15. Februar 1921.* Volume 1: *I. Teil.* Prague: Státní Úřad Statistický, 1924.

———— ———— *Statistická ročenka Republiky Československé* [Statistical Annual of the Republic of Czechoslovakia]. Prague: Státní Úřad Statistický, 1937-1938.

———— ———— *Sčítání lidu v Republice Československé ze dne 1. prosince 1930* [The Census of the Population of Czechoslovakia of 1 December 1930]. Volume 1: *Růst, koncentrace a hustota obyvatelstva, pohlaví, věkové rozvrstvení, rodinny stav, státní příslušnost, národnost, náboženské vyznání* [Growth, Concentration, and Density of the Population, Sex, Age Structure, Family Status, Citizenship, Nationality and Religion]. Československá statistika svazek 98. Prague: Státní Úřad Statistický, 1934.

———— Ústřední Komise Lidové Kontroly a Statistiky [Central Commission of People's Control and Statistics]. *Dvacet let rozvoje Československé Socialistické Republiky* [20 Years of Development of the Czechoslovak Socialist Republic]. Prague: Nakladatelství Politické Literatury, 1965.

———— ———— *Sčítání lidu, domů a bytů v Československé Socialistické Republice k 1. březnu 1961* [Census of the Population, Dwellings and Apartments, March, 1961]. Volume 1: *Demografické charackteristiky obyvatelstva* [Demographic Characteristics of the Population]. *Československá statistika, nová řada,* svazek 35. Prague: Ústřední Komise Lidové Kontroly a Statistiky, 1965. Volume 2: *Socialní, ekonomická a profesionální skladba obyvatelstva* [Social, Economic and Professional Structure of the Population]. *Československá statistika, nová řada,* svazek 36. Prague: Ústřední Komise Lidové Kontroly a Statistiky, 1965.

———— ———— *Vývoj společnosti ČSSR v číslech: rozbory výsledků sčítání lidu, domů, a bytů.* [The Development of the Society of the CSR in Figures: Summary Results of the Census of Population, Dwellings and Apartments]. Prague: SEVT, 1965.

Dellin, L.E.D., ed. *East Central Europe Under the Communists: Bulgaria.* New York: Praeger, 1957.

X s'ezd Vengerskoĭ Sofsialisticheskoĭ Rabocheĭ Partii [X Congress of the Hungarian Socialist Workers' Party]. Moscow: Gosudarstvennoe Izdatel'stvo Politicheskoĭ Literatury, 1971.

IX s'ezd Vengerskoĭ Sofsialisticheskoĭ Rabocheĭ Partii [IX Congress of the Hungarian Socialist Workers' Party]. Moscow: Gosudarstvennoe Izdatel'stvo Politicheskoĭ Literatury, 1967.

Dilo, Jani I. *The Communist Party Leadership in Albania.* Washington, D.C.: Georgetown University Institute of Ethnic Studies, 1961.

Enciklopedija Jugoslavije [Yugoslav Encyclopedia]. Zagreb: Leksikografski Zavod FNRJ, 1955-1971.

Enciklopedija Leksikografskog Zavoda [Encyclopedia of the Lexicographic Society]. Zagreb: Jugoslovenski Leksikografski Zavod, 1966-1969.

Einheit, No. 10, 1973, p. 1189.

"Endgültige Ergebnisse der Volks- und Berufszählung vom 29. Oktober 1946." *Statistische Praxis*, no. 3 (Oct., 1948), entire issue.

Federal Republic of Germany. Bundesministerium für Gesamtdeutschen Fragen. *A bis Z: Ein Taschen-und Nachschlagebuch über den anderen Teil Deutschlands.* Bonn: Deutscher Bundes-Verlag, 1969.

———— ———— *DDR Handbuch.* Cologne: Verlag Wissenschaft und Politik, 1975.

———— ———— *SBZ Biographie.* Berlin: n.p., 1964.

Fischer-Galati, Stephen, ed. *East Central Europe Under the Communists: Romania.* New York: Praeger, 1957.

Food and Agricultural Organization. *Provisional Food Balance Sheets, 1972-1974 Average.* Rome, FAO, 1977.

Foreign Broadcast Information Service. *Daily Report.* Washington, D.C.: GPO, 1976-1979.

Fortsch, Eckart. *Die SED.* Stuttgart: W. Kohlhammer Verlag, 1969.

25 Jahre Deutsche Demokratische Republik: Eine Bilanz in Tatsachen und Zahlen. Berlin: Dietz Verlag, 1974.

Geilke, Georg, ed. *Fragen des Mitteleuropäischen Minderheitenrechts.* Munich: Institut für Ostrecht, 1967.

Gorá, Władysław. *Polska Rzeczpospolita Ludowa 1944-1974* [The Polish People's Republic]. Warsaw: Książka i Wiedza, 1974.

German Democratic Republic. Staatliche Zentralverwaltung für Statistik. *Ergebnisse der Volks-und Berufszählung am 31. Dezember 1964.* Berlin: Staatsverlag der Deutschen Demokratischen Republik, 1967.

———— ———— *Ergebnisse über die Struktur der wirtschaftlich tätigen Wohnbevölkerung.* Berlin: Staatsverlag der Deutschen Demokratischen Republik, 1966.

_____ _____ *Statistisches Jahrbuch der Deutschen Demokratischen Republik*. Berlin: Staatsverlag der Deutschen Demokratischen Republik, 1955-1976.

_____ _____ *Volks-, Beruf-, and Gebäudezählung am 1. Januar 1971*, vol. 1. Berlin: Staatsverlag der Deutschen Demokratischen Republik, 1971.

Gheorghiu-Dej, Gheorghe. *Raportul C.C. al P.M.R. cu privire la activitatea partidului în perioda dintre congresul al II-lea și congresul al III-lea al partidului* [The Report of the C.C. of the Romanian Workers' Party in Consideration of the Activity of the Party Between the Second and Third Congress of the Party]. Bucharest: Editura Politică, 1960.

Ginić, Ivanka. *Dinamika i struktura gradskog stanovništva Jugoslavije: Demografski aspekt urbanizacije* [The Dynamics and Structure of the Urban Population of Yugoslavia: The Demographic Aspects of Urbanization]. Belgrade: Institut Društvenih Nauka, 1967.

Habel, Walter, ed. *Wer ist Wer*, vol. 2. Berlin: Arani Verlag, 1965.

Hafner, Vinko. "Kako menjati socijalni sastav Saveza Komunista [How to Change the Social Composition of the League of Communists]. *Komunist*, no. 846 (June 4, 1973), p. 10.

Halecki, Oscar, ed. *East Central Europe Under the Communists: Poland*. New York: Praeger, 1957.

Haupt, Georges and Marie, Jean Jacques. *Makers of The Russian Revolution*. Ithaca: Cornell University Press, 1974.

Helmreich, Ernst C., ed. *East Central Europe Under the Communists: Hungary*. New York: Praeger, 1957.

Herod, Czesław. "Kształtowanie się składu i struktury społeczno-zawodowej PZPR [The Formation of the Socio-Occupational Composition and Structure of the PUWP]," *Nowe drogi*, no. 2 (1971), pp. 79-86.

Hoover Institution. *Yearbook on International Communist Affairs*. Stanford: Hoover Institution, 1966-1978.

Hoxha, Enver. *Rapport d'Activite du Comite Central du Parti du Travail d'Albanie*. Tirana: Naim Frashëri, 1971.

_____ *Report on the Activity of the Central Committee of The Party of Labour of Albania Held at the 4th Congress of the PLA on February 13, 1961*. Tirana: Naim Frasheri, 1961.

_____ *Report on the Activity of the Central Committee of The Party of Labour of Albania*. Tirana: Naim Frasheri, 1971.

_____ *Report to the 7th Congress of the Albanian Party of Labor*. New York: Gamma Publishing Co., 1976.

Human Relations Area Files. *Contemporary Poland: Society, Politics, Economy*. Chicago, HRAF, 1955.

Hungary. Hungarian Statistical Office. *Statistical Yearbook/Statisticheskii ezhegodnik*. Budapest: Hungarian Central Statistical Office, 1966-1975.

_____ Központi Statisztikai Hivatal [Hungarian Statistical Office]. *Annuaire statistique Hongrois*. Budapest: Központi Statisztikai Hivatal, 1932-1934.

_____ _____ *Demográfiai évkönyv* [Demographic Annual]. Budapest: Központi Statisztikai Hivatal, 1975.

_____ _____ *Munkaügyi adattár 1949-1966* [Labor Statistics, 1949-1966]. Budapest: Központi Statisztikai Hivatal, 1968.

_____ _____ *Recensement général de la population en 1930*. Volume 1: *Données démographiques*. Budapest: Imprimerie Stephaneum Société Anonyme, 1933.

_____ _____ *1941 évi népszámlálás. Demográfiai adatok* [The Census of 1941. Demographic Data]. Budapest: Stephaneum Nyomda Részvénytársaság, 1947.

_____ _____ *1949 évi népszámlálás* [The 1949 Census]. Volume 6: *Foglalkozásstatisztikai eredmények* [Occupational Statistics Results]. Budapest: Állami Nyomda, 1950.

_____ _____ *1960 évi népszámlálás* [The 1960 Census]. Volume 2: *Személyi és családi adatok képviseleti minta alapján* [Individual and Family Data on the Basis of a Representative Sample]. Budapest: Központi Statisztikai Hivatal, 1960. Volume 13: *Összefoglaló adatok* [Summary of the Data]. Budapest: Központi Statisztikai Hivatal, 1964. Volume 33: *Az adatfelvétel és feldoglozás összefoglaló ismertetése* [Summary Description of the Collection and Evaluation of the Data]. Budapest: Központi Statisztikai Hivatal, 1965.

_____ _____ *1970 évi népszámlálás* [The 1970 Census]. Volume 2: *Részletes adatok az 1%-os képviseleti minta alapján* [Detailed Data on the Basis of the 1% Representative Sample]. Budapest: Központi Statisztikai Hivatal, 1971. Volume 24: *Foglalkozási adatok I.* [Occupational Data I.]. Budapest: Központi Statisztikai Hivatal, 1973.

"Increase of Urban Population." *Yugoslav Survey*, vol. 5, no. 18 (July–Sept., 1964), pp. 2559-66.

Institute for the Study of the USSR. *Biographic Directory of the USSR*. New York: Scarecrow Press, 1958.

_____ *Party and Government Officials of the Soviet Union, 1917-1967*. Metuchen, N.J.: Scarecrow Press, 1969.

_____ *Prominent Personalities in the USSR*. Metuchen, N.J.: Scarecrow Press, 1968.

_____ *Who Was Who in the USSR*. Metuchen, N.J.: Scarecrow Press, 1972.

International Labour Office. *International Standard Classification of Occupations. Revised Edition 1948*. Geneva: International Labour Office, 1969.

_____ *Labour Force Estimates and Projections*, 2d ed. Volume 4: *Northern America, Europe, Oceania and USSR*. Geneva: International Labour Office, 1977.

_____ *Year Book of Labour Statistics*. Geneva: International Labour Office, 1943-1977.

I͡udin, I. N. *Sofsial'nai͡a baza rosta KPSS* [Social Basis of the Growth of the CPSU]. Moscow: Izdatel'stvo Politicheskoĭ Literatury, 1973.

Ivanov, K. *Chlenstvoto v partii͡ata i reguliraneto na neĭnii͡a sustav* [Membership in the Party and Regulating its Composition]. Sofia: BKP, 1956.

Jarzabek, William A. *A Volume of Interpretive Codebooks: Archive on Political Elites in Eastern Europe*. Pittsburgh: University Center for International Studies, 1972.

Joint Publications Research Service, No. 69438 (1977).

Kadar, I͡a. *O politicheskom polozhenii i zadachakh partii* [On the Political Position and Tasks of the Party]. Moscow: Gosudarstvennoe Izdatel'stvo Politicheskoĭ Literatury, 1960.

Kdo je kdo v Československu [Who's Who in Czechoslovakia]. Prague: Československá Tisková Kancelář, 1969.

Ki kicsoda [Who's Who], 1st ed. Budapest: Kossuth Könyvkiadó, 1969.

Ki kicsoda [Who's Who], 2d ed. Budapest: Kossuth Könyvkiadó, 1972.

Kalynowych, Wasyl. "The Top Elite of the Communist Party of the USSR in 1919-1971: A Comparative Study." PhD: Indiana University, 1972.

Ko je ko u Jugoslaviji [Who's Who in Yugoslavia]. Belgrade: Sedme Sile, 1957.

_____ Belgrade: Savez Lekarskih Društava Jugoslavije, 1968.

Komunistické Strany Československa. Ústřední Výbor [Communist Party of Czechoslovakia, Central Committee]. *XII sjezd Komunistické Strany Československa* [XII Congress of the Communist Party of Czechoslovakia]. Prague: Nakladatelství Politické Literatury, 1963.

_____ _____ *Protokol IX sjezdu Komunistické Strany Československa* [Minutes of the 9th Congress of the Communist Party of Czechoslovakia]. Prague: Ústřední Výbor KSČ, 1950.

_____ _____ *XIII sjezd Komunistické Strany Československa* [XIII Congress of the Communist Party of Czechoslovakia]. Prague: Svoboda, 1967.

_____ _____ *Usnesení a dokumenty ÚV KSČ* [Resolutions and Documents of the CC of the CPC]. Prague: Nakladatelství Politické Literatury, 1964.

Kovrig, Bennett. "Hungary." *Communism in Eastern Europe*, Teresa Rakowska Harmstone and Andrew Gyorgy, eds., pp. 71-79. Bloomington: Indiana University Press, 1979.

Kozlov, V. I. *Nafsional'nosti SSSR (Etnodemografskii obzor)* [Nationalities of the USSR (Ethnographic Survey)]. Moscow: Statistika, 1975.

"KPSS v fsifrakh (1956-1961 gg.) [The CPSU in figures (1956-1961)]." *Partiinai͡a zhizn*, no. 1 (Jan., 1962), pp. 44-54.

"KPSS v fsifrakh (1961-1964 gody) [The CPSU in Figures (1961-1964)]," *Partiinai͡a zhizn*, no. 10 (May, 1965), pp. 8-17.

"KPSS v fsifrakh [The CPSU in Figures]," *Partiinai͡a zhizn*, no. 19 (Oct., 1967), pp. 8-20.

"KPSS v fsifrakh [The CPSU in Figures]." *Partiinai͡a zhizn*, no. 14 (July, 1973), pp. 11-26.

Kraterski, Andrzej. "Konsekwencja warunkiem prawidłowego wzrostu szeregów partyjnych [Consistency as the Condition of the Appropriate Increase of Party Membership]." *Życie partii*, no. 9 (1974), pp. 6-7.

Kratka Bŭlgarska entsiklopedii͡a [Short Bulgarian Encyclopedia]. Sofia: Bŭlgarska Akademii͡a na Naukite, 1963-1969.

Kuhn, Heinrich. *Biographisches Handbuch der Tschechoslowakei*. 5th ed. Munich: Verlag Robert Lerche, 1975.

Kwilecki, Andrzej. "Mniejszości narodowe w Polsce Ludowej [National Minorities in People's Poland]." *Kultura i społeczeństwo*, vol. 7, no. 4 (1963), pp. 85-103.

Landy-Tołwińska, Joanna. *Analfabetyzm w Polsce i na świecie* [Illiteracy in Poland and in the World]. Warsaw: Wiedza Powszechna, 1961.

League of Nations. *Monthly Bulletin of Statistics*, Aug., 1943, p. 208.

_____ *Statistical Yearbook*. Geneva: League of Nations, 1938-1939.

Levytsky, Boris. *The Soviet Political Elite*. Stanford: Hoover Institution, 1970.

Lewytzkyj, Borys, and Stroynowski, Juliusz, eds. *Who's Who in the Socialist Countries*. New York and Munich: K. G. Saur Publishing Co., 1978.

"Liczby dotyczące składu partii [Figures Concerning the Make-Up of the Party]. *Nowe drogi*, vol. 11, no. 7 (July, 1957), pp. 125–27.

Lorimer, Frank. *The Population of the Soviet Union: History and Prospects*. Geneva: League of Nations, 1946.

McCartney, C. A. *National States and National Minorities*. London: Oxford University Press, 1934.

Markert, Werner, ed. *Osteuropa Handbuch: Jugoslawien*. Cologne: Böhlau Verlag, 1954.

Magyar életrajzi lexikon [Hungarian Biographical Dictionary], 2 vols. Budapest: Akadémiai Kiadó, 1969.

Máté, György. "Gondolatok pártunk összetételének alakulásáról [Thoughts About the Development of the Composition of the Party]." *Társadalmi szemle*, vol. 19, no. 2 (Feb., 1964), pp. 33–82.

Materiali III s'ezda Albanskoĭ Partii Truda (25 Maiâ–3 Iiûniâ 1956 goda) [Material from the III Congress of the Albanian Party of Labor (25 May–3 June 1956)]. Moscow: Gosudarstvennoe Izdatel'stvo Politicheskoĭ Literatury, 1957.

"Membership of the League of Communists of Yugoslavia." *Yugoslav Survey*, vol. 3, no. 4 (1967), pp. 39–48.

Milić, Vladimir and Tozi, Djoko. "Preobražaj i socijalna struktura Saveza Komunista Jugoslavije [Transformation and Social Structure of the League of Communists of Yugoslavia]." *Socijalizam*, vol. 14, no. 7–8 (1971), pp. 832–48.

Milo, Pasko, "Popullsia e Republikës Popullore të Shqipërisë sipas regjistrimit të tetorit 1955 [The Population of the People's Republic of Albania According to the Census of October 1955]. *Ekonomia Popullore*, no. 5 (1957), pp. 53–69.

National Committee for a Free Europe, Research and Publications Service. *Organization and Strategy of the Hungarian Workers' Party*. New York: Radio Free Europe, Oct. 1952.

"Nekotorye itogi perepisi naseleniiâ 1939 g. [Some Results of the Census of the Population of 1939]." *Vestnik statistiki*, no. 6 (1956), pp. 89–90.

Népszabadság, March 16, 1975, Supplement, p. 2.

Neues Deutschland, May 19, 1976, p. 12.

Nikolić, Miloš, ed. *Savez Komunista u uslovima samoupravljanja: Zbornik tekstova* [The League of Communists Under Conditions of Self-Management: Collection of Texts]. Belgrade: Kultura, 1967.

NIN, October 8, 1972, p. 10.

"O statisticheskikh pokazataliâkh urovniâ obrazovaniiâ i gramotnosti naseleniiâ [On the Statistical Indicators of the Level of Education and Literacy of the Population]." *Vestnik statistiki*, no. 2 (1972), pp. 39–43.

XI s'ezd Kommunisticheskoĭ Partii Chekhoslovakii [The XI Congress of the Communist Party of Czechoslovakia]. Moscow: Gosudarstvennoe Izdatel'stvo Politicheskoĭ Literatury, 1959.

Ostrowski, Krzysztof, and Suflin, Zbigniew. "Problemy rozwoju partii między IV a V zjazdem [Problems of the Development of the Party Between the IV and V Congress]. *Nowe drogi*, vol. 23, no. 1 (Jan., 1969), pp. 30–36.

Partia e Punës se Shqipërisë [The Albanian Party of Labor]. *Kongresi IV i Partisë së Punës se Shqipërisë* [The IVth Party Congress of the Albanian Party of Labor]. Tirana: Naim Frashëri, 1961.

Partidul Comunist Român [The Romanian Communist Party]. *Congresul al IX-lea al Partidului Comunist Român 19–24 iulie 1965* [IXth Congress of the Romanian Communist Party 19–24 July, 1965]. Bucharest: Editura Politică, 1966.

_____ *Die Landeskonferenz der Rumänischen Kommunistischen Partei 19–21. Juli 1972* [The National Conference of the Romanian Communist Party 19–21 July 1972]. Bucharest: Politischer Verlag, 1972.

Partidul Muncitoresc Romîn [Romanian Workers' Party]. *Congesul al II-lea al Partidului Muncitoresc Romîn 23–28 decembrie 1955* [IInd Congress of the Romanian Workers' Party 23–28 December 1955]. Bucharest: Literatura Politică, 1956.

_____ *Raportul C.C. al P.M.R. cu privire la activitațae partidului in perioda dintre congresul al II-lea și congesul al III-lea al Partidului* [Report of the C.C. of the R.W.P. in Respect to the Activity of the Party in the Period Between the IInd Congress and the IIIrd Congress of the Party]. Bucharest: Editura Politică, 1960.

"Pismenost i školska sprema stanovništva [Literacy and Schooling of the Population]," *Jugoslovenski pregled*, vol. 8, no. 3 (March, 1964), pp. 9–16.

Poland. Główny Urząd Statystyczny [Main Statistical Office]. *Drugi powszechny spis ludności z dn. 9 XII 1931 r. Mieszkania i gospodarstwa domowe. Ludność. Stosunki zawodowe. Polska (dane skrócone)* [Second General Census of the Population of 9 XII 1931. Apartments and Households. Population. Professional Relationships. Poland. Abridged Data]. Warsaw: Główny Urząd Statystyczny, 1937.

_____ _____ *Concise Statistical Yearbook of Poland*. Warsaw. Główny Urząd Statystyczny, 1938.

_____ _____ *Drugi powszechny spis ludności z dn. 9 XII 1931 r.. Mieszkania i gospodarstwa domowe. Ludność* [Second General Census of the Population of 9 XII 1931. Apartments and Households. Population]. Warsaw: Główny Urząd Statystyczny, 1938.

_____ _____ *Kobieta w Polsce* [Women in Poland]. Warsaw: Główny Urząd Statystyczny, 1975.

_____ _____ *Ludność Polski w latach 1945-1965* [The Population of Poland 1945-1965]. *Seria studia i prace statystyczne*, zeszyt 1. Warsaw: Główny Urząd Statystyczny, 1966.

_____ _____ *Narodowy spis powszechny 8 XII 1970. Wyniki ostateczne* [General National Census of 8 XII 1970. Final Results]. Volumes consulted include: *Struktura demograficzna i zawodowa ludności. Gospodarstwa domowe. Polska* [Demographic and Occupational Structure of the Population. Households. Poland]. *Seria ludność*, zeszyt 23. Warsaw: Główny Urząd Statystyczny, 1976.

_____ _____ *Polska w liczbach* [Poland in Figures]. Warsaw: Główny Urząd Statystyczny, 1976.

_____ _____ *Powszechny sumaryczny spis ludności z dn. 14. II. 1946 r.* [General Summary Census of the Population of 14 II 1946]. Warsaw: Główny Urząd Statystyczny, 1947.

_____ _____ *Rocznik demograficzny 1945-1966* [Demographic Yearbook 1945-1966]. Warsaw: Główny Urząd Statystyczny, 1966.

_____ _____ *Rocznik demograficzny* [Demographic Yearbook]. Warsaw: Główny Urząd Statystyczny, 1967-1975.

_____ _____ *Rocznik statystyczny* [Statistical Annual]. Warsaw: Główny Urząd Statystyczny, 1947-1977.

_____ _____ *Rocznik statystyczny pracy 1945-1968* [Yearbook of Labor Force Statistics 1945-1968]. Warsaw: Główny Urząd Statystyczny, 1970.

_____ _____ *Spis ludności i mieszkań metodą reprezentacyjną. Stan w dniu 30 III 1974. Struktura demograficzna i społeczno-zawodowa ludności, gospodarstwa domowe i rodziny* [Population and Housing Census According to a Representative Sample. Situation as of 30 III 1974. Demographic and Socio-Occupational Structure of the Population, Households and Families]. Warsaw: Główny Urząd Statystyczny, 1975.

_____ _____ *Spis powszechny z dnia 6 grudnia 1960 r. Wyniki ostateczne: Ludność, gospodarstwa domowe, Polska* [General Census of December 6, 1960. Final Results: Population, Households, Poland]. Warsaw: Główny Urząd Statystyczny, 1965.

_____ _____ *Wybrane dane o kwalifikacjach i dojazdach do pracy zatrudnionych w gospodarce uspołecznionej. Wyniki spisu kadrowego 1973 r.* [Selected Data on the Qualifications and the Commuting of Persons Employed in the Socialist Economy. Results of the Cadre Census of 1973]. Warsaw: Główny Urząd Statystyczny, 1976.

Politika, April 14, 1978, p. 6.

"Poljoprivredno stanovništvo [Agricultural Population]." *Jugoslovenski Pregled*, vol. 21, no. 10 (Oct., 1977), pp. 13-18.

"Prehlad najvyšších organov KSS v rokoch 1944-1966 [Review of the Highest Organs of the SCP in the Years 1944-1966]." *Příspěvky k Dějinám KSČ*, vol. 6, no. 5 (1966), pp. 736-64.

Rabotnichesko Delo, Dec. 30, 1975.

Radio Free Europe. "An Albanian Case Study of Party Composition and Problems." *Radio Free Europe Research, Albania*, Sept. 4, 1967.

_____ "The BCP Congress: Changes in the Politburo and Secretariat." *Radio Free Europe Research, Bulgaria*, no. 11 (April 5, 1976).

_____ "Biographies of Trade Union Leaders in Eastern Europe." *Radio Free Europe Research, Eastern Europe*, no. 8 (May 17, 1973).

_____ "The Bulgarian Party Leadership." *Radio Free Europe Research, Bulgaria*, no. 10 (Sept. 8, 1972).

_____ "The Czechoslovak Party Leadership." *Radio Free Europe Research, Czechoslovakia*, no. 2 (Aug. 28, 1972).

_____ "Eastern Europe's Communist Leaders: Hungary." *Radio Free Europe Research, Hungary*, June 20, 1966.

_____ "Eastern Europe's Communist Leaders, Part II: Poland." *Radio Free Europe Research, Poland*, Sept. 1, 1966.

_____ "Eastern Europe's Communist Leaders, Part III: Rumania," *Radio Free Europe Research, Rumania*, Sept. 1, 1966.

_____ "Eastern Europe's Communist Leaders: Part V, Bulgaria." *Radio Free Europe Research, Bulgaria*, Sept. 1, 1966.

_____ Eastern Europe's Communist Leaders: Bulgaria, Addenda." *Radio Free Europe Research, Bulgaria*, March 20, 1967.

_____ "The HSWP: A Statistical Profile." *Radio Free Europe Research, Hungary*, no. 29 (Nov. 20, 1970).

_____ "The Hungarian Party Leadership." *Radio Free Europe Research, Hungary*, no. 16 (Sept. 11, 1972).

_____ "Latest Figures on Party Structure." *Radio Free Europe Research, Rumania*, no. 19 (May 18, 1971).

_____ "Poland's Communist Leaders." *Radio Free Europe Research, Poland*, no. 19 (June 2, 1972).

_____ "Selected Demographic Data on Eastern Europe." *RAD Background Report*, no. 225 (Nov. 3, 1976).

Rigby, T. H. *Communist Party Membership in the USSR 1917-1967*. Princeton: Princeton University Press, 1968.

_____ "The Soviet Politburo, A Comparative Profile, 1951-1971." *Soviet Studies*, vol. 24, no. 1 (July, 1972), pp. 3-23.

"Raspredelenie postoĭannogo naseleniiâ SSSR po istochnikam sredstv sushchestvovaniiâ [Distribution of the Population of the USSR According to Sources of Means of Support]." *Vestnik statistiki*, no. 3 (1973), pp. 83-94.

"Rise in the Urban Population, 1969-1971" *Yugoslav Survey*, vol. 14, no. 2 (May, 1973), pp. 45-54.

Rocznik polityczny i gospodarczy [Political and Economic Almanac]. Warsaw: Polskie Wydawnictwa Gospodarcze, 1958-1975.

Romania. Direcţiunea Centrală de Statistică [Central Statistical Office]. *Anuarul statistic al Republicii Socialiste Romania* [Statistical Annual of the Socialist Republic of Romania]. Bucharest: Editura Ştiinţifică, 1957-1976.

_____ _____ *Recensămîntul populaţiei din 21 februarie 1956* [The Population Census of 21 February 1956]. Volume 1: *Rezultate generale* [General Results]. Bucharest: Direcţia Centrală de Statistică, 1959. Volume 2: *Structura social-economică a populaţiei—Populaţia activă, populaţia pasivă; grupe sociale; ramuri, subramuri de activitate* [Socio-Economic Structure of the Population—Active Population, Passive Population; Social Groups; Branches, Subbranches of Activity]. Bucharest: Direcţia Centrală de Statistică, n.d. Volume 3: *Structura demografică a populaţiei* [Demographic Structure of the Population]. Bucharest: Direcţia Centrală de Statistică, n.d.

_____ _____ *Recensămîntul populaţiei şi locuinţelor din 15 martie 1966* [Census of the Population and Dwellings of 15 March 1966]. Volume 1: *Rezultate generale, Part I; Populaţie* [General Results, Part I; Population]. Bucharest: Direcţia Centrală de Statistică, 1969.

_____ Direcţia Centrală de Comisia Natională de Statistică, Comisia Natională de Demografie [Central Office of the National Commission for Statistics, National Commission for Demography]. *Anuarul demografia al Republici Socialiste România* [Demographic Yearbook of the Socialist Republic of Romania]. Bucharest: Direcţia Centrală de Statistică, 1967-1977.

_____ Institut Central de Statistică [Central Statistical Institute]. *Anuarul statistic al Romaniei 1937 si 1938* [Statistical Annual of Romania 1937 and 1938]. Bucharest: Imprimeria Natională, 1939.

_____ _____ *Recensământul general al populaţiei României din 29 decemvrie 1930* [General Census of the Population of Romania of 29 December 1930]. Volume 2: *Neam, limba maternă, religie* [Nationality, Maternal Language, Religion]. Bucharest: Tiparit la Monitorul Oficial, Imprimeria Natională, 1938.

Rudé právo, 1966.

Sadowski, Michał. *Przemiany społeczne a system partyjny PRL* [Social Change and the Party System in the PPR]. Warsaw: Książka i Wiedza, 1969.

_____ "Przemiany społeczne a partie polityczne PRL [Social Change and Political Parties in the PPR]. *Studia socjologiczne*, vol. 8, no. 3 (1968), pp. 89-113.

Sándor, József. "Pártunk szervezeti fejlődésének néhány kérdése [Our Party Organization and Development a Few Questions]." *Társadalmi szemle*, vol. 16, no. 6 (June, 1961), pp. 37-47.

Savez Komunista Jugoslavije [League of Communists of Yugoslavia]. *Deveti kongres Saveza Komunista Jugoslavije* [Ninth Congress of the League of Communists of Yugoslavia]. Belgrade: Kultura, 1969.

_____ *Osmi kongres Saveza Komunista Jugoslavije* [Eighth Congress of the League of Communists]. Belgrade: Kultura, 1964.

_____ *VII kongres SKJ: Izveštaj Centralnog Komiteta i Centralne Revizione Komisije SKJ o radu od sedmog do osmog kongresa SKJ* [VIIth Congress of the LCY: Report of the Central Committee and the Central Revision Commission of the LCY on the Work from the Seventh to the Eighth Congress of the LCY]. Belgrade: Kultura, 1964.

_____ *VI kongres Komunističke Partije Jugoslavije (Savez Komunista Jugoslavije)* [VIth Congress of the Communist Party of Yugoslavia (League of Communists of Yugoslavia)]. Belgrade: Kultura, 1953.

Schueller, G. K. *The Politburo*. Stanford: Stanford University Press, 1951.

Schulz, Heinrich and Taylor, Stephen S. *Who's Who in the USSR 1965-1966*. New York: Scarecrow Press, 1966.

Scînteia, 1961-1975.

VII s'ezd Bolgarskoĭ Kommunisticheskoĭ Partii [VIIth Congress of the Bulgarian Communist Party]. Moscow: Gosudarstvennoe Izdatel'stvo Politicheskoĭ Literatury, 1958.

VII s'ezd Vengerskoĭ Sofsialisticheskoĭ Rabocheĭ Partii [VIIth Congress of the Hungarian Socialists Worker's Party]. Moscow: Gosudarstvennoe Izdatel'stvo Politicheskoĭ Literatury, 1958.

Sivignon, Michel. "Quelques données démographiques sur la République Populaire d'Albanie." *Revue de Géographie de Lyon*, no. 1 (1970), pp. 60-74.

Sheri, F. *Popullsia e Shqipërisë* [The Population of Albania]. Tirana: Shëpia Botuse "Naim Frashëri," 1970.

Shoup, Paul. *Communism and the Yugoslav National Question*. New York: Columbia University Press, 1968.

Sovet Ekonomicheskoĭ Vzaimopomoshchi. Sekretariat [Council for Mutual Economic Assistance. Secretariat]. *Statisticheskiĭ ezhegodnik stran-chlenov Soveta Ekonomicheskoĭ Vzaimopomoshchi* [Statistical Annual of the Member Countries of the Council for Mutual Economic Assistance]. Moscow: Statistika, 1974-1977.

Sozialistische Einheitspartei Deutschlands [Socialist Unity Party of Germany]. *Protokoll der Verhandlungen des VIII. Parteitages der Sozialistischen Einheitspartei Deutschlands*. Berlin: Dietz Verlag, 1971.

_____ *Protokoll der Verhandlungen des III. Parteitages der Sozialistischen Einheitspartei Deutschlands*. Berlin: Dietz Verlag, 1951.

_____ *Protokoll der Verhandlungen des V. Parteitages der Sozialistischen Einheitspartei Deutschlands*. Berlin: Dietz Verlag, 1959.

_____ *Protokoll der Verhandlungen des VI. Parteitages der Sozialistischen Einheitspartei Deutschlands*. Berlin: Dietz Verlag, 1963.

_____ *Protokoll der Verhandlungen des VII. Parteitages der Sozialistischen Einheitspartei Deutschlands*. Berlin: Dietz Verlag, 1967.

Srb, Vladimir. *Demografická příručka* [Demographic Handbook]. Prague: Nakladatelství Svoboda, 1967.

Stefanov, Iv., ed. *Demografiiâ na Bŭlgariiâ* [Demography in Bulgaria]. Sofia: Nauka i Izkustvo, 1974.

Stern, Carola. *Porträt einer bolschewistischen Partei*. Cologne: Verlag für Politik und Wirtschaft, 1957.

Strzelecki, Jan. *La Question de L'Habitation Urbaine en Pologne*. Geneva: League of Nations, 1936.

"Tendencje rozwojowe partii w pierwszym półroczu 1974 r. [Developmental Tendencies in the Party in the First Half of 1974]." *Życie partii*, no. 8 (1974), pp. 11-13.

Tomasic, D. A. "The Rumanian Communist Leadership." *Slavic Review*, vol. 20, no. 3 (Oct., 1961), pp. 477-94.

30 let budovaní ČSSR [30 Years of Building the CSR]. Prague: Nakladatelství Svoboda, 1975.

Trybuna ludu, 1956-1975.

USSR. Tsentral'noe Statisticheskoe Upravlenie [Central Statistical Administration]. *Itogi vsesoiûznoĭ perepisi naseleniiâ 1959 goda: Svodnyĭ tom* [Results of the All-Union Census of the Population of 1959: Introductory Volume]. (Hereafter referred to as volume 1.) Moscow: Gosstatizdat, 1962. *Armiânskaiâ SSR* [Armenian SSR]. Moscow: Gosstatizdat, 1963. *Azerbaĭdzhanskaiâ SSR* [Azerbaidzan SSR]. Moscow: Gosstatizdat, 1963. *Belorusskaiâ SSR* [Belorussian SSR]. Moscow: Gosstatizdat, 1963. *Estonskaiâ SSR* [Estonian SSR]. Moscow: Gosstatizdat, 1962. *Gruzinskaiâ SSR* [Georgian SSR]. Moscow: Gosstatizdat, 1963. *Kazakhskaiâ SSR* [Kazakh SSR]. Moscow: Gosstatizdat, 1962. *Kirgizskaiâ SSR* [Kirgiz SSR]. Moscow: Gosstatizdat, 1963. *Latviĭskaiâ SSR* [Latvian SSR]. Moscow: Gosstatizdat, 1962. *Litovskaiâ SSR* [Lithuanian SSR]. Moscow: Gosstatizdat, 1963. *Moldavskaiâ SSR* [Moldavian SSR]. Moscow: Gosstatizdat, 1962. *RSFSR* [RSFSR]. Moscow: Gosstatizdat, 1963. *Tadzhikskaiâ SSR* [Tadzhik SSR]. Moscow: Gosstatizdat, 1963. *Turkmenskaiâ SSR* [Turkmen SSR]. Moscow: Gosstatizdat, 1963. *Ukrainskaiâ SSR* [Ukrainian SSR]. Moscow: Gosstatizdat, 1963. *Uzbekskaiâ SSR* [Uzbek SSR]. Moscow: Gosstatizdat, 1962.

_____ _____ *Itogi vsesoiûznoĭ perepisi naseleniiâ 1970 goda* [Results of the All-Union Census of the Population of 1970]. Volume 3: *Uroven' obrazovaniiâ naseleniiâ SSSR* [Level of Education of the Population of the USSR]. Moscow: Statistika, 1972. Volume 4: *Nafsional'nyĭ sostav naseleniiâ SSSR, soiûznykh i avtonomnykh respublik, kraev, oblasteĭ i nafsional'nykh okrugov* [National Composition of the Population of the USSR, Union and Autonomous Republics, Kraj, Oblasts and National Okrugs]. Moscow: Statistika, 1973. Volume 5: *Raspredelenie naseleniiâ SSSR, soiûznykh i avtonomnykh respublik, kraev i oblasteĭ po obshchestvennym gruppam, istochnikam sredstv sushchestvovaniiâ i otrasliâm narodnogo khoziâĭstva* [Distribution of the Population of the USSR, Union and Autonomous Republics, Kraj and Oblasts by Social Groups, Sources of Means of Support and Branches of the National Economy]. Moscow: Statistika, 1973. Volume 6: *Raspredelenie naseleniiâ SSSR i soiûznykh respublik po zaniâtiiâm* [The Distribution of the Population of the USSR and the Union Republics by Occupation]. Moscow: Statistika, 1973.

_____ _____ *Narodnoe khoziâĭstvo SSSR* [The National Economy of the USSR]. Moscow: Statistika, 1973-1975.

____ ____ *Narodnoe khozíaĭstvo SSSR 1922-1972* [The National Economy of the USSR, 1922-1972]. Moscow: Statistika, 1972.

____ ____ *Naselenie SSSR po dannym vsesoíuznoĭ perepisi naseleniía 1979 goda*. Moscow: Politizdat, 1980.

____ ____ *Trud v SSSR* [Labor in the USSR]. Moscow: Statistika, 1968.

____ ____ *Vsesoíuznaía perepis naseleniía: 17 dekabría 1926 g. Kratkie svodki* [The All-Union Census of the Population: 17 December 1926. Short Summary]. Volume 3: *Naselenie SSSR* [Population of the USSR]. Moscow: Ts. S. U. Soíuza SSR, 1927. Volume 4: *Narodnost i rodnoĭ íazyk naseleniía SSSR* [Nationality and Native Tongue of the Population of the USSR]. Moscow: Ts.S.U. Soíuza SSR, 1928. Volume 7: *Vozrast i gramotnost naseleniía SSSR* [Age and Literacy of the Population of the USSR]. Moscow: Ts.S.U. Soíuza SSR, 1928.

____ ____ *Vsesoíuznaía perepis naseleniía 1926 goda* [All-Union Census of the Population of 1926]. Volume 17: *Narodnost, rodnoĭ íazyk, vozrast, gramotnost* [Native Tongue, Age, Literacy]. Moscow: Plankhozgiza, 1928. Volume 34: *Zaníatíía* [Occupations]. Moscow: Plankhozgiza, 1930.

United Nations. Department of Economic and Social Affairs. *Compendium of Social Science Statistics*. New York: United Nations, 1968.

____ ____ *Demographic Yearbook*. New York: United Nations, 1948-1975.

____ ____ *Growth of the World's Urban and Rural Population, 1920-2000*. Population Studies No. 44. New York: United Nations, 1969.

____ ____ *Statistical Yearbook*. New York: United Nations, 1956-1977.

____ ____ *Yearbook of National Account Statistics 1976*. New York: United Nations, 1977.

____ Economic Commission for Europe. *Economic Survey of Europe in 1974, Part II: Post-War Demographic Trends in Europe and the Outlook Until the Year 2000*. New York: United Nations, 1975.

____ ____ *A Statistical Survey of the Housing Situation in the ECE Countries Around 1970*. New York: United Nations, 1978.

United Nations Scientific, Educational and Cultural Organization. *Progress of Literacy in Various Countries*. Paris: UNESCO, 1953.

____ *Statistical Yearbook*. Paris: UNESCO, 1962-1977.

____ *Statistics of Educational Attainment and Illiteracy, 1945-1974*. Statistical Reports and Studies, No. 22. Paris: UNESCO, 1977.

____ *World Illiteracy at Mid Century. A Statistical Study*. Paris: UNESCO, 1957.

United States. Department of Agriculture. Economics, Statistics and Cooperative Services. *Agricultural Statistics of Eastern Europe and the Soviet Union 1950-1970*. Washington, D.C., GPO, 1973.

____ Department of the Army. *Who's Who in Eastern Europe*. Washington, D.C.: n.d.

____ Department of Commerce. Bureau of the Census. Foreign Demographic Analysis Division. *The Labor Force of Bulgaria*, by Zora Prochazka. International Population Statistics Reports, Series P-90, No. 16. Washington, D.C.: GPO, 1962.

____ ____ *The Labor Force of Czechoslovakia*, by James N. Ypsilantis. International Population Statistics Reports Series P-90, No. 13. Washington, D.C.: GPO, 1960.

____ ____ *The Labor Force of the Soviet Zone of Germany and the Soviet Sector of Berlin*, by Samuel Baum and Jerry W. Combs, Jr. International Population Statistics Reports Series P-90, No. 11. Washington, D.C.: GPO, 1959.

____ ____ *The Labor Force of Yugoslavia*, by Andrew Elias. International Population Statistics Reports Series P-90, No. 22. Washington, D.C.: GPO, 1965.

____ ____ *The Population of Poland*, by W. Parker Mauldin and Donald S. Akers. International Population Statistics Reports Series P-90, No. 4. Washington, D.C.: GPO, 1954.

____ ____ *The Population of Yugoslavia*, by Paul F. Myers. International Population Statistics Reports Series P-90, No. 5. Washington, D.C.: GPO, 1954.

____ ____ *Projections of the Population of the Communist Countries of Eastern Europe by Age and Sex: 1975 to 2000*, by Godfrey Baldwin. International Population Statistics Reports Series P-91, No. 25. Washington, D.C.: GPO, 1976.

____ Department of Commerce. Bureau of the Census. Population Division. *World Population 1977: Recent Demographic Estimates for the Countries and Regions of the World*. Washington, D.C.: GPO, 1978.

____ ____ Social and Economic Statistics Administration, Bureau of Economic Analysis. Foreign Demographic Analysis Division. *Estimates and Projections of the Population of the USSR by Age and Sex: 1950-2000*, by Godfrey Baldwin. International Population Reports, Series P-91, No. 23. Washington, D.C.: GPO, 1973.

_____ State Department. Bureau of Intelligence and Research. *World Strength of the Communist Party Organizations*. Washington, D.C.: GPO, 1958-1973.

United States Congress. House of Representatives. Committee on Foreign Affairs. *The Strategy and Tactics of World Communism*, Supplement IV: *Five Hundred Leading Communists (In the Eastern Hemisphere, Excluding the U.S.S.R.)*. Washington, D.C.: GPO, 1948.

_____ Joint Economic Committee. *Reorientation and Commercial Relations of the Economies of Eastern Europe*. Washington, D.C.: GPO, 1974.

_____ _____ *Soviet Economy in a New Perspective*. Washington, D.C.: GPO, 1976.

"Uroven obrazovaniia naseleniia zaniatogo fizicheskim i umstvennym trudom [The Level of Education of the Population Employed in Physical and Mental Work]." *Vestnik statistiki*, No. 2 (1973), pp. 72-95.

Vsesoiuznaia Kommunisticheskaia Partiia (Bol'sh). Statisticheskiĭ otdel Tsentral'nogo Komiteta [All Union Communist Party (Bolsheviks). Statistical Section of the Central Committee]. *Vsesoiuznaia partiĭnaia perepis 1927 goda* [All Union Party Census of 1927]. Moscow: Izdanie Statisticheskogo Otdela TsK VKP(b), 1927.

Vušković, Boris. "Gibanja u socijalnoj strukturi članstva SKJ [Fluctuation in the Social Structure of the Membership of the LCY]." *Socijalizam*, vol. 17, no. 7-8 (1974), pp. 679-708.

Weber, Hermann. *Die Sozialistische Einheitspartei Deutschlands 1946-1971*. Hannover: Verlag für Literatur und Zeitgeschehen, 1971.

Wer ist wer in der SBZ [Who's Who in the SBZ]. Berlin: Verlag für Internationalen Kulturaustausch, 1958.

"Wer ist wer? in der Tschechischen und Slowakischen Politik," *Osteuropa*, vol. 9, no. 9 (1959), pp. 557-80.

Wiadomości statystyczne, vol. 16, no. 5 (May, 1971), back cover.

Wielka encyklopedia powszechna [The Great General Encyclopedia]. Warsaw: PWN, 1962-1970.

Wightman, G. and Brown, A. H. "Changes in the Level of Membership and Social Composition of the Communist Party of Czechoslovakia, 1945-1973." *Soviet Studies*, vol. 27, no. 3 (July, 1975), pp. 396-417.

World Bank. *1978 World Bank Atlas*. Washington, D.C.: World Bank, 1979.

World Health Organization. *World Health Statistics Annual*. Geneva: World Health Organization, 1971-1978.

Yugoslavia. Direkcija Državne Statistike [Office of State Statistics]. *Definitivni rezultati popisa stanovništva od 31 januara 1921 god*. [Definitive Results of the Census of the Population of 31 January 1921]. Sarajevo: Državna Štamparija, 1932.

_____ _____ *Statistički godišnjak*. Belgrade: Državna Štamparija, 1936-1938.

Yugoslavia. Opšta Državna Statistika [General State Statistics]. *Definitivni rezultati popisa stanovništva od 31 marta 1931 godine* [Definitive Results of the Census of the Population of 31 March 1931]. Volume 3: *Prisutno stanovništvo po pismenosti i starosti* [Resident Population According to Literacy and Age]. Belgrade: Državna Štamparija, 1938.

Yugoslavia. Savezni Zavod za Statistiku [Federal Statistical Office]. *Demografska statistika 1974* [Demographic Statistics 1974]. Belgrade: Savezni Zavod za Statistiku, 1976.

_____ _____ *Konačni rezultati popisa stanovništva od 15 marta 1948 godine* [Final Results of the Census of the Population of 15 March 1948]. Volume 3: *Stanovništvo po zanimanju* [Population According to Occupation]. Belgrade: Savezni Zavod za Statistiku, 1954. Volume 4: *Stanovništvo po školskoj spremi* [Population According to Level of Education]. Belgrade: Savezni Zavod za Statistiku, 1952. Volume 5: *Stanovništvo po pismenosti* [Population According to Literacy]. Belgrade: Savezni Zavod za Statistiku, 1955. Volume 9: *Stanovništvo po narodnosti* [Population According to Nationality]. Belgrade: Savezni Zavod za Statistiku, 1954.

_____ _____ "Konačni rezultati popisa stanovništva od 31 III 1953 g. [Final Results of the Census of the Population of 31 III 1953]." *Statistički Bilten* No. 73. Belgrade: Savezni Zavod za Statistiku, 1957.

_____ _____ "Nacionalni sastav stanovništva po opštinama [National Composition of the Population by Opstina]." *Statistički Bilten* No. 727. Belgrade: Savezni Zavod za Statistiku, 1972.

_____ _____ *Popis stanovništva 1953* [Census of the Population of 1953]. Volume 1: *Vitalna i etnička obeležja* [Vital and Ethnic Characteristics]. Belgrade: Savezni Zavod za Statistiku, 1959. Volume 2: *Ekonomska obeležja stanovništva* [Economic Characteristics of the Population]. Belgrade: Savezni Zavod za Statistiku, 1960. Volume 3: *Pismenost i školska sprema* [Literacy and Levels of Education]. Belgrade: Savezni Zavod za Statistiku, 1960. Volume 5: *Stanovništvo po pismenosti* [Population According to Literacy]. Belgrade: Savezni Zavod za Statistiku, 1955. Volume 8: *Narodnost i maternji jezik* [Nationality and Mother Tongue]. Belgrade: Savezni Zavod za Statistiku, 1959.

_____ _____ *Popis stanovništva 1961* [Census of the Population of 1961]. Volume 2: *Pismenost i školovanost* [Literacy and Schooling]. Belgrade: Savezni Zavod za Statistiku, 1971. Volume 3, Book 1: *Ekonomske karakteristike I deo (Ukupno i aktivno stanovništvo)* [Economic Characteristics Part I

(Total and Active Population)]. Belgrade: Savezni Zavod za Statistiku, 1970. Volume 4, Book 2: *Ekonomska obeležja stanovništva (radnicislužbenici)* [Economic Characteristics of the Population (Workers-Employees)]. Belgrade: Savezni Zavod za Statistiku, 1969. Volume 6: *Vitalna, etnička i migraciona obeležja* [Vital, Ethnic and Migration Characteristics]. Belgrade: Savezni Zavod za Statistiku, 1967.

_____ _____ *Popis stanovništva i stanova 1971* [Census of the Population and Dwellings of 1971]. Volume 1: *Stanovništvo: vitalna, etnička i migraciona obeležja* [Population: Vital, Ethnic and Migration Characteristics]. Belgrade: Savezni Zavod za Statistiku, 1974. Volume 2: *Pismenost i školovanost* [Literacy and Schooling]. Belgrade: Savezni Zavod za Statistiku, 1974. Volume 4: *Ekonomske karakteristike II deo. Zaposleno osoblje* [Economic Characteristics II Part. Employed Persons]. Belgrade: Savezni Zavod za Statistiku, 1974.

_____ _____ "Prosveta, nauka i kultura [Education, Science and Culture]," *Statistički bilten* No. 2. Belgrade: Savezni Zavod za Statistiku, 1950.

_____ _____ "Stanovništvo po zanimanju, školskoj spremi i delatnosti [Population by Occupation, Schooling and Activity]." *Statistički Bilten* No. 73. Belgrade: Savezni Zavod za Statistiku, 1957.

_____ _____ *Statistički godišnjak Jugoslavije.* Belgrade: Savezni Zavod za Statistiku, 1953-1978.

Za nauchnostta v partiĭno-organizatsionnata rabota [For a Scientific Approach to Party-Organizational Work]. Sofia: Partizdat, 1975.

Zbornik narodnih heroja Jugoslavije [Collection (of Biographies) of Peoples' Heroes]. Belgrade: Omladina, 1957.

Zëri i popullit, 1952.

Zinner, Paul. *Revolution in Hungary.* New York: Columbia University Press, 1962.

Zhivkov, Todor. *Eighth Congress of the Bulgarian Communist Party.* Sofia: Foreign Languages Press, 1973.

_____ *Ninth Congress of the Bulgarian Communist Party.* Sofia: Foreign Languages Press, 1967.

Život strany, 1956-1968.

SUMMARY OF SOURCES

The following account provides a summary of sources used for the tables presented in *The Handbook*. Sources cited in abbreviated form in this summary are given in full in the bibliography. For statistical annuals and other official statistical publications cited below, the complete entry in the bibliography will be found under the country in question and its statistical office; other sources cited in this account will be found under the name of the author, or title if no author is given.

Data on population in census years, given in Tables A-1 through A-5, are taken from results of censuses cited in the bibliography, as well as from statistical annuals for the countries in question. Data on the prewar Albanian population are those cited in the postwar Albanian *Anuari statistikor* (Statistical Annual) for 1966; preliminary results of the 1979 census are those reported by the British Broadcasting Service. Data on population in census years for the GDR are taken from Bundesministerium für Gesamtdeutschen Fragen, *DDR Handbuch*, and for the USSR for 1979, from *Naselenie SSSR . . . 1979 goda*. For the source of the estimate of the prewar Polish population in postwar boundaries, see the introduction to Section A. Data on annual population estimates and vital rates in Tables A-6 through A-14 are taken from U.S. Department of Commerce, Bureau of the Census, *Projections of the Population of the Communist Countries of Eastern Europe by Age and Sex: 1975-2000*, by Godrey Baldwin, supplemented by data for 1975 to be found in statistical and demographic annuals of the countries in question, and by data supplied by the Foreign Demographic Analysis Division of the Bureau of the Census. For sources on estimates of the Albanian population for 1975, see the introduction to Section A.

Data on Tables A-15 through A-23, on distribution of the population by age groups and sex, are based on data published by the International Labour Office, *Labour Force Estimates and Projections, 1950-2000* (1977), adjusted to agree with population figures given in Tables A-6 through A-14. For 1975, official estimates are utilized where available, based on data to be found in statistical and demographic annuals of the countries in question. Data on urban and rural birthrates and on urban and rural infant mortality rates in Tables A-24 and A-25, are taken from the statistical and demographic annuals of the countries in question; data for Yugoslavia, for 1959, are from Ginić, *Dinamika i struktura gradskog stanovništva Jugoslavije* (1967); for Hungary, data have been sup-

plied by the Hungarian statistical office. Tables A-26 through A-34, on age specific fertility rates and total fertility rates utilize data drawn from the UN Economic Commission for Europe, *Postwar Demographic Trends in Europe*, Vol. 2. Table A-35, giving projections of the population to the year 2000, are based on data supplied by the Foreign Demographic Analysis Division, U.S. Bureau of the Census; projections for Eastern Europe were prepared in March 1978; those for Soviet Union, in March 1977.

Table B-1, on the number of members in the Communist parties of Eastern Europe and the Soviet Union, is based on a number of different sources, including data on the party reported at party congresses cited in the bibliography, newspaper accounts, secondary sources in Eastern European languages and Russian, and several English language sources. Of special importance for party membership in the Soviet Union generally are "KPSS v t͡sifrakh [The CPSU in Figures]," *Partiinai͡a zhizn* (1973); "The CPSU in Figures," *Soviet Law and Government* (1976-1977); and "KPSS v t͡sifrakh [The CPSU in Figures]," *Partiinai͡a zhizn* (1967). Secondary sources in English used in Table B-1 include U.S. State Department, *World Strength of Communist Party Organizations*; Hoover Institution, *Yearbook on International Communist Affairs*; and Wightman and Brown, "Changes in the Level of Membership," *Soviet Studies* (1975). Data on the size of the Polish United Workers Party are taken largely from the *Rocznik statystyczny* [Statistical Annual].

Data for Tables B-2 through B-12, dealing with the social composition of the parties, are drawn from the aforementioned sources, as well as from the Polish *Rocznik polityczny i gospodarczy* [Political and Economic Annual]; articles appearing in the Yugoslav journal *Jugoslovenski pregled*, "Članstvo Saveza Komunista" [Membership of the League of Communists] in 1964 and in 1976; the Czech party journal *Život strany*, and, in the case of Romania, articles appearing in the newspaper, *Scînteia*. Data on the social composition of the Hungarian Workers' Party for 1951 are taken from National Committee for a Free Europe, *Organization and Strategy of the Hungarian Workers' Party* (1952), and for other years from reports of party congresses, articles appearing in *Nepszabadsag* and from Mate, "Gondolatok pártunk összetételének alakulásáról [Thoughts about the Development of the Composition of the Party]," *Társadalmi szemle* (1964). Data on the German SED draw largely on reports of party congresses; articles appearing in *Neues Deutschland*, and *Einheit*; and Stern,*Porträt einer Bolschewistischen Partei* (1957). For Poland, data are published on the social composition of the party in various editions of *Rocznik statystyczny* and *Rocznik politycny i gospodarczy* [Political and Economic Annual]. Data on the social composition of the Bulgarian party are drawn exclusively from reports of party congresses, and in the case of the Albanian party, from reports of Enver Hohxa to the Albanian Party of Labor.

Tables B-13 through B-17, dealing with the number of white collar employees in the parties, utilize the sources cited above. For Czechoslovakia, note especially the two articles appearing in *Život strany*, no. 24, 1962; and no. 18, 1966. For Poland, in addition to sources already cited, data were taken from Sadowski, "Przemiany społeczny [Social Changes]," *Studia socjologiczne* (1968). Yugoslav data draw on the articles from *Jugoslovenski pregled* cited above, as well as from Milić and Tozi, "Preobražaj i struktura Saveza Komunista Jugoslavije [The Transformation and Structure of the League of Communists of Yugoslavia]," *Socijalizam* (1971) and other sources. For the data on the education of party members given in Tables B-18 through B-22, see the sources cited above. For the USSR, data are also taken from Rigby, *Communist Party Membership*, Table 42. For the data on the age of party members see the above sources; for Poland, Herod's contribution to *Nowe Drogi* (1971), is an important source, as is Human Relations Area Files,*Contemporary Poland* (1955), which gives data for earlier years otherwise not available. Data on nationalities draw on the sources cited above; for Yugoslavia, an important source is *Borba Reflektor*, Jan. 24, 1970, as well as Shoup, *Communism and the Yugoslav National Question* (1968).

All data in Section C are taken from censuses cited in the bibliography, with the exception of the data for Albania, which is to be found in Milo, "Popullsia e Republikës Popullore [The Population of the Peoples Republic of Albania]," *Ekonomia Popullore* (1957); the data from the Polish census of 1946, which is taken from the 1947 *Rocznik Statystyczny*; the estimates for the minority population in Poland, cited in the introduction to Section C; the figures for Romania for 1977, which appeared in *Scînteia*, 14 June, 1977, and have been translated in *Joint Publications Research Service*, No. 69438 (1977); and data for the Soviet Union for 1939, which were published in Kozlov, *Natsional'nosti SSSR* [Nationalities of the USSR] (1975). In addition, a useful source for the data on Yugoslavia, by republic, is the publication of the Yugoslav Statistical Office, "Nacionalni sastav Stanovništva [National Composition of the Population]," *Statistički Bilten*, No. 727 (1972). For the data on the Hungarian minorities in 1970,

see Radio Free Europe, "Selected Demographic Data on Eastern Europe" (1976).

Data on literacy, in Tables D-1 through D-6, are to be found in the censuses cited in the bibliography, as well as in the United Nations 1960 *Demographic Yearbook*, an important source for data on literacy, and UNESCO, *Progress of Literacy in Various Countries* (1953) and *World Illiteracy at Mid-Century* (1957). Data for Albania are from the article by Pasko Milo cited above. For Poland, data are drawn from the UN sources cited above, from various editions of the *Rocznik demograficzny* [Demographic Annual], and from Landy-Tołwinska, *Analfabetyzm w Polsce* [Illiteracy in Poland] (1961). Soviet data are from census sources supplemented by statistics published in "Nekotorye itogi perepisis naseleniiâ 1939 [Some Results of the Census of 1939]," *Vestnik statistiki* (1956). For Yugoslavia, see "Pismenost i školska sprema [Literacy and Schooling]," *Jugoslovenski pregled* (1964), and the 1973 *Statistički godišnjak*, Table 103-4, in which data on the number of illiterates for 1961 are adjusted significantly upward. Data for Hungary have been supplied by the Hungarian Statistical Office.

Data on levels of education in Tables D-7 through D-26 are drawn largely from results of censuses. For Bulgaria, an additional source is Stefanov, *Demografiiâ na Bŭlgariiâ* [Demography in Bulgaria] (1974), and for Czechoslovakia, Srb,*Demografická příručka* [Demographic Handbook] (1967). Data for the GDR for 1970 and for Poland for 1960 are not taken directly from census sources, but are to be found in the *Statistisches Jahrbuch* and various editions of *Rocznik statystyczny*. Especially important is Table 13 of the 1974 *Statistisches Jahrbuch*, the only source of any completeness for data on levels of educational attainment in the GDR. Data for Table D-27, on levels of educational attainment measured by international standards, are taken from UNESCO, *Statistics of Educational Attainment and Literacy* (1977).

Tables E-1 through E-9, on the class structure of the population, utilize census sources cited in the bibliography. For Albania, the data are taken from the 1958 *Anuari statistikor* and the volume *30 vjet Shqipëri socialiste* [30 Years of Socialist Albania]. Sources for the GDR, in addition to the census of 1964, include the 1955 *Statistisches Jahrbuch*, which gives data from the 1950 census. For Poland, data on classes for the period 1930–1960 are taken from the very important Table 18 (55) of the 1969 *Rocznik statystyczny*, as well as from censuses for 1970 and 1974. Data on classes in Czechoslovakia make use of census sources for 1961 and 1970, and also the excellent volume on the 1960 census issued by the Czech Statistical Office, *Vývoj společnosti ČSSR v číslech* [The Development of Czech Society in Figures] (1965). Data for Hungary, Series III, 1949–1973, are based on data given in the *Statistical Yearbook/Statisticheskiĭ Ezhegodnik*. Data on the class structure of the population in the USSR are based on census sources, but also make use of the volume *Narodnoe Khoziaĭstvo SSSR 1922–1972* (National Economy of the USSR 1922–1972), as well as *Bol'shevik*, 1939. Data on the class composition of the population of Yugoslavia, Romania, and Bulgaria are drawn exclusively from census sources cited in the bibliography.

Data on the class structure of Active Earners, given in Tables E-10 through E-17, are drawn from census sources and other sources cited immediately above. Data on the GDR utilize, in addition to census sources, statistics on the civilian labor force taken from various editions of the *Statistisches Jahrbuch*. Data on the class structure of Active Earners for Poland for the years 1950 and 1960 are taken from the 1965 *Rocznik Statystyczny*'s Table 18 (55).

Table E-18, giving the breakdown of the Hungarian population according to the Manual, Nonmanual, and Independent Population, is based on materials from the 1960 and 1970 Hungarian censuses. Tables E-19 through E-27, on education and class, are taken from census sources cited in the bibliography, with the exception of the data on Poland given in Table E-26, on the education of Manual and Nonmanual Employees, which are civilian labor force data drawn from the excellent volume, *Rocznik statystyczny prace, 1945–1968* [Labor Force Annual, 1945–1968] (1970). Table E-27, on the level of education of Manual and Nonmanual Active Earners in the USSR, is based on data reported in census sources, as well as "Uroven obrazovaniĭa naseleniĭa [The Level of Education of the Population]," *Vestnik statistiki* (1973).

Data on the agricultural population, given in Tables E-28 through E-35, are taken from census sources cited in the bibliography, and, for the GDR and Hungary, from civilian labor force data appearing in various editions of the *Statistisches Jahrbuch*, the *Statisztikai evkönyv* [Statistical Annual] and the Hungarian statistical annual, *Statistical Yearbook/Statisticheskiĭ ezhegodnik*. Data on the agricultural population in Czechoslovakia are also taken from the basic work by Srb cited above, *Demografická příručka*.

Table E-36, in which the class structure of the population is reported for the CMEA countries, is based on data given in the 1977 CMEA handbook, Sovet Ekonomicheskoĭ Vzaimopomoshchi [Council for Mutual Economic Assistance], *Statisticheskiĭ ezhegodnik* [Statistical Annual]. Data for Table E-37, on the population by type of economic activity according to international standard classifications, are drawn from various editions of the ILO, *Year Book of Labour Statistics*, and from the remainder of the tables in Section E.

For the data in Section F, on the background characteristics of party leaders, the reader is referred to the *Who's Who* volumes appearing in the bibliography, the various Radio Free Europe bulletins dealing with the East European leadership, and the volumes dealing with the Soviet leaders published by the Institute for the Study of the USSR cited in the bibliography. Especially important for biographical information on the leadership in Eastern Europe immediately after the war are the volumes edited by Busek (1957), Dellin (1957), Fischer-Galati (1957), Halecki (1957), and Helmreich (1957) on *East Central Europe Under the Communists*. For the background of the Yugoslav party leadership the two editions of *Ko je ko* [Who's Who] (1957 and 1968) are basic, as well as the volume *Zbornik narodnih heroja Jugoslavije* [Collection (of Biographies) of Peoples' Heroes] (1957). For the Bolshevik leaders, use was made of Haupt, *Makers of the Russian Revolution* (1974), and the very useful volume, Institute for the Study of the USSR, *Who Was Who in the USSR* (1972). For Bulgaria, Czechoslovakia, Hungary, Poland, and Romania, the data gathered from the abovementioned sources have been compared and combined with those available from the *Archive on Political Elites in Eastern Europe*, the product of the pathbreaking study of East European elites carried out by the University of Pittsburgh Project on Elites in Eastern Europe. Finally, in selected cases the data include information provided by individuals familiar with the leaders in question.

Data in Section G on occupations are taken in the greatest part from census sources. In addition, data on occupations in the GDR in 1950 are drawn from the 1955 *Statistisches Jahrbuch* and for Poland, for 1960, from the back cover of *Wiadomości statystyczne* no. 5 (May, 1971). For occupations in Yugoslavia in 1953, use was also made of the publication of the Yugoslav statistical office, "Stanovništvo po zanimanju [Population by Occupation], *Statistički Bilten* No. 73 (1957). Table G-20, which gives data on occupations according to international standard classifications, was based on data appearing in various editions of the ILO *Year Book of Labour Statistics*.

Table H-1, which gives selected indicators of development for Eastern Europe and the Soviet Union, is based on data from the remainder of *The Handbook*, as well as statistics on infant mortality in the interwar period published in the League of Nations *Monthly Bulletin of Statistics*, Aug., 1943. Data on national income in Tables H-2 through H-4 originate in the CMEA Handbooks cited earlier (for NMP data); in the data published by Thad Alton and the Research Project on National Income in East Central Europe, especially *Occasional Papers* No. 53; in the *World Bank Atlas* for 1978 and the CIA *Handbook of Economic Statistics* for 1978, and in two of the Joint Economic Committee of the U.S. Congress reports, *Soviet Economy in a New Perspective* (1976), and *Reorientation and Commercial Relations of the Economies of Eastern Europe* (1974). Data on NMP for Yugoslavia are drawn from the 1977 *Statistički godisnjak*. Data on GNP for years prior to 1978 in Series I, Table H-3, have been provided by the World Bank. For a discussion of methodology, see the *1978 World Bank Atlas*, pp. 31–32, and Thad Alton et al., *Statistics on East European Economic Structure and Growth*, Occasional Papers of the Research Project on National Income in East Central Europe, No. 48 (1975).

Data on the number of persons in agriculture, given in Tables H-5 through H-12, are taken from census results and from several volumes providing data on the labor force in Eastern Europe. For Bulgaria, data for the prewar period are taken from the 1938 *Statisticheski godishnik* [Statistical Annual]. Data for Czechoslovakia for 1946–47 are from U.S. Department of Commerce, Bureau of the Census, *The Labor Force of Czechoslovakia*, and Srb, *Demografická příručka*, as well as from census sources. Data for the GDR and Hungary include civilian labor force data reported in various editions of the *Statistisches Jahrbuch* and the Hungarian statistical annual, *Statistical Yearbook/ Statisticheskiĭ ezhegodnik*. For Poland, data for 1930 and 1950 are those to be found in Table 18 (55) of the 1969 *Rocznik statystyczny*. In addition to census results, the data on Romania draw on the ILO *Year Book of Labour Statistics, 1943– 44*, for data on Active Earners in 1930. Data on the Soviet Union are taken from the results of the 1926, 1959, and 1970 censuses. For Yugoslavia, data for the prewar period are from the 1936 *Statistički godišnjak*; official estimates for the agricultural population in 1976 are to be found in "Poljoprivredno stanovništvo [Agricultural Population]," *Jugoslovenski pregled* (1975); remaining data are from the postwar census sources.

Statistics on urbanization in Tables H-13 through H-21 are based on census sources, official estimates for intercensal years appearing in statistical annuals, and data published in the United Nations *Demographic Yearbook*. For Albania, a key source for urbanization data is Table 1, p. 27, of the 1966 *Anuari statistikor*. Excellent data on urbanization in Bulgaria are to be found in various editions of *Statisticheski godishnik* [Statistical Annual]; data are also drawn from the 1960 *Demografska statistika* [Demographic Statistics] and the 1974 *Nase-*

lenie [Population], as well as from the urbanization statistics appearing in the 1960 United Nations *Demographic Yearbook*. Czechoslovak data on urbanization are taken from the results of the prewar and postwar censuses, the *Statistická ročenka* [Statistical Annual], and Srb, *Demografická příručka*. Data on the GDR are drawn exclusively from various editions of the *Statistisches Jahrbuch*. Data on urbanization for Hungary have been provided by the Hungarian Statistical Office. Data for the urban population in Poland prewar are drawn from Strzelecki, *La Question de Habitation Urbaine en Pologne* (1936), and for the postwar period, the demographic and statistical annuals *Rocznyk statystyczny* and *Rocznik demograficzny 1945–1966* [Demographic Annual 1945–1966]. Romanian data are based on statistics appearing in the *Anuarul statistic* [Statistical Annual] and the *Anuarul demografia* [Demographic Annual]. Soviet data on urbanization are taken from prewar and postwar census sources, and from various editions of *Narodnoe khoziaĭstvo SSSR* [National Economy of the USSR]. For Yugoslavia, urbanization statistics for 1953, 1961, and 1971 are to be found in "Increase of Urban Population," *Yugoslav Survey* (1964), and "Rise in the Urban Population, 1969–1971," *Yugoslav Survey* (1973); for earlier years use was made of U.S. Department of Commerce, Bureau of the Census, *The Population of Yugoslavia* (1954), as well as census sources.

Data on housing, appearing in Tables H-22 through H-28, are taken from the United Nations, Economic Commission for Europe, *A Statistical Survey of the Housing Situation in the ECE Countries Around 1970* (1978).

Food consumption statistics, appearing in Tables H-29 and H-30, are drawn from U.S. Department of Agriculture, *Agricultural Statistics of Eastern Europe and the Soviet Union, 1950–1970*; Food and Agricultural Organization, *Provisional Food Balance Sheets, 1972–1974 Average* (1977), and data supplied by the Centrally Planned Countries Program Area, Foreign Demand and Competition Division, U.S. Department of Agriculture.

Data on developmental indicators relating to communications, transport, health, and culture are taken from various editions of the *United Nations Yearbook*, the United Nations Scientific, Educational, and Cultural Organization, *Statistical Yearbook*, the World Health Organization, *World Health Statistics Annual*, and the United Nations, *Compendium of Social Science Statistics* (1967).

SOURCES FOR INDIVIDUAL TABLES

Sources are given in abbreviated form by author, or by title if an author is lacking. For official statistical publications, the complete entry in the bibliography will be found under the country in question and its statistical office. The following abbreviations for official statistical publications are used in the references to follow. Sources are alphabetized in right-hand column.

Anuari statistikor	Albania. Drejtoria e Statistikës. *Anuari statistikor i R.P.SH.*
30 vjet	____ ____ *30 vjet Shqipëri socialiste.*
Vjetari statistikor	____ ____ *Vjetari statistikor i RP SH.*
Prebroĭavane 1926	Bulgaria. Glavna direkt͡sii͡a na Statistikata. *Obshti rezultati ot prebroĭavaneto . . . 1926 god.*
Stat. god. T͡s. Bŭlgarii͡a	____ ____ *Statisticheski godishnik na T͡sarstvo Bulgarii͡a.*
Stat. godishnik NRB	____ ____ *Statisticheski godishnik na Narodna Republika Bŭlgarii͡a.*
Stat. ezhegodnik	____ ____ *Statisticheskiĭ ezhegodnik–Statistical Yearbook.*
Prebroĭavane 1956	____ ____ *Prebroĭavane na naselenieto . . . 1956.*
Prebroĭavane 1965, tri prot͡s. repr. raz.	____ ____ *Rezultati ot prebroĭavaneto na naselenieto na . . . 1965 godina (tri prot͡sentova reprezentativna razrabotka).*
Prebroĭavane 1965	____ ____ *Rezultati ot prebroĭavaneto 1965 g.*
Prebroĭavane 1946	____ ____ *Predvaritelni rezultati prebroĭavaneto 1946.*
Výsledky sčítání lidu 1970	Czechoslovakia. Federální Statistický Úřad. *Předběžné výsledky sčítání lidu . . . 1970.*
Stat. ročenka	____ ____ *Statistická ročenka ČSSR.*
Volkzählung 1921	____ Státní Úřad Statistický. *Volkzählung in der Tschechoslowakischen Republik vom . . . 1921.*
Stat. ročenka RC	____ ____ *Statistická ročenka Republiky Československé.*
Sčítání lidu 1930	____ ____ *Sčítání lidu v Republice Československé . . . 1930.*
Sčítání lidu 1961	____ ____ *Sčítání lidu . . . k l breznu 1961.*
Volkszählung 1964	German Democratic Republic. Staatliche Zentralverwaltung für Statistik. *Ergebnisse der Volks und Berufszählung . . . 1964.*
Stat. Jahrbuch	____ ____ *Statistisches Jahrbuch der Deutschen Demokratischen Republik.*
Stat. Yrbk.	Hungary. Hungarian Statistical Office. *Statistical Yearbook/Statisticheskiĭ ezhegodnik.*
Recensement 1930	Központi Statisztikai Hivatal . . . *Recensement général de la population en 1930.*
1941 népszámlálás	____ *1941 évi népszámlálás.*
1949 népszámlálás	____ *1949 évi népszámlálás.*
1960 népszámlálás	____ *1960 évi népszámlálás.*
1970 népszámlálás	____ *1970 évi népszámlálás.*
ILO Yrbk.	International Labour Office. *Year Book of Labour Statistics.*
Spis ludności 1931 (dane skrócone)	Poland. Główny Urząd Statystyczny. *Drugi powszechny spis . . . 1931 (dane skrócone).*
Spis ludności 1931	____ ____ *Drugi powszechny spis . . . 1931.*
Spis powszechny 1970	____ ____ *Narodowy spis powszechny . . . 1970.*
Spis ludności 1946	____ ____ *Powszechny spis ludności . . . 1946.*
Rocznik dem.	____ ____ *Rocznik demograficzny.*
Rocznik stat.	____ ____ *Rocznik statystyczny.*
Spis ludności 1974	____ ____ *Spis ludności i mieszkan . . . 1974.*
Spis powszechny 1960	____ ____ *Spis powszechny . . . 1960.*
Anuarul stat.	Romania. Direcţiunea Centrală de Statistică. *Anuarul statistic al Republicii Socialiste Romania.*
Recensămîntul 1956	____ ____ *Recensămîntul populaţiei . . . 1956.*
Recensămîntul 1966	____ ____ *Recensămîntul populaţiei . . . 1966.*
Anuarul dem.	____ ____ *Anuarul demografia al Republici Socialiste România.*

Recensămantul 1930	____ Institut Central de Statistică. *Recensământul general . . . 1930.*
Stat. ezhegodnik SEV	Sovet Ekonomicheskoĭ Vzaimopomoschi. Sekretariat. *Statisticheskiĭ ezhegodnik.*
Itogi perepisi 1959	USSR. T͡sentral'noe Statisticheskoe Upravlenie. *Itogi vsesoi͡uznoĭ perepisi 1959.*
Itogi perepisi 1970	____ ____ *Itogi vsesoi͡uznoĭ perepisi naselenii͡a SSSR 1970 goda.*
Nar. khoz.	____ ____ *Narodnoe khozi͡aĭstvo SSSR.*
Perepis naselenii͡a 1926: Kratkie sv.	____ ____ *Vsesoi͡uzna͡ia perepis naselenii͡a 1926 g.: Kratkie svodki.*
Perepis naselenii͡a 1926	____ ____ *Vsesoi͡uzna͡ia perepis naselenii͡a 1926 goda.*
UN Dem. Yrbk.	United Nations. *Demographic Yearbook.*
UN Stat. Yrbk.	____ *Statistical Yearbook.*
Popis 1921	Yugoslavia. Direkcija Državne Statistike. *Definitivni rezultati popisa . . . 1921.*
Popis 1931	____ *Definitivni rezultati popisa stanovništva . . . 1931.*
Popis 1948	____ Savezni Zavod za Statistiku. *Konačni rezultati popisa stanovništva . . . 1948.*
Popis 1953	____ *Popis stanovništva 1953.*
Popis 1961	____ *Popis stanovništva 1961.*
Popis 1971	____ *Popis stanovništva i stanova 1971.*
Stat. godišnjak	____ *Statistički godišnjak Jugoslavije*

SECTION A

A-1   *UN Dem. Yrbk. 1948*, Table 1, pp. 82–85. League of Nations, *Statistical Yearbook 1938/39*, Table 2, p. 18. *Vjetari statistikor 1969-1970*, Table 1, p. 23. *Prebroi͡avane 1926*, Table 1, p. 1. *Prebroi͡avane 1934*, vol. 1, Table 1, p. 1. Balevski, pp. 35-36. *Stat. godishnik NRB 1977*, Table 8, p. 32.

A-2   Federal Republic of Germany, *DDR Handbuch*, Table 1, p. 148. *Stat. Jahrbuch 1977*, Table 1, p. 1. *Volkszählung 1921*, I Teil, Table 1, p. 16. *Stat. ročenka 1957*, Table 3-1, p. 35.

A-3   *Recensement 1930*, vol. 1, Table 5, p. 2. *1941 népszámlálás*, Table 4, p. 12. *Demográfiai évkönyv 1975*, Table 1.3, p. 12. *Spis ludności 1931*, p. 1. *Rocznik stat. 1976*, Table 1 (49), p. 28. *Spis powszechny 1970*, Table A, p. 3. U.S. Dept. of Commerce, *The Population of Poland*, Table 22, p. 122.

A-4   *Anuarul stat. 1937 si 1938*, Table 29, p. 46. *Anuarul stat. 1974*, Table 7, p. 9. *Recensămîntul 1956*, vol. 1, p. xv. *Anuarul stat. 1978*, Table 13, p. 45. *Perepis naselenii͡a 1926: Kratkie sv.*, vol. 3, Table 1, pp. 2-3. *Itogi perepisi 1970*, vol. 2, Table 1, p. 5. *Nar. khoz. 1922-1972*, p. 30. "Nekotorye itogi," pp. 88–89. Foreign Broadcast Information Service, *Soviet Union*, vol. 3, no. 085 (May, 1979), p. R-1.

A-5   U.S. Dept. of Commerce, *The Population of Yugoslavia*, Table 3, p. 117. *Stat. godišnjak 1976*, Table 104-1, p. 101.

A-6   U.S. Dept. of Commerce, *Projections of the Population of the Communist Countries of Eastern Europe*, Table 1a, p. 14.

A-7   U.S. Dept. of Commerce, *Projections of the Population of the Communist Countries of Eastern Europe*, Table 1b, p. 16. *Stat. Ezhegodnik 1976*, Table 8, p. 33.

A-8   U.S. Dept. of Commerce, *Projections of the Population of the Communist Countries of Eastern Europe*, Table 1c, p. 18. *Stat. ročenka 1977*, Table 4-5, pp. 94-95. *Stat. ročenka 1976*, Table 3-2, p. 82.

A-9   U.S. Dept. of Commerce, *Projections of the Population of the Communist Countries of Eastern Europe*, Table 1d, p. 20. *Stat. Jahrbuch 1977*, Tables 1 and 2, pp. 395-96.

A-10   U.S. Dept. of Commerce, *Projections of the Population of the Communist Countries of Eastern Europe*, Table 1e, p. 22. *Stat. Yrbk. 1975*, Table 1.

A-11   U.S. Dept. of Commerce, *Projections of the Population of the Communist Countries of Eastern Europe*, Table 1f, p. 24. *Rocznik stat. 1976*, Table 20 (83), p. 43.

A-12   U.S. Dept. of Commerce, *Projections of the Population of the Communist Countries of Eastern Europe*, Table 1g, p. 26. *Anuarul stat. 1976*, Table 12, p. 15.

A-13   U.S. Dept. of Commerce, *Estimates and Projections of the Population of the USSR*, Table 3, p. 17. *Nar. khoz. 1975*, pp. 7, 40–41. *Nar. khoz. za 60 let*, pp. 69–70.

A-14   U.S. Dept. of Commerce, *Projections of the Population of the Communist Countries of Eastern Europe*, Table 1h, p. 28. *Stat. godišnjak 1977*, Table 104-2, p. 102.

A-15   International Labour Office, *Labour Force Estimates and Projections*, Table 2, p. 27 and Table 5, p. 94.

A-16   International Labour Office, *Labour Force Estimates and Projections*, Table 2, p. 12. *Stat. ezhegodnik 1975*, Table 7, p. 18. *Stat. ezhegodnik 1976*, Table 7, p. 32.

A-17   International Labour Office, *Labour Force Estimates and Projections*, Table 2, p. 13. *Stat. ročenka 1977*, Table 4-6, p. 96.

A-18   International Labour Office, *Labour Force Estimates and Projections*, Table 2, p. 14. *Stat. Jahrbuch 1975*, Table 1, p. 390. *Stat. Jahrbuch 1976*, Table 1, p. 389.

A-19   International Labour Office, *Labour Force Estimates and Projections*, Table 2, p. 15. *Stat. Yrbk. 1974*, Table 4, p. 32. *Stat. Yrbk. 1975*, Table 4, p. 30.

A-20   International Labour Office, *Labour Force Estimates and Projections*, Table 2, p. 16. *Rocznik stat. 1975*, Table 8 (51), p. 32.

A-21   International Labour Office, *Labour Force Estimates and Projections*, Table 2, p. 17. *Anuarul stat. 1976*, Table 12, p. 15.

A-22   International Labour Office, *Labour Force Estimates and Projections*, Table 2, p. 54, and Table 5, p. 121.

A-23   International Labour Office, *Labour Force Estimates and Projections*, Table 2, p. 33. *Demografska statistika 1974*, Table 1-6, p. 24.

A-24   *Vjetari statistikor 1971–1972*, Table 9, p. 31, and Table 10, p. 32. *Stat. ezhegodnik 1976*, Table 9, pp. 34–36. *Stat. ročenka 1960*, Table 4-1, pp. 62–63. *Stat. ročenka 1971*, Table 4-6, pp. 104–05. *Stat. ročenka 1977*, Table 4-5, pp. 94–95. *Stat. Jahrbuch 1977*, Table 2, p. 396. *Stat. Yrbk. 1966*, Table 2, p. 12. *Stat. Yrbk. 1975*, Table 1, pp. 6–7. *Rocznik dem. 1945–1966*, Table 1 (52), p. 197. *Rocznik stat. 1971*, Table 1 (17), p. 54. *Rocznik stat. 1976*, Table 21 (69), p. 43. *Anuarul stat. 1974*, Table 15, pp. 22–23. *Nar. kh. 1975*, p. 41. *Nar. kh. 1965*, p. 42. *Nar. kh. 1960*, p. 60. *Stat. godišnjak 1976*, Table 104-2, p. 101. Ginić, p. 66. *UN Dem. Yrbk. 1970*, Table 13, pp. 623–24. *UN Dem. Yrbk 1972*, Table 16, pp. 476–78. *UN Dem. Yrbk. 1974*, Table 9, pp. 247–53.

A-25   *UN Dem. Yrbk. 1961*, Table 12, pp. 230–35. *UN Dem. Yrbk. 1964*, Table 19, pp. 555–57. *UN Dem. Yrbk. 1970*, Table 16, pp. 646–52. *UN Dem. Yrbk. 1974*, Table 20, pp. 348–63. *Stat. ezhegodnik 1961*, Table 14, pp. 48–50. *Stat. ezhegodnik 1976*, Table 21, p. 64. *Stat. ročenka 1960*, Table 4-1, pp. 62–63. *Stat. ročenka 1971*, Table 4-6, p. 105. *Stat. ročenka 1977*, Table 4-5, p. 94. *Stat. Jahrbuch 1960/61*, Table 4, p. 39. *Stat. Jahrbuch 1977*, Table 1, p. 395. *Stat. Yrbk. 1966*, Table 2, p. 12. *Stat. Yrbk. 1975*, Table 1, pp. 6–7. *Rocznik dem. 1945–1966*, Table 1 (52), p. 197. *Rocznik dem. 1971*, Table 1 (17), p. 54. *Rocznik stat. 1976*, Table 21 (69), p. 43. *Anuarul dem. 1974*, Table 55, p. 306. *Nar. kh. 1960*, p. 60. *Nar. kh. 1965*, p. 42. *Nar. kh. 1975*, p. 40. *Stat. godišnjak 1976*, Table 104-2, p. 101.

A-26   United Nations, Economic Commission for Europe, *Economic Survey of Europe in 1974*, Table A.V.2., pp. 232–33.

A-27   United Nations, Economic Commission for Europe, *Economic Survey of Europe in 1974*, Table A.V.2. pp. 232–33.

A-28   United Nations, Economic Commission for Europe, *Economic Survey of Europe in 1974*, Table A.V.2., pp. 232–33.

A-29   United Nations, Economic Commission for Europe, *Economic Survey of Europe in 1974*, Table A.V.2., pp. 232–33.

A-30   United Nations, Economic Commission for Europe, *Economic Survey of Europe in 1974*, Table A.V.2., pp. 232–33.

A-31 United Nations, Economic Commission for Europe, *Economic Survey of Europe in 1974*, Table A.V.2., pp. 232-33.

A-32 United Nations, Economic Commission for Europe, *Economic Survey of Europe in 1974*, Table A.V.2., pp. 238-39.

A-33 United Nations, Economic Commission for Europe, *Economic Survey of Europe in 1974*, Table A.V.2., pp. 238-39.

A-34 United Nations, Economic Commission for Europe, *Economic Survey of Europe in 1974*, Table V.2., p. 81.

A-35 United Nations, Economic Commission for Europe, *Economic Survey of Europe in 1974*, Table A.VII.1., pp. 249-52.

SECTION B

B-1 U.S. State Dept., *World Strength of the Communist Party Organizations*, 1958-1973. Hoover Institution, *Yearbook 1978*, pp. 36, 50, 58. Wightman and Brown, pp. 396-417. Zinner, p. 75. *Materiali III s'ezda*, p. 119. Hoxha, *Report* (1961), p. 135. "BKP v t͡sifri," p. 37. *Kratkie Bŭlgarska entsiklopediia*, vol. 1, p. 41. Bŭlgarska Komunisticheska Partiia, *Peti kongres*, p. 209; *Shesti kongres*, p. 71. *VII s'ezd Vengerskoĭ Sot͡sialisticheskoĭ Rabocheĭ Partii*, p. 142. Sozialistische Einheitspartei Deutschlands, *Protokoll des III Parteitages*, p. 82; *Protokoll des V Parteitages*, p. 1,608; *Protokoll des VI Parteitages*, p. 253; *Protokoll des VII Parteitages*, p. 226; *Protokoll des VIII Parteitages*, pp. 100-1. *Neues Deutschland*, May 19, 1976. *X s'ezd Vengerskoĭ SRP*, p. 20. *IX s'ezd Vengerskoĭ SRP*, p. 71. Sandor, p. 41. *Politika*, April 14, 1978. "KPSS v t͡sifrakh" (1967), p. 9. "KPSS v t͡sifrakh" (1973), pp. 9-10. Human Relations Area Files, p. 316. Alster, p. 236. Fischer-Galati, p. 76. "Membership of the League of Communists," p. 40. "Članstvo Saveza komunista" (1976), p. 121. *Stat. godišnjak 1975*, Table 103-5, p. 100. *Stat. godišnjak 1976*, Table 103-5, p. 100. Kovrig, p. 76. Also see sources cited under *Rocznik Stat.* and *Rocznik polityczny i gospodarczy* for Table B-7, and sources cited under *Scînteia* for Table B-8.

B-2 *Materialy III s'ezd*, pp. 118-19. Hoxha, *Report on the Activity* (1961), pp. 134-38. Hoxha, *Rapport d'Activité du Comité Central*, p. 188. Partia e Punës se Shqipërisë, The Institute of Marxist Leninist Studies, vol. 2, pp. 210-11. Hoxha, *Report to the 7th Congress*, pp. 7-8.

B-3 Bŭlgarska Komunisticheska Partiia. *Peti kongres*, p. 209; *Shesti kongres*, pp. 71-72; *Osmi kongres*, p. 142; *IX kongres*, p. 95; *Deseti kongres*, p. 102. *VII s'ezd Bolgarskoĭ Kommunisticheskoĭ Partii*, p. 108. Foreign Broadcast Information Service, *Eastern Europe*, vol. 2, no. 61 (March, 1976), p. c-11. Ivanov, p. 67.

B-4 *Život strany*, no. 10, 1956, p. 10; no. 24, 1962, p. 1,504; no. 18, 1966, p. 11. Komunistické Strany Československa, *XIII sjezd*, p. 911.

B-5 Sozialistische Einheitspartei Deutschlands, *Protokoll des V Parteitages*, p. 1,068; *Protokoll des VI Parteitages*, p. 253; *Protokoll des VII Parteitages*, pp. 226-27; *Protokoll des VIII Parteitages*, p. 101. *Einheit*, no. 10, 1973, p. 1,189. Fortsch, p. 104. *Neues Deutschland*, May 19, 1976.

B-6 A Magyar Dolgozók Pártja, *II kongresszusának*, pp. 50-51. A Magyar Szocialista Munkáspárt, *VII kongresszusának*, p. 64; *IX kongresszusának*, p. 67; *X kongresszusának*, p. 24. Radio Free Europe, "The HSWP," p. 9. *Népszabadság*, March 16, 1975, Supplement.

B-7 Góra, p. 466. Alster & Andrzejewski, p. 239. "Liczby dotyczace składu partii," p. 125. Sadowski, "Przemiany społeczne," p. 93. *Nowe drogi*, no. 4, 1967, p. 15. Bukowski, p. 4. *Rocznik stat. 1969*, Table 12 (31), p. 19; *1970*, Table 9 (28), p. 16; *1971*, Table 8 (27), p. 61; *1972*, Table 9 (28), p. 62; *1973*, Table 6 (25), p. 59; *1974*, Table 5 (23), p. 59; *1975*, Table 5 (40), p. 21; *1976*, Table 6 (44), p. 24. *Rocznik polityczny i gospodarczy 1958*, p. 341; *1959*, p. 163; *1961*, p. 182; *1962*, p. 108; *1963*, p. 98; *1964*, pp. 128-29; *1965*, p. 130; *1966*, p. 162; *1969*, p. 296; *1970*, p. 171; *1971*, p. 137; *1972*, p. 165; *1973*, p. 132; *1974*, p. 178; *1976*, p. 136.

B-8 *Scînteia*, Dec. 13, 1961; April 17, 1965; April 14, 1966; Dec. 7, 1967; March 12, 1969; Aug. 7, 1969; April 3, 1974; Aug. 8, 1969; Nov. 26, 1974; Aug. 8, 1969; Nov. 26, 1974; July 25, 1975. Partidul Comunist Român, *Congresul al IX-lea*, p. 72; *Die Landeskonferenz*, p. 60; *Raportul*, p. 87. Fischer Galati, p. 76. U.S. State Dept, *World Strength of the Communist Party Organizations 1962*, p. 29; *1963*, p. 31.

B-9   Íudin, pp. 128 and 164. Rigby, *Communist Party Membership*, Table 2, p. 116.

B-10   Nikolić, p. 41. Milić & Tozi, p. 836. *Vušković*, pp. 679–702. *Borba*, Jan. 24, 1970 "Članstvo Saveza Komunista," (1976), pp. 453–58. Hafner, p. 10. "Membership of the League of Communists," pp. 39–47. "Članstvo Saveza komunista" (1964), pp. 293–95.

B-11   A Mágyar Dolgozók Pártja, *II kongresszusának*, p. 35. National Committee for a Free Europe, p. 35. Kadar, p. 27. Sandor, p. 41. *X s'ezd Vengerskoĭ SRP*, p. 98. *Népszabadság*, March 16, 1975.

B-12   Vsesoíuznaîa Kommunisticheskaîa Partiîa (Bol'sh), pp. 12–13. *Bol'shaîa Soveîskaîa entsiklopediîa*, vol. 11 (1930), p. 534. "The CPSU in Figures," p. 7; "KPSS v ísifrakh," (1967), p. 13. "KPSS v ísifrakh" (1973), p. 13. "KPSS v ísifrakh" (1962), p. 47. Rigby, *Communist Party Membership*, pp. 116, 199, 325.

B-13   Komunistické Strany Československa, *XIII sjezd*, p. 911. *Život strany*, no. 24, 1962, p. 1,505; no. 18, 1966, p. 11.

B-14   Sadowski, "Przemiany społeczne," p. 93. Also see sources cited in *Rocznik stat.* and *Rocznik polityczny i gospodarczy* under Table B-7.

B-15   "KPSS v ísifrakh" (1962), p. 48. "KPSS v ísifrakh" (1965), p. 11. "KPSS v ísifrakh" (1967), p. 13. "KPSS v ísifrakh" (1973), p. 16.

B-16   "Membership of the League of Communists," p. 44.

B-17   Milić & Tozi, p. 836. *NIN*, Oct. 8, 1972, p. 10. *Komunist*, May 1, 1969. "Članstvo Saveza Komunista" (1976), p. 124.

B-18   *Materialy III s'ezd*, p. 152. Hoxha, *Rapport d'Activité du Comité Central*, p. 197. *Zëri i popullit*, April 1, 1952. Bulgarska Komunisticheska Partiîa, *Peti kongres*, p. 211. *Za nauchnostta*, p. 185.

B-19   Sožialistische Einheitspartei Deutschlands, *Protokoll der Verhandlungen des VII Parteitages*, p. 225. *Einheit*, no. 10 (1973), p. 1,189. Weber, p. 137. Foreign Broadcast Information Service, *Eastern Europe*, vol. 2, no. 100 (May 21, 1976), pp. E-41-42.

B-20   A Magyar Dolgozók Pártja, *X kongresszusának*, p. 24.

B-21   *Trybuna ludu*, June 29, 1956. See also tables cited in *Rocznik stat.* under Table B-7.

B-22   Vsesoíuznaîa Kommunisticheskaîa Partiîa (Bol'sh), p. 56. "KPSS v ísifrakh" (1965), p. 11. "KPSS v ísifrakh" (1967), p. 14. "The CPSU in Figures," p. 8. Rigby, *Communist Party Membership*, Table 42, p. 401.

B-23   "Članstvo Saveza Komunista" (1964), Table 6, p. 34. "Membership of the League of Communists," pp. 39–47. *Borba*, Jan. 24, 1970. *NIN*, Oct. 8, 1972, p. 10.

B-24   Wightman & Brown, p. 400. Komunistické Strany Československa, *Protokol IX sjezdu*, p. 150. *XIII sjezd*, p. 910. Radio Free Europe, "Latest Figures on Party Structure," p. 5.

B-25   Stern, p. 284. Sozialistische Einheitspartei Deutschlands, *Protokoll des V Parteitages*, p. 1,609; *Protokoll des VII Parteitages*, p. 226; *Protokoll des VIII Parteitages*, p. 101. *Neues Deutschland*, May 19, 1976.

B-26   Human Relations Area Files, p. 325. *Trybuna ludu*, June 29, 1956. Herod, p. 85. See also tables cited in *Rocznik stat.* under Table B-7.

B-27   Vsesoíuznaîa Kommunisticheskaîa Partiîa (Bol'sh), pp. 62–63. "KPSS v ísifrakh" (1965), p. 13. "KPSS v ísifrakh" (1967), p. 16. "KPSS v ísifrakh" (1973), p. 19. A Magyar Dolgozók Pártja, *II kongresszusának*, p. 50. *X s'ezd Vengerskoĭ SRP*, p. 20.

B-28   "Članstvo Saveza Komunista" (1964), p. 294. "Članstvo Saveza Komunista" (1976), p. 454. "Membership of the League of Communists," p. 42.

B-29   *X s'ezd Vengerskoĭ SRP*, p. 20. *XIII sjezd*, p. 912. *Život strany*, no. 24, 1962, p. 1,506; no. 3, 1968, p. 35; no. 12, 1968, p. 699. *Rude pravo* Aug. 31, 1966. *Scînteia*, April 25, 1968.

B-30   Vsesoíuznaîa Kommunisticheskaîa Partiîa (Bol'sh), pp. 48–49. "KPSS v ísifrakh" (1962), p. 49. "KPSS v ísifrakh" (1967), p. 15. "KPSS v ísifrakh" (1973), p. 19. "The CPSU in Figures," p. 10.

B-31   Herod, pp. 85–86. "Članstvo Saveza Komunista" (1964), p. 34. *Borba*, Jan. 24, 1970. "Membership of the League of Communists," p. 43.

B-32 Partidul Comunist Român, *Congresul al IX -lea*, p. 72; *Die Landeskonferenz*, p. 61. *XIII sjezd*, p. 911. *Život strany*, no. 24, 1962, p. 1,506; no. 18, 1966, p. 21.

B-33 "KPSS v fsifrakh" (1962), p. 49. "KPSS v fsifrakh" (1967), pp. 14-15. "KPSS v fsifrakh" (1973), p. 18. "The CPSU in Figures," p. 8. Vsesoîuznaîa Kommunisticheskaîa Partiîa (Bol'sh), pp. 66-71.

B-34 Shoup, Appendix B, p. 270. "Članstvo Saveza Komunista" (1964), p. 294. *NIN*, Oct. 8, 1972, p. 10. *Borba*, Jan. 24, 1970. Nikolić, p. 50.

SECTION C

C-1 Milo, p. 63. Czechoslovakia, *Vývoj společnosti ČSSR*, Table 12, p. 199. Czechoslovakia, *Statistisches Jahrbuch 1937*, Table II-7, p. 9. *Výsledky sčítání lidu 1970*, vol. 2, Table 15, p. 71. Srb, p. 11.

C-2 *Prebroîavane 1934*, vol. 1, Table 6, pp. 22-23. *Prebroîavane 1965, tri profs. repr. raz.*, Table 28, p. 45. *Prebroîavane 1965*, vol. 1, p. 12.

C-3 *Recensement 1930*, vols. 4 and 5, Table 21, pp. 235-37. *1960 népszámlálás*, vol. 13, Table 1.20, pp. 28-29. *1941 népszámlálás*, Table 3, p. 696. Radio Free Europe, "Selected Demographic Data," Appendix C. Data also supplied by the Hungarian Statistical Office.

C-4 *Spis ludności 1931*, Table 10. *Rocznik stat. 1947*, Table 8, p. 20. Gielke, p. 130. Breyer, pp. 265-74. Kwilecki, p. 87. Radio Free Europe, "Selected Demographic Data," Appendix C.

C-5 *Recensămîntul 1930*, vol. 2, p. xxiv. *Recensămîntul 1966*, Table 19, p. 75. *Joint Publications Research Service*, no. 69438, p. 47. *Anuarul stat. 1966*, Table 19, p. 75.

C-6 *Perepis naseleniîa 1926*, vol. 17, Table VI, p. 8. *Itogi perepisi 1959*, vol. 1, pp. 184-89. *Itogi perepisi 1970*, vol. 4, Table 1, pp. 9-11. Kozlov, Table 37, pp. 249-50. *Nar. khoz. 1922-1972*, p. 31.

C-7 Markert, Table 3, p. 16. *Popis 1948*, vol. 9, pp. 2-7. *Popis 1953*, vol. 1, Table G, p. lxviii. *Popis 1961*, vol. 6, p. xxix. *Popis 1971*, vol. 1, Table 2, p. 12.

C-8 See sources cited for Czechoslovakia under Table C-1.

C-9 *Perepis naseleniîa 1926*, vol. 17, Table X, pp. 38-41. *Itogi perepisi 1959*, vol. 1, Table 54, pp. 202-10. *Itogi perepisi 1959: Tadzhikskaîa SSR*, Table 53, pp. 116-17; *Kirgizskaîa SSR*, Table 53, pp. 128-29; *Armianskaîa SSR*, Table 53, pp. 102-3; *Gruzinskaîa SSR*, Table 53, pp. 134-35; *Turkmenskaîa SSR*, Table 53, pp. 128-29; *Estonskaîa SSR*, Table 53, pp. 94-95; *Azerbaîdzanskaîa SSR*, Table 53, pp. 134-35; *RSFSR*, Table 53, pp. 300-1; *Moldavskaîa SSR*, Table 53, pp. 90-91; *Litovskaîa SSR*, Table 53, pp. 160-61; *Latviîskaîa SSR*, Table 53, pp. 92-93; *Ukrainskaîa SSR*, Table 53, pp. 168-69. *Belorusskaîa SSR*, Table 53, pp. 124-25; *Kazakhskaîa SSR*, Table 53, pp. 162-63. *Tadzhikskaîa SSR*, Table 53, pp. 116-17. *Turkmenskaîa SSR*, pp. 128-29. *Uzbekskaîa SSR*, Table 53, pp. 138-39. *Itogi perepis 1970*, vol. 4, p. 43, 152, 202, 222-23, 263, 276, 280, 284, 295, 303, 307, 321-330. Kozlov, Table 13, pp. 108-12 and Table 1, p. 62.

C-10 Yugoslavia, "Nacionalni sastav," entire. *Popis 1971*, vol. 6, Table 1-1, p. 3. Also see sources cited for Table C-7.

C-11 *Prebroîavane 1965*, p. 10. *Popis 1953*, vol. 1, Table 10, p. 266. *Recensămantul 1930*, vol. 1, p. 562. *Recensămîntul 1966*, vol. 1, Table 14, p. 173. Also see sources cited for Tables C-2, C-5, and C-7.

C-12 *Perepis naseleniîa 1926*, vol. 17, Table IX, pp. 35-37. *Itogi perepisi 1959*, vol. 1, pp. 226-31. *Itogi perepisi 1970*, vol. 4, Table 31, p. 331. Also see sources cited for Table C-6.

C-13 *Prebroîavane 1934*, Table 6, p. 22. *Sčítání lidu 1930*, vol. 1, Table 12, pp. 104-7. *Recensămantul 1930*, vol. 2, p. xxiv. *Annuaire statistique Hongrois 1932*, Table 15, p. 16. *Spis ludności 1931*, Table 10. Markert, Tables 4 and 5, p. 17. *Stat. godišnjak 1937-1938*, Table 14, p. 73. *Popis 1953*, vol. 1, Table 11, p. 278. *Stat. Jahrbuch 1955*, p. 33. *Volkszählung 1964*, p. 92.

C-14 *Prebroîavane 1934*, vol. 1, Table 6, p. 22.

C-15 *Annuaire statistique Hongrois 1934*, Table 15, p. 13. *Sčítání lidu 1930*, vol. 1, Table 12, p. 107.

C-16 *Spis ludności 1931*, Table 10.

C-17 Markert, Tables 4 and 5, p. 16. *Popis 1953*, vol. 1, Table 11, pp. 278-79.

SECTION D

D-1   *UNESCO Statistical Yearbook 1977*, Table 1.3, p. 48. *Prebroǐavane 1965, tri profs. repr. raz.*, Table 26, p. 44. *Stat. god. Ts̃. Bŭlgariiǎ 1940*, Table 15, p. 5. *Stat. god. NRB 1956*, Table 4, p. 13.

D-2   Data provided by the Hungarian Statistical Office.

D-3   Landy-Tołwinska, Table 4, p. 96, and Table 5, p. 98. *Rocznik dem. 1973*, Table 23, p. 76. *Concise Statistical Yearbook of Poland 1938*, Table 20, p. 28.

D-4   *Recensămantul 1930*, vol. 3, Table A, p. xxviii; Table B, p. xxxviii; Table C, p. xlviii. *Recensămîntul 1956*, vol. 1, Table 14, p. xxi; Table 15, p. xxii; pp. 426–29. *Anuarul dem. 1974*, Table 6, p. 22. *UN Dem. Yrbk. 1960*, Table 11, p. 448. UNESCO, *World Illiteracy*, p. 101.

D-5   *Perepis naseleniiǎ 1926: Kratkie sv.*, vol. 7, Table I, p. 8. *Itogi perepisi 1959*, vol. 1, Table 25, p. 88, and Table 26, p. 89. *Itogi perepisi 1970*, vol. 3, Table 8, pp. 570–71. "Nekotorye itogi," p. 90.

D-6   Yugoslavia, "Prosveta, nauka i kultura," Table 18, p. 25. *Popis 1971*, vol. 2, Table 1, p. 2. "Pismenost i školska sprema," Table 1, p. 101, and Table 3, p. 102.

D-7   Tables D-13 though D-26.

D-8   Stefanov, Table 7.11, p. 368. Also see sources cited for Table D-13.

D-9   Tables D-14, D-15, and D-16.

D-10   Tables D-22 and D-23 and *1960 népszámlálás*, vol. 13, Table 1.11, p. 17.

D-11   Tables D-20, D-21, and D-24.

D-12   Tables D-25 and D-26.

D-13   *Prebroǐavane 1956*, vol. 2, Table 5, p. 124. *Prebroǐavane 1965*, vol. 1, p. 13.

D-14   Srb, Table 1-24, p. 39. *Stat. ročenka 1957*, Table 3-14, p. 43. Czechoslovakia, *Vývoj společnosti ČSSR*, p. 100 and Table 14, pp. 204–5. *Výsledky sčítání lidu 1970*, vol. 2, p. 28.

D-15   *Výsledky sčítání lidu 1970*, vol. 2, Table 13, p. 65, and Table 14, p. 68.

D-16   *Stat. Jahrbuch 1974*, Table 13, p. 84. *Volkszählung 1964*, p. 275.

D-17   *1960 népszámlálás*, vol. 13, Table 1.13, p. 22.

D-18   *1960 népszámlálás*, vol. 13, Table 1.13, p. 22.

D-19   *1970 népszámlálás*, vol. 2, Table 2.1.5, p. 101.

D-20   *Rocznik stat. 1975*, Table 13 (56), p. 35. *Rocznik stat. 1976*, Table 13 (61) p. 39.

D-21   *Spis ludności 1974*, Table 6, pp. 38–39. *Rocznik stat. 1975*, Table 13 (56), p. 35.

D-22   *Anuarul dem. 1974*, Table 11, pp. 104–5. *Recensămîntul 1956*, vol. 1, pp. 482–85.

D-23   *Anuarul dem. 1974*, Table 11, pp. 104–5. *Recensămîntul 1966*, vol. 1, Table 12, pp. 191–95.

D-24   *Itogi perepisi 1959*, vol. 1, Table 20, pp. 74–75. *Itogi perepisi 1970*, vol. 3, pp. 6–7.

D-25   *Popis 1948*, vol. 4, pp. 2–3. *Popis 1953*, vol. 3, Table E, p. L and Table 3, p. 32.

D-26   *Popis 1961*, vol. 2, Table 1–2, p. 2. *Popis 1971*, vol. 2, Table 2, p. 6.

D-27   United Nations Scientific, Cultural, and Educational Organization, *Statistics of Educational Attainment*, pp. 108–28.

SECTION E

E-1   *30 vjet*, Table 14, p. 28. *Anuari statistikor 1958*, Table 13, p. 23.

E-2   *Prebroǐavane 1965, tri profs. repr. raz.*, Table 79, p. 88. *Prebroǐavane 1965*, vol. 1, p. 408, and pp. 418–20.

E-3   Czechoslovakia, *Vývoj společnosti ČSSR*, Table 15, p. 210. *Sčítání lidu 1961*, vol. 1, Table 1, p. 10; vol. 2, Tables 1 and 2, p. 2. *Výsledky sčítání lidu 1970*, vol. 2, Table 1, p. 31; Table 3, p. 35; Table 29, p. 33. *Stat. ročenka 1967*, Table 3.7, p. 77. *Stat. ročenka 1972*, Table 4.4, p. 103.

E-4   *Stat. Jahrbuch 1955*, Table 21, p. 33. *Stat. Jahrbuch 1971*, Table 1, p. 52. *Stat. Jahrbuch 1977*, Table 1, p. 52, and Table 4, p. 15. *Volkszählung 1964*, p. 96, pp. 110-11, and pp. 172-74.

E-5   *1949 népszámlálás*, vol. 8, Table 1, pp. 2-7. *1970 népszámlálás*, vol. 2, Table 1.2.13, p. 75; vol. 24, Table 1.12, p. 64; Table 2.5, p. 108. *Stat. Yrbk. 1975*, Tables 9, 10, 11, pp. 35-37.

E-6   *Rocznik stat. 1969*, Table 14 (51), p. 45, and Table 18 (55), p. 47. *Spis powszechny 1970*, p. xxvii; Table D, p. 15; Table 7, p. 80; Table 13, p. 194; Table 25, p. 324. *Spis ludności 1974*, Table 3, pp. 10-14.

E-7   *Recensămîntul 1956*, vol. 1, pp. 628-29 and p. 1,034. *Recensămîntul 1966*, vol. 1, Table 23, p. 364, and Table 37, p. 846.

E-8   *Perepis naseleniia 1926*, vol. 34, Table 1, pp. 2-3. *Nar. khoz. 1922-1972*, p. 35. *Bol'shevik*, no. 15-16, 1939, p. 113. *Itogi perepisi 1959*, vol. 1, Table 28, p. 72; Table 29, p. 93; Table 31, pp. 98-99; Table 33, pp. 104-5. *Itogi perepisi 1970*, vol. 5, Table 2, pp. 8-9; Table 3, p. 83; Table 9, pp. 146-47; Table 11, p. 162.

E-9   *Popis 1953*, vol. 2, Table V, pp. civ and xlviii; vol. 2, Table 4, p. 382. *Popis 1961*, vol. 4, Table 4, p. lviii; vol. 3, Table 1-3, p. 9; Table 1-5, p. 104; Table 1-10, p. 284. *Popis 1971*, vol. 3, Table 1, p. 3; Table 3, p. 16; Table 6, p. 63.

E-10   *Prebroiavane 1956*, vol. 3, Table 1, pp. 6-281; vol. 4, Table 2, p. 24. *Prebroiavane 1965, tri profs. repr. raz.*, Table 73, p. 85; Table 79, p. 88. *Prebroiavane 1965*, vol. 1, p. 408. *Joint Publications Research Service*, no. 67830, p. 2.

E-11   Czechoslovakia, *Vývoj společnosti ČSSR*, Table 51, p. 75. *Sčítání lidu 1961*, vol. 2, Table 6, p. 5. *Výsledky sčítání lidu 1970*, vol. 2, Table 2a, p. 33; Table 7, p. 44.

E-12   *Stat. Jahrbuch 1955*, Table 21, p. 33. *Volkszählung 1964*, p. 96. Also see sources cited for Table E-4.

E-13   *1949 népszámlálás*, vol. 8, Table 1, pp. 2-7. *1970 népszámlálás*, vol. 2, Table 1.2.13, p. 75; vol. 24, Table 1.12, p. 64, and Table 2.5, p. 108. *Stat. Yrbk. 1975*, Table 10, p. 35.

E-14   *Rocznik stat. 1969*, Table 18 (55), p. 47. *Spis powszechny 1960*, Tables 10 and 11, p. 54. *Spis powszechny 1970*, Table 15, p. 224; Table 16, p. 239; Table 30, pp. 366-67. *Spis ludności 1974*, Table 11, p. 92, and Table 15, p. 120.

E-15   *Recensămîntul 1956*, vol. 2, pp. 138-39. *Recensămîntul 1966*, vol. 1, Table 23, pp. 364-67, and Table 30, pp. 548-55.

E-16   *Perepis naseleniia 1926*, vol. 34, Table I, pp. 2-3, and Table VI, pp. 174-83. *Itogi perepisi 1959*, vol. 1, Table 33, pp. 104-9. *Itogi perepisi 1970*, vol. 5, Table 11, pp. 162-63, and Table 12, pp. 194-203.

E-17   *Stat. godišnjak 1954*, Table 55, p. 93. *Popis 1961*, vol. 3, Table 1-5, p. 104. *Popis 1971*, vol. 3, Table 8, pp. 112-14.

E-18   *1960 népszámlálás*, vol. 13, Table 1.45, p. 51. *1970 népszámlálás*, vol. 24, Table 1.12, p. 64; Table 2.5, p. 108; Table 2.8, p. 142.

E-19   *Prebroiavane 1956*, vol. 4, Table 2, pp. 24-25.

E-20   *Prebroiavane 1965, tri profs. repr. raz.*, Table 70, p. 82.

E-21   *1949 népszámlálás*, vol. 8, Table 3, p. 10. *1960 népszámlálás*, vol. 2, Table 19, pp. 106-17. *1970 népszámlálás*, vol. 24, Table 1.17, p. 70.

E-22   *Spis powszechny 1970*, Table 30, p. 366.

E-23   *Recensămîntul 1956*, vol. 3, pp. 346-47.

E-24   "Raspredelenie postoiannogo naseleniia SSSR," Table 5, p. 86. *Itogi perepisi 1959*, vol. 1, Table 33, pp. 104-5, and Table 36, p. 115. *Itogi perepisi 1970*, vol. 5, Table 4, p. 26. *Nar. khoz. 1973*, p. 41.

E-25   *1960 népszámlálás*, vol. 13, Table 1.58, p. 74; *1970 népszámlálás*, vol. 2, Table 1.2.16, p. 78.

E-26   Poland, *Rocznik pracy*, Table 2 (89), p. 253. Poland, *Wybrane dane o kwalifikacjach*, Table 2, p. 65.

E-27   *Itogi perepisi 1959*, vol. 1, Table 41, p. 130, and Table 50, p. 174. "Uroven obrazovaniíâ naseleniíâ," Table 2, p. 73.

E-28   *Prebroíâvane 1956*, vol. 2, Table 9, p. 55. *Prebroíâvane 1965*, vol. 1, p. 418.

E-29   Srb, Tables 1-18 and 1-19, pp. 34-35. Czechoslovakia, *Vývoj společnosti ČSSR*, Table 55, p. 80. *Sčítání lidu 1961*, vol. 1, Table 2, p. 80. *Výsledky sčítání lidu 1970*, vol. 2, Table 7, pp. 44-45, and Table 11, p. 57.

E-30   *Stat. Jahrbuch 1956*, Table 7, p. 158. *Stat. Jahrbuch 1974*, Table 5, p. 57. *Volkszählung 1964*, p. 110, 172, 216.

E-31   Hungary, *Munkaugyi adattar*, Table 24, p. 113. Also see sources cited for Tables E-5 and E-13.

E-32   *Rocznik stat. 1959*, Table 39 (59), p. 40. *Rocznik stat. 1966*, Table 19 (38), p. 39. *Rocznik stat. 1969*, Table 18 (55), p. 47. *Rocznik stat. 1973*, Table 18 (49), p. 83. *Spis powszechny 1960*, Table 14, p. 92. *Spis powszechny 1970*, Table 19, p. 269; Table 20, p. 271; Table 21, pp. 274-80. *Spis ludności 1974*, Table 22, p. 185.

E-33   *Recensămîntul 1956*, vol. 2, pp. 138 and 628. *Recensămîntul 1966*, vol. 1, Table 23, p. 366; Table 30, pp. 550-63; Table 38, p. 852.

E-34   *Perepis naseleniíâ 1926: Kratkie sv.*, vol. 10. p. 8. *Perepis naseleniíâ 1926*, vol. 34, p. 2. *Itogi perepisi 1959*, vol. 1, table 33, p. 104; Table 34, p. 110; Table 39, p. 117-18. *Itogi perepisi 1970*, vol. 5, Table 12, pp. 194-96.

E-35   *Stat. godišnjak 1954*, Table 25, p. 56. *Popis 1953*, vol. 5, p. 2. *Popis 1961*, vol. 3, Table 1-11, p. 294; Table 1-12, p. 296. *Popis 1971*, vol. 3, Table 1, p. 3; Table 8, p. 112; vol. 11, Table 3.5, p. 1.

E-36   *Stat. ezhegodnik SEV 1977*, Table 10, p. 17.

SECTION F

General Archive on Political Elites in Eastern Europe. United States, Dept. of the Army, *Who's Who in Eastern Europe*. United States Congress, House of Representatives, *Five Hundred Leading Communists*. Lewytzkyj, *Who's Who in the Socialist Countries*. Burks, pp. 20-21 and 26-27.

F-1   Congresses of the Albanian Party of Labor; see entries in the bibliography under Partia e Punës se Shqipërisë, and *Materialy III s'ezd*. Skendi, pp. 323-45.

F-2   Congresses of the Bulgarian Communist Party; see entries in the bibliography under Bulgarska Komunisticheska Partiíâ, and *VII s'ezd Bolgarskoĭ Kommunisticheskoĭ Partiĭ*. Radio Free Europe, "The Bulgarian Party Leadership" and "East Europe's Communist Leaders: Bulgaria." Dellin, pp. 386-99.

F-3   Congresses of the Czechoslovak Communist Party; see entries in the bibliography under Komunistické Strany Československa. *Kdo je kdo*. Radio Free Europe, "The Czechoslovak Party Leadership." Busek, pp. 418-32.

F-4   Congresses of the Socialist Unity Party; see entries in the bibliography under Sozialistische Einheitspartei Deutschlands. Federal Republic of Germany, *A bis Z*. Buch, *Namen and Daten*. Habel, *Wer ist wer*. Weber, pp. 131-51. *Wer ist wer in der SBZ*.

F-5   Congresses of the Hungarian Worker's Party and the Hungarian Socialist Workers' Party; see entries in the bibliography under A Magyar Dolgozók Pártja and A Magyar Szocialista Munkáspárt, and *X s'ezd Vengerskoĭ SRP*. *Magyar életrajzi lexikon. Ki kicsoda*. Radio Free Europe, "Eastern Europe's Communist Leaders: Hungary," and "The Hungarian Party Leadership." Helmreich, pp. 392-409.

F-6   *Rocznik polityczny i gospodarczy. Wielka encyklopedia powszechna. Trybuna ludu*, Dec. 14, 1975. Radio Free Europe, "Poland's Communist Leaders," and "Eastern Europe's Communist Leaders: Poland." Halecki, pp. 516-34.

F-7   Congresses of the Romanian Workers' Party and the Romanian Communist Party; see entries in the bibliography under Partidul Comunist Român and Partidul Muncitoresc Romîn. Academia Republici Populare Romîne, *Dictionar. Scanteia*, Feb. 27, 1948. *Scînteia*, Dec. 29, 1955. *Scînteia*, Aug. 13, 1969. Tomasic, "The Rumanian Communist Leadership." Radio Free Europe, "Eastern Europe's Communist Leaders: Rumania." Fischer-Galati, pp. 344-50.

F-8   Haupt, *Makers of the Russian Revolution. Bol'shaia Sovetskaia entsiklopediia*. Institut for the Study of the USSR, *Who Was Who in the USSR* and *Party and Government Officials of the Soviet Union*. Schueller, *The Politburo*.

F-9   *Bol'shaia Sovetskaia entsiklopediia*. Institute for the Study of the USSR, *Biographic Dictionary of the USSR*, also *Prominent Personalities in the USSR*, and *Who Was Who in the USSR*. Levytsky, *The Soviet Political Elite*. Rigby, "The Soviet Politburo."

F-10   *Ko je Ko. Zbornik narodnih heroja. Enciklopedija Jugoslavije. Enciklopedija leksikografskog zavoda*. Byrnes, pp. 410-11.

F-11   Tables F-1 and F-2.

F-12   Table F-3.

F-13   Tables F-4 and F-5.

F-14   Table F-6.

F-15   Table F-7.

F-16   Tables F-8 and F-9.

F-17   Table F-10.

SECTION G

G-1   *Prebroiavane 1956*, vol. 3, Table 1, pp. 6-98. *Prebroiavane 1965*, vol. 1, pp. 383-90, 398-405.

G-2   *Sčítání lidu 1961*, vol. 2, Table 1, pp. 154-67.

G-3   *Stat. Jahrbuch 1955*, Table 19, p. 30. *Volkszählung 1964*, pp. 221-44.

G-4   *1960 népszámlálás*, vol. 10, Table 4, pp. 110-32. *1970 népszámlálás*, vol. 24, Table 2.14, pp. 188-93.

G-5   *Wiadomości statystyczne* (1971), back cover. *Spis ludności 1974*, Table 16, pp. 121-22.

G-6   *Recensămînul 1956*, vol. 1, pp. 840-41. *Recensămîntul 1966*, vol. 1, Table 31, pp. 630-31.

G-7   *Itogi perepisi 1959*, vol. 1, Table 47, pp. 161-66; Table 49, pp. 171-73. *Itogi perepisi 1970*, vol. 6, Table 2, pp. 6-23; Table 18, pp. 165-69; Table 43, pp. 167-69.

G-8   *Popis 1953*, vol. 2, Table 4, pp. 368-83. *Popis 1961*, vol. 3, Table 1-7, pp. 124-26. *Popis 1971*, vol. 3, Table 8, pp. 112-14.

G-9   *Prebroiavane 1956*, vol. 3, Table 2, pp. 282-319.

G-10   *Prebroiavane 1965, tri profs. repr. raz.*, Table 64, pp. 71-76.

G-11   *1960 népszámlálás*, vol. 10, Table 4, pp. 110-26.

G-12   *1970 népszámlálás*, vol. 24, Table 2.17, pp. 212-16.

G-13   *Recensămîntul 1956*, vol. 1, pp. 936-47.

G-14   *Recensămîntul 1966*, vol. 1, Table 33, pp. 674-87.

G-15   *Itogi perepisi 1959*, vol. 1, Table 47, pp. 164-65; Table 52, pp. 177-83; *Itogi perepisi 1970*, vol. 6, Table 2, pp. 20-22; Table 6, p. 408; Table 8, p. 559; Table 68, pp. 628-31.

G-16   See sources for Table G-15.

G-17   Yugoslavia, "Stanovništvo po zanimanju," Table 2, pp. 10-14.

G-18   *Popis 1961*, vol. 3, Table 1-4, p. 11, and Table 1-9, pp. 130-32.

G-19   *Popis 1971*, vol. 4, Table 8, pp. 210-17.

G-20   International Labour Office, *Year Book 1967*, Table 2B, pp. 226-27, 240-41; *Year Book 1970*, Table 2B, pp. 244-45, 266-67, 270-71; *Year Book 1976*, Table 2B, pp. 242-45, 254-55, 264-67, 271-76.

SECTION H

H-1 League of Nations, *Monthly Bulletin of Statistics*, vol. 24, No. 8a (Aug., 1943), p. 208. U.S. Dept. of Commerce, *The Labor Force of the Soviet Zone of Germany*, Table A-1, p. 25. Data also drawn from the remainder of the tables in Section H.

H-2 U.S. Congress, Joint Economic Committee, *Soviet Economy in a New Perspective*, Table 1, p. 271; also *Reorientation and Commercial Relations*, Table 9, p. 270. *Stat. godišnjak 1977*, Table 102-6, p. 81. *Stat. ezhegodnik SEV 1974*, Table 11, pp. 27-42. *Stat. ezhegodnik SEV 1975*, Table 11, pp. 21-28. *Stat. ezhegodnik 1977*, Table 11, pp. 21-29. *United Nations Yearbook of National Account Statistics 1976*, p. 3. Alton, "Economic Growth in Eastern Europe," Tables 1 through 6, pp. 6-10.

H-3 Central Intelligence Agency, *Handbook of Economic Statistics 1978*, Table 7, p. 17. *1978 World Bank Atlas*, pp. 29-30, and data supplied by the World Bank. Alton, "Economic Growth in Eastern Europe," Table 8, p. 13.

H-4 Table H-3 and Section A, Tables A-6 through A-14. U.S. Dept. of Commerce, *World Population 1977*.

H-5 U.S. Dept. of Commerce, *The Labor Force of Bulgaria*, Table A-1, p. 32. *Stat. god. T͡s. Bŭlgarii͡a 1938*, Table 25, p. 40. *Prebroi͡avane 1956*, vol. 3, Table 1, pp. 6-99; vol. 4, Table 1, p. 6, and Table 2, p. 24. *Prebroi͡avane 1965, tri profs. repr. raz.*, Table 47, p. 58; Table 53, p. 61, and Table 55, p. 63. *Prebroi͡avane 1965*, vol. 1, pp. 284-91.

H-6 *Sčítání lidu 1930*, vol. 2, Part 2, Table 3, p. 270. U.S. Dept. of Commerce, *The Labor Force of Czechoslovakia*, Table A-1, p. 25. Srb, Table 1-19, p. 35. *Sčítání lidu 1961*, Part 1, Table 1, p. 10; Part 2, Table 6, p. 5. *Výsledky sčítání lidu 1970*, Table 11, p. 57; Table 12, pp. 59-60. U.S. Dept. of Commerce, *The Population of Czechoslovakia*, Table 25, p. 68, and Table 14, p. 62.

H-7 Federal Republic of Germany, *DDR Handbuch*, Table 1, p. 148. *Stat. Jahrbuch 1956*, Table 7, p. 158. *Stat. Jahrbuch 1977*, Table 4, pp. 15-16. *Volkszählung 1964*, pp. 172-74.

H-8 *Stat. Yrbk. 1974*, Table 1, p. 103. *Stat. Yrbk 1975*, Table 1, pp. 6-7. *1970 népszámlálás*, vol. 2, Table 1.2.7, p. 69; Table 1.2.8, p. 70; Table 2.2.2, p. 106; vol. 24, Table 2.5, p. 108, and Table 2.8, p. 142.

H-9 *Rocznik stat. 1969*, Table 18 (55), p. 47. *Rocznik stat. 1975*, Table 16 (59), p. 37, and Table 17 (60), p. 37. *Spis powszechny 1960*, Table 10, p. 54. *Spis powszechny 1970*, Tables C & D, pp. 14-15, and Table 13, p. 194. *Spis ludności 1974*, Table 3, pp. 10-14, and Table 11, p. 92.

H-10 *Recensămantul 1930*, vol. 5, p. xiv and pp. 3-4. *Recensămîntul 1956*, vol. 1, pp. 628-29, 680; vol. 2, p. 578. *Recensămîntul 1966*, Table 23, pp. 364-66; Table 25, p. 402; Table 30, pp. 550-51; Table 35, p. 816; Table 38, p. 852.

H-11 *Perepis naselenii͡a 1926*, vol. 34, Table 1, pp. 2-3. *Itogi perepisi 1959*, vol. 1, Table 30, p. 96; Table 33, p. 104; Table 29, p. 94. *Itogi perepisi 1970*, vol. 5, pp. 162-63; pp. 146-47, 194-95.

H-12 *Stat. godišnjak 1936*, Table 1, pp. 33-35. *Stat. godišnjak 1957*, Table 4-5, p. 73. *Stat. godišnjak 1971*, Table 103-8, p. 76. *Popis 1948*, vol. 3, Table 12, p. xxx. *Popis 1953*, vol. 2, Table D, p. xlviii. *Popis 1961*, vol. 3, Table 1-5, p. 104, and Table 1-3, p. 9. *Popis 1971*, vol. 3, Table 3, p. 16; Table 6, p. 63; vol. 11, Table 3-5, p. 1. "Poljoprivredno stanovništvo," Table 5, p. 374.

H-13 *Vjetari statistikor 1966*, Table 1, p. 27; Table 2, pp. 28-29. *30 vjet*, Table 12, p. 22.

H-14 Bulgaria. *Predvaritelni rezultati prebroi͡avane 1946*, Table G, pp. xi-xii. *Stat. godishnik NRB 1960*, Table 4, p. 19. *Stat. godishnik NRB 1971*, Table 5, p. 16. *Stat. godishnik NRB 1975*, Table 3, p. 14. *Stat. godishnik NRB 1977*, Table 3, p. 28. Bulgaria, *Demografska statistika 1960*, Table 4, pp. 221-23. Bulgaria. *Naselenie 1974*, Table 6, pp. 20-37. *UN Dem. Yrbk 1960*, Table 8, p. 363.

H-15 *Stat. ročenka 1957*, Table 3-5, p. 37. *Stat. ročenka 1967*, Table 3-10, p. 79. *Stat. ročenka 1974*, Table 4-4, p. 100. *Stat. ročenka 1975*, Table 4-4, p. 106. *Stat. ročenka 1976*, Table 3-2, p. 82; Table 3-4, p. 83. *Volkszählung 1921*, Part 1, Table 15, p. 44. *Sčítání lidu 1930*, vol. 1, Table 3, p. 25. Czechoslovakia. *Vývoj společnosti ČSSR*, Table 2, p. 171. Srb, Table 1-7, p. 23. *UN Dem. Yrbk. 1952*, Table 6, p. 179. *UN Dem. Yrbk 1960*, Table 7, p. 326. *UN Dem. Yrbk 1977*, Table 6, p. 175.

H-16   *Stat. Jahrbuch 1975*, Table 5, p. 8. *Stat. Jahrbuch 1977*, Table 4, p. 7.

H-17   Data supplied by the Hungarian Statistical Office.

H-18   Strzelecki, Table III, p. 176, and Table 4, p. 179. *Rocznik stat. 1947*, Table 10, p. 21. *Rocznik stat. 1970*, Table 2 (35), p. 21. *Rocznik stat. 1977*, Table 5 (46), p. 30. *Rocznik dem. 1976*, Table 4, p. 5.

H-19   *Anuarul stat. 1937 si 1938*, Table 30, p. 48. *Anuarul stat. 1966*, Table 13, p. 65. *Anuarul stat. 1971*, Table 18, p. 69. *Anuarul stat. 1976*, Table 7, p. 9, and Table 11, p. 14. *Anuarul stat. 1978*, Table 14, p. 45, and Table 19, p. 54. *Anuarul dem. 1974*, Table 7, pp. 30-37, and Table 9, pp. 100-1.

H-20   *Perepis naseleniîa 1926*, vol. 17, Table IV, pp. 6-7. *Itogi perepisi 1959*, vol. 1, Table 7, p. 35. *Itogi perepisi 1970*, vol. 1, Table 4, p. 61. *Nar. khoz.* 1975, p. 7. *Foreign Broadcast Information Service, Soviet Union*, p. R-1.

H-21   U.S. Dept. of Commerce, *The Population of Yugoslavia*, Table 5, p. 119. *Popis 1948*, vol. 1, pp. lxxii-lxxvii. *Popis 1961*, vol. 10, Table 4, p. xxiv. "Increase of Urban Population," Table 1, p. 2,561. "Rise in the Urban Population," Table VI, p. 49.

H-22   United Nations, *A Statistical Survey of the Housing Situation*, Table I.2, p. 28; Table III.3, p. 91; Table III.5, p. 118; Table III.7, p. 134.

H-23   United Nations, *A Statistical Survey of the Housing Situation*, Table I.2, p. 29; Table III.3, p. 92; Table III.5, p. 119; Table III.7, p. 134.

H-24   United Nations, *A Statistical Survey of the Housing Situation*, Table I.2, p. 31; Table III.3, p. 94; Table III.5, p. 120; Table III.7, p. 136.

H-25   United Nations, *A Statistical Survey of the Housing Situation*, Table I.2, p. 32; Table III.3, p. 95; Table III.5, p. 121; Table III.7, p. 137.

H-26   United Nations, *A Statistical Survey of the Housing Situation*, Table I.2, p. 34; Table III.3, p. 98; Table III.5, p. 123; Table III.7, p. 139.

H-27   United Nations, *A Statistical Survey of the Housing Situation*, Table I.2, p. 35; Table III.3, p. 99; Table III.5, p. 123; Table III.7, p. 139.

H-28   United Nations, *A Statistical Survey of the Housing Situation*, Table I.2, p. 37; Table III.3, pp. 101-02; Table III.5, p. 125; Table III.7, p. 141.

H-29   U.S. Dept. of Agriculture, *Agricultural Statistics of Eastern Europe*, Tables 93-99, pp. 100-6, and data supplied by the Centrally Planned Program Area, Foreign Demand and Competition Division, U.S. Dept. of Agriculture.

H-30   Food and Agricultural Organization, *Provisional Food Balance Sheets*, no page numbers in original.

H-31   *UN Stat. Yrbk. 1956*, Table 148, p. 378. *UN Stat. Yrbk. 1962*, Table 140, pp. 362-63, and Table 150, pp. 417-18. *UN Stat. Yrbk. 1967*, Table 152, pp. 416-17. *UN Stat. Yrbk. 1970*, Table 162, pp. 485-86. *UN Stat. Yrbk. 1976*, Table 156, p. 491. *UN Stat. Yrbk. 1977*, Table 159, pp. 542-43. *UNESCO Stat. Yrbk. 1963*, Table 39, pp. 432-33, 450-51, 454-61. *UNESCO Stat. Yrbk. 1975*, Table 15.2, pp. 712-13, and Table 16.2, pp. 723-31. *UNESCO Stat. Yrbk. 1977*, Table 15-2, p. 1,006, and Table 16.2, pp. 1,009-18.

H-32   *UN Stat. Yrbk. 1956*, Table 176, pp. 571-72, and Table 179, pp. 602-3. *UN Stat. Yrbk. 1962*, Table 175, pp. 603-6, and Table 178, pp. 641-44. *UN Stat. Yrbk. 1967*, Table 201, pp. 696-99, and Table 206, pp. 756-60. *UN Stat. Yrbk. 1971*, Table 201, pp. 713-15, and Table 207, pp. 785-89. *UN Stat. Yrbk. 1977*, Table 209, pp. 889-91, and Table 213, pp. 926-28. *Compendium of Social Statistics*, Table 17, pp. 211-12. *World Health Statistics Annual 1971*, Table 4, pp. 138-68. *World Health Statistics Annual 1973-1976*, vol. 3, Table 5, pp. 234-87. *UNESCO Stat. Yrbk., 1963*, Table 27, pp. 346-55.